The Definitive Guide to HTML5

Adam Freeman

The Definitive Guide to HTML5

Copyright © 2011 by Adam Freeman

ISBN-13 (pbk): 978-1-4302-3960-4

ISBN-13 (electronic): 978-1-4302-3961-1

President and Publisher: Paul Manning
Lead Editor: Ben Renow-Clarke
Development Editor: Ewan Buckingham
Technical Reviewers: Kevin Grant and Andy Olsen
Editorial Board: Steve Anglin, Mark Beckner, Ewan Buckingham, Gary Cornell, Morgan Ertel, Jonathan Gennick, Jonathan Hassell, Robert Hutchinson, Michelle Lowman, James Markham, Matthew Moodie, Jeff Olson, Jeffrey Pepper, Douglas Pundick, Ben Renow-Clarke, Dominic Shakeshaft, Gwenan Spearing, Matt Wade, Tom Welsh
Coordinating Editor: Jennifer L. Blackwell
Copy Editors: Lori Cavanaugh, Roger LeBlanc, Ralph Moore, Vanessa Moore, Marilyn Smith, Kim Wimpsett
Compositor: Bytheway Publishing Services
Indexer: BIM Indexing & Proofreading Services
Artist: SPI Global
Cover Designer: Anna Ishchenko

Distributed to the book trade worldwide by Springer Science+Business Media, LLC., 233 Spring Street, 6th Floor, New York, NY 10013. Phone 1-800-SPRINGER, fax (201) 348-4505, e-mail orders-ny@springer-sbm.com, or visit www.springeronline.com.

For information on translations, please e-mail rights@apress.com, or visit www.apress.com.

Apress and friends of ED books may be purchased in bulk for academic, corporate, or promotional use. eBook versions and licenses are also available for most titles. For more information, reference our Special Bulk Sales–eBook Licensing web page at www.apress.com/bulk-sales.

The source code for this book is available to readers at www.apress.com. You will need to answer questions pertaining to this book in order to successfully download the code.

Dedicated to my lovely wife, Jacqui Griffyth
–Adam Freeman

Contents at a Glance

iv

Contents

About the Author

 **Adam Freeman** is an experienced IT professional who has held senior positions in a range of companies, most recently serving as Chief Technology Officer and Chief Operating Officer of a global bank. Now retired, he spends his time writing and running. This is his thirteenth technology book.

About the Technical Reviewers

Kevin Grant is a full time PHP Developer, living and working in the Sheffield area, UK. His current role involves maintaining Zend Framework based websites for clients (thanks to a book on ZF from Apress!) and during the day he enjoys a mixture of coding, server admin, performance profiling, and/or advising others on implementing scalability technologies like memcached or load balancing. On weekends he spends time with his family, occasionally does odd jobs around the house and frequently complains about not going climbing enough, despite the proximity of several local climbing walls and crags. His first computer was a ZX Spectrum 48K+ but his all time favorite game remains Parsec.

Andy Olsen is a freelance consultant based in the UK, and spends most of his working time immersed in web/mobile technologies, .NET, and Java. Andy had been working in IT for 25 years (where do the years go?) and would like to play professional football when he grows up. Andy lives by the seaside in Swansea in South Wales with his family, and enjoys running, skiing, and watching the Swans. You can reach Andy at andyo@olsensoft.com.

Acknowledgments

I would like to thank everyone at Apress for working so hard to bring this book to print. In particular, I would like to thank Jennifer Blackwell for keeping me on track (and for putting up with my refusal to use SharePoint), and Ewan Buckingham and Ben Renow-Clarke for commissioning and editing this book. I would also like to thank Kevin, Andy, Roger, Vanessa, Lori, Ralph, Kim, and Marilyn for their reviews and copyediting.

PART I

Getting Started

Before you can begin to explore HTML5, you have some preparation to do. In the next five chapters, I'll describe the structure of the book, show you how to get set up for HTML5 development, and give you a refresher in basic HTML, CSS, and JavaScript.

CHAPTER 1

Putting HTML5 in Context

The *Hypertext Markup Language* (HTML) has been around since the early 1990s. My earliest encounter was somewhere around 1993 or 1994, when I was working at a university research lab not far from London. There was only one browser—NCSA Mosaic—and the number of web servers could be counted on one hand.

When I think back to those days, I wonder why we were so excited about HTML and the World Wide Web. (We had to laboriously type all three words in those days. There wasn't the critical mass or current sense of importance to refer to just "the Web."

Everything was very basic. I remember some images of gemstones that we could watch load...slowly. This was before the broadband revolution and the entire university had the kind of bandwidth that is common on a mobile phone these days. But we *were* excited. Grant proposals were hurriedly rewritten to embrace the new world, and there was a real sense that the world of technology had fractured into before-Web and after-Web periods, even if all we could do was see pictures of a coffee pot in *another* university not far from London (but too far to go for coffee).

Since then, the Web has become indistinguishable from the Internet for many users and we are long past the point of being excited about pictures of gems. Along the way, HTML has been extended, enhanced, twisted, tortured, fought over, litigated over, ignored, embraced, denigrated for being too simple, hailed as being the future and, ultimately, settling into its current position as part of the indispensable plumbing in the daily lives of billions of people.

This book is about HTML5—the latest version of the HTML standard and an attempt to bring order, structure, and enhancement to a critical technology that has finally matured after years of difficult adolescence.

The History of HTML

All HTML books have a section titled *The History of HTML,* and most use this section to give a careful timeline of the HTML standard from the moment it was created until the present day.

If you need that information, I encourage you to find it on Wikipedia—although it isn't very interesting or useful. To understand how HTML has been shaped and how we ended up at HTML5, we care about a small number of key turning points and one long-lived trend.

The Introduction of JavaScript

JavaScript (which, despite the name, has very little to do with the Java programming language) was developed by a company called Netscape. It marked the start of client-side scripting embedded in the web browser, moving HTML from a carrier of static content into something a little richer. I say a *little* richer because it took a while for the kind of complex interactions we see in the browser today to emerge.

JavaScript isn't part of the core HTML specification, but the association between web browsers, HTML, and JavaScript is so close that it makes no sense to tease them apart. The HTML5 specification assumes that JavaScript is available, and we need to use JavaScript to use some of the most interesting new features that have been added to HTML5.

The End of the Browser Wars

There was a period where the browser market was hotly contested. The main competitors were Microsoft and Netscape, and these companies competed by adding unique features to their web browsers. The idea was that these features would be so compelling that web developers would build their content so that it would work only on a particular browser—and this content would be so compelling that users would prefer one browser over another and market domination would follow.

It didn't quite work out that way. Web developers ended up using only features that were available in all browsers or coming up with elaborate workarounds that used roughly comparable features in each. It was pretty painful, and web development still bears the scars of this period.

In the end, Microsoft was found guilty of antitrust violations after giving away Internet Explorer for free, undercutting Netscape's paid-for Navigator product. Microsoft has been blamed for Netscape going out of business. There may be some truth in this, but I consulted for Netscape for 18 months or so during this period, and I have never encountered a company so bent on self-destruction. Some companies are destined to be lessons to others, and Netscape is one such company.

The destruction of Netscape and the penalties given to Microsoft ended the browser wars and set the scene for standards-based web browsing. The HTML specification was improved, and adherence to it became the norm. These days, browsers compete on their level of compliance to the standards—a complete turnabout that has made life easier for developers and users alike.

The Dominance of Plugins

Plugins have been a good thing for the web. They have allowed companies to provide support for advanced features and rich content that cannot be easily achieved using HTML alone. Some of these plugins have become so feature rich and so widely installed that many sites are just vehicles for that plugin's content. This is especially true for Adobe Flash, and I often encounter sites that are completely implemented in Flash. There is nothing intrinsically wrong with this, but it does mean that the browser and HTML are not being used beyond their ability to act as a Flash container.

Plugins make the creators of browsers uncomfortable because it puts control in the hands of the plugin maker, and one key area of enhancement in HTML5 is an attempt to put the kind of rich content that Flash is used for directly into the browser. Two companies in particular are driving the move away from Flash: Apple and Microsoft. Apple does not support Flash in its iOS, and Microsoft has disabled Flash from the Metro-style version of Internet Explorer in Windows 8.

The Emergence of Semantic HTML

Early versions of the HTML standard didn't do much to separate the significance of content from the way it was presented. If you wanted to indicate that a span of text was important, you applied an HTML element that made the text bold. It was up to the user to make the association that bold content is important content. This is something that humans do very easily and that automated agents find very hard to do. The automated processing of content has become important in the years since HTML was first introduced, and there has been a gradual effort to separate the significance of HTML elements from the way that content is presented in the browser.

The Trend: The HTML Standard Lags Behind HTML Use

The process for creating a standard is always a long one, especially for something as widely used as HTML. There are a lot of stakeholders, and each wants to influence new versions of the standard to their commercial benefit or particular point of view. Standards are not laws, and standards bodies fear fragmentation above all else—which leads to a lot of time-consuming reconciliation around how potential features and enhancements may work.

The standards body for HTML is the World Wide Web Consortium (known as W3C). They have a difficult job, and it takes a long time for a proposal to become a standard. It takes a very long time for a revision to the core HTML specification to be approved.

The consequence of the lengthy standards process is that the W3C has always been following the curve, trying to standardize what has already become accepted practice. The HTML specification has been a reflection of leading-edge thinking about web content from several years ago. This has reduced the importance of the HTML standard because the real innovation was happening away from the W3C, partly in the browsers and partly in plugins.

Introducing HTML5

HTML5 isn't just the latest version of the HTML specification. It is also an umbrella term that describes a set of related technologies that are used to make modern, rich web content. I'll introduce you to these technologies in later chapters, but the three most important ones are the core HTML5 specification, Cascading Style Sheets (CSS), and JavaScript.

The core HTML5 specification defines the elements we use to mark up content, indicating its significance. CSS allows us to control the appearance of marked-up content as it is presented to the user. JavaScript allows us to manipulate the contents of an HTML document, respond to user interaction, and take advantage of some programming-centric features of the new HTML5 elements.

▪ **Tip** Don't worry if none of this makes sense—I'll introduce you to HTML elements in Chapter 3, familiarize you with CSS in Chapter 4, and refresh your JavaScript in Chapter 5.

Some people (picky, obsessive, detail-oriented people) will point out that HTML5 refers to just the HTML elements. Ignore these people—they are missing a fundamental shift in the nature of web content. The technologies used in web pages have become so interconnected that you need to understand them all to create content. If you use HTML elements without CSS, you create content that users find hard to parse. If you use HTML and CSS without JavaScript, you miss the opportunity to give users immediate feedback on their actions and the ability to take advantage of some of the new advanced features that HTML5 specifies.

The New Standard(s)

To deal with the long standardization process and the way that the standard lags behind common usage, HTML5 and related technologies are defined by a larger number of small standards. Some are just a handful of pages focused on a very particular aspect of a single feature. Others, of course, are still hundreds of pages of dense text that cover whole swathes of functionality.

The idea is that smaller groups can cooperate in developing and standardizing features that are important to them and that less contentious topics can be standardized without being held up by arguments about other features.

There are some positive and negative consequences to this approach. The positives are that standards *are* being developed more quickly. The main negative is that it is hard to keep track of all of the different standards in development and how they relate to one another. The quality of the specifications has also fallen—there is ambiguity in some of standards, which leads to inconsistent implementations in the browsers.

Perhaps the biggest drawback is that there is no baseline against which HTML5 compliance can be assessed. We are still in the early days, but we can't rely on features being implemented in all of the browsers that our users might employ. This makes adopting features problematic and requires a careful assessment of how widely adopted a standard has become. The W3C has released an official HTML5 logo, shown in Figure 1-1, but it doesn't indicate support for any particular aspect of the HTML5 standard or its related technologies.

Figure 1-1. The official W3C HTML5 logo

Embracing Native Multimedia

A key enhancement in HTML5 is the support for playing video and audio files natively in the browser that is, without needing a plugin). This is one part of the response from the W3C to the dominance of plugins, and the integration between the native multimedia support and the rest of the HTML features offers a lot of promise. I explain these features in Chapter 34.

Embracing Programmatic Content

One of the biggest changes in HTML5 is the addition of the canvas element, a feature that I describe in Chapters 35 and 36. The canvas is another response to the domination of plugins, and it provides a general-purpose drawing surface we can use to achieve some of the tasks that Adobe Flash is commonly used for.

Part of the significance of this feature arises because we have to use JavaScript to work with the canvas element. This makes programming a first-class activity in an HTML document, which is an important change.

Embracing the Semantic Web

HTML5 introduces a number of features and rules to separate the meaning of elements from the way that content is presented. This is an important concept in HTML5, and I cover it in more detail in Chapter 6. This is a theme I will return to several times in this book, and it marks a new maturity in HTML and reflects the diversity of ways in which HTML content is produced and consumed. This change (which has been gradually introduced in earlier versions of HTML) creates slightly more work for the web developer because we have to mark up content and then define its presentation, but there are some useful new enhancements to make this process less burdensome.

The Current State of HTML5

The core HTML5 standard is still under development, and it is not expected to be finalized for some time. This means there are likely to be some changes between the features I describe in this book and the final standard. However, the standard is unlikely to be finished for several years and the changes are likely to be minor.

Browser Support for HTML5

The most popular web browsers already implement many HTML5 features, and throughout this book I show you how examples are displayed by viewing HTML5 documents in browsers such as Google Chrome or Mozilla Firefox. Not all browsers support all features, however, and it is worth checking whether support exists before using a feature in a real project. Some browsers, such as Chrome ad Firefox, are updated on an almost continuous basis. I have lost count of the number of browser updates I applied as I wrote this book, and each update brings some new feature or bug fix. This means I have been unable to give definitive information about which features are supported by which browsers. But given the fragmented nature of the HTML5 standards, it makes sense to check for features using a JavaScript library such as *Modernizr* (http://www.modernizr.com). Modernizr allows you to programmatically check to see if the browser the user has employed supports key HTML5 features, giving you the ability to make decisions in the document about which features you rely on.

If you want to plan in advance, I recommend the site *When Can I Use?* (http://caniuse.com), which provides detailed information about browser support and adoption rates and seems to be very well maintained.

Site Support for HTML5

The number of sites that use HTML5 features is growing rapidly. Some are simply demonstration sites, showing how a given HTML5 features appears, but there is an increasing number of more substantial sites that can take advantage of an HTML5 browser. A good example is YouTube, which now offers native HTML5 video support—although, of course, Flash video is used for older browsers.

The Structure of This Book

I have split this book into five parts. This part, Part I, contains the information you need to get ready to use this book and a refresher in basic HTML, CSS, and JavaScript. If you haven't done any web development recently, you will find these chapters bring you up to speed.

Part II covers the HTML elements, including those that are new or modified in HTML5. Each element is described and demonstrated, and you'll find information about the default presentation for elements.

Part III covers *Cascading Style Sheets* (CSS). These chapters describe all of the CSS selectors and properties available for styling content, and you'll find plenty of examples and demonstrations to help put everything in context. In these chapters, I cover the latest version of CSS (CSS3), but I also show you which features were introduced in CSS1 and CSS2.

Part IV describes the *Document Object Model* (DOM), which allows you to explore and manipulate HTML content using JavaScript. The DOM contains a set of features that are essential to creating rich web content.

Part V contains information about advanced HTML5 features, such as Ajax, multimedia, and the canvas element. These are features that require more programming skill but offer significant enhancements to your web content. You don't have to use these features to take advantage of HTML5, but they are worth considering for complex projects.

■ **Note** One HTML5-related technology I have not covered in this book is Scalable Vector Graphics (SVG). SVG allows you to create two-dimensional vector graphics using either markup or JavaScript. SVG is not a topic to be taken on lightly. If you are interested in SVG, I recommend *SVG Programming* by Kurt Cagle, which is also published by Apress.

Finding More Information About HTML5

I tried to be comprehensive in this book, but it is inevitable that you will encounter a problem I don't address or have a question that I don't answer. When this happens, the first place to look is the W3C site (w3c.org). Here you can peruse the standards and work out what should be happening in the browser. The standards can be hard to read (and tend toward being self-referential), but they offer some useful insights.

A friendlier, but less authoritative, resource is the Mozilla Developer Network (developer.mozilla.org). There is a lot of useful information available about the different HTML features, including some good HTML5 content.

Summary

In this chapter, I provided some context in which to explain HTML5, setting out the key turning points in the history of HTML and explaining how HTML5 attempts to address them. In the next chapter, I'll tell you how to prepare for working through the many examples in this book. After that, we will start our exploration of HTML5, beginning with the HTML elements themselves.

Getting Ready

Before you start, you need to do a small amount of preparation. You need some basic tools for all web development, and there is one piece of software you will need if you want to re-create some of the advanced examples later in the book.

The good news about web development tools is that there are plenty of free and open-source choices available. All of the tools I used when developing the examples for this book are available freely. Once you have made you selections, you can begin your HTML5 journey.

Selecting a Browser

The most important tool you'll need for this book is a browser. Throughout this book, I refer to the mainstream browsers, by which I mean the desktop versions of the following:

- Google Chrome
- Mozilla Firefox
- Opera
- Apple Safari
- Internet Explorer

These browsers are the most widely used, and the desktop versions are more frequently updated and more feature rich than their mobile counterparts. Your preferred browser may not be on this list, which doesn't mean it won't support the HTML5 features I demonstrate, but my advice is to stick to one of the browsers on the list.

My favorite browser is Google Chrome. I like its simplicity, and it has pretty good developer tools. For this reason, most of the figures in this book show Google Chrome displaying an HTML5 document. If you are not a fan of Chrome, I suggest Firefox or Opera because their HTML5 support is on a par with Chrome. Safari and Internet Explorer seem to lag behind.

Internet Explorer is in an interesting state at the moment. As I write this, Internet Explorer 9 is in production and has some reasonable support for basic HTML5 features. There is a preview version of Internet Explorer 10, which is much improved, but it is still missing support for key features. However, it is becoming clear that Microsoft's proposition for Windows 8 includes application development based on HTML5 and JavaScript, which suggests that we can expect good levels of HTML5 support in the Internet Explorer engine as we approach the Windows 8 release.

■ **Note** Please don't write to me explaining why your preferred browser is better than my preferred browser. I am sure your browser is lovely and your choice is well made, and I wish you many years of browsing happiness. If you really can't let this go, I am prepared to sell you a remediation kit for only $50—it contains a pack of paper, a pair of scissors, and some glue. These will allow you to print and cut out a template you can stick over all of the figures in this book, showing your browser instead of Chrome. I think you will agree that this is a small price to pay for peace of mind.

Selecting an HTML Editor

You will need an editor to write HTML documents. Any text editor will do, but I recommend an editor that has specific support for HTML (and ideally HTML5). These usually offer syntax checking for your markup, autocomplete to reduce the amount of typing you have to do, and a preview panel that shows you the effect of changes as you type.

For this book, I used *Komodo Edit* from ActiveState (available from activestate.com)—a free, open-source editor that has some pretty good HTML support and which suits my personal preferences about how an editor should work. I have no relationship with ActiveState and no reason to promote Komodo Edit, other than I have found it useful for this book and some other projects.

Selecting a Web Server

A web server isn't essential to follow this book, but some features work differently if you load the HTML documents from disk. Any web server is suitable for the examples in this book, and plenty of free and open-source options are available. I used IIS 7.5, which is Microsoft's web and application server. This isn't a free option, but I have a development server that runs Windows Server 2008 R2, so I already had all the features I needed.

Obtaining Node.js

For a few of the chapters in this book, I needed to write code for a back-end server that the web browser could communicate with. I chose Node.js for this task. Node.js has become something of a phenomenon recently. It offers simple, event-driven I/O, which is ideally suited for high-volume, low-data-rate web requests.

You don't need to know about or worry about any of this. The reason I chose Node.js is that I write server scripts using JavaScript, which means that I don't have to introduce a second programming language in this book. I am not going to explain how Node.js works—or even explain the detail of my server scripts—but you should be able to use your JavaScript skills to figure out how they work if you can't treat them as a black box.

You can download Node.js from nodejs.org. I used version 0.4.11 in this book. Node.js seems to be evolving very quickly, so you may find that there are later versions available by the time you read this. I use Windows, and I obtained the precompiled binaries from http://node-js.prcn.co.cc.

Obtaining the Multipart Module

Not all of the functionality you need is included in the core Node.js package. You also need the `multipart` module, which is available from `https://github.com/isaacs/multipart-js`. Follow the instructions to install this module—you will need it for Chapters 32 and 33 when we take a look at Ajax.

Getting the Sample Code

All of the example HTML documents I create in this book are available free of charge from apress.com. You will find the examples organized by chapter, and they are provided with their supported resources (except for the video and audio content I used in Chapter 34, because clearing media content is very difficult).

Summary

In this chapter, I outlined the simple steps required to get ready for the chapters that follow. Web development requires only a few simple tools, the most important of which is the browser and all of which can be obtained free of charge. The next three chapters refresh your basic skills in HTML, Cascading Style Sheets (CSS), and JavaScript.

CHAPTER 3

Getting Started with HTML

Every developer knows at least something about HTML. It has become all-pervasive in recent years, and the chances are good that you have at least *seen* some HTML, even if you have never needed to write any. In this chapter, I am going back to the basics of HTML to make sure you get the fundamentals right—beginning with what HTML is for and how it works. I'll define the basic terminology HTML uses and show you some of the core HTML elements that pretty much every web page uses.

As its name suggests, HTML is a markup language. This markup takes the form of *elements* applied to *content*, typically text. In the following sections, I'll explain the different aspects of HTML elements, explain how you can configure the elements with attributes, and describe the set of global attributes that can be used on all HTML elements. Table 3-1 provides the summary for this chapter.

Table 3-1. Chapter Summary

Problem	Solution	Listing
Apply markup to content.	Use an HTML element.	1-5
Fine-tune the way that a browser handles HTML elements.	Apply one or more attributes to the element.	6-10
Declare that a document contains HTML.	Use the DOCTYPE and html elements.	11
Describe an HTML document.	Use the head element to contain one or more of the metadata elements (which are described in Chapter 7).	12
Add content to an HTML document.	Use the body element to contain text and other HTML elements.	13
Add a shortcut key to select an element.	Use the accesskey global attribute.	14
Classify elements together, either so that a consistent style can be applied or so that the elements can be located programmatically.	Use the class global attribute.	15-17

Allow the user to edit the content of an element.	Use the `contenteditable` global attribute.	18
Add a context menu to an element.	Use the `contextmenu` global attribute. (Note that this attribute has no browser support currently.)	-
Specify the layout direction of an element's content.	Use the `dir` global attribute.	19
Specify that an element can be dragged.	Use the `draggable` global attribute. (See Chapter 37 for details of HTML5 drag and drop.)	-
Specify that an element can be used as a target on which to drop other elements .	Use the `dropzone` global attribute. (See Chapter 37 for details of HTML5 drag and drop.)	-
Indicate that an element and its contents are not relevant.	Use the `hidden` global attribute.	20
Assign a unique identifier to an element so that a style can be applied or so that the element can be selected programmatically.	Use the `id` global attribute.	21
Specify the language in which the content of an element is expressed.	Use the `lang` global attribute.	22
Specify whether the contents of an element should be checked for spelling errors.	Use the `spellcheck` global attribute.	23
Define a style directly to an element.	Use the `style` global attribute.	24
Specify the order in which the Tab key moves between elements in an HTML document.	Use the `tabindex` global attribute.	25
Provide additional information about an element (which will typically be used to in a tool tip).	Use the `title` global attribute.	26

Using Elements

Listing 3-1 shows a simple example of an HTML element applied to some text.

Listing 3-1. Example of an HTML Element

`I like `**`<code>`**`apples`**`</code>`**` and oranges.`

I have shown the element in bold—it has three parts. The first two are called *tags*. The start tag is `<code>`, and the end tag is `</code>`. Between the tags is the element's content (in this case, the word *apples*). Together, the tags and the content form the code element, as shown in Figure 3-1.

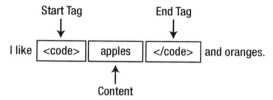

Figure 3-1. The anatomy of an HTML element

Elements are the way you tell the browser about your content. The effect of the element is applied to the element contents. Each of the HTML elements has a different and quite specific meaning—the code element, for example, represents a fragment of computer code.

■ **Tip** Element names are not case sensitive—browsers will recognize `<CODE>` and `<code>`, and even `<CoDe>`, as start tags for the code element. In general, the convention is to adopt a single case format and stick to it. In recent years, the more common style has been to use lowercase characters throughout. This is the format I will use in this book.

HTML defines different types of element that fulfill various roles in an HTML document—the code element is an example of a *sematic element*. Semantic elements allow us to define the meaning of our content and the relationships between different parts of the content. I'll explain more about this in Chapter 8. You can see the effect of the code element in Figure 3-2.

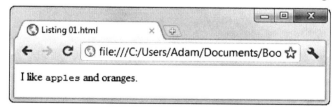

Figure 3-2. The effect of the code element displayed in a broswer

Notice that the browser doesn't display the element tags—its job is to interpret your HTML and render a view to the user that takes your elements into account.

THE SEPARATION OF PRESENTATION AND CONTENT

Some HTML elements have an impact on presentation—meaning that when the browser encounters one of these elements, it will change the way the content is displayed to the user. The code element is a good example. As Figure 3-1 shows, when the browser encounters the code element, it displays the enclosed content using a fixed-width font.

The use of HTML elements to manage the way content is presented is now strongly discouraged. The idea is that you use HTML elements to define the structure and meaning of your content and Cascading Style Sheets (CSS) to control the way the content is presented to the user. We'll come to CSS in Chapter 4.

The elements that do affect presentation tend to be those that originated in the early versions of HTML, when the idea of separating presentation and content were not so rigorously enforced. Browsers will apply a default presentation style to these elements, such as the fixed-width font that is typically used for the code element. As I'll explain in Chapter 4, you can use CSS to override those default styles.

Understanding the Elements Used in This Chapter

To provide a refresher on HTML, I need to use some elements that I don't describe until later chapters. Table 3-2 lists these elements, along with a brief description and the chapter in which you can find full details.

Table 3-2. Element Summary

Element	Description	Chapter
a	Creates a hyperlink	8
body	Denotes the content of an HTML document	7
button	Creates a button for submitting forms	12
code	Denotes a fragment of computer code	8
DOCTYPE	Denotes the start of an HTML document	7
head	Denotes the header section of an HTML document	7
hr	Denotes a thematic break	9
html	Denotes the HTML section of a document	7
input	Denotes input supplied by a user	8
label	Creates a label for another element	12

p	Denotes a paragraph	9
style	Defines a CSS style	7
table	Denotes tabular data	11
td	Denotes a table cell	11
textarea	Creates a multiline text box to gather input from the user	14
th	Creates a table header cell	11
title	Defines the title for an HTML document	7
tr	Denotes a table row	11

Using Empty Elements

You are not required to place any content between the start and end tags. If you don't, you create an *empty element*, like the one shown in Listing 3-2.

Listing 3-2. An Empty HTML Element

```
I like <code></code> apples and oranges.
```

Not all elements make sense when they are empty (and code is one of these), but even so, this is still valid HTML.

Using Self-Closing Tags

You can express empty elements more concisely by using a single tag, as shown in Listing 3-3.

Listing 3-3. Expressing an Empty Element Using a Single Tag

```
I like <code/> apples and oranges.
```

You combine the start and end tag into one—the stroke character (/), which is usually used to signify the start of the end tag, is placed at the end of the single tag. The element in Listing 3-2 and the element in Listing 3-3 are equivalent—the single tag is a more concise way of expressing the empty element.

Using Void Elements

There are some elements that *must* be expressed using a single tag—the HTML specification makes it illegal to place any content in them. These are known as *void elements*. One such element is hr, which is a *grouping element* and is used to denote a paragraph-level break in the content. (You'll see the other grouping elements in Chapter 9.) You can use void elements in one of two ways—the first is to specify only a start tag, as shown in Listing 3-4.

Listing 3-4. Specifying a Void Element Using Just a Start Tag

```
I like apples and oranges.
<hr>
Today was warm and sunny.
```

The browser knows that hr is a void element and doesn't expect to see a closing tag. You can also include a stroke to make the element consistent with empty elements, as shown in Listing 3-5.

Listing 3-5. Expressing Void Elements Using the Empty Element Structure

```
I like apples and oranges.
<hr />
Today was warm and sunny.
```

This is the format I prefer and will use in this book. As an aside, the hr element is another example of an element that had presentational meaning—in this case, to display a horizontal rule (hence the name). You can see the default interpretation of the hr element in Figure 3-3.

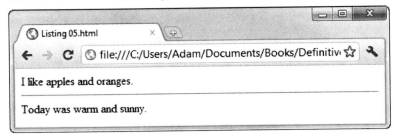

Figure 3-3. The default presentation of the hr element

(NOT) USING OPTIONAL START AND END TAGS

Many HTML5 elements have special rules under which you can choose to omit one of the tags. As an example, the html element (which I describe in Chapter 7) permits its end tag to be omitted if "*the element is not immediately followed by a comment and the element contains a body element that is either not empty or whose start tag has not been omitted*". The text in italics comes from one of the official HTML5 specification documents. I encourage you to read these specifications (which you can get at w3c.org), but be warned: they are all written in this lively style.

I think it is great that there is such flexibility in the markup, but I also think it is confusing and leads to maintenance problems. The elements you apply to HTML are not just processed by browsers—they have to be read by your colleagues and by future versions of yourself when you come back to maintain and update your application. The browser may be able to determine why a given tag has been omitted, but it won't be as obvious to your colleagues or when you return to the HTML to make changes. To that end, I don't detail these special rules in this book and I use the start and end tags of an element unless there is a compelling reason not to (in which case, I'll explain why).

Using Element Attributes

You can configure your elements by using *attributes*. Listing 3-6 shows an attribute that applies to the a element. This element lets you create a hyperlink that, when it's clicked on, loads a different HTML document.

Listing 3-6. Using an Element Attribute

```
I like <a href="/apples.html">apples</a> and oranges.
```

Attributes can be added only to start tags or single tags—they can never be added to end tags. Attributes have a name and a value, as shown in Figure 3-4.

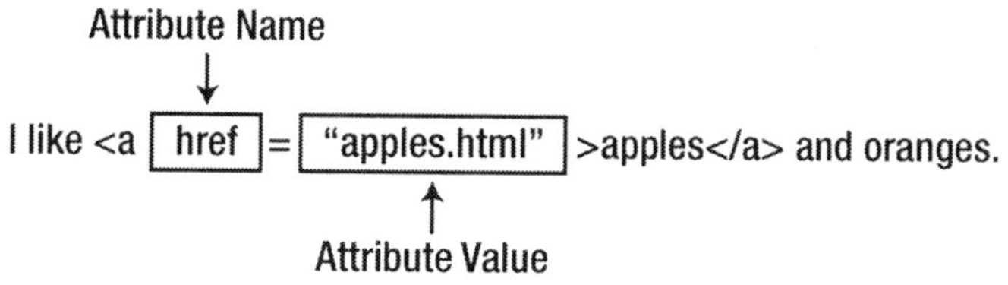

Figure 3-4. Applying attributes to HTML elements

There are a set of global attributes that can be applied to any HTML element—I describe these in later in this chapter. In addition to these global attributes, elements can define their own attributes that provide configuration information that is specific to the role of the element. The href attribute is local to the a element, and it configures the URL that is the destination of the hyperlink. The a element defines a number of specific attributes, which I describe in Chapter 8.

▪ **Tip** I have used double quotes ("myvalue") to delimit the attribute value in the listing, but you can also use single quotes ('myvalue'). If you want to specify a value for an attribute that itself must contain quotes, you use both styles ("my'quoted'value" or 'my"quoted"value').

Applying Multiple Attributes to an Element

You can apply multiple attributes to an element by separating them with one or more space characters. Listing 3-7 provides an example.

Listing 3-7. Defining Multiple Attributes in an Element

```
I like <a class="link" href="/apples.html" id="firstlink">apples</a> and oranges.
```

19

The order of the attributes is not important, and you can freely mix global attributes with the ones that are element specific, which is what I have done in the listing. The class and id attributes are global. (I explain these attributes later in this chapter.)

Using Boolean Attributes

Some attributes are *Boolean attributes*. You don't have to specify a value for these attributes—just add the attribute name to the element, as shown in Listing 3-8.

Listing 3-8. A Boolean Attribute

```
Enter your name: <input disabled>
```

The Boolean attribute in this example is disabled, and I have just added the attribute name to the element. The input element provides a means for the user to enter data into an HTML form (which I describe in Chapter 12). Adding the disabled attribute stops the user from entering data. Boolean attributes are a little odd because it is the *presence* of the attribute that configures the element, not the value you assign to the attribute. I didn't specify disabled="true"—I just added the word disabled. You can achieve the same effect by assigning the empty string ("") or by setting the value to be the name of the attribute, as shown in Listing 3-9.

Listing 3-9. A Boolean Attribute Assigned the Empty String Value

```
Enter your name: <input disabled="">
Enter your name: <input disabled="disabled">
```

Using Custom Attributes

You can define your own attributes as long as the name you use is prefixed with data-. Listing 3-10 shows the use of such attributes.

Listing 3-10. Applying Custom Attributes to an Element

```
Enter your name: <input disabled="true" data-creator="adam" data-purpose="collection">
```

The proper name for these attributes is *author defined attributes*, which are sometimes referred to as *expando attributes*, but I prefer the more commonly used term *custom attribute*.

Custom attributes are a formal definition of a widely used HTML4 technique where browsers would ignore any attribute they didn't recognize. You prefix these attributes with data- to avoid clashing with attribute names that might be created by future versions of HTML. Custom attributes are useful when working with CSS (introduced in Chapter 4) and with JavaScript (introduced in Chapter 5).

Creating an HTML Document

Elements and attributes don't exist in isolation—you use them to mark up your content in an *HTML document*. The simplest way to create an HTML document is to create a text file—the convention is that these files have the .html file extension. You can then load the file into a browser, either directly from the disk or via a web server. (In this book, I generally use a web server. My server is called titan, and you'll often see this name in browser windows shown in screenshots.)

BROWSERS AND USER AGENTS

Throughout this chapter (and for most of this book), I refer to the browser as the target for the HTML we create. This is a convenient way of thinking about HTML and is the most common way that HTML is consumed, but it doesn't tell the full story. The collective name for software components and components that might consume HTML is *user agents*. Although browsers are the most prevalent kind of user agent, they are not the only kind.

Nonbrowser user agents are still quite rare, but they are expected to become more popular. The increased emphasis on separating content and presentation in HTML5 is important because it recognizes that not all HTML content is displayed to users. I'll still refer to the browser in this book (because browsers are the most important and dominant category of user agent), but it is useful to keep in mind that some other kind of software might be what your HTML5 is delivering service to.

An HTML document has a particular structure—you need to have some key elements in place as a minimum. Most of the examples in this book are shown as complete HTML documents—this means you can quickly and easily see how an element is applied and the effect it has. I explain all of the elements in the listings in later chapters, but as a quick jump start I am going to give you a tour of a basic HTML document. I will also provide references to the later chapters where you can get more detail.

HTML VS. XHTML

Although this is a book about HTML, I would be remiss if I didn't also mention *XHTML* (that's *HTML* preceded with an *X*). The HTML syntax allows you to do things that make for illegal XML documents. This means it can be difficult to process an HTML document using a standard XML parser.

To solve this problem, you can use XHTML, which is an XML serialization of HTML (that is, you express your content and HTML elements and attributes in a way that makes for valid XML and can be readily handled by an XML parser). You can also create *polyglot documents*, which are valid HTML *and* valid XML, although this requires using a subset of the HTML syntax. I don't cover XHTML in this book, but you can get more information about XHTML at the following URL: http://wiki.whatwg.org/wiki/HTML_vs._XHTML.

The Outer Structure

There are two elements that provide the outer structure of an HTML document—the DOCTYPE and html elements, as shown in Listing 3-11.

Listing 3-11. The Outer Structure of an HTML Document

```
<!DOCTYPE HTML>
<html>
    <!-- elements go here -->
</html>
```

The DOCTYPE element tells the browser it is dealing with an HTML document. This is expressed through the HTML boolean attribute:

```
<!DOCTYPE HTML>
```

You follow the DOCTYPE element with the start tag of the html element. This tells the browser that the contents of the element should be treated as HTML all the way through until the html close tag. It may seem odd that you use the DOCTYPE element and then immediately use the html element, but back when HTML emerged as a standard there were other markup languages that were given equal weight and it was expected that documents would contain a mix of markup types.

These days, HTML is the dominant markup language and most browsers will assume they are dealing with HTML even if you omit the DOCTYPE element and html elements. That doesn't mean you should leave them out. These elements serve an important purpose, and relying on the default behavior of a browser is like trusting strangers—things will be fine most of the time, but every now and again something will go very badly wrong. See Chapter 7 for more details of the DOCTYPE and html elements.

The Metadata

The metadata region of an HTML document allows you to provide information about your document to the browser. The metadata is contained inside a head element, as shown in Listing 3-12.

Listing 3-12. Adding the head Element to an HTML Document

```
<!DOCTYPE HTML>
<html>
    <head>
        <!-- metadata goes here -->
        <title>Example</title>
    </head>
</html>
```

In the listing, I have provided the minimum amount of metadata, which is the title element. All HTML documents are expected to contain a title element, although browsers will generally ignore any omissions. Most browsers display the contents of the title element in the menu bar of the browser window or at the top of the tab that displays the page. The head and title elements are described fully in Chapter 7, along with all of the other metadata elements that can be placed in the head element.

■ **Tip** The listing demonstrates how you create comments in HTML document. You begin with the tag `<!--` and end with `-->`. The browser will ignore anything you put inside these tags.

In addition to containing elements that describe the HTML document, the head element is also used to define relationships to external resources (such as CSS stylesheets), define inline CSS styles, and define and load scripts. All of these activities are demonstrated in Chapter 7.

The Content

The third and final part of the document is the content, which you put inside a body element, as shown in Listing 3-13.

Listing 3-13. Adding the body Element to an HTML Document

```
<!DOCTYPE HTML>
<html>
    <head>
        <!-- metadata goes here -->
        <title>Example</title>
    </head>
    <body>
        <!-- content and elements go here -->
        I like <code>apples</code> and oranges.
    </body>
</html>
```

The body element tells the browser which part of the document is to be displayed to the user—and, of course, a lot of this book is given over to what you can put inside the body element. With the addition of the body element, you have the skeletal HTML document I will use for most of the examples in this book.

Understanding Parents, Children, Descendants, and Siblings

HTML elements have defined relationships with the other elements in an HTML document. An element that contains another element is the *parent* of the second element. In Listing 3-13, the body element is the parent to the code element, because the code element is contained between the start and end tags of the body element. Conversely, the code element is a *child* of the body element. An element can have multiple children, but only one parent.

Elements can contain elements that, in turn, contain other elements. You can also see this in Listing 3-13: the html element contains the body element, which contains the code element. The body and code elements are *descendents* of the html element, but only the body element is a child of the html element. Children are direct descendants. Elements that share the same parent are known as *siblings*. In Listing 3-13, the head and body elements are siblings because they are both children of the html element.

The importance of the relationship between elements runs through HTML. As you'll see in the following section, elements have restrictions as to which other elements can be their parents or children. These restrictions are expressed through *element types*. Element relationships are also essential in CSS—which I introduce in Chapter 4—and one of the ways you select elements to apply styles to is through their parent/child relationships. Finally, when you read about the Document Object Model (DOM) in Part IV, you will find specific elements in a document by navigating through the *document tree*, which is a representation of the relationships between elements. Knowing your siblings from your descendants is an important skill in the world of HTML.

Understanding Element Types

The HTML5 specification groups elements into three categories: *metadata elements, flow elements,* and *phrasing elements.*

Metadata elements are used to create the basic structure of an HTML document and to provide information and direction to the browser about how the document should be processed. I describe the metadata elements in Chapter 7.

The other two categories are slightly different—you use them to specify the valid set of parents and children for an element. The phrasing elements are the basic building blocks of HTML. Chapter 8 contains descriptions of the most commonly used phrasing elements. The flow elements category is a super-set of the phrasing elements—which is to say that all phrasing elements are also flow elements, but not all flow elements are phrasing elements.

Not all elements belong to one of the element categories—those that don't either have special significance or can be used only in very restrictive circumstances. An example of a restricted element is the li element, which denotes a list item and is limited to one of three parent elements: ol (which denotes an ordered list), ul (which denotes an unordered list), and menu (which denotes a menu). You can learn more about the li element in Chapter 9. I tell you which category each element belongs to as part of the element descriptions that start in Chapter 6.

Using HTML Entities

As you can see from the examples in this chapter, there are some characters that have special meaning in HTML document—the obvious ones being the < and > characters. You will sometimes need to use these characters in your content without wanting them to be interpreted as HTML. To do this, you use *HTML entities.* An entity is a code the browser substitutes for the special character. You can see some common entities in Table 3-3.

Table 3-3. Commonly Used HTML Entities

Character	Entity Name	Entity Number
<	<	<
>	>	>
&	&	&#30;
€	€	€
£	£	£
§	§	§
©	©	©
®	®	®

™	™	™

Each special character has an entity number that you can include in your content to represent the character—for example, the ampersand character is &#30;. The more popular special characters also have a name—for example, &#30; and & have the same meaning to the browser.

The HTML5 Global Attributes

Earlier in this chapter, I showed you how to configure elements using attributes. Each element can define its own attributes—these are known as *local attributes*. When I begin describing elements in detail in Chapter 6, I will give you a list of each of the local attributes that an element defines and show you how to use them. Each local attribute gives you the ability to control some aspect of the unique behavior of an element.

There is a second category of attributes—the *global attributes*. These configure the behavior that is common to *all* elements. You can apply every global attribute to every element, although this doesn't always lead to a meaningful or useful behavior change. In the following sections, I describe each of the global attributes and give a demonstration. Some of these attributes are linked to broader HTML features that I cover in more depth later in this book. In these cases, I give a reference to the relevant chapters.

The accesskey Attribute

The accesskey attribute lets you specify one or more keyboard shortcuts that will select the element on the page. Listing 3-14 shows the use of this attribute in a simple form. Forms are the topic of Chapters 12 through 14, so you might want to come back to this example after reading those chapters.

Listing 3-14. Using the accesskey Attribute

```
<!DOCTYPE HTML>
<html>
    <head>
        <title>Example</title>
    </head>
    <body>
        <form>
            Name: <input type="text" name="name" accesskey="n"/>
            <p/>
            Password: <input type="password" name="password" accesskey="p"/>
            <p/>
            <input type="submit" value="Log In" accesskey="s"/>
        </form>
    </body>
</html>
```

In this example, I have added the accesskey attribute to three input elements. (I describe the input element in Chapters 12 and 13.) The idea is to enable users who are regular users of a page or site to use keyboard shortcuts to move between commonly used elements. The key combination required to trigger the accesskey setting differs between platforms—for Windows, it is the Alt key and the accesskey value pressed together. You can see the effect of the accesskey attribute in Figure 3-5. I press Alt+n to focus on the first input element and enter my name. I then press Alt+p to focus on the second input element and enter my password. Alt+s presses the Log In button, which submits the form.

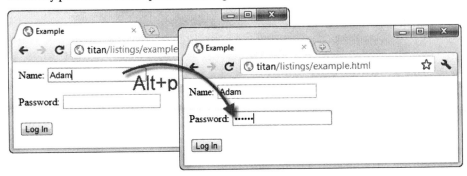

Figure 3-5. The effect of the accesskey attribute

The class Attribute

The class attribute is used to classify or categorize elements. You usually do this so that you can locate elements in the document that belong to a given class or to apply a CSS style. Listing 3-15 shows how you can apply the class attributes.

Listing 3-15. Applying the class Attribute

```
<!DOCTYPE HTML>
<html>
    <head>
        <title>Example</title>
    </head>
    <body>
        <a class="class1 class2" href="http://apress.com">Apress web site</a>
        <p/>
        <a class="class2 otherclass" href="http://w3c.org">W3C web site</a>
    </body>
</html>
```

You can apply multiple classes to each element by separating the class names with a space. The names of the classes that you create are arbitrary, but it is a good idea to make the names meaningful, especially if you have a document that contains many classes. On its own, the class attribute doesn't do anything. Figure 3-6 shows the HTML displayed in a browser. As you can see, you just get a couple of hyperlinks.

Figure 3-6. A pair of a elements to which the class attribute has been applied

The first way you can take advantage of the class attribute is to create a style that targets one of more of the classes you have defined. Listing 3-16 provides an example.

Listing 3-16. Defining a Style That Relies on Classes

```
<!DOCTYPE HTML>
<html>
    <head>
        <title>Example</title>
        <style type="text/css">
            .class2 {
                background-color:grey;
                color:white;
                padding:5px;
                margin:2px;
            }
            .class1 {
                font-size:x-large;
            }
        </style>
    </head>
    <body>
        <a class="class1 class2" href="http://apress.com">Apress web site</a>
        <p/>
        <a class="class2 otherclass" href="http://w3c.org">W3C web site</a>
    </body>
</html>
```

In this example, I used a style element to define two styles—the first is applied to elements that are assigned to class2 and the second is applied to class1.

I explain the style element in Chapter 7, and I provide an introduction to styles and how they can be used to target elements in different ways in Chapter 4.

When you load the HTML in a browser, the styles are applied to the elements. The effect is shown in Figure 3-7. The advantage of using classes to assign styles is that you don't have to duplicate the same style settings on each element.

Figure 3-7. Using the class attribute to apply styles

Another way to use the class attribute is in a script. Listing 3-17 provides a demonstration.

Listing 3-17. Using the class Attribute in a Script

```
<!DOCTYPE HTML>
<html>
    <head>
        <title>Example</title>
    </head>
    <body>
        <a class="class1 class2" href="http://apress.com">Apress web site</a>
        <p/>
        <a class="class2 otherclass" href="http://w3c.org">W3C web site</a>
        <script type="text/javascript">
            var elems = document.getElementsByClassName("otherclass");
            for (i = 0; i < elems.length; i++) {
                var x = elems[i];
                x.style.border = "thin solid black";
                x.style.backgroundColor = "white";
                x.style.color = "black";
            }
        </script>
    </body>
</html>
```

The script in this example finds all of the elements that have been assigned to the otherclass class and applies some styling. I explain the script element in Chapter 7, each of the style properties in Chapters 19 through 24, and how to find elements in the document in Chapter 26. The effect of this script is shown in Figure 3-8.

Figure 3-8. Using the class attribute in a script

The contenteditable Attribute

The `contenteditable` attribute is new in HTML5 and allows the user to change the content in the page. Listing 3-18 provides a simple demonstration.

Listing 3-18. Using the contenteditable Attribute

```
<!DOCTYPE HTML>
<html>
    <head>
        <title>Example</title>
    </head>
    <body>
        <p contenteditable="true">It is raining right now</p>
    </body>
</html>
```

I have applied the `contenteditable` attribute to a p element (which I describe in Chapter 9). Setting the attribute value to `true` allows the user to edit the element contents, and setting it to `false` disables this feature. (If you don't specify a value, the element inherits the setting for this property from its parent.) You can see the effect that the attribute has in Figure 3-9. The user clicks on the text and starts to type.

Figure 3-9. Enabling editing with the contenteditable attribute

29

The contextmenu Attribute

The contextmenu attribute allows you to define context menus for elements. These menus pop up when the user triggers them (for example, when a Windows PC user right-clicks). At the time of this writing, no browser supports the contextmenu attribute.

The dir Attribute

The dir attribute specifies the direction of an element's text. The two supported values are ltr (for left-to-right text) and rtl (for right-to-left text). Listing 3-19 shows both values being used.

Listing 3-19. Using the dir Attribute

```
<!DOCTYPE HTML>
<html>
    <head>
        <title>Example</title>
    </head>
    <body>
        <p dir="rtl">This is right-to-left</p>
        <p dir="ltr">This is left-to-right</p>
    </body>
</html>
```

You can see the effect of the dir attribute in Figure 3-10.

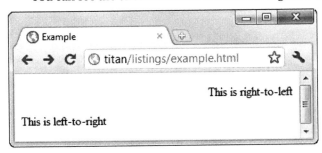

Figure 3-10. Displaying left-to-right and right-to-left text

The draggable Attribute

The draggable attribute is part of the HTML5 support for drag and drop, and it is used to indicate whether an element can be dragged. I explain drag and drop in detail in Chapter 37.

The dropzone Attribute

The dropzone attribute is part of the HTML5 support for drag and drop. It is the counterpart to the draggable attribute I just described. I explain both elements in Chapter 37.

The hidden Attribute

The hidden attribute is a Boolean attribute that indicates an element is not presently relevant. Browsers interpret this attribute by hiding the element from view. Listing 3-20 shows the effect of the hidden attribute.

Listing 3-20. Using the hidden Attribute

```
<!DOCTYPE HTML>
<html>
    <head>
        <title>Example</title>
        <script>
            var toggleHidden = function() {
                var elem = document.getElementById("toggle");
                if (elem.hasAttribute("hidden")) {
                    elem.removeAttribute("hidden");
                } else {
                    elem.setAttribute("hidden", "hidden");
                }
            }
        </script>
    </head>
    <body>
        <button onclick="toggleHidden()">Toggle</button>
        <table>
            <tr><th>Name</th><th>City</th></tr>
            <tr><td>Adam Freeman</td><td>London</td></tr>
            <tr id="toggle" hidden><td>Joe Smith</td><td>New York</td></tr>
            <tr><td>Anne Jones</td><td>Paris</td></tr>
        </table>
    </body>
</html>
```

I made this example somewhat more elaborate than it needs to be. I defined a table element that contains a tr element (which represents a row in the table) for which the hidden attribute is present. I also defined a button element that, when pressed, invokes the toggleHidden JavaScript function defined in the script element. This script removes the hidden attribute when it is present and adds it otherwise. Don't worry about how this all works for the moment. I explain the table, tr, th, and td elements in Chapter 11, the script element in Chapter 7, and events in Chapter 30.

I put this all in place to demonstrate what happens when the hidden attribute is applied, You can see the effect of pressing the button in Figure 3-11.

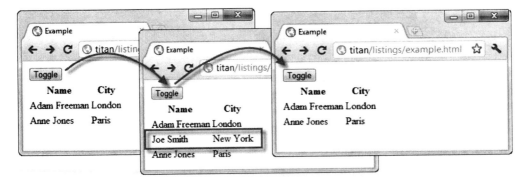

Figure 3-11. The effect of removing and adding the hidden element

When the hidden attribute is applied to an element, the browser doesn't render it at all. It is as though it were not contained in the HTML, so the table is rendered with the reduced number of rows.

The id Attribute

The id attribute is used to assign a unique identifier to an element. These identifiers are commonly used to apply styles to an element or to select an element with JavaScript. Listing 3-21 demonstrates how to apply a style based on the value of the id attribute.

Listing 3-21. Using the id Attribute

```
<!DOCTYPE HTML>
<html>
    <head>
        <title>Example</title>
    </head>
    <style>
        #w3clink {
            background:grey;
            color:white;
            padding:5px;
            border: thin solid  black;
        }
    </style>
    <body>
        <a href="http://apress.com">Apress web site</a>
        <p/>
        <a id="w3clink" href="http://w3c.org">W3C web site</a>
    </body>
</html>
```

To apply a style based on an id attribute value, you prefix id with the # character when defining the style. I give more details about CSS selectors in Chapters 17 and 18, and I describe the various styles that can be applied in Chapters 19 through 24. You can see the effect of applying the style in Figure 3-12.

Figure 3-12. Applying a style based on an element's id attribute value

---

⬛ **Tip** The id attribute can also be used to navigate to a particular section in a document. If you imagine a document called example.html that contains an element with an id attribute value of myelement, you can navigate directly to the element by requesting example.html#myelement. This last part of the URL (the # plus the element id) is known as the *URL fragment identifier*.

The lang Attribute

The lang attribute is used to specify the language of an element's contents. Listing 3-22 demonstrates how to use this attribute.

Listing 3-22. Using the lang Attribute

```
<!DOCTYPE HTML>
<html>
    <head>
        <title>Example</title>
    </head>
    <body>
        <p lang="en">Hello - how are you?</p>
        <p lang="fr">Bonjour - comment êtes-vous?</>
        <p lang="es">Hola - ¿cómo estás?</p>
    </body>
</html>
```

The value for the lang attribute must be a valid ISO language code. You can get full details of how to specify languages at http://tools.ietf.org/html/bcp47. Be warned, though: dealing with languages can be a complex and technical business.

The lang attribute is intended to allow the browser to adjust its approach to displaying an element. This can mean changing quotation marks, for example, and also having to properly pronounce text when a text-to-speech reader (or other accessibility) tool is used.

You can also use the lang attribute to select content of a given language—perhaps to apply a style or display only content in a language the user selects.

The spellcheck Attribute

The spellcheck attribute is used to specify if the browser should check the spelling of an element's content. Using this attribute makes sense only when it is applied to an element the user can edit, as shown in Listing 3-23. I describe the textarea element in Chapter 14.

Listing 3-23. Using the spellcheck Attribute

```
<!DOCTYPE HTML>
<html>
    <head>
        <title>Example</title>
    </head>
    <body>
        <textarea spellcheck="true">This is some mispelled text</textarea>
    </body>
</html>
```

The permitted values for the spellcheck attribute are true (spellchecking is enabled) and false (spellchecking is disabled). The way that spellchecking is implemented differs between browsers. In Figure 3-13, you can see how Google Chrome handles this feature, which is a check-as-you-type approach. Other browsers require the user to explicitly perform a spellcheck.

Figure 3-13. Spellchecking as implemented by Chrome

Caution The current implementation of spellchecking in the most commonly used browsers ignores the lang element I just described. Spellchecking will be performed using the language defined by the user's operating system or by a separate browser setting.

The style Attribute

The style attribute allows you to define a CSS style directly on an element (as opposed to in a style element or external stylesheet). Listing 3-24 provides a demonstration.

Listing 3-24. Using the style Attribute

```
<!DOCTYPE HTML>
<html>
```

```
    <head>
        <title>Example</title>
    </head>
    <body>
        <a href="http://apress.com" style="background: grey; color:white; padding:10px">
            Visit the Apress site
        </a>
    </body>
</html>
```

I describe CSS styles in more detail in Chapter 5, and you can learn about the different style options available in Chapters 19 through 24.

The tabindex Attribute

The tabindex attribute allows you to control the order in which the Tab key moves the focus through the HTML page, overriding the default order. Listing 3-25 demonstrates how to use this attribute.

Listing 3-25. Using the tabindex Attribute

```
<!DOCTYPE HTML>
<html>
    <head>
        <title>Example</title>
    </head>
    <body>
        <form>
            <label>Name: <input type="text" name="name" tabindex="1"/></label>
            <p/>
            <label>City: <input type="text" name="city" tabindex="-1"/></label>
            </p>
            <label>Country: <input type="text" name="country" tabindex="2"/></label>
            </p>
            <input type="submit" tabindex="3"/>
        </form>
    </body>
</html>
```

The first element that will be selected is the one that has the tabindex value of 1. When the user presses the Tab key, the element with a tabindex of 2 will be selected, and so on. A tabindex value of -1 ensures that an element will not be selected when the user presses the Tab key. The effect of the tabindex values in the listing is that, as the Tab key is pressed, the focus shifts from the first input element to the third and then to the Submit button, as shown in Figure 3-14.

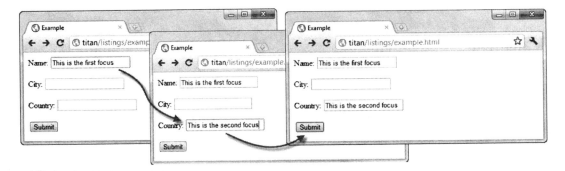

Figure 3-14. Controlling the focus sequence with the tabindex attribute

The title Attribute

The title attribute provides additional information about an element, which is commonly used by the browser to display tool tip information. Listing 3-26 shows how the title attribute is used.

Listing 3-26. Using the title Attribute

```
<!DOCTYPE HTML>
<html>
    <head>
        <title>Example</title>
    </head>
    <body>
        <a title="Apress Publishing" href="http://apress.com">Visit the Apress site</a>
    </body>
</html>
```

Figure 3-15 shows how this value is handled by Google Chrome.

Figure 3-15. A title attribute value displayed as a tool tip

Useful HTML Tools

There are only two tools that I think help when working with HTML. The first is a good HTML editor, which will highlight invalid elements and attributes and generally keep you on the right path. As I mentioned in Chapter 2, I get on well with Komodo Edit, but there are innumerable editors available and you are bound to find one that suits your working style (just be sure that it supports HTML5).

The other tool is the View Source menu (or its equivalent), which is built into most browsers. Being able to see the HTML markup behind a document is a great way to validate your own work and to learn new techniques from others.

Summary

In this chapter, I gave you a quick tour through the structure and nature of an HTML document and showed you how to apply HTML elements to mark up content and create an HTML document. I explained how you can configure the way that elements are interpreted by the browser with attributes and described the difference between local and global attributes. I described each of the global attributes and briefly explained the basic elements and structure that make up an HTML document.

CHAPTER 4

Getting Started with CSS

Cascading Style Sheets (CSS) are the means by which you specify the presentation (the appearance and the formatting) of an HTML document. In this chapter, I'll show you how to create and apply CSS styles, explain why they are called *cascading* style sheets, and provide an overall foundation for future chapters. Table 4-1 provides the summary for this chapter.

Table 4-1. Chapter Summary

Problem	Solution	Listing
Define a style.	Use a property/value declaration.	1
Apply a style directly to an element.	Use the style attribute to create an inline style.	2
Create a style that can be applied to multiple elements.	Use the style element, and specify a selector and a number of style declarations.	3, 4
Create styles that can be applied to multiple HTML documents.	Create an external stylesheet, and reference it using the link element.	5-9
Determine which style properties will be used for a given element.	Apply the cascade order to your source of styles, and calculate style specificity for tie-breaks.	10-12, 14-16
Override the normal style cascade.	Create an important style.	13
Use a style property defined by a parent.	Use property inheritance.	17, 18
Specify a property value in terms of another property.	Use a relative unit of measure.	19-23

| Calculate a property value dynamically. | Use the calc function. | 24 |

Defining and Applying a Style

A CSS style is made up of one or more declarations separated by a semi-colon. Each declaration consists of a CSS property and a value for that property separated by a colon. Listing 4-1 shows a simple style.

Listing 4-1. A Simple CSS Style

```
background-color:grey; color:white
```

Figure 4-1 shows the declarations, properties, and values in this style.

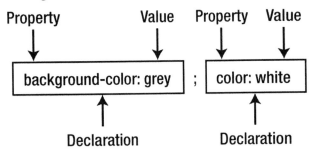

Figure 4-1. The anatomy of a CSS style

In this example, the style has two declarations. The first sets the value grey for the background-color property, and the second sets the value white for the color property.

There is a wide range of CSS properties available, and each controls some aspect of the appearance of the elements to which it is applied. In Chapters 19 through 24, I describe the available CSS properties and demonstrate their effect.

Understanding the CSS Properties Used in This Chapter

To demonstrate how CSS operates, I need to use some CSS properties that I don't describe fully until later chapters. Table 4-2 lists these properties, gives a very brief description of them, and shows you which chapter contains full details.

Table 4-2. CSS Property Summary

Property	Description	Chapter
background-color	Sets the background color of an element	19
border	Defines the border that surrounds an element	19

color	Sets the foreground color of an element	24
font-size	Sets the font size of an element's text	22
height	Sets the height of an element	20
padding	Specifies the amount of space between an element's content and its border	20
text-decoration	Sets the decoration applied to an element's text—including underlining, as used in this chapter	22
width	Sets the width of an element	20

Applying a Style Inline

It isn't enough to just define a style— you also need to apply it, effectively telling the browser which elements the style should affect. The most direct way to apply a style to an element is by using the style global attribute (described in Chapter 3), as shown in Listing 4-2.

Listing 4-2. Applying a Style Using the Style Global Attribute

```
<!DOCTYPE HTML>
<html>
    <head>
        <title>Example</title>

    </head>
    <body>
        <a href="http://apress.com" style="background-color:grey; color:white">
            Visit the Apress website
        </a>
        <p>I like <span>apples</span> and oranges.</p>
        <a href="http://w3c.org">Visit the W3C website</a>
    </body>
</html>
```

There are four content elements in this HTML document—two hyperlinks (created with the a element) and a p element that contains a span element. I used the style global attribute to apply the style to the first a element—the one that links to the Apress web site. (You can learn more about the a, p, and span elements in Chapters 8 and 9. For the moment, you are interested only in applying styles.) The style attribute acts upon only the element to which it has been applied, as you can see in Figure 4-2.

Figure 4-2. Applying a style directly to an element

The impact of the two CSS properties used in the example can be seen in the figure. The background-color property sets the color of the background of the element, and the color property sets the color of the foreground. The other two content elements in the HTML document are unaffected by the style.

THE ISSUE OF CSS RELIGION

CSS is a topic that seems to attract zealots. If you start reading any online discussion about how to achieve a certain effect with CSS, you soon see an argument about which is the *right* way. I have no time for people who make such arguments—the only right way to solve any problem is to use the knowledge and tools you have available to support as many of your users as possible. Tying yourself in knots to achieve CSS perfection is foolish. My advice is to ignore these arguments and adapt and develop the tricks and techniques that suit you and that you find pleasing and effective.

Creating an Embedded Style

Applying styles to individual elements can be a useful technique, but it is an inefficient approach when applied to a complex document that might require dozens of different styles. Not only do you have to apply the correct style to each element, but you have to be careful to correctly apply updates, which is an error-prone process. Instead, you can use the style element (as opposed to the style *attribute*) to define an *embedded* style and direct the browser to apply the style using a *CSS selector*. Listing 4-3 shows how you can use the style element with a simple CSS selector.

Listing 4-3. Using the Style Element

```
<!DOCTYPE HTML>
<html>
    <head>
        <title>Example</title>
        <style type="text/css">
            a {
                background-color:grey;
                color:white
```

```
            }
        </style>
    </head>
    <body>
        <a href="http://apress.com">Visit the Apress website</a>
        <p>I like <span>apples</span> and oranges.</p>
        <a href="http://w3c.org">Visit the W3C website</a>
    </body>
</html>
```

I describe the style element and its attributes in Chapter 7. In this chapter, we are interested in how to specify a style inside of the style element. You still use declarations, but they are wrapped in braces (the { and } characters) and follow a selector, as shown in Figure 4-3.

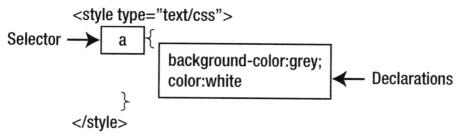

Figure 4-3. The anatomy of a style defined inside a style element

The selector in this example is a, which instructs the browser to apply the style to *every* a element in the document. You can see how the browser does this in Figure 4-4.

Figure 4-4. The effect of the a selector

You can define multiple styles in a single style element—you just repeat the process of defining a selector and a set of declarations. Listing 4-4 shows a style element that has two styles.

Listing 4-4. Defining Multiple Styles in a Single Style Element

```
<!DOCTYPE HTML>
<html>
    <head>
        <title>Example</title>
        <style type="text/css">
            a {
                background-color:grey;
                color:white
            }
            span {
                border: thin black solid;
                padding: 10px;
            }
        </style>
    </head>
    <body>
        <a href="http://apress.com">Visit the Apress website</a>
        <p>I like <span>apples</span> and oranges.</p>
        <a href="http://w3c.org">Visit the W3C website</a>
    </body>
</html>
```

This new style has a selector of span (which means the browser will apply the style to all span elements in the document and use the border and padding properties). The border property defines a border around the targeted element, and the padding property creates some space around it. You can see the effect in Figure 4-5. The selectors and the properties in these examples are very basic. I describe the full range of selectors in Chapters 17 and 18 and the properties in Chapters 19 and 20.

Figure 4-5. Applying multiple styles

Using an External Stylesheet

Rather than define the same set of styles in each of your HTML pages, you can create a separate stylesheet. This is an independent file, conventionally one that has the .css file extension, into which you put your styles. Listing 4-5 shows the contents of the file styles.css, which you can find in the source code download that accompanies this chapter and which is available from apress.com.

Listing 4-5. The styles.css File

```
a {
    background-color:grey;
    color:white
}
span {
    border: thin black solid;
    padding: 10px;
}
```

You don't need to use a style element in a stylesheet— you just use the selector, followed by the declarations for each style that you require. You can then use the link element to bring the styles into your document, as shown in Listing 4-6.

Listing 4-6. Importing an External Stylesheet

```
<!DOCTYPE HTML>
<html>
    <head>
        <title>Example</title>
        <link rel="stylesheet" type="text/css" href="styles.css"></link>
    </head>
    <body>
        <a href="http://apress.com">Visit the Apress website</a>
        <p>I like <span>apples</span> and oranges.</p>
        <a href="http://w3c.org">Visit the W3C website</a>
    </body>
</html>
```

You can link to as many stylesheets as you need—one per link element. I describe the link element fully in Chapter 7. As with the style element, the order in which you import stylesheets is important if you define two styles with the same selector. The one that is loaded last will be the one that is applied.

Importing from Another Stylesheet

You can import styles from one stylesheet into another using the @import statement. To demonstrate this feature, I created a second stylesheet called combined.css, the contents of which are shown in Listing 4-7.

Listing 4-7. The combined.css File

```
@import "styles.css";
span {
    border: medium black dashed;
    padding: 10px;
}
```

You can import as many stylesheets as you want, using one @import statement per stylesheet. The @import statements must appear at the top of the stylesheet, before any new styles are defined. In the combined.css stylesheet, I imported styles.css and then defined a new style for span elements. Listing 4-8 shows the combined.css stylesheet being linked from an HTML document.

Listing 4-8. Linking to a Stylesheet That Contains Imports

```
<!DOCTYPE HTML>
<html>
    <head>
        <title>Example</title>
        <link rel="stylesheet" type="text/css" href="combined.css"/>
    </head>
    <body>
        <a href="http://apress.com">Visit the Apress website</a>
        <p>I like <span>apples</span> and oranges.</p>
        <a href="http://w3c.org">Visit the W3C website</a>
    </body>
</html>
```

The @import statement in combined.css has the effect of importing both of the styles defined in the styles.css stylesheet and then overriding the style that will be applied to span elements. You can see the effect shown in Figure 4-6.

Figure 4-6. Importing styles from another stylesheet

The @import statement isn't widely used. This is partly because its existence isn't well known, but it is also because browser implementations have tended to deal with @import statements in such a way as to offer slower performance than using multiple link elements and relying on the way that styles cascade (which I explain in the next section).

Specifying the Character Encoding of a Stylesheet

The only thing that can come before an @import statement in a CSS stylesheet is an @charset statement, which specifies the character encoding used by the stylesheet. Listing 4-9 demonstrates how to specify the UTF-8 encoding (which is the most prevalent).

Listing 4-9. Specifying a Type of Character Encoding in a Stylesheet

```
@charset "UTF-8";
@import "styles.css";
span {
    border: medium black dashed;
    padding: 10px;
}
```

If you don't specify a type of character encoding, the browser will use the encoding specified in the HTML document that loaded the stylesheet. If there is no encoding specified for the HTML document, UTF-8 will be used by default.

Understanding How Styles Cascade and Inherit

The key to understanding stylesheets is to understand how they *cascade* and *inherit*. Cascading and inheritance are the means by which the browser determines which values should be used for properties when they display an element. Each element has a number of CSS properties that will be used when the browser needs to render the page. For each of those properties, the browser needs to navigate through all of the sources of styles it has. You have seen three different ways you can define styles (inline, embedded, and from an external stylesheet), but there are two other sources of styles that you need to know about.

Understanding Browser Styles

The *browser styles* (more properly known as the *user agent styles*) are the default styles a browser applies to an element if no other style has been specified. These styles vary slightly between browsers, but they tend to be broadly similar. As an example, consider how a browser displays an a element—a hyperlink—when there are no other styles defined in the HTML document. Listing 4-10 shows a simple HTML document that contains no styles.

Listing 4-10. An HTML Document That Contains No Styles

```
<!DOCTYPE HTML>
<html>
    <head>
        <title>Example</title>
    </head>
    <body>
        <a href="http://apress.com">Visit the Apress website</a>
        <p>I like <span>apples</span> and oranges.</p>
        <a href="http://w3c.org">Visit the W3C website</a>
    </body>
</html>
```

This listing is just a variation of the previous example, without any styles. You can see how the browser renders the a elements in Figure 4-7.

Figure 4-7. The default style for hyperlink elements

We are so accustomed to seeing the style that browsers apply to links that it becomes invisible. However, if you stop and consider what you are looking at, you can see details of the style. The text content of the link is displayed in blue and is underlined. You can extrapolate from what you see and assume the browser is applying a style similar to the one shown in Listing 4-11.

Listing 4-11. Extrapolating to Create the Default Browser Style for a Elements

```
a {
    color: blue;
    text-decoration: underline;
}
```

Browsers don't have default styles for every HTML element, but many elements are displayed using such styles. In each chapter of this book that describes HTML elements, I include the typical default style you can expect common browsers to apply. You can see the description for the a element in Chapter 8.

Understanding User Styles

Most browsers allow users to define their own stylesheets. The styles that these stylesheets contain are called *user styles*. This isn't a widely used feature, but users who define their own stylesheets often attach great importance in being able to do so—not least, because it provides a way of making pages more accessible.

Each browser has its own mechanism for user styles. Google Chrome, for example, creates a file in the user's profile directory called Default\User StyleSheets\Custom.css. Any styles added to this file are applied to *any* site the user visits, subject to the cascading rules I describe in the following section. As a simple demonstration, Listing 4-12 shows a style I added to my Custom.css file.

Listing 4-12. Adding a Style to the User Stylesheet

```
a {
    color: white;
    background:grey;
    text-decoration: none;
    padding: 2px;
}
```

This style applies to a elements and overrides the default browser style. Figure 4-8 shows the effect of my user style if I reload the HTML document in Listing 4-9.

Figure 4-8. Defining user styles

Understanding How Styles Cascade

Now that you have seen all of the sources of styles that a browser has to consider, you can look at the order in which the browser will look for a property value when it comes to display an element. The order is very specific:

1.   Inline styles (styles that are defined using the style global attribute on an element)

2.   Embedded styles (styles that are defined in a style element)

3.   External styles (styles that are imported using the link element)

4.   User styles (styles that have been defined by the user)

5.   Browser styles (the default styles applied by the browser)

Imagine that the user needs to display an a element. One of the things the browser needs to know is what color the text should be displayed in. To answer this question, it will need to find a value for the CSS color property. First, it will check to see if the element it is trying to render has an inline style that defines a value for color, like this:

```
<a style="color: red" href="http://apress.com">Visit the Apress website</a>
```

If there is no inline style, the browser will look for a style element that contains a style that applies to the element, like this:

```
<style type="text/css">
    a {
        color: red;
    }
</style>
```

If there is no such style element, the browser looks at the stylesheets that have been loaded via the link element, and so on, until the browser either finds a value for the color property—and that means using the value defined in the default browser styles if no other value is available.

The first three sources of properties (inline styles, embedded styles, and stylesheets) are collectively referred to as the *author styles*. The styles defined in the user stylesheet are known as the *user styles*, and the styles defined by the browser are known as the *browser styles*.

Tweaking the Order with Important Styles

You can override the normal cascade order by marking your property values as *important*, as shown in Listing 4-13.

Listing 4-13. Marking Style Properties as Important

```
<!DOCTYPE HTML>
<html>
    <head>
        <title>Example</title>
        <style type="text/css">
            a {
                color: black !important;
            }
        </style>
    </head>
    <body>
        <a style="color:red" href="http://apress.com">Visit the Apress website</a>
        <p>I like <span>apples</span> and oranges.</p>
        <a href="http://w3c.org">Visit the W3C website</a>
    </body>
</html>
```

You mark individual values as important by appending !important to the declaration. The browser gives preference to important styles, regardless of where they are defined. You can see the effect of property importance in Figure 4-9, where the embedded value for the color property overrides the inline value. (This may be a little hard to see on the printed page.)

Figure 4-9. Important property values overriding inline property values

▨ **Tip** The only thing that will take precedence over an important value that you define is an important value defined in the user stylesheet. For regular values, the author styles are used before the user styles, but this is reversed when dealing with important values.

Tie-Breaking with Specificity and Order Assessments

You enter a tie-break situation if there are two styles that can applied to an element defined at the same level and they both contain values for the CSS property the browser is looking for. To decide which value to use, the browser assesses the specificity of each style and selects the one that is most specific. The browser determines the specificity of a style by counting three different characteristics:

1. The number of id values in the style's selector

2. The number of other attributes and pseudo-classes in the selector

3. The number of element names and pseudo-elements in the selector

I explain how to create selectors that contain all of these different characteristics in Chapters 17 and 18. The browser combines the values from each assessment and applies the property value from the style that is most specific. You can see a very simple example of specificity in Listing 4-14.

Listing 4-14. Specificity in Styles

```
<!DOCTYPE HTML>
<html>
    <head>
        <title>Example</title>
        <style type="text/css">
            a {
                color: black;
            }
            a.myclass {
                color:white;
                background:grey;
            }
        </style>
    </head>
    <body>
        <a href="http://apress.com">Visit the Apress website</a>
        <p>I like <span>apples</span> and oranges.</p>
        <a class="myclass" href="http://w3c.org">Visit the W3C website</a>
    </body>
</html>
```

When assessing specificity, you create a number in the form a-b-c, where each letter is the total from one of the three characteristics that are counted. This is not a three-digit number—a style is more specific if its a value is the greatest. Only if the a values are equal does the browser compare b values—the style with the greater b value is more specific in this case. Only if both the a and b values are the same does the browser consider the c value. This means that a specificity score of 1-0-0 is more specific than 0-5-5.

In this case, the selector a.myclass includes a class attribute, which means that the specificity of the style is 0-1-0 (0 id values + 1 other attributes + 0 element names). The other style has a specificity of 0-0-0 (that is, it contains no id values, other attributes or element names). The browser finds a value for the color property when rendering an a element that has been assigned to the myclass class. For all other a elements, the value from the other style will be used. You can see how the browser selects and applies values for this example in Figure 4-10.

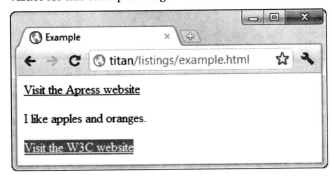

Figure 4-10. Applying values from styles based on specificity

When there are values defined in styles with the same specificity, the browser selects the value it uses based on the order in which the values are defined—the one that is defined last is the one that will be used. Listing 4-15 shows a document that contains two equally specific styles.

Listing 4-15. Styles That Are Equally Specific

```
<!DOCTYPE HTML>
<html>
    <head>
        <title>Example</title>
        <style type="text/css">
            a.myclass1 {
                color: black;
            }
            a.myclass2 {
                color:white;
                background:grey;
            }
        </style>
    </head>
    <body>
        <a href="http://apress.com">Visit the Apress website</a>
        <p>I like <span>apples</span> and oranges.</p>
        <a class="myclass1 myclass2" href="http://w3c.org">Visit the W3C website</a>
    </body>
</html>
```

Both styles defined in the style element have the same specificity score. When the browser is rendering the second a element in the page, it will select the white property for the color property because that is the value defined in the latter style. You can see this in Figure 4-11.

Figure 4-11. Selecting property values based on the order in which styles are defined

You can reverse the order of the styles to prove that this is the way the browser has selected the value for the color property, as shown in Listing 4-16.

Listing 4-16. Reversing the Order in Which Styles Are Defined

```
<!DOCTYPE HTML>
<html>
    <head>
        <title>Example</title>
        <style type="text/css">
            a.myclass2 {
                color:white;
                background:grey;
            }
            a.myclass1 {
                color: black;
            }
        </style>
    </head>
    <body>
        <a href="http://apress.com">Visit the Apress website</a>
        <p>I like <span>apples</span> and oranges.</p>
        <a class="myclass1 myclass2" href="http://w3c.org">Visit the W3C website</a>
    </body>
</html>
```

As expected, the value the browser selects for the color property is now black, as shown in Figure 4-12.

Figure 4-12. The effect of changing the order in which styles are defined

The notion of selecting a value is based on the specificity and order performed on a property-by-property basis. In the examples in this section, I defined a value for the background property as well. Because this value was not defined in both styles, there was no conflict and thus no need to look for alternative values.

Understanding Inheritance

If the browser can't find a value for a property in one of the available styles, it will use *inheritance*, which means taking the value for the property defined by the parent element. Listing 4-17 provides a demonstration.

Listing 4-17. CSS Property Inheritance

```
<!DOCTYPE HTML>
<html>
    <head>
        <title>Example</title>
        <style type="text/css">
            p {
                color:white;
                background:grey;
                border: medium solid black;
            }
        </style>
    </head>
    <body>
        <a href="http://apress.com">Visit the Apress website</a>
        <p>I like <span>apples</span> and oranges.</p>
        <a class="myclass1 myclass2" href="http://w3c.org">Visit the W3C website</a>
    </body>
</html>
```

In this example, we are interested in the properties the browser applies to the span element, whose parent is a p element. You can see how the browser renders this document in Figure 4-13.

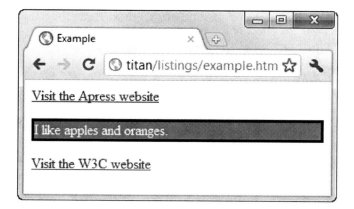

Figure 4-13. The application of inherited CSS property values

Nowhere in this document have I defined a value for the color property in a style that is applied to the span element, yet the browser has used the value white to display the text content. This value has been inherited from the parent p element.

Confusingly, not all CSS properties are inherited. As a rule of thumb, those that relate to the appearance of an element are inherited (text color, font details, and so forth) and those that relate to the layout of the element on the page are not inherited. You can force inheritance by using the special value inherit in a style, which explicitly instructs the browser to use the parent element's value for the property. Listing 4-18 shows the inherit value being used.

Listing 4-18. Using the Special Inherit Value

```
<!DOCTYPE HTML>
<html>
    <head>
        <title>Example</title>
        <style type="text/css">
            p {
                color:white;
                background:grey;
                border: medium solid black;
            }
            span {
                border: inherit;
            }
        </style>
    </head>
    <body>
        <a href="http://apress.com">Visit the Apress website</a>
        <p>I like <span>apples</span> and oranges.</p>
        <a class="myclass1 myclass2" href="http://w3c.org">Visit the W3C website</a>
    </body>
</html>
```

In this example, I created a style that will be applied to span elements and inherit whatever the parent's value for the border property is. You can see the effect of this in Figure 4-14. There is now a border around the span element and the containing p element.

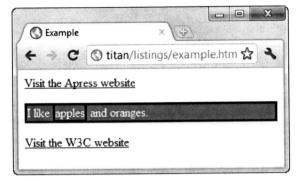

Figure 4-14. Using the inherit property

Working with CSS Colors

Colors are very important in web pages, and when using CSS you can specify colors in a range of different ways. The simplest ways are to use one of the predefined color names or to use a decimal or hexadecimal value for each of the red, green, and blue components. Decimal values are separated by a comma, and hex values are usually prefixed with #—such as #ffffff, which represents white. You can see some of the predefined names for colors and their decimal and hex equivalents in Table 4-3.

Table 4-3. Selected CSS Colors

Color Name	Hex	Decimal	Color Name	Hex	Decimal
black	#000000	0,0,0	green	#008000	0,128,0
silver	#C0C0C0	192,192,192	lime	#00FF00	0,255,0
gray	#808080	128,128,128	olive	#808000	128,128,0
white	#FFFFFF	255,255,255	yellow	#FFFF00	255,255,0
maroon	#800000	128,0,0	navy	#000080	0,0,128
red	#FF0000	255,0,0	blue	#0000FF	0,0,255
purple	#800080	128,0,128	teal	#008080	0,128,128
fushia	#FF00FF	255,0,255	aqua	#00FFFF	0,255,255

These are known as the basic color names—CSS defines the extended colors as well. There are too many color names to list here, but a complete list can be found at www.w3.org/TR/css3-color. There are a lot of new shades defined by the extended colors, including slight variations on the colors in the basic list. As an example, Table 4-4 shows the extended set of gray shades that can be used.

Table 4-4. Selected CSS Colors

Color Name	Hex	Decimal
darkgray	#a9a9a9	169,169,169
darkslategray	#2f4f4f	47,79,79
dimgray	#696969	105,105,105
gray	#808080	128,128,128
lightgray	#d3d3d3	211,211,211
lightslategray	#778899	119,136,153
slategray	#708090	112,128,144

Specifying More Complex Colors

Color names and simple hex values aren't the only way you can specify colors. There are a number of functions that allow you to select a color. Table 4-5 describes each of the functions available.

Table 4-5. CSS Color Functions

Function	Description	Example
rgb(r, g, b)	Specifies a color using the RGB model.	color: rgb(112, 128, 144)
rgba(r, g, b, a)	Specifies a color using the RGB model, with the addition of an alpha value to specify opacity. A value of 0 is fully transparent; a value of 1 is fully opaque.	color: rgba(112, 128, 144, 0.4)
hsl(h, s, l)	Specifies a color using the hue, saturation, and lightness (HSL) model.	color: hsl(120, 100%, 22%)
hsla(h, s, l, a)	The same as for HSL, but with the addition of an alpha value to specify opacity.	color: hsla(120, 100%, 22%, 0.4)

Understanding CSS Lengths

Many CSS properties require you to specify a *length*. A couple of examples are the width property, which is used to specify the width of an element, and the font-size property, which is used to specify the size of font used to render an element's content. Listing 4-19 shows a style that uses both of these properties.

Listing 4-19. Specifying Units of Measurement in Properties

```
<!DOCTYPE HTML>
<html>
    <head>
        <title>Example</title>
        <style type="text/css">
            p {
                background: grey;
                color:white;
                width: 5cm;
                font-size: 20pt;
            }
        </style>
    </head>
    <body>
        <a href="http://apress.com">Visit the Apress website</a>
        <p>I like <span>apples</span> and oranges.</p>
        <a class="myclass1 myclass2" href="http://w3c.org">Visit the W3C website</a>
    </body>
</html>
```

When you specify a length, you concatenate the number of units and the unit identifier together, without any spaces or other characters between them. In the listing, I specified the value of the width property as 5cm, which means 5 of the units represented by the cm identifier (centimeters). Equally, I specified the value of the font-size property as 20pt, which means 20 of the units represented by the pt identifier (points, which are explained in the following sections). CSS defines two kinds of length unit— those that are absolute, and those that are relative to another property. I'll explain both in the sections that follow.

Working with Absolute Lengths

In the preceding listing, I used the cm and pt units, both of which are examples of *absolute units*. These units are real-world measurements. CSS supports five types of absolute units, which are described in Table 4-6.

Table 4-6. CSS absolute units of measurement

Unit Identifier	Description
in	Inches
cm	Centimeters

mm	Millimeters
pt	Points (1 point is 1/72 of an inch)
pc	Picas (1 pica is 12 points)

You can mix and match units in a style and also mix absolute and relative units. Absolute units can be useful if you have some prior knowledge of how the content will be rendered, such as when designing for print. I don't use the absolute units that much in my CSS styles. I find the relative units more flexible and easier to maintain, and I rarely create content that has to correspond to real-world measurements.

■ **Tip** You might be wondering where pixels are in the table of absolute units. In fact, CSS tries to make pixels a relative unit of measurement—although, as I explain later in this chapter, this hasn't been how things worked out. You can learn more in the "Working with Pixels" section.

Working with Relative Lengths

Relative lengths are more complex to specify and implement than absolute units, and they require tight and concise language to define their meaning unambiguously. A relative unit is measured in terms of some other unit. Unfortunately, the language in the CSS specifications isn't precise enough (a problem that has plagued CSS for years). This means that CSS defines a wide range of interesting and useful relative measurements, but you can't use some of them because they don't have widespread or consistent browser support. Table 4-7 shows the relative units that CSS defines and that can be relied on in mainstream browsers.

Table 4-7. CSS relative units of measurement

Unit Identifier	Description
em	Relative to the font size of the element
ex	Relative to "x-height" of the element's font
rem	Relative to the font size of the root element
px	A number of CSS pixels (assumed to be on a 96dpi display)
%	A percentage of the value of another property

In the following sections, I show you how to use these units to express lengths.

Working Relative to Font Size

When you use a relative unit, you are effectively specifying a multiple of another measurement. The first units we will look at are relative to font size. Listing 4-20 gives an example.

Listing 4-20. Using a Relative Unit

```
<!DOCTYPE HTML>
<html>
    <head>
        <title>Example</title>
        <style type="text/css">
            p {
                background: grey;
                color:white;
                font-size: 15pt;
                height: 2em;
            }
        </style>
    </head>
    <body>
        <a href="http://apress.com">Visit the Apress website</a>
        <p>I like <span>apples</span> and oranges.</p>
        <p style="font-size:12pt">I also like mangos and cherries.</p>
        <a class="myclass1 myclass2" href="http://w3c.org">Visit the W3C website</a>
    </body>
</html>
```

In this example, I specified the value of the height property to be 2em, which means that p elements should be rendered so that the height of the element on the screen is twice the font size. This multiple is calculated for each element as it is displayed. I defined a default font-size of 15pt in the style element and specified an inline value of 12pt on the second p element in the document. You can see how the browser displays these elements in Figure 4-15.

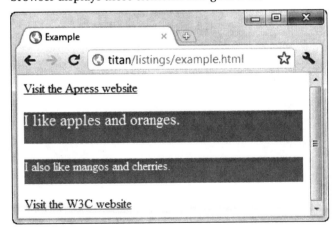

Figure 4-15. The effect of using relative measurements

You can use relative units to express a multiple of another relative measure. Listing 4-21 gives an example where the height property is expressed in em units. The em units are derived from the value of the font-size property, which I have expressed using rem units.

Listing 4-21. Using Units That Are Derived from Other Relative Values

```
<!DOCTYPE HTML>
<html>
    <head>
        <title>Example</title>
        <style type="text/css">
            html {
                font-size: 0.2in;
            }
            p {
                background: grey;
                color:white;
                font-size: 2rem;
                height: 2em;
            }
        </style>
    </head>
    <body style="font-size: 14pt">
        <a href="http://apress.com">Visit the Apress website</a>
        <p>I like <span>apples</span> and oranges.</p>
        <a class="myclass1 myclass2" href="http://w3c.org">Visit the W3C website</a>
    </body>
</html>
```

The rem unit is relative to the font size of the html element—also known as the root element. In this example, I assigned an absolute font size of 0.2 inches using a style (although I also could have created an inline style by defining the style attribute on the html element directly). The font-size value in the other style is expressed as 2rem, which means that the font size in every element that this value is applied to will be twice the size of the root element font—0.4 inches. The height property in the same style is specified as 2em, which is twice as much again. This means the browser will display p elements using a font that is 0.4 inches high and the overall element will be 0.8 inches high. You can see how the browser handles these styles in Figure 4-16.

Figure 4-16. Defining relative units in terms of other relative units

The third font-related relative unit is ex, which is the current font's *x-height*. This is the distance from the typeface baseline and the midline, but it is generally about the height of the letter x (hence the name). As a rule of thumb, 1ex is approximately 0.5em.

Working with Pixels

Pixels in CSS are not what you might expect. The usual meaning of the term *pixel* refers to the smallest addressable unit on a display—one picture element. CSS tries to do something different and defines a pixel as follows:

The reference pixel is the visual angle of one pixel on a device with a pixel density of 96dpi and a distance from the reader of an arm's length.

This is the kind of vague definition that plagues CSS. I don't want to rant, but specifications that are dependent on the length of a user's arm are problematic. Fortunately, the mainstream browsers ignore the difference between pixels as defined by CSS and pixels in the display, and they treat 1 pixel to be 1/96th of an inch. (This is the standard Windows pixel density. Browsers on platforms with displays that have a different pixel density usually implement a translation so that 1 pixel is still roughly 1/96th of an inch).

■ **Tip** Although it isn't much use, you can read the full definition of a CSS pixel at www.w3.org/TR/CSS21/syndata.html#length-units.

The net effect of this is that although CSS pixels are intended to be a relative unit of measure, they are treated as an absolute unit by browsers. Listing 4-22 demonstrates specifying pixels in a CSS style.

Listing 4-22. Using Pixel Units in a Style

```
<!DOCTYPE HTML>
<html>
    <head>
        <title>Example</title>
        <style type="text/css">
            p {
                background: grey;
                color:white;
                font-size: 20px;
                width: 200px;

            }
        </style>
    </head>
    <body>
        <a href="http://apress.com">Visit the Apress website</a>
        <p>I like <span>apples</span> and oranges.</p>
        <a class="myclass1 myclass2" href="http://w3c.org">Visit the W3C website</a>
    </body>
</html>
```

In this example, I expressed both the font-size and the width properties in pixels. You can see how the browser applies this style in Figure 4-17.

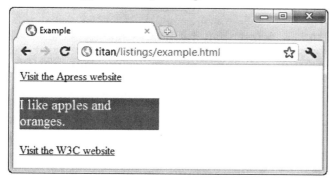

Figure 4-17. Specifying units in pixels

■ **Tip** Although I often use pixels as units in CSS, it tends to be a matter of habit. I find em units more flexible. This is because I only have to alter the size of the font when I need to make a change and the rest of the style works seamlessly. Remember that although CSS pixels were intended to be relative units, they are absolute units in practice and can become a little inflexible as a consequence.

Working with Percentages

You can express a unit of measurement as a percentage of another property value. You do this using the % (percent) unit, as demonstrated in Listing 4-23.

Listing 4-23. Expressing Units as a Percentage of Another Property Value

```
<!DOCTYPE HTML>
<html>
    <head>
        <title>Example</title>
        <style type="text/css">
            p {
                background: grey;
                color:white;
                font-size: 200%;
                width: 50%;
            }
        </style>
    </head>
    <body>
        <a href="http://apress.com">Visit the Apress website</a>
        <p>I like <span>apples</span> and oranges.</p>
        <a class="myclass1 myclass2" href="http://w3c.org">Visit the W3C website</a>
    </body>
</html>
```

There are two complications in using percentages as units. The first complication is that not all properties can be expressed in this way. The second is that each property that *can* be expressed as a percentage individually defines which *other* property the percentage refers to. For example, the font-size property uses the inherited font-size value and the width property uses the width of the containing block.

This isn't as confusing as it might seem. I'll explain what *containing block* means in Chapter 16. (It is an important and recurring concept.) I'll also tell you which CSS properties support percentage units and what the percentage is calculated from as I describe each CSS property starting in Chapter 19.

CSS Units Without Wide Support

In addition to the relative units I listed, CSS defines some units that have yet to get wide support. Table 4-8 lists these new units. These will be useful when they are implemented widely and consistently, but they should be avoided until this happens.

Table 4-8. CSS relative units of measurement without browser support

Unit Identifier	Description
gd	Relative to a grid—not widely supported because it depends on some properties that are not well defined in the CSS specifications.
vw	Relative to the viewport width—each vw is 1/100th of the width display area for the document (typically the browser window).
vh	Relative to the viewport height—each vh is 1/100th of the height of the display area.
vm	Each wm unit is 1/100th of the shortest viewport axis (either the height or the width, whichever is the smallest).
ch	Relative to the average width of a character displayed using the current typeface. This is poorly defined in the CSS specifications and is not consistently implemented.

The vw, vh, and wm units have the potential to be useful in a wide range of situations, but at present they are implemented only in Internet Explorer. Even then, my brief testing suggested that the implementation doesn't quite match the CSS specification.

CSS Unit Calculations

CSS3 defines an interesting feature that lets you calculate units. This is a flexible approach that gives you both control and precision when you create styles. Listing 4-24 provides an example.

Listing 4-24. Calculating Units

```
<!DOCTYPE HTML>
<html>
    <head>
        <title>Example</title>
        <style type="text/css">
            p {
                background: grey;
                color:white;
                font-size: 20pt;
                width: calc(80% - 20px);
            }
        </style>
    </head>
    <body>
        <a href="http://apress.com">Visit the Apress website</a>
        <p>I like <span>apples</span> and oranges.</p>
```

```
        <a class="myclass1 myclass2" href="http://w3c.org">Visit the W3C website</a>
    </body>
</html>
```

You use the calc keyword and parentheses to encompass a calculation. You can mix other units and perform basic arithmetic. Before you get too excited, I should point out that, as I write this, only Internet Explorer implements support for the calc() feature. I generally avoid describing features in this book that are not widely supported, but I am hopeful this particular feature will get traction and I believe it is worth tracking its adoption.

Other CSS Units

Lengths aren't the only CSS units. In fact, there are lots of different units, but only a small number of them are used widely. In the following sections, I describe the units we'll use in this book.

Using CSS Angles

You will need to use angles when you come to transforms in Chapter 23. You express angles as a number followed by a unit—for example, 360deg. Table 4-9 shows the set of supported angle units.

Table 4-9. CSS angle units

Unit Identifier	Description
deg	Specifies the angle in degrees (values are from 0deg to 360deg)
grad	Specifies the angle in gradians (values are from 0grad to 400grad)
rad	Specifies the angle in radians (values are from 0rad to 6.28rad)
turn	Specifies the angle in complete turns (1turn is equal to 360deg)

Using CSS Times

You can measure intervals using the CSS time used. You express times as a number of units followed by a time unit—for example, 100ms. Table 4-10 shows the supported time units.

Table 4-10. CSS time units

Unit Identifier	Description
s	Specifies time in seconds
ms	Specifies time in milliseconds (1s is equal to 1000ms)

Testing for CSS Feature Support

The fragmented nature of the CSS specification and its patchy implementation in browsers means you might find it hard to figure out which CSS features are available. I find a couple of tools are useful in determining support.

The first is the web site `http://caniuse.com`, which provides a comprehensive analysis of which versions of which browsers support HTML5 and CSS3 features. Detailed information is available on a wide range of desktop and mobile browsers on a range of operating systems. Also, there are some simple decision-support tools that are tied to browser popularity and market penetration. I find this web site very useful when starting a new project to get a feel for which features I can reasonably rely on. It makes tracking the fragmented standard process and browser implementation reasonably simple.

The second tool is `Modernizr` (`www.modernizr.com`), which tests for individual features dynamically. It takes the form of a small JavaScript library that tests for the presence of key HTML5 and CSS features, allowing you to adapt to the features that the user's browser supports. It also has some other nice features, such as enabling the styling of the new HTML5 semantic elements (described in Chapter 10) in older versions of Internet Explorer.

Useful CSS Tools

There are some tools I don't discuss in this book but that you might find useful when working with CSS. Each of the following sections describes one of these tools. All of these tools are freely available or included in mainstream browsers.

Browser Style Reporting

All mainstream browsers include style inspection as part of their developer tools. The implementations differ slightly, but the basic premise is that you can select an element from the rendered document or the document markup and see the styles the browser has applied.

These style inspectors show the order in which styles have been cascaded and the *computed style* (which is the overall style applied to the element by processing all of the cascaded and inherited styles). They even let you edit and create new styles to see their effect. You can see the Google Chrome style inspector in Figure 4-18.

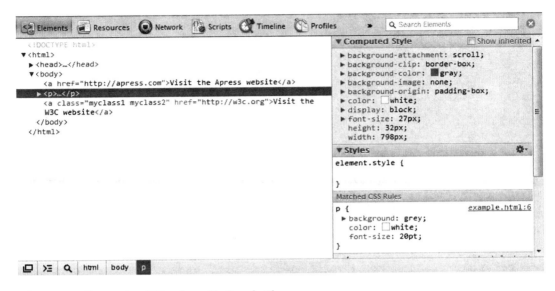

Figure 4-18. Inspecting CSS styles with Google Chrome

Creating Selectors with SelectorGadget

In Chapters 17 and 18, I explain all of the different selectors that CSS supports. There are a lot of them, and they can be combined to create powerful and flexible effects. Mastering CSS selectors takes time, and one of the most helpful tools I have found to help in this area is *SelectorGadget*, which is a JavaScript bookmarklet available at www.selectorgadget.com.

This tool hasn't been updated for a while, but it still works on modern browsers. Follow the installation instructions. When you load the script, you are able to click on elements in the browser to create CSS selectors. Figure 4-19 shows SelectorGadget at work.

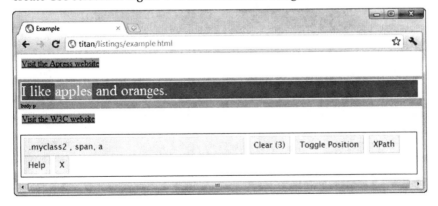

Figure 4-19. Using SelectorGadget to create CSS selectors

Enhancing CSS with LESS

When you start working with CSS, you will quickly realize that it is a verbose and repetitive way of expressing styles. There is a lot of duplication, which can make long-term maintenance of your styles time consuming and error prone.

You can extend CSS using *LESS*, which uses JavaScript to enhance CSS. It supports some nice features, such as variables, inheritance from one style to another, and functions. I have been using LESS a lot lately, and I have been pleased with the results. You can get details and download the JavaScript library at *http://lesscss.org*.

Using a CSS Framework

A number of high-quality CSS frameworks are available that you can use as the foundation for web sites and web applications. These frameworks contain sets of styles, which mean you don't have to reinvent the wheel. The better frameworks also smooth out the differences in implementation between browsers.

The CSS framework that I recommend is Blueprint, which is available for download at www.blueprintcss.org. It is simple to use and very flexible, and it has an excellent system for creating grid layouts.

Summary

In this chapter, I described how you create and apply styles, how these styles cascade, and how CSS handles units of measurements. I also mentioned some useful tools for determining and detecting support for particular CSS features in browsers and some additional resources that can be useful when working with CSS.

CHAPTER 5

Getting Started with JavaScript

JavaScript has had a hard life—a difficult birth, followed by a painful adolescence—and it is only in the last few years that JavaScript has earned a reputation for being a useful and flexible programming language. You can do a lot with JavaScript, and although it is far from perfect, it deserves to be taken seriously. In this chapter, I am going to top up your knowledge of JavaScript and, in doing so, describe the functions and features you will need later in this book.

Tip To get the best from this book, you will need some programming experience and an understanding of concepts such as variables, functions, and objects. If you are new to programming, a good starting point is a series of articles posted on the popular website lifehacker.com, where no programming knowledge is assumed and all of the examples are conveniently in JavaScript. The guide is available here: `http://lifehacker.com/5744113/learn-to-code-the-full-beginners-guide`.

My focus in this chapter is on the core JavaScript features you need for web programming. If you want to go further with JavaScript, there are a couple of books I recommend. For general language information, I like *JavaScript: The Definitive Guide* by David Flanagan, published by O'Reilly. For more advanced concepts and features, I recommend *Pro JavaScript Design Patterns* by Ross Harmes and Dustin Diaz, published by Apress. Table 5-1 provides the summary for this chapter.

Table 5-1. Chapter Summary

Problem	Solution	Listing
Define an inline script in a document.	Use the script element.	1
Execute a statement immediately.	Define a statement directly in the script element.	2
Define a JavaScript function.	Use the function keyword.	3-5
Define a primitive variable.	Use the var keyword, and express the value literally.	6-9

Create an object.	Use new `Object()` or the object literal syntax.	10-11
Add methods to an object.	Create a new property, and assign a function to it.	12
Get or set a property from an object.	Use dot or array-index style notation.	13
Enumerate the properties in an object.	Use the `for...in` statement.	14
Add a property or method to an object.	Assign a value to the property name that you require.	15, 16
Delete a property from an object.	Use the `delete` keyword.	17
Determine if an object defines a property.	Use the `in` expression.	18
Determine if two variables have the same value, regardless of type.	Use the equality operator (`==`).	19, 21
Determine if two variables have the same value and type.	Use the identity operator (`===`).	20, 22
Explicitly convert from one type to another.	Use the `Number` or `String` functions.	23-25
Create an array.	Use new `Array()` or the array literal syntax.	26, 27
Read or modify the contents of an array.	Use index notation to retrieve or assign a new value to a position in the array.	28, 29
Enumerate the contents of an array.	Use a `for` loop.	30
Handle errors.	Use a `try...catch` statement.	31, 32
Compare `null` and `undefined` values.	Coerce a value to the boolean type, or use the equality operator (`==`) to treat null and undefined as being the same and the identity operator (`===`) to treat them as different values.	33-36

Getting Ready to Use JavaScript

There are a couple of ways you can define scripts in an HTML document. You can define an *inline script*, where the content of the script is part of the HTML document. You can also define an *external script*, where the JavaScript is contained in a separate file and referenced via a URL. Both of these approaches rely on the script element, which I describe fully in Chapter 7. In this chapter, I use inline scripts for simplicity. You can see an example of this style of script in Listing 5-1.

Listing 5-1. A Simple Inline Script

```
<!DOCTYPE HTML>
<html>
    <head>
        <title>Example</title>
    </head>
    <body>
        <script type="text/javascript">
            document.writeln("Hello");
        </script>
    </body>
</html>
```

This is a trivially simple script that appends the word Hello to the document. The script element appears after the other content in the document so that the browser has parsed the other elements before the script is executed. I explain why this is important (and how to exert some control over script execution) in Chapter 7.

▪ **Tip** As I introduce JavaScript, many of the examples I show will use the document.writeln method as a simple way of showing a result from a script. This method simply appends a line of text to the HTML document. You can learn more about the document object and its writeln method in Chapter 26.

You can see how the browser renders the content and the effect of the script in Figure 5-1.

Figure 5-1. Using JavaScript to append content to an HTML document

In this chapter, I won't show screenshots, just the result from some of the examples. So, for example, for Listing 5-1, the output is as follows:

```
Hello
```

I formatted some of the results to make them easier to read. In the sections that follow, I'll show you the core features of the JavaScript language. If you have had any experience programming in any other modern language, you will find the JavaScript syntax and style familiar.

Using Statements

The basic JavaScript building block is the statement. Each statement represents a single command, and statements are usually terminated by a semicolon (;). In fact, semicolons are optional, but using them makes your code easier to read and allows for multiple statements on a single line. Listing 5-2 shows a couple of statements in a script.

Listing 5-2. Using JavaScript Statements

```html
<!DOCTYPE HTML>
<html>
    <head>
        <title>Example</title>
    </head>
    <body>
        <script type="text/javascript">
            document.writeln("This is a statement");
            document.writeln("This is also a statement");
        </script>
    </body>
</html>
```

The browser executed each statement in turn. In this example, I just write out a pair of simple messages. The results are as follows (you may see the result on a single line):

```
This is a statement

This is also a statement
```

Defining and Using Functions

If you define statements directly in the script element, as I did in Listing 5-2 earlier, the browser will execute those statements as soon as it reaches them. As an alternative, you can package up multiple statements into a *function*, which won't be executed until the browser encounters a statement that invokes the function, as shown in Listing 5-3.

Listing 5-3. Defining a JavaScript Function

```html
<!DOCTYPE HTML>
<html>
    <head>
        <title>Example</title>
    </head>
    <body>
        <script type="text/javascript">
```

```
        function myFunc() {
            document.writeln("This is a statement");
        };

        myFunc();
    </script>
    </body>
</html>
```

The statements contained by a function are encompassed by braces ({ and }) and are referred to as the *code block*. This listing defines a function called myFunc, which contains a single statement in the code block. JavaScript is a case-sensitive language, which means that the keyword function must be lowercase. The statement in the function won't be executed until the browser reaches another statement that calls the myFunc function, like this:

```
myFunc();
```

This example isn't especially useful because the function is invoked immediately after it has been defined. You can see some examples where functions are much more useful when you look at events later in the chapter.

Defining Functions with Parameters

In common with most programming languages, JavaScript allows you to define parameters for functions, as shown in Listing 5-4.

Listing 5-4. Defining Functions with Parameters

```
<!DOCTYPE HTML>
<html>
    <head>
        <title>Example</title>
    </head>
    <body>
        <script type="text/javascript">

            function myFunc(name, weather) {
                document.writeln("Hello " + name + ".");
                document.writeln("It is " + weather + " today");
            };

            myFunc("Adam", "sunny");
        </script>
    </body>
</html>
```

In this listing, I added two parameters to the myFunc function: name and weather. JavaScript is a loosely typed language, which means you don't have to declare the data type of the parameters when you define the function. I'll come back to loose-typing later in the chapter when you look at JavaScript variables. To invoke a function with parameters, you provide values as arguments when you invoke the function, like this:

```
myFunc("Adam", "sunny");
```

The results from this listing are as follows:

```
Hello Adam. It is sunny today
```

The number of arguments used when you invoke a function doesn't need to match the number of parameters in the function. If you call the function with fewer arguments than it has parameters, the value of any parameters you have not supplied values for is undefined. If you call the function with more arguments than there are parameters, the additional arguments are simply ignored. The consequence of this is that you can't create two functions with the same name and different parameters and expect JavaScript to differentiate between them based on the arguments you provide when invoking the function. If you define two functions with the same name, the second definition replaces the first.

Defining Functions That Return Results

You can return results from functions using the return keyword. Listing 5-5 shows a function that returns a result.

Listing 5-5. Returning a Result from a Function

```
<!DOCTYPE HTML>
<html>
    <head>
        <title>Example</title>
    </head>
    <body>
        <script type="text/javascript">

            function myFunc(name) {
                return ("Hello " + name + ".");
            };

            document.writeln(myFunc("Adam"));
        </script>
    </body>
</html>
```

This function defines one parameter and uses it to generate a simple result. I invoke the function and pass the result as the argument to the document.writeln function, like this:

```
document.writeln(myFunc("Adam"));
```

Notice that you don't have to declare that the function will return a result or denote the data type of the result. The result from this listing is as follows:

```
Hello Adam.
```

Using Variables and Types

You define variables using the var keyword, and you can optionally assign a value to the variable as you assign it in a single statement. Variables that are defined in a function are *local variables* and are available for use only within that function. Variables that are defined directly in the script element are *global variables* and can be accessed anywhere, including in other scripts. Listing 5-6 demonstrates the use of local and global variables.

Listing 5-6. Using Local and Global Variables

```
<!DOCTYPE HTML>
<html>
    <head>
        <title>Example</title>
    </head>
    <body>
        <script type="text/javascript">
            var myGlobalVar = "apples";

            function myFunc(name) {
                var myLocalVar = "sunny";
                return ("Hello " + name + ". Today is " + myLocalVar + ".");
            };
            document.writeln(myFunc("Adam"));
        </script>
        <script type="text/javascript">
            document.writeln("I like " + myGlobalVar);
        </script>
    </body>
</html>
```

JavaScript is a loosely typed language. This doesn't mean JavaScript doesn't have types—it just means that you don't have to explicitly declare the type of a variable and that you can assign different types to the same variable without any difficulty. JavaScript determines the type based on the value you assign to a variable and freely converts between types based on the context in which they are used. The result from Listing 5-6 is as follows:

```
Hello Adam. Today is sunny. I like apples
```

Using the Primitive Types

JavaScript defines a small set of primitive types. These are string, number, and boolean. This may seem like a short list, but JavaScript manages to fit a lot of flexibility into these three types.

Working with Strings

You define string values using either the double quote or single quote characters, as shown in Listing 5-7.

Listing 5-7. Defining String Variables

```
<!DOCTYPE HTML>
<html>
    <head>
        <title>Example</title>
    </head>
    <body>
        <script type="text/javascript">
            var firstString = "This is a string";
            var secondString = 'And so is this';
        </script>
    </body>
</html>
```

The quote characters you use must match. You can't start a string with a single quote and finish with a double quote, for example.

Working with Booleans

The boolean type has two values: true and false. Listing 5-8 shows both values being used, but this type is most useful when used in conditional statements, which I describe later in this chapter.

Listing 5-8. Defining boolean Values

```
<!DOCTYPE HTML>
<html>
    <head>
        <title>Example</title>
    </head>
    <body>
        <script type="text/javascript">
            var firstBool = true;
            var secondBool = false;
        </script>
    </body>
</html>
```

Working with Numbers

The number type is used to represent both *integer* and *floating-point* numbers (also known as *real numbers*). Listing 5-9 provides a demonstration.

Listing 5-9. Defining Number Values

```
<!DOCTYPE HTML>
<html>
    <head>
        <title>Example</title>
```

```
    </head>
    <body>
        <script type="text/javascript">
            var daysInWeek = 7;
            var pi = 3.14;
            var hexValue = 0xFFFF;
        </script>
    </body>
</html>
```

You don't have to specify which kind of number you are using—you just express the value you require, and JavaScript will act accordingly. In the listing, I defined an integer value and a floating-point value, and I prefixed a value with 0x to denote a hexadecimal value.

Creating Objects

JavaScript supports the notion of objects, and there are different ways you can create them. Listing 5-10 gives a simple example.

Listing 5-10. Creating an Object

```
<!DOCTYPE HTML>
<html>
    <head>
        <title>Example</title>
    </head>
    <body>
        <script type="text/javascript">
            var myData = new Object();
            myData.name = "Adam";
            myData.weather = "sunny";

            document.writeln("Hello " + myData.name + ". ");
            document.writeln("Today is " + myData.weather + ".");
        </script>
    </body>
</html>
```

I create an object by calling new Object(), and I assign the result (the newly created object) to a variable called myData. After the object is created, I can define properties on the object just by assigning values, like this:

```
myData.name = "Adam";
```

Prior to this statement, my object doesn't have a property called name. After the statement has executed, the property does exist and it has been assigned the value Adam. You can read the value of a property by combining the variable name and the property name with a period, like this:

```
document.writeln("Hello " + myData.name + ". ");
```

79

Using Object Literals

You can define an object and its properties in one step using the *object literal* format. Listing 5-11 shows how this is done.

Listing 5-11. Using the Object Literal Format

```
<!DOCTYPE HTML>
<html>
    <head>
        <title>Example</title>
    </head>
    <body>
        <script type="text/javascript">
            var myData = {
                name: "Adam",
                weather: "sunny"
            };

            document.writeln("Hello " + myData.name + ". ");
            document.writeln("Today is " + myData.weather + ".");
        </script>
    </body>
</html>
```

Each property you want to define is separated from its value using a colon (:), and properties are separated using a comma (,).

Using Functions as Methods

Just as you can add properties to an object, you can add functions to an object too. A function that belongs to an object is known as a *method*. This is one of the JavaScript features I like most. I don't know why, but I find this elegant and endlessly pleasing. Listing 5-12 shows how you can add methods in this manner.

Listing 5-12. Adding Methods to an Object

```
<!DOCTYPE HTML>
<html>
    <head>
        <title>Example</title>
    </head>
    <body>
        <script type="text/javascript">
            var myData = {
                name: "Adam",
                weather: "sunny",
                printMessages: function() {
                    document.writeln("Hello " + this.name + ". ");
                    document.writeln("Today is " + this.weather + ".");
                }
```

```
        };

        myData.printMessages();

    </script>
    </body>
</html>
```

In this example, I used a function to create a method called `printMessages`. Notice that to refer to the properties defined by the object, I have to use the `this` keyword. When a function is used as a method, the function is implicitly passed the object on which the method has been called as an argument through the special variable `this`. The output from the listing is as follows:

```
Hello Adam. Today is sunny.
```

> ▪ **Tip** JavaScript has a lot more to offer when it comes to creating and managing objects, but you don't need those features to work with HTML5. Take a look at the books I recommended at the start of the chapter if you want to delve deeper into the language.

Working with Objects

After you have created objects, you can do a number of things with them. In the following sections, I'll describe the activities that will be useful later in this book.

Read and Modify the Property Values

The most obvious thing to do with an object is read or modify the values assigned to the properties that the object defines. You can use two different syntax styles, both of which are shown in Listing 5-13.

Listing 5-13. Reading and Modifying Object Properties

```
<!DOCTYPE HTML>
<html>
    <head>
        <title>Example</title>
    </head>
    <body>
        <script type="text/javascript">
            var myData = {
                name: "Adam",
                weather: "sunny",
            };

            myData.name = "Joe";
```

```
        myData["weather"] = "raining";

        document.writeln("Hello " + myData.name + ".");
        document.writeln("It is " + myData["weather"]);

    </script>
    </body>
</html>
```

The first style is the one most programmers will be familiar with, and it's the one I used in earlier examples. You concatenate the object name and the property name together with a period, like this:

```
myData.name = "Joe";
```

The second style is an array-style index, which looks like this:

```
myData["weather"] = "raining";
```

In this style, you specify the name of the property you want between square braces ([and]). This can be a very convenient way to access a property because you can pass the property you are interested in using a variable, like this:

```
var myData = {
    name: "Adam",
    weather: "sunny",
};

var propName = "weather";
myData[propName] = "raining";
```

This is the basis for how you enumerate the properties of an object, which I describe next.

Enumerating an Object's Properties

You enumerate the properties an object has using the for...in statement. Listing 5-14 shows how you can use this statement.

Listing 5-14. Enumerating an Object's Properties

```
<!DOCTYPE HTML>
<html>
    <head>
        <title>Example</title>
    </head>
    <body>
        <script type="text/javascript">
            var myData = {
                name: "Adam",
                weather: "sunny",
                printMessages: function() {
                    document.writeln("Hello " + this.name + ". ");
                    document.writeln("Today is " + this.weather + ".");
                }
```

```
            };

            for (var prop in myData) {
                document.writeln("Name: " + prop + " Value: " + myData[prop]);
            }

        </script>
    </body>
</html>
```

The `for...in` loop performs the statement in the code block for each property in the `myData` object. In each iteration, the prop variable is assigned the name of the property being processed. I use an array-style index (that is, using the [and] brackets) to retrieve the value of the property from the object. The output from this listing is as follows (I formatted the results to make them easier to read):

```
Name: name Value: Adam

Name: weather Value: sunny

Name: printMessages Value: function () { document.writeln("Hello " + this.name + ". ");
document.writeln("Today is " + this.weather + "."); }
```

From the result, you can see that the function I defined as a method is also enumerated. This is as a result of the flexible way JavaScript handles functions and because methods are themselves considered to be properties of an object.

Adding and Deleting Properties and Methods

You are still able to define new properties for an object, even when you have used the object literal style. Listing 5-15 gives a demonstration.

Listing 5-15. Adding a New Property to an Object

```
<!DOCTYPE HTML>
<html>
    <head>
        <title>Example</title>
    </head>
    <body>
        <script type="text/javascript">
            var myData = {
                name: "Adam",
                weather: "sunny",
            };

            myData.dayOfWeek = "Monday";
        </script>
    </body>
</html>
```

In this listing, I added a new property to the object called dayOfWeek. – I used the dot-notation (concatenating the object and property names with a period), but I could as readily used the array-style index notation.

As you might expect by now, you can also add new methods to an object by setting the value of a property to be a function, as shown in Listing 5-16.

Listing 5-16. Adding a New Method to an Object

```
<!DOCTYPE HTML>
<html>
    <head>
        <title>Example</title>
    </head>
    <body>
        <script type="text/javascript">
            var myData = {
                name: "Adam",
                weather: "sunny",
            };

            myData.sayHello = function() {
              document.writeln("Hello");
            };

        </script>
    </body>
</html>
```

You can delete a property or method from an object using the delete keyword, as shown in Listing 5-17.

Listing 5-17. Deleting a Property from an Object

```
<!DOCTYPE HTML>
<html>
    <head>
        <title>Example</title>
    </head>
    <body>
        <script type="text/javascript">
            var myData = {
                name: "Adam",
                weather: "sunny",
            };

            myData.sayHello = function() {
              document.writeln("Hello");
            };


            delete myData.name;
            delete myData["weather"];
```

```
            delete myData.sayHello;
        </script>
    </body>
</html>
```

Determine If an Object Has a Property

You can check to see if an object has a property using the in expression, as shown in Listing 5-18.

Listing 5-18. Checking Whether an Object Has a Property

```
<!DOCTYPE HTML>
<html>
    <head>
        <title>Example</title>
    </head>
    <body>
        <script type="text/javascript">
            var myData = {
                name: "Adam",
                weather: "sunny",
            };

            var hasName = "name" in myData;
            var hasDate = "date" in myData;

            document.writeln("HasName: " + hasName);
            document.writeln("HasDate: " + hasDate);

        </script>
    </body>
</html>
```

In this example, I test for a property that exists and one that doesn't. The value of the hasName variable will be true, and the value of the hasDate property will be false.

Using JavaScript Operators

JavaScript defines a largely standard set of operators. I've summarized the most useful ones in Table 5-2.

Table 5-2. Useful JavaScript Operators

Operator	Description
++, --	Pre- or post- increment and decrement
+, -, *, /, %	Addition, subtraction, multiplication, division, remainder
<, <=, >, >=	Less than, less than or equal to, more than, more than or equal to

==, !=	Equality and inequality tests
===, !==	Identity and nonidentity tests
&&, ||	Logical AND and OR
=	Assignment
+	String concatenation
?:	Three operand conditional statement

Using the Equality and Identity Operators

The equality and identity operators are of particular note. The equality operators attempt to coerce operands to the same type in order to assess equality. This is a handy feature as long as you are aware of its actions. Listing 5-19 shows the equality operator in action.

Listing 5-19. Using the Equality Operator

```
<!DOCTYPE HTML>
<html>
    <head>
        <title>Example</title>
    </head>
    <body>
        <script type="text/javascript">

            var firstVal = 5;
            var secondVal = "5";

            if (firstVal == secondVal) {
                document.writeln("They are the same");
            } else {
                document.writeln("They are NOT the same");
            }
        </script>
    </body>
</html>
```

The output from this script is as follows:

```
They are the same
```

JavaScript is converting the two operands into the same type and comparing them—in essence, the equality operator tests that values are the same regardless of their type. If you want to test to ensure that the values *and* the types are the same, you need to use the identity operator (===, which is three equals signs rather than the two of the equality operator), as shown in Listing 5-20.

Listing 5-20. Using the Identity Operator

```
<!DOCTYPE HTML>
<html>
    <head>
        <title>Example</title>
    </head>
    <body>
        <script type="text/javascript">

            var firstVal = 5;
            var secondVal = "5";

            if (firstVal === secondVal) {
                document.writeln("They are the same");
            } else {
                document.writeln("They are NOT the same");
            }
        </script>
    </body>
</html>
```

In this example, the identity operator considers the two variables to be different—this operator doesn't coerce types. The result from this script is as follows:

```
They are NOT the same
```

▓ **Tip** Notice that I have used the `if` conditional statement in Listings 5-19 and 5-20. This statement evaluates a condition and, if the condition evaluates to `true`, executes the statements in the code block. The `if` statement can be used with an optional `else` clause, which contains a code block whose statements will be executed if the condition is `false`.

JavaScript primitives (the built-in types, such as strings and numbers) are compared by value, but JavaScript objects are compared by reference. Listing 5-21 shows how JavaScript handles equality and identity tests for objects.

Listing 5-21. Performing Equality and Identity Tests on Objects

```
<!DOCTYPE HTML>
<html>
    <head>
        <title>Example</title>
```

```
    </head>
    <body>
        <script type="text/javascript">

            var myData1 = {
                name: "Adam",
                weather: "sunny",
            };

            var myData2 = {
                name: "Adam",
                weather: "sunny",
            };

            var myData3 = myData2;

            var test1 = myData1 == myData2;
            var test2 = myData2 == myData3;
            var test3 = myData1 === myData2;
            var test4 = myData2 === myData3;

            document.writeln("Test 1: " + test1 + " Test 2: " + test2);
            document.writeln("Test 3: " + test3 + " Test 4: " + test4);
        </script>
    </body>
</html>
```

The results from this script are as follows:

```
Test 1: false Test 2: true

Test 3: false Test 4: true
```

Listing 5-22 shows the same tests performed on primitives.

Listing 5-22. Performing Equality and Identity Tests on Primitives

```
<!DOCTYPE HTML>
<html>
    <head>
        <title>Example</title>
    </head>
    <body>
        <script type="text/javascript">

            var myData1 = 5;
            var myData2 = "5";
            var myData3 = myData2;

            var test1 = myData1 == myData2;
```

```
            var test2 = myData2 == myData3;
            var test3 = myData1 === myData2;
            var test4 = myData2 === myData3;

            document.writeln("Test 1: " + test1 + " Test 2: " + test2);
            document.writeln("Test 3: " + test3 + " Test 4: " + test4);
        </script>
    </body>
</html>
```

The results from this script are as follows:

```
Test 1: true Test 2: true

Test 3: false Test 4: true
```

Explicitly Converting Types

The string concatenation operator (+) has a higher precedence than the addition operator (also +). This can cause confusion because JavaScript converts types freely to produce a result, and it isn't always the result that is expected. Listing 5-23 shows an example.

Listing 5-23. String Concatenation Operator Precedence

```
<!DOCTYPE HTML>
<html>
    <head>
        <title>Example</title>
    </head>
    <body>
        <script type="text/javascript">

            var myData1 = 5 + 5;
            var myData2 = 5 + "5";

            document.writeln("Result 1: " + myData1);
            document.writeln("Result 2: " + myData2);

        </script>
    </body>
</html>
```

The result from this script is as follows:

```
Result 1: 10

Result 2: 55
```

89

The second result is the kind that causes confusion. What might be intended to be an addition operation is interpreted as string concatenation through a combination of operator precedence and overeager type conversion. To avoid this, you can explicitly convert the types of values to ensure you perform the right kind of operation. Table 5-3 describes the most useful conversion methods.

Converting Numbers to Strings

If you are working with multiple number variables and you want to concatenate them as strings, you can convert the numbers to strings with the toString method, as shown in Listing 5-24.

Listing 5-24. Using the Number.toString Method

```
<!DOCTYPE HTML>
<html>
    <head>
        <title>Example</title>
    </head>
    <body>
        <script type="text/javascript">
            var myData1 = (5).toString() + String(5);
            document.writeln("Result: " + myData1);
        </script>
    </body>
</html>
```

Notice that I placed the numeric value in parentheses and then called the toString method. This is because you have to allow JavaScript to convert the literal value into a number before you can call the methods that the number type defines. I also showed an alternative approach to achieve the same effect as calling toString, which is to call the String function and pass in the numeric value as an argument. Both of these techniques have the same effect, which is to convert a number to a string, meaning that the + operator is used for string concatenation and not addition. The output from this script is as follows:

```
Result: 55
```

There are some other methods that allow us to exert more control over how a number is represented as a string. I briefly describe these in Table 5-3. All of the methods shown in the table are defined by the number type.

Table 5-3. Useful Number-to-String Methods

Method	Description	Returns
toString()	Represents a number in base 10	string
toString(2) toString(8) toString(16)	Represents a number in binary, octal, or hexadecimal notation	string

toFixed(n)	Represents a real number with n digits after the decimal point	string
toExponential(n)	Represents a number using exponential notation with one digit before the decimal point and n digits after	string
toPrecision(n)	Represents a number with n significant digits, using exponential notation if required	string

Converting Strings to Numbers

The opposite problem is to convert strings to numbers so that you can perform addition rather than concatenation. You can do this with the Number function, as shown in Listing 5-25.

Listing 5-25. Converting Strings to Numbers

```
<!DOCTYPE HTML>
<html>
    <head>
        <title>Example</title>
    </head>
    <body>
        <script type="text/javascript">

            var firstVal = "5";
            var secondVal = "5";

            var result = Number(firstVal) + Number(secondVal);

            document.writeln("Result: " + result);
        </script>
    </body>
</html>
```

The output from this script is as follows:

```
Result: 10
```

The Number function is quite strict in the way that it parses string values, but you can use two other functions that are more flexible and will ignore trailing non-number characters: parseInt and parseFloat. I described all three functions in Table 5-4.

Table 5-4. *Useful String-to-Number Functions*

Method	Description
Number(<str>)	Parses the specified string to create an integer or real value
parseInt(<str>)	Parses the specified string to create an integer value
parseFloat(<str>)	Parses the specified string to create an integer or real value

Working with Arrays

JavaScript arrays work pretty much like arrays in most other programming languages. Listing 5-26 shows how you can create and populate an array.

Listing 5-26. Creating and Populating an Array

```
<!DOCTYPE HTML>
<html>
    <head>
        <title>Example</title>
    </head>
    <body>
        <script type="text/javascript">

            var myArray = new Array();
            myArray[0] = 100;
            myArray[1] = "Adam";
            myArray[2] = true;

        </script>
    </body>
</html>
```

I created a new array by calling new Array(). This creates an empty array, which I assign to the variable myArray. In the subsequent statements, I assign values to various index positions in the array.

There are a couple of things to note in this example. First, I didn't need to declare the number of items in the array when I created it. JavaScript arrays resize themselves to hold any number of items. The second point to note is that I didn't have to declare the data types that the array will hold. Any JavaScript array can hold any mix of data types. In the example, I assigned three items to the array: a number, a string, and a boolean.

Using an Array Literal

The array literal style lets you create and populate an array in a single statement, as shown in Listing 5-27.

Listing 5-27. Using the Array Literal Style

```
<!DOCTYPE HTML>
<html>
    <head>
        <title>Example</title>
    </head>
    <body>
        <script type="text/javascript">

            var myArray = [100, "Adam", true];

        </script>
    </body>
</html>
```

In this example, I specified that the myArray variable should be assigned a new array by specifying the items I wanted in the array between square brackets ([and]).

Reading and Modifying the Contents of an Array

You read the value at a given index using square braces ([and]), placing the index you require between the braces, as shown in Listing 5-28. JavaScript uses zero-based array indexes.

Listing 5-28. Reading Data from an Array Index

```
<!DOCTYPE HTML>
<html>
    <head>
        <title>Example</title>
    </head>
    <body>
        <script type="text/javascript">
            var myArray = [100, "Adam", true];
            document.writeln("Index 0: " + myArray[0]);
        </script>
    </body>
</html>
```

You can modify the data held in any position in a JavaScript array simply by assigning a new value to the index. Just as with regular variables, you can switch the data type at an index without any problems. Listing 5-29 demonstrates modifying the contents of an array.

Listing 5-29. Modifying the Contents of an Array

```
<!DOCTYPE HTML>
<html>
    <head>
        <title>Example</title>
    </head>
    <body>
```

```
        <script type="text/javascript">
            var myArray = [100, "Adam", true];
            myArray[0] = "Tuesday";
            document.writeln("Index 0: " + myArray[0]);
        </script>
    </body>
</html>
```

In this example, I assigned a `string` to position 0 in the array—a position that was previously held by a `number`.

Enumerating the Contents of an Array

You enumerate the content of an array using a `for` loop. Listing 5-30 shows how to apply the loop to display the contents of a simple array.

Listing 5-30. Enumerating the Contents of an Array

```
<!DOCTYPE HTML>
<html>
    <head>
        <title>Example</title>
    </head>
    <body>
        <script type="text/javascript">
            var myArray = [100, "Adam", true];
            for (var i = 0; i < myArray.length; i++) {
                document.writeln("Index " + i + ": " + myArray[i]);
            }
        </script>
    </body>
</html>
```

The JavaScript loop works just the same way as loops in many other languages. You determine how many elements are in the array by using the `length` property. The output from the listing is as follows:

```
Index 0: 100 Index 1: Adam Index 2: true
```

Using the Built-in Array Methods

The JavaScript `Array` object defines a number of methods you can use to work with arrays. Table 5-5 describes the most useful of these methods.

Table 5-5. Useful Array Methods

Method	Description	Returns
concat(<otherArray>)	Concatenates the contents of the array with the array specified by the argument. Multiple arrays can be specified.	Array
join(<separator>)	Joins all of the elements in the array to form a string. The argument specifies the character used to delimit the items.	string
pop()	Treats an array like a stack, and removes and returns the last item in the array.	object
push(<item>)	Treats an array like a stack, and appends the specified item to the array.	void
reverse()	Reverses the order of the items in the array in place.	Array
shift()	Like pop, but operates on the first element in the array.	object
slice(<start>,<end>)	Returns a sub-array.	Array
sort()	Sorts the items in the array in place.	Array
unshift(<item>)	Like push, but inserts the new element at the start of the array.	void

Handling Errors

JavaScript uses the try...catch statement to deal with errors. For the most part, you won't be worrying about errors in this book because my focus is on explaining the features of HTML5 and not core programming skills. Listing 5-31 shows how to use this kind of statement.

Listing 5-31. Handling an Exception

```
<!DOCTYPE HTML>
<html>
    <head>
        <title>Example</title>
    </head>
    <body>
        <script type="text/javascript">
            try {
                var myArray;
                for (var i = 0; i < myArray.length; i++) {
```

95

```
                document.writeln("Index " + i + ": " + myArray[i]);
            }
        } catch (e) {
            document.writeln("Error: " + e);
        }
    </script>
    </body>
</html>
```

The problem in this script is a common one—I am trying to use a variable that has not been initialized properly. I wrapped the code that I suspect will cause an error in the try clause of the statement. If no problems arise, the statements execute normally and the catch clause is ignored.

However, if there is an error, execution of the statements in the try clause stops immediately and control passes to the catch clause. The error you encountered is described by an Error object, which is passed to the catch clause. Table 5-6 shows the properties defined by the Error object.

Table 5-6. The Error Object

Property	Description	Returns
message	A description of the error condition.	string
name	The name of the error. This is Error, by default.	string
number	The error number, if any, for this kind of error.	number

The catch clause is your opportunity to recover from the error or clean up after it. If there are statements that need to be executed whether or not there has been an error, you can place them in the optional finally clause, as shown in Listing 5-32.

Listing 5-32. Using a finally Clause

```
<!DOCTYPE HTML>
<html>
    <head>
        <title>Example</title>
    </head>
    <body>
        <script type="text/javascript">
            try {
                var myArray;
                for (var i = 0; i < myArray.length; i++) {
                    document.writeln("Index " + i + ": " + myArray[i]);
                }
            } catch (e) {
                document.writeln("Error: " + e);
            } finally {
                document.writeln("Statements here are always executed");
            }
        </script>
    </body>
```

```
</html>
```

Comparing the undefined and null Values

There are a couple of special values JavaScript defines that you need to be careful with when you compare them: undefined and null. The undefined value is returned when you read a variable that hasn't had a value assigned to it or try to read an object property that doesn't exist. Listing 5-33 shows how undefined is used in JavaScript.

Listing 5-33. The Undefined Special Value

```
<!DOCTYPE HTML>
<html>
    <head>
        <title>Example</title>
    </head>
    <body>
        <script type="text/javascript">
            var myData = {
                name: "Adam",
                weather: "sunny",
            };
            document.writeln("Prop: " + myData.doesntexist);
        </script>
    </body>
</html>
```

The output from this listing is as follows:

```
Prop: undefined
```

JavaScript is odd in that it also defines null—another special value. The null value is slightly different from undefined. The undefined value is returned when no value is defined, and null is used when you want to indicate you have assigned a value but that value is not a valid object, string, number, or boolean (that is, you have defined a value of *no value*). To help clarify this, Listing 5-34 shows the transition from undefined to null.

Listing 5-34. Using undefined and null

```
<!DOCTYPE HTML>
<html>
    <head>
        <title>Example</title>
    </head>
    <body>
        <script type="text/javascript">

            var myData = {
                name: "Adam",
```

```
            };

            document.writeln("Var: " + myData.weather);
            document.writeln("Prop: " + ("weather" in myData));

            myData.weather = "sunny";
            document.writeln("Var: " + myData.weather);
            document.writeln("Prop: " + ("weather" in myData));

            myData.weather = null;
            document.writeln("Var: " + myData.weather);
            document.writeln("Prop: " + ("weather" in myData));

        </script>
    </body>
</html>
```

I create an object and then try to read the value of the weather property, which is not defined in the early part of the code fragment:

```
document.writeln("Var: " + myData.weather);
document.writeln("Prop: " + ("weather" in myData));
```

There is no weather property yet, so the value returned by calling myData.weather is undefined and using the in keyword to determine if the object contains the property returns false. The output from these two statements is as follows:

```
Var: undefined

Prop: false
```

I then assign a value to the weather property, which has the effect of adding the property to the object:

```
myData.weather = "sunny";
document.writeln("Var: " + myData.weather);
document.writeln("Prop: " + ("weather" in myData));
```

I read the value of the property and check to see if the property exists in the object again. As you might expect, you learn that the object *does* define the property and that its value is sunny:

```
Var: sunny

Prop: true
```

Now I set the value of the property to null, like this:

```
myData.weather = null;
```

This has a very specific effect—the property is still defined by the object, but I indicated it doesn't contain a value. When I perform my checks again, I get the following results:

```
Var: null

Prop: true
```

Checking Whether a Variable or Property Is null or undefined

If you want to check whether a property is null or undefined (and you don't care which), you can simply use an if statement and the negation operator (!), as shown in Listing 5-35.

Listing 5-35. Checking Whether a Property Is null or undefined

```
<!DOCTYPE HTML>
<html>
    <head>
        <title>Example</title>
    </head>
    <body>
        <script type="text/javascript">

            var myData = {
                name: "Adam",
                city: null
            };

            if (!myData.name) {
                document.writeln("name IS null or undefined");
            } else {
                document.writeln("name is NOT null or undefined");
            }

            if (!myData.city) {
                document.writeln("city IS null or undefined");
            } else {
                document.writeln("city is NOT null or undefined");
            }

        </script>
    </body>
</html>
```

This technique relies on the type coercion that JavaScript performs such that the values you are checking are treated as boolean values. If a variable or property is null or undefined, the coerced boolean value is false.

Differentiating Between null and undefined

If you want to compare two values, you have a choice. If you want to treat an undefined value as being the same as a null value, you can use the equality operator (==) and rely on JavaScript converting the types—an undefined variable will be regarded as being equal to a null variable, for example. If you want to differentiate between null and undefined, you need to use the identity operator (===). Both comparisons are shown in Listing 5-36.

Listing 5-36. Equality and Identity Comparisons for null and undefined Values

```
<!DOCTYPE HTML>
<html>
    <head>
        <title>Example</title>
    </head>
    <body>
        <script type="text/javascript">

            var firstVal = null;
            var secondVal;

            var equality = firstVal == secondVal;
            var identity = firstVal === secondVal;

            document.writeln("Equality: " + equality);
            document.writeln("Identity: " + identity);

        </script>
    </body>
</html>
```

The output from this script is as follows:

```
Equality: true

Identity: false
```

Useful JavaScript Tools

There are a lot of tools available to help make working with JavaScript simpler. There are two that I think are particularly worthy of note.

Using a JavaScript Debugger

The current generation of browsers includes sophisticated JavaScript debuggers (or supports them through plug-ins like Firebug for Mozilla Firefox). These can be used to set breakpoints, detect errors, and step through a script as it is executing. When you get into difficulty with a script, the debugger is the first place to turn to. My preferred browser is Google Chrome, and I get on well with the built-in debugger. However, when I have a particularly intractable problem, I find myself using Firebug on Firefox. The Firebug debugger seems more robust when dealing with complex issues.

Using a JavaScript Library

One of the easiest ways of using JavaScript is through a JavaScript toolkit or library. There is no shortage of such toolkits, but there are two that I recommend in particular. The first one, and the one I have the most experience with, is jQuery. jQuery and its companion jQuery UI are immensely popular, actively developed, and packed with useful features. jQuery makes working with JavaScript simpler and more pleasurable than it would otherwise be.

The other toolkit—and the main competitor to jQuery—is Dojo. Dojo has very similar functionality to jQuery and is equally well supported and widely used. I have had less experience with Dojo than jQuery, but my time spent with Dojo has been positive. You can download jQuery at `jquery.com` and Dojo is available at `http://dojotoolkit.org`. At the risk of being seen as shilling for my own books, if you want more detail about jQuery, consider reading *Pro jQuery*, which is also published by Apress.

Summary

In this chapter, I showed you the core JavaScript features you will use throughout this book. JavaScript is an integral part of HTML5, and a basic understanding of the language and its use is essential.

PART II

The HTML Elements

Now that you are set up and your knowledge of the basics is refreshed, you can begin to look at HTML5. In this part of the book, I'll introduce you to the HTML elements, including those that are new or changed in HTML5.

CHAPTER 6

HTML Elements in Context

In the chapters that follow, I describe the elements defined by HTML5. Many of these are elements that also existed in HTML4, but in many cases the meaning of the element has changed or the way in which the element can be used is different. Before we look at the elements, I want to put them in context and set the foundation for what follows. Knowing how to use the elements is as important as understanding their significance.

Understanding the Sematic/Presentation Divide

One of the major changes in HTML5 is a philosophical one—the separation between the semantic significance of an element and the effect an element has on the presentation of content. In principle, this is a sensible idea—you use HTML elements to give structure and meaning to your content and then control the presentation of that content by applying CSS styles to the elements. Not every consumer of HTML documents needs to display them, and by keeping presentation as a separate endeavor you make HTML easier to process and draw meaning from automatically.

Most of the new elements that have been added to HTML5 add a specific meaning to your content. You can use the `article` element (described in Chapter 10) to denote a self-contained piece of content suitable for syndication or the `figure` element to denote, well, a figure.

A large number of elements that existed in HTML4 originated when there was no notion of separating presentation from meaning—and that puts us in an odd situation. A great example is the b element. Until HTML5, the b element instructed the browser to show the content contained by the start and end tags as bold text. In HTML5, you don't want elements to be just presentational, so you have a new definition. Here it is:

> *The b element represents a span of text offset from its surrounding content without conveying any extra emphasis or importance, and for which the conventional typographic presentation is bold text; for example, keywords in a document abstract, or product names in a review.*
>
> – HTML: The Markup Language, w3c.org

This is a long-winded way of telling us that the b element tells the browser to make text bold. There is no semantic significance to the b element; it is all about presentation. And this weasel-worded definition tells us something important about HTML5: we are in a period of transition. We need to preserve the old elements because they are so widely used, and dumping the HTML4 elements in HTML5 is unthinkable because it would certainly slow adoption. So we have a two-speed standard. Some of the elements, especially the new ones, have only sematic significance. Other elements, largely those with one letter tags, are so well established that we are willing to bend the presentation/semantic divide, even if we are not willing to admit this as openly as we might.

As you read through the descriptions of elements, starting in the next chapter, you will find it helpful to keep this tension between the new way of thinking and the old way in mind. It will certainly help explain some of the minor oddities you will encounter.

My advice is to err on the side of semantics and, where sensible, try to avoid elements that are largely (or solely) presentational. It is a simple matter to define a custom class and apply the required style. As long as you use the style based on the type of content (and not just the way you want the content to appear), you will preserve at least the semantic spirit.

Understanding How to Select Elements

Even if you leave the presentation issues aside, the HTML5 specification has some ambiguities. Some of the elements are very generic, and you might find this off-putting at first.

The elements *are* generic, but that's because HTML elements are used to mark up so many different kinds of content. Most of my writing is for books like this, so when I hear terms like *section, article, heading,* and *figure,* I think of the structure and styles that Apress requires from authors. The same terms have different meanings when applied to other kinds of content. A specification, legal contract, and blog post might all have sections, for example, but the meaning of that term for each is radically different. Rather than having a definition for a book section, a specification section, a contract section, and a blog section, we just have the general term and some degree of interpretation is required. There are some basic rules that I recommend you follow when selecting elements to apply to your content. They are described in the following sections.

Less Can Be More

It is very easy to get carried away and end up with a lot of markup in a document. You just need to add the markup to give the semantic significance your content demands. If you don't need to define complex titles, you don't need the hgroup element (described in Chapter 10), and detailed citations with the cite element (Chapter 8) are required only in documents where citations are important (such as journal articles).

Judging how much markup to apply is a matter of experience, but here is a rule of thumb: ask yourself how the semantics of an element are going to be used. I don't apply the element if I don't have an immediate answer.

Don't Abuse Elements

Each element denotes a particular kind of content, even those tricky presentation-only elements like b. When marking up content, use the elements only for their defined purpose and avoid creating private semantics. If you can't find an element that has the significance you require, consider using one of the generic elements (such as span or div) and using the class global attribute to denote the meaning in your document. Classes don't have to be used just for CSS styles.

Be Specific and Consistent

You need to pick the most specific element to represent your content. This means resisting the temptation to construct your page using generic elements when there are elements that denote the appropriate type of content. There has been a tendency in HTML4 to rely on div elements (described in Chapter 9) to build structure in a page, but the problem is that the semantics are not immediately apparent to anyone trying to process your content. You might decide to create a class called article and apply your styles using that class, but this doesn't impart the same meaning to others as using the article element.

Equally, when you use an element, make sure you apply it consistently throughout your page, site, or web application. This will make it easier for you to maintain your HTML markups and for others to process your HTML.

Don't Make Assumptions About the Audience

It is easy to assume that the consumers of your HTML care only about how the page is rendered in the browser and, as a consequence, you don't have to worry about the semantic accuracy of your markup. The whole point of the semantic/presentation divide is to make HTML easier to process programmatically and, as a consequence, you can expect this style of HTML consumption to gradually increase as HTML5 is more widely adopted and implemented. By assuming you don't have to worry about the accuracy or consistency of your markups, you make it harder to process your HTML, which will limit the range of purposes the user can find for your content.

Understanding Element Descriptions

As I describe each element, I provide a summary table with the key facts you need to know and which you can refer back to as you apply markup to content. Table 6-1 is an example of such a summary—it describes the ol element, which is used to denote an ordered list. (You can see full details of HTML lists in Chapter 9.)

Table 6-1. The ol Element

Element:	**ol**
Element Type:	Flow
Permitted Parents:	Any element that can contain flow elements
Local Attributes:	start, reversed, type
Contents:	Zero or more li elements
Tag Style:	Start and end tags
New in HTML5?	No

Changes in HTML5	The reversed attribute has been added in HTML5. The start and type attributes, which were deprecated in HTML4, have been restored in HTML5, but with sematic (rather than presentational) significance. The compact attribute is now obsolete.

Style Convention	`ol { display: block; list-style-type: decimal;`
	`      margin-before: 1em; margin-after: 1em;`
	`      margin-start: 0; margin-end: 0;`
	`      padding-start: 40px; }`

The tables in this chapter tell you which parents are suitable for the element, the kind of content an element can contain, the style of tag that is required, the default presentation style, and whether the element is new or changed in HTML5. The information about suitable parents and content is based on the element categories I described in Chapter 3—principally *flow* and *phrasing* elements.

Element Quick Reference

The following tables are a quick reference for all of the HTML5 elements that I describe in the following chapters.

The Document and Metadata Elements

Table 6-2 summarizes the document and metadata elements, which are described in detail in Chapter 7. These elements are used to create the superstructure of an HTML document, to provide information to the browser about the document, and to define scripts and CSS styles and content that will be displayed if scripts are disabled in the browser.

Table 6-2. *The Document/Metadata Elements*

Element	Description	Type	New/Changed
base	Sets the base for relative URLs	Metadata	Unchanged
body	Denotes content in an HTML document	N/A	Changed
DOCTYPE	Denotes the start of an HTML document	N/A	Changed
head	Contains document metadata	N/A	None
html	Indicates the start of HTML in a document	N/A	Changed
link	Defines a relationship with an external resource, usually a stylesheet or a favicon	Metadata	Changed

meta	Provides information about the document	Metadata	Changed
noscript	Contains content that will be displayed when scripting is disabled or unavailable in the browser	Metadata/Phrasing	Unchanged
script	Defines a script block, either inline or in an external file	Metadata/Phrasing	Changed
style	Defines a CSS style	Metadata	Changed
title	Sets the title for the document	Metadata	No

The Text Elements

The text elements are applied to content to give basic structure and meaning. Table 6-3 summarizes these elements, which are described fully in Chapter 8.

Table 6-3. *The Text Elements*

Element	Description	Type	New/Changed
a	Creates a hyperlink	Phrasing/Flow	Changed
abbr	Denotes an abbreviation	Phrasing	Unchanged
b	Offsets a span of text without additional emphasis or importance	Phrasing	Changed
br	Denotes a line break	Phrasing	Unchanged
cite	Denotes the title of another work	Phrasing	Changed
code	Denotes a fragment of computer code	Phrasing	Unchanged
del	Denote text that has been removed from the document	Phrasing/Flow	New
dfn	Denotes the definition of a term	Phrasing	Unchanged
em	Denotes a span of text with emphatic stress	Phrasing	Unchanged
i	Denotes a span of text that is of a different nature than the surrounding content, such as a word from another language	Phrasing	Changed

ins	Denotes text that has been added to the document	Phrasing/Flow	New
kbd	Denotes user input	Phrasing	Unchanged
mark	Denotes content that is highlighted because of its relevance in another context	Phrasing	New
q	Denotes content quoted from another source	Phrasing	Unchanged
rp	Denotes parameters for use with the ruby element	Phrasing	New
rt	Denotes a notation for use with the ruby element	Phrasing	New
ruby	Denotes a notation to be placed above or to the right of characters in a logographic language	Phrasing	New
s	Denotes text that is no longer accurate	Phrasing	Changed
samp	Denotes output from a computer program	Phrasing	Unchanged
small	Denotes fine print	Phrasing	Changed
span	A generic element that does not have semantic meaning of its own. Use this element to apply global attributes without imparting additional semantic significance.	Phrasing	Unchanged
strong	Denotes text that is important	Phrasing	Unchanged
sub	Denotes subscript text	Phrasing	Unchanged
sup	Denotes superscript text	Phrasing	Unchanged
time	Denotes a time or date	Phrasing	New
u	Offsets a span of text without additional emphasis or importance	Phrasing	Changed
var	Denotes a variable from a program or computer system	Phrasing	Unchanged
wbr	Denotes a place where a line break can be safely placed	Phrasing	New

Grouping Content

The elements in Table 6-4 are used to associate related content in groups. The full details of these elements can be found in Chapter 9.

Table 6-4. The Grouping Elements

Element	Description	Type	New/Changed
blockquote	Denotes a block of content quoted from another source	Flow	Unchanged
dd	Denotes a definition within a dl element	N/A	Unchanged
div	A generic element that doesn't have any pre-defined semantic significance. This is the flow equivalent of the span element.	Flow	Unchanged
dl	Denotes a description list that contains a series of terms and definitions	Flow	Unchanged
dt	Denotes a term within a dl element	N/A	Unchanged
figcaption	Denotes a caption for a figure element	N/A	New
figure	Denotes a figure	Flow	New
hr	Denotes a paragraph-level thematic break	Flow	Changed
li	Denotes an item in a ul, ol, or menu element	N/A	Changed
ol	Denotes an ordered list of items	Flow	Changed
p	Denotes a paragraph	Flow	Changed
pre	Denotes content whose formatting should be preserved	Flow	Unchanged
ul	Denotes an unordered list of items	Flow	Changed

Sectioning Content

The elements in Table 6-5 are used to break down the content so that each concept, idea, or topic is isolated. Many of these elements are new, and they provide a lot of the foundation for separating the meaning of elements from their appearance. You can learn more about these elements in Chapter 10.

Table 6-5. The Section Elements

Element	Description	Type	New/Changed
address	Denotes contact information for a document or article	Flow	New
article	Denotes an independent block of content	Flow	New
aside	Denotes content that is tangentially related to the surrounding content	Flow	New
details	Creates a section the user can expand to get additional details	Flow	New
footer	Denotes a footer region	Flow	New
h1-h6	Denotes a heading	Flow	Unchanged
header	Denotes a heading region	Flow	New
hgroup	Hides all but the first of a set of headings from the document outline	Flow	New
nav	Denotes a significant concentration of navigation elements	Flow	New
section	Denotes a significant concept or topics	Flow	New
summary	Denotes a title or description for the content in an enclosing details element	N/A	New

Creating Tables

The elements in Table 6-6 are used to create tables to show data in a grid. The main change in HTML5 is that you can no longer use tables to manage the layout of pages. Instead, you must use the CSS table features, which I described in Chapter 21.

Table 6-6. The Table Elements

Element	Description	Type	New/Changed
caption	Adds a caption to a table	N/A	Changed
col	Denotes a single column	N/A	Changed

colgroup	Denotes a group of columns	N/A	Changed
table	Denotes a table	Flow	Changed
tbody	Denotes the body of a table	N/A	Changed
td	Denotes an individual table cell	N/A	Changed
tfoot	Denotes a footer for a table	N/A	Changed
th	Denotes an individual header cell	N/A	Changed
thead	Denotes a header for a table	N/A	Changed
tr	Denotes a row of table cells	N/A	Changed

Creating Forms

The elements in Table 6-7 are used to create HTML forms you can use to solicit input from the user. This area of HTML has received a lot of attention in HTML5, and it has many new elements and features, including the ability to validate input on the client before the user is able to submit the form. I describe the HTML form elements in Chapters 12, 13, and 14. Of particular interest are the new types of input element, which I introduce in Chapter 12 and cover in depth in Chapter 13.

Table 6-7. The Form Elements

Element	Description	Type	New/Changed
button	Denotes a button that will submit or reset the form (or that can be used as a generic button)	Phrasing	Changed
datalist	Defines a set of suggested values for the user	Flow	Changed
fieldset	Denotes a group of form elements	Flow	Changed
form	Denotes an HTML form	Flow	Changed
input	Denotes a control to gather data from the user	Phrasing	Changed
keygen	Generates a public/private key pair	Phrasing	New
label	Denotes a label for a form element	Phrasing	Changed
legend	Denotes a descriptive label for a fieldset element	N/A	Unchanged

optgroup	Denotes a group of related option elements	N/A	Unchanged
option	Denotes an option to be presented to the user	N/A	Unchanged
output	Denotes the result of a calculation	Phrasing	New
select	Presents the user with a fixed set of options	Phrasing	Changed
textarea	Allows the user to enter multiple lines of text	Phrasing	Changed

Embedding Content

The elements in Table 6-8 are used to embed content into an HTML document. Some of these elements are described in Chapter 15, and others are covered in later parts of this book.

Table 6-8. The Embedding Elements

Element	Description	Type	New/Changed
area	Denotes an area for a client-side image map	Phrasing	Changed
audio	Denotes an audio resource	N/A	New
canvas	Provides a dynamic graphics canvas	Phrasing/Flow	New
embed	Embeds content in an HTML document using a plugin	Phrasing	New
iframe	Embeds one document in another by creating a browsing context	Phrasing	Changed
img	Embeds an image	Phrasing	Changed
map	Denotes the definition of a client-side image map	Phrasing/Flow	Changed
meter	Embeds a representation of a numeric value displayed within the range of possible values	Phrasing	New
object	Embeds content in an HTML document, and can also be used to create browsing contexts and to create client-side image maps	Phrasing/Flow	Changed
param	Denotes a parameter that will be passed to a plugin through the object element	N/A	Unchanged

progress	Embeds a representation of progress toward a goal or completion of a task	Phrasing	New
source	Denotes a media resource	N/A	New
svg	Denotes structured vector content	N/A	New
track	Denotes a supplementary media track, such as a subtitle	N/A	New
video	Denotes a video resource	N/A	New

Unimplemented Elements

There are two elements that no browser currently implements and that are only vaguely described in the HTML5 specifications. These elements are command and menu. At a high level, they are intended to make working with menus and user-interface elements simpler, but I am unable to present any detailed information in this book. I hope that subsequent versions of browsers will start to form a de facto consensus as to the meaning of these elements.

Summary

In this chapter, I provided some context for the detailed descriptions of the HTML5 elements that appear in the chapters that follow. I also provided a quick reference so that you can find the description of an element when you need to refresh your memory in the future. As you start to learn about the elements and attributes in HTML, you should remember the core advice I offered at the start of the chapter: use the most specific element possible, don't misuse elements, and use elements consistently within your documents and across your web site or web application.

CHAPTER 7

Creating HTML Documents

In this chapter, you are going to look at the most fundamental elements defined by HTML5: the *document* and *metadata elements*. These are the elements that you use to create an HTML document and to describe its contents.

These are the least interesting elements that HTML defines, and yet they are critically important. By all means, feel free to skip over this chapter and come back later—but please do come back. Every HTML document uses at least some of these elements (and often all of them) and knowing how to use them properly is essential to creating standards-compliant HTML5 documents. Table 7-1 provides the summary for this chapter.

Table 7-1. *Chapter Summary*

Problem	Solution	Listing
Denote that a document contains HTML5.	Use the doctype element.	7-1
Denote the start of the HTML markup in a document.	Use the html element.	7-2
Denote the start of the metadata section of an HTML document.	Use the head element.	7-3
Denote the start of the content section of an HTML document.	Use the body element.	7-4
Specify the title of an HTML document.	Use the title element.	7-5
Define the URL against which relative URLs contained in the HTML document will be resolved.	Use the base element.	7-6
Add descriptions of the data contained in an HTML document.	Use the meta element.	7-7
Specify the character encoding of an HTML	Use the meta element with the charset	7-8

document.	attribute.	
Specify a default stylesheet for an HTML document or refresh the content of a page periodically.	Use the meta element with the http-equiv attribute.	7-9
Define inline styles.	Use the style element.	7-10 through 7-12
Load an external resource, including a stylesheet or a favicon.	Use the link element.	7-13 through 7-15
Preemptively load a resource that is expected to be needed soon.	Use the link element with the rel attribute value prefetch.	7-16
Define a script inline.	Use the script element.	7-17
Load an external script file.	Use the script element with the src attribute.	7-18 and 7-19
Control when and how a script is executed.	Use the script element with the async or defer attributes.	7-20 through 7-24
Display content when JavaScript isn't supported or is disabled.	Use the noscript element.	7-25 and 7-26

Setting Up the Basic Document Structure

Let's begin with the *document elements*. These are the building blocks that define the shape of your HTML document and set the initial context for the browser. There are only four document elements, but they are always required in any HTML document.

The doctype Element

The doctype element is unique and in a category of its own. You are required to begin every HTML document that you create with a doctype element; this is the element that tells the browser that it will be dealing with HTML. Most browsers will still display your content correctly if you omit the doctype element, but it is bad practice to rely on browsers to behave in this way. Table 7-2 summarizes the doctype element.

Table 7-2. The doctype Element

Element	doctype
Element Type	N/A

Permitted Parents	None
Local Attributes	None
Contents	None
Tag Style	Single open tag
New in HTML5	No
Changes in HTML5	The DTD that was required in HTML4 is obsolete in HTML5
Style Convention	None

There is only one way to use the doctype element in HTML5, and that is shown in Listing 7-1. As you work through this chapter, you'll apply each element to create a simple, but complete, HTML5 document. Listing 7-1 shows the first line.

Listing 7-1. Using the doctype Element

```
<!DOCTYPE HTML>
```

This element tells the browser two things: it is dealing with HTML, and which version of the HTML specification the content has been annotated with. You don't have to supply a version number. The browser will automatically detect that you are using HTML5 (this is because this element has a slightly different form in HTML5 than in earlier HTML versions). There is no end tag for this element. You simply put a single tag at the start of the document.

The html Element

The html element, which is more properly called the *root element*, indicates the start of the HTML inside of your document. Table 7-3 summarizes the html element.

Table 7-3. The html Element

Element	html
Element Type	N/A
Permitted Parents	None
Local Attributes	manifest—see Chapter 40 for details
Contents	One head and one body element

Tag Style	Start and end tag enclosing other elements
New in HTML5	No
Changes in HTML5	The manifest attribute has been added in HTML5; the HTML4 version attribute is now obsolete
Style Convention	`html { display: block; }` `html:focus { outline: none;}`

The html element indicates the start of the HTML markup in the document. Listing 7-2 shows the html element in use.

Listing 7-2. Using the html Element

```
<!DOCTYPE HTML>
<html>
    ...content and elements omitted...
</html>
```

The head Element

The head element contains the metadata for the document. In HTML, metadata provides the browser with information about the content and markup in the document, but can also include scripts and references to external resources (such as CSS stylesheets). You will see the metadata elements later in this chapter. Table 7-4 summarizes the head element.

Table 7-4. *The head Element*

Element	head
Element Type	N/A
Permitted Parents	html
Local Attributes	None
Contents	One title element is required; other metadata elements are optional
Tag Style	Start and end tag enclosing other elements
New in HTML5	No
Changes in HTML5	None

Style Convention	None

Listing 7-3 shows the head element in use. Every HTML document should contain a head element and it, in turn, must contain a `title` element, as shown in the listing. The full details of the `title` element are shown later in this chapter.

Listing 7-3. Using the head Element

```
<!DOCTYPE HTML>
<html>
    <head>
        <title>Hello</title>
    </head>
</html>
```

The body Element

The body element encapsulates the content of an HTML document, as opposed to the head element, which encapsulates metadata and document information. The body element always follows the head element so that it is the second child of the `html` element. Table 7-5 describes the body element.

Table 7-5. The body Element

Element	body
Element Type	N/A
Permitted Parents	html
Local Attributes	None
Contents	All phrasing and flow elements
Tag Style	Start and end tag required
New in HTML5	No
Changes in HTML5	The alink, background, bgcolor, link, margintop, marginbottom, marginleft, marginrightm, marginwidth, text, and vlink attributes are obsolete; the effect that these attributes had can be achieved with CSS
Style Convention	body { display: block; margin: 8px; }
	body:focus { outline: none; }

121

Listing 7-4 shows the body element in use.

Listing 7-4. Using the body Element

```
<!DOCTYPE HTML>
<html>
    <head>
        <title>Example</title>
    </head>
    <body>
        <p>
            I like <code id="applecode">apples</code> and oranges.
        </p>
        <a href="http://apress.com">Visit Apress.com</a>
    </body>
</html>
```

I have added some simple content to the body element. The individual elements that I used (p, code, and a) are described in Chapters 8 and 9. You have reached the point where you have a simple, but complete, HTML document. You can see how the browser displays this document in Figure 7-1.

Figure 7-1. Displaying a simple HTML document in the browser

Describing Documents with the Metadata Elements

The metadata elements let you provide information about the HTML document. They are not content themselves, but they provide information about the content that follows. Metadata elements are added to the head element.

Setting the Document Title

The title element sets the document's title or name. Browsers usually display the contents of this element at the top of the browser window or tab. Table 7-6 describes the title element.

Table 7-6. The title Element

Element	`title`
Element Type	Metadata
Permitted Parents	`head`
Local Attributes	None
Contents	The title of the document or a meaningful description of its contents
Tag Style	Start and end tag enclosing text
New in HTML5	No
Changes in HTML5	None
Style Convention	`title { display: none; }`

Every HTML document should have exactly one `title` element, and the text enclosed by the start and end tags should be meaningful to the user. At the very least, it should allow the user to differentiate between browser tabs or windows and recognize which of them belong to your web application. Listing 7-5 shows the head element in use.

Listing 7-5. Using the head Element

```
<!DOCTYPE HTML>
<html>
    <head>
        <title>Example</title>
    </head>
    <body>
        <p>
            I like <code id="applecode">apples</code> and oranges.
        </p>
        <a href="http://apress.com">Visit Apress.com</a>
    </body>
</html>
```

You can see the way that a browser handles the head element in Figure 7-2. The figure shows Google Chrome, but other browsers do something broadly similar.

Figure 7-2. The effect of using the title element

Setting the Base for Relative URLs

The base element sets a base URL against which relative links, contained in the HTML document, will be resolved. A relative link is one that omits the protocol, host, and port parts of the URL and is evaluated against some other URL—either one specified by the base element or the URL used to load the current document. The base element also specifies how links are opened when a user clicks them, and how the browser acts after a form has been submitted (I explain HTML5 forms in Chapter 12). Table 7-7 summarizes the base element.

Table 7-7. The base Element

Element	base
Element Type	Metadata
Permitted Parents	head
Local Attributes	href, target
Contents	None
Tag Style	Void
New in HTML5	No
Changes in HTML5	None
Style Convention	None

An HTML document should contain, at most, one base element. It is typically one of the first elements you place inside of the head element. This ensures that the base URL is applied to the relative URLs used in subsequent metadata elements.

Using the href Attribute

The href attribute specifies the base URL against which relative URLs in the rest of the document will be resolved. Listing 7-6 shows the base element in use.

Listing 7-6. Using the href Attribute in the base Element

```
<!DOCTYPE HTML>
<html>
    <head>
        <title>Example</title>
        <base href="http://titan/listings/"/>
    </head>
    <body>
        <p>
            I like <code id="applecode">apples</code> and oranges.
        </p>
        <a href="http://apress.com">Visit Apress.com</a>
        <a href="page2.html">Page 2</a>
    </body>
</html>
```

In this example, I have set the base URL to http://titan/listings/. Titan is the name of my development server, and listings is the directory on the server that contains the examples for this book.

Later in the document, I have added an a element to create a hyperlink using the relative URL page2.html (I explain how to use the a element in Chapter 8). When the user clicks the hyperlink, the browser combines the base URL and the relative URL to create the combined URL http://titan/listings/page2.html.

▪ **Tip** If you do not use the base element, or specify a base URL using the href attribute, then the browser will assume that it should resolve any relative links against the URL of the current document. So, for example, if you load a document from the URL http://myserver.com/app/mypage.html and it contains a hyperlink with a relative URL of myotherpage.html, then the browser will attempt to load the second page from the fully qualified URL http://myserver.com/app/myotherpage.html.

Using the target Attribute

The target attribute tells the browser how to open URLs. The values you specify for this attribute represent a *browsing context.* You'll see some examples of these contexts and how to use them in Chapters 8 and 15, when you look at the a and iframe elements.

Using Metadata to Describe the Document

The meta element allows you to define different kinds of metadata in your document. You can use this element in a number of different ways, and an HTML document can contain multiple meta elements. Table 7-8 provides the summary for the meta element.

Table 7-8. The meta Element

Element	`meta`
Element Type	Metadata
Permitted Parents	**head**
Local Attributes	`name, content, charset, http-equiv`
Contents	None
Tag Style	Void
New in HTML5	No
Changes in HTML5	The charset attribute is new in HTML5. In HTML4, the `http-equiv` attribute could have any number of different values. In HTML5, this has been changed so that only the values I describe in this table are permitted. The HTML4 scheme attribute is now obsolete. You no longer specify the language for the page using a `meta` element (I'll show you how to do this in HTML5 later in this chapter).
Style Convention	None

In the sections that follow, I'll show you the different ways that you can use the meta element. Note that each instance of the meta element can be used for only one of these purposes. If you want to take advantage of more than one of these features, you must add multiple meta elements to the head element.

Specifying Name/Value Metadata Pairs

The first use for the meta element is to define metadata in name/value pairs, for which you use the name and content attributes. Listing 7-7 provides a demonstration.

Listing 7-7. Using the meta Element to Define Metadata in Name/Value Pairs

```
<!DOCTYPE HTML>
<html>
    <head>
        <title>Example</title>
        <base href="http://titan/listings/"/>
        <meta name="author" content="Adam Freeman"/>
        <meta name="description" content="A simple example"/>
```

```
    </head>
    <body>
        <p>
            I like <code id="applecode">apples</code> and oranges.
        </p>
        <a href="http://apress.com">Visit Apress.com</a>
        <a href="page2.html">Page 2</a>
    </body>
</html>
```

You use the name attribute to specify which type of metadata the element refers to, and the content attribute to provide a value. Table 7-9 lists the predefined metadata types that you can use with the meta element.

Table 7-9. The Predefined Metadata Types for Use with the meta Element

Metadata Name	Description
application name	The name of the web application that the current page is part of
author	The name of the author of the current page
description	A description of the current page
generator	The name of the software that generated the HTML (this is usually used when using some kind of server framework to generate HTML pages, such as Ruby on Rails, ASP.NET, etc.)
keywords	A set of comma-separated strings that describe the content of the page

In addition to the five predefined metadata names, you can also use metadata extensions. Go to http://wiki.whatwg.org/wiki/MetaExtensions to see a list of these extensions, which change over time. Some of the extensions are widely used, while others are fairly specialized and hardly used at all. The robots metadata type is an example of an extension that is very widely used. It allows the author of an HTML document to specify how the document should be treated by search engines. For example:

```
<meta name="robots" content="noindex">
```

The three values that most search engines will recognize are noindex (don't index this page), noarchive (don't create archives or cached versions of this page), and nofollow (don't follow links from this page). There are many more metadata extensions available, and I recommend you read through the online list to see what is suitable for your project.

■ **Tip** In the past, the keywords metadata was the main way to tell a search engine how it should categorize and rank your content. These days, search engines pay far less attention to the keywords metadata because it can be abused to give a false impression of the relevance and contents of a page. The best way to improve the way that search engines consider your content is to take the advice of the search engines themselves—most of them provide guidance for optimizing your pages or entire site. You can find Google's guide at http://google.com/support/webmasters/bin/topic.py?topic=15260.

Declaring a Character Encoding

Another use for the meta element is to declare the character encoding that the HTML document content uses. An example of this is shown in Listing 7-8.

Listing 7-8. Using the meta Element to Declare a Character Encoding

```
<!DOCTYPE HTML>
<html>
    <head>
        <title>Example</title>
        <base href="http://titan/listings/"/>
        <meta name="author" content="Adam Freeman"/>
        <meta name="description" content="A simple example"/>
        <meta charset="utf-8"/>
    </head>
    <body>
        <p>
            I like <code id="applecode">apples</code> and oranges.
        </p>
        <a href="http://apress.com">Visit Apress.com</a>
        <a href="page2.html">Page 2</a>
    </body>
</html>
```

In this case, I have specified that my page uses the UTF-8 encoding. UTF-8 is a common character encoding because it can represent all of the Unicode characters in the smallest number of bytes. (As I write this, around 50 percent of all web pages use UTF-8 encoding.)

Simulate an HTTP Header

The final use for the meta element is to override the value of one of the HTTP (Hypertext Transfer Protocol) headers. HTTP is what you usually use to transport HTML data between the server and the browser. I am not going to describe HTTP any further, other than to say that each response from the server contains a series of headers that describe the content to the browser, and that you can use the meta element to simulate or replace three of those headers. Listing 7-9 shows the general form of this use of the meta element.

Listing 7-9. Using the meta Element to Simulate an HTTP Header

```
<!DOCTYPE HTML>
<html>
    <head>
```

```
        <title>Example</title>
        <base href="http://titan/listings/"/>
        <meta name="author" content="Adam Freeman"/>
        <meta name="description" content="A simple example"/>
        <meta charset="utf-8"/>
        <meta http-equiv="refresh" content="5"/>
    </head>
    <body>
        <p>
            I like <code id="applecode">apples</code> and oranges.
        </p>
        <a href="http://apress.com">Visit Apress.com</a>
        <a href="page2.html">Page 2</a>
    </body>
</html>
```

You use the http-equiv attribute to specify which header you want to simulate, and the content attribute to provide the value you want to use. In this case, I have specified the refresh header and a value of 5, which has the effect of asking the browser to reload the page every five seconds.

■ **Tip** If you follow the refresh interval with a semicolon and a URL, the browser will load the specified URL after the interval has passed. See the section "The noscript Element" for an example.

There are three permitted values for the http-equiv attribute, which I describe in Table 7-10.

Table 7-10. Permitted Values for the http-equiv Attribute in the meta Element

Attribute Value	Description
refresh	This specifies a period, in seconds, after which the current page should reload from the server. You can also specify a different URL to be loaded. For example: `<meta http-equiv="refresh" content="5; http://www.apress.com"/>`
default-style	This specifies the preferred stylesheet that should be used with this page. The value of the content attribute must match the title attribute on a script or link element in the same document.
content-type	This is an alternative way of specifying the character encoding of the HTML page. For example: `<meta http-equiv="content-type" content="text/html charset=UTF-8"/>`

Defining CSS Styles

The style element lets you define CSS styles inline in your HTML document (as opposed to the link element, which lets you import styles from an external stylesheet). Table 7-11 summarizes the style element.

Table 7-11. The style Element

Element	style
Element Type	N/A
Permitted Parents	Any element that can contain metadata plus, head, div, noscript, section, article, aside
Local Attributes	type, media, scoped
Contents	CSS styles
Tag Style	Start and end tag enclosing text
New in HTML5	No
Changes in HTML5	The scoped attribute has been added in HTML5
Style Convention	None

Listing 7-10 gives an example of the style element in use.

Listing 7-10. Using the style Element

```
<!DOCTYPE HTML>
<html>
    <head>
        <title>Example</title>
        <base href="http://titan/listings/"/>
        <meta name="author" content="Adam Freeman"/>
        <meta name="description" content="A simple example"/>
        <meta charset="utf-8"/>
        <style type="text/css">
            a {
                background-color: grey;
                color: white;
                padding: 0.5em;
            }
        </style>
    </head>
    <body>
```

```
    <p>
        I like <code id="applecode">apples</code> and oranges.
    </p>
    <a href="http://apress.com">Visit Apress.com</a>
    <a href="page2.html">Page 2</a>
</body>
</html>
```

In this example, I have created a new style for the a element. It displays the link with a grey background, white text, and some padding. (If you are new to CSS, you can get a quick primer in Chapter 4, and full coverage begins in Chapter 16.) You can see the effect of this style in Figure 7-3.

Figure 7-3. Using the style element to create an inline style

You can use the `style` element throughout an HTML document, and a single document can contain multiple `style` elements. This means that you don't have to define all of your styles in the head section. This can be useful if you are generating your pages through a template engine because it means you can supplement the styles defined by the template with styles that are specific to a particular page.

Specifying the Style Type

The `type` attribute lets you tell the browser what kind of style you are going to define; however, the only style mechanism that browsers support is CSS, so the value of this attribute will always be text/css.

Specifying the Scope of the Style

If the `scoped` attribute is present in a style element, then the styles are applied to only the element's parent and the parent's child elements. Without the `scoped` attribute, a style defined anywhere in an HTML document is applied to all elements in the document.

■ **Caution** As I write this, none of the major browsers support the `scoped` attributes for styles.

Specifying the Media for a Style

The media attributes lets you specify when a style should be applied to the document. Listing 7-11 gives an example of how you can use this attribute.

Listing 7-11. Using the media Attribute of the style Element

```
<!DOCTYPE HTML>
<html>
    <head>
        <title>Example</title>
        <base href="http://titan/listings/"/>
        <meta name="author" content="Adam Freeman"/>
        <meta name="description" content="A simple example"/>
        <meta charset="utf-8"/>
        <style media="screen" type="text/css">
            a {
                background-color: grey;
                color: white;
                padding: 0.5em;
            }
        </style>
        <style media="print">
            a{
                color:Red;
                font-weight:bold;
                font-style:italic
            }
        </style>
    </head>
    <body>
        <p>
            I like <code id="applecode">apples</code> and oranges.
        </p>
        <a href="http://apress.com">Visit Apress.com</a>
        <a href="page2.html">Page 2</a>
    </body>
</html>
```

In the listing, I have defined two style elements that have different values for the media attribute. The browser will apply the first style when the HTML is displayed onscreen, and the second style when the page is printed.

You can create very specific conditions in which to use a style. First, you can specify the device that you are interested in. I have summarized the supported values in Table 7-12.

Table 7-12. The Defined Device Values for the media Attribute of the style Element

Device	Description
all	Apply this style to any device (this is the default).

aural	Apply this style to speech synthesizers.
braille	Apply this style to Braille devices.
handheld	Apply this style to handheld devices.
projection	Apply this style to projectors.
print	Apply this style in print preview and when the page is printed.
screen	Apply this style when the content is shown on a computer screen.
tty	Apply this style to fixed-width devices, such as teletypes.
tv	Apply this style to televisions.

The browser interprets which category a device falls into. Browsers handle some device types (such as screen and print) consistently, but other devices (such as the handheld device type) may get a more liberal interpretation. It is worth checking that your target browsers have the same interpretation of specific devices that you do. Using the media features allows you to be even more specific. Listing 7-12 provides an example.

Listing 7-12. Adding Specificity to a style Element

```
<!DOCTYPE HTML>
<html>
    <head>
        <title>Example</title>
        <base href="http://titan/listings/"/>
        <meta name="author" content="Adam Freeman"/>
        <meta name="description" content="A simple example"/>
        <meta charset="utf-8"/>
        <style media="screen AND (max-width:500px)" type="text/css">
            a {
                background-color: grey;
                color: white;
                padding: 0.5em;
            }
        </style>
        <style media="screen AND (min-width:500px)" type="text/css">
            a {color:Red; font-style:italic}
        </style>
    </head>
    <body>
        <p>
            I like <code id="applecode">apples</code> and oranges.
        </p>
        <a href="http://apress.com">Visit Apress.com</a>
```

```
            <a href="page2.html">Page 2</a>
        </body>
</html>
```

In this listing, I have used the width feature to differentiate between two styles. The first will be used when the browser window is narrower than 500 pixels, and the second when the window is wider than 500 pixels. If you display the HTML from Listing 7-12 in a browser, and then drag the window to change its size, you can see the effect of this feature, as shown in Figure 7-4.

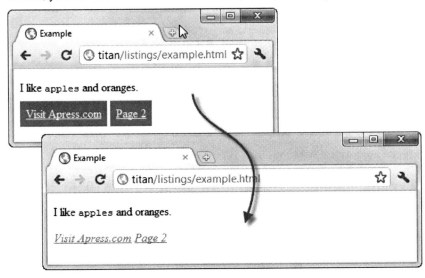

Figure 7-4. Different styles applied, based on browser window width

Notice how I have used AND to combine a device with a feature. In addition to AND, you can also use NOT, or a comma (,) to represent OR. This allows you to create complex and quite specific conditions in which to apply a style.

You usually use features such as width with the min and max modifiers to make them more flexible; although you can apply styles based on very specific window conditions by omitting them. I have listed and described the available features, along with their modifiers, in Table 7-13. Unless otherwise noted, you can modify these features with min- or max- to create thresholds rather than specific values.

Table 7-13. Features for the media Attribute of the style Element

Feature	Description	Example
width height	Specifies the width or height of the browser window. Units are expressed as px for pixels.	width:200px
device-width device-height	Specifies the width or height of the entire device (and not just the browser window). Units are expressed as px for pixels.	min-device-height:200px

resolution	Specifies the pixel density of the device. Units are dpi (dots per inch) or dpcm (dots per centimeter).	max-resolution:600dpi
orientation	Specifies the orientation of the device. The supported values are portrait and landscape. There are no modifiers for this feature.	orientation:portrait
aspect-ratio device-aspect-ratio	Specifies the pixel ratio of the browser window or the entire device. Values are expressed as the number of width pixels over the number of height pixels.	min-aspect-ratio:16/9
color monochrome	Specifies the number of bits per pixel of color or monochrome devices.	min-monochrome:2
color-index	Specifies the number of colors that the display can show.	max-color-index:256
scan	Specifies the scanning mode of a TV. The supported values are progressive and interlace. There are no modifiers for this feature.	scan:interlace
grid	Specifies the type of device. Grid devices use fixed grids to display content; for example, character-based terminals and one-line pager displays. The supported values are 0 and 1, where 1 is a grid device. There are no modifiers for this feature.	grid:0

As with the devices, the interpretation of each of the features is left to the browser, and there can be variations in which features are recognized and when they are considered to be present and available. If you rely on the features to apply styles, you should test thoroughly and define a fall-back style that will be applied if your expected features are not available.

Denoting External Resources

The link element creates a relationship between an HTML document and an external resource, most typically a CSS stylesheet. Table 7-14 summarizes the link element.

Table 7-14. The link Element

Element	link

Element Type	Metadata
Permitted Parents	head, noscript
Local Attributes	href, rel, hreflang, media, type, sizes
Contents	None
Tag Style	Void element
New in HTML5	No
Changes in HTML5	The sizes attribute has been added; the attributes charset, rev and target are obsolete in HTML5
Style Convention	None

The link element defines six local attributes, which I summarize in Table 7-15. The most important of these attributes is rel, which defines the nature of the relationship between the HTML page and the resource that the link items relates to. I'll show you some of the most common types of relationships shortly.

Table 7-15. *Local Attributes of the link Element*

Attribute	Description
href	Specifies the URL of the resource that the link element refers to.
hreflang	Specifies the language of the linked resource.
media	Specifies the device that the linked content is intended for. This attribute uses the same device and feature values that I described in Tables 7-10 and 7-11.
rel	Specifies the kind of relationship between the document and the linked resource.
sizes	Specifies the size of icons. I show you an example of using the link element to load a favicon later in the chapter.
type	Specifies the MIME type of the linked resource, such as text/css or image/x-icon.

The value assigned to the rel attribute determines how the browser deals with the link element. Table 7-16 shows some of the more common values for the rel attribute and describes each of them. There are additional rel values defined, but this is still a volatile area of HTML5. You can find the most complete definition of rel values at http://iana.org/assignments/link-relations/link-relations.xml.

Table 7-16. Selected Values for the rel Attribute of the link Element

Value	Description
alternate	Links to an alternative version of the document, such as a translation to another language.
author	Links to the author of the document.
help	Links to help related to the current document.
icon	Specifies an icon resource. See Listing 7-14 for an example.
license	Links to a license associated with the current document.
pingback	Specifies a pingback server, which allows a blog to be notified automatically when other web sites link to it.
prefetch	Preemptively fetches a resource. See Listing 7-15 for an example.
sylesheet	Loads an external CSS stylesheet. See Listing 7-13 for an example.

Loading a Stylesheet

To demonstrate the link element in this way, I have created a stylesheet called styles.css, the contents of which are shown in Listing 7-13.

Listing 7-13. The styles.css File

```
a {
    background-color: grey;
    color: white;
    padding: 0.5em;
}
```

This is the CSS style previously applied using a style element, but placed into an external stylesheet. To take advantage of this stylesheet, use the link element, as shown in Listing 7-14.

Listing 7-14. Using the link Element for an External Stylesheet

```
<!DOCTYPE HTML>
<html>
    <head>
        <title>Example</title>
        <base href="http://titan/listings/"/>
        <meta name="author" content="Adam Freeman"/>
        <meta name="description" content="A simple example"/>
```

```
        <meta charset="utf-8"/>
        <link rel="stylesheet" type="text/css" href="styles.css"/>
    </head>
    <body>
        <p>
            I like <code id="applecode">apples</code> and oranges.
        </p>
        <a href="http://apress.com">Visit Apress.com</a>
        <a href="page2.html">Page 2</a>
    </body>
</html>
```

You can use multiple link elements to load multiple external resources. The advantage of using an external stylesheet is that you can use one set of styles in multiple documents without having to duplicate the styles. The browser loads and applies the styles just as if you had set the CSS properties in a style element, as shown in Figure 7-5.

Figure 7-5. Applying styles obtained through an external stylesheet

Defining a Favicon for Your Page

After CSS stylesheets, the most common use for the link element is to define an icon that will be associated with your page. Different browsers handle the icon in different ways, but typically the icon appears on a page tab, and when the user adds your page to the favorites list. To demonstrate this, I have taken the favicon that Apress uses at www.apress.com. This is a 32-pixel by 32-pixel image file in the .ico format. Browsers universally support this format. You can see how the image appears in Figure 7-6. The image file is favicon.ico.

Figure 7-6. The Apress favicon

You can then use this favicon by adding a link element to your page, as shown in Listing 7-15.

Listing 7-15. Adding a Favicon Using a link Element

```
<!DOCTYPE HTML>
<html>
    <head>
        <title>Example</title>
        <base href="http://titan/listings/"/>
        <meta name="author" content="Adam Freeman"/>
        <meta name="description" content="A simple example"/>
        <link rel="stylesheet" type="text/css" href="styles.css"/>
        <link rel="shortcut icon" href="favicon.ico" type="image/x-icon" />
    </head>
    <body>
        <p>
            I like <code id="applecode">apples</code> and oranges.
        </p>
        <a href="http://apress.com">Visit Apress.com</a>
        <a href="page2.html">Page 2</a>
    </body>
</html>
```

When the HTML page is loaded, the browser will load and display the favicon, as shown in Figure 7-7. The figure shows Google Chrome, which displays the favicon at the top of the page tab.

Figure 7-7. The favicon displayed at the top of the browser tab

___

■ **Tip** You don't have to use the link element if the favicon is located at /favicon.ico (i.e., in the root directory of the web server). Most browsers will automatically request this file when a page is loaded, even without the link element being present.

___

Preemptively Fetching a Resource

You can ask the browser to preemptively fetch a resource that you expect to be needed soon. Listing 7-16 shows the use of the link element to specify prefetching.

Listing 7-16. Prefetching a Linked Resource

```
<!DOCTYPE HTML>
<html>
    <head>
        <title>Example</title>
        <base href="http://titan/listings/"/>
        <meta name="author" content="Adam Freeman"/>
        <meta name="description" content="A simple example"/>
        <link rel="stylesheet" type="text/css" href="styles.css"/>
        <link rel="shortcut icon" href="favicon.ico" type="image/x-icon" />
        <link rel="prefetch" href="/page2.html"/>
    </head>
    <body>
        <p>
            I like <code id="applecode">apples</code> and oranges.
        </p>
        <a href="http://apress.com">Visit Apress.com</a>
        <a href="page2.html">Page 2</a>
    </body>
</html>
```

I have set the rel attribute to prefetch and specified that an HTML page, page2.html, be loaded in the expectation that the user will click a link to perform some other action that requires this page.

▓ **Note** At the time of writing, only Firefox supports link prefetching.

Using the Scripting Elements

There are two scripting elements. The first, script, allows you to define scripts and control their execution. The second, noscript, allows you to define what happens when a browser doesn't support scripting or has it disabled.

▓ **Tip** You usually use the script element inside the head element, but you may use it anywhere in an HTML document. I recommend putting all of your script elements together in the head section of a document because it makes them easier to track and because that's where most people expect to find script definitions.

The script Element

The script element lets you include scripting in your pages, either defined inline in the document or referenced to an external file. The most commonly used type of script is JavaScript—and that's the type

I'll be focusing on—but browsers do support other scripting languages, including some remnants from the browser wars that I described in Chapter 1 Table 7-17 describes the `script` element. You use one `script` element for each script that you need to define or import.

Table 7-17. The script Element

Element	`script`
Element Type	Metadata/phrasing
Permitted Parents	**Any element that can contain metadata or phrasing elements**
Local Attributes	`type`, `src`, `defer`, `async`, `charset`
Contents	Script language statements or empty if an external JavaScript library is specified
Tag Style	A start and end tag are required; self-closing tags are not permitted, even when referencing an external JavaScript library
New in HTML5	No
Changes in HTML5	The `type` attribute is optional in HTML5; the `async` and `defer` attributes have been added; the HTML4 `language` attribute is obsolete in HTML5
Style Convention	None

The type of this element varies based on where it is used. `script` elements defined within the head element are metadata, but `script` elements defined in other elements (such as `body` or `section`) are phrasing elements.

In the following sections, I'll show you how to use the `script` element to achieve different effects. Table 7-18 describes the attributes that the `script` element defines.

Table 7-18. Local Attributes of the script Element

Attribute	Description
type	Specifies the type of the script that is references or defined. This attribute can be omitted for JavaScript scripts.
src	Specifies the URL for an external script file. See the following demonstration.
defer async	Specifies how the script will be executed. See the following demonstration. These attributes can only be used in conjunction with the `src` attribute.

141

charset   Specifies the character encoding of an external script file. This attribute can only be
                           used in conjunction with the src attribute.

Defining an Inline Script

The simplest way to define a script is to do so inline. This means that you include the JavaScript
statements in the HTML page. Listing 7-17 provides a demonstration.

Listing 7-17. Defining a Script Inline

```
<!DOCTYPE HTML>
<html>
    <head>
        <title>Example</title>
        <base href="http://titan/listings/"/>
        <meta name="author" content="Adam Freeman"/>
        <meta name="description" content="A simple example"/>
        <link rel="stylesheet" type="text/css" href="styles.css"/>
        <link rel="shortcut icon" href="favicon.ico" type="image/x-icon" />
        <script>
            document.write("This is from the script");
        </script>
    </head>
    <body>
        <p>
            I like <code id="applecode">apples</code> and oranges.
        </p>
        <a href="http://apress.com">Visit Apress.com</a>
        <a href="page2.html">Page 2</a>
    </body>
</html>
```

If you don't use the type attribute, the browser will assume that you are using JavaScript. This
simple script adds some text to the HTML document. By default, scripts are executed as soon as they are
encountered in the page. You can see the effect of this in Figure 7-8 where the text from the script
appears in the browser window before the p element contained in the body.

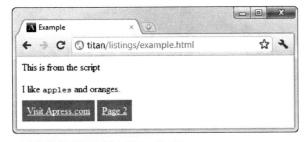

Figure 7-8. The effect of a simple script

Loading an External Scripting Library

You can separate scripts into separate files and load them using the script element. These files can be as simple (such as the demonstration that follows) or as complex (such as sophisticated libraries such as jQuery) as you like. To demonstrate an external script, I have created a file called simple.js, the contents of which are shown in Listing 7-18.

Listing 7-18. Contents of the simple.js Script File

```
document.write("This is from the external script");
```

The file contains a single statement, similar to the one that I used in the inline script. Listing 7-19 shows how you can use the src attribute in the script element to reference this file.

▪ **Tip** A script element must be empty if it uses the src attribute. You can't use the same script element to define an inline script and an external script.

Listing 7-19. Loading an External Script Using the src Attribute

```
<!DOCTYPE HTML>
<html>
    <head>
        <title>Example</title>
        <base href="http://titan/listings/"/>
        <meta name="author" content="Adam Freeman"/>
        <meta name="description" content="A simple example"/>
        <link rel="stylesheet" type="text/css" href="styles.css"/>
        <link rel="shortcut icon" href="favicon.ico" type="image/x-icon" />
        <script src="simple.js"></script>
    </head>
    <body>
        <p>
            I like <code id="applecode">apples</code> and oranges.
        </p>
        <a href="http://apress.com">Visit Apress.com</a>
        <a href="page2.html">Page 2</a>
    </body>
</html>
```

The value for the src attribute is the URL of the script file that you want to load. I created the simple.js file in the same directory as the HTML file, so I am able to use a relative URL in this example. You can see the effect of the script in Figure 7-9.

143

Figure 7-9. The effect of an external script

■ **Tip** Notice that I have included an end tag for the `script` element, even though the element has no content. If you use a self-closing tag when referencing an external script, the browsers will ignore the element and not load the file.

Deferring Execution of a Script

You can exert some control over the execution of a script by using the `async` and `defer` attributes. The `defer` attribute tells the browser not to execute the script until the page has been loaded and parsed. To understand the benefit that the `defer` attribute can offer, you need to look at the problem that it solves. Listing 7-20 shows the contents of the `simple2.js` script file, which contains a single statement.

Listing 7-20. The Statement Contained in the simple2.js Script File

```
document.getElementById("applecode").innerText = "cherries";
```

I'll break down the various parts of this statement in Part IV of this book , but for now it is enough to know that when this script runs, it will find an element with an `id` attribute value of `applecode` and change the inner text of that element to `cherries`. Listing 7-21 shows an HTML document that references the script file using a `script` element.

Listing 7-21. Referencing a Script File

```
<!DOCTYPE HTML>
<html>
    <head>
        <title>Example</title>
        <base href="http://titan/listings/"/>
        <meta name="author" content="Adam Freeman"/>
        <meta name="description" content="A simple example"/>
        <link rel="stylesheet" type="text/css" href="styles.css"/>
        <link rel="shortcut icon" href="favicon.ico" type="image/x-icon" />
        <script src="simple2.js"></script>
    </head>
```

```
<body>
    <p>
        I like <code id="applecode">apples</code> and oranges.
    </p>
    <a href="http://apress.com">Visit Apress.com</a>
    <a href="page2.html">Page 2</a>
</body>
</html>
```

When you load the preceding HTML page, you don't get the desired result, as shown in Figure 7-10.

Figure 7-10. A script timing issue

The default behavior for a browser when it encounters a `script` element is to stop processing the HTML document, load the script file, and execute its contents. It is only after the script execution completes that the browser resumes parsing the HTML. This means that the browser loads and executes the statement in `simple2.js` before it has parsed the rest of the HTML, and discovered the code element. The script doesn't find the element it is looking for, and so no changes are applied. After the script completes, the browser continues parsing the HTML, and finds the code element. However, by then it is too late for the script, which isn't executed again. One obvious way of solving this problem is to put the `script` element at the end of the document, as shown in Listing 7-22.

Listing 7-22. Solving the Script Timing Issue by Moving the script Element

```
<!DOCTYPE HTML>
<html>
    <head>
        <title>Example</title>
        <base href="http://titan/listings/"/>
        <meta name="author" content="Adam Freeman"/>
        <meta name="description" content="A simple example"/>
        <link rel="stylesheet" type="text/css" href="styles.css"/>
        <link rel="shortcut icon" href="favicon.ico" type="image/x-icon" />
    </head>
    <body>
        <p>
            I like <code id="applecode">apples</code> and oranges.
        </p>
        <a href="http://apress.com">Visit Apress.com</a>
        <a href="page2.html">Page 2</a>
        <script src="simple2.js"></script>
```

```
    </body>
</html>
```

This approach takes the way in which the browser responds to script elements into account, ensuring that the script isn't loaded and executed until the elements that the script is interested in have been parsed. As you can see in Figure 7-11, you get the result that you want from the script.

Figure 7-11. The effect of the script, applied to an a element

This approach is perfectly valid, but in HTML5 you can achieve the same effect by using the defer attribute. When a browser encounters a script element in which the defer attribute is present, it holds off loading and executing the script until all of the elements in the HTML document have been parsed. Listing 7-23 shows a script element that uses the defer element.

Listing 7-23. Using a script Element with the defer Attribute

```
<!DOCTYPE HTML>
<html>
    <head>
        <title>Example</title>
        <base href="http://titan/listings/"/>
        <meta name="author" content="Adam Freeman"/>
        <meta name="description" content="A simple example"/>
        <link rel="stylesheet" type="text/css" href="styles.css"/>
        <link rel="shortcut icon" href="favicon.ico" type="image/x-icon" />
        <script defer src="simple2.js"></script>
    </head>
    <body>
        <p>
            I like <code id="applecode">apples</code> and oranges.
        </p>
        <a href="http://apress.com">Visit Apress.com</a>
        <a href="page2.html">Page 2</a>
    </body>
</html>
```

Loading this page into the browser gives the same effect as moving the script element to the end of the page. The script is able to locate the code element and change the text contents, producing the same effect as you saw in Figure 7-11.

■ **Tip** You can use the `defer` attribute on external script files only. It doesn't work for inline scripts.

Executing a Script Asynchronously

You can solve a different problem using the `async` attribute. As I mentioned earlier, the default browser behavior when it encounters a `script` element is to stop processing the page while it loads and executes the script. Each script element is executed synchronously (i.e., nothing else happens when the script is loading and running) and in turn (i.e., in the order in which they are defined).

Synchronous and sequential execution makes sense as a default way of handling scripts, but there are some scripts for which this isn't required and you can improve performance by using the `async` attribute. A good example is a tracking script. This type of script could, for example, report which sites you visit so that advertisers could profile and target you based on your browsing habits, or it could gather visitor statistics for site analytics. Such scripts are self-contained and tend not to interact with the elements in the HTML document. Delaying the rendering of the page while you wait for this kind of script to load and then report back to its server doesn't make any sense at all.

When you use the `async` attribute, the browser loads and executes the script asynchronously while it continues to parse the other elements in the HTML, including other `script` elements. For the right kind of script, this can improve overall load performance significantly. Listing 7-24 shows the async attribute applied to a `script` element.

Listing 7-24. Using the async Element

```
<!DOCTYPE HTML>
<html>
    <head>
        <title>Example</title>
        <base href="http://titan/listings/"/>
        <meta name="author" content="Adam Freeman"/>
        <meta name="description" content="A simple example"/>
        <link rel="stylesheet" type="text/css" href="styles.css"/>
        <link rel="shortcut icon" href="favicon.ico" type="image/x-icon" />
        <script async src="simple2.js"></script>
    </head>
    <body>
        <p>
            I like <code id="applecode">apples</code> and oranges.
        </p>
        <a href="http://apress.com">Visit Apress.com</a>
        <a href="page2.html">Page 2</a>
    </body>
</html>
```

One important effect of using the `async` attribute is that the scripts in a page might not be executed in the order in which they are defined. This makes the `async` feature unsuitable for scripts that depend on functions or values defined by other scripts.

The noscript Element

The noscript element allows you to display content to users who have disabled JavaScript or who are using a browser that doesn't support it. Table 7-19 summarizes the noscript element.

Table 7-19. The noscript Element

Element	noscript
Element Type	Metadata/phrasing/flow
Permitted Parents	Any element that can contain metadata, phrasing, or flow elements
Local Attributes	None
Contents	Phrasing and flow elements
Tag Style	A start and end tag are both required
New in HTML5	No
Changes in HTML5	None
Style Convention	None

As with the script element, the type of the noscript element depends on where it is placed in the document.

Although JavaScript support is widespread these days, there are still some specialized browsers that don't support it. Even when the browser does implement JavaScript, the user could have disabled it—many large corporations enforce a no-JavaScript rule on their computer users. The noscript element lets you deal with these users by displaying content that doesn't require JavaScript to operate or, at the very least, explains that they can't use your site or page unless they enable JavaScript. Listing 7-25 shows the noscript element set up to display a simple message.

Listing 7-25. Using the noscript Element

```
<!DOCTYPE HTML>
<html>
    <head>
        <title>Example</title>
        <base href="http://titan/listings/"/>
        <meta name="author" content="Adam Freeman"/>
        <meta name="description" content="A simple example"/>
        <link rel="stylesheet" type="text/css" href="styles.css"/>
        <link rel="shortcut icon" href="favicon.ico" type="image/x-icon" />
        <script defer src="simple2.js"></script>
        <noscript>
```

```
            <h1>Javascript is required!</h1>
            <p>You cannot use this page without Javascript</p>
        </noscript>
    </head>
    <body>
        <p>
            I like <code id="applecode">apples</code> and oranges.
        </p>
        <a href="http://apress.com">Visit Apress.com</a>
        <a href="page2.html">Page 2</a>
    </body>
</html>
```

You can see the effect of the noscript element in Figure 7-12. To achieve this effect, I disabled JavaScript support in Google Chrome and loaded the HTML in the listing.

Figure 7-12. The effect of the noscript element

Notice that the remainder of the page is processed as normal, and the content elements are still displayed.

■ **Tip** You can add multiple noscript elements to a page so that they correspond to individual areas of functionality that require scripting. This approach is most useful for providing fallback markup that doesn't rely on JavaScript.

An alternative approach is to redirect the user's browser to a different URL if it doesn't support JavaScript. You do this by placing a meta element inside the noscript element, as shown in Listing 7-26.

Listing 7-26. Using the noscript Element to Redirect the User's Browser

```
<!DOCTYPE HTML>
<html>
    <head>
        <title>Example</title>
        <base href="http://titan/listings/"/>
        <meta name="author" content="Adam Freeman"/>
        <meta name="description" content="A simple example"/>
        <link rel="stylesheet" type="text/css" href="styles.css"/>
        <link rel="shortcut icon" href="favicon.ico" type="image/x-icon" />
        <script defer src="simple2.js"></script>
        <noscript>
            <meta http-equiv="refresh" content="0; http://www.apress.com"/>
        </noscript>
    </head>
    <body>
        <p>
            I like <code id="applecode">apples</code> and oranges.
        </p>
        <a href="http://apress.com">Visit Apress.com</a>
        <a href="page2.html">Page 2</a>
    </body>
</html>
```

This will redirect the user to the www.apress.com site when a browser that doesn't support JavaScript, or that has JavaScript disabled, tries to load this page.

Summary

In this chapter, I have introduced you to the document and metadata elements. These are not the most dynamic and exciting of elements defined by HTML5, but they are incredibly important. Understanding how to define the core building blocks of an HTML document is essential to getting the best result—especially when it comes to aspects such as controlling script execution with the script element and managing styles with the style and link elements.

CHAPTER 8

Marking Up Text

We are going to switch track from the big structural document elements to something much finer grained: the *text-level elements* (text elements, for brevity). When you add these elements to your text, you add structure and meaning. This will become evident as you work through the examples in this chapter.

The HTML5 specification makes it clear that you should only use elements for their semantic value. However, to make life easier, the specification also makes it clear that the traditional styling associated with these elements is part of the semantic meaning for some elements. This is a bit of a fudge, but a helpful one that maintains compatibility with older HTML versions.

Some of these elements have very specific meanings. For example, the cite element is used only to cite the title of another work, such as a book or film. However, many other elements are more ambiguous and, despite the intention of the HTML5 standard, essentially related to presentation.

My advice is to take a pragmatic approach. First, use a task-specific element if there is one available. Second, consider avoiding those elements that were formerly presentational only and that have had semantic meaning applied in retrospect—such as the b element—and manage presentation using CSS. Finally, irrespective of which elements you choose to use, use them consistently throughout your HTML. Table 8-1 provides the summary for this chapter.

Table 8-1. Chapter Summary

Problem	Solution	Listing
Create a hyperlink to another document.	Use the a element, with either an absolute or relative URL as the href attribute value.	8-1, 8-2
Create a hyperlink to an element in the same document.	Use the a element, with a CSS-style ID selector for the target element.	8-3
Denote text without imparting any additional importance or significance.	Use the b or u elements.	8-4, 8-9
Denote emphatic stress.	Use the em element.	8-5
Denote scientific or foreign-language terms.	Use the i element.	8-6

Denote inaccurate or incorrect content.	Use the s element.	8-7
Denote importance.	Use the strong element.	8-8
Denote fine print.	Use the small element.	8-10
Denote superscript or subscript.	Use the sup or sub elements.	8-11
Denote a line break or an opportunity for a line break.	Use the br or wbr elements.	8-12, 8-13
Represent computer code, the output from a program, or a variable or input from a user.	Use the code, var, samp, or kbd elements.	8-14
Denote an abbreviation.	Use the abbr element.	8-15
Denote a definition of a term.	Use the dfn element.	8-16
Denote quoted content.	Use the q element.	8-17
Cite the title of another work.	Use the cite element.	8-18
Denote ruby annotations for East-Asian languages.	Use the ruby, rt, and rp elements.	8-19
Specify the directionality for a span of content.	Use the bdo element.	8-20
Isolate a span of text for the purposes of directionality.	Use the bdi element.	8-21, 8-22
Apply a global attribute to content.	Use the span element.	8-23
Denote content that has relevance in another context.	Use the mark element.	8-24
Denote text that has been added or removed from the document.	Use the ins and del elements.	8-25
Denote a time or date.	Use the time element.	8-26

Creating Hyperlinks

Hyperlinks are a critical feature in HTML, and provide the basis by which users can navigate through content, both within the same document and across pages. You create hyperlinks using the a element, which is summarized in Table 8-2.

Table 8-2. *The a Element*

Element	a
Element Type	The a element is considered as a phrasing element when it contains phrasing content, and as a flow element when it contains flow content
Permitted Parents	Any element that can contain phrasing content
Local Attributes	href, hreflang, media, rel, target, type
Contents	Phrasing content and flow elements
Tag Style	Start and end tag required
New in HTML5	No
Changes in HTML5	This element can now contain flow as well as phrasing content. The media attribute has been added. The target attribute, which was deprecated in HTML4, has now been reinstated. In HTML5, an a element without an href value is a placeholder for a hyperlink. The id, coords, shape, urn, charset, methods, and rev attributes are obsolete.

Style Convention	`a:link, a:visited {`
	`    color: blue;`
	`    text-decoration: underline; cursor: auto;`
	`}`
	
	`a:link:active, a:visited:active {`
	`    color: blue;`
	`}`

The a element defines six local attributes, described in Table 8-3. The most important of these attributes is href, as you'll see later in this section.

Table 8-3. Local Attributes of the a Element

Attribute	Description
href	Specifies the URL of the resource that the a element refers to.
hreflang	Specifies the language of the linked resource.
media	Specifies the device that the linked content is intended for. This attribute uses the same device and feature values that I described in Chapter 7.
rel	Specifies the kind of relationship between the document and the linked resource. This attribute uses the same values as the rel attribute of the link element, as described in Chapter 7.
target	Specifies the browsing context in which the linked resource should be opened.
type	Specifies the MIME type of the linked resource, such as text/html.

Creating External Hyperlinks

You can create hyperlinks to other HTML documents by setting the href attribute to a URL that starts with http://. When the user clicks the hyperlink, the browser will load the specified page. Listing 8-1 shows the a element being used to link to external content.

Listing 8-1. Using the a Element to Link to an External Resource

```
<!DOCTYPE HTML>
<html>
    <head>
        <title>Example</title>
        <base href="http://titan/listings/"/>
        <meta name="author" content="Adam Freeman"/>
        <meta name="description" content="A simple example"/>
        <link rel="shortcut icon" href="favicon.ico" type="image/x-icon" />
    </head>
    <body>
        I like <a href="http://en.wikipedia.org/wiki/Apples">apples</a> and
        <a href="http://en.wikipedia.org/wiki/Orange_(fruit)">oranges</a>.
    </body>
</html>
```

In this example, I have created two a elements that link to Wikipedia articles. Clicking either link will cause the appropriate article to be loaded and displayed to the user. You can see the default style convention for hyperlinks in Figure 8-1.

Figure 8-1. The default appearance of hyperlinks

Not all URLs have to refer to other web pages. Although the http protocol is the most widely used form of URL, browsers also support other protocols such as https and ftp. If you want to reference an e-mail address, you can use the mailto protocol; for example, mailto:adam@mydomain.com.

■ **Tip** You can use the a element to create image-based hyperlinks (where the user clicks an image, rather than text, to follow a hyperlink). This requires the use of the img element. You can find the details of the img element and a demonstration of an image-based hyperlink in Chapter 15.

Creating Relative URLs

If the value of the href attribute doesn't start with a recognized protocol, such as http://, then the browser treats the hyperlink as a relative reference. By default, this means that the browser assumes that a target resource is available in the same location as the current document. Listing 8-2 gives an example of a relative URL.

Listing 8-2. Using a Relative URL in a Hyperlink

```
<!DOCTYPE HTML>
<html>
    <head>
        <title>Example</title>
        <base href="http://titan/listings/"/>
        <meta name="author" content="Adam Freeman"/>
        <meta name="description" content="A simple example"/>
        <link rel="shortcut icon" href="favicon.ico" type="image/x-icon" />
    </head>
    <body>
        I like <a href="http://en.wikipedia.org/wiki/Apples">apples</a> and
        <a href="http://en.wikipedia.org/wiki/Orange_(fruit)">oranges</a>.
        You can see other fruits I like <a href="fruitlist.html">here</a>.
    </body>
</html>
```

In this example, I have set the value of the href attribute to fruitlist.html. When the user clicks the link, the browser uses the URL of the current document to determine how to load the linked page. As an example, if the current document had been loaded from http://www.mydomain.com/docs/example.html, then the browser would load the target page from http://www.mydomain.com/doc.fruitlist.html.

■ **Tip** You can override this default behavior and provide an alternative base URL through the base element, which I described in Chapter 7.

Creating Internal Hyperlinks

You can create hyperlinks that bring another element into view in the browser window. You do this using the CSS-style ID selector, #<id>, as shown in Listing 8-3.

Listing 8-3. Creating an Internal Hyperlink

```
<!DOCTYPE HTML>
<html>
    <head>
        <title>Example</title>
        <meta name="author" content="Adam Freeman"/>
        <meta name="description" content="A simple example"/>
        <link rel="shortcut icon" href="favicon.ico" type="image/x-icon" />
    </head>
    <body>
        I like <a href="http://en.wikipedia.org/wiki/Apples">apples</a> and
        <a href="http://en.wikipedia.org/wiki/Orange_(fruit)">oranges</a>.
        You can see other fruits I like <a href="#fruits">here</a>.

        <p id="fruits">
            I also like bananas, mangoes, cherries, apricots, plums, peaches and grapes.
        </p>
    </body>
</html>
```

I have created a hyperlink with the href value of #fruits. When the user clicks the link, the browser will look for an element in the document whose id attribute has a value of fruits. If the element isn't already visible on the screen, the browser will scroll the document so that it is.

■ **Tip** If the browser can't find an element with the desired id attribute value, it will search again, looking for a name attribute that matches the target.

Targeting a Browsing Context

The target attribute lets you tell the browser where you want the linked resource to be displayed. By default, the browser uses the window, tab, or frame in which the current document is displayed, meaning that the new document replaces the existing one. However, you do have other choices. Table 8-4 describes the supported values for the target attribute.

Table 8-4. *Values for the target Attribute of the a Element*

Attribute	Description
_blank	Open the document in a new window (or tab).
_parent	Open the document in the parent frameset.
_self	Open the document in the current window (this is the default behavior).
_top	Open the document in the full body of the window.
<frame>	Open the document in the specified frame.

Each of these values represents a *browsing context*. The _blank and _self values are self-evident; the others relate to the use of frames, which I explain in Chapter 15.

Annotating Content with the Basic Text Elements

The first set of text elements that you will look at have been around in HTML for a while. Some of these elements represented text formatting in the past, but as HTML has evolved, the separation of presentation from broader semantics has meant that they now have more generalized significance.

Denoting Keywords and Product Names

The b element is used to offset a span of text without indicating any extra emphasis or importance. The examples given in the HTML5 specification are keywords in a document abstract and product names in a review. Table 8-5 describes the b element.

Table 8-5. *The b Element*

Element	b
Element Type	Phrasing
Permitted Parents	Any element that can contain phrasing content

Local Attributes	None
Contents	Phrasing content
Tag Style	Start and end tag required
New in HTML5	No
Changes in HTML5	The b element had only presentational meaning in HTML4; in HTML5, it has the semantic meaning described previously, and the presentation aspect has been downgraded to being the style convention
Style Convention	`b { font-weight: bolder; }`

The b element is very simple: content contained between the start and end tags is offset from the surrounding content. You would usually do this by showing the content in bold, but you can use CSS to change the style applied to b elements. Listing 8-4 shows the b element in use.

Listing 8-4. Using the b Element

```
<!DOCTYPE HTML>
<html>
    <head>
        <title>Example</title>
        <base href="http://titan/listings/"/>
        <meta name="author" content="Adam Freeman"/>
        <meta name="description" content="A simple example"/>
        <link rel="stylesheet" type="text/css" href="styles.css"/>
        <link rel="shortcut icon" href="favicon.ico" type="image/x-icon" />
    </head>
    <body>
        I like <b>apples</b> and <b>oranges</b>.
    </body>
</html>
```

You can see the default style convention for the b element in Figure 8-2.

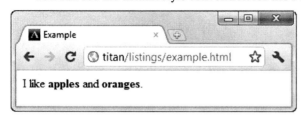

Figure 8-2. Using the b element

Adding Emphasis

The em element represents a span of text with emphatic stress. You use this to give a kind of context to the reader about the meaning of a sentence or paragraph. I'll show you what this means following Table 8-6, which describes the em element.

***Table 8-6.** The em Element*

Element	em
Element Type	Phrasing
Permitted Parents	Any element that can contain phrasing content
Local Attributes	None
Contents	Phrasing content
Tag Style	Start and end tag required
New in HTML5	No
Changes in HTML5	None
Style Convention	em { font-style: italic; }

Listing 8-5 shows the em element in use.

Listing 8-5. Using the em Element

```
<!DOCTYPE HTML>
<html>
    <head>
        <title>Example</title>
        <base href="http://titan/listings/"/>
        <meta name="author" content="Adam Freeman"/>
        <meta name="description" content="A simple example"/>
        <link rel="stylesheet" type="text/css" href="styles.css"/>
        <link rel="shortcut icon" href="favicon.ico" type="image/x-icon" />
    </head>
    <body>
        <em>I</em> like <b>apples</b> and <b>oranges</b>.
    </body>
</html>
```

The styling convention for this element is to use italics, as shown in Figure 8-3.

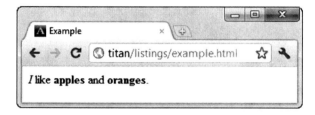

Figure 8-3. Using the em element

In this example, I have placed the emphasis on I, at the start of the sentence. When thinking about the em element, it helps to read the sentence aloud and consider a question that the sentence might be an answer to. For example, imagine that I asked, "Who likes apples and oranges?" Your answer would be, "*I* like apples and oranges." (When you read this aloud and put emphasis on *I*, you are making it clear that you are the person who likes these fruits.)

But if I asked, "You like apples and what else?" you might answer, "I like apples and *oranges*." In this case, the weight of your emphasis would be on the last word, emphasizing that oranges are the other fruit you like. You would represent this variation as follows in HTML:

```
I like apples and <em>oranges</em>.
```

Denoting Foreign or Technical Terms

The i element denotes a span of text that has a different nature from the surrounding content. This is a fairly loose definition, but common examples include words from other languages, a technical or scientific term, and even a person's thoughts (as opposed to speech). Table 8-7 describes the i element.

Table 8-7. The i Element

Element	i
Element Type	Phrasing
Permitted Parents	Any element that can contain phrasing content
Local Attributes	None
Contents	Phrasing content
Tag Style	Start and end tag required
New in HTML5	No
Changes in HTML5	The i element had only presentational meaning in HTML4; in HTML5, it has the semantic meaning described previously, and the presentation aspect has been downgraded to being the style

convention

Style Convention   i { font-style: italic; }

Listing 8-6 shows the i element in use.

Listing 8-6. Using the i Element

```
<!DOCTYPE HTML>
<html>
    <head>
        <title>Example</title>
        <base href="http://titan/listings/"/>
        <meta name="author" content="Adam Freeman"/>
        <meta name="description" content="A simple example"/>
        <link rel="stylesheet" type="text/css" href="styles.css"/>
        <link rel="shortcut icon" href="favicon.ico" type="image/x-icon" />
    </head>
    <body>
        <em>I</em> like <b>apples</b> and <b>oranges</b>.
        My favorite kind of orange is the mandarin, properly known
        as <i>citrus reticulata</i>.
    </body>
</html>
```

You can see the effect of the i element in Figure 8-4. Notice that the style convention for the i element is the same as for the em element. This is a great example of how the meaning of an element differs from its appearance.

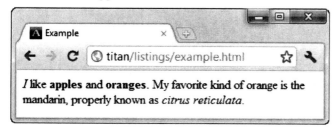

Figure 8-4. Using the i element

Showing Inaccuracies or Corrections

You use the s element to denote a span of text that is no longer correct or accurate. The style convention is to display the text with a line drawn through it. Table 8-8 describes the s element.

161

Table 8-8. The s Element

Element	s
Element Type	Phrasing
Permitted Parents	Any element that can contain phrasing content
Local Attributes	None
Contents	Phrasing content
Tag Style	Start and end tag required
New in HTML5	No
Changes in HTML5	The s element had only presentational meaning in HTML4; in HTML5, it has the semantic meaning described previously, and the presentation aspect has been downgraded to being the style convention
Style Convention	s { text-decoration: line-through; }

Listing 8-7 shows the s element in use.

Listing 8-7. Using the s Element

```
<!DOCTYPE HTML>
<html>
    <head>
        <title>Example</title>
        <base href="http://titan/listings/"/>
        <meta name="author" content="Adam Freeman"/>
        <meta name="description" content="A simple example"/>
        <link rel="stylesheet" type="text/css" href="styles.css"/>
        <link rel="shortcut icon" href="favicon.ico" type="image/x-icon" />
    </head>
    <body>
        <em>I</em> like <b>apples</b> and <b>oranges</b>.
        My favorite kind of orange is the mandarin, properly known
        as <i>citrus reticulata</i>.
        Oranges at my local store cost <s>$1 each</s> $2 for 3.
    </body>
</html>
```

You can see the default style convention of the s element in Figure 8-5.

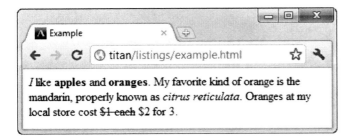

Figure 8-5. Using the s element

Denoting Important Text

The strong element denotes a span of text that is important. Table 8-9 describes this element.

Table 8-9. The strong Element

Element	strong
Element Type	Phrasing
Permitted Parents	Any element that can contain phrasing content
Local Attributes	None
Contents	Phrasing content
Tag Style	Start and end tag required
New in HTML5	No
Changes in HTML5	None
Style Convention	strong { font-weight: bolder; }

Listing 8-8 shows the strong element in use.

Listing 8-8. Using the strong Element

```
<!DOCTYPE HTML>
<html>
    <head>
        <title>Example</title>
        <base href="http://titan/listings/"/>
```

```
        <meta name="author" content="Adam Freeman"/>
        <meta name="description" content="A simple example"/>
        <link rel="stylesheet" type="text/css" href="styles.css"/>
        <link rel="shortcut icon" href="favicon.ico" type="image/x-icon" />
    </head>
    <body>
        I like apples and oranges.
        <strong>Warning:</strong> Eating too many oranges can give you heart burn.
    </body>
</html>
```

I have removed some of the text from the earlier examples to make the listing easier to read. You can see the default style convention of the strong element in Figure 8-6. The strong element has the same style convention as the b element. However, it is important to pick the right element when marking up your content; notice that the b element doesn't assign any importance to the text it encompasses.

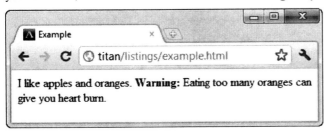

Figure 8-6. Using the strong element

Underlining Text

The u element offsets a span of text from the surrounding content without implying any increased importance or emphasis. This is a vague description because the u element previously had a presentational impact only (to underline text) and no real semantic significance. In effect, this is still a presentational element and the effect it has is to underline text (although you could potentially change this behavior using CSS, I don't recommend repurposing elements in this way; look at using the span element instead). Table 8-10 summarizes the u element.

Table 8-10. The u Element

Element	u
Element Type	Phrasing
Permitted Parents	Any element that can contain phrasing content
Local Attributes	None
Contents	Phrasing content

Tag Style	Start and end tag required
New in HTML5	No
Changes in HTML5	The u element had only presentational meaning in HTML4; in HTML5, it has the semantic meaning described previously, and the presentation aspect has been downgraded to being the style convention
Style Convention	`u { text-decoration:underline; }`

The style convention for the u element is similar to that for the a element, which means that users will often mistake underlined text as being a hyperlink. To prevent this confusion, avoid the u element when possible. Listing 8-9 shows the u element in use.

Listing 8-9. Using the u Element

```
<!DOCTYPE HTML>
<html>
    <head>
        <title>Example</title>
        <base href="http://titan/listings/"/>
        <meta name="author" content="Adam Freeman"/>
        <meta name="description" content="A simple example"/>
        <link rel="stylesheet" type="text/css" href="styles.css"/>
        <link rel="shortcut icon" href="favicon.ico" type="image/x-icon" />
    </head>
    <body>
        I like apples and oranges.
        <strong>Warning:</strong> Eating <u>too many</u> oranges can give you heart burn.
    </body>
</html>
```

You can see how the browser displays this element using the default style convention in Figure 8-7.

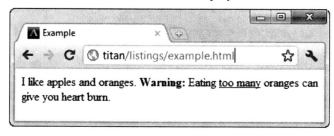

Figure 8-7. Using the u element

Adding Fine Print

The small element denotes fine print and is often used for disclaimers and clarifications. Table 8-11 summarizes the small element.

Table 8-11. The small Element

Element	small
Element Type	Phrasing
Permitted Parents	Any element that can contain phrasing content
Local Attributes	None
Contents	Phrasing content
Tag Style	Start and end tag required
New in HTML5	No
Changes in HTML5	The small element had only presentational meaning in HTML4; in HTML5, it has the semantic meaning described previously, and the presentation aspect has been downgraded to being the style convention
Style Convention	small { font-size: smaller; }

Listing 8-10 shows the small element in use.

Listing 8-10. Using the small Element

```
<!DOCTYPE HTML>
<html>
    <head>
        <title>Example</title>
        <meta name="author" content="Adam Freeman"/>
        <meta name="description" content="A simple example"/>
        <link rel="shortcut icon" href="favicon.ico" type="image/x-icon" />
    </head>
    <body>
        Oranges at my local store are $1 each <small>(plus tax)</small>
    </body>
</html>
```

You can see how the browser applies the default style convention in Figure 8-8.

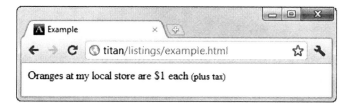

Figure 8-8. Using the small element

Adding Superscript and Subscript

You use the sub and sup elements to denote subscripts and superscripts, respectively. Superscripts are required in some languages and both superscripts and subscripts are used in simple mathematical expressions. Table 8-12 summarizes these elements.

Table 8-12. The sub and sup Elements

Element	sub and sup
Element Type	Phrasing
Permitted Parents	Any element that can contain phrasing content
Local Attributes	None
Contents	Phrasing content
Tag Style	Start and end tag required
New in HTML5	No
Changes in HTML5	None
Style Convention	sub { vertical-align: sub;font-size: smaller; } sup { vertical-align: super;font-size: smaller;}

Listing 8-11 shows the sub and sup elements in use.

Listing 8-11. Using the sub and sup Elements

```
<!DOCTYPE HTML>
<html>
    <head>
        <title>Example</title>
```

```
        <meta name="author" content="Adam Freeman"/>
        <meta name="description" content="A simple example"/>
        <link rel="shortcut icon" href="favicon.ico" type="image/x-icon" />
    </head>
    <body>
        The point x<sub>10</sub> is the 10<sup>th</sup> point.
    </body>
</html>
```

You can see how the browser applies the default style convention in Figure 8-9.

Figure 8-9. Using the sub and sup elements

Creating Breaks

There are two elements that you can use to deal with line breaks in content: the br and wbr elements.

Forcing a Line Break

The br element introduces a line break. The style convention is to move subsequent content onto a new line. Table 8-13 summarizes the br element.

Table 8-13. The br Element

Element	br
Element Type	Phrasing
Permitted Parents	Any element that can contain phrasing content
Local Attributes	None
Contents	N/A
Tag Style	Void
New in HTML5	No

Changes in HTML5	No
Style Convention	Display subsequent content on a new line (not possible through CSS)

Listing 8-12 shows the br element in use.

■ **Note** The br element may be used only when line breaks are part of the content, as in Listing 8-12. You must not use the br element to create paragraphs or other groupings of content; there are other elements for that task, which I describe in Chapters 9 and 10.

Listing 8-12. Using the br Element

```
<!DOCTYPE HTML>
<html>
    <head>
        <title>Example</title>
        <meta name="author" content="Adam Freeman"/>
        <meta name="description" content="A simple example"/>
        <link rel="shortcut icon" href="favicon.ico" type="image/x-icon" />
    </head>
    <body>
        I WANDERED lonely as a cloud<br/>
        That floats on high o'er vales and hills,<br/>
        When all at once I saw a crowd,<br>
        A host, of golden daffodils;
    </body>
</html>
```

You can see how the use of the br element causes the browser to display the content in Figure 8-10.

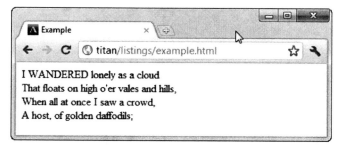

Figure 8-10. Using the br element

Indicating an Opportunity for a Safe Line Break

The wbr element is new to HTML5 and indicates where the browser could reasonably insert a line break to wrap content that is larger than the current browser window. It is the browser that makes the decision as to whether or not a line break is *actually* used. The wbr element is simply a guide to suitable places to break content. Table 8-14 summarizes the wbr element.

Table 8-14. The wbr Element

Element	wbr
Element Type	Phrasing
Permitted Parents	Any element that can contain phrasing content
Local Attributes	None
Contents	N/A
Tag Style	Void
New in HTML5	Yes
Changes in HTML5	N/A
Style Convention	Display subsequent content on a new line when wrapping content is required

Listing 8-13 shows the use of the wbr element to help the browser display a long word.

Listing 8-13. Using the wbr Element

```
<!DOCTYPE HTML>
<html>
    <head>
        <title>Example</title>
        <meta name="author" content="Adam Freeman"/>
        <meta name="description" content="A simple example"/>
        <link rel="shortcut icon" href="favicon.ico" type="image/x-icon" />
    </head>
    <body>
        This is a very long word: Super<wbr>califragilistic<wbr>expialidocious.
        We can help the browser display long words with the <code>wbr</code> element.
    </body>
</html>
```

To understand the value of the wbr element, you have to see how the browser operates with and without the use of the element. Figure 8-11 shows how the browser deals with content when the wbr element isn't present.

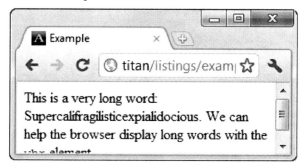

Figure 8-11. Wrapping content without the wbr element

Without the wbr element, the browser encounters the long word and treats it as a single unit. This means that you end up with a large amount of wasted space at the end of the first line of text. If you add the wbr element, as in Listing 8-13, then you give the browser more options, as Figure 8-12 shows.

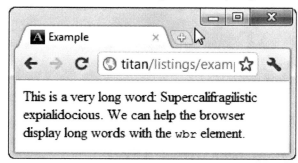

Figure 8-12. Wrapping content with the wbr element

With the wbr element, the browser is able to treat the very long word as a series of smaller segments, and can wrap the content more elegantly. When you use the wbr element, you are telling the browser where breaking a word would be most appropriate.

Representing Inputs and Outputs

There are four elements that betray the geeky origins of HTML. You use these elements to represent inputs and outputs of a computer. Table 8-15 summarizes these elements. None of these elements define local attributes and none of them are new or changed in HTML5.

Table 8-15. *The Input and Output Text Elements*

Element	Description	Style Convention
code	Denotes a fragment of computer code.	`code { font-family: monospace; }`
var	Denotes a variable in a programming context or a placeholder for the reader to mentally insert a specific value.	`var { font-style: italic; }`
samp	Denotes output from a program or computer system.	`samp { font-family: monospace; }`
kbd	Denotes user input.	`kbd { font-family: monospace; }`

Listing 8-14 shows these four elements used in a document.

Listing 8-14. Using the code, var, samp, and kbd Elements

```
<!DOCTYPE HTML>
<html>
    <head>
        <title>Example</title>
        <meta name="author" content="Adam Freeman"/>
        <meta name="description" content="A simple example"/>
        <link rel="shortcut icon" href="favicon.ico" type="image/x-icon" />
    </head>
    <body>
        <p>
        <code>var fruits = ["apples", "oranges", "mangoes", "cherries"];<br>
            document.writeln("I like " + fruits.length + " fruits");</code>
        </p>
        <p>The variable in this example is <var>fruits</var></p>
        <p>The output from the code is: <samp>I like 4 fruits</samp></p>
        <p>When prompted for my favorite fruit, I typed: <kbd>cherries</kbd>
    </body>
</html>
```

You can see the default style conventions for these elements in Figure 8-13. Notice that three of these elements have the same style convention. I have used the p element to add some structure to the content (I describe the p element in Chapter 9).

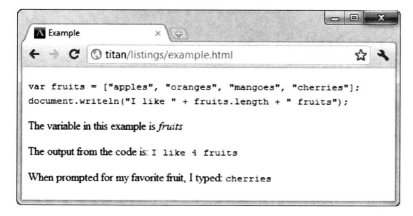

Figure 8-13. Using the code, var, samp, and kbd elements

Creating Citations, Quotations, Definitions, and Abbreviations

The next four elements that you will look at allow you to denote citations, quotations, definitions, and abbreviations. These are widely used in scientific and academic documents.

Denoting Abbreviations

The abbr element allows you to denote an abbreviation. When using this element, you use the `title` attribute to provide the expanded text that the abbreviation represents. Table 8-16 summarizes this element.

Table 8-16. The abbr Element

Element	abbr
Element Type	Phrasing
Permitted Parents	Any element that can contain phrasing content
Local Attributes	None, but the global `title` attribute has special meaning
Contents	Phrasing content
Tag Style	Start and end tag
New in HTML5	No

Changes in HTML5	None
Style Convention	None

Listing 8-15 shows the abbr element in use.

Listing 8-15. Using the abbr Element

```
<!DOCTYPE HTML>
<html>
    <head>
        <title>Example</title>
        <meta name="author" content="Adam Freeman"/>
        <meta name="description" content="A simple example"/>
        <link rel="shortcut icon" href="favicon.ico" type="image/x-icon" />
    </head>
    <body>
        I like apples and oranges.
        The <abbr title="Florida Department of Citrus">FDOC</abbr> regulates the Florida
        citrus industry.
    </body>
</html>
```

There is no style convention for the abbr element, so content contained in this element is not offset in any way.

Defining Terms

The dfn element denotes the defining instance of a term. This is the instance that explains the meaning or significance of a word or phrase. Table 8-17 summarizes this element.

Table 8-17. The dfn Element

Element	dfn
Element Type	Phrasing
Permitted Parents	Any element that can contain phrasing content
Local Attributes	None, but the global title attribute has special meaning
Contents	Text or one abbr element
Tag Style	Start and end tag

New in HTML5	No
Changes in HTML5	None
Style Convention	None

There are some rules about how to use the dfn element. If the dfn element has a title attribute, then the value of the title attribute must be the term that is being defined. You can see an example of a dfn element being used this way in Listing 8-16.

Listing 8-16. Using the dfn Element

```
<!DOCTYPE HTML>
<html>
    <head>
        <title>Example</title>
        <meta name="author" content="Adam Freeman"/>
        <meta name="description" content="A simple example"/>
        <link rel="shortcut icon" href="favicon.ico" type="image/x-icon" />
    </head>
    <body>
        I like apples and oranges.
        The <abbr title="Florida Department of Citrus">FDOC</abbr> regulates the Florida
        citrus industry.

        <p>
            The <dfn title="apple">apple</dfn> is the pomaceous fruit of the apple tree,
            species Malus domestica in the rose family.
        </p>
    </body>
</html>
```

If the dfn element contains an abbr element, then the abbreviation is the term that is being defined. If there is no title attribute and the contents of the element are text, then the text represents the term being defined. There is no style convention associated with this element, so the content of this element is not offset in any way.

Quoting Content from Another Source

The q element denotes content quoted from another source. Table 8-18 summarizes the q element.

Table 8-18. The q Element

Element	q
Element Type	Phrasing

Permitted Parents	Any element that can contain phrasing content
Local Attributes	cite
Contents	Phrasing content
Tag Style	Start and end tag
New in HTML5	No
Changes in HTML5	None
Style Convention	q { display: inline; }
	q:before { content: open-quote; }
	q:after { content: close-quote; }

The definition of the term *apple* in the previous section comes from Wikipedia, and should be properly attributed. The cite attribute is used to specify the URL of the source document, as shown in Listing 8-17.

Listing 8-17. Using the q Element

```
<!DOCTYPE HTML>
<html>
    <head>
        <title>Example</title>
        <meta name="author" content="Adam Freeman"/>
        <meta name="description" content="A simple example"/>
        <link rel="shortcut icon" href="favicon.ico" type="image/x-icon" />
    </head>
    <body>
        I like apples and oranges.
        The <abbr title="Florida Department of Citrus">FDOC</abbr> regulates the Florida
        citrus industry.
        <p>
            <q cite="http://en.wikipedia.org/wiki/Apple">The
            <dfn title="apple">apple</dfn> is the pomaceous fruit of the apple tree,
            species Malus domestica in the rose family.</q>
        </p>
    </body>
</html>
```

Here, the style convention for the q element uses the CSS :before and :after pseudo-element selectors to surround the quoted text with quotation marks, as shown in Figure 8-14. You can learn about pseudo-element selectors in Chapters 17 and 18.

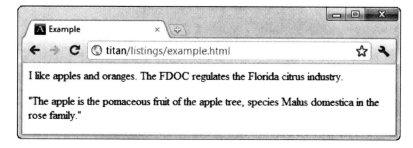

I like apples and oranges. The FDOC regulates the Florida citrus industry.

"The apple is the pomaceous fruit of the apple tree, species Malus domestica in the rose family."

Figure 8-14. Using the q element

Citing the Title of Another Work

The cite element denotes the title of a cited work, such a book, article, film, or poem. Table 8-19 summarizes the cite element.

Table 8-19. The cite Element

Element	cite
Element Type	Phrasing
Permitted Parents	Any element that can contain phrasing content
Local Attributes	None
Contents	Phrasing content
Tag Style	Start and end tag
New in HTML5	No
Changes in HTML5	The cite element may no longer be used to cite the name of a person, but rather the title of a cited work only
Style Convention	cite { font-style: italic; }

Listing 8-18 shows the use of the cite element.

Listing 8-18. Using the cite Element

```
<!DOCTYPE HTML>
<html>
    <head>
```

```
        <title>Example</title>
        <meta name="author" content="Adam Freeman"/>
        <meta name="description" content="A simple example"/>
        <link rel="shortcut icon" href="favicon.ico" type="image/x-icon" />
    </head>
    <body>
        I like apples and oranges.
        The <abbr title="Florida Department of Citrus">FDOC</abbr> regulates the Florida
        citrus industry.
        <p>
            <q cite="http://en.wikipedia.org/wiki/Apple">The
            <dfn title="apple">apple</dfn> is the pomaceous fruit of the apple tree,
            species Malus domestica in the rose family.</q>
        </p>
        My favorite book on fruit is <cite>Fruit: Edible, Inedible, Incredible</cite>
        by Stuppy & Kesseler
    </body>
</html>
```

You can see the application of the default style convention in Figure 8-15.

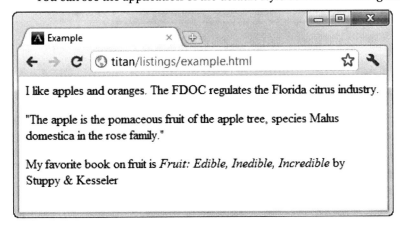

Figure 8-15. Using the cite element

Working with the Language Elements

There are five HTML elements, four of which are new in HTML5, that provide support for working with non-Western languages. The following sections describe these elements.

The ruby, rt, and rp Elements

Ruby characters are notations placed above or to the right of characters in logographic languages (such as Chinese or Japanese), and that aid the reader in correctly pronouncing characters. The ruby element denotes a span of text that contains a ruby. Table 8-20 summarizes this element.

Table 8-20. The ruby Element

Element	ruby
Element Type	Phrasing
Permitted Parents	Any element that can contain phrasing content
Local Attributes	None
Contents	Phrasing content and rt and rp elements
Tag Style	Start and end tag
New in HTML5	Yes
Changes in HTML5	N/A
Style Convention	ruby { text-indent: 0; }

You use the ruby element in conjunction with the rt and rp elements, which are also new in HTML5. The rt element marks the ruby notation, and the rp element denotes parentheses around an annotation that can be displayed by browsers that don't support ruby annotations.

I don't speak any logographic languages, which means that I don't have a basis on which to create an example using logograms. The best that I can do in this section is to use English text to demonstrate how ruby annotations are displayed by the browser. Listing 8-19 contains such an annotation.

Listing 8-19. Using the ruby, rt, and rp Elements

```
<!DOCTYPE HTML>
<html>
    <head>
        <title>Example</title>
        <meta name="author" content="Adam Freeman"/>
        <meta name="description" content="A simple example"/>
        <link rel="shortcut icon" href="favicon.ico" type="image/x-icon" />
    </head>
    <body>
        I like apples and oranges.
        The <abbr title="Florida Department of Citrus">FDOC</abbr> regulates the Florida
        citrus industry.
        <p>
            <q cite="http://en.wikipedia.org/wiki/Apple">The
            <dfn title="apple">apple</dfn> is the pomaceous fruit of the apple tree,
            species Malus domestica in the rose family.</q>
        </p>
        <p>
```

179

```
            Oranges are often made
            into<ruby> OJ <rp>(</rp><rt>Orange Juice</rt><rp>)</rp></ruby>
        </p>
    </body>
</html>
```

When the document is displayed in a browser that supports ruby annotations, the rp elements and their contents are ignored, and the contents of the rt element is displayed as an annotation, as shown in Figure 8-16.

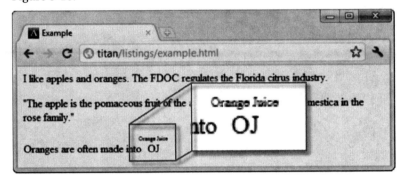

Figure 8-16. Using the ruby, rt, and rp elements

If you display the document in a browser that doesn't support ruby annotations, then the contents of the rp and rt elements are displayed. As I write this chapter, Firefox doesn't support ruby annotations; you can see how it would display the content in Figure 8-17.

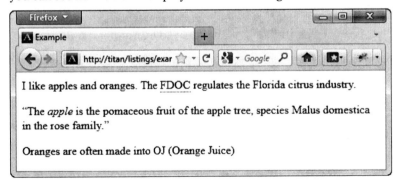

Figure 8-17. Rubies in a browser that doesn't support annotations

The bdo Element

The bdo element specifies an explicit text direction for its content, overriding the automatic directionality that would usually be applied. Table 8-21 summarizes the bdo element.

Table 8-21. The bdo Element

Element	bdo
Element Type	Phrasing
Permitted Parents	Any element that can contain phrasing content
Local Attributes	None, but the dir global attribute is required
Contents	Phrasing content
Tag Style	Start and end tag
New in HTML5	No
Changes in HTML5	None
Style Convention	None

You must use the bdo element with the dir attribute, which has the allowed values of rtl (for right-to-left layout) and ltr (for left-to-right layout). Listing 8-20 shows the bdo element in use.

Listing 8-20. Using the bdo Element

```
<!DOCTYPE HTML>
<html>
    <head>
        <title>Example</title>
        <meta name="author" content="Adam Freeman"/>
        <meta name="description" content="A simple example"/>
        <link rel="shortcut icon" href="favicon.ico" type="image/x-icon" />
    </head>
    <body>
        I like apples and oranges.
        The <abbr title="Florida Department of Citrus">FDOC</abbr> regulates the Florida
        citrus industry.
        <p>
            This is left-to-right: <bdo dir="ltr">I like oranges</bdo>
        </p>
        <p>
            This is right-to-left: <bdo dir="rtl">I like oranges</bdo>
        </p>
    </body>
</html>
```

181

You can see how the browser displays the content of this element in Figure 8-18.

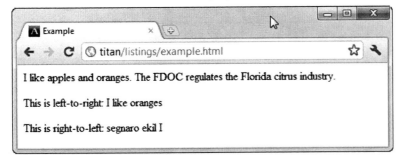

Figure 8-18. Using the bdo element

The bdi Element

The bdi element denotes a span of text that is isolated from other content for the purposes of text directionality. Table 8-22 summarizes this element.

Table 8-22. The bdi Element

Element	bdi
Element Type	Phrasing
Permitted Parents	Any element that can contain phrasing content
Local Attributes	None
Contents	Phrasing content
Tag Style	Start and end tag
New in HTML5	Yes
Changes in HTML5	N/A
Style Convention	None

You use this element when displaying content for which there is no directionality information available. When this happens, the browser determines the directionality automatically, and that can upset the formatting of the page. Listing 8-21 gives a simple example of the problem.

Listing 8-21. Dealing with Text Without the bdi Element

```
<!DOCTYPE HTML>
<html>
    <head>
        <title>Example</title>
        <meta name="author" content="Adam Freeman"/>
        <meta name="description" content="A simple example"/>
        <meta charset="utf-8"/>
        <link rel="shortcut icon" href="favicon.ico" type="image/x-icon" />
    </head>
    <body>
        I like apples and oranges.

        Here are some users and the fruit they purchased this week:

        <p>Adam: 3 applies and 2 oranges</p>
        <p>أبو كريم: 2 apples</p>
        <p>Joe: 6 apples</p>
    </body>
</html>
```

When you display this document, the Arabic name causes the text directionality algorithm in the browser to display the number 2 before the name, and not after it, as shown in Figure 8-19.

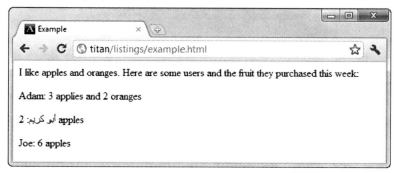

Figure 8-19. The effect of the bidirectional text algorithm when mixing formats

You can address this problem using the bdi element, as shown in Listing 8-22.

Listing 8-22. Using the bdi Element

```
<!DOCTYPE HTML>
<html>
    <head>
        <title>Example</title>
        <meta name="author" content="Adam Freeman"/>
        <meta name="description" content="A simple example"/>
        <meta charset="utf-8"/>
```

```
            <link rel="shortcut icon" href="favicon.ico" type="image/x-icon" />
        </head>
        <body>
            I like apples and oranges.

            Here are some users and the fruit they purchased this week:

            <p><bdi>Adam</bdi>: 3 applies and 2 oranges</p>
            <p><bdi>مير ك وبأ</bdi> : 2 apples</p>
            <p><bdi>Joe</bdi>: 6 apples</p>
        </body>
</html>
```

You can see the corrective effect of this element in Figure 8-20.

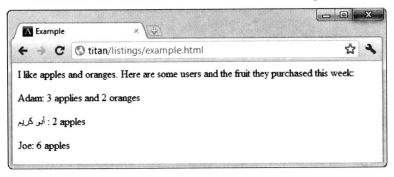

Figure 8-20. Using the bdi element

Wrapping Up: The Other Text Elements

There are four other elements that don't fit neatly into one of the other groups. I describe them in the following sections.

Denoting a Generic Span of Content

The span element has no meaning in its own right. You would use it to apply one of the global attributes to a region of content. Table 8-23 summarizes the span element.

Table 8-23. The span Element

Element	span
Element Type	Phrasing
Permitted Parents	Any element that can contain phrasing content

Local Attributes	None
Contents	Phrasing content
Tag Style	Start and end tag
New in HTML5	No
Changes in HTML5	None
Style Convention	None

Listing 8-23 shows the span element used with the class attribute, so that I can target content with a CSS style.

Listing 8-23. Using the span Element

```
<!DOCTYPE HTML>
<html>
    <head>
        <title>Example</title>
        <meta name="author" content="Adam Freeman"/>
        <meta name="description" content="A simple example"/>
        <link rel="shortcut icon" href="favicon.ico" type="image/x-icon" />
        <style>
            .fruit {
                border: thin solid black;
                padding: 1px;
            }
        </style>
    </head>
    <body>
        I like <span class="fruit">apples</span> and <span class="fruit">oranges</span>.
    </body>
</html>
```

You can see the application of the style in Figure 8-21.

Figure 8-21. Using the span element to target styles

Highlighting Text

The mark element is new to HTML5 and represents a span of text that is highlighted due to its relevance in another context. Table 8-24 summarizes the mark element.

Table 8-24. The mark Element

Element	mark
Element Type	Phrasing
Permitted Parents	Any element that can contain phrasing content
Local Attributes	None
Contents	Phrasing content
Tag Style	Start and end tag
New in HTML5	Yes
Changes in HTML5	N/A
Style Convention	mark { background-color: yellow; color: black; }

Listing 8-24 demonstrates the mark element.

Listing 8-24. Using the mark Element

```
<!DOCTYPE HTML>
<html>
    <head>
        <title>Example</title>
        <meta name="author" content="Adam Freeman"/>
        <meta name="description" content="A simple example"/>
        <link rel="shortcut icon" href="favicon.ico" type="image/x-icon" />
    </head>
    <body>

        Homophones are words which are pronounced the same, but have different spellings
        and meanings. For example:
        <p>
            I would like a <mark>pair</mark> of <mark>pears</mark>
        </p>
    </body>
</html>
```

You can see the style convention in Figure 8-22.

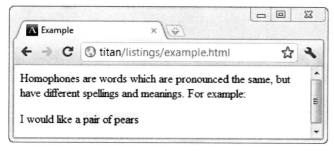

Figure 8-22. Using the mark element

Denoting Added or Removed Content

You can denote text that has been added or removed from the document using the ins and del elements. The ins element denotes inserted content and is summarized in Table 8-25.

Table 8-25. *The ins Element*

Element	ins
Element Type	This element is considered as a phrasing element when it is a child of a phrasing element, and as a flow element when it is the child of a flow element
Permitted Parents	Any element that can contain phrasing or flow content
Local Attributes	cite, datetime
Contents	Phrasing or flow content, depending on the type of the parent element
Tag Style	Start and end tag
New in HTML5	Yes
Changes in HTML5	N/A
Style Convention	ins { text-decoration: underline; }

You denote text that has been removed from the document using the del element, which is summarized in Table 8-26.

187

Table 8-26. The del Element

Element	`del`
Element Type	This element is considered as a phrasing element when it is a child of a phrasing element, and as a flow element when it is the child of a flow element
Permitted Parents	Any element that can contain phrasing or flow content
Local Attributes	`cite`, `datetime`
Contents	Phrasing or flow content, depending on the type of the parent element
Tag Style	Start and end tag
New in HTML5	Yes
Changes in HTML5	N/A
Style Convention	`del { text-decoration: line-through; }`

The ins and del elements defined the same local attributes. The cite attribute specifies a URL to a document that explains why the text was added or removed, and the datetime attribute specifies when the modification was made. You can see the ins and del elements in use in Listing 8-25.

Listing 8-25. Using the del and ins Elements

```
<!DOCTYPE HTML>
<html>
    <head>
        <title>Example</title>
        <meta name="author" content="Adam Freeman"/>
        <meta name="description" content="A simple example"/>
        <link rel="shortcut icon" href="favicon.ico" type="image/x-icon" />
    </head>
    <body>

        Homophones are words which are pronounced the same, but have different spellings
        and meanings. For example:
        <p>
            I would like a <mark>pair</mark> of <mark>pears</mark>
        </p>
        <p>
            <del>I can <mark>sea</mark> the <mark>see</mark></del>
```

```
            <ins>I can <mark>see</mark> the <mark>sea</mark></ins>
        </p>
    </body>
</html>
```

The default style convention is shown in Figure 8-23.

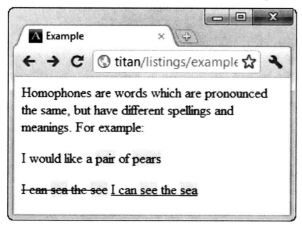

Figure 8-23. Using the ins and del elements

Denoting Times and Dates

You use the `time` element to represent a time of day or a date. Table 8-27 summarizes the `time` element.

Table 8-27. The time Element

Element	time
Element Type	Phrasing
Permitted Parents	Any element that can contain phrasing content
Local Attributes	datetime, pubdate
Contents	Phrasing content
Tag Style	Start and end tag
New in HTML5	Yes
Changes in	N/A

HTML5

Style Convention	None

If the Boolean pubdate attribute is present, then the time element is assumed to be the publication date of the entire HTML document or the nearest article element (I describe the article element in Chapter 10). The datetime attribute specifies the date or time in a format specified by RFC3339, which you can find at http://tools.ietf.org/html/rfc3339. Using the datetime attribute means you can specify a date in a human-readable form within the element and still ensure that a computer can unambiguously parse the date or time. Listing 8-26 shows the time element in use.

Listing 8-26. Using the time Element

```
<!DOCTYPE HTML>
<html>
    <head>
        <title>Example</title>
        <meta name="author" content="Adam Freeman"/>
        <meta name="description" content="A simple example"/>
        <link rel="shortcut icon" href="favicon.ico" type="image/x-icon" />
    </head>
    <body>
        I still remember the best apple I ever tasted.
        I bought it at <time datetime="15:00">3 o'clock</time>
        on <time datetime="1984-12-7">December 7th</time>.
    </body>
</html>
```

Summary

In this chapter, I have taken you on a tour of the text elements—those elements that you use to give structure and meaning to your content. These elements range from the basic to the complex, and you can see the tension between the desire to divorce meaning from presentation in HTML5 and the desire to preserve compatibility with HTML4.

Make sure you select text elements based on their meaning, and not the default style convention with which they are associated. You can apply the CSS style to your content in ways that you did not expect, and users will get odd results if you don't mark up your content correctly and consistently.

CHAPTER 9

Grouping Content

In this chapter, I describe the HTML elements that you can use to group related content together, which will add further structure and meaning to the content in your document. The elements in this chapter are largely flow elements. There is one exception: the a element, which has the distinction of its element category being determined by the content it contains. Table 9-1 provides the summary for this chapter.

Table 9-1. Chapter Summary

Problem	Solution	Listing
Denote a paragraph.	Use the p element.	9-2
Apply global attributes to a region of content without denoting any other content grouping.	Use the div element.	9-3
Preserve layout in the HTML source document.	Use the pre element.	9-4
Denote content quoted from another source.	Use the blockquote element.	9-5
Denote a paragraph-level thematic break.	Use the hr element.	9-6
Create a list in which the order of items is significant.	Use the ol and li elements.	9-7
Create a list in which the order of items is not significant.	Use the ul and li elements.	9-8
Create an ordered list in which the numbering of items is nonsequential.	Use the value attribute of the li element contained within an ol element.	9-9
Create a list of terms and their definitions.	Use the dl, dt, and dd elements.	9-10
Create a list that has custom item	Use the ul element in conjunction	9-11

| numbering. | with the CSS :before selector and counter feature. | |
| Denote a figure (and optionally, a caption). | Use the figure and figcaption elements. | 9-12 |

Understanding the Need to Group Content

HTML requires browsers to *collapse* multiple whitespace characters into a single space. This is generally a useful feature, because it separates the layout of your HTML document from the layout of the content in the browser window. Listing 9-1 shows a longer block of content than I have used in examples so far.

Listing 9-1. A Longer Content Section in an HTML Document

```
<!DOCTYPE HTML>
<html>
    <head>
        <title>Example</title>
        <meta name="author" content="Adam Freeman"/>
        <meta name="description" content="A simple example"/>
        <link rel="shortcut icon" href="favicon.ico" type="image/x-icon" />
    </head>
    <body>

        I like apples and oranges.

        I also like bananas, mangoes, cherries, apricots, plums, peaches and grapes.
        You can see other fruits I like <a href="fruitlist.html">here</a>.

        <strong>Warning:</strong> Eating too many oranges can give you heart burn.

        My favorite kind of orange is the mandarin, properly known
            as <i>citrus reticulata</i>.
        Oranges at my local store cost <s>$1 each</s> $2 for 3.

        The <abbr title="Florida Department of Citrus">FDOC</abbr> regulates the Florida
            citrus industry.

        I still remember the best apple I ever tasted.
        I bought it at <time datetime="15:00">3 o'clock</time>
            on <time datetime="1984-12-7">December 7th</time>.
    </body>
</html>
```

The text in the body element spreads over multiple lines. Some of those lines are indented, and there are line breaks between groups of lines. The browser will ignore all of this structure and display all of the content as a single line, as shown in Figure 9-1.

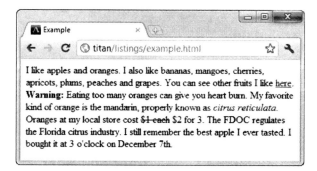

Figure 9-1. The browser collapses whitespace in an HTML document

The elements in the sections that follow will help you add structure to a document by grouping together related regions of content. There are many different approaches to grouping content, from a simple paragraph to sophisticated lists.

Creating Paragraphs

The p element represents a paragraph. Paragraphs are blocks of text containing one or more related sentences that address a single point or idea. Paragraphs can also be comprised of sentences that address different points, but share some common theme. Table 9-2 summarizes the p element.

Table 9-2. The p Element

Element	p
Element Type	Flow
Permitted Parents	Any element that can contain flow elements
Local Attributes	**None**
Contents	Phrasing content
Tag Style	Start and end tag required
New in HTML5	No
Changes in HTML5	The align attribute is obsolete in HTML5 (it was deprecated in HTML4)

Style Convention	p { display: block; margin-before: 1em;
	     margin-after: 1em; margin-start: 0;
	     margin-end: 0; }

Listing 9-2 shows the application of the p element to the example content.

Listing 9-2. Using the p Element

```
<!DOCTYPE HTML>
<html>
    <head>
        <title>Example</title>
        <meta name="author" content="Adam Freeman"/>
        <meta name="description" content="A simple example"/>
        <link rel="shortcut icon" href="favicon.ico" type="image/x-icon" />
    </head>
    <body>
        <p>I like apples and oranges.

        I also like bananas, mangoes, cherries, apricots, plums, peaches and grapes.
        You can see other fruits I like <a href="fruitlist.html">here</a>.</p>

        <p><strong>Warning:</strong> Eating too many oranges can give you heart burn.</p>

        <p>My favorite kind of orange is the mandarin, properly known
            as <i>citrus reticulata</i>.
        Oranges at my local store cost <s>$1 each</s> $2 for 3.</p>

        <p>The <abbr title="Florida Department of Citrus">FDOC</abbr> regulates the
            Florida citrus industry.</p>

        <p>I still remember the best apple I ever tasted.
        I bought it at <time datetime="15:00">3 o'clock</time>
            on <time datetime="1984-12-7">December 7th</time>. </p>
    </body>
</html>
```

I've added a number of p elements to the body element to group related sentences together and give the content some structure. Multiple whitespace within a p element is still collapsed to a single character, as you can see in Figure 9-2.

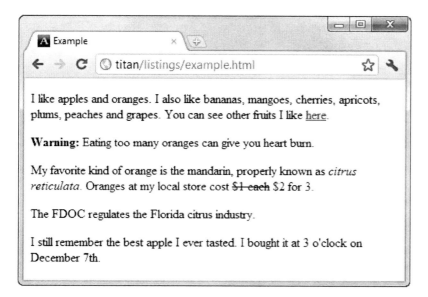

Figure 9-2. The effect of the p element

Using the div Element

The div element doesn't have a specific meaning. You use it to create structure and give meaning to content when the other HTML elements are insufficient. You add this meaning by applying the global attributes (described in Chapter 3), typically the class or id attributes. Table 9-3 summarizes the div element.

▨ **Caution** You should use the div element only as a last resort, when those elements that do have semantic significance are not appropriate. Before using the div element, consider using the new HTML5 elements, such as article and section (described in Chapter 10). There is nothing intrinsically wrong with div, but you should strive to include semantic information wherever possible in your HTML5 documents.

Table 9-3. The div Element

Item	Description
Element	div
Element Type	Flow
Permitted	Any element that can contain flow elements

Parents	
Local Attributes	**None**
Contents	Phrasing content
Tag Style	Start and end tag required
New in HTML5	No
Changes in HTML5	None, although elements added in HTML5, such as article and section, should be used in preference to this element
Style Convention	div { display: block; }

The div element is the flow equivalent of the span element. It is an element that has no specific meaning, and can, therefore, be used to add customized structure to a document. The problem with creating custom structure is that the significance is specific to your web page or web application, and the meaning is not evident to others. This can be problematic when your HTML is being processed or styled by third parties. Listing 9-3 shows the div element in use.

Listing 9-3. Using the div Element

```
<!DOCTYPE HTML>
<html>
    <head>
        <title>Example</title>
        <meta name="author" content="Adam Freeman"/>
        <meta name="description" content="A simple example"/>
        <link rel="shortcut icon" href="favicon.ico" type="image/x-icon" />
        <style>
            .favorites {
                background:grey;
                color:white;
                border: thin solid black;
                padding: 0.2em;
            }
        </style>
    </head>
    <body>

        <div class="favorites">

        <p>I like apples and oranges.

        I also like bananas, mangoes, cherries, apricots, plums, peaches and grapes.
        You can see other fruits I like <a href="fruitlist.html">here</a>.</p>

        <p>My favorite kind of orange is the mandarin, properly known
```

```
                as <i>citrus reticulata</i>.
            Oranges at my local store cost <s>$1 each</s> $2 for 3.</p>

        </div>

        <p><strong>Warning:</strong> Eating too many oranges can give you heart burn.</p>

        <p>The <abbr title="Florida Department of Citrus">FDOC</abbr> regulates the
            Florida citrus industry.</p>

        <p>I still remember the best apple I ever tasted.
        I bought it at <time datetime="15:00">3 o'clock</time>
            on <time datetime="1984-12-7">December 7th</time>. </p>
    </body>
</html>
```

In this example, I have shown a slightly different use for the div element, which is to group multiple elements of a different type together so that they can be styled consistently. I could have added a class attribute to both of the p elements contained within the div, but this approach can be simpler and relies on the way that styles are inherited (as described in Chapter 4).

Working with Preformatted Content

The pre element lets you change the way that the browser deals with content, so that whitespace is not collapsed and formatting is preserved. This can be useful when the original formatting of a section of content is significant. However, you should not use this element otherwise, since it undermines the flexibility that comes with using elements and styles to control presentation. Table 9-4 summarizes the pre element.

Table 9-4. The pre Element

Element	pre
Element Type	Flow
Permitted Parents	Any element that can contain flow elements
Local Attributes	**None**
Contents	Phrasing content
Tag Style	Start and end tag required
New in HTML5	No
Changes in HTML5	None

Style Convention   pre { display: block; font-family: monospace;
                         white-space: pre; margin: 1em 0; }

The pre element can be particularly useful when you use it with the code element. The formatting in programming languages, for example, is usually significant and you would not want to have to recreate that formatting using elements. Listing 9-4 shows the pre element in use.

Listing 9-4. Using the pre Element

```
<!DOCTYPE HTML>
<html>
    <head>
        <title>Example</title>
        <meta name="author" content="Adam Freeman"/>
        <meta name="description" content="A simple example"/>
        <link rel="shortcut icon" href="favicon.ico" type="image/x-icon" />
        <style>
            .favorites {
                background:grey;
                color:white;
                border: thin solid black;
                padding: 0.2em;
            }
        </style>
    </head>
    <body>

        <pre><code>
var fruits = ["apples", "oranges", "mangoes", "cherries"];
for (var i = 0; i < fruits.length; i++) {
    document.writeln("I like " + fruits[i]);
}

        </code></pre>

        <div class="favorites">

        <p>I like apples and oranges.

        I also like bananas, mangoes, cherries, apricots, plums, peaches and grapes.
        You can see other fruits I like <a href="fruitlist.html">here</a>.</p>

        <p>My favorite kind of orange is the mandarin, properly known
            as <i>citrus reticulata</i>.
        Oranges at my local store cost <s>$1 each</s> $2 for 3.</p>

        </div>
    </body>
</html>
```

In Listing 9-4, I have used the pre element with some JavaScript code. This code won't be executed because it is not in a script element, but the formatting of the code will be preserved. The browser won't do anything to reformat the content within the pre element, which means that the leading spaces or tabs for each line will be displayed in the browser window. This is why the individual statements in the pre element are not indented to match the structure of the HTML document. You can see how the browser displays the formatted content in Figure 9-3.

Figure 9-3. Displaying preformatted content with the pre element

Quoting from Other Sources

The blockquote element denotes a block of content that is quoted from another source. This element is similar in purpose to the q element described in Chapter 8, but is generally applied to larger amounts of quoted content. Table 9-5 summarizes the blockquote element.

Table 9-5. The blockquote Element

Element	blockquote
Element Type	Flow
Permitted Parents	Any element that can contain flow elements
Local Attributes	cite
Contents	Flow content
Tag Style	Start and end tag required
New in HTML5	No

Changes in HTML5	None
Style Convention	blockquote { display: block; margin-before: 1em; margin-after: 1em; margin-start: 40px; margin-end: 40px; }

The cite attribute can be used to supply a URL for the original source of the content, as shown in Listing 9-5.

Listing 9-5. Using the blockquote Element

```
<!DOCTYPE HTML>
<html>
    <head>
        <title>Example</title>
        <meta name="author" content="Adam Freeman"/>
        <meta name="description" content="A simple example"/>
        <link rel="shortcut icon" href="favicon.ico" type="image/x-icon" />
    </head>
    <body>

        <p>I like apples and oranges.

        I also like bananas, mangoes, cherries, apricots, plums, peaches and grapes.
        You can see other fruits I like <a href="fruitlist.html">here</a>.</p>

        <p>My favorite kind of orange is the mandarin, properly known
            as <i>citrus reticulata</i>.
        Oranges at my local store cost <s>$1 each</s> $2 for 3.</p>

        <blockquote cite="http://en.wikipedia.org/wiki/Apple">
        The apple forms a tree that is small and deciduous, reaching 3 to 12 metres
        (9.8 to 39 ft) tall, with a broad, often densely twiggy crown.
        The leaves are alternately arranged simple ovals 5 to 12 cm long and 3-6
        centimetres (1.2-2.4 in) broad on a 2 to 5 centimetres (0.79 to 2.0 in) petiole
        with anacute tip, serrated margin and a slightly downy underside. Blossoms are
        produced in spring simultaneously with the budding of the leaves.
        The flowers are white with a pink tinge that gradually fades, five petaled,
        and 2.5 to 3.5 centimetres (0.98 to 1.4 in) in diameter.
        The fruit matures in autumn, and is typically 5 to 9 centimetres (
        2.0 to 3.5 in) in diameter.
        The center of the fruit contains five carpels arranged in a five-point star,
        each carpel containing one to three seeds, called pips.</blockquote>

        <p><strong>Warning:</strong> Eating too many oranges can give you heart burn.</p>

        <p>The <abbr title="Florida Department of Citrus">FDOC</abbr> regulates the
            Florida citrus industry.</p>
```

```
            <p>I still remember the best apple I ever tasted.
            I bought it at <time datetime="15:00">3 o'clock</time>
                on <time datetime="1984-12-7">December 7th</time>. </p>
        </body>
    </html>
```

You can see how the browser applies the style convention in Figure 9-4.

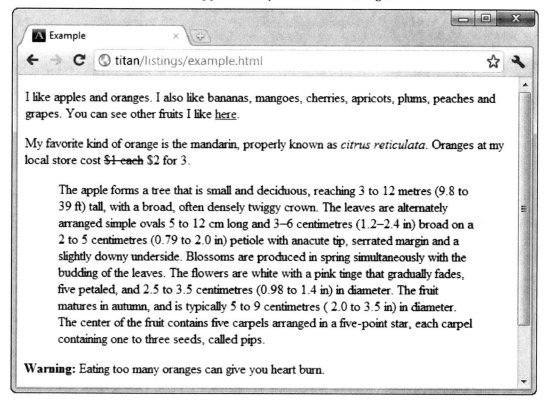

Figure 9-4. Using the blockquote element

■ **Tip** You can see in Figure 9-4 that the browser ignores any formatting inside of the blockquote element. You can add structure to quoted content by adding other grouping elements, such as p or hr (as shown in the following example).

Adding Thematic Breaks

The hr element represents a paragraph-level thematic break. This is another oddly specified term that arises from the need to separate semantics from presentation. In HTML4, the hr element represented a horizontal rule (literally a line across the page). In HTML5, the hr element represents a transition to a separate, but related, topic. The style convention in HTML5 is a line across the page. Table 9-6 summarizes the hr element.

Table 9-6. The hr Element

Element	hr
Element Type	Flow
Permitted Parents	Any element that can contain flow elements
Local Attributes	**None**
Contents	None
Tag Style	Void element
New in HTML5	No
Changes in HTML5	The hr element had only presentational meaning in HTML4. In HTML5, it has the semantic meaning described previously, and the presentation aspect has been downgraded to being the style convention. In addition, the following local attributes are obsolete in HTML5: align, width, noshade, size, color.
Style Convention	hr { display: block; margin-before: 0.5em; margin-after: 0.5em; margin-start: auto; margin-end: auto; border-style: inset; border-width: 1px; }

The HTML5 specification is somewhat vague about what constitutes a valid use for the hr element, but two examples are given: a scene change in a story, or a transition to another topic within a section in a reference book. Listing 9-6 shows the hr element applied to content.

Listing 9-6. Using the hr Element

```
<!DOCTYPE HTML>
<html>
    <head>
        <title>Example</title>
        <meta name="author" content="Adam Freeman"/>
        <meta name="description" content="A simple example"/>
```

```
        <link rel="shortcut icon" href="favicon.ico" type="image/x-icon" />
    </head>
    <body>

        <p>I like apples and oranges.

        I also like bananas, mangoes, cherries, apricots, plums, peaches and grapes.
        You can see other fruits I like <a href="fruitlist.html">here</a>.</p>

        <p>My favorite kind of orange is the mandarin, properly known
            as <i>citrus reticulata</i>.
        Oranges at my local store cost <s>$1 each</s> $2 for 3.</p>

        <blockquote cite="http://en.wikipedia.org/wiki/Apple">
        The apple forms a tree that is small and deciduous, reaching 3 to 12 metres
        (9.8 to 39 ft) tall, with a broad, often densely twiggy crown.
        <hr>
        The leaves are alternately arranged simple ovals 5 to 12 cm long and 3-6
        centimetres (1.2-2.4 in) broad on a 2 to 5 centimetres (0.79 to 2.0 in) petiole
        with anacute tip, serrated margin and a slightly downy underside. Blossoms are
        produced in spring simultaneously with the budding of the leaves.
        <hr>
        The flowers are white with a pink tinge that gradually fades, five petaled,
        and 2.5 to 3.5 centimetres (0.98 to 1.4 in) in diameter.
        The fruit matures in autumn, and is typically 5 to 9 centimetres (
        2.0 to 3.5 in) in diameter.
        <hr>
        The center of the fruit contains five carpels arranged in a five-point star,
        each carpel containing one to three seeds, called pips.</blockquote>

        <p><strong>Warning:</strong> Eating too many oranges can give you heart burn.</p>

        <p>The <abbr title="Florida Department of Citrus">FDOC</abbr> regulates the
            Florida citrus industry.</p>

        <p>I still remember the best apple I ever tasted.
        I bought it at <time datetime="15:00">3 o'clock</time>
            on <time datetime="1984-12-7">December 7th</time>. </p>
    </body>
</html>
```

In this example, I have added some hr elements to a blockquote to add some structure. You can see how this affects the default appearance of the HTML in Figure 9-5.

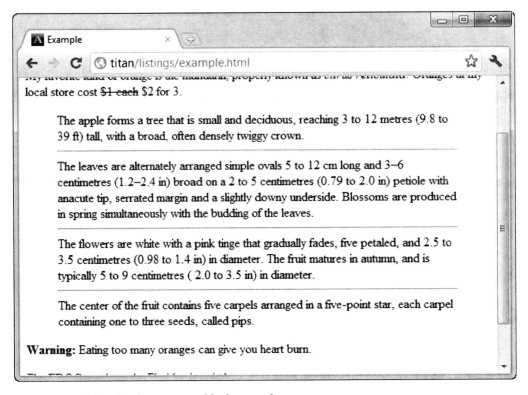

Figure 9-5. Adding hr elements to a blockquote element

Grouping Content into Lists

HTML defines a number of elements that you can use to create lists of content items. As I describe in the following sections, you can create ordered, unordered, and descriptive lists.

The ol Element

The ol element denotes an ordered list. The items in the list are denoted using the li element, which is described in the following section. Table 9-7 summarizes the ol element.

Table 9-7. The ol Element

Element	ol
Element Type	Flow
Permitted Parents	Any element that can contain flow elements

Local Attributes	start, reversed, type
Contents	Zero or more li elements
Tag Style	Start and end tag
New in HTML5	No
Changes in HTML5	The reversed attribute has been added in HTML5. The start and type attributes, which were deprecated in HTML4, have been restored in HTML5, but with semantic (rather than presentational) significance. The compact attribute is now obsolete.
Style Convention	ol { display: block; list-style-type: decimal; margin-before: 1em; margin-after: 1em; margin-start: 0; margin-end: 0; padding-start: 40px; }

Listing 9-7 shows the ol element being used to create a simple ordered list.

Listing 9-7. Creating a Simple List with the ol Element

```
<!DOCTYPE HTML>
<html>
    <head>
        <title>Example</title>
        <meta name="author" content="Adam Freeman"/>
        <meta name="description" content="A simple example"/>
        <link rel="shortcut icon" href="favicon.ico" type="image/x-icon" />
    </head>
    <body>

        I like apples and oranges.

        I also like:
        <ol>
            <li>bananas</li>
            <li>mangoes</li>
            <li>cherries</li>
            <li>plums</li>
            <li>peaches</li>
            <li>grapes</li>
        </ol>

        You can see other fruits I like <a href="fruitlist.html">here</a>.

    </body>
</html>
```

You can see how the browser displays this list in Figure 9-6.

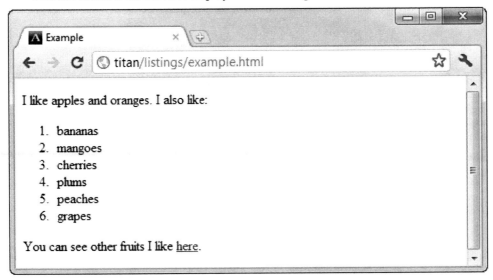

Figure 9-6. A simple ordered list

You can control the way that the items in the list are managed using the attributes defined by the ol element. You use the start attribute to define the ordinal value of the first item in the list. If this attribute is not defined, the first item is assigned the ordinal value of 1. You use the type attribute to indicate which marker should be displayed next to each item. Table 9-8 shows the supported values for this attribute.

Table 9-8. The Supprted Values for the type Attribute of the ol Element

Value	Description	Example
1	Decimal numbers (default)	1., 2., 3., 4.
a	Lowercase Latin characters	a., b., c., d.
A	Uppercase Latin characters	A., B., C., D.
i	Lowercase Roman characters	i., ii., iii., iv.
I	Uppercase Roman characters	I., II., III., IV.

If the reversed attribute is defined, then the list is numbered in descending order. However, as I write this, none of the mainstream browsers implement the reversed attribute.

The ul Element

You use the ul element to denote unordered lists. As with the ol element, items in the ul element are denoted using the li element, which is described next. Table 9-9 summarizes the ul element.

Table 9-9. The ul Element

Element	ul
Element Type	Flow
Permitted Parents	Any element that can contain flow elements
Local Attributes	None
Contents	Zero or more li elements
Tag Style	Start and end tag
New in HTML5	No
Changes in HTML5	The type and compact attributes are obsolete
Style Convention	ul { display: block; list-style-type: disc; margin-before: 1em; margin-after: 1em; margin-start: 0; margin-end: 0; padding-start: 40px; }

The ul element contains a number of li items. The element doesn't define any attributes and you control the presentation of the list using CSS. You can see the ul element in use in Listing 9-8.

Listing 9-8. Using the ul Element

```
<!DOCTYPE HTML>
<html>
    <head>
        <title>Example</title>
        <meta name="author" content="Adam Freeman"/>
        <meta name="description" content="A simple example"/>
        <link rel="shortcut icon" href="favicon.ico" type="image/x-icon" />
    </head>
    <body>

        I like apples and oranges.

        I also like:
        <ul>
```

```
            <li>bananas</li>
            <li>mangoes</li>
            <li>cherries</li>
            <li>plums</li>
            <li>peaches</li>
            <li>grapes</li>
        </ul>

        You can see other fruits I like <a href="fruitlist.html">here</a>.

    </body>
</html>
```

Each list item is displayed with a bullet. You can control which style bullet is used through the list-style-type CSS property, which is described in Chapter 24. You can see the default style convention (which uses the disc bullet style) in Figure 9-7.

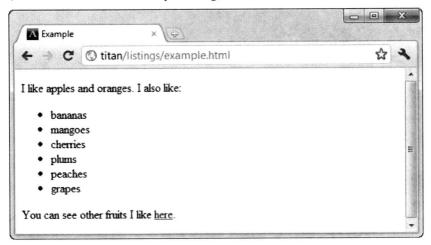

Figure 9-7. The style convention applied to the ul element

The li Element

The li element denotes an item in a list. You can use it with the ul, ol, and menu elements (the menu element is not yet supported in the main stream browsers). Table 9-10 summarizes the li item.

Table 9-10. The li Element

Element	li
Element Type	N/A
Permitted Parents	ul, ol, menu

Local Attributes	value (only permitted when child of ol element)
Contents	Flow content
Tag Style	Start and end tag
New in HTML5	No
Changes in HTML5	The value attribute was deprecated in HTML4, but has been restored in HTML5
Style Convention	li { display: list-item; }

The li item is very simple. It denotes a list item within its parent element. You can, however, use the value attribute to create nonconsecutive ordered lists, as shown in Listing 9-9.

Listing 9-9. Creating Nonconsecutive Ordered Lists

```
<!DOCTYPE HTML>
<html>
    <head>
        <title>Example</title>
        <meta name="author" content="Adam Freeman"/>
        <meta name="description" content="A simple example"/>
        <link rel="shortcut icon" href="favicon.ico" type="image/x-icon" />
    </head>
    <body>

        I like apples and oranges.

        I also like:
        <ol>
            <li>bananas</li>
            <li value="4">mangoes</li>
            <li>cherries</li>
            <li value="7">plums</li>
            <li>peaches</li>
            <li>grapes</li>
        </ol>

        You can see other fruits I like <a href="fruitlist.html">here</a>.

    </body>
</html>
```

When the browser encounters a li element with a value attribute, the counter for the list items is advanced to the attribute value. You can see this effect in Figure 9-8.

209

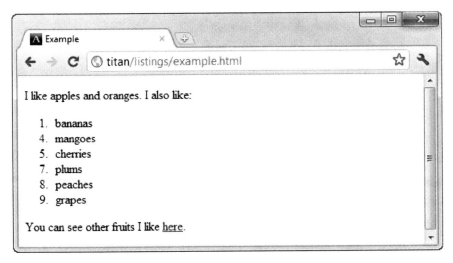

Figure 9-8. Creating nonconsecutive ordered lists

Creating Description Lists

A description list consists of a set of term/description groupings (i.e., a number of terms, each of which is accompanied by a definition of that term). You use three elements to define description lists: the dl, dt, and dd elements. These elements do not define attributes and have not changed in HTML5. Table 9-11 summarizes these elements.

Table 9-11. The Description List Elements

Element	Description	Style Convention

dl	Denotes a description list.	dl { display: block;
		    margin-before: 1em;
		    margin-after: 1em;
		    margin-start: 0;
		    margin-end: 0; }

dt	Denotes a term within a description list.	dt { display: block; }
dd	Denotes a definition within a description list.	dd { display: block; margin-start: 40px; }

You can see these elements used in Listing 9-10. Notice that multiple dd elements can be used for a single dt element, which allows you to provide multiple definitions for a single term.

Listing 9-10. Creating Description Lists

```
<!DOCTYPE HTML>
<html>
```

```
<head>
    <title>Example</title>
    <meta name="author" content="Adam Freeman"/>
    <meta name="description" content="A simple example"/>
    <link rel="shortcut icon" href="favicon.ico" type="image/x-icon" />
</head>
<body>

    I like apples and oranges.

    I also like:

    <dl>
        <dt>Apple</dt>
            <dd>The apple is the pomaceous fruit of the apple tree</dd>
            <dd><i>Malus domestica</i></dd>
        <dt>Banana</dt>
            <dd>The banana is the parthenocarpic fruit of the banana tree</dd>
            <dd><i>Musa acuminata</i></dd>
        <dt>Cherry</dt>
            <dd>The cherry is the stone fruit of the genus <i>Prunus</i></dd>
    </dl>

    You can see other fruits I like <a href="fruitlist.html">here</a>.
</body>
</html>
```

Creating Custom Lists

The HTML support for lists is more flexible than it might appear. You can create complex arrangements of lists using the ul element, combined with two features of CSS: the counter feature and the :before selector. I describe the counter feature and the :before selector (and its companion, :after) in Chapter 17. I don't want to get too far into CSS in this chapter, so I present this example as a self-contained demonstration for you to come back to when you have read the CSS chapters later in this book, or when you have a pressing need for some advanced lists. Listing 9-11 shows a list that contains two nested lists. All three lists are numbered using custom values.

Listing 9-11. Nesting Lists with Custom Counters

```
<!DOCTYPE HTML>
<html>
    <head>
        <title>Example</title>
        <meta name="author" content="Adam Freeman"/>
        <meta name="description" content="A simple example"/>
        <link rel="shortcut icon" href="favicon.ico" type="image/x-icon" />
        <style>
            body {
                counter-reset: OuterItemCount 5 InnerItemCount;
            }
```

```
            #outerlist > li:before {
                content: counter(OuterItemCount) ". ";
                counter-increment: OuterItemCount 2;
            }

            ul.innerlist > li:before {
                content: counter(InnerItemCount, lower-alpha) ". ";
                counter-increment: InnerItemCount;
            }
        </style>
    </head>
<body>

    I like apples and oranges.

    I also like:

    <ul id="outerlist" style="list-style-type: none">
        <li>bananas</li>
        <li>mangoes, including: </li>
            <ul class="innerlist">
                <li>Haden mangoes</li>
                <li>Keitt mangoes</li>
                <li>Kent mangoes</li>
            </ul>
        <li>cherries</li>
        <li>plums, including:
            <ul class="innerlist">
                <li>Elephant Heart plums</li>
                <li>Stanley plums</li>
                <li>Seneca plums</li>
            </ul>
        </li>
        <li>peaches</li>
        <li>grapes</li>
    </ul>

    You can see other fruits I like <a href="fruitlist.html">here</a>.
    </body>
</html>
```

You can see how the browser displays the lists in Figure 9-9.

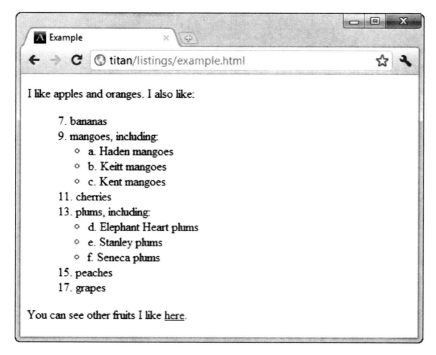

Figure 9-9. Custom lists using CSS features

There are a few things to note in the preceding example. All of the lists in this HTML document are unordered, and created using the ul element. This is so I can disable the standard bullet (using the list-style-type property) and rely on the content generated by the :before selector.

Notice also that the numbering of the outer list (the list of fruits) starts at 7 and goes up in steps of 2. This is something that you can't arrange using the standard ol element. The CSS counter feature is a little awkward to use, but is very flexible.

The final point to note is that the numbering of the inner lists (the varieties of mangoes and plums) is continuous. You could achieve a similar effect by using either the value attribute of the li element, or the start attribute of the ol element. However, both of those approaches require you to know how many list items you are working with in advance, which isn't always possible when working with web applications.

Dealing with Figures

The last of the grouping elements relates to figures. HTML5 defines figures as "a unit of content, optionally with a caption, that is self-contained, that is typically referenced as a single unit from the main flow of the document, and that can be moved away from the main flow of the document without affecting the document's meaning." This is a fairly general definition and can be applied more widely than the traditional idea of a figure, which is some form of illustration or diagram. You define figures using the figure element, which is summarized in Table 9-12.

Table 9-12. The figure Element

Element	figure
Element Type	Flow
Permitted Parents	Any element that can contain flow elements
Local Attributes	None
Contents	Flow content and, optionally, one figcaption element
Tag Style	Start and end tag
New in HTML5	Yes
Changes in HTML5	N/A
Style Convention	figure { display: block; margin-before: 1em; margin-after: 1em; margin-start: 40px; margin-end: 40px; }

The figure element can optionally contain a figcaption element, which denotes a caption for the figure. Table 9-13 summarizes the figcaption element.

Table 9-13. The figcaption Element

Element	figcaption
Element Type	N/A
Permitted Parents	figure
Local Attributes	None
Contents	Flow content
Tag Style	Start and end tag
New in HTML5	Yes
Changes in	N/A

HTML5

Style Convention   figcaption { display: block; }

You can see the figure and figcaption elements used together in Listing 9-12.

Listing 9-12. Using the figure and figcaption Elements

```
<!DOCTYPE HTML>
<html>
    <head>
        <title>Example</title>
        <meta name="author" content="Adam Freeman"/>
        <meta name="description" content="A simple example"/>
        <link rel="shortcut icon" href="favicon.ico" type="image/x-icon" />
    </head>
    <body>

        I like apples and oranges.

        <figure>
            <figcaption>Listing 23. Using the code element</figcaption>
            <code>var fruits = ["apples", "oranges", "mangoes", "cherries"];<br>
                document.writeln("I like " + fruits.length + " fruits");
            </code>
        </figure>

        You can see other fruits I like <a href="fruitlist.html">here</a>.
    </body>
</html>
```

In this example, I have used the figure element to create a figure around a code element. I have used the figcaption element to add a caption. Note that the figcaption element must be the first or last child of the figure element. You can see how the browser applies the style conventions for these elements in Figure 9-10.

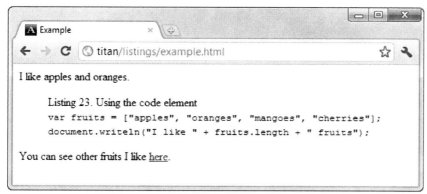

Figure 9-10. Using the figure and figcaption elements

Summary

In this chapter, I have shown you the HTML elements that let you group related content together—be it in a paragraph, a lengthy quotation from another source, or a list of related items. The elements described in this chapter are endlessly useful and simple to use, although some of the more sophisticated list options can require some practice to perfect.

CHAPTER 10

Creating Sections

In this chapter, I show you the elements you use to denote sections in your content—in effect, how to separate your content so that each topic or concept is isolated from the others. Many of the elements in this chapter are new, and they form a significant foundation in the effort to separate the meaning of elements from their presentation. Unfortunately, this means these elements are hard to demonstrate, because they have little or no visual impact on the content. To this end, I added some CSS styles to many of the examples in this chapter to emphasize the structure and changes these elements bring.

I don't explain the meaning of the CSS styles in this chapter. Chapter 4 contains a reminder of the key features of CSS, and the individual CSS properties are described from Chapter 16 onwards. Table 10-1 provides the summary for this chapter.

Table 10-1. Chapter Summary

Problem	Solution	Listing
Denote a heading.	Use the h1–h3 elements.	1
Denote a group of headings, only the first of which should be reflected in the document outline.	Use the hgroup element.	2, 3
Denote a significant topic or concept.	Use the section element.	4
Denote headers and footers.	Use the header and footer elements.	5
Denote a concentration of navigation elements.	Use the nav element.	6
Denote a major topic or concept that could be distributed independently.	Use the article element.	7
Denote content that is tangentially related to the surrounding content.	Use the aside element.	8
Denote contact information for a document or article.	Use the address element.	9
Create a section the user can expand to get additional details.	Use the details and summary elements.	10

Adding Basic Headings

The h1 element represents a heading. HTML defines a hierarchy of heading elements, with h1 being the highest ranked. The other heading elements are h2, h3, through to h6. Table 10-2 summarizes the h1–h6 elements.

Table 10-2. *The h1–h6 Elements*

Element:	h1–h6
Element Type:	Flow
Permitted Parents:	The hgroup element or any element that can contain flow elements. These elements cannot be descendants of the address element.
Local Attributes:	None
Contents:	**Phrasing content**
Tag Style:	Start and end tags
New in HTML5?	No
Changes in HTML5	None
Style Convention	See Table 10-3.

Headings of the same rank are typically used to break up content so that each topic is in its own section. Headings of descending rank are typically used to represent different aspects of the same topic. An additional benefit of these elements is that they create a document outline, where the user can get a sense of the overall nature and structure of the document simply by looking at the headings and more rapidly navigate to an area of interest by following the heading hierarchy. Listing 10-1 shows the h1–h3 elements in use.

Listing 10-1. *Using the h1–h3 Elements*

```
<!DOCTYPE HTML>
<html>
    <head>
        <title>Example</title>
        <meta name="author" content="Adam Freeman"/>
        <meta name="description" content="A simple example"/>
        <link rel="shortcut icon" href="favicon.ico" type="image/x-icon" />
    </head>
    <body>
        <h1>Fruits I like</h1>
```

```
I like apples and oranges.
<h2>Additional fruits</h2>
I also like bananas, mangoes, cherries, apricots, plums, peaches and grapes.
<h3>More information</h3>
You can see other fruits I like <a href="fruitlist.html">here</a>.

<h1>Activities I like</h1>
<p>I like to swim, cycle and run. I am in training for my first triathlon,
but it is hard work.</p>
<h2>Kinds of Triathlon</h2>
There are different kinds of triathlon - sprint, Olympic and so on.
<h3>The kind of triathlon I am aiming for</h3>
I am aiming for Olympic, which consists of the following:
<ol>
    <li>1.5km swim</li>
    <li>40km cycle</li>
    <li>10km run</li>
</ol>
    </body>
</html>
```

I showed only the h1, h2, and h3 headings in the listing because it is rare to have content that warrants any additional depth. The exceptions tend to be very technical and precise content, such as contracts and specifications. Most content requires two or three levels of heading at most. As an example, I use three levels of heading in my Apress books. Although the Apress template defines five levels of heading, the copy editors become uncomfortable if I use the fourth and fifth levels.

You can see how the browser displays the h1, h2, and h3 elements in the listing in Figure 10-1.

Figure 10-1. Displaying the h1, h2, and h3 elements using the default style conventions

As you can see in the figure, each level of header has a different style convention. Table 10-3 shows the style convention for each header element.

Table 10-3. The Style Conventions for the h1–h6 Elements

Element	Style Convention
h1	h1 { display: block; font-size: 2em; margin-before: 0.67em; margin-after: 0.67em; margin-start: 0; margin-end: 0; font-weight: bold; }
h2	h2 { display: block; font-size: 1.5em; margin-before: 0.83em; margin-after: 0.83em; margin-start: 0; margin-end: 0; font-weight: bold; }
h3	h3 { display: block; font-size: 1.17em; margin-before: 1em; margin-after: 1em; margin-start: 0; margin-end: 0; font-weight: bold; }
h4	h4 { display: block; margin-before: 1.33em; margin-after: 1.33em; margin-start: 0; margin-end: 0; font-weight: bold; }

h5	h5 { display: block; font-size: .83em; margin-before: 1.67em; margin-after: 1.67em; margin-start: 0; margin-end: 0; font-weight: bold; }
h6	h6 { display: block; font-size: .67em; margin-before: 2.33em; margin-after: 2.33em; margin-start: 0; margin-end: 0; font-weight: bold; }

You don't have to respect the h1–h6 element hierarchy, but you run the risk of confusing the user if you deviate from it. Hierarchical headings are so prevalent that users have a fixed expectation of how they work.

Hiding Subheadings

The hgroup element allows you to treat multiple header elements as a single item without affecting the outline of your HTML document. Table 10-4 summarizes the hgroup element.

Table 10-4. The hgroup Element

Element:	hgroup
Element Type:	Flow
Permitted Parents:	Any element that can contain flow elements
Local Attributes:	None
Contents:	**One or more header elements** (h1–h6)
Tag Style:	Start and end tags
New in HTML5?	**Yes**
Changes in HTML5	N/A
Style Convention	hgroup { display: block; }

The most common problem that the hgroup solves is subtitles. Imagine that I want to create a section in my document with the title "Fruits I Like" with the subtitle "How I Learned to Love Citrus". I could use the h1 and h2 elements, as shown in Listing 10-2.

Listing 10-2. Using the h1 and h2 Elements to Create a Title with a Subtitle

```
<!DOCTYPE HTML>
<html>
    <head>
        <title>Example</title>
        <meta name="author" content="Adam Freeman"/>
        <meta name="description" content="A simple example"/>
        <link rel="shortcut icon" href="favicon.ico" type="image/x-icon" />
    </head>
    <body>
        <h1>Fruits I Like</h1>
        <h2>How I Learned to Love Citrus</h2>
        I like apples and oranges.
        <h2>Additional fruits</h2>
        I also like bananas, mangoes, cherries, apricots, plums, peaches and grapes.
        <h3>More information</h3>
        You can see other fruits I like <a href="fruitlist.html">here</a>.

        <h1>Activities I Like</h1>
        <p>I like to swim, cycle and run. I am in training for my first triathlon,
        but it is hard work.</p>
        <h2>Kinds of Triathlon</h2>
        There are different kinds of triathlon - sprint, Olympic and so on.
        <h3>The kind of triathlon I am aiming for</h3>
        I am aiming for Olympic, which consists of the following:
        <ol>
            <li>1.5km swim</li>
            <li>40km cycle</li>
            <li>10km run</li>
        </ol>
    </body>
</html>
```

The problem here is that you haven't been able to differentiate between the h2 element that is the subtitle and the h2 element that is a lower-level heading. If you wrote a script that went through your document to build an outline based on the h1–h6 elements, you would get a distorted result, like this:

```
Fruits I Like
    How I Learned to Love Citrus
    Additional fruits
        More information
Activities I Like
    Kinds of Triathlon
        The kind of triathlon I am aiming for
```

This gives the appearance that How I Learned to Love Citrus is a section header, not a subtitle. You can address this problem using the hgroup element, as shown in Listing 10-3.

Listing 10-3. Using the hgroup Element

```
<!DOCTYPE HTML>
<html>
    <head>
        <title>Example</title>
        <meta name="author" content="Adam Freeman"/>
        <meta name="description" content="A simple example"/>
        <link rel="shortcut icon" href="favicon.ico" type="image/x-icon" />
        <style>
            h1, h2, h3 { background: grey; color: white; }

            hgroup > h1 { margin-bottom: 0px;}

            hgroup > h2 { background: grey; color: white; font-size: 1em;
                          margin-top: 0px; }
        </style>
    </head>
    <body>
            <hgroup>
                <h1>Fruits I Like</h1>
                <h2>How I Learned to Love Citrus</h2>
            </hgroup>
            I like apples and oranges.
            <h2>Additional fruits</h2>
            I also like bananas, mangoes, cherries, apricots, plums, peaches and grapes.
            <h3>More information</h3>
            You can see other fruits I like <a href="fruitlist.html">here</a>.

            <h1>Activities I like</h1>
            <p>I like to swim, cycle and run. I am in training for my first triathlon,
            but it is hard work.</p>
            <h2>Kinds of Triathlon</h2>
            There are different kinds of triathlon - sprint, Olympic and so on.
            <h3>The kind of triathlon I am aiming for</h3>
            I am aiming for Olympic, which consists of the following:
            <ol>
                <li>1.5km swim</li>
                <li>40km cycle</li>
                <li>10km run</li>
            </ol>
    </body>
</html>
```

The position in the h1–h6 hierarchy of an hgroup element is determined by the first heading element child within the hgroup. For example, the hgroup in the listing is equivalent to an h1 element because that is the first child. Only the first h1–h6 element is included in the outline of a document, which gives you an outline like this:

```
Fruits I Like
    Additional fruits
```

```
        More information
Activities I Like
    Kinds of Triathlon
        The kind of triathlon I am aiming for
```

There is no longer confusion about the subtitle h2 element—the hgroup element tells you to ignore it. The second issue you have to deal with is making the subtitle visually distinctive from regular h2 elements. You can see that I applied some simple styles in the listing, the effect of which can be seen in Figure 10-2. You can learn how the CSS selectors in the listing work in Chapter 17.

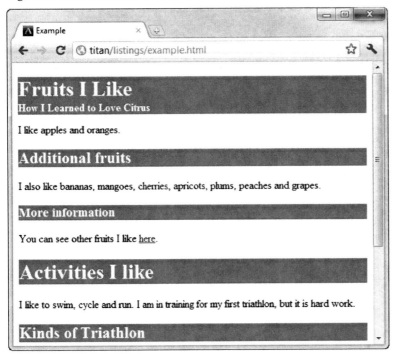

Figure 10-2. Making the relationship between elements in an hgroup visually explicit

I don't suggest that you adopt such a stark style, but you can see that you can make the relationship between elements in an hgroup element visually explicit by applying styles that eliminate some of the margins of the heading elements and bringing the elements together with a common background color.

Creating Sections

The section element is new to HTML5 and, as its name suggests, denotes a section of a document. When you use heading elements, you create *implied* sections, but this element lets you make them explicit and also allows you to divorce the sections of your document from the h1–h6 elements. There are no hard-and-fast rules about when to use the section element, but as a rule of thumb, the section element should be used to contain content that would be listed in a document's outline or table of contents. Section elements usually contain of one or more paragraphs of content and a heading, although the heading is optional. Table 10-5 summarizes the section element.

Table 10-5. The section Element

Element:	section
Element Type:	Flow
Permitted Parents:	Any element that can contain flow elements. The section element cannot be a child of the address element.
Local Attributes:	None
Contents:	style elements and flow content.
Tag Style:	Start and end tags
New in HTML5?	**Yes**
Changes in HTML5	N/A
Style Convention	section { display: block; }

Listing 10-4 shows the section element in use.

Listing 10-4. Using the section Element

```
<!DOCTYPE HTML>
<html>
    <head>
        <title>Example</title>
        <meta name="author" content="Adam Freeman"/>
        <meta name="description" content="A simple example"/>
        <link rel="shortcut icon" href="favicon.ico" type="image/x-icon" />
        <style>
            h1, h2, h3 { background: grey; color: white; }
            hgroup > h1 { margin-bottom: 0px; }
            hgroup > h2 { background: grey; color: white; font-size: 1em;
                          margin-top: 0px;}
        </style>
    </head>
    <body>
        <section>
            <hgroup>
                <h1>Fruits I Like</h1>
                <h2>How I Learned to Love Citrus</h2>
            </hgroup>
            I like apples and oranges.
            <section>
```

225

```
            <h1>Additional fruits</h1>
            I also like bananas, mangoes, cherries, apricots, plums,
            peaches and grapes.
            <section>
                <h1>More information</h1>
                You can see other fruits I like <a href="fruitlist.html">here</a>.
            </section>
        </section>
    </section>

    <h1>Activities I like</h1>
    <p>I like to swim, cycle and run. I am in training for my first triathlon,
            but it is hard work.</p>
    <h2>Kinds of Triathlon</h2>
    There are different kinds of triathlon - sprint, Olympic and so on.
    <h3>The kind of triathlon I am aiming for</h3>
    I am aiming for Olympic, which consists of the following:
    <ol>
        <li>1.5km swim</li>
        <li>40km cycle</li>
        <li>10km run</li>
    </ol>
    </body>
</html>
```

I have defined three section elements in this listing, one of which is nested within the other. Notice that the heading element in each is an h1. When using the section element, the browser is responsible for figuring out the hierarchy of heading elements, freeing you from having to determine and maintain the appropriate sequence of h1–h6 elements—at least in principle. The actual browser implementations differ slightly. Google Chrome, Internet Explorer 9 (IE9), and Firefox are able to derive the implied hierarchy and work out the relative rankings for each h1 element, as shown in Figure 10-3.

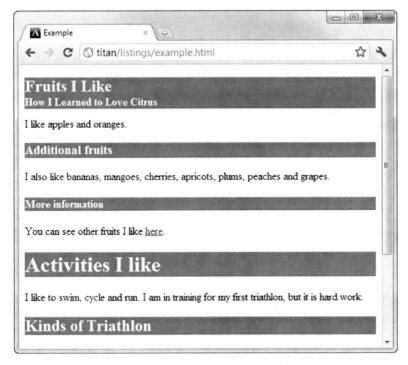

Figure 10-3. Using the section element with nested h1 elements in Chrome

This is good, but if you are observant, you noticed that the font used to display the h1 element whose content is Fruits I Like is smaller than the font used for the other h1 element at the same level—the Activities I like element. This is because some browsers (including Chrome and Firefox) apply a different style to h1 (and h2–h6) elements when they appear within section, article, aside, and nav elements. (The last three are described later in this chapter.) This new style is the same as the style convention for the h2 element. IE9 doesn't apply a special style, as shown in Figure 10-4. This is the correct behavior.

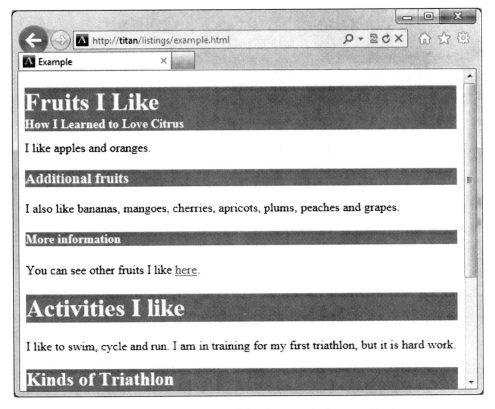

Figure 10-4. Using the section element with h1 elements in Internet Explorer

Further, not all browsers properly support creating an implied hierarchy of nested heading elements of the same type. You can see how Opera deals with these elements in Figure 10-5. Safari deals these elements in the same way—by ignoring the hierarchy implementations created by the section elements.

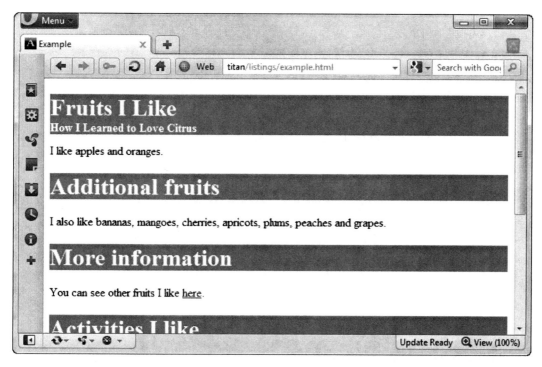

Figure 10-5. Using the section element with h1 elements in Opera

You can overcome the special style that Chrome and Firefox apply by creating your own styles, which take precedence over the styles defined by the browser (as I explained in Chapter 4). Internet Explorer does what you would expect. But you can't do much about Opera and Safari—and until the browser implementations become more consistent, this handy feature should be used with caution.

Adding Headers and Footers

The header element denotes the header of a section. It can contain any content that you wish to denote as being the header, including a masthead or logo. In terms of other elements, a header element typically contains one h1–h6 element or an hgroup element, and it can also contain navigation elements for the section. See the nav element (discussed in the upcoming "Adding Navigation Blocks" section) for details of navigation. Table 10-6 summarizes the header element.

Table 10-6. *The header Element*

Element:	`header`
Element Type:	Flow
Permitted Parents:	Any element that can contain flow elements. The header element cannot be a descendent of the `address` or `footer` element and cannot be a descendant of another `header` element.
Local Attributes:	None
Contents:	Flow content.
Tag Style:	Start and end tags
New in HTML5?	**Yes**
Changes in HTML5	N/A
Style Convention	`header { display: block; }`

The `footer` element is the complement to `header` and represents the footer for a section. A `footer` usually contains summary information about a section and can include details of the author, rights information, links to associated content, and logos and disclaimers. Table 10-7 summarizes the `footer` element.

Table 10-7. *The footer Element*

Element:	`footer`
Element Type:	Flow
Permitted Parents:	Any element that can contain flow elements. The `footer` element cannot be a descendent of the `address` or `header` element and cannot be a descendant of another `footer` element.
Local Attributes:	None
Contents:	Flow content.
Tag Style:	Start and end tags

New in HTML5?	**Yes**
Changes in HTML5	N/A
Style Convention	`footer { display: block; }`

You can see the header and footer elements in Listing 10-5.

Listing 10-5. Using the header and footer Elements

```html
<!DOCTYPE HTML>
<html>
    <head>
        <title>Example</title>
        <meta name="author" content="Adam Freeman"/>
        <meta name="description" content="A simple example"/>
        <link rel="shortcut icon" href="favicon.ico" type="image/x-icon" />
        <style>
            h1, h2, h3 { background: grey; color: white; }
            hgroup > h1 { margin-bottom: 0; margin-top: 0}
            hgroup > h2 { background: grey; color: white; font-size: 1em;
                        margin-top: 0px; margin-bottom: 2px}

            body > header  *, footer > * { background:transparent; color:black;}
            body > section, body > section > section,
            body > section > section > section {margin-left: 10px;}

            body > header, body > footer {
                border: medium solid black; padding-left: 5px; margin: 10px 0 10px 0;
            }
        </style>
    </head>
    <body>
        <header>
            <hgroup>
                <h1>Things I like</h1>
                <h2>by Adam Freeman</h2>
            </hgroup>
        </header>
        <section>
            <header>
                <hgroup>
                    <h1>Fruits I Like</h1>
                    <h2>How I Learned to Love Citrus</h2>
                </hgroup>
            </header>
            I like apples and oranges.
            <section>
                <h1>Additional fruits</h1>
```

```
                    I also like bananas, mangoes, cherries, apricots, plums,
                    peaches and grapes.
                    <section>
                        <h1>More information</h1>
                        You can see other fruits I like <a href="fruitlist.html">here</a>.
                    </section>
                </section>
            </section>

            <section>
                <header>
                    <h1>Activities I like</h1>
                </header>
                <section>
                    <p>I like to swim, cycle and run. I am in training for my first
                    triathlon, but it is hard work.</p>
                    <h1>Kinds of Triathlon</h1>
                    There are different kinds of triathlon - sprint, Olympic and so on.
                    <section>
                        <h1>The kind of triathlon I am aiming for</h1>
                        I am aiming for Olympic, which consists of the following:
                        <ol>
                            <li>1.5km swim</li>
                            <li>40km cycle</li>
                            <li>10km run</li>
                        </ol>
                    </section>
                </section>
            </section>
            <footer id="mainFooter">
                &#169;2011, Adam Freeman. <a href="http://apress.com">Visit Apress</a>
            </footer>
        </body>
</html>
```

I defined three header elements in this example. When a header is a child of the body element, it is assumed to be the header for the entire document (but be careful—this is not the same as the head element, which I described in Chapter 7). When the header element is part of a section (either implied or explicitly defined using the section element), it is the header for that section. I added some styles to the document to make it easier to see the hierarchical relationship between the various sections and headings. You can see this in Figure 10-6.

Notice the relative sizes of the fonts. This is presumably why Google Chrome and Firefox redefine the h1–h6 elements when they are in a section element. It is to differentiate between the top-level h1 header and those that are nested in sections. This doesn't excuse the gratuitous redefinition of styles, but it does put it in context.

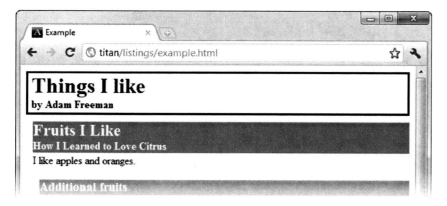

Figure 10-6. Using the header element

You can see the effect of the footer in Figure 10-7.

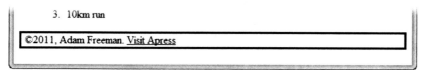

Figure 10-7. Adding a footer element

Adding Navigation Blocks

The nav element denotes a section of the document that contains links to other pages or to other parts of the same page. Obviously, not all hyperlinks have to be in a nav element. The purpose of this element is to identify the major navigation sections of a document. Table 10-8 describes the nav element.

Table 10-8. The nav Element

Element:	nav
Element Type:	Flow
Permitted Parents:	Any element that can contain flow elements, but this element cannot be a descendant of the address element.
Local Attributes:	None
Contents:	Flow content.
Tag Style:	Start and end tags
New in HTML5?	**Yes**

Changes in HTML5	N/A
Style Convention	nav { display: block; }

Listing 10-6 shows the use of the nav element.

Listing 10-6. Using the nav Element

```
<!DOCTYPE HTML>
<html>
    <head>
        <title>Example</title>
        <meta name="author" content="Adam Freeman"/>
        <meta name="description" content="A simple example"/>
        <link rel="shortcut icon" href="favicon.ico" type="image/x-icon" />
        <style>
            h1, h2, h3 { background: grey; color: white; }
            hgroup > h1 { margin-bottom: 0; margin-top: 0}
            hgroup > h2 { background: grey; color: white; font-size: 1em;
                        margin-top: 0px; margin-bottom: 2px}

            body > header  *, body > footer * { background:transparent; color:black;}
            body > section, body > section > section,
            body > section > section > section {margin-left: 10px;}

            body > header, body > footer {
                border: medium solid black; padding-left: 5px; margin: 10px 0 10px 0;
            }

            body > nav { text-align: center; padding: 2px; border : dashed thin black;}
            body > nav > a {padding: 2px; color: black}
        </style>
    </head>
    <body>
        <header>
            <hgroup>
                <h1>Things I like</h1>
                <h2>by Adam Freeman</h2>
            </hgroup>
            <nav>
                <h1>Contents</h1>
                <ul>
                    <li><a href="#fruitsilike">Fruits I Like</a></li>
                    <ul>
                        <li><a href="#morefruit">Additional Fruits</a></li>
                    </ul>
                    <li><a href="#activitiesilike">Activities I Like</a></li>
                    <ul>
                        <li><a href="#tritypes">Kinds of Triathlon</a></li>
```

234

```
                <li><a href="#mytri">The kind of triathlon I am
                    aiming for</a></li>
            </ul>
        </ul>
    </nav>
</header>
<section>
    <header>
        <hgroup>
            <h1 id="fruitsilike">Fruits I Like</h1>
            <h2>How I Learned to Love Citrus</h2>
        </hgroup>
    </header>
    I like apples and oranges.
    <section>
        <h1 id="morefruit">Additional fruits</h1>
        I also like bananas, mangoes, cherries, apricots, plums,
        peaches and grapes.
        <section>
            <h1>More information</h1>
            You can see other fruits I like <a href="fruitlist.html">here</a>.
        </section>
    </section>
</section>

<section>
    <header>
        <h1 id="activitiesilike">Activities I like</h1>
    </header>
    <section>
        <p>I like to swim, cycle and run. I am in training for my first
        triathlon, but it is hard work.</p>
        <h1 id="tritypes">Kinds of Triathlon</h1>
        There are different kinds of triathlon - sprint, Olympic and so on.
        <section>
            <h1 id="mytri">The kind of triathlon I am aiming for</h1>
            I am aiming for Olympic, which consists of the following:
            <ol>
                <li>1.5km swim</li>
                <li>40km cycle</li>
                <li>10km run</li>
            </ol>
        </section>
    </section>
</section>
<nav>
    More Information:
    <a href="http://fruit.org">Learn More About Fruit</a>
    <a href="http://triathlon.org">Learn More About Triathlons</a>
</nav>
<footer id="mainFooter">
    &#169;2011, Adam Freeman. <a href="http://apress.com">Visit Apress</a>
```

```
            </footer>
        </body>
</html>
```

I added a couple of nav elements to the document to give a sense of the flexibility of this element. The first nav element provides the user with navigation within the document. I used ul, li, and a elements to create a hierarchical set of relative hyperlinks. You can see how this is displayed by the browser in Figure 10-8.

Figure 10-8. Using a nav element to create a content navigation section

I placed this nav element inside the main header element for the document. This is not compulsory, but I like to do this to indicate that this is the main nav element. Notice that I mixed the h1 element in with the other content. The nav element can contain any flow content, not just hyperlinks. I added the second nav element to the end of the document, providing the user with some links to get more information. You can see how the browser renders this in Figure 10-9.

Figure 10-9. Using a nav element to provide external navigation

In both instances of the nav element, I added styles to the style element in the document to make the additions visually distinctive. The style conventions for the nav element don't explicitly denote the nav element's content.

Working with Articles

The article element represents a self-contained piece of content in an HTML document that could, in principle, be distributed or used independently from the rest of the page (such as through an RSS feed). That's not to say you *have* to distribute it independently, just that independence is the guidance for when to use this element. Good examples include a new article and a blog entry. Table 10-9 summarizes the article element.

Table 10-9. The article Element

Element:	article
Element Type:	Flow
Permitted Parents:	Any element that can contain flow elements, but this element cannot be a descendant of the address element.
Local Attributes:	None
Contents:	style elements and flow content.
Tag Style:	Start and end tags
New in HTML5?	**Yes**
Changes in HTML5	N/A
Style Convention	article { display: block; }

Listing 10-7 shows the article element in use.

Listing 10-7. Using the article Element

```
<!DOCTYPE HTML>
<html>
    <head>
        <title>Example</title>
        <meta name="author" content="Adam Freeman"/>
        <meta name="description" content="A simple example"/>
        <link rel="shortcut icon" href="favicon.ico" type="image/x-icon" />
        <style>
            h1, h2, h3, article > footer { background: grey; color: white; }
            hgroup > h1 { margin-bottom: 0; margin-top: 0}
```

```
            hgroup > h2 { background: grey; color: white; font-size: 1em;
                    margin-top: 0px; margin-bottom: 2px}

            body > header  *, body > footer * { background:transparent; color:black;}

            article {border: thin black solid; padding: 10px; margin-bottom: 5px}
            article > footer {padding:5px; margin: 5px; text-align: center}
            article > footer > nav > a {color: white}

            body > article > section,
            body > article > section > section {margin-left: 10px;}

            body > header, body > footer {
                border: medium solid black; padding-left: 5px; margin: 10px 0 10px 0;
            }
            body > nav { text-align: center; padding: 2px; border : dashed thin black;}
            body > nav > a {padding: 2px; color: black}
        </style>
    </head>
    <body>
        <header>
            <hgroup>
                <h1>Things I like</h1>
                <h2>by Adam Freeman</h2>
            </hgroup>
            <nav>
                <h1>Contents</h1>
                <ul>
                    <li><a href="#fruitsilike">Fruits I Like</a></li>
                    <li><a href="#activitiesilike">Activities I Like</a></li>
                </ul>
            </nav>
        </header>

        <article>
            <header>
                <hgroup>
                    <h1 id="fruitsilike">Fruits I Like</h1>
                    <h2>How I Learned to Love Citrus</h2>
                </hgroup>
            </header>
            I like apples and oranges.
            <section>
                <h1 id="morefruit">Additional fruits</h1>
                I also like bananas, mangoes, cherries, apricots, plums,
                peaches and grapes.
                <section>
                    <h1>More information</h1>
                    You can see other fruits I like <a href="fruitlist.html">here</a>
                </section>
            </section>
            <footer>
```

```
            <nav>
                More Information:
                <a href="http://fruit.org">Learn More About Fruit</a>
            </nav>
        </footer>
    </article>

    <article>
        <header>
            <hgroup>
                <h1 id="activitiesilike">Activities I like</h1>
                <h2>It hurts, but I keep doing it</h2>
            </hgroup>
        </header>
        <section>
            <p>I like to swim, cycle and run. I am in training for my first
            triathlon, but it is hard work.</p>
            <h1 id="tritypes">Kinds of Triathlon</h1>
            There are different kinds of triathlon - sprint, Olympic and so on.
            <section>
                <h1 id="mytri">The kind of triathlon I am aiming for</h1>
                I am aiming for Olympic, which consists of the following:
                <ol>
                    <li>1.5km swim</li>
                    <li>40km cycle</li>
                    <li>10km run</li>
                </ol>
            </section>
        </section>
        <footer>
            <nav>
                More Information:
                <a href="http://triathlon.org">Learn More About Triathlons</a>
            </nav>
        </footer>
    </article>

    <footer id="mainFooter">
        &#169;2011, Adam Freeman. <a href="http://apress.com">Visit Apress</a>
    </footer>
</body>
</html>
```

In this example, I restructured my document to be more consistent with the general style of a blog, although perhaps it's not the most interesting blog available. The main part of the document is broken down into three parts. The first is the header, which transcends individual entries and provides an anchor point for the rest of document. The second part is the footer, which balances the header and provides the user with some basic information that applies to the rest of the content. The new addition is the third part: the article elements. In this example, each article describes a kind of thing I like. This meets the independence test because each description of a thing I like is self-contained and can be distributed on its own while still making some kind of sense. Once again, I added some styles to highlight the section effect of the element, which you can see in Figure 10-10.

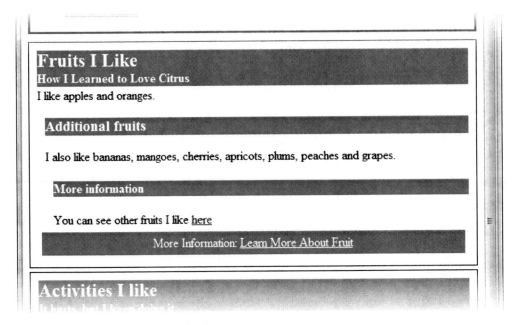

Figure 10-10. Applying the article element

The article element can be applied as flexibly as the other new semantic elements. For example, you could nest article elements to indicate the original article and then each update or comment that you received. As with some of the other elements, the value of article is contextual—that which adds meaningful structure in one kind of content may not add value in another. Judgment (and consistency) is required.

Creating Sidebars

The aside element denotes content that is only tangentially related to the surrounding element. This is similar to a sidebar in a book or magazine. The content has something to do with the rest of the page, article, or section, but it isn't part of the main flow. It could be some additional background, a set of links to related articles, and so on. Table 10-10 summarizes the aside element.

Table 10-10. The aside Element

Element:	`aside`
Element Type:	Flow
Permitted Parents:	Any element that can contain flow elements, but this element cannot be a descendant of the `address` element.
Local Attributes:	None
Contents:	`style` elements and flow content
Tag Style:	Start and end tags
New in HTML5?	**Yes**
Changes in HTML5	N/A
Style Convention	`aside { display: block; }`

Listing 10-8 shows the `aside` element in use. I added an aside to one of the articles and added styles to give it the appearance of a simple magazine-style sidebar.

Listing 10-8. Adding and Styling the asideEeement

```
<!DOCTYPE HTML>
<html>
    <head>
        <title>Example</title>
        <meta name="author" content="Adam Freeman"/>
        <meta name="description" content="A simple example"/>
        <link rel="shortcut icon" href="favicon.ico" type="image/x-icon" />
        <style>
            h1, h2, h3, article > footer { background: grey; color: white; }
            hgroup > h1 { margin-bottom: 0; margin-top: 0}
            hgroup > h2 { background: grey; color: white; font-size: 1em;
                    margin-top: 0px; margin-bottom: 2px}

            body > header  *, body > footer * { background:transparent; color:black;}

            article {border: thin black solid; padding: 10px; margin-bottom: 5px}
            article > footer {padding:5px; margin: 5px; text-align: center}
            article > footer > nav > a {color: white}

            body > article > section,
            body > article > section > section {margin-left: 10px;}
```

```
        body > header, body > footer {
            border: medium solid black; padding-left: 5px; margin: 10px 0 10px 0;
        }
        body > nav { text-align: center; padding: 2px; border : dashed thin black;}
        body > nav > a {padding: 2px; color: black}

        aside { width:40%; background:white; float:right; border: thick solid black;
            margin-left: 5px;}
        aside > section { padding: 5px;}
        aside > h1 {background: white; color: black; text-align:center}
    </style>
</head>
<body>
    <header>
        <hgroup>
            <h1>Things I like</h1>
            <h2>by Adam Freeman</h2>
        </hgroup>
        <nav>
            <h1>Contents</h1>
            <ul>
                <li><a href="#fruitsilike">Fruits I Like</a></li>
                <li><a href="#activitiesilike">Activities I Like</a></li>
            </ul>
        </nav>
    </header>

    <article>
        <header>
            <hgroup>
                <h1 id="fruitsilike">Fruits I Like</h1>
                <h2>How I Learned to Love Citrus</h2>
            </hgroup>
        </header>
        <aside>
            <h1>Why Fruit is Healthy</h1>
                <section>
                Here are three reasons why everyone should eat more fruit:
                <ol>
                    <li>Fruit contains lots of vitamins</li>
                    <li>Fruit is a source of fibre</li>
                    <li>Fruit contains few calories</li>
                </ol>
            </section>
        </aside>
        I like apples and oranges.
        <section>
            <h1 id="morefruit">Additional fruits</h1>
            I also like bananas, mangoes, cherries, apricots, plums,
            peaches and grapes.
            <section>
```

```
            <h1>More information</h1>
            You can see other fruits I like <a href="fruitlist.html">here</a>
        </section>
    </section>
    <footer>
        <nav>
            More Information:
            <a href="http://fruit.org">Learn More About Fruit</a>
        </nav>
    </footer>
</article>
<article>
    <header>
        <hgroup>
            <h1 id="activitiesilike">Activities I like</h1>
            <h2>It hurts, but I keep doing it</h2>
        </hgroup>
    </header>
    <section>
        <p>I like to swim, cycle and run. I am in training for my first
        triathlon, but it is hard work.</p>
        <h1 id="tritypes">Kinds of Triathlon</h1>
        There are different kinds of triathlon - sprint, Olympic and so on.
        <section>
            <h1 id="mytri">The kind of triathlon I am aiming for</h1>
            I am aiming for Olympic, which consists of the following:
            <ol>
                <li>1.5km swim</li>
                <li>40km cycle</li>
                <li>10km run</li>
            </ol>
        </section>
    </section>
    <footer>
        <nav>
            More Information:
            <a href="http://triathlon.org">Learn More About Triathlons</a>
        </nav>
    </footer>
</article>
<footer id="mainFooter">
    &#169;2011, Adam Freeman. <a href="http://apress.com">Visit Apress</a>
</footer>
</body>
</html>
```

You can see the effect of the aside element and the additional styles in Figure 10-11. I added some filler text to the document shown in the figure to make the flow of content more apparent.

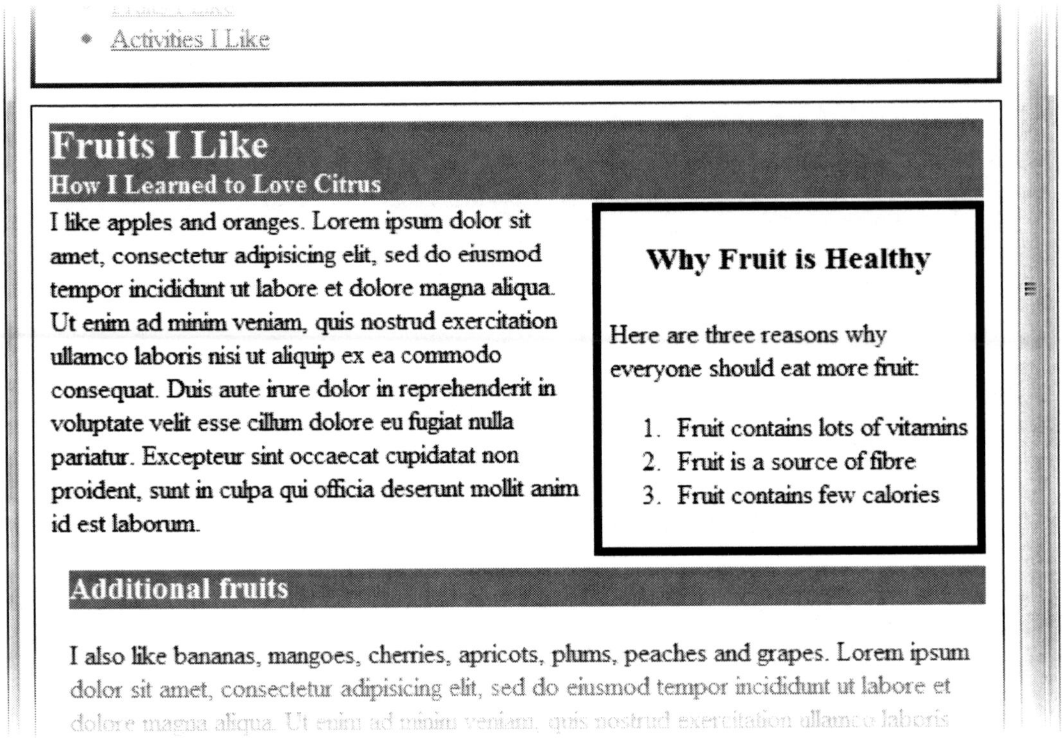

Figure 10-11. Applying and styling the aside element

Providing Contact Information

The address element is used to denote contact information for a document or article element. Table 10-11 summarizes the address element.

Table 10-11. The address Element

Element:	address
Element Type:	Flow
Permitted Parents:	Any element that can contain flow elements
Local Attributes:	None
Contents:	Flow content, but the h1–h6, section, header, footer, nav, article, and aside elements may not be used as descendants of

this element.

Tag Style:	Start and end tags
New in HTML5?	**Yes**
Changes in HTML5	N/A
Style Convention	`address { display: block; font-style: italic; }`

When the address element is a descendant of an article element, it is assumed to provide contact information for that article. Otherwise, when an address element is a child of a body element (and there is no article element between the body and address elements), the address is assumed to provide contact information for the entire document.

The address element must not be used to denote addresses that are not contact information for a document or article. For example, you can't use this element to denote addresses of customers or users in the content of a document. Listing 10-9 shows the address element in use.

Listing 10-9. Using the address Element

```
...
<body>
    <header>
        <hgroup>
            <h1>Things I like</h1>
            <h2>by Adam Freeman</h2>
        </hgroup>
        <address>
            Questions and comments? <a href="mailto:adam@myboringblog.com">Email me</a>
        </address>
        <nav>
            <h1>Contents</h1>
            <ul>
                <li><a href="#fruitsilike">Fruits I Like</a></li>
                <li><a href="#activitiesilike">Activities I Like</a></li>
            </ul>
        </nav>
    </header>

    <article>
        <header>
            <hgroup>
...
```

I added the address element to the header for the document. In this case, I provided an email address for users/readers to contact me. You can see the addition in Figure 10-12.

Figure 10-12. Adding an address element

Creating a Details Section

The details element creates a section of the document that the user can expand to get further details about a topic. Table 10-12 summarizes the details element.

Table 10-12. The details Element

Element:	details
Element Type:	Flow
Permitted Parents:	Any element that can contain flow elements
Local Attributes:	open
Contents:	An (optional) summary element and flow content
Tag Style:	Start and end tags
New in HTML5?	**Yes**
Changes in HTML5	N/A
Style Convention	details { display: block; }

The details element usually contains a summary element, which creates a label or title for the details section. Table 10-13 describes the summary element.

Table 10-13. The summary Element

Element:	summary
Element Type:	N/A
Permitted Parents:	The details element
Local Attributes:	None
Contents:	Phrasing content
Tag Style:	Start and end tags
New in HTML5?	**Yes**
Changes in HTML5	N/A
Style Convention	summary { display: block; }

You can see both the details and summary elements used in Listing 10-10.

Listing 10-10. Using the summary and details Elements

```
<!DOCTYPE HTML>
<html>
    <head>
        <title>Example</title>
        <meta name="author" content="Adam Freeman"/>
        <meta name="description" content="A simple example"/>
        <link rel="shortcut icon" href="favicon.ico" type="image/x-icon" />
        <style>
            h1, h2, h3, article > footer { background: grey; color: white; }
            hgroup > h1 { margin-bottom: 0; margin-top: 0}
            hgroup > h2 { background: grey; color: white; font-size: 1em;
                        margin-top: 0px; margin-bottom: 2px}
            body > header  *, body > footer * { background:transparent; color:black;}
            body > article > section,
            body > article > section > section {margin-left: 10px;}
            body > header {
                border: medium solid black; padding-left: 5px; margin: 10px 0 10px 0;
            }
            article {border: thin black solid; padding: 10px; margin-bottom: 5px}
            details {border: solid thin black; padding: 5px}
            details > summary { font-weight: bold}
        </style>
    </head>
```

```
<body>
    <header>
        <hgroup>
            <h1>Things I like</h1>
            <h2>by Adam Freeman</h2>
        </hgroup>
    </header>
    <article>
        <header>
            <hgroup>
                <h1 id="activitiesilike">Activities I like</h1>
                <h2>It hurts, but I keep doing it</h2>
            </hgroup>
        </header>
        <section>
            <p>I like to swim, cycle and run. I am in training for my first
            triathlon, but it is hard work.</p>
            <details>
                <summary>Kinds of Triathlon</summary>
                There are different kinds of triathlon - sprint, Olympic and so on.
                I am aiming for Olympic, which consists of the following:
                <ol>
                    <li>1.5km swim</li>
                    <li>40km cycle</li>
                    <li>10km run</li>
                </ol>
            </details>
        </section>
    </article>
</body>
</html>
```

You can see how the browser displays these elements in Figure 10-13. Not all browsers support the details element properly. IE9 has difficulties, for example.

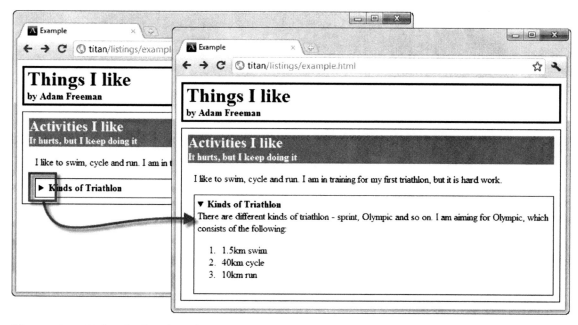

Figure 10-13. Using the details and summary attributes

As you can see from the figure, the browser provides an interface control which, when activated, opens and displays the contents of the details element. When the details element is closed, only the contents of the summary element are visible. To have the details element open when the page is first displayed, apply the open attribute.

Summary

In this chapter, I introduced you to the elements that you use to create sections in your documents and to isolate unrelated content. Most of these elements are new to HTML5. Although you are not compelled to use them to create compliant HTML5 documents, these new elements are one of the major enhancements in the effort to bring semantics to HTML.

CHAPTER 11

Table Elements

In this chapter, I will show you the HTML elements you can use to create tables. The main use for tables is to display two-dimensional data in a grid, but in earlier versions of HTML, it became common to use tables to control the layout of content in the page. In HTML5, this is no longer permitted, and the new CSS table feature (described in Chapter 21) must be used instead. Table 11-1 provides the summary for this chapter.

Table 11-1. Chapter Summary

Problem	Solution	Listing
Create a basic table.	Use the table, tr, and td elements.	1, 2
Add header cells to a table.	Use the th element.	3
Differentiate between column and row headers.	Use the thead and tbody elements.	4, 5
Add a footer to a table.	Use the tfoot element.	6
Create irregular table grids.	Use the span attribute defined by the th and td elements.	7-9
Associate cells with headers for assistive technology.	Use the headers attribute defined by the td and th element.	10
Add a caption to a table.	Use the caption element.	11
Work with columns instead of rows in a table.	Use the colgroup and col elements.	12, 13
Denote that a table is not being used to lay out a page.	Use the border attribute defined by the table element.	14

Creating a Basic Table

There are three elements that every table must contain: table, tr, and td. There are other elements—and I'll explain them later in this chapter—but these are the three you must start with. The first, table, is at the heart of support for tabular content in HTML and denotes a table in an HTML document. Table 11-2 summarizes the table element.

Table 11-2. The table Element

Element:	table
Element Type:	Flow
Permitted Parents:	Any element that can contain flow elements
Local Attributes:	border
Contents:	The caption, colgroup, thead, tbody, tfoot, tr, th, and td elements
Tag Style:	Start and end tags
New in HTML5?	No
Changes in HTML5	The summary, align, width, bgcolor, cellpadding, cellspacing, frame, and rules attributes are obsolete. You must use CSS instead.
	The value of the border attribute must be 1. The thickness of the border must then be set using CSS.
Style Convention	table { display: table; border-collapse: separate; border-spacing: 2px; border-color: gray; }

The next core table element is tr, which denotes a table row. HTML tables are row, rather than column, oriented and you must denote each row separately. Table 11-3 summarizes the tr element.

Table 11-3. The tr Element

Element:	tr
Element Type:	N/A
Permitted Parents:	The table, thead, tfoot, and tbody elements

Local Attributes:	None
Contents:	One or more td or th elements
Tag Style:	Start and end tags
New in HTML5?	No
Changes in HTML5	The align, char, charoff, valign, and bgcolor attributes are obsolete. You must use CSS instead.
Style Convention	tr { display: table-row; vertical-align: inherit; border-color: inherit;}

The last of our three core elements is td, which denotes a table cell. Table 11-4 summarizes the td element.

***Table 11-4.** The td Element*

Element:	td
Element Type:	N/A
Permitted Parents:	The tr element
Local Attributes:	colspan, rowspan, headers
Contents:	Flow content
Tag Style:	Start and end tags
New in HTML5?	No
Changes in HTML5	The scope attribute is obsolete. See the scope attribute on the th element instead.
	The abbr, axis, align, width, char, charoff, valign, bgcolor, height, and nowrap attributes are obsolete, and you must use CSS instead.
Style Convention	td { display: table-cell; vertical-align: inherit; }

Having defined these three elements, you can combine them to create tables, as shown in Listing 11-1.

Listing 11-1. Using the table, tr, and td Elements to Create a Table

```
<!DOCTYPE HTML>
<html>
    <head>
        <title>Example</title>
        <meta name="author" content="Adam Freeman"/>
        <meta name="description" content="A simple example"/>
        <link rel="shortcut icon" href="favicon.ico" type="image/x-icon" />
    </head>
    <body>
        <table>
            <tr>
                <td>Apples</td>
                <td>Green</td>
                <td>Medium</td>
            </tr>
            <tr>
                <td>Oranges</td>
                <td>Orange</td>
                <td>Large</td>
            </tr>
        </table>
    </body>
</html>
```

In this example I defined a table element that has two rows (denoted by the two tr elements). Each row has three columns, each of which is represented by a td element. The td element can contain any flow content, but I stuck to simple text in this example. You can see how the default style conventions are applied to display the table in Figure 11-1.

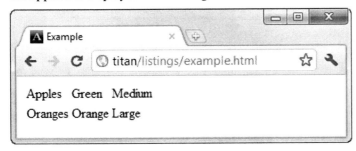

Figure 11-1. Displaying a simple table

This is a very simple table, but you can see the basic structure. The browser is responsible for sizing the rows and columns to maintain the table. As an example, see what happens when I add some longer content, as in Listing 11-2.

254

Listing 11-2. Adding Some Longer Cell Content

```html
<!DOCTYPE HTML>
<html>
    <head>
        <title>Example</title>
        <meta name="author" content="Adam Freeman"/>
        <meta name="description" content="A simple example"/>
        <link rel="shortcut icon" href="favicon.ico" type="image/x-icon" />
    </head>
    <body>
        <table>
            <tr>
                <td>Apples</td>
                <td>Green</td>
                <td>Medium</td>
            </tr>
            <tr>
                <td>Oranges</td>
                <td>Orange</td>
                <td>Large</td>
            </tr>
            <tr>
                <td>Pomegranate</td>
                <td>A kind of greeny-red</td>
                <td>Varies from medium to large</td>
            </tr>
        </table>
    </body>
</html>
```

The content of each of the newly added td elements is longer than in the previous two rows. You can see how the browser resizes the other cells to make them the same size in Figure 11-2.

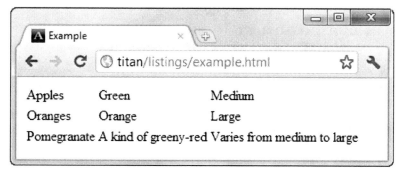

Figure 11-2. Cells resized to accommodate longer content

One of the nicest features of the table element is that you don't have to worry about the sizing issues. The browser makes sure that the columns are wide enough for the longest content and that the rows are tall enough for the tallest cell.

Adding Headers Cells

The th element denotes a header cell, allowing us to differentiate between data and the descriptions of that data. Table 11-5 summarizes the th element.

Table 11-5. The th Element

Element:	th
Element Type:	N/A
Permitted Parents:	The tr element
Local Attributes:	colspan, rowspan, scope, headers
Contents:	Phrasing content
Tag Style:	Start and end tags
New in HTML5?	No
Changes in HTML5	The scope attribute is obsolete. See the scope attribute on the th element instead.
	The abbr, axis, align, width, char, charoff, valign, bgcolor, height, and nowrap attributes are obsolete, and you must use CSS instead.
Style Convention	th { display: table-cell; vertical-align: inherit; font-weight: bold; text-align: center; }

You can see how I added th elements to the table in Listing 11-3 to provide some context for the data values contained in the td elements.

Listing 11-3. Adding Header Cells to a Table

```
<!DOCTYPE HTML>
<html>
    <head>
        <title>Example</title>
        <meta name="author" content="Adam Freeman"/>
        <meta name="description" content="A simple example"/>
        <link rel="shortcut icon" href="favicon.ico" type="image/x-icon" />
```

```
    </head>
    <body>
        <table>
            <tr>
                <th>Rank</th><th>Name</th>
                <th>Color</th><th>Size</th>
            </tr>
            <tr>
                <th>Favorite:</th>
                <td>Apples</td><td>Green</td><td>Medium</td>
            </tr>
            <tr>
                <th>2nd Favorite:</th>
                <td>Oranges</td><td>Orange</td><td>Large</td>
            </tr>
            <tr>
                <th>3rd Favorite:</th>
                <td>Pomegranate</td><td>A kind of greeny-red</td>
                <td>Varies from medium to large</td>
            </tr>
        </table>
    </body>
</html>
```

You can see that I am able to mix the th and td elements together in a row and also create a row that just contains th elements. You can see how the browser renders these in Figure 11-3.

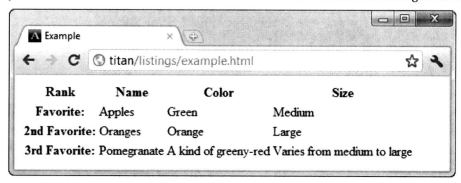

Figure 11-3. Adding header cells to a table

Adding Structure to a Table

You have a basic table, but you have managed to create a problem for yourself. When you go to style the table, you will find it hard to differentiate between the th elements that are on their own row and those that are mixed in with the data. It is not impossible it just requires close attention.. Listing 11-4 shows how you might do this.

Listing 11-4. Differentiating Between th Elements in a Table

```
<!DOCTYPE HTML>
<html>
    <head>
        <title>Example</title>
        <meta name="author" content="Adam Freeman"/>
        <meta name="description" content="A simple example"/>
        <link rel="shortcut icon" href="favicon.ico" type="image/x-icon" />
        <style>
            tr > th { text-align:left; background:grey; color:white}
            tr > th:only-of-type {text-align:right; background: lightgrey; color:grey}
        </style>
    </head>
    <body>
        <table>
            <tr>
                <th>Rank</th><th>Name</th><th>Color</th><th>Size</th>
            </tr>
            <tr>
                <th>Favorite:</th><td>Apples</td><td>Green</td><td>Medium</td>
            </tr>
            <tr>
                <th>2nd Favorite:</th><td>Oranges</td><td>Orange</td><td>Large</td>
            </tr>
            <tr>
                <th>3rd Favorite:</th><td>Pomegranate</td><td>A kind of greeny-red</td>
                <td>Varies from medium to large</td>
            </tr>
        </table>
    </body>
</html>
```

In this example, I created one selector that matches all of the th elements and a second style that matches only those th elements that are the only children of that type in a tr element. You can see the effect of the styles in Figure 11-4.

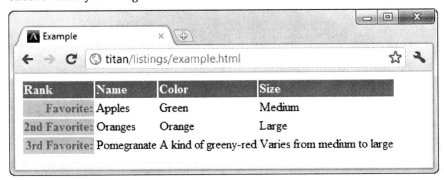

Figure 11-4. Adding styles that match the th rows in the table

This is a perfectly workable approach, but it lacks flexibility. If I add additional th elements to the rows of the table, my second selector won't work anymore. I don't really want to have to tweak my selectors every time I change the table.

To solve this problem in a flexible way, you can use the thead, tbody, and tfoot elements. These elements allow you to add structure to a table, and the major benefit of this structure is that it makes working with the different parts of the table simpler, especially when it comes to CSS selectors.

Denoting the Headings and the Table Body

The tbody element denotes the set of rows that comprise the body of our table—as opposed to the header and footer rows, which you denote with the thead and tfoot elements and which we'll get to shortly. Table 11-6 summarizes the tbody element.

Table 11-6. *The tbody Element*

Element:	tbody
Element Type:	N/A
Permitted Parents:	The table element
Local Attributes:	None
Contents:	Zero or more tr elements
Tag Style:	Start and end tags
New in HTML5?	No
Changes in HTML5	The align, char, charoff, and valign attributes are obsolete.
Style Convention	thead { display: table-header-group; vertical-align: middle; border-color: inherit; }

As a related aside, most browsers automatically insert the tbody element when they process a table element, even if it has not been specified in the document. This means that CSS selectors that assume the table layout is as written can fail. For example, a selector such as table > tr won't work, because the browser has inserted a tbody element between the table and tr elements. To address this, you must use a selector such as table > tbody > tr, table tr (no > character), or even just tbody > tr.

The thead element defines one or more rows that are the column labels for a table element. Table 11-7 summarizes the thead element.

Table 11-7. The thead Element

Element:	th
Element Type:	N/A
Permitted Parents:	The table element
Local Attributes:	None
Contents:	Zero or more tr elements
Tag Style:	Start and end tags
New in HTML5?	No
Changes in HTML5	The align, char, charoff, and valign attributes are obsolete.
Style Convention	thead { display: table-header-group; vertical-align: middle; border-color: inherit; }

Without the thead element, all of your tr elements are assumed to belong to the *body* of the table. Listing 11-5 shows the addition of the thead and tbody elements to the example table, and the more flexible CSS selectors you can use as a consequence.

Listing 11-5. Adding thead and tbody Elements to a Table

```
<!DOCTYPE HTML>
<html>
    <head>
        <title>Example</title>
        <meta name="author" content="Adam Freeman"/>
        <meta name="description" content="A simple example"/>
        <link rel="shortcut icon" href="favicon.ico" type="image/x-icon" />
        <style>
            thead th { text-align:left; background:grey; color:white}
            tbody th { text-align:right; background: lightgrey; color:grey}
        </style>
    </head>
    <body>
        <table>
            <thead>
                <tr>
                    <th>Rank</th><th>Name</th><th>Color</th><th>Size</th>
                </tr>
            </thead>
```

```
        <tbody>
            <tr>
                <th>Favorite:</th><td>Apples</td><td>Green</td><td>Medium</td>
            </tr>
            <tr>
                <th>2nd Favorite:</th><td>Oranges</td><td>Orange</td><td>Large</td>
            </tr>
            <tr>
                <th>3rd Favorite:</th><td>Pomegranate</td>
                <td>A kind of greeny-red</td><td>Varies from medium to large</td>
            </tr>
        </tbody>
    </table>
  </body>
</html>
```

This may not seem like a big deal, but the structure you added to the table makes dealing with the different kinds of cells much easier and less likely to fail if you modify the design of the table.

Adding a Footer

The tfoot element denotes the block of rows that form the footer for the table. Table 11-8 summarizes the tfoot element.

Table 11-8. The tfoot Element

Element:	tfoot
Element Type:	N/A
Permitted Parents:	The table element
Local Attributes:	None
Contents:	Zero or more tr elements
Tag Style:	Start and end tags
New in HTML5?	No
Changes in HTML5	The tfoot element can now appear before or after the tbody or tr elements. In HTML4, the tfoot element could appear only before these elements.
	The align, char, charoff, and valign attributes are obsolete.
Style Convention	tfoot { display: table-footer-group; vertical-align: middle; border-color: inherit; }

Listing 11-6 shows how the tfoot element can be used to create a footer for a table element. Prior to HTML5, the tfoot element had to appear before the tbody element (or the first tr element if the tbody had been omitted). In HTML5, you can instead put the tfooter element after the tbody or the last tr element, which is more consistent with the way the table will be displayed by the browser. In Listing 11-6, I show the tfoot element in the first position—either is acceptable. My feeling is that the above-the-tbody approach is generally more helpful when generating HTML programmatically using templates and the below-the-tbody approach feels more natural when writing HTML manually.

Listing 11-6. Using the tfoot Element

```
<!DOCTYPE HTML>
<html>
    <head>
        <title>Example</title>
        <meta name="author" content="Adam Freeman"/>
        <meta name="description" content="A simple example"/>
        <link rel="shortcut icon" href="favicon.ico" type="image/x-icon" />
        <style>
            thead th, tfoot th { text-align:left; background:grey; color:white}
            tbody th { text-align:right; background: lightgrey; color:grey}
        </style>
    </head>
    <body>
        <table>
            <thead>
                <tr>
                    <th>Rank</th><th>Name</th><th>Color</th><th>Size</th>
                </tr>
            </thead>
            <tfoot>
                <tr>
                    <th>Rank</th><th>Name</th><th>Color</th><th>Size</th>
                </tr>
            </tfoot>
            <tbody>
                <tr>
                    <th>Favorite:</th><td>Apples</td><td>Green</td><td>Medium</td>
                </tr>
                <tr>
                    <th>2nd Favorite:</th><td>Oranges</td><td>Orange</td><td>Large</td>
                </tr>
                <tr>
                    <th>3rd Favorite:</th><td>Pomegranate</td>
                    <td>A kind of greeny-red</td><td>Varies from medium to large</td>
                </tr>
            </tbody>
        </table>
    </body>
</html>
```

I duplicated the set of rows in the header to be in the footer. We'll come back and make the footer more interesting later in the chapter. I also added a second selector to one of the styles so that the th elements in the thead and tfoot elements are styled in the same way. You can see the addition of the footer shown in Figure 11-5.

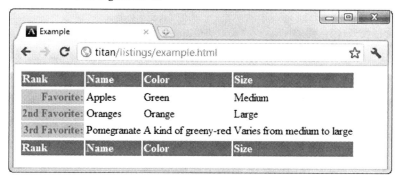

Figure 11-5. Adding a footer to a table

Creating Irregular Tables

Most tables are straightforward grids, where each cell occupies one position in the grid. However, to represent more complicated data, you sometimes need to create irregular tables, where cells are spread across multiple rows and columns. You create such tables using the colspan and rowspan attributes of the td and th elements. Listing 11-7 shows how to use these attributes to create an irregular table.

Listing 11-7. Creating an Irregular Table

```
<!DOCTYPE HTML>
<html>
    <head>
        <title>Example</title>
        <meta name="author" content="Adam Freeman"/>
        <meta name="description" content="A simple example"/>
        <link rel="shortcut icon" href="favicon.ico" type="image/x-icon" />
        <style>
            thead th, tfoot th { text-align:left; background:grey; color:white}
            tbody th { text-align:right; background: lightgrey; color:grey}
            [colspan], [rowspan] {font-weight:bold; border: medium solid black}
            thead [colspan], tfoot [colspan] {text-align:center; }
        </style>
    </head>
    <body>
        <table>
            <thead>
                <tr>
                    <th>Rank</th><th>Name</th><th>Color</th>
                    <th colspan="2">Size & Votes</th>
                </tr>
            </thead>
            <tbody>
                <tr>
```

```
            <th>Favorite:</th><td>Apples</td><td>Green</td>
            <td>Medium</td><td>500</td>
        </tr>
        <tr>
            <th>2nd Favorite:</th><td>Oranges</td><td>Orange</td>
            <td>Large</td><td>450</td>
        </tr>
        <tr>
            <th>3rd Favorite:</th><td>Pomegranate</td>
            <td colspan="2" rowspan="2">
                Pomegranates and cherries can both come in a range of colors
                and sizes.
            </td>
            <td>203</td>
        </tr>
        <tr>
            <th rowspan="2">Joint 4th:</th>
            <td>Cherries</td>
            <td rowspan="2">75</td>
        </tr>
        <tr>
            <td>Pineapple</td>
            <td>Brown</td>
            <td>Very Large</td>
        </tr>
    </tbody>
    <tfoot>
        <tr>
            <th colspan="5">&copy; 2011 Adam Freeman Fruit Data Enterprises</th>
        </tr>
    </tfoot>
    </table>
    </body>
</html>
```

If you want a cell to span multiple rows, you can use the rowspan attribute. The value you assign to this attribute is the number of rows to span. Similarly, if you want a cell to span multiple columns, you use the colspan attribute.

▪ **Tip** The values assigned to the rowspan and colspan must be integers. Some browsers will understand the value 100% to mean all of the rows or columns in a table, but this is not part of the HTML5 standard and is not consistently implemented.

I added some additional styles to the example document to highlight the cells that span multiple rows or columns, as shown in Figure 11-6. The affected cells are shown with a thick border.

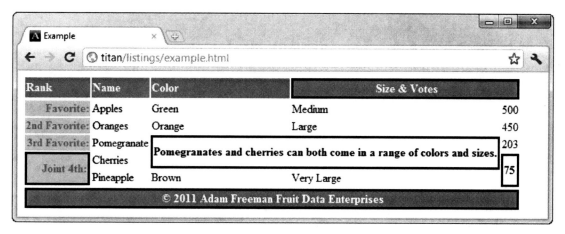

Figure 11-6. Spanning multiple rows and columns

You apply the colspan and rowspan attributes to the cell that is the uppermost and leftmost of the part of the grid you want to cover. You omit the td or tr elements that you would have included normally. As an example, consider the simple table shown in Listing 11-8.

Listing 11-8. A Simple Table

```
<!DOCTYPE HTML>
<html>
    <head>
        <title>Example</title>
        <meta name="author" content="Adam Freeman"/>
        <meta name="description" content="A simple example"/>
        <link rel="shortcut icon" href="favicon.ico" type="image/x-icon" />
        <style>
            td {border: thin solid black; padding: 5px; font-size:x-large};
        </style>
    </head>
    <body>
        <table>
            <tr>
                <td>1</td>
                <td>2</td>
                <td>3</td>
            </tr>
            <tr>
                <td>4</td>
                <td>5</td>
                <td>6</td>
            </tr>
            <tr>
                <td>7</td>
                <td>8</td>
                <td>9</td>
```

265

```
            </tr>
        </table>
    </body>
</html>
```

The table in this example is a 3x3 regular grid, as shown in Figure 11-7.

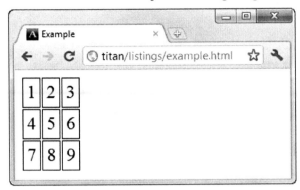

Figure 11-7. A regular grid

If you want one cell in the middle column to span all three rows, you apply the rowspan attribute to cell 2, which is the uppermost (and leftmost, but that doesn't matter in this example) cell of the area of the grid you want to cover. You also have to remove the cell elements that the expanded cell will cover—cells 5 and 8, in this case. You can see the changes in Listing 11-9.

Listing 11-9. Expanding a Cell to Cover Multiple Rows

```
<!DOCTYPE HTML>
<html>
    <head>
        <title>Example</title>
        <meta name="author" content="Adam Freeman"/>
        <meta name="description" content="A simple example"/>
        <link rel="shortcut icon" href="favicon.ico" type="image/x-icon" />
        <style>
            td {border: thin solid black; padding: 5px; font-size:x-large};
        </style>
    </head>
    <body>
        <table>
            <tr>
                <td>1</td>
                <td rowspan="3">2</td>
                <td>3</td>
            </tr>
            <tr>
                <td>4</td>
                <td>6</td>
            </tr>
```

```
            <tr>
                <td>7</td>
                <td>9</td>
            </tr>
        </table>
    </body>
</html>
```

You can see the result of these changes in Figure 11-8.

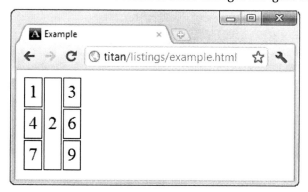

Figure 11-8. Expanding a cell to cover three rows

The browser is responsible for working out how the other cells you define should be fitted around the expanded cell.

■ **Caution** Be careful not to create overlapping cells by having two cells expand into the same area. The purpose of the table element is to represent tabular data. The only reason for using overlapping cells is to have the table element lay out other elements, which is something that should be done using the CSS table feature (described in Chapter 21).

Associating Headers with Cells

The td and th elements define the headers attribute, which can be used to make tables easier to process with screen readers and other assistive technology. The value of the headers attribute is the ID attribute value of one or more th cells. Listing 11-10 shows how you can use this attribute.

Listing 11-10. Using the headers Attribute

```html
<!DOCTYPE HTML>
<html>
    <head>
        <title>Example</title>
        <meta name="author" content="Adam Freeman"/>
        <meta name="description" content="A simple example"/>
        <link rel="shortcut icon" href="favicon.ico" type="image/x-icon" />
        <style>
            thead th, tfoot th { text-align:left; background:grey; color:white}
            tbody th { text-align:right; background: lightgrey; color:grey}
            thead [colspan], tfoot [colspan] {text-align:center; }
        </style>
    </head>
    <body>
        <table>
            <thead>
                <tr>
                    <th id="rank">Rank</th>
                    <th id="name">Name</th>
                    <th id="color">Color</th>
                    <th id="sizeAndVotes" colspan="2">Size & Votes</th>
                </tr>
            </thead>
            <tbody>
                <tr>
                    <th id="first" headers="rank">Favorite:</th>
                    <td headers="name first">Apples</td>
                    <td headers="color first">Green</td>
                    <td headers="sizeAndVote first">Medium</td>
                    <td headers="sizeAndVote first">500</td>
                </tr>
                <tr>
                    <th id="second" headers="rank">2nd Favorite:</th>
                    <td headers="name second">Oranges</td>
                    <td headers="color second">Orange</td>
                    <td headers="sizeAndVote second">Large</td>
                    <td headers="sizeAndVote second">450</td>
                </tr>
            </tbody>
            <tfoot>
                <tr>
                    <th colspan="5">&copy; 2011 Adam Freeman Fruit Data Enterprises</th>
                </tr>
            </tfoot>
        </table>
    </body>
</html>
```

I added the global id attribute to each of the th elements in the thead and the th elements that appear in the tbody. For each td and th in the tbody, I used the headers attribute to associate the cell with the column header. For the td elements, I also specified the row header (the header that appears in the first column).

Adding a Caption to a Table

The caption element lets you define a caption and associate it with a table element. Table 11-9 summarizes the caption element.

Table 11-9. The caption Element

Element:	caption
Element Type:	N/A
Permitted Parents:	The table element
Local Attributes:	None
Contents:	Flow content (but no table elements)
Tag Style:	Start and end tags
New in HTML5?	No
Changes in HTML5	The align attribute is obsolete.
Style Convention	caption { display: table-caption; text-align: center; }

Listing 11-11 shows the caption element in use.

Listing 11-11. Using the caption Element

```
<!DOCTYPE HTML>
<html>
    <head>
        <title>Example</title>
        <meta name="author" content="Adam Freeman"/>
        <meta name="description" content="A simple example"/>
        <link rel="shortcut icon" href="favicon.ico" type="image/x-icon" />
        <style>
            thead th, tfoot th { text-align:left; background:grey; color:white}
            tbody th { text-align:right; background: lightgrey; color:grey}
            [colspan], [rowspan] {font-weight:bold; border: medium solid black}
            thead [colspan], tfoot [colspan] {text-align:center; }
```

```
            caption {font-weight: bold; font-size: large; margin-bottom:5px}
        </style>
    </head>
    <body>
        <table>
            <caption>Results of the 2011 Fruit Survey</caption>
            <thead>
                <tr>
                    <th>Rank</th><th>Name</th><th>Color</th>
                    <th colspan="2">Size & Votes</th>
                </tr>
            </thead>
            <tbody>
                <tr>
                    <th>Favorite:</th><td>Apples</td><td>Green</td>
                    <td>Medium</td><td>500</td>
                </tr>
                <tr>
                    <th>2nd Favorite:</th><td>Oranges</td><td>Orange</td>
                    <td>Large</td><td>450</td>
                </tr>
                <tr>
                    <th>3rd Favorite:</th><td>Pomegranate</td>
                    <td colspan="2" rowspan="2">
                        Pomegranates and cherries can both come in a range of colors
                        and sizes.
                    </td>
                    <td>203</td>
                </tr>
                <tr>
                    <th rowspan="2">Joint 4th:</th>
                    <td>Cherries</td>
                    <td rowspan="2">75</td>
                </tr>
                <tr>
                    <td>Pineapple</td>
                    <td>Brown</td>
                    <td>Very Large</td>
                </tr>
            </tbody>
            <tfoot>
                <tr>
                    <th colspan="5">&copy; 2011 Adam Freeman Fruit Data Enterprises</th>
                </tr>
            </tfoot>
        </table>
    </body>
</html>
```

A table can contain only one caption element, but it doesn't have to be the first element contained in the table. However, it will always be displayed above the table, regardless of where the element is defined. You can see the effect of the caption (and the style I applied to it) in Figure 11-9.

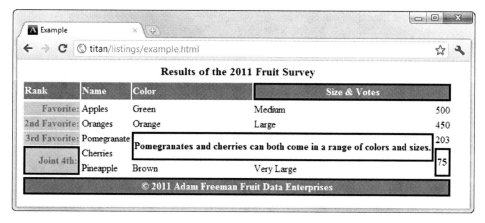

Figure 11-9. Applying a caption to a table

Working with Columns

The HTML approach to tables is oriented around rows. You place the definitions of your cells inside of tr elements and build up tables row by row. This can make it awkward to apply styles to columns, especially when working with tables that contain irregular cells. The solution to this is to use the colgroup and col elements.

The colgroup element represents a set of columns. Table 11-10 summarizes the colgroup element.

Table 11-10. The colgroup Element

Element:	colgroup
Element Type:	N/A
Permitted Parents:	The table element
Local Attributes:	span
Contents:	Zero or more col elements (can be used only when the span attribute is not applied)
Tag Style:	Void if used with the span attribute; otherwise, start and end tags
New in HTML5?	No
Changes in HTML5	The width, char, charoff, and valign attributes are obsolete.
Style Convention	colgroup { display: table-column-group; }

Listing 11-12 shows the use of the colgroup element.

Listing 11-12. Using the colgroup Element

```
<!DOCTYPE HTML>
<html>
    <head>
        <title>Example</title>
        <meta name="author" content="Adam Freeman"/>
        <meta name="description" content="A simple example"/>
        <link rel="shortcut icon" href="favicon.ico" type="image/x-icon" />
        <style>
            thead th, tfoot th { text-align:left; background:grey; color:white}
            tbody th { text-align:right; background: lightgrey; color:grey}
            [colspan], [rowspan] {font-weight:bold; border: medium solid black}
            thead [colspan], tfoot [colspan] {text-align:center; }
            caption {font-weight: bold; font-size: large; margin-bottom:5px}
            #colgroup1 {background-color: red}
            #colgroup2 {background-color: green; font-size:small}
        </style>
    </head>
    <body>
        <table>
            <caption>Results of the 2011 Fruit Survey</caption>
            <colgroup id="colgroup1" span="3"/>
            <colgroup id="colgroup2" span="2"/>
            <thead>
                <tr>
                    <th>Rank</th><th>Name</th><th>Color</th>
                    <th colspan="2">Size & Votes</th>
                </tr>
            </thead>
            <tbody>
                <tr>
                    <th>Favorite:</th><td>Apples</td><td>Green</td>
                    <td>Medium</td><td>500</td>
                </tr>
                <tr>
                    <th>2nd Favorite:</th><td>Oranges</td><td>Orange</td>
                    <td>Large</td><td>450</td>
                </tr>
                <tr>
                    <th>3rd Favorite:</th><td>Pomegranate</td>
                    <td colspan="2" rowspan="2">
                        Pomegranates and cherries can both come in a range of colors
                        and sizes.
                    </td>
                    <td>203</td>
                </tr>
                <tr>
                    <th rowspan="2">Joint 4th:</th>
                    <td>Cherries</td>
```

```
                        <td rowspan="2">75</td>
                    </tr>
                    <tr>
                        <td>Pineapple</td>
                        <td>Brown</td>
                        <td>Very Large</td>
                    </tr>
                </tbody>
                <tfoot>
                    <tr>
                        <th colspan="5">&copy; 2011 Adam Freeman Fruit Data Enterprises</th>
                    </tr>
                </tfoot>
            </table>
        </body>
</html>
```

In this example, I defined two colgroup elements. The span attribute specifies how many columns the colgroup element applies to. The first colgroup in the listing applies to the first three columns in the table, and the other element applies to the next two columns. I applied the global id attribute to each colgroup element and defined CSS styles that use the id values as selectors. You can see the effect in Figure 11-10.

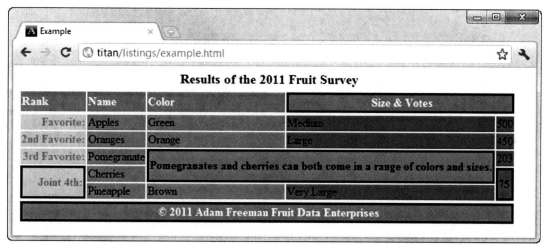

Figure 11-10. Using the colgroup element

The figure demonstrates some of the important aspects of using the colgroup element. The first thing to know is that CSS styles that are applied to colgroups have lower specificity than styles applied to tr, td, and th elements directly. You can see this in the way that the styles applied to the thead, tfoot, and first column of th elements are not affected by the styles that match the colgroups. If I remove all of the styles except those that target the colgroup elements, all of the cells are modified, as shown in Figure 11-11.

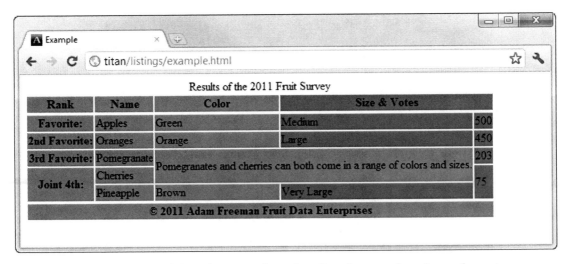

Figure 11-11. Removing all of the styles except those that directly target the colspan elements

The second point to note is that irregular cells are counted as part of the column they start in. You can see this in the third row, where a cell that is matched by the first style extends into the area covered by the other colgroup element.

The final point to be aware of is that the colgroup element includes all of the cells in a column, even those that are in thead and tfoot elements, and it matches both th and td elements. The colgroup element is special because it relates to elements that are not contained within the element. This means you can't use the colgroup element as the basis for more focused selectors (for example, a selector such as #colgroup1 > td doesn't match any elements).

Calling Out Individual Columns

You can use the col element instead of the span attribute of the colgroup element. This allows you to define a group and the distinct columns that exist within it. Table 11-11 summarizes the col element.

Table 11-11. The col Element

Element:	col
Element Type:	N/A
Permitted Parents:	The colgroup element
Local Attributes:	span
Contents:	None
Tag Style:	Void

New in HTML5?	No
Changes in HTML5	The align, width, char, charoff, and valign attributes are obsolete.
Style Convention	col { display: table-column; }

The advantage of using the col element is greater control. You can apply styles to groups of columns and the individual columns in that group. The col element is placed inside the colgroup element, as shown in Listing 11-13, and each instance of col represents one column in the group.

Listing 11-13. Using the col Element

```
<!DOCTYPE HTML>
<html>
    <head>
        <title>Example</title>
        <meta name="author" content="Adam Freeman"/>
        <meta name="description" content="A simple example"/>
        <link rel="shortcut icon" href="favicon.ico" type="image/x-icon" />
        <style>
            thead th, tfoot th { text-align:left; background:grey; color:white}
            tbody th { text-align:right; background: lightgrey; color:grey}
            [colspan], [rowspan] {font-weight:bold; border: medium solid black}
            thead [colspan], tfoot [colspan] {text-align:center; }
            caption {font-weight: bold; font-size: large; margin-bottom:5px}
            #colgroup1 {background-color: red}
            #col3 {background-color: green; font-size:small}
        </style>
    </head>
    <body>
        <table>
            <caption>Results of the 2011 Fruit Survey</caption>
            <colgroup id="colgroup1">
                <col id="col1And2" span="2"/>
                <col id="col3"/>
            </colgroup>
            <colgroup id="colgroup2" span="2"/>
            <thead>
                <tr>
                    <th>Rank</th><th>Name</th><th>Color</th>
                    <th colspan="2">Size & Votes</th>
                </tr>
            </thead>
            <tbody>
                <tr>
                    <th>Favorite:</th><td>Apples</td><td>Green</td>
                    <td>Medium</td><td>500</td>
                </tr>
                <tr>
```

```
            <th>2nd Favorite:</th><td>Oranges</td><td>Orange</td>
            <td>Large</td><td>450</td>
        </tr>
        <tr>
            <th>3rd Favorite:</th><td>Pomegranate</td>
            <td colspan="2" rowspan="2">
                Pomegranates and cherries can both come in a range of colors
                and sizes.
            </td>
            <td>203</td>
        </tr>
        <tr>
            <th rowspan="2">Joint 4th:</th>
            <td>Cherries</td>
            <td rowspan="2">75</td>
        </tr>
        <tr>
            <td>Pineapple</td>
            <td>Brown</td>
            <td>Very Large</td>
        </tr>
    </tbody>
    <tfoot>
        <tr>
            <th colspan="5">&copy; 2011 Adam Freeman Fruit Data Enterprises</th>
        </tr>
    </tfoot>
</table>
</body>
</html>
```

You can use the span attribute to create a col element that represents two columns in the colgroup. The col element represents a single column if you don't use the span attribute. In this example, I applied a style to the colgroup and to one of the col elements it contains. You can see the effect in Figure 11-12.

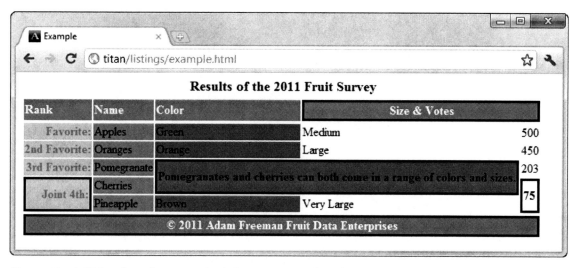

Figure 11-12. Using the colgroup and col elements to apply styling to a table

Applying Borders to the table Element

The table element defines the border attribute. When you apply this attribute, it tells the browser you are using the table to represent tabular data, rather than to lay out other elements. Most browsers respond to the border attribute by drawing borders around the table and each individual cell. Listing 11-14 shows the application of the border element.

Listing 11-14. Using the border Attribute

```
<!DOCTYPE HTML>
<html>
    <head>
        <title>Example</title>
        <meta name="author" content="Adam Freeman"/>
        <meta name="description" content="A simple example"/>
        <link rel="shortcut icon" href="favicon.ico" type="image/x-icon" />
    </head>
    <body>
        <table border="1">
            <caption>Results of the 2011 Fruit Survey</caption>
            <colgroup id="colgroup1">
                <col id="col1And2" span="2"/>
                <col id="col3"/>
            </colgroup>
            <colgroup id="colgroup2" span="2"/>
            <thead>
                <tr>
                    <th>Rank</th><th>Name</th><th>Color</th>
                    <th colspan="2">Size & Votes</th>
                </tr>
```

277

```
            </thead>
            <tbody>
                <tr>
                    <th>Favorite:</th><td>Apples</td><td>Green</td>
                    <td>Medium</td><td>500</td>
                </tr>
                <tr>
                    <th>2nd Favorite:</th><td>Oranges</td><td>Orange</td>
                    <td>Large</td><td>450</td>
                </tr>
                <tr>
                    <th>3rd Favorite:</th><td>Pomegranate</td>
                    <td colspan="2" rowspan="2">
                        Pomegranates and cherries can both come in a range of colors
                        and sizes.
                    </td>
                    <td>203</td>
                </tr>
                <tr>
                    <th rowspan="2">Joint 4th:</th>
                    <td>Cherries</td>
                    <td rowspan="2">75</td>
                </tr>
                <tr>
                    <td>Pineapple</td>
                    <td>Brown</td>
                    <td>Very Large</td>
                </tr>
            </tbody>
            <tfoot>
                <tr>
                    <th colspan="5">&copy; 2011 Adam Freeman Fruit Data Enterprises</th>
                </tr>
            </tfoot>
        </table>
    </body>
</html>
```

The value assigned to the border attribute must be 1 or the empty string (""). This attribute doesn't control the style of the border. You do that via CSS. You can see how Google Chrome responds to the presence of the border attribute in Figure 11-13. (Notice that I removed the style element from this example to emphasize the effect of the border attribute.)

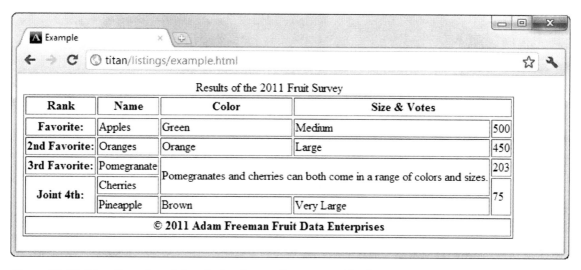

Figure 11-13. The effect of applying the border attribute to a table element

The default border that browsers apply isn't especially appealing, so you typically have to use CSS in addition to the border attribute.

■ **Tip** You don't have to apply the border attribute to a table to be able to define borders using CSS. However, if you don't apply the border attribute, the browser is free to assume you are using the table for layout purposes, and it may display the table in an unexpected way. As I write this, mainstream browsers don't pay much attention to the border attribute (aside from applying the default border), but that may change in the future.

Even though the border attribute causes the browser to apply a border to the table *and* each cell, you still have to target each kind of element individually in your CSS selectors to replace. You are not short of choices when it comes to creating CSS selectors: you can target the outer border of the table through the table element; the header, body, and footer with the thead, tbody, and tfoot elements; columns through the colspan and col elements; and individual cells using the th and td elements. And, if all else fails, you can still explicitly create targets using the id and class global attributes.

Summary

In this chapter, I took you on a tour of the HTML5 support for tables. The most important change in HTML5 is that you can no longer use tables to handle page layouts—for that you must rely on the CSS table support, which I describe in Chapter 21. This limitation aside, tables are endlessly flexible, are easy to style, and can be a pleasure to work with.

CHAPTER 12

Working with Forms

Forms are the HTML mechanism for gathering input from the user. Forms are incredibly important to web applications, but for many years the functionality defined in HTML has lagged behind the way forms are used. In HTML5, the entire form system has been overhauled and spruced up, aligning the standard with the way forms have evolved in use.

In this chapter, I describe the basics of HTML forms. I start by defining a very simple form and build on it to demonstrate how you configure and control the way the form operates. I introduce a Node.js script you can use to test your forms and see the data that is sent from the browser to the server.

In the chapter that follows, I cover the advanced form features, including the HTML5 changes that have attracted the most attention—the new ways of gathering specific data types from the user, and the ability to validate the data in the browser. These are important enhancements, but a lot of other changes are worthy of note as well. This chapter and the next are worthy of close attention.

As I write this, the mainstream browser support for HTML5 forms is good, but not perfect, and it is worth checking how widely implemented each feature is before adopting it. Table 12-1 provides the summary for this chapter.

Table 12-1. Chapter Summary

Problem	Solution	Listing
Create a basic form.	Use the form, input, and button elements.	1
Specify the URL that the form data is sent to.	Use the action attribute on the form element (or the formaction attribute on the button element).	3 (and 15)
Specify the way in which the form data is encoded for transmission to the server.	Use the enctype attribute on the form element (or the formenctype attribute on the button element).	4 (and 15)
Control auto-completion.	Use the autocomplete attribute on the form or input element.	5, 6
Specify where the response from the server should be displayed.	Use the target attribute on the form element (or the formtarget attribute on the button element).	7
Specify a name for the form	Use the name attribute on the form element.	8

Add a label for an input element.	Use the `label` element.	9
Automatically focus on an input element when the form is loaded.	Use the `autofocus` attribute on the `input` element.	10
Disable an individual input element.	Apply the `disabled` attribute to the `input` element.	11
Group input elements together.	Use the `fieldset` element.	12
Add a descriptive label to a `fieldset` element.	Use the `legend` element.	13
Disable a group of input elements.	Apply the `disabled` attribute to the `fieldset` element.	14
Use the button element to submit a form.	Set the value of the type attribute to `submit`.	15
Use the button element to reset a form.	Set the value of the type attribute to `reset`.	16
Use the button element as a generic button control.	Set the value of the type attribute to `button`.	17
Associate an element with a form that is not an antecedent.	Use the `form` attribute.	18

Creating a Basic Form

To create a basic form, you need three elements: the `form`, `input`, and `button` elements. Listing 12-1 shows an HTML document that contains a simple form.

Listing 12-1. A Simple HTML Form

```
<!DOCTYPE HTML>
<html>
    <head>
        <title>Example</title>
        <meta name="author" content="Adam Freeman"/>
        <meta name="description" content="A simple example"/>
        <link rel="shortcut icon" href="favicon.ico" type="image/x-icon" />
    </head>
```

```
<body>
    <form method="post" action="http://titan:8080/form">
        <input name="fave"/>
        <button>Submit Vote</button>
    </form>
</body>
</html>
```

You can see how this appears in the browser in Figure 12-1.

Figure 12-1. Displaying a basic form in the browser

This form is so simple that it isn't much use, but after you've looked at each of the three core elements, you can start to add to the form and make it more meaningful and useful.

Defining the Form

The starting point is the form element, which denotes the presence of a form in an HTML page. Table 12-2 summarizes the form element.

Table 12-2. *The table Element*

Element:	form
Element Type:	Flow
Permitted Parents:	Any element that can contain flow elements, but the form element cannot be a descendant of another form.
Local Attributes:	action, method, enctype, name, accept-charset, novalidate, target, autocomplete
Contents:	Flow content (but particularly label and input elements)
Tag Style:	Start and end tags
New in HTML5?	No

Changes in HTML5	The `novalidate` and `autocomplete` attributes are new in HTML5.
Style Convention	`form { display: block; margin-top: 0em; }`

I'll come back and show you how to use the element attributes to configure the `form` element later in this chapter. For the moment, it is enough to know that the `form` element tells the browser that it is dealing with an HTML form.

The second critical element is `input`, which allows you to gather input from the user. You can see in Figure 12-1 that the `input` element has been displayed by the browser as a simple text box, into which the user can type. This is the most basic type of `input` element and, as you'll see, there are lots of options for how you gather input from the user (including some nice new additions in HTML5). I explain these in Chapter 13. Table 12-3 summarizes the `input` element.

Table 12-3. The input Element

Element:	input
Element Type:	Phrasing
Permitted Parents:	Any element that can contain phrasing elements
Local Attributes:	`name`, `disabled`, `form`, `type`, plus other attributes based on the value of the type attribute
Contents:	None
Tag Style:	Void
New in HTML5?	No, but there are some new types of input, which are accessed through the type attribute. (See Chapter 13 for details.)
Changes in HTML5	There are new values for the type attribute in HTML5, and there are several new attributes that are used with specific values for the type attribute.
Style Convention	None. The appearance of this element is determined by the type attribute.

There are 29 attributes that can be applied to the `input` element, depending on the value of the `type` attribute. I'll show these attributes and explain their use when we look at the different ways you can gather data from the user in Chapter 13.

■ **Tip** You can use elements other than `input` to collect data from the user. I explain and demonstrate these in Chapter 14.

The final element in the example is `button`. You need some means for the user to indicate to the browser that all of the data has been entered and that the browser should send the data to the server. The `button` element is the most commonly used way of doing this (although, as you'll see in Chapter 13, there is another mechanism you can use). Table 12-4 summarizes the `button` element.

Table 12-4. The button Element

Element:	`button`
Element Type:	Phrasing
Permitted Parents:	Any parent that can contain phrasing elements
Local Attributes:	`name`, `disabled`, `form`, `type`, `value`, `autofocus`, plus other attributes based on the value of the `type` attribute
Contents:	Phrasing Content
Tag Style:	Start and end tags
New in HTML5?	No
Changes in HTML5	There are new attributes, which are available depending on the value of the `type` attribute. (See the "Using the `button` Element" section for details.)
Style Convention	None

The `button` element is a multipurpose element, and I'll explain the uses it can be put to in the "Using the `button` Element" section, later in this chapter. When used inside a `form` element and without any attributes, the `button` element tells the browser to submit the data collected from the user to the server.

Seeing the Form Data

You need a server for the browser to send the data to. To this end, I wrote a simple Node.js script that generates an HTML page containing the data that the form collects from the user. See Chapter 2 for details of obtaining and setting up Node.js. Listing 12-2 shows the script we'll be using. As I mentioned in Chapter 2, I won't be digging into the details of the server-side scripts, but because Node.js is JavaScript-based, you can easily see what the script does by following the descriptions of the JavaScript language features in Chapter 5 and reading some of the documentation available at `http://nodejs.org`.

Listing 12-2. The formecho.js Script

```
var http = require('http');
var querystring = require('querystring');

http.createServer(function (req, res) {
  switch(req.url) {
    case '/form':
        if (req.method == 'POST') {
          console.log("[200] " + req.method + " to " + req.url);
          var fullBody = '';
          req.on('data', function(chunk) {
            fullBody += chunk.toString();
          });
          req.on('end', function() {
            res.writeHead(200, "OK", {'Content-Type': 'text/html'});
            res.write('<html><head><title>Post data</title></head><body>');
            res.write('<style>th, td {text-align:left; padding:5px; color:black}\n');
            res.write('th {background-color:grey; color:white; min-width:10em}\n');
            res.write('td {background-color:lightgrey}\n');
            res.write('caption {font-weight:bold}</style>');
            res.write('<table border="1"><caption>Form Data</caption>');
            res.write('<tr><th>Name</th><th>Value</th>');
            var dBody = querystring.parse(fullBody);
            for (var prop in dBody) {
              res.write("<tr><td>" + prop + "</td><td>" + dBody[prop] + "</td></tr>");
            }
            res.write('</table></body></html>');
            res.end();
          });
        } else {
          console.log("[405] " + req.method + " to " + req.url);
          res.writeHead(405, "Method not supported", {'Content-Type': 'text/html'});
          res.end('<html><head><title>405 - Method not supported</title></head><body>' +
                  '<h1>Method not supported.</h1></body></html>');
        }
      break;
    default:
      res.writeHead(404, "Not found", {'Content-Type': 'text/html'});
      res.end('<html><head><title>404 - Not found</title></head><body>' +
              '<h1>Not found.</h1></body></html>');
      console.log("[404] " + req.method + " to " + req.url);
  };
}).listen(8080);
```

This script collects together the data that the browser has submitted and returns a simple HTML document that displays that data in an HTML table. (I described the table element in Chapter 11.) This script listens for browser connections on port 8080 and deals only with forms that are sent from the browser using the HTTP POST method and to the /form URL. You'll see the significance of port 8080 and the /form URL when you look at the attributes supported by the form element later in this chapter. I saved this script to a file called formecho.js. To start the script, I opened a command prompt on titan and typed the following:

```
bin\node.exe formecho.js
```

Titan runs Windows Server 2008 R2, so the exact command to start Node.js will be different if you are using another operating system. Figure 12-2 shows the browser displaying the output that is produced by entering `Apples` into the text box in the example form and pressing the `Submit Vote` button.

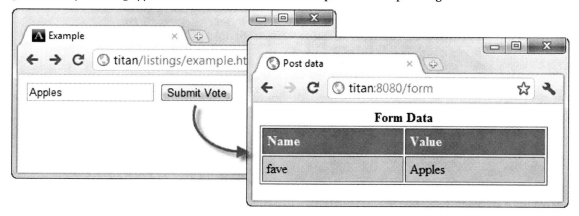

Figure 12-2. Viewing the form data submitted by the browser using Node.js

There is only one item of data because there is only one `input` element in the example form. The value in the `Name` column is `fave` because that is the value I assigned to the `name` attribute in the `input` element. The value in the `Value` column is `Apples` because that is what I entered into the text box before pressing the `Submit Vote` button. I'll show the tabular output from the Node.js script as we create more complex forms.

Configuring the Form

We've created an HTML document that contains a basic form, and we've used Node.js to display the data that is sent to the server. Now it is time for me to show you the basic configuration options you can apply to the form and its contents.

Configuring the Form action Attribute

The `action` attribute specifies where the browser should send the data collected from the user when the `form` is submitted. I want the data to be submitted to my Node.js script, which means I want the form to post to the `/form` URL on port 8080 of my development server, `titan`. You can see that I already express this in the original form in Listing 12-1, like this:

```
...
<form method="post" action="http://titan:8080/form">
...
```

If you don't apply the `action` attribute to the `form` element, the browser will send the form data to the same URL that the HTML document was loaded from. This isn't as useless as it might initially appear, and several popular web application development frameworks depend on this feature.

If you specify a relative URL, this value is appended to the URL of the current page or—if you used the base element described in Chapter 7—to the value of the href attribute of that element. Listing 12-3 shows how you can use the base element to set the destination for the form data.

Listing 12-3. Using the base Element to Set a Destination for Form Data

```
<!DOCTYPE HTML>
<html>
    <head>
        <title>Example</title>
        <meta name="author" content="Adam Freeman"/>
        <meta name="description" content="A simple example"/>
        <link rel="shortcut icon" href="favicon.ico" type="image/x-icon" />
        <base href="http://titan:8080"/>
    </head>
    <body>
        <form method="post" action="/form">
            <input name="fave"/>
            <button>Submit Vote</button>
        </form>
    </body>
</html>
```

■ **Caution** The base element affects *all* relative URLs in an HTML document, not just the form element.

Configuring the HTTP method Attribute

The method attribute specifies which HTTP method will be used to send the form data to the server. The allowed values are get and post, which correspond to the HTTP GET and POST methods. The default used when you don't apply the method attribute is get, which is unfortunate because most forms require HTTP POST. You can see that I specified the post value for the form in the example, as follows:

```
...
<form method="post" action="http://titan:8080/form">
...
```

GET requests are for *safe interactions*, which means you can make the same request as many times as you want and there will be no side effects. POST requests are for *unsafe interactions*, where the act of submitting the data changes some kind of state. This is most commonly the case when dealing with web applications. These conventions are set by the World Wide Web Consortium (W3C), which you can read about at www.w3.org/Provider/Style/URI.

The rule of thumb is that GET requests should be used for all read-only information retrieval, while POST requests should be used for any operation that changes the application state. It is important to use the right kind of requests. If you are unsure, err on the side of caution and use the POST method.

■ **Tip** The Node.js script I use in this chapter will respond only to POST requests.

Configuring the Data Encoding

The enctype attribute specifies how the browser encodes and presents the data to the server. There are three allowed values for this attribute, which are described in Table 12-5.

Table 12-5. The Allowed Values for the enctype Attribute

Value	Description
application/x-www-form-urlencoded	This is the default encoding that is used when you don't apply the enctype attribute. This encoding cannot be used to upload files to the server.
multipart/form-data	This encoding is used to upload files to the server.
text/plain	This encoding varies between browsers. See the following text for more details.

To understand how the different encodings work, you need to add a second input element to your form, as shown in Listing 12-4.

Listing 12-4. Adding an input Element to the Form

```
<!DOCTYPE HTML>
<html>
    <head>
        <title>Example</title>
        <meta name="author" content="Adam Freeman"/>
        <meta name="description" content="A simple example"/>
        <link rel="shortcut icon" href="favicon.ico" type="image/x-icon" />
    </head>
    <body>
        <form method="post" action="http://titan:8080/form">
            <input name="fave"/>
            <input name="name"/>
            <button>Submit Vote</button>
        </form>
    </body>
</html>
```

You need the second input element so that you can collect two items of data from the user. As you may have guessed, you are building up a form that will allow users to vote for their favorite fruits. The new input element will be used to gather their names. As you can see from this listing, I set the name value of this element to be name. To demonstrate the effect of the different form encodings, I added the enctype attribute to the form and set it to each of the supported encoding types. In each instance, I entered the same data into the text boxes. In the first text box I entered Apples, and in the second I entered Adam Freeman (with the space between my first and second names).

The application/x-www-form-urlencoded Encoding

This is the default encoding, and it is suitable for every kind of form except those that upload files to the server. The name and value of each data item is encoded using the same scheme that is used to encode URLs (hence, the urlencoded part of the name). This is how the encoding is applied to the data in the example form:

```
fave=Apples&name=Adam+Freeman
```

Special characters are replaced with their HTML entity counterpart. The name of the data item and the value are separated by the equals sign (=) and data/value tuples are separated by the ampersand character (&).

The multipart/form-data Encoding

The multipart/form-data encoding takes a different approach. It is more verbose and more complex to process, which is why it tends to be used only for forms that need to upload files to the server—something that can't be done using the default encoding. Here is how the data from the example form is encoded:

```
------WebKitFormBoundary2qgCsuH4ohZ5eObF

Content-Disposition: form-data; name="fave"

Apples

------WebKitFormBoundary2qgCsuH4ohZ5eObF

Content-Disposition: form-data; name="name"

Adam Freeman

------WebKitFormBoundary2qgCsuH4ohZ5eObF--

fave=Apple

name=Adam Freeman
```

The text/plain Encoding

This encoding should be used with caution. There is no formal specification as to how data should be encoded when using this scheme, and the mainstream browsers encode data in different ways. For example, Google Chrome encodes data in the same way as for the `application/x-www-form-urlencoded` scheme, whereas Firefox encodes the data as follows:

```
fave=Apple

name=Adam Freeman
```

Each data item is placed on a line, and special characters are not encoded. I recommend avoiding this encoding. The variations between browsers make it unpredictable.

Controlling Form Completion

Browsers aid the user by remembering the data they have entered into forms and offering to reuse that data automatically when a similar form is seen again. This technique reduces the need for the user to enter the same data over and over again. A good example is the name and shipping details a user enters when purchasing goods or services online. Every web site has its own shopping cart and registration process, but my browser uses the data I have entered in *other* forms to speed up the checkout process. Browsers use different techniques to figure out what data to reuse, but a common approach is to look for the `name` attribute of `input` elements.

In general, completing forms automatically is beneficial to the user and makes little difference to the web application. But there are times when you don't want the browser to fill out the form. Listing 12-5 shows how you can do this, using the `autocomplete` attribute on the `form` element.

Listing 12-5. Disabling the form Element autocomplete Attribute

```html
<!DOCTYPE HTML>
<html>
    <head>
        <title>Example</title>
        <meta name="author" content="Adam Freeman"/>
        <meta name="description" content="A simple example"/>
        <link rel="shortcut icon" href="favicon.ico" type="image/x-icon" />
    </head>
    <body>
        <form autocomplete="off" method="post" action="http://titan:8080/form">
            <input name="fave"/>
            <input name="name"/>
            <button>Submit Vote</button>
        </form>
    </body>
</html>
```

There are two allowed values for the `autocomplete` attribute: on and off. The on value permits the browser to fill out the form and is the default value that is assumed when you don't apply the attribute.

You can be more specific by applying the autocomplete attribute to individual input elements, as shown in Listing 12-6.

Listing 12-6. Applying the autocomplete Attribute to input Elements

```
<!DOCTYPE HTML>
<html>
    <head>
        <title>Example</title>
        <meta name="author" content="Adam Freeman"/>
        <meta name="description" content="A simple example"/>
        <link rel="shortcut icon" href="favicon.ico" type="image/x-icon" />
    </head>
    <body>
        <form autocomplete="off" method="post" action="http://titan:8080/form">
            <input autocomplete="on" name="fave"/>
            <input name="name"/>
            <button>Submit Vote</button>
        </form>
    </body>
</html>
```

The autocomplete attribute on the form element sets the default policy for the input elements in the form. However, as the listing shows, you can override that policy for individual elements. In this example, the attribute on the form element disabled autocomplete, but the same attribute applied to the first input element switches it back on—but just for that element. The second input element, to which the autocomplete attribute has not been applied, is subject to the form-wide policy.

In general, you should leave autocomplete enabled—users are accustomed to populating forms automatically and are typically faced with several forms during any kind of web transaction. For you to take this feature away intrudes into the preferences and work habits of your users. I know from my own experience that it is jarring when I try to buy items from sites that disable autocompletion, especially when the form I am trying to fill in wants very basic information such as my name and address. Some sites disable autocomplete for credit card data, which makes more sense—but even then, this approach should be used with caution and the reasons for using this feature should be fully thought through.

Specifying a Target for the Form Response

The default behavior of a browser is to replace the page that contains the form with the response that the server returns after the form has been submitted. You can change this behavior by using the target attribute on the form element. This attribute works in the same way as the target attribute on the a element, and you can select from the range of targets shown in Table 12-6.

Table 12-6. Values for the target Attribute of the form Element

Attribute	Description
_blank	Opens the server response in a new window (or tab)
_parent	Opens the server response in the parent frameset

_self	Opens the server response in the current window (which is the default behavior)
_top	Opens the server response in the full body of the window.
<frame>	Opens the server response in the specified frame

Each of these values represents a *browsing context*. The _blank and _self values are self-evident. The others relate to the use of frames, which I explain in Chapter 15. Listing 12-7 shows the target attribute applied to a form element.

Listing 12-7. Using the target Attribute

```
<!DOCTYPE HTML>
<html>
    <head>
        <title>Example</title>
        <meta name="author" content="Adam Freeman"/>
        <meta name="description" content="A simple example"/>
        <link rel="shortcut icon" href="favicon.ico" type="image/x-icon" />
    </head>
    <body>
        <form target="_blank" method="post" action="http://titan:8080/form">
            <input autocomplete="on" name="fave"/>
            <input name="name"/>
            <button>Submit Vote</button>
        </form>
    </body>
</html>
```

In this example, I specified the _blank target, which tells the browser to display the response from the server in a new window or tab. You can see the effect of this change in Figure 12-3.

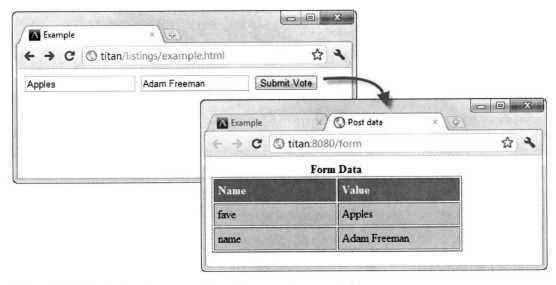

Figure 12-3. Displaying the response from the server in a new tab

Setting the Name of the Form

The name attribute lets you set a unique identifier for a form so that you can distinguish between forms when working with the Document Object Model (DOM). I introduce the DOM in Chapter 25. The name attribute is distinct from the id global attribute, and in most cases, HTML documents use the id attribute for CSS selectors. Listing 12-8 shows a form element to which the name and id attributes have been applied. I used the same value for both attributes for the sake of simplicity.

Listing 12-8. Using the name and id Attributes on a form Element

```
<!DOCTYPE HTML>
<html>
    <head>
        <title>Example</title>
        <meta name="author" content="Adam Freeman"/>
        <meta name="description" content="A simple example"/>
        <link rel="shortcut icon" href="favicon.ico" type="image/x-icon" />
    </head>
    <body>
        <form name="fruitvote" id="fruitvote"
                method="post" action="http://titan:8080/form">
            <input name="fave"/>
            <input name="name"/>
            <button>Submit Vote</button>
        </form>
    </body>
</html>
```

The value of the name attribute is not sent to the server when the form is posted, which is why this attribute has value only in the DOM and is not as important as the name attribute on the input element. If an input element doesn't have a name attribute, the data that the user has entered will not be sent to the server when the form is submitted.

Adding Labels to a Form

You have a form that collects data from the user, but it isn't very easy to use. You can see how the input element added in the previous section is displayed by the browser in Figure 12-4.

Figure 12-4. The example form

The obvious problem is a complete lack of guidance for the user, who would have to read the source HTML to figure out what each of the text boxes is for. You can address this problem by using the label element, which lets you provide some context for each element in a form. Table 12-7 summarizes the label element.

Table 12-7. The label Element

Element:	label
Element Type:	Phrasing
Permitted Parents:	Any parent that can contain phrasing elements
Local Attributes:	for, form
Contents:	Phrasing Content
Tag Style:	Start and end tags
New in HTML5?	No
Changes in HTML5	The form attribute has been added in HTML5. See the "Working with Elements Outside the Form" section of this chapter for details of this attribute.

Style Convention   `label { cursor: default; }`

Listing 12-9 shows how you can give the user some context.

Listing 12-9. Using the label Element

```
<!DOCTYPE HTML>
<html>
    <head>
        <title>Example</title>
        <meta name="author" content="Adam Freeman"/>
        <meta name="description" content="A simple example"/>
        <link rel="shortcut icon" href="favicon.ico" type="image/x-icon" />
    </head>
    <body>
        <form method="post" action="http://titan:8080/form">
            <p><label for="fave">Fruit: <input id="fave" name="fave"/></label></p>
            <p><label for="name">Name: <input id="name" name="name"/></label></p>
            <button>Submit Vote</button>
        </form>
    </body>
</html>
```

I added a label for each of the input elements. Notice that I added an id attribute to the input elements and used these ids as the value for the for attributes on the label elements. This is how you associate labels with inputs, which makes processing forms simpler for screen readers and other assistive technologies. You can see how the labels appear in Figure 12-5.

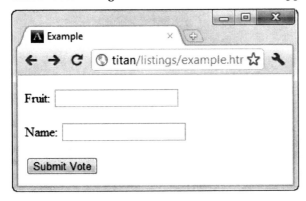

Figure 12-5. Adding labels to a form

In the listing, I placed the input elements as contents of the label elements. This isn't a requirement, and the two elements can be defined independently of one another. It is common to define the labels independently of the inputs when laying out complex forms.

■ **Note** I added some p elements to the form to provide a very basic layout. This is something I'll do for most of the examples in this chapter because it will make it easier to see the presentation impact of additions to the HTML document. To create prettier layouts for form elements, you can use the CSS table feature, which I describe in Chapter 21. The p element is described in Chapter 9.

Automatically Focusing on an input Element

You can select which input element the browser focuses on when the form is displayed. This means the user can start typing directly into the selected field without having to explicitly select it first. You specify which input element the focus should be applied to with the autofocus attribute, as shown in Listing 12-10.

Listing 12-10. Using the autofocus Attribute

```
<!DOCTYPE HTML>
<html>
    <head>
        <title>Example</title>
        <meta name="author" content="Adam Freeman"/>
        <meta name="description" content="A simple example"/>
        <link rel="shortcut icon" href="favicon.ico" type="image/x-icon" />
    </head>
    <body>
        <form method="post" action="http://titan:8080/form">
            <p>
                <label for="fave">Fruit: <input autofocus id="fave" name="fave"/></label>
            </p>
            <p><label for="name">Name: <input id="name" name="name"/></label></p>
            <button>Submit Vote</button>
        </form>
    </body>
</html>
```

As soon as the browser displays the page, it will focus on the first input element. You can see the visual cue Google Chrome gives to the user to indicate a focused element in Figure 12-6.

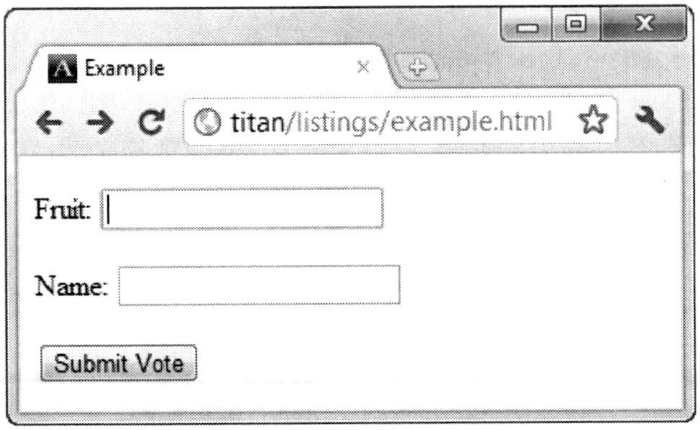

Figure 12-6. Autofocusing on an input element

You can apply the autofocus attribute only to one input element. If you try to apply the element more than once, the browser will focus on the last element in the document that has the element.

Disabling Individual input Elements

You can disable input elements so that the user cannot enter data into them. This isn't as odd as it might sound. You might want to present a consistent interface that is used for several related tasks, but for which not all of the input elements are germane. You can also use JavaScript to enable the elements based on a user's actions. A common example is enabling a set of input elements to capture an address when the user selects an option to ship to an address that is not the user's billing address. (You would enable the elements through the DOM, which is described in Chapters 25-31. Presenting users with check boxes is described in Chapter 13.)

You disable input elements by applying the disabled attribute, as shown in Listing 12-11.

Listing 12-11. Using the disabled Attribute on input Elements

```
<!DOCTYPE HTML>
<html>
    <head>
        <title>Example</title>
        <meta name="author" content="Adam Freeman"/>
        <meta name="description" content="A simple example"/>
        <link rel="shortcut icon" href="favicon.ico" type="image/x-icon" />
    </head>
    <body>
        <form method="post" action="http://titan:8080/form">
            <p>
                <label for="fave">Fruit: <input autofocus id="fave" name="fave"/></label>
            </p>
            <p>
                <label for="name">Name: <input disabled id="name" name="name"/></label>
            </p>
            <button>Submit Vote</button>
        </form>
```

```
    </body>
</html>
```

In this example, I applied the `disabled` attribute to the `input` element that gathers the user's name. You can see how Google Chrome displays a disabled `input` element in Figure 12-7. The other browsers use a similar style.

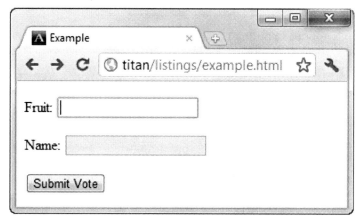

Figure 12-7. Disabling an input element

Grouping Form Elements Together

As you build more complex forms, it can be convenient to group some of the elements together, which you can do using the `fieldset` element. Table 12-8 summarizes this element.

Table 12-8. The fieldset Element

Element:	`fieldset`
Element Type:	Flow
Permitted Parents:	Any parent that can contain flow elements, usually as a descendent of a `form` element
Local Attributes:	`name, form, disabled`
Contents:	An optional `legend` element, followed by flow content
Tag Style:	Start and end tags
New in HTML5?	No
Changes in HTML5	The `form` attribute has been added in HTML5. See the "Working with Elements Outside the Form" section of this chapter for

details of this attribute.

Style Convention
```
fieldset { display: block; margin-start: 2px;
          margin-end: 2px; padding-before: 0.35em;
          padding-start: 0.75em; padding-end: 0.75em;
          padding-after: 0.625em; border: 2px groove; }
```

You can see how the `fieldset` element is applied in Listing 12-12. I added additional input elements to this example to demonstrate that a `fieldset` can be applied to a subset of the elements in a form.

Listing 12-12. Using the fieldset Element

```
<!DOCTYPE HTML>
<html>
    <head>
        <title>Example</title>
        <meta name="author" content="Adam Freeman"/>
        <meta name="description" content="A simple example"/>
        <link rel="shortcut icon" href="favicon.ico" type="image/x-icon" />
    </head>
    <body>
        <form method="post" action="http://titan:8080/form">
            <fieldset>
                <p><label for="name">Name: <input id="name" name="name"/></label></p>
                <p><label for="name">City: <input id="city" name="city"/></label></p>
            </fieldset>
            <fieldset>
                <p><label for="fave1">#1: <input id="fave1" name="fave1"/></label></p>
                <p><label for="fave2">#2: <input id="fave2" name="fave2"/></label></p>
                <p><label for="fave3">#3: <input id="fave3" name="fave3"/></label></p>
            </fieldset>
            <button>Submit Vote</button>
        </form>
    </body>
</html>
```

I used a `fieldset` element to group together two `input` elements that gather details about the user, and another `fieldset` to group three `input` elements that allow the user to vote for her three favorite fruits. You can see how the browser shows the default style convention for the `fieldset` element in Figure 12-8.

Figure 12-8. Using the fieldset element to group input elements together

Adding a Descriptive Label to a fieldset Element

You grouped your input elements together, but you still lack context for the user. You can remedy this by adding a legend element to each of your fieldset elements. Table 12-9 summarizes this element.

Table 12-9. The legend Element

Element:	legend
Element Type:	N/A
Permitted Parents:	The fieldset element
Local Attributes:	None
Contents:	Phrasing Content
Tag Style:	Start and end tags
New in HTML5?	No

Changes in HTML5	None
Style Convention	legend { display: block; padding-start: 2px; padding-end: 2px; border: none; }

The legend element must be the first child of a fieldset element, as shown in Listing 12-13.

Listing 12-13. Using the legend Element

```
<!DOCTYPE HTML>
<html>
    <head>
        <title>Example</title>
        <meta name="author" content="Adam Freeman"/>
        <meta name="description" content="A simple example"/>
        <link rel="shortcut icon" href="favicon.ico" type="image/x-icon" />
    </head>
    <body>
        <form method="post" action="http://titan:8080/form">
            <fieldset>
                <legend>Enter Your Details</legend>
                <p><label for="name">Name: <input id="name" name="name"/></label></p>
                <p><label for="name">City: <input id="city" name="city"/></label></p>
            </fieldset>
            <fieldset>
                <legend>Vote For Your Three Favorite Fruits</legend>
                <p><label for="fave1">#1: <input id="fave1" name="fave1"/></label></p>
                <p><label for="fave2">#2: <input id="fave2" name="fave2"/></label></p>
                <p><label for="fave3">#3: <input id="fave3" name="fave3"/></label></p>
            </fieldset>
            <button>Submit Vote</button>
        </form>
    </body>
</html>
```

You can see how the browser displays the legend elements in Figure 12-9.

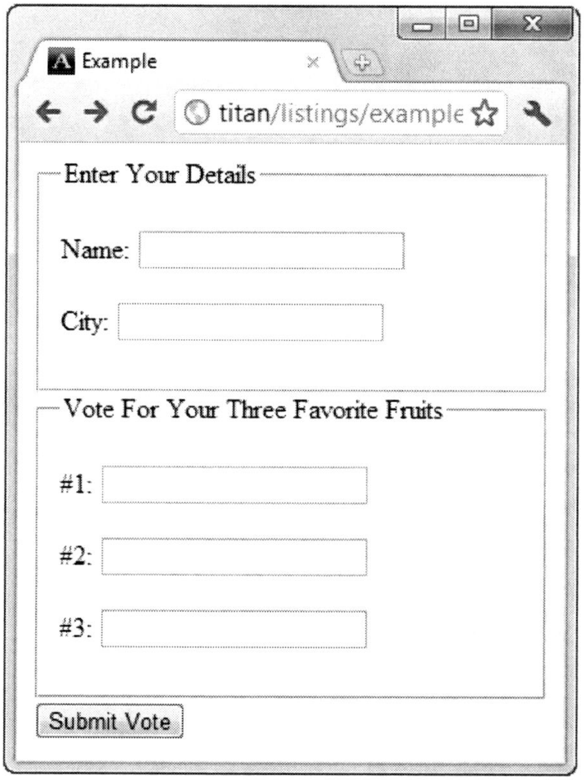

Figure 12-9. Using the legend element

Disabling Groups of Inputs Using the fieldset Element

I showed you how to disable *individual* input elements earlier in the chapter. You can also disable *multiple* input elements in a single step by applying the `disabled` attribute to the `fieldset` element. When you do this, all of the input elements contained by `fieldset` will be disabled, as shown in Listing 12-14.

Listing 12-14. Disabling the input Elements Using the fieldset Element

```
<!DOCTYPE HTML>
<html>
    <head>
        <title>Example</title>
        <meta name="author" content="Adam Freeman"/>
        <meta name="description" content="A simple example"/>
        <link rel="shortcut icon" href="favicon.ico" type="image/x-icon" />
    </head>
    <body>
        <form method="post" action="http://titan:8080/form">
```

```
        <fieldset>
            <legend>Enter Your Details</legend>
            <p><label for="name">Name: <input id="name" name="name"/></label></p>
            <p><label for="name">City: <input id="city" name="city"/></label></p>
        </fieldset>
        <fieldset disabled>
            <legend>Vote For Your Three Favorite Fruits</legend>
            <p><label for="fave1">#1: <input id="fave1" name="fave1"/></label></p>
            <p><label for="fave2">#2: <input id="fave2" name="fave2"/></label></p>
            <p><label for="fave3">#3: <input id="fave3" name="fave3"/></label></p>
        </fieldset>
        <button>Submit Vote</button>
    </form>
</body>
</html>
```

You can see the effect of disabling the input elements in Figure 12-10.

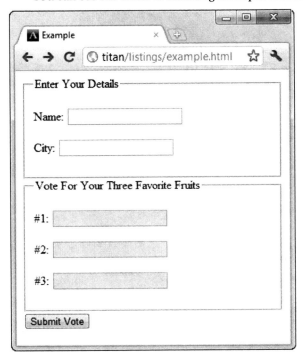

Figure 12-10. Disabling input elements through the fieldset element

Using the button Element

The button element is more flexible than it might first appear. There are three ways you can use button. The key to these different modes of operation is the type attribute, which has three values. These are described in Table 12-10.

Table 12-10. *Values for the type Attribute of the button Element*

Value	Description
submit	Specifies that the button will be used to submit a form
reset	Specifies that the button will be used to reset a form
button	Specifies that the button has no specific semantic significance

I describe each of these values and the functionality they offer in the following sections.

Using the button Element to Submit Forms

When you set the type attribute to submit, pressing the button will submit the form that contains the button. This is the default behavior when you have not applied the type attribute. When you use the button in this way, you have access to some additional attributes, which are described in Table 12-11.

Table 12-11. *Additional Attributes when the type Attribute of a Button Is Set to submit*

Attribute	Description
form	Specifies the form (or forms) with which the button is associated. See the "Working with Elements Outside the Form" section for details.
formaction	Overrides the action attribute on the form element, and specifies a new URL to which the form will be submitted. See the "Configuring the Form Action" section earlier in this chapter for details of the action attribute.
formenctype	Overrides the enctype attribute on the form element, and specifies the encoding scheme for the form data. See the "Configuring the Data Encoding" section earlier in this chapter for details of the enctype attribute.
formmethod	Overrides the method attribute on the form element. See the "Configuring the HTTP Method" section earlier in this chapter for details of the method attribute.
formtarget	Overrides the target attribute on the form element. See the "Specifying a Target for the Form Response" section earlier in this chapter for details of the target attribute.
formnovalidate	Overrides the novalidate attribute on the form element to specify whether client-side validation should be performed. See Chapter 14 for details of input validation.

For the most part, these attributes allow you to override or supplement the configuration of the form element and specify the action, method, encoding scheme, and target and to control client-side validation. These elements are new in HTML5. Listing 12-15 shows how you can apply these attributes to the button element.

Listing 12-15. Using the button Element Attributes

```
<!DOCTYPE HTML>
<html>
    <head>
        <title>Example</title>
        <meta name="author" content="Adam Freeman"/>
        <meta name="description" content="A simple example"/>
        <link rel="shortcut icon" href="favicon.ico" type="image/x-icon" />
    </head>
    <body>
        <form>
            <p>
                <label for="fave">Fruit: <input autofocus id="fave" name="fave"/></label>
            </p>
            <p>
                <label for="name">Name: <input id="name" name="name"/></label>
            </p>
            <button type="submit" formaction="http://titan:8080/form"
                    formmethod="post">Submit Vote</button>
        </form>
    </body>
</html>
```

In this example, I omitted the action and method attributes from the form element and provided the configuration through the formaction and formmethod attributes on the button element.

Using the button Element to Reset Forms

If you set the type attribute to reset, pressing the button causes all of the input elements in the form to be reset to their initial state. There are no additional attributes available when you use the button element in this way. Listing 12-16 shows the addition of a reset button to the HTML document.

Listing 12-16. Using the button Element to Reset a Form

```
<!DOCTYPE HTML>
<html>
    <head>
        <title>Example</title>
        <meta name="author" content="Adam Freeman"/>
        <meta name="description" content="A simple example"/>
        <link rel="shortcut icon" href="favicon.ico" type="image/x-icon" />
    </head>
    <body>
        <form method="post" action="http://titan:8080/form">
            <p>
                <label for="fave">Fruit: <input autofocus id="fave" name="fave"/></label>
            </p>
            <p>
                <label for="name">Name: <input id="name" name="name"/></label>
            </p>
```

```
                <button type="submit">Submit Vote</button>
                <button type="reset">Reset</button>
            </form>
        </body>
    </html>
```

You can see the effect of resetting a form in Figure 12-11.

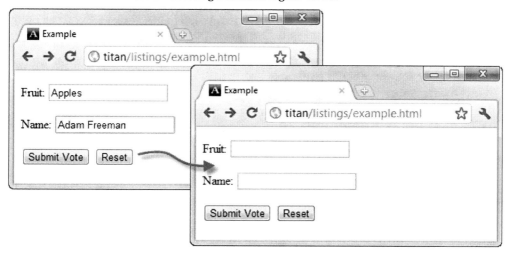

Figure 12-11. Resetting a form

Using button as a Generic Element

If you set the type attribute to button, you create a button element that is, well...just a button. It has no special meaning and won't do anything when you press it. Listing 12-17 shows the addition of such a button to the example HTML document.

Listing 12-17. Using a Generic Button

```
<!DOCTYPE HTML>
<html>
    <head>
        <title>Example</title>
        <meta name="author" content="Adam Freeman"/>
        <meta name="description" content="A simple example"/>
        <link rel="shortcut icon" href="favicon.ico" type="image/x-icon" />
    </head>
    <body>
        <form method="post" action="http://titan:8080/form">
            <p>
                <label for="fave">Fruit: <input autofocus id="fave" name="fave"/></label>
            </p>
            <p>
                <label for="name">Name: <input id="name" name="name"/></label>
```

```
                    </p>
                    <button type="submit">Submit Vote</button>
                    <button type="reset">Reset</button>
                    <button type="button">Do <strong>NOT</strong> press this button</button>
            </form>
        </body>
</html>
```

This may not seem like a useful way to use the element, but as I explain in Chapter 30, you can use JavaScript to perform actions when a button is pressed. This allows you to create customized behaviors in your web pages.

Notice that I styled the text contained in the button element. You can use any phrasing elements to mark up the text. You can see the effect of this markup in Figure 12-12.

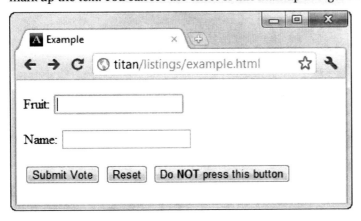

Figure 12-12. Adding a generic button element

Working with Elements Outside the Form

In HTML4, the input, button, and other form-related elements had to be contained within the form element, just as I demonstrated in all of the examples so far in this chapter. In HTML5, that restriction has been removed, and you can associate elements with forms anywhere in the document. You do this using the form attribute, which is defined by input, button, and the other form-related elements I describe in Chapter 14. To associate an element with a form that is not an antecedent, you simply set the form attribute to the id value of the form. Listing 12-18 gives an example.

Listing 12-18. Using the form Attribute

```
<!DOCTYPE HTML>
<html>
    <head>
        <title>Example</title>
        <meta name="author" content="Adam Freeman"/>
        <meta name="description" content="A simple example"/>
        <link rel="shortcut icon" href="favicon.ico" type="image/x-icon" />
    </head>
    <body>
```

```
<form id="voteform" method="post" action="http://titan:8080/form">
    <p>
        <label for="fave">Fruit: <input autofocus id="fave" name="fave"/></label>
    </p>
</form>
<p>
    <label for="name">Name: <input form="voteform" id="name" name="name"/>
    </label>
</p>

<button form="voteform" type="submit">Submit Vote</button>
<button form="voteform" type="reset">Reset</button>
</body>
</html>
```

In this example, only one of the input elements is a descendent of the form element. The other input element and both of the button elements are outside of the form element, but they use the form attribute to associate themselves with the form.

Summary

In this chapter, I showed you the basics of the HTML5 support for forms. You saw how to use the form element to denote a form and configure the way that the form functions. I showed you the basic input element, which lets you gather simple text data from the user, and the button element, which lets the user submit or reset a form (and which you can use as a generic button).

There are some useful new form features in HTML5. The headline items are covered in the next chapter, but even the basic form operations have been improved. The ability to associate an element with a form that is not an antecedent, the support for automatically focusing on an element, and the enhancements to the button element are all welcome additions.

CHAPTER 13

Customizing the Input Element

In the previous chapter, I showed you the basic use of the input element, which produced a simple text box in which the user can enter data. The problem with this approach is that the user can enter *any* data. This can be fine in some situations, but in other cases you might want a *specific* kind of data value from the user. In such cases, you can configure the input element to collect data from users in different ways. You configure the input element through the type attribute, for which there are 23 different values in HTML5. After you have selected the type value you want, you have access to additional attributes. There are 30 attributes available for the input element in total, and many of these can be used with only certain type values. I'll explain all of the different types and the associated attributes in this chapter. Table 13-1 provides the summary for this chapter.

Table 13-1. Chapter Summary

Problem	Solution	Listing
Set the size and capacity of an input element.	Use the size and maxlength attributes.	13-1
Set an initial value for an input element or a hint as to the kind of data required.	Use the value and placeholder attributes.	13-2
Provide suggested values to the user.	Use the datalist element and the list attribute on the input element.	13-3
Create read-only or disabled input elements.	Use the disabled and readonly attributes.	13-4
Hide the characters that a user enters from view.	Use the password type of input element.	13-5
Create buttons using an input element.	Use the submit, reset, or button types of input element.	13-6
Restrict the user to a numeric value.	Use the number type of input element.	13-7
Restrict the user to a range of numeric values.	Use the range type of input element.	13-8

Restrict the user to a true/false response.	Use the checkbox type of input element.	13-9
Restrict the user to a limited number of choices.	Use the radio type of input element.	13-10
Restrict the user to a specific format of string.	Use the email, tel, or url types of input element.	13-11
Restrict the user to a time or date.	Use the datetime, datetime-local, date, month, time, or week types of input element.	13-12
Restrict the user to selecting a color.	Use the color type of input element.	13-13
Restrict the user to entering terms for a search.	Use the search type of input element.	13-14
Create an input element that is not displayed to the user.	Use the hidden type of input element.	13-15
Create image buttons that submit the form.	Use the image type of input element.	13-16
Upload a file to the server.	Use the file type of input element and set the encoding for the form to multipart/form-data.	13-17

Using the input Element for Text Input

If you set the type attribute to text, the browser will display a single-line text box. This is the same style for the input element that you saw in the last chapter, and the style that is used when you omit the type attribute entirely. Table 13-2 summarizes the attributes that are available for this input element type (these attributes are in addition to those described in the previous chapter).

Table 13-2. Additional Attributes Available for the text Type

Attribute	Description	New in HTML5
dirname	Specifies a value for the name of the directionality of the text. See the section "Specifying Text Directionality" for details.	No
list	Specifies the id of a datalist element that provides values for this element. See the section "Using a Data List" for details.	Yes
maxlength	Specifies the maximum number of characters that the user can enter into the text box. See the section "Specifying the Element Size" for	No

details.

pattern	Specifies a regular expression pattern for the purposes of input validation. See Chapter 14 for details.	Yes
placeholder	Specifies a hint to the user as to the kind of input that you expect. See the section "Setting Values and Using Placeholders" for details.	Yes
readonly	If present, this attribute makes the text box read-only, and the user cannot edit the content. See the section "Creating Read-Only and Disabled Text Boxes" for details.	No
required	Specifies that the user must enter a value for the purposes of input validation. See Chapter 14 for details.	Yes
size	Specifies the width of the element, expressed as the number of characters that are visible in the text box. See the section "Specifying the Element Size" for details.	No
value	Specifies the initial value for the text box. See the section "Settings Values and Using Placeholders" for details.	No

In the following sections, I describe the attributes that are available for this text type of input.

■ **Tip** For multiline text boxes, use the textarea element, which I describe in Chapter 14.

Specifying the Element Size

There are two attributes that have an effect on the size of the text box. The maxlength attribute specifies an upper limit for the number of characters that the user can enter, and the size attribute specifies how many characters the text box can display. For both attributes, the number of characters is expressed as a positive integer value. Listing 13-1 shows both of these attributes in use.

Listing 13-1. Using the maxlength and size Attributes

```
<!DOCTYPE HTML>
<html>
    <head>
        <title>Example</title>
        <meta name="author" content="Adam Freeman"/>
        <meta name="description" content="A simple example"/>
        <link rel="shortcut icon" href="favicon.ico" type="image/x-icon" />
    </head>
    <body>
        <form method="post" action="http://titan:8080/form">
```

```
        <p>
            <label for="name">
                Name: <input maxlength="10" id="name" name="name"/>
            </label>
        </p>
        <p>
            <label for="city">
                City: <input size="10" id="city" name="city"/>
            </label>
        </p>
        <p>
            <label for="fave">
                Fruit: <input size="10" maxlength="10" id="fave" name="fave"/>
            </label>
        </p>
        <button type="submit">Submit Vote</button>
    </form>
</body>
</html>
```

For the first input element, I have applied the maxlength attribute with a value of 10. This means that the browser is free to determine the amount of space that the text box occupies on the screen, but the user can only enter up to ten characters. If the user tries to enter more than ten characters, the browser will discard the input.

For the second input element, I have applied the size attribute, also with a value of 10. This means that the browser must ensure that it sizes the text box so that it can display ten characters. The size attribute doesn't apply any restriction on the number of characters that the user can enter.

I have applied both attributes to the third input element. This has the effect of fixing the size onscreen and limiting the number of characters that the user can enter. You can see how these attributes affect the display and data entry in Figure 13-1.

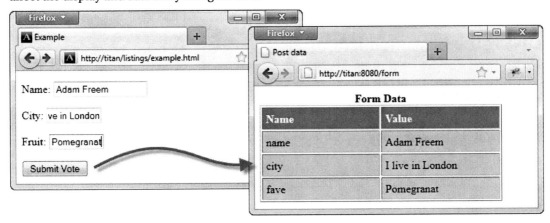

Figure 13-1. Using the maxlength and size attributes

In Figure 13-1, you can see the layout in the browser and the data that is passed to the server when the form is submitted. I have used Firefox for this example because my preferred browser, Chrome, doesn't properly implement the size attribute. When looking at the data that has been submitted to the server, notice that the city data item contains more characters than are displayed on the screen. As I mentioned, this is because the size attribute doesn't limit the number of characters that the user can enter, just the number that the browser can display.

Setting Values and Using Placeholders

The text box has been empty in all of the form examples so far, but this need not be the case. You can use the value attribute to specify a default value and the placeholder attribute to give the user a helpful hint about the kind of data that they should enter. Listing 13-2 shows these attributes in use.

Listing 13-2. Using the value and placeholder Attributes

```
<!DOCTYPE HTML>
<html>
    <head>
        <title>Example</title>
        <meta name="author" content="Adam Freeman"/>
        <meta name="description" content="A simple example"/>
        <link rel="shortcut icon" href="favicon.ico" type="image/x-icon" />
    </head>
    <body>
        <form method="post" action="http://titan:8080/form">
            <p>
                <label for="name">
                    Name: <input placeholder="Your name" id="name" name="name"/>
                </label>
            </p>
            <p>
                <label for="city">
                    City: <input placeholder="Where you live" id="city" name="city"/>
                </label>
            </p>
            <p>
                <label for="fave">
                    Fruit: <input value="Apple" id="fave" name="fave"/>
                </label>
            </p>
            <button type="submit">Submit Vote</button>
        </form>
    </body>
</html>
```

Use the placeholder attribute when you need the user to enter data, and you want to provide some context to help the user decide what data to provide. Use the value attribute to provide a default value, either because the user has previously provided this information, or because it is a common choice that is likely to be correct. You can see how the browser represents the values specified by these attributes in Figure 13-2.

Figure 13-2. Providing placeholders and default values

■ **Tip** When you use the button element to reset the form (as described in Chapter 12), the browser restores the placeholders and the default values.

Using a Data List

The list attribute allows you to specify the id value of a datalist element, which will be used to suggest options to the user when they enter data into the text box. Table 13-3 describes the datalist element.

Table 13-3. The datalist Element

Element:	datalist
Element Type:	Phrasing
Permitted Parents:	Any parent that can contain phrasing elements
Local Attributes:	None
Contents:	option elements and phrasing content
Tag Style:	Start and end
New in HTML5?	Yes

Changes in HTML5:	N/A
Style Convention:	None

The datalist element is new in HTML5 and allows you to define a set of values that assist the user in providing the data you require. Different types of input elements use the datalist element in slightly different ways. For the text type, the values are presented as autocomplete suggestions. You specify the values you want to give to the user through the option element, which is described in Table 13-4.

Table 13-4. The option Element

Element:	option
Element Type:	N/A
Permitted Parents:	datalist, select, optgroup
Local Attributes:	disabled, selected, label, value
Contents:	Character data
Tag Style:	Void or start and end
New in HTML5?	No
Changes in HTML5:	None
Style Convention:	None

Listing 13-3 shows the datalist and option elements used to create a set of values for a text box.

■ **Tip** You'll see the option element again when you look at the select and optgroup elements in Chapter 14.

Listing 13-3. Using the datalist Element

```
<!DOCTYPE HTML>
<html>
    <head>
        <title>Example</title>
        <meta name="author" content="Adam Freeman"/>
```

```
        <meta name="description" content="A simple example"/>
        <link rel="shortcut icon" href="favicon.ico" type="image/x-icon" />
    </head>
    <body>
        <form method="post" action="http://titan:8080/form">
            <p>
                <label for="name">
                    Name: <input placeholder="Your name" id="name" name="name"/>
                </label>
            </p>
            <p>
                <label for="city">
                    City: <input placeholder="Where you live" id="city" name="city"/>
                </label>
            </p>
            <p>
                <label for="fave">
                    Fruit: <input list="fruitlist" id="fave" name="fave"/>
                </label>
            </p>
            <button type="submit">Submit Vote</button>
        </form>

        <datalist id="fruitlist">
            <option value="Apples" label="Lovely Apples"/>
            <option value="Oranges">Refreshing Oranges</option>
            <option value="Cherries"/>
        </datalist>

    </body>
</html>
```

Each option element contained inside of the datalist represents a value that you want to propose to the user. The value attribute specifies the data value that will be used in the input element if that option is selected. You can use a different label to describe the option by using the label attribute or by defining content within the option element. You can see that I have done this for the Apples and Oranges option elements in Listing 13-3. Figure 13-3 shows how the browser uses the option elements defined in the datalist.

Figure 13-3. Using a datalist with a text input element

Take care when using a different label when working with the text input type; the user might not understand why clicking an item called Lovely Apples leads to just Apples being entered in the text box. Some browsers, such as Opera, take a slightly different approach when the label and value are different, as shown in Figure 13-4.

Figure 13-4. Opera displaying different value and labels

This is an improvement (although notice that the label attribute is detected, but the content of the option element is ignored), but can still be confusing.

Creating Read-Only and Disabled Text Boxes

The readonly and disabled attributes allow you to create text boxes that the user cannot edit. Each creates a different visual effect. Listing 13-4 shows both attributes.

Listing 13-4. Using the readonly and disabled Attributes

```
<!DOCTYPE HTML>
<html>
    <head>
        <title>Example</title>
        <meta name="author" content="Adam Freeman"/>
        <meta name="description" content="A simple example"/>
        <link rel="shortcut icon" href="favicon.ico" type="image/x-icon" />
    </head>
    <body>
        <form method="post" action="http://titan:8080/form">
            <p>
                <label for="name">
                    Name: <input value="Adam" disabled id="name" name="name"/>
                </label>
            </p>
            <p>
                <label for="city">
                    City: <input value="Boston" readonly id="city" name="city"/>
                </label>
            </p>
            <p>
                <label for="fave">
                    Fruit: <input id="fave" name="fave"/>
                </label>
            </p>
            <button type="submit">Submit Vote</button>
        </form>
    </body>
</html>
```

You can see how the browser deals with these attributes in Figure 13-5.

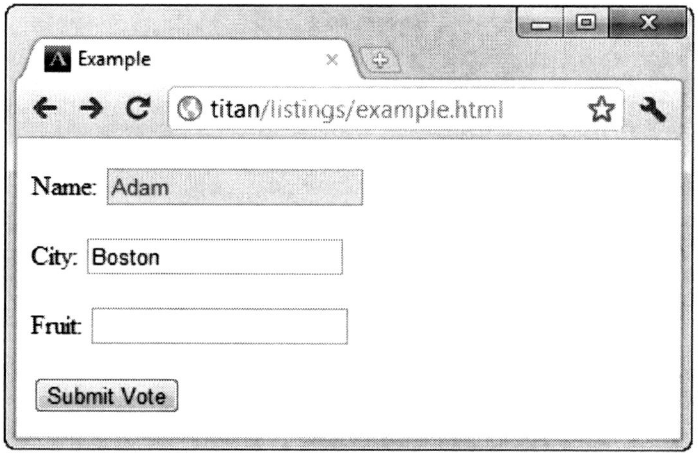

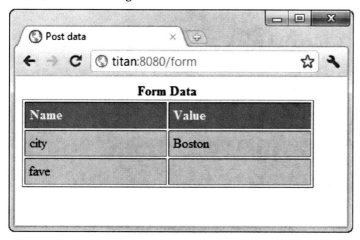

Figure 13-5. Using the disabled and readonly attributes

The first input element in Listing 13-4 has the disabled attribute, which has the effect of graying out the text box and preventing the user from editing the text. The second input element has the readonly attribute, which prevents the user from editing the text, but doesn't affect the appearance of the text box. When you submit the forms, the values that were defined with the value attribute are submitted to the server, as shown in Figure 13-6.

Figure 13-6. Form data from input elements with the disabled and readonly attributes

Notice that the data from the input element, with the disabled attribute, is not submitted to the server. If you want to use this attribute and you need to ensure that the server receives a value for the input element, then consider adding a hidden type input element (see the section "Using the input Element to Create Hidden Data Items," later in this chapter).

My advice is to use the readonly attribute with caution. Although the data is submitted to the user, there is no visual cue to the user that the field isn't editable; the browser simply ignores the keystrokes, which can cause confusion.

Specifying Text Directionality

The dirname attribute allows you to specify the name of the data value submitted to the server, and contains the text direction for the data that the user has entered. At the time of writing, none of the mainstream browsers support this attribute.

Using the input Element for Password Input

The password value for the type attribute creates an input element for entering a password. The characters that the user types are represented by a masking character, such as an asterisk (*). Table 13-5 lists the additional attributes that are available when the type attribute is set to password. Many of these are shared with the text type and work in the same way.

Table 13-5. Additional Attributes Available for the password Type

Attribute	Description	New in HTML5
maxlength	Specifies the maximum number of characters that the user can enter into the password box. See the section "Specifying the Element Size," earlier in this chapter, for details.	No
pattern	Specifies a regular expression pattern for the purposes of input validation. See Chapter 14 for details.	Yes
placeholder	Specifies a hint to the user as to the kind of input that you expect. See the section "Setting Values and Using Placeholders," earlier in this chapter, for details.	Yes
readonly	If present, this attribute makes the password box read-only, and the user cannot edit the content. See the section "Creating Read-Only and Disabled Text Boxes," earlier in this chapter, for details.	No
required	Specifies that the user must enter a value for the purposes of input validation. See Chapter 14 for details.	Yes
size	Specifies the width of the element, expressed as the number of characters that are visible in the password box. See the section "Specifying the Element Size," earlier in this chapter, for details.	No
value	Specifies the initial value for the password.	No

Listing 13-5 shows the password type in use.

Listing 13-5. Using the password Type

```
<!DOCTYPE HTML>
<html>
    <head>
        <title>Example</title>
        <meta name="author" content="Adam Freeman"/>
        <meta name="description" content="A simple example"/>
        <link rel="shortcut icon" href="favicon.ico" type="image/x-icon" />
    </head>
    <body>
        <form method="post" action="http://titan:8080/form">
            <p>
                <label for="name">
                    Name: <input value="Adam" id="name" name="name"/>
                </label>
            </p>
            <p>
                <label for="password">
                    Password: <input type="password" placeholder="Min 6 characters"
                        id="password" name="password"/>
                </label>
            </p>
            <p>
                <label for="fave">
                    Fruit: <input value="Apples" id="fave" name="fave"/>
                </label>
            </p>
            <button type="submit">Submit Vote</button>
        </form>
    </body>
</html>
```

In Listing 13-5, I have used the placeholder attribute to give the user some guidance about the kind of password that I am expecting. When the user starts to type, the browser removes the placeholder and replaces each typed character with a circular bullet (different browsers use different masking characters). You can see this effect in Figure 13-7.

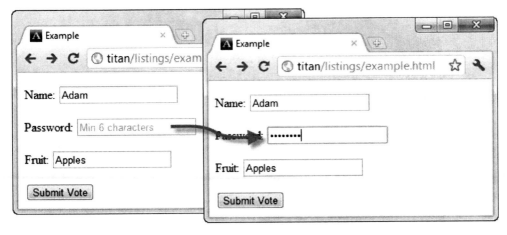

Figure 13-7. Using the password type of the input element

At the risk of stating the obvious, the masking applies only to the display of the text that the user enters. When you submit the form, the server receives the password in clear text, as you can see in Figure 13-8, which shows the response from the Node.js script.

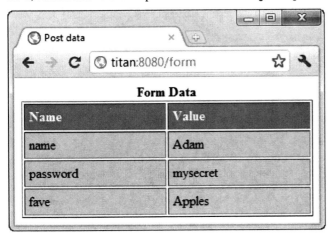

Figure 13-8. Submitting a form that contains a password field

---

■ **Caution** The password type of the input element doesn't protect the password when it is submitted to the server. The value that the user entered is transmitted as clear text. If security is important to your site and application (and it should be), you should consider using SSL/HTTPS to encrypt communications between the browser and your server.

Using the input Element to Create Buttons

The submit, reset, and button types of input element create buttons that are very similar to those created when using the button element, described in Chapter 12. Table 13-6 summarizes these input types.

Table 13-6. The input Element Types That Create Buttons

Type	Description	Additional Attributes
submit	Creates a button that submits the form.	formaction, formenctype, formmethod, formtarget, formnovalidate
reset	Creates a button that resets the form.	None
button	Creates a button that performs no action.	None

The additional attributes that are available when you use the submit type are the same as when you use the button element. You can find descriptions and demonstrations of these attributes in Chapter 12. The reset and button types don't define any additional attributes.

For all three of these input types, the label that is displayed on the button is taken from the value attribute, as shown in Listing 13-6.

Listing 13-6. Using the input Element to Create Buttons

```
<!DOCTYPE HTML>
<html>
    <head>
        <title>Example</title>
        <meta name="author" content="Adam Freeman"/>
        <meta name="description" content="A simple example"/>
        <link rel="shortcut icon" href="favicon.ico" type="image/x-icon" />
    </head>
    <body>
        <form method="post" action="http://titan:8080/form">
            <p>
                <label for="name">
                    Name: <input value="Adam" id="name" name="name"/>
                </label>
            </p>
            <p>
                <label for="password">
                    Password: <input type="password" placeholder="Min 6 characters"
                        id="password" name="password"/>
                </label>
            </p>
            <p>
                <label for="fave">
                    Fruit: <input value="Apples" id="fave" name="fave"/>
                </label>
```

```
            </p>
            <input type="submit" value="Submit Vote"/>
            <input type="reset" value="Reset Form"/>
            <input type="button" value="My Button"/>
        </form>
    </body>
</html>
```

You can see how the browser displays these buttons in Figure 13-9. As you can see, they have the same appearance as when you use the button element.

Figure 13-9. Using input elements to create buttons

The difference between using the input element to create buttons and using the button element is that you can use the button element to display marked up text (you can see an example of this in Chapter 12). Some older browsers, notably IE6, do odd things to button elements, which is why most web sites tend toward using input elements—they have traditionally been handled more consistently.

Using the input Element to Restrict Data Entry

HTML5 introduces some new values for the input element's type attribute that let you be more specific about the kind of data that you want from the user. In the following sections, I'll introduce each new type value and demonstrate its use. Table 13-7 summarizes these new type values.

Table 13-7. Restricted Data type Values

Type	Description	New in HTML5
checkbox	Restricts the input to a true/false check box.	No
color	Restricts the input to a color.	Yes
date	Restricts the input to a date.	Yes
datetime	Restricts the input to a global date and time with time zone.	Yes
datetime-local	Restricts the input to a global date and time without time zone.	Yes
email	Restricts the input to a properly formatted e-mail address.	Yes
month	Restricts the input to a year and month.	Yes
number	Restricts the input to an integer or floating-point number.	Yes
radiobutton	Restricts the input to a fixed set of choices.	No
range	Restricts the input to a specified range.	Yes
tel	Restricts the input to a properly formatted telephone number.	Yes
time	Restricts the input to a time of day.	Yes
week	Restricts the input to a year and week.	Yes
url	Restricts the input to a fully qualified URL.	Yes

Some of these input types present users with strong visual cues as to the kind of restrictions on the data that they may enter or choose (e.g., the checkbox and radiobutton types). Others, such as the email and url types, rely on input validation, which I describe in Chapter 14.

Using the input Element to Obtain a Number

The number value for the type attribute creates an input box that will only accept numeric values. Some browsers, notably Chrome, will also display selector arrows that will increment and decrement the numeric value. Table 13-8 describes the additional attributes that are available when using this input type.

Table 13-8. Additional Attributes Available for the number Type

Attribute	Description	New in HTML5
list	Specifies the id of a datalist element that provides values for this element. See the section "Using a Data List," earlier in this chapter, for details of the datalist element.	Yes
min	Specifies the minimum acceptable value for the purposes of input validation (and sets the limits for the decrement button, if displayed). See Chapter 14 for details of input validation.	Yes
max	Specifies the maximum acceptable value for the purposes of input validation (and sets the limits for the increment button, if displayed). See Chapter 14 for details of input validation.	Yes
readonly	If present, this attribute makes the input box read-only, and the user cannot edit the content. See the section "Creating Read-Only and Disabled Text Boxes," earlier in this chapter, for details.	No
required	Specifies that the user must provide a value for the purposes of input validation. See Chapter 14 for details.	Yes
step	Specifies the granularity of increments and decrements to the value.	Yes
value	Specifies the initial value for the element.	No

The values for the min, max, step, and value attributes can be expressed as integer or decimal numbers; for example, 3 and 3.14 are both valid. Listing 13-7 shows the number type of input in use.

Listing 13-7. Using the number Type of the input Element

```
<!DOCTYPE HTML>
<html>
    <head>
        <title>Example</title>
        <meta name="author" content="Adam Freeman"/>
        <meta name="description" content="A simple example"/>
        <link rel="shortcut icon" href="favicon.ico" type="image/x-icon" />
    </head>
    <body>
        <form method="post" action="http://titan:8080/form">
            <p>
                <label for="name">
                    Name: <input value="Adam" id="name" name="name"/>
                </label>
            </p>
            <p>
```

```
        <label for="password">
            Password: <input type="password" placeholder="Min 6 characters"
                id="password" name="password"/>
        </label>
    </p>
    <p>
        <label for="fave">
            Fruit: <input value="Apples" id="fave" name="fave"/>
        </label>
    </p>

    <p>
        <label for="price">
            $ per unit in your area:
            <input type="number" step="1" min="0" max="100"
                value="1" id="price" name="price"/>
        </label>
    </p>
    <input type="submit" value="Submit Vote"/>
    </form>
</body>
</html>
```

In Listing 13-7, I solicit the price that the user pays for their favorite fruit in their area. I have specified a minimum value of 1, a maximum value of 100, a step of 1, and a starting value of 1. You can see how the browser displays this type of input element in Figure 13-10. I have shown both Firefox and Chrome in this figure; notice that Chrome displays the small arrow buttons that can be used to increment the numeric value, but Firefox does not.

Figure 13-10. Chrome and Firefox displaying the number type of the input element

Using the input Element to Obtain a Number in a Given Range

An alternative approach to obtaining a numeric value is to use the range type of input element, which restricts the user to selecting a value from a predetermined range. The range type supports the same set of attributes as the number type (shown in Table 13-8), but the way that the browser displays the element is different. Listing 13-8 shows the range type in use.

Listing 13-8. Using the range Type of the input Element

```
<!DOCTYPE HTML>
<html>
    <head>
        <title>Example</title>
        <meta name="author" content="Adam Freeman"/>
        <meta name="description" content="A simple example"/>
        <link rel="shortcut icon" href="favicon.ico" type="image/x-icon" />
    </head>
    <body>
        <form method="post" action="http://titan:8080/form">
            <p>
                <label for="name">
                    Name: <input value="Adam" id="name" name="name"/>
                </label>
            </p>
            <p>
                <label for="password">
                    Password: <input type="password" placeholder="Min 6 characters"
                        id="password" name="password"/>
                </label>
            </p>
            <p>
                <label for="fave">
                    Fruit: <input value="Apples" id="fave" name="fave"/>
                </label>
            </p>

            <p>
                <label for="price">
                    $ per unit in your area: 1
                    <input type="range" step="1" min="0" max="100"
                        value="1" id="price" name="price"/>100
                </label>
            </p>
            <input type="submit" value="Submit Vote"/>
        </form>
    </body>
</html>
```

You can see how the browser displays the range type in Figure 13-11.

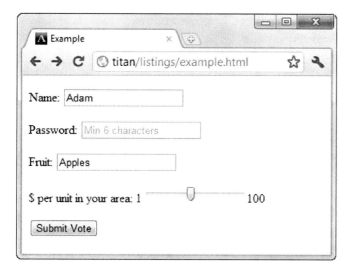

Figure 13-11. Using the range type of input element

Using the input Element to Obtain a Boolean Response

The checkbox type of the input element creates a check box that allows the user to make a true/false choice. This value for the type attribute supports the additional attributes shown in Table 13-9.

Table 13-9. Additional Attributes Available for the checkbox Type

Attribute	Description	New in HTML5
checked	If applied, this attribute ensures that the check box is checked when initially displayed to the user or when the form is reset.	No
required	Specifies that the user must check the check box for the purposes of input validation. See Chapter 14 for details.	Yes
value	Specifies the data value that is submitted to the server when the check box is checked; defaults to on.	No

Listing 13-9 shows the checkbox type of input element in use.

Listing 13-9. Using an input Element to Create a Check Box

```
<!DOCTYPE HTML>
<html>
    <head>
        <title>Example</title>
        <meta name="author" content="Adam Freeman"/>
        <meta name="description" content="A simple example"/>
```

```
            <link rel="shortcut icon" href="favicon.ico" type="image/x-icon" />
        </head>
        <body>
            <form method="post" action="http://titan:8080/form">
                <p>
                    <label for="name">
                        Name: <input value="Adam" id="name" name="name"/>
                    </label>
                </p>
                <p>
                    <label for="password">
                        Password: <input type="password" placeholder="Min 6 characters"
                            id="password" name="password"/>
                    </label>
                </p>
                <p>
                    <label for="fave">
                        Fruit: <input value="Apples" id="fave" name="fave"/>
                    </label>
                </p>
                <p>
                    <label for="veggie">
                        Are you vegetarian: <input type="checkbox" id="veggie" name="veggie"/>
                    </label>
                </p>
                <input type="submit" value="Submit Vote"/>
            </form>
        </body>
    </html>
```

You can see how the browser displays this kind of input element in Figure 13-12.

Figure 13-12. Creating a check box with an input element

The wrinkle that arises with the checkbox type is that when the form is submitted, a data value is sent to the server only if the user has checked the check box. So, if I submit the form as it is shown in Figure 13-12, I get the response from the Node.js script shown in Figure 13-13.

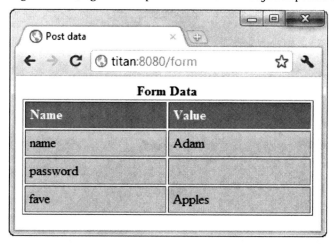

Figure 13-13. The data items submitted by the form shown in the previous figure

Notice that there is a value for the password element, but not for the checkbox. The absence of a data item for a checkbox type input element indicates that the user has not checked the box; the presence of a data value indicates the user has checked the box, as shown in Figure 13-14.

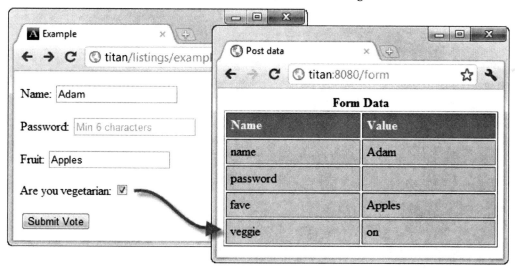

Figure 13-14. Submitting a form where a check box is checked

Using the input Element to Create Fixed Choices

The radio type of the input element allows you to create a group of radio buttons that let the user pick from a fixed set of options. This is useful when there are a small number of valid data values that you can work with. Table 13-10 describes the additional attributes that are support by this type of input element.

Table 13-10. Additional Attributes Available for the radio Type

Attribute	Description	New in HTML5
checked	If applied, this attribute ensures that the radio button is selected when initially displayed to the user or when the form is reset.	No
required	Specifies that the user must select one of the radio buttons for the purposes of input validation. See Chapter 14 for details.	Yes
value	Specifies the data value that is submitted to the server when the check box is checked.	No

Each input element with the type radio represents a single option to the user. You create a set of exclusive options by ensuring that the input elements all have the same value for the name attribute. You can see how this works in Listing 13-10.

Listing 13-10. Using the radio Type to Create Fixed Choices

```
<!DOCTYPE HTML>
<html>
    <head>
        <title>Example</title>
        <meta name="author" content="Adam Freeman"/>
        <meta name="description" content="A simple example"/>
        <link rel="shortcut icon" href="favicon.ico" type="image/x-icon" />
    </head>
    <body>
        <form method="post" action="http://titan:8080/form">
            <p>
                <label for="name">
                    Name: <input value="Adam" id="name" name="name"/>
                </label>
            </p>
            <p>
                <label for="password">
                    Password: <input type="password" placeholder="Min 6 characters"
                        id="password" name="password"/>
                </label>
            </p>
            <p>
                <fieldset>
                    <legend>Vote for your favorite fruit</legend>
                    <label for="apples">
```

```
                        <input type="radio" checked value="Apples" id="apples"
                            name="fave"/>
                        Apples
                    </label>
                    <label for="oranges">
                        <input type="radio" value="Oranges" id="oranges" name="fave"/>
                        Oranges
                    </label>
                    <label for="cherries">
                        <input type="radio" value="Cherries" id="cherries" name="fave"/>
                        Cherries
                    </label>
                </fieldset>
            </p>
            <input type="submit" value="Submit Vote"/>
        </form>
    </body>
</html>
```

In this example, I have created three input elements that are of the radio type. The value of the name attribute for all three is fave, which means that the browser will treat them as related to one another. This means that selecting one of the buttons will cause the other two to be unselected. I use the value attribute to specify the data value to send to the server when the form is submitted, and I have used fieldset and legend attributes to give the user a visual cue that the three buttons are related (this is optional; both the fieldset and legend elements are described in Chapter 12). I have applied the checked attribute on the first of the radio elements so that there is always a value selected. You can see how the browser displays these input elements in Figure 13-15.

Figure 13-15. Using the input element to create a set of radio buttons

At most, one of the radio buttons will be checked. There can be no checked buttons if the checked attribute is not applied and the user doesn't make a selection. Like the checkbox type of input element, no value will be submitted to the server if the element isn't checked, which means that no data item will be present if the user doesn't make a selection.

Using the input Element to Obtain Formatted Strings

The email, tel, and url type values configure the input element to accept only input that is a valid e-mail address, telephone number, or URL, respectively. All three of these types support the additional attributes shown in Table 13-11.

Table 13-11. Additional Attributes Available for the email, tel, and url Types

Attribute	Description	New in HTML5
list	Specifies the id of a datalist element that provides values for the element. See the section "Using a Data List," earlier in this chapter, for details	Yes
maxlength	Specifies the maximum number of characters that the user can enter into the text box. See the section "Specifying the Element Size," earlier in this chapter, for details.	No
pattern	Specifies a regular expression pattern for the purposes of input validation. See Chapter 14 for details.	Yes
placeholder	Specifies a hint to the user as to the kind of input that you expect. See the section "Setting Values and Using Placeholders," earlier in this chapter, for details.	Yes
readonly	If present, this attribute makes the text box read-only, and the user cannot edit the content.	No
required	Specifies that the user must provide a value for the purposes of input validation. See Chapter 14 for details.	Yes
size	Specifies the width of the element, expressed as the number of characters that are visible in the text box. See the section "Specifying the Element Size," earlier in this chapter, for details.	No
value	Specifies the initial value for the element. See the section "Setting Values and Using Placeholders," earlier in this chapter, for details. For the email type, this can be a single address, or multiple addresses separated by commas.	No

The email type also supports the multiple attribute which, when applied, allows the input element to accept multiple e-mail addresses. You can see all three types of input elements used in Listing 13-11.

Listing 13-11. Using the email, tel, and url input Types

```
<!DOCTYPE HTML>
<html>
    <head>
        <title>Example</title>
        <meta name="author" content="Adam Freeman"/>
        <meta name="description" content="A simple example"/>
        <link rel="shortcut icon" href="favicon.ico" type="image/x-icon" />
    </head>
    <body>
        <form method="post" action="http://titan:8080/form">
            <p>
                <label for="name">
                    Name: <input value="Adam" id="name" name="name"/>
                </label>
            </p>
            <p>
                <label for="password">
                    Password: <input type="password" placeholder="Min 6 characters"
                        id="password" name="password"/>
                </label>
            </p>
            <p>
                <label for="email">
                    Email: <input type="email" placeholder="user@domain.com"
                        id="email" name="email"/>
                </label>
            </p>
            <p>
                <label for="tel">
                    Tel: <input type="tel" placeholder="(XXX)-XXX-XXXX"
                        id="tel" name="tel"/>
                </label>
            </p>
            <p>
                <label for="url">
                    Your homepage: <input type="url" id="url" name="url"/>
                </label>
            </p>
            <input type="submit" value="Submit Vote"/>
        </form>
    </body>
</html>
```

These input types appear as regular text boxes to the user, and only validate the data that the user has entered when the form is submitted. This is part of the new HTML5 support for input validation, which I describe in Chapter 14. The quality of the validation is variable. All of the mainstream browsers cope well with the email type and properly detect valid e-mail addresses. The url type is a bit hit and miss. Some browsers simply prepend http:// to whatever the user enters, some require the user to enter a value that begins with http:// but don't validate the rest of the value, and some just let the user submit any value without validation. The tel input type is the least well supported. None of the mainstream browsers apply any kind of useful validation, as I write this.

Using the input Element to Obtain Times and Dates

HTML5 has also introduced some input element types to gather dates and times from the user. Table 13-12 describes these input types.

Table 13-12. The input Element Types for Obtaining Times and Dates

Type	Description	Example
datetime	Obtains a global date and time, including time zone.	2011-07-19T16:49:39.491Z
datetime-local	Obtains a local date and time, (with no time zone information).	2011-07-19T16:49:39.491
date	Obtains a local date (with no time or time zone).	2011-07-20
month	Obtains a year and month (no day, time, or time zone information).	2011-08
time	Obtains a time.	17:49:44.746
week	Obtains the current week.	2011-W30

Dates and times are notoriously difficult to deal with and, sadly, the specification of these new input element type falls far short of the ideal. The date formats are taken from RFC 3339 (available at http://tools.ietf.org/html/rfc3339), which describes timestamps that are rigidly described and formatted. This is a very different expression of dates from the many regional variations that are actually in use and which users will expect. As an example, few users will realize that the T in the datetime format denotes the start of the time segment, and that the Z represents the invariant *Zulu* Time Zone. All of the input element types described in Table 13-12 support the additional attributes described in Table 13-13.

Table 13-13. Additional Attributes Available for the Date and Time input Element Types

Attribute	Description	New in HTML5
list	Specifies the id of a datalist element that provides values for the element. See the section "Using a Data List," earlier in this chapter, for details.	Yes
min	Specifies the minimum acceptable value for the purposes of input validation (and sets the limits for the decrement button, if displayed). See Chapter 14 for details of input validation.	Yes
max	Specifies the maximum acceptable value for the purposes of input validation (and sets the limits for the increment button, if displayed).	Yes

See Chapter 14 for details of input validation.

readonly	If present, this attribute makes the text box read-only, and the user cannot edit the content.	No
required	Specifies that the user must provide a value for the purposes of input validation. See Chapter 14 for details.	Yes
step	Specifies the granularity of increments and decrements to the value.	Yes
value	Specifies the initial value for the element.	No

Listing 13-12 shows the date type in use.

Listing 13-12. Using the date Type of the input Element

```
<!DOCTYPE HTML>
<html>
    <head>
        <title>Example</title>
        <meta name="author" content="Adam Freeman"/>
        <meta name="description" content="A simple example"/>
        <link rel="shortcut icon" href="favicon.ico" type="image/x-icon" />
    </head>
    <body>
        <form method="post" action="http://titan:8080/form">
            <p>
                <label for="name">
                    Name: <input value="Adam" id="name" name="name"/>
                </label>
            </p>
            <p>
                <label for="password">
                    Password: <input type="password" placeholder="Min 6 characters"
                        id="password" name="password"/>
                </label>
            </p>
            <p>
                <label for="fave">
                    Fruit: <input value="Apples" id="fave" name="fave"/>
                </label>
            </p>
            <p>
                <label for="lastbuy">
                    When did you last buy: <input type="date"
                        id="lastbuy" name="lastbuy"/>
                </label>
            </p>
            <input type="submit" value="Submit Vote"/>
        </form>
```

```
        </body>
    </html>
```

The browser support for these new input types is still very limited. As I write this, Opera has the best support and provides a date-picker widget, as shown in Figure 13-16.

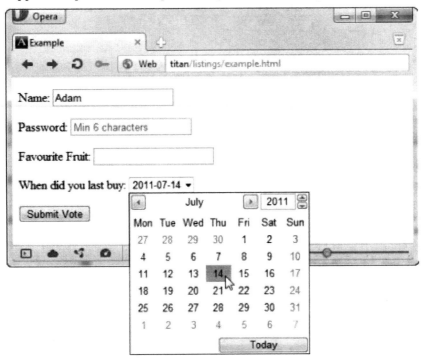

Figure 13-16. Selecting a date with Opera

The next best implementation is in Chrome, which presents the same kind of text box as for the number type of input element, with small up and down buttons to increment and decrement the time. The other mainstream browsers simply preset a single-line text box and leave the user to figure everything out. I am sure that this situation will improve, but until then I recommend looking at the calendar pickers that are available with popular JavaScript libraries such as jQuery.

Using the input Element to Obtain a Color

The color type of input element restricts the user to selecting a color. This input type supports the additional attribute list, which I describe in the section "Using a Data List," earlier in this chapter.

Color values are expressed as exactly seven characters: a leading #, followed by three two-digit hexadecimal values representing the red, green, and blue values (for example, #FF1234). CSS color names, such as red or black, are not supported. You can see this type of input element in use in Listing 13-13.

Listing 13-13. Using the color Type of the input Element

```
<!DOCTYPE HTML>
<html>
    <head>
        <title>Example</title>
        <meta name="author" content="Adam Freeman"/>
        <meta name="description" content="A simple example"/>
        <link rel="shortcut icon" href="favicon.ico" type="image/x-icon" />
    </head>
    <body>
        <form method="post" action="http://titan:8080/form">
            <p>
                <label for="name">
                    Name: <input value="Adam" id="name" name="name"/>
                </label>
            </p>
            <p>
                <label for="password">
                    Password: <input type="password" placeholder="Min 6 characters"
                        id="password" name="password"/>
                </label>
            </p>
            <p>
                <label for="fave">
                    Favorite Fruit: <input type="text" id="fave" name="fave"/>
                </label>
            </p>
            <p>
                <label for="color">
                    Color: <input type="color" id="color" name="color"/>
                </label>
            </p>
            <input type="submit" value="Submit Vote"/>
        </form>
    </body>
</html>
```

Most of the browsers don't implement any special support for this type of the input element. Google Chrome lets the user type in a value and reports formatting problems when performing input validation (which I describe in Chapter 14). The best support is available in Opera, which displays a simple color picker that can be expanded to a full-range color selector dialog, as shown in Figure 13-17.

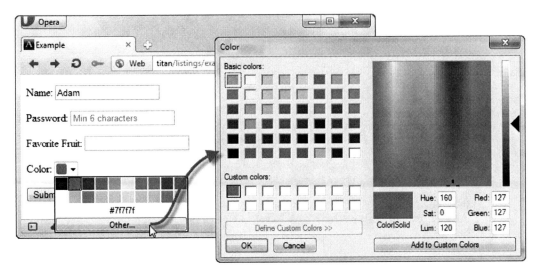

Figure 13-17. The color picker support in Opera

Using the input Element to Obtain Search Terms

The search type of input element presents the user with a single-line text box for entering search terms. This is an unusual input type because it doesn't really do anything. There are no built-in restrictions on the data that the user can enter, and there are no special features, such as searching the local page or using the user's default search engine to perform a search. This type of input element supports the same additional attributes as the text type, and you can see it in use in Listing 13-14.

Listing 13-14. Using the search Type of the input Element

```
<!DOCTYPE HTML>
<html>
    <head>
        <title>Example</title>
        <meta name="author" content="Adam Freeman"/>
        <meta name="description" content="A simple example"/>
        <link rel="shortcut icon" href="favicon.ico" type="image/x-icon" />
    </head>
    <body>
        <form method="post" action="http://titan:8080/form">
            <p>
                <label for="name">
                    Name: <input value="Adam" id="name" name="name"/>
                </label>
            </p>
            <p>
                <label for="password">
                    Password: <input type="password" placeholder="Min 6 characters"
                        id="password" name="password"/>
```

```
            </label>
        </p>
        <p>
            <label for="fave">
                Favorite Fruit: <input type="text" id="fave" name="fave"/>
            </label>
        </p>
        <p>
            <label for="search">
                Search: <input type="search" id="search" name="search"/>
            </label>
        </p>
        <input type="submit" value="Submit Vote"/>
    </form>
</body>
</html>
```

Browsers can choose to display the text box in a way that makes it obvious that you are gathering search terms. Google Chrome presents a standard text box until the user starts typing, at which point a cancel icon is displayed, as shown in Figure 13-18. At the time of writing, the other mainstream browsers simply treat this type of input as though it were a regular text type.

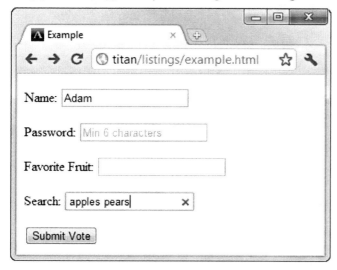

Figure 13-18. The search type of input, as displayed by Google Chrome

Using the input Element to Create Hidden Data Items

There are occasions when you want to ensure that data items are sent to the server when the form is submitted, without showing them to the user, or allowing them to be edited. A common example is when a web application is displaying a database record to a user for editing. You often need to include the primary key in the web page so you know which record the user is editing in a simple and easy manner, but you don't want to display that information to the user. You use the hidden type of input element to achieve this effect. Listing 13-15 shows how you can use this type of input element.

Listing 13-15. Creating a hidden Type input Element

```
<!DOCTYPE HTML>
<html>
    <head>
        <title>Example</title>
        <meta name="author" content="Adam Freeman"/>
        <meta name="description" content="A simple example"/>
        <link rel="shortcut icon" href="favicon.ico" type="image/x-icon" />
    </head>
    <body>
        <form method="post" action="http://titan:8080/form">
            <input type="hidden" name="recordID" value="1234"/>
            <p>
                <label for="name">
                    Name: <input value="Adam" id="name" name="name"/>
                </label>
            </p>
            <p>
                <label for="password">
                    Password: <input type="password" placeholder="Min 6 characters"
                        id="password" name="password"/>
                </label>
            </p>
            <p>
                <label for="fave">
                    Favorite Fruit: <input type="text" id="fave" name="fave"/>
                </label>
            </p>
            <input type="submit" value="Submit Vote"/>
        </form>
    </body>
</html>
```

In this example, I have created a hidden input element whose name attribute has a value of recordID and whose value attribute is 1234. When the page is displayed, the browser doesn't provide any visual representation of the input element, as you can see in Figure 13-19.

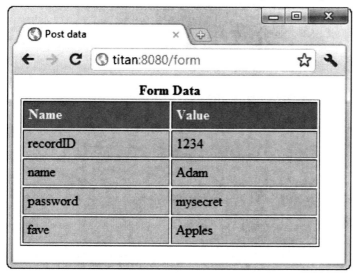

Figure 13-19. A web page with a hidden input element

When the user submits the form, the browser includes a data item using the name and value we have provided for the hidden input element. You can see this in Figure 13-20, which shows the response from the Node.js script when the form shown in the previous figure is submitted.

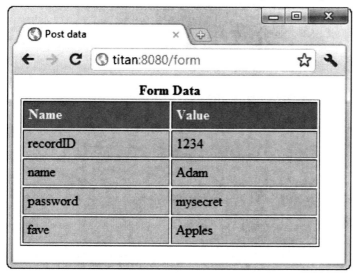

Figure 13-20. The response from the server showing the hidden data value

---

■ **Caution** This kind of input element is only suitable for data that is being hidden for convenience or usability, and not because it is sensitive or has an impact on security. The user can see hidden input elements by looking at the HTML for a page, and the data value is sent from the browser to the server as clear text. Most web application frameworks have support for keeping sensitive data securely at the server and associating it with the requests based on sessions identifiers, most typically expressed as cookies.

Using the input Element to Create Image Buttons and Maps

The image type of input element allows you to create buttons that display an image and submit the form when clicked. This type of input element supports the additional attributes shown in Table 13-14.

Table 13-14. Additional Attributes Available for the image Type of the input Element

Attribute	Description	New in HTML5
alt	Provides a text description of the element. This is useful for users who require assistive technologies.	No
formaction	As for the button element, described in Chapter 12.	Yes
formenctype	As for the button element, described in Chapter 12.	Yes
formmethod	As for the button element, described in Chapter 12.	Yes
formtarget	As for the button element, described in Chapter 12.	Yes
formnovalidate	As for the button element, described in Chapter 12.	Yes
height	Specifies the height of the image in pixels (the image will be displayed at its natural height if this attribute is not applied).	No
src	Specifies the URL for the image that should be displayed.	No
width	Specifies the width of the image in pixels (the image will be displayed at its natural width if this attribute is not applied).	No

Listing 13-16 shows the image type of the input element in use.

Listing 13-16. Using the image Type of the input Element

```
<!DOCTYPE HTML>
<html>
    <head>
        <title>Example</title>
```

```
        <meta name="author" content="Adam Freeman"/>
        <meta name="description" content="A simple example"/>
        <link rel="shortcut icon" href="favicon.ico" type="image/x-icon" />
    </head>
    <body>
        <form method="post" action="http://titan:8080/form">
            <input type="hidden" name="recordID" value="1234"/>
            <p>
                <label for="name">
                    Name: <input value="Adam" id="name" name="name"/>
                </label>
            </p>
            <p>
                <label for="password">
                    Password: <input type="password" placeholder="Min 6 characters"
                        id="password" name="password"/>
                </label>
            </p>
            <p>
                <label for="fave">
                    Favorite Fruit: <input type="text" id="fave" name="fave"/>
                </label>
            </p>
            <input type="image" src="accept.png" name="submit"/>
        </form>
    </body>
</html>
```

You can see how the browser displays this type of input element in Figure 13-21.

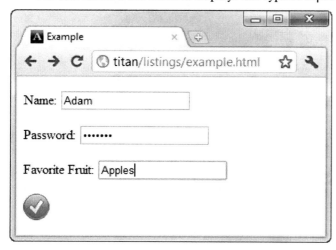

Figure 13-21. Using the image type of input element

When the user clicks the image, the browser submits the form and includes two data items representing the image input element. These represent the x and y coordinates where the user clicked, relative to the top-left corner of the image. You can see how the data values are submitted in Figure 13-22, which shows the response from the Node.js script when the form in the previous figure was submitted.

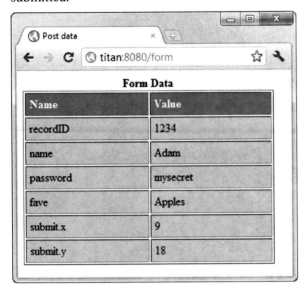

Figure 13-22. The Node.js response to a form containing an image input element

The fact that the coordinates are provided means that you can use images that contain regions representing different actions and responses to the user depending on where on the image they clicked.

Using the input Element to Upload Files

The final type of input element is file, which allows you to upload files to the server as part of the form submission. This type of input supports the additional attributes shown in Table 13-15.

Table 13-15. Additional Attributes Available for the file Type of the input Element

Attribute	Description	New in HTML5
accept	Specifies the set of mime-types that will be accepted. RFC2046 defines MIME types (http://tools.ietf.org/html/rfc2046).	No
multiple	When applied, this attribute specifies that the input element can upload multiple files. At the time of writing, none of the mainstream browsers have implemented this attribute.	Yes
required	Specifies that the user must provide a value for the purposes of input validation. See Chapter 14 for details.	Yes

Listing 13-17 shows the file type of input element in use.

Listing 13-17. Using the file Type of the input Element to Upload Files

```
<!DOCTYPE HTML>
<html>
    <head>
        <title>Example</title>
        <meta name="author" content="Adam Freeman"/>
        <meta name="description" content="A simple example"/>
        <link rel="shortcut icon" href="favicon.ico" type="image/x-icon" />
    </head>
    <body>
        <form method="post" action="http://titan:8080/form"
            enctype="multipart/form-data">
            <input type="hidden" name="recordID" value="1234"/>
            <p>
                <label for="name">
                    Name: <input value="Adam" id="name" name="name"/>
                </label>
            </p>
            <p>
                <label for="password">
                    Password: <input type="password" placeholder="Min 6 characters"
                        id="password" name="password"/>
                </label>
            </p>
            <p>
                <label for="fave">
                    Favorite Fruit: <input type="text" id="fave" name="fave"/>
                </label>
            </p>
            <p>
                <input type="file" name="filedata"/>
            </p>
            <input type="submit" value="Submit"/>
        </form>
    </body>
</html>
```

You can upload files only when the encoding type for the form is multipart/form-data. As you can see, I have used the enctype attribute of the form element to set the encoding. You can see how the browser displays the input element in Figure 13-23.

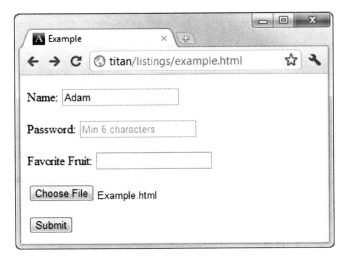

Figure 13-23. The file type of the input element

When the user clicks the Choose File button, they are presented with a dialog that allows a file to be selected. When the form is submitted, the contents of the file will be sent to the server.

Summary

In this chapter, I have shown you the many different types of input elements available. No other HTML element has so many different functions, and any web page or web application that requires interaction with the user will depend heavily on the input element.

In the next chapter, I'll show you some other kinds of elements you can use in forms. I'll also demonstrate the new HTML5 input validation feature, which allows you to check that the user has entered the kind of data you want to work with before the form is submitted.

CHAPTER 14

Other Form Elements and Input Validation

In this chapter, I complete the tour of the HTML form features. There are five further elements that you can use in HTML forms, and I describe each of them in turn. I also explain the new input validation features that have been introduced in HTML5. These new features allow you to apply constraints to the data that a user enters, and prevent a form from being submitted until those constrains are satisfied. Table 14-1 provides the summary for this chapter.

Table 14-1. Chapter Summary

Problem	Solution	Listing
Create a list of options to present to the user.	Use the select element.	14-1, 14-2
Add structure to the list of options in a select element.	Use the optgroup element.	14-3
Obtain multiple lines of text from the user.	Use the textarea element.	14-4
Denote the result of a calculation.	Use the output element.	14-5
Generate a public/private key pair.	Use the keygen element.	—
Ensure that the user provides a value for a form element.	Use the required attribute.	14-6
Ensure that a value is within bounds.	Use the min and max attributes.	14-7
Ensure that a value matches a regular expression.	Use the pattern attribute.	14-8, 14-9
Disable input validation.	Use the novalidate or formnovalidate attributes.	14-10

Using the Other Form Elements

In the following sections, I describe the five other elements you can use in a form. These are select, optgroup, textarea, output, and keygen.

Creating Lists of Options

The select element lets you create lists of options from which the user can make a selection. This is a more compact alternative to the radiobutton type of the input element that you saw in Chapter 13, and is ideally suited for larger sets of options. Table 14-2 summarizes the select element.

Table 14-2. The select Element

Element:	select
Element Type:	Phrasing
Permitted Parents:	Any element that can contain phrasing elements
Local Attributes:	name, disabled, form, size, multiple, autofocus, required
Contents:	option and optgroup elements
Tag Style:	Start and end tag
New in HTML5?	No
Changes in HTML5:	The form, autofocus and required attributes are new in HTML5
Style Convention:	None, the appearance of this element is platform- and browser-specific

The name, disabled, form, autofocus, and required attributes work in the same way as for the input elements. The size attribute specifies how many choices you want to show to the user and when the multiple attribute is applied, the user is able to select more than one value.

You use the option element to define the choices that you want to present to the user. This is the same option element used with the datalist element in Chapter 12. Listing 14-1 shows how you use the select and option elements.

Listing 14-1. Using the select and option Elements

```
<!DOCTYPE HTML>
<html>
    <head>
        <title>Example</title>
```

```
        <meta name="author" content="Adam Freeman"/>
        <meta name="description" content="A simple example"/>
        <link rel="shortcut icon" href="favicon.ico" type="image/x-icon" />
    </head>
    <body>
        <form method="post" action="http://titan:8080/form">
            <input type="hidden" name="recordID" value="1234"/>
            <p>
                <label for="name">
                    Name: <input value="Adam" id="name" name="name"/>
                </label>
            </p>
            <p>
                <label for="password">
                    Password: <input type="password" placeholder="Min 6 characters"
                        id="password" name="password"/>
                </label>
            </p>
            <p>
                <label for="fave">
                    Favorite Fruit:
                    <select id="fave" name="fave">
                        <option value="apples" selected label="Apples">Apples</option>
                        <option value="oranges" label="Oranges">Oranges</option>
                        <option value="cherries" label="Cherries">Cherries</option>
                        <option value="pears" label="Pears">Pears</option>
                    </select>
                </label>
            </p>
            <input type="submit" value="Submit"/>
        </form>
    </body>
</html>
```

In Listing 14-1, I have used the select element and defined four option elements to represent the choices that I want to offer to the user. I have applied the selected attribute to the first of the option elements so that it is selected automatically when the page is displayed. You can see the initial appearance of the select element and how the browser displays the option elements in Figure 14-1.

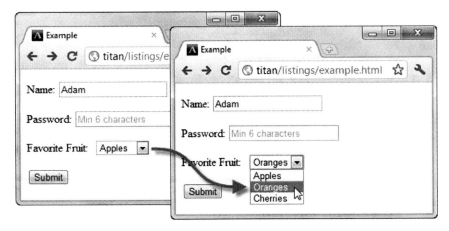

Figure 14-1. Using the select element to preset the user with a list of options

You can use the `size` attribute on the `select` element to show more than one option to the user, and the `multiple` attribute to allow the user to select more than one option, as shown in Listing 14-2.

Listing 14-2. Using the size and multiple Attributes on the select Element

```
<!DOCTYPE HTML>
<html>
    <head>
        <title>Example</title>
        <meta name="author" content="Adam Freeman"/>
        <meta name="description" content="A simple example"/>
        <link rel="shortcut icon" href="favicon.ico" type="image/x-icon" />
    </head>
    <body>
        <form method="post" action="http://titan:8080/form">
            <input type="hidden" name="recordID" value="1234"/>
            <p>
                <label for="name">
                    Name: <input value="Adam" id="name" name="name"/>
                </label>
            </p>
            <p>
                <label for="password">
                    Password: <input type="password" placeholder="Min 6 characters"
                        id="password" name="password"/>
                </label>
            </p>
            <p>
                <label for="fave" style="vertical-align:top">
                    Favorite Fruit:
                    <select id="fave" name="fave" size="5" multiple>
                        <option value="apples" selected label="Apples">Apples</option>
                        <option value="oranges" label="Oranges">Oranges</option>
```

```
                    <option value="cherries" label="Cherries">Cherries</option>
                    <option value="pears" label="Pears">Pears</option>
                </select>
            </label>
        </p>
        <input type="submit" value="Submit"/>
    </form>
</body>
</html>
```

In Listing 14-2, I have applied the `size` and `multiple` attributes, which creates the effect you can see in Figure 14-2. You can select multiple options by pressing the Ctrl button while clicking. I have also applied an inline style (as described in Chapter 4) to change the vertical alignment so that the `label` is aligned with the top of the `select` element (by default, it aligns to the bottom, which looks a little odd).

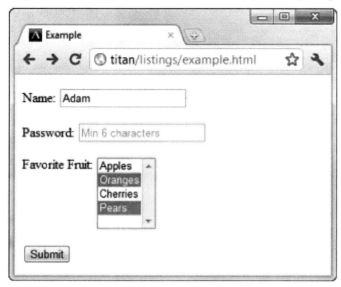

Figure 14-2. Using the select element to display and select multiple items

Adding Structure to a select Element

You can add some structure to a `select` element by using the `optgroup` element. Table 14-3 describes this element.

Table 14-3. The optgroup Element

Element:	optgroup
Element Type:	N/A
Permitted	The select element

Parents:

Local Attributes: label, disabled

Contents: option elements

Tag Style: Start and end tag

New in HTML5?   No

Changes in   None
HTML5:

Style Convention: None

You use the optgroup element to group option elements together. The label attribute lets you create a title for the grouped options and the disabled attribute lets you prevent the user from selecting any of the option elements that are contained in the optgroup. Listing 14-3 shows the optgroup element in use.

Listing 14-3. Using the optgroup Element

```
<!DOCTYPE HTML>
<html>
    <head>
        <title>Example</title>
        <meta name="author" content="Adam Freeman"/>
        <meta name="description" content="A simple example"/>
        <link rel="shortcut icon" href="favicon.ico" type="image/x-icon" />
    </head>
    <body>
        <form method="post" action="http://titan:8080/form">
            <input type="hidden" name="recordID" value="1234"/>
            <p>
                <label for="name">
                    Name: <input value="Adam" id="name" name="name"/>
                </label>
            </p>
            <p>
                <label for="password">
                    Password: <input type="password" placeholder="Min 6 characters"
                        id="password" name="password"/>
                </label>
            </p>
            <p>
                <label for="fave" style="vertical-align:top">
                    Favorite Fruit:
                    <select id="fave" name="fave">
                        <optgroup label="Top Choices">
                            <option value="apples" label="Apples">Apples</option>
                            <option value="oranges" label="Oranges">Oranges</option>
```

```
                    </optgroup>
                    <optgroup label="Others">
                        <option value="cherries" label="Cherries">Cherries</option>
                        <option value="pears" label="Pears">Pears</option>
                    </optgroup>
                </select>
            </label>
        </p>
        <input type="submit" value="Submit"/>
    </form>
</body>
</html>
```

You can see how the optgroup element adds structure to a list of option elements in Figure 14-3. The optgroup labels are purely for structure; the user cannot select these as values.

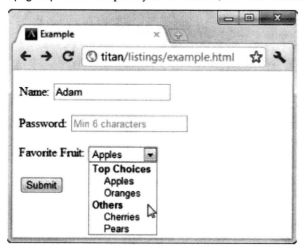

Figure 14-3. Using the optgroup element

Capturing Multiple Lines of Text

The textarea element creates a multiline text box into which the user can enter more than one line of text. Table 14-4 summarizes the textarea element.

Table 14-4. *The textarea Element*

Element:	textarea
Element Type:	Phrasing
Permitted Parents:	Any element that can contain phrasing elements, but most typically a form

Local Attributes:	name, disabled, form, readonly, maxlength, autofocus, required, placeholder, dirname, rows, wrap, cols
Contents:	Text, which represents the content for the element
Tag Style:	Start and end tag
New in HTML5?	No
Changes in HTML5	The form, autofocus, required, placeholder, and wrap attributes are new in HTML5
Style Convention	None

The rows and cols attributes specify the dimensions of the textarea, and you can set the wrap attribute to hard or soft to control how line breaks are added to the text entered by the user. The other attributes work in the same way as the corresponding attributes on the input element, described in Chapters 12 and 13. Listing 14-4 show the textarea element in use.

Listing 14-4. Using the textarea Element

```
<!DOCTYPE HTML>
<html>
    <head>
        <title>Example</title>
        <meta name="author" content="Adam Freeman"/>
        <meta name="description" content="A simple example"/>
        <link rel="shortcut icon" href="favicon.ico" type="image/x-icon" />
    </head>
    <body>
        <form method="post" action="http://titan:8080/form">
            <input type="hidden" name="recordID" value="1234"/>
            <p>
                <label for="name">
                    Name: <input value="Adam" id="name" name="name"/>
                </label>
            </p>
            <p>
                <label for="password">
                    Password: <input type="password" placeholder="Min 6 characters"
                        id="password" name="password"/>
                </label>
            </p>
            <p>
                <label for="fave" style="vertical-align:top">
                    Favorite Fruit:
                    <select id="fave" name="fave">
                        <optgroup label="Top Choices">
                            <option value="apples" label="Apples">Apples</option>
```

```
                    <option value="oranges" label="Oranges">Oranges</option>
                </optgroup>
                <optgroup label="Others">
                    <option value="cherries" label="Cherries">Cherries</option>
                    <option value="pears" label="Pears">Pears</option>
                </optgroup>
            </select>
        </label>
    </p>
    <p>
        <textarea cols="20" rows="5" wrap="hard" id="story"
            name="story">Tell us why this is your favorite fruit</textarea>
    </p>
    <input type="submit" value="Submit"/>
</form>
</body>
</html>
```

In Listing 14-4, I have added a textarea that is 20 columns wide and 5 rows high. You can see how the browser displays this in Figure 14-4.

Figure 14-4. Using the textarea element

The wrap attribute controls how line breaks are inserted into the text when the form is submitted. If you set the wrap attribute to hard, the content will have line breaks inserted so that no line in the submitted text has more characters than the value of the cols attribute.

Denoting the Result of a Calculation

The output element represents the result of a calculation. Table 14-5 summarizes this element.

Table 14-5. The output Element

Element:	output
Element Type:	Phrasing
Permitted Parents:	Any element that can contain phrasing elements
Local Attributes:	name, form, for
Contents:	Phrasing content
Tag Style:	Start and end tag
New in HTML5?	Yes
Changes in HTML5:	N/A
Style Convention:	output { display: inline; }

Listing 14-5 shows the output element in use.

Listing 14-5. Using the output Element

```
<!DOCTYPE HTML>
<html>
    <head>
        <title>Example</title>
        <meta name="author" content="Adam Freeman"/>
        <meta name="description" content="A simple example"/>
        <link rel="shortcut icon" href="favicon.ico" type="image/x-icon" />
    </head>
    <body>
        <form onsubmit="return false"
            oninput="res.value = quant.valueAsNumber * price.valueAsNumber">
            <fieldset>
                <legend>Price Calculator</legend>
                <input type="number" placeholder="Quantity" id="quant" name="quant"/> x
                <input type="number" placeholder="Price" id="price" name="price"/> =
                <output for="quant name" name="res"/>
            </fieldset>
        </form>
    </body>
</html>
```

```
</html>
```

In Listing 14-5, I have used the JavaScript event system to create a simple calculator (you can learn more about events in Chapter 30. There are two `number` type `input` elements and as the user types, the values of the `input` elements are multiplied and the result is displayed in the `output` element. You can see how this appears in the browser in Figure 14-5.

Figure 14-5. Using the output element

Creating Public/Private Key Pairs

You use the keygen element to generate a public/private pair of keys. This is an important function of public key cryptography, which underpins much of web security, including client certificates and SSL. When the form is submitted, a new pair of keys is created. The public key is sent to the server, and the private key is retained by the browser and added to the user's key store. Table 14-6 summarizes the keygen element.

Table 14-6. The keygen Element

Element:	keygen
Element Type:	Phrasing
Permitted Parents:	Any element that can contain phrasing elements
Local Attributes:	`challenge, keytype, autofocus, name, disabled, form`
Contents:	None
Tag Style:	Void
New in HTML5?	Yes
Changes in HTML5:	N/A
Style Convention:	None

The name, disabled, form, and autofocus attributes work just as they do for the input element, as described in Chapter 12. The keytype attribute specifies the algorithm that will be used to generate the key pair, but the only supported value is RSA. The challenge attribute specifies a challenge phrase that is sent to the server along with the public key.

The browser support for this element is patchy, and those browsers that do support the element present it to the user in different ways. My recommendation is to avoid using this element until support improves.

Using Input Validation

When you solicit input from users, you run the risk of receiving data that you can't use. This can be because the user has made a mistake, or you have failed to clearly communicate the kind of response you were looking for.

HTML5 introduces support for *input validation,* which is where you provide the browser with some basic information about the kind of data you require. The browser uses this information to check that the user has entered usable data before the form is submitted. If the data is problematic, the user is prompted to correct the problem and can't submit the form until the issue is resolved.

Performing validation in the browser is not a new idea, but prior to HTML5 you had to use a JavaScript library, such as the excellent jQuery validation plugin. Having built-in validation support with HTML5 is certainly convenient but, as you shall see, the support is rudimentary and inconsistent across browsers.

The benefit of input validation in the browser is that the user gets immediate feedback about problems. Without this feature, the user has to submit the form, wait for the server to respond, and then deal with any problems that are reported. On a low-performing network and an over-utilized server, this can be a slow and frustrating process.

■ **Caution** Input validation in the browser complements, rather than replaces, validation at the server. You cannot rely on users to employ browsers that properly support input validation, and it is a small matter for a malicious user to craft a script that will send input directly to your server without any form of validation at all.

You manage input validation through attributes. Table 14-7 shows which elements (and input types) support the different validation attributes.

Table 14-7. Support for Input Validation

Validation Attribute	Elements
required	textarea, select, input (the text, password, checkbox, radio, file, datetime, datetime-local, date, month, time, week, number, email, url, search, and tel types)
min, max	input (the datetime, datetime-local, date, month, time, week, number, and range types)
pattern	input (the text, password, email, url, search, and tel types)

Ensuring the User Provides a Value

The simplest kind of input validation is to ensure that the user provides a value. You do this with the required attribute. The user cannot submit the form until a value has been provided, although no limits are placed on what the value can be. Listing 14-6 shows the required attribute in use.

Listing 14-6. Using the required Attribute

```
<!DOCTYPE HTML>
<html>
    <head>
        <title>Example</title>
        <meta name="author" content="Adam Freeman"/>
        <meta name="description" content="A simple example"/>
        <link rel="shortcut icon" href="favicon.ico" type="image/x-icon" />
    </head>
    <body>
        <form method="post" action="http://titan:8080/form">
            <input type="hidden" name="recordID" value="1234"/>
            <p>
                <label for="name">
                    Name:
                    <input type="text" required id="name" name="name"/>
                </label>
            </p>
            <p>
                <label for="password">
                    Password: <input type="password" required
                        placeholder="Min 6 characters" id="password" name="password"/>
                </label>
            </p>
            <p>
                <label for="accept">
                    <input type="checkbox" required id="accept" name="accept"/>
                    Accept Terms & Conditions
                </label>
            </p>
            <input type="submit" value="Submit"/>
        </form>
    </body>
</html>
```

In Listing 14-6, I have applied the required attribute to three types of input elements. The user will not be able to submit the form until they have provided values for all three. For the text and password types, this means that the user has to enter text into the text box, and the box has to be checked for the checkbox type.

■ **Tip** An initial value set with the value attribute will satisfy the required validation attribute. If you want to force the user to enter a value, consider using the placeholder attribute instead. See Chapter 12 for details of both the value and the placeholder attributes.

Each browser that supports input validation does so in a slightly different way, but the effect is much the same: when the user clicks the button to submit the form, the first element that has the required attribute and that does not have a value is flagged for the user's attention. The user can then correct the omission and submit the form again. If there are other omissions, then the next problem element is flagged. The process continues until the user has provided a value for all of the elements with the required attribute. You can see how Google Chrome attracts the user's attention to a problem in Figure 14-6.

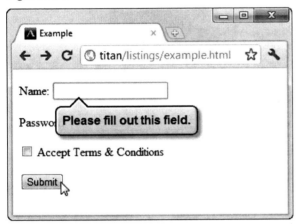

Figure 14-6. Google Chrome attracting the user's attention to a required field

The HTML5 input validation support is fairly basic, especially if you are used to the richer functionality available through libraries such as jQuery. For example, each problem is highlighted to the user in turn, meaning that if there are multiple problems in a form, the user is forced to undertake a voyage of gradual discovery by repeatedly submitting the form and fixing one problem at a time. There is no summary of all of the validation errors and you have no control over the appearance of the validation error warning.

Ensuring a Value Is Within Bounds

You use the min and max attributes to ensure that numeric and date values are within a specific range. Listing 14-7 shows these attributes applied to the number type of the input element.

Listing 14-7. Using the min and max Attributes

```
<!DOCTYPE HTML>
<html>
```

```
<head>
    <title>Example</title>
    <meta name="author" content="Adam Freeman"/>
    <meta name="description" content="A simple example"/>
    <link rel="shortcut icon" href="favicon.ico" type="image/x-icon" />
</head>
<body>
    <form method="post" action="http://titan:8080/form">
        <input type="hidden" name="recordID" value="1234"/>
        <p>
            <label for="name">
                Name:
                <input type="text" id="name" name="name"/>
            </label>
        </p>
        <p>
            <label for="password">
                Password: <input type="password"
                    placeholder="Min 6 characters" id="password" name="password"/>
            </label>
        </p>
        <p>
            <label for="price">
                $ per unit in your area:
                <input type="number" min="0" max="100"
                        value="1" id="price" name="price"/>
            </label>
        </p>
        <input type="submit" value="Submit"/>
    </form>
</body>
</html>
```

You need not apply both attributes. You create an upper limit for the value if you apply just the max attribute, and a lower limit if you apply just the min attribute. When you apply both, you constrain the upper and lower values to create a range. The min and max values are inclusive, meaning that if you specify a max value of 100, then any value up to *and including* 100 is allowed.

You can see how the browser reports a range validation error in Figure 14-7.

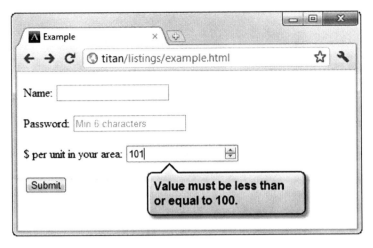

Figure 14-7. A range validation error

■ **Tip** The min and max attributes only result in validation when the user provides a value. The browser will allow the user to submit the form if the text box is empty. For this reason, the mix and max attributes are often used in conjunction with the required attribute, described in the previous section.

Ensuring a Value Matches a Pattern

The pattern attribute ensures that a value matches a regular expression. Listing 14-8 shows the pattern attribute in use.

Listing 14-8. Using the pattern Attribute

```
<!DOCTYPE HTML>
<html>
    <head>
        <title>Example</title>
        <meta name="author" content="Adam Freeman"/>
        <meta name="description" content="A simple example"/>
        <link rel="shortcut icon" href="favicon.ico" type="image/x-icon" />
    </head>
    <body>
        <form method="post" action="http://titan:8080/form">
            <input type="hidden" name="recordID" value="1234"/>
            <p>
                <label for="name">
                    Name:
                    <input type="text" id="name" name="name" pattern="^.* .*$"/>
                </label>
```

```
            </p>
            <p>
                <label for="password">
                    Password: <input type="password"
                        placeholder="Min 6 characters" id="password" name="password"/>
                </label>
            </p>
            <input type="submit" value="Submit"/>
        </form>
    </body>
</html>
```

In Listing 14-8, I have applied a simple pattern to ensure that the user enters two names, separated by a space. This is not a sensible way of validating that a value is a name, because it ignores all of the regional variations for names, but it does provide a suitable example of the validation support. You can see how the browser displays a pattern validation error in Figure 14-8.

Figure 14-8. A pattern validation error

■ **Tip** The `pattern` attribute only results in validation when the user provides a value. The browser will allow the user to submit the form if the text box is empty. For this reason, this attribute is often used in conjunction with the `required` attribute, described earlier in the chapter.

Ensuring a Value Is an E-mail Address or URL

The `email` and `url` types of the `input` element, which I described in Chapter 13, ensure that the user has entered a valid e-mail address or fully qualified URL, respectively (well, almost—the browser support for the `email` type is fairly decent, but the `url` type is somewhat sketchy).

We can combine the `pattern` attribute with these types of `input` elements to further restrict the values that the user can enter; for example, limiting e-mail address to a particular domain. Listing 14-9 provides a demonstration.

Listing 14-9. Using the pattern Attribute with the email input Element Type

```
<!DOCTYPE HTML>
<html>
    <head>
        <title>Example</title>
        <meta name="author" content="Adam Freeman"/>
        <meta name="description" content="A simple example"/>
        <link rel="shortcut icon" href="favicon.ico" type="image/x-icon" />
    </head>
    <body>
        <form method="post" action="http://titan:8080/form">
            <input type="hidden" name="recordID" value="1234"/>
            <p>
                <label for="name">
                    Name:
                    <input type="text" id="name" name="name" pattern="^.* .*$"/>
                </label>
            </p>
            <p>
                <label for="password">
                    Password: <input type="password"
                        placeholder="Min 6 characters" id="password" name="password"/>
                </label>
            </p>
            <p>
                <label for="email">
                    Email: <input type="email" placeholder="user@mydomain.com" required
                        pattern=".*@mydomain.com$" id="email" name="email"/>
                </label>
            </p>
            <input type="submit" value="Submit"/>
        </form>
    </body>
</html>
```

In Listing 14-9, I have used three of the validation features. The email type of the input element ensures that use enters a valid e-mail address. The required attribute ensures that the user provides a value. The pattern attribute ensures that the user enters an e-mail address that belongs to a specific domain (mydomain.com). The use of the email input type and the pattern attribute might seem redundant, but the input element is still responsible for ensuring that everything before the @ character is valid as an e-mail address.

Disabling Input Validation

There are times when you want to allow the user to submit the form without validating the contents. A good example is when the user needs to save progress through an incomplete process. You want the user to be able to save whatever they have entered so that they can resume the process later. This would be a frustrating process if all errors had to be corrected before progress could be saved.

You can submit the form without validation either by applying the novalidate attribute to the form element, or the formnovalidate attribute to the types of the button and input elements that can submit forms. Listing 14-10 shows how you can disable form validation.

Listing 14-10. Disabling Input Validation

```
<!DOCTYPE HTML>
<html>
    <head>
        <title>Example</title>
        <meta name="author" content="Adam Freeman"/>
        <meta name="description" content="A simple example"/>
        <link rel="shortcut icon" href="favicon.ico" type="image/x-icon" />
    </head>
    <body>
        <form method="post" action="http://titan:8080/form">
            <input type="hidden" name="recordID" value="1234"/>
            <p>
                <label for="name">
                    Name:
                    <input type="text" id="name" name="name" pattern="^.* .*$"/>
                </label>
            </p>
            <p>
                <label for="password">
                    Password: <input type="password"
                        placeholder="Min 6 characters" id="password" name="password"/>
                </label>
            </p>
            <p>
                <label for="email">
                    Email: <input type="email" placeholder="user@mydomain.com" required
                        pattern=".*@mydomain.com$" id="email" name="email"/>
                </label>
            </p>
            <input type="submit" value="Submit"/>
            <input type="submit" value="Save" formnovalidate/>
        </form>
    </body>
</html>
```

In this example, I have added an input element to the HTML document that will submit the form without validation, allowing the user to save progress (assuming of course, that there is a corresponding feature implemented at the server that will accept values from the browser without applying further validation).

Summary

In this chapter, I have shown you the remaining elements that you can use in a form, and I demonstrated the new input validation features that have been introduced in HTML5.

CHAPTER 15

Embedding Content

In this chapter, I introduce the elements you can use to embed content in your HTML document. Until now, I have largely focused on using HTML elements to create structure and meaning in your documents. The elements in this chapter allow you to enrich those documents.

Note Some of the HTML5 elements for embedding content are covered elsewhere in this book. See the "Other Embedding Elements" section at the end of this chapter for details.

Table 15-1 provides the summary for this chapter.

Table 15-1. Chapter Summary

Problem	Solution	Listing
Embed an image into an HTML document.	Use the img or object element.	1, 9
Create an image-based hyperlink.	Use an img element inside an a element.	2
Create a client-side image map.	Use the img or object element in conjunction with the map and area elements.	3, 4, 10
Embed another HTML document.	Use the iframe element.	5
Embed content using a plugin.	Use the embed or object element.	6-8
Create a browsing context.	Use the object element with the name attribute defining the name of the browsing context.	11

| Embed audio and video without needing to use a plugin. | Use the audio, video, source, and track elements. See Chapter 34. | - |
| Embed graphics into an HTML document. | Use the canvas element. See Chapters 35 & 36. | - |

Embedding an Image

The img element allows you to embed an image into an HTML document. Table 15-2 summarizes this element, which is one of the most widely used in HTML.

Table 15-2. The img Element

Element:	img
Element Type:	Phrasing
Permitted Parents:	Any element that can contain phrasing content
Local Attributes:	src, alt, height, width, usemap, ismap
Contents:	None
Tag Style:	Void
New in HTML5?	No
Changes in HTML5	The border, longdesc, name, align, hspace, and vspace attributes are obsolete in HTML5.
Style Convention	None

To embed an image, you need to use the src and alt attributes, as shown in Listing 15-1.

Listing 15-1. Embedding an Image

```
<!DOCTYPE HTML>
<html>
    <head>
        <title>Example</title>
        <meta name="author" content="Adam Freeman"/>
        <meta name="description" content="A simple example"/>
        <link rel="shortcut icon" href="favicon.ico" type="image/x-icon" />
    </head>
```

```
<body>
    Here is a common form for representing the three activities in a triathlon.
    <p>
        <img src="triathlon.png" alt="Triathlon Image" width="200" height="67"/>
    </p>
    The first icon represents swimming, the second represents cycling and the third
    represents running.
</body>
</html>
```

The src attribute specifies the URL for the image you want to embed. In this case, I specified a relative URL for the image file triathlon.png. The alt attribute defines the *fallback content* for the img element. This content will be shown if the image cannot be displayed (either because the image can't be located, because the image format is not supported by the browser, or because the browser or the device the user is using cannot display images). You can see the image in Figure 15-1.

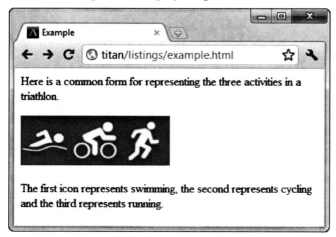

Figure 15-1. Embedding an image with the img element

You use the width and height attributes to specify the size (in pixels) of an image displayed by the img element. Images are not loaded until after the HTML markup has been processed, which means that if you omit the width and height attributes, the browser doesn't know how much space on the screen to allocate to the image. As a consequence, the browser has to determine the size from the image file itself and then reposition content on the screen to accommodate it. This can be jarring to the user, who may have already started to read the content contained directly in the HTML. Specifying the width and height attributes gives the browser the opportunity to lay out the elements on the page correctly, even though the image has yet to be loaded.

■ **Caution** The width and height attributes tell the browser what the size of the image is, not what you would like it to be. You should not use these attributes to dynamically resize images.

Embedding an Image in a Hyperlink

A common use of the img element is to create an image-based hyperlink in conjunction with the a element (which I described in Chapter 8). This is the counterpart to the image-based submit button for forms (described in Chapter 12). Listing 15-2 shows how you can use the img and a elements together.

Listing 15-2. Using the img and a Elements to Create a Server-Side Image Map

```html
<!DOCTYPE HTML>
<html>
    <head>
        <title>Example</title>
        <meta name="author" content="Adam Freeman"/>
        <meta name="description" content="A simple example"/>
        <link rel="shortcut icon" href="favicon.ico" type="image/x-icon" />
    </head>
    <body>
        Here is a common form for representing the three activities in a triathlon.
        <p>
            <a href="otherpage.html">
                <img src="triathlon.png" ismap alt="Triathlon Image"
                    width="200" height="67"/>
            </a>
        </p>
        The first icon represents swimming, the second represents cycling and the third
        represents running.
    </body>
</html>
```

The browser doesn't display the image any differently, as you can see in Figure 15-2. It is important, therefore, to give the user visual cues that particular images represent hyperlinks. This can be done with CSS or, preferably, by the content of the images.

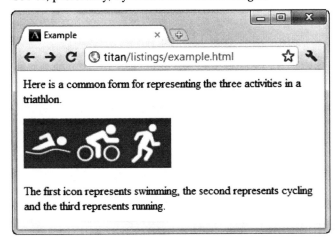

Figure 15-2. Embedding an image in a hyperlink

If you click on the image, the browser will navigate to the URL specified by the href attribute of the parent a element. If you apply the ismap attribute to the img element, you create a *server-side image map*, which means that the position you clicked on the image is appended to the URL. For example, if you clicked 4 pixels from the top and 10 pixels from the left edges of the images, the browser will navigate to the following:

```
http://titan/listings/otherpage.html?10,4
```

(Obviously, this URL is based on the fact that I loaded the original HTML document from my development server, titan, and the href attribute on the a element is a relative URL.) Listing 15-3 show the contents of otherpage.html, which contains a simple script that displays the coordinates of the click.

Listing 15-3. The Contents of otherpage.html

```html
<!DOCTYPE HTML>
<html>
    <head>
        <title>Other Page</title>
    </head>
    <body>
        <p>The X-coordinate is <b><span id="xco">??</span></b></p>
        <p>The Y-coordinate is <b><span id="yco">??</span></b></p>
        <script>
            var coords = window.location.href.split('?')[1].split(',');
            document.getElementById('xco').innerHTML = coords[0];
            document.getElementById('yco').innerHTML = coords[1];
        </script>
    </body>
</html>
```

You can see the effect of the mouse click in Figure 15-3.

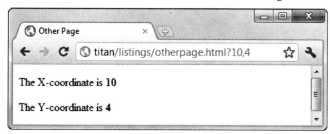

Figure 15-3. Displaying the coordinates of a mouse click on an image embedded in a hyperlink

The presumption with a server-side image map is that the server will act differently when the user clicks in different regions of the image, perhaps returning different responses. If you omit the ismap attribute from the img element, the coordinates of the mouse click are not included in the requested URL.

Creating a Client-Side Image Map

You can create a *client-side image map*, where clicking on regions in an image cause the browser to navigate to different URLs. This is done without needing any direction from the server, meaning that you need to define the regions for the image and the actions they lead to using elements. The key element for a client-side image map is map, which is summarized in Table 15-3.

Table 15-3. *The map Element*

Element:	map
Element Type:	The map element is considered as a phrasing element when it contains phrasing content and as a flow element when it contains flow content.
Permitted Parents:	Any element that can contain phrasing or flow content
Local Attributes:	name
Contents:	One or more area elements
Tag Style:	Start and end tags
New in HTML5?	No
Changes in HTML5	If the id attribute is used, it must have the same value as the name attribute.
Style Convention	None

The map element contains one or more area elements, each of which denotes a region in the image that can be clicked on. Table 15-4 summarizes the area element.

Table 15-4. *The area Element*

Element:	area
Element Type:	Phrasing
Permitted Parents:	The map element
Local Attributes:	alt, href, target, rel, media, hreflang, type, shape, coords
Contents:	None

Tag Style:	Void
New in HTML5?	No
Changes in HTML5	The rel, media, and hreflang attributes are new in HTML5. The nohref attribute is now obsolete.
Style Convention	area { display: none; }

The attributes for the area element can be broken into two categories, the first of which deals with the URL that will be navigated to by the browser if the user clicks in the region of the image that area represents. These are described in Table 15-5 and are similar to corresponding attributes you have seen on other elements.

Table 15-5. Attributes of the area Element That Relate to the Target

Attribute	Description
href	The URL that the browser should load when the region is clicked on
alt	The alternative content. See the corresponding attribute on the img element.
target	The browsing content in which the URL should be displayed. See the corresponding attribute on the base element in Chapter 7.
rel	Describes the relationship between the current and target documents. See the corresponding attribute on the link element in Chapter 7.
media	The media for which the area is valid. See the corresponding attribute on the style element in Chapter 7.
hreflang	The language of the target document
type	The MIME type of the target document

The more interesting attributes form the second category: the shape and coords attributes. You use these to denote the regions of an image the user can click on. The shape and coords attributes work together. The meaning of the coords attribute depends on the value of the shape attribute, as described in Table 15-6.

Table 15-6. Values for the shape and coords Attributes

Shape Value	Nature and Meaning of the coords Value
rect	This value represents a rectangular area. The coords attribute must consist of **four** comma-separated integers representing the distance from the following:

- The left edge of the image to the left side of the rectangle

- The top edge of the image to the top side of the rectangle

- The left edge of the image to the right side of the rectangle

- The top edge of the image to the bottom side of the rectangle

circle   This value represents a circular area. The coords attribute must consist of **three** comma-separated integers representing the following:

- The distance from the left edge of the image to the circle center

- The distance from the top edge of the image to the circle center

- The radius of the circle

poly   This value represents a polygon. The coords attribute must be at least six comma-separated integers, each pair of which represents a point on the polygon.

default   This value is the default area, which covers the entire image. No coords value is required when using this value for the shape attribute.

Now that I've described the elements, we can move on to an example. One of the difficulties in demonstrating image maps is that area elements are invisible on the browser screen. To that end, Figure 15-4 illustrates two of the regions I intend to define in the example, using the triathlon.png image from the previous section. For simplicity, I make both areas rectangular.

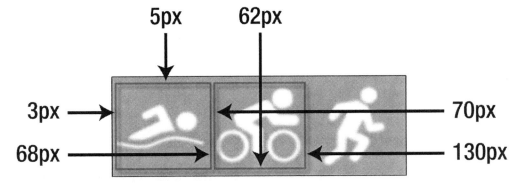

Figure 15-4. Planning the areas of an image map

From this diagram, you can create the map and area elements, as shown in Listing 15-4.

Listing 15-4. Creating an Image Map

```
<!DOCTYPE HTML>
<html>
    <head>
        <title>Example</title>
```

```
        <meta name="author" content="Adam Freeman"/>
        <meta name="description" content="A simple example"/>
        <link rel="shortcut icon" href="favicon.ico" type="image/x-icon" />
    </head>
    <body>
        Here is a common form for representing the three activities in a triathlon.
        <p
            <img src="triathlon.png" usemap="#mymap" alt="Triathlon Image"/>
        </p>
        The first icon represents swimming, the second represents cycling and the third
        represents running.

        <map name="mymap">
            <area href="swimpage.html" shape="rect" coords="3,5,68,62" alt="Swimming"/>
            <area href="cyclepage.html" shape="rect" coords="70,5,130,62" alt="Running"/>
            <area href="otherpage.html" shape="default" alt="default"/>
        </map>
    </body>
</html>
```

Notice the addition of the usemap attribute on the img element. The value of this attribute must be a *hash-name reference*, which means a string that starts with a # character, followed by the value of the name attribute of the map you want to use—in this case, #mymap. This is how you associate the map element with the image.

If the user clicks on the swimming part of the image, the browser navigates to swimpage.html. If the user clicks on the cycling part of the image, they browser navigates to cyclepage.html. Clicking anywhere else on the image causes the browser to navigate to otherpage.html.

■ **Tip** Notice that you don't need to use the a element to explicitly create a hyperlink when working with client-side image maps.

Embedding Another HTML Document

The iframe element allows you to embed another HTML document within the existing one. Table 15-7 summarizes this element.

Table 15-7. The iframe Element

Element:	iframe
Element Type:	Phrasing
Permitted Parents:	Any element that can contain phrasing content

Local Attributes:	`src, srcdoc, name, width, height, sandbox, seamless`
Contents:	Character data
Tag Style:	Start and end tags
New in HTML5?	No
Changes in HTML5	The `sandbox` and `seamless` attributes are new in HTML5.
	The `longdesc, align, allowtransparency, frameborder, marginheight, marginwidth`, and `scrolling` attributes are obsolete.
Style Convention	`iframe { border: 2px inset; }`

Listing 15-5 shows how the `iframe` element can be used.

Listing 15-5. Using the iframe Element

```
<!DOCTYPE HTML>
<html>
    <head>
        <title>Example</title>
        <meta name="author" content="Adam Freeman"/>
        <meta name="description" content="A simple example"/>
        <link rel="shortcut icon" href="favicon.ico" type="image/x-icon" />
    </head>
    <body>
        <header>
          <h1>Things I like</h1>
          <nav>
            <ul>
                <li>
                    <a href="fruits.html" target="frame">Fruits I Like</a>
                </li>
                <li>
                    <a href="activities.html" target="frame">Activities I Like</a>
                </li>
            </ul>
          </nav>
        </header>

        <iframe name="myframe" width="300" height="100">
        </iframe>
    </body>
</html>
```

In this example, I created an `iframe` with a `name` attribute value of frame. This creates a *browsing context* called `myframe`. I can then use this browsing context with the target attribute of other elements—

specifically, a, form, button, input, and base. I use the a element to create a pair of hyperlinks which, when followed, will load the URLs specified in their href attributes into the iframe. You can see how this works in Figure 15-5.

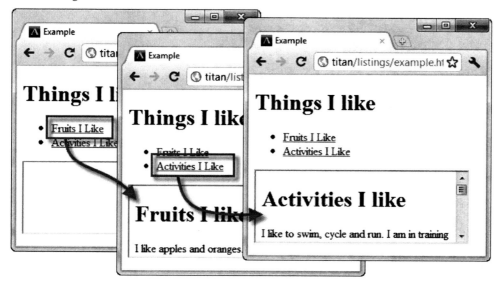

Figure 15-5. Using an iframe to embed external HTML documents

The width and height attributes specify the size in pixels. The src attribute specifies a URL that should be loaded and displayed in the iframe initially, and the srcdoc attribute allows you to define an HTML document to display inline.

HTML5 introduces two new attributes for the iframe element. The first, seamless, instructs the browser to display the iframe contents as though they were an integral part of the main HTML document. You can see from the figure that a border is applied by default and that a scrollbar is present if the content is larger than the size specified by the width and height attributes.

The second attribute, sandbox, applies restrictions to the HTML document. When the attribute is applied with no value, like this:

```
...
<iframe sandbox name="myframe" width="300" height="100">
</iframe>
...
```

the following are disabled:

- scripts
- forms
- plugins
- links that target other browsing contexts

In addition, the content in the iframe is treated as though it originated from a different source than the rest of the HTML document, which enforces additional security measures. You can enable individual features by defining values for the sandbox attribute, like this:

```
...
<iframe sandbox="allow-forms" name="myframe" width="300" height="100">
</iframe>
...
```

The set of values that can be used is described in Table 15-8. Unfortunately, none of the mainstream browsers support the sandbox and seamless attributes as I write this, so I am unable to demonstrate either.

Table 15-8. The allow Values for the iframe sandbox Attribute

Value	Description
allow-forms	Enables forms
allow-scripts	Enables scripts
allow-top-navigation	Allows links that target the top-level browsing contexts, which allows the entire document to be replaced with another, or for a new tab or window to be created
allow-same-origin	Allows content in the iframe to be treated as though it originated from the same location as the rest of the document

Embedding Content Using Plugins

The object and embed elements both originated as a way to extend the capabilities of browsers by adding support for plugins that could process content the browser didn't support directly. These elements were introduced during the browser wars I mentioned in Chapter 1, and each was conceived by a different camp.

More recently, the object element has been part of the HTML4 specification, but the embed element has not—even though the embed element has been widely used. To bring parity to these two elements, HTML5 adds support for the embed element. This gives you two very similar elements for the sake of compatibility.

Although the object and embed elements are generally used for plugins, they can also be used to embed content that the browser can handle directly, such as images. I'll give you a demonstration of why this can be useful later in this section.

Using the embed Element

I will start with the embed element, which is summarized by Table 15-9.

Table 15-9. The embed Element

Element:	embed
Element Type:	Phrasing
Permitted Parents:	Any element that can contain phrasing content
Local Attributes:	src, type, height, width
Contents:	None
Tag Style:	Void
New in HTML5?	Yes, although this has been a widely used unofficial element for some years.
Changes in HTML5	N/A
Style Convention	None

Listing 15-6 shows the embed element in use. For this example, I embedded a video from www.youtube.com, showing a talk from some Google engineers about HTML5.

Listing 15-6. Using the embed Element

```
<!DOCTYPE HTML>
<html>
    <head>
        <title>Example</title>
        <meta name="author" content="Adam Freeman"/>
        <meta name="description" content="A simple example"/>
        <link rel="shortcut icon" href="favicon.ico" type="image/x-icon" />
    </head>
    <body>
        <embed src="http://www.youtube.com/v/qzA60hHca9s?version=3"
               type="application/x-shockwave-flash" width="560" height="349"
               allowfullscreen="true"/>
    </body>
</html>
```

The src attribute specifies the location of the content, and the type attribute specifies the MIME type of the content so that the browser knows what to do with it. The width and height attributes determine the size that the embedded content will occupy on screen. Any other attributes you apply are considered parameters for the plugin or the content. In this case, I applied an attribute called `allowfullscreen`, which the YouTube video player uses to enable full-screen viewing. You can see how the browser renders this content in Figure 15-6.

Figure 15-6. Embedding a YouTube video

Using the object and param Elements

The `object` element achieves the same result as the `embed` element, but it works in a slightly different way and has some additional features. Table 15-10 summarizes the `object` element.

Table 15-10. The object Element

Element:	`object`
Element Type:	This element is considered as a phrasing element when it contains phrasing content and as a flow element when it contains flow content.
Permitted Parents:	Any element that can contain phrasing or flow content
Local Attributes:	`data`, `type`, `height`, `width`, `usemap`, `name`, `form`
Contents:	Zero or more `param` elements and, optionally, phrasing or flow content to be used as a fallback. See later in this section for an

example.

Tag Style:	Start and end tags
New in HTML5?	No
Changes in HTML5	The `form` attribute is new in HTML5.
	The `archive`, `classid`, `code`, `codebase`, `codetype`, `declare`, `standby`, `align`, `hspace`, `vspace`, and `border` attributes are obsolete.
Style Convention	None

Listing 15-7 shows how you can use the `object` element to embed the same YouTube video as in the previous example.

Listing 15-7. Using the object and param Attributes

```
<!DOCTYPE HTML>
<html>
    <head>
        <title>Example</title>
        <meta name="author" content="Adam Freeman"/>
        <meta name="description" content="A simple example"/>
        <link rel="shortcut icon" href="favicon.ico" type="image/x-icon" />
    </head>
    <body>
        <object width="560" height="349"
            data="http://www.youtube.com/v/qzA60hHca9s?version=3"
            type="application/x-shockwave-flash">
            <param name="allowFullScreen" value="true"/>
        </object>
    </body>
</html>
```

The `data` attribute provides the location for the content, and the `type`, `width`, and `height` attributes have the same meaning as for the `embed` element. You define the parameters that will be passed to the plugin using the `param` element. You use one `param` element for each parameter you need to define. The element is summarized in Table 15-11. As you might imagine, the `name` and `value` attributes define the name and value of the parameter.

Table 15-11. The param Element

Element:	`param`
Element Type:	N/A
Permitted Parents:	The `object` element

Local Attributes:	name, value
Contents:	None
Tag Style:	Void
New in HTML5?	No
Changes in HTML5	None
Style Convention	param { display: none; }

Specifying Fallback Content

One of the advantages of the object element is that you can include content that will be displayed if the content you specify is not available. Listing 15-8 provides a simple demonstration.

Listing 15-8. Using the Fallback Content Feature of the object Element

```
<!DOCTYPE HTML>
<html>
    <head>
        <title>Example</title>
        <meta name="author" content="Adam Freeman"/>
        <meta name="description" content="A simple example"/>
        <link rel="shortcut icon" href="favicon.ico" type="image/x-icon" />
    </head>
    <body>
        <object width="560" height="349" data="http://titan/myimaginaryfile">
            <param name="allowFullScreen" value="true"/>
            <b>Sorry!</b> We can't display this content
        </object>
    </body>
</html>
```

In this example, I used the data attribute to refer to a file that doesn't exist. The browser will attempt to load this nonexistent content and, when it fails to do so, display the content inside the object element instead. The param elements are ignored, leaving just your phrasing and flow content to be displayed, as shown in Figure 15-7.

Figure 15-7. Relying on fallback content in an object element

Notice that I removed the type attribute in the listing. When there is no type attribute present, the browser tries to determine the type of content from the data itself. For some combinations of browsers and plugins, the plugin will still be loaded even when the data isn't available. This means that an empty region is displayed on screen and the fallback content isn't used.

Other Uses for the object Element

Although the object element is mostly used to embed content for plugins, it was originally intended as a more generic alternative to several elements, including img. In the following sections, I describe some of the other ways you can use the object element. Even though these features have been in the HTML specification for some time, not all of the browsers support all of the features. I include these sections for completeness, but I recommend that you stick to the more specific elements, such as s.

■ **Tip** The form attribute allows the object element to be associated with HTML forms (which are the topic of Chapter 12). This is a new addition in HTML5. Currently, none of the browsers support this attribute and the HTML5 specification is vague as to how this feature will work.

Using the object Element to Embed Images

As I mentioned, one of the elements that object was intended to replace is img. As a consequence, you can use the object element to embed images in your HTML documents. Listing 15-9 gives a demonstration.

Listing 15-9. Embedding an Image with the object Element

```
<!DOCTYPE HTML>
<html>
    <head>
        <title>Example</title>
        <meta name="author" content="Adam Freeman"/>
        <meta name="description" content="A simple example"/>
        <link rel="shortcut icon" href="favicon.ico" type="image/x-icon" />
    </head>
```

```
<body>
    <object data="triathlon.png" type="image/png">
    </object>
</body>
</html>
```

In this example, I used the data attribute to refer to the image I used earlier in the chapter. The browser embeds and displays the image just as it does when you use the img element, as shown by Figure 15-8.

Figure 15-8. Embedding an image with the object element

Using the object Element to Create Client-Side Image Maps

You can use the object element to create client-side image maps as well. The usemap attribute can be used to associate a map element with an object element, as shown in Listing 15-10. I used the same map and area elements as I did when performing the same task with the img element.

Listing 15-10. Creating a Client-Side Image Map with the object Element

```
<!DOCTYPE HTML>
<html>
    <head>
        <title>Example</title>
        <meta name="author" content="Adam Freeman"/>
        <meta name="description" content="A simple example"/>
        <link rel="shortcut icon" href="favicon.ico" type="image/x-icon" />
    </head>
    <body>
        <map name="mymap">
            <area href="swimpage.html" shape="rect" coords="3,5,68,62" alt="Swimming"/>
            <area href="cyclepage.html" shape="rect" coords="70,5,130,62" alt="Running"/>
            <area href="otherpage.html" shape="default" alt="default"/>
        </map>

        <object data="triathlon.png" type="image/png" usemap="#mymap">
        </object>
    </body>
</html>
```

■ **Caution** Not all browsers support image maps created with the object element. At the time of this writing, Google Chrome and Apple Safari do not support this feature.

Using the object Element as a Browsing Context

You can use the object element to embed one HTML document inside of another, just as you did with the iframe element. If you apply the name attribute, you create a browsing context you can use with the target attribute of elements, such as a and form. Listing 15-11 shows how you can do this.

Listing 15-11. Creating a Browsing Context with the object Element

```
<!DOCTYPE HTML>
<html>
    <head>
        <title>Example</title>
        <meta name="author" content="Adam Freeman"/>
        <meta name="description" content="A simple example"/>
        <link rel="shortcut icon" href="favicon.ico" type="image/x-icon" />
    </head>
    <body>
        <header>
            <h1>Things I like</h1>
            <nav>
                <ul>
                    <li>
                        <a href="fruits.html" target="frame">Fruits I Like</a>
                    </li>
                    <li>
                        <a href="activities.html" target="frame">Activities I Like</a>
                    </li>
                </ul>
            </nav>
        </header>

        <object type="text/html" name="frame" width="300" height="100">
        </object>
    </body>
</html>
```

This feature works only if you set the type attribute to text/html—even then, browser support is not universal. At the time of this writing, Google Chrome and Apple Safari are the only mainstream browsers that support this feature.

Embedding Numeric Representations

There are two elements that are new to HTML5 that allow you to embed representations of numeric values in your documents.

Showing Progress

The progress element can be used to indicate the gradual completion of a task. Table 15-12 summarizes the progress element.

Table 15-12. The progress Element

Element:	progress
Element Type:	Phrasing
Permitted Parents:	Any element that can contain phrasing elements
Local Attributes:	value, max, form
Contents:	Phrasing content
Tag Style:	Start and end tags
New in HTML5?	**Yes**
Changes in HTML5	N/A
Style Convention	None

The value attribute defines the current progress, which is on a scale between zero and the value of the max attribute. When the max attribute is omitted, the scale is between zero and 1. You express progress using floating-point numbers, such as 0.3 for 30%.

Listing 15-12 shows the progress element and some buttons. Pressing a button updates the value displayed by the progress element. I connected the buttons and the progress element together using some simple JavaScript. I describe the techniques I use in Part IV of this book.

Listing 15-12. Using the progress Element

```
<!DOCTYPE HTML>
<html>
    <head>
        <title>Example</title>
        <meta name="author" content="Adam Freeman"/>
```

```
    <meta name="description" content="A simple example"/>
    <link rel="shortcut icon" href="favicon.ico" type="image/x-icon" />
</head>
<body>

    <progress id="myprogress" value="10" max="100"></progress>
    <p>
        <button type="button" value="30">30%</button>
        <button type="button" value="60">60%</button>
        <button type="button" value="90">90%</button>
    </p>

    <script>
        var buttons = document.getElementsByTagName('BUTTON');
        var progress = document.getElementById('myprogress');
        for (var i = 0; i < buttons.length; i++) {
            buttons[i].onclick = function(e) {
                progress.value = e.target.value;
            };
        }
    </script>
</body>
</html>
```

You can see how the progress element is used to display different values in Figure 15-9.

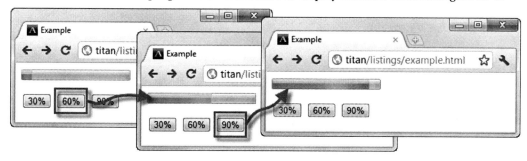

Figure 15-9. Using the progress element

Showing a Ranged Value

The meter element shows a value displayed in the context of the range of possible values. Table 15-13 summarizes this element.

Table 15-13. The meter Element

Element:	meter
Element Type:	Phrasing

391

Permitted Parents:	Any element that can contain phrasing elements
Local Attributes:	value, min, max, low, high, optimum, form
Contents:	Phrasing content
Tag Style:	Start and end tags
New in HTML5?	**Yes**
Changes in HTML5	N/A
Style Convention	None

The min and max attributes set the bounds for the range of possible values. These can be expressed using floating-point numbers. The display for the meter element can be broken into three segments: too low, too high, and just right. The low attribute sets the value under which a value is considered to be too low, and the high attribute sets the value over which a value is considered to be too high. The optimum attribute specifies the "just right" value. You can see these attributes applied to the meter element in Listing 15-13.

Listing 15-13. Using the meter Element

```
<!DOCTYPE HTML>
<html>
    <head>
        <title>Example</title>
        <meta name="author" content="Adam Freeman"/>
        <meta name="description" content="A simple example"/>
        <link rel="shortcut icon" href="favicon.ico" type="image/x-icon" />
    </head>
    <body>
        <meter id="mymeter" value="90"
               min="10" max="100" low="40" high="80" optimum="60"></meter>

        <p>
            <button type="button" value="30">30</button>
            <button type="button" value="60">60</button>
            <button type="button" value="90">90</button>
        </p>

        <script>
            var buttons = document.getElementsByTagName('BUTTON');
            var meter = document.getElementById('mymeter');
            for (var i = 0; i < buttons.length; i++) {
                buttons[i].onclick = function(e) {
                    meter.value = e.target.value;
```

```
            };
        }
    </script>
  </body>
</html>
```

In this example, the `button` elements set the `value` attribute of the `meter` element to values that are in the too-low and too-high ranges and to the optimum value. You can see how this appears in the browser in Figure 15-10.

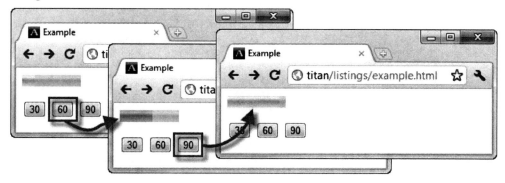

Figure 15-10. Using the meter element

The `optimum` attribute doesn't have any visual effect on the appearance of the meter element as it is currently implemented. Browsers that support the `meter` element differentiate only values that are lower than the `low` value and higher than the `high` value, as the figure shows.

Other Embedding Elements

There are further elements that can be used to embed content in an HTML document. These are covered in depth in later chapters, but they are mentioned here for completeness.

Embedding Audio and Video

HTML5 defines several new attributes that support embedding audio and video into an HTML document without the need for plugins. These elements (`audio`, `video`, `source`, and `track`) are covered in depth in Chapter 34.

Embedding Graphics

The `canvas` element is another major area of functionality introduced in HTML5, allowing the addition of dynamic graphics in an HTML document. The `canvas` element is covered in Chapters 35 & 36. .

Summary

In this chapter, I introduced the elements that allow you to enrich your HTML documents with embedded content. These elements range from simple additions, such as images, to rich and extensible technologies available through plugins.

Cascading Style Sheets

In this part of the book, I will show you how to use *Cascading Style Sheets* (CSS) to control the way that content is presented to users in the browser. CSS can be surprisingly subtle and expressive, and allows you to exert a very high degree of control over your content with very little effort.

CSS in Context

In the chapters that follow, I describe the properties defined by CSS, more properly known as *Cascading Style Sheets*. Chapter 4 provided a quick refresher in the basics of CSS, and this chapter provides some additional context before we start digging into the details.

Understanding CSS Standardization

CSS has had a difficult past. During the period when browsers were seen as tools to fragment the market, browser-makers used CSS as a key tool to create features that were unique to their software. It was a mess—properties with the same name were handled in different ways, and browser-specific properties were used to access browser-specific functionality. The idea was to force web developers to make their site or application work on just one browser.

The good news is that browsers mostly differentiate themselves on speed, ease-of-use and, to a growing extent, compliance with standards such as CSS. The bad news is that the standardization process for CSS isn't ideal.

As you'll see in the following chapters, there is a lot of functionality in CSS. Rather than try to create a monolithic standard, the W3C (the standards body for CSS as well as for HTML) decided to break CSS3S into *modules* and let each one follow its own timeline. This is a great idea—it certainly beats the monolithic approach—but it means that there is no overall standard for CSS3 compliance. Instead, you have to consider each module in turn and decide whether or not it has broad enough support to use.

A further complication is that very few of the CSS3 modules have reached the end of the standardization process. Some modules, especially those that introduce new areas of functionality to CSS, are still in an early stage of the process and are subject to change. Properties might be added, changed, or removed; modules might be merged or killed off; and the relationship between modules might change (because modules often depend on properties or units defined in other modules). This means you might find that some of the newer properties have changed since I wrote this book.

In the chapters that follow, I included properties from modules that seem stable and are expected to be implemented by the mainstream browsers reasonably quickly. For the most part, these features are stable and can be relied on in recent browser releases. To help you decide if using a property is suitable for your project, I included the CSS version to which each property was added in the "Properties Quick Reference" section later in this chapter.

During the more volatile stages of a module's definition, browsers will implement a feature using a browser-specific prefix. This isn't like the bad old days—these are trial implementations that allow early adopters to test out a browser's implementation of a particular set of properties. I generally avoid properties that are available this way, but some CSS3 features are so important that I used the prefixes in the example. In all cases, the browser-specific implementations are very close to the specification. Each browser has a different prefix. You can see the prefixes for the most popular browsers in Table 16-1.

Table 16-1. The Browser-Specific Prefixes

Browser	Prefix
Chrome Safari	-webkit-
Opera	-o-
Firefox	-moz-
Internet Explorer	-ms-

Understanding the Box Model

One of the fundamental concepts in CSS is the *box model*. If an element is visible, it will occupy a rectangular region of the page. This is known as the element's *box*. There are four parts to this box, as shown in Figure 16-1.

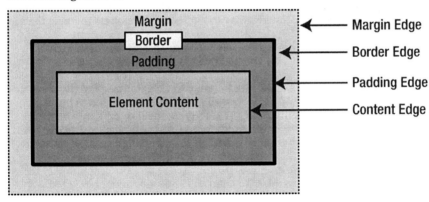

Figure 16-1. The CSS box model

Two of the parts can be visible: the contents and the border. Padding is the amount of space between the content and the border, and the margin is the space between the border and the other elements on the page. Understanding how these four parts relate to one another is essential to getting the best out of CSS. In the following chapters, I'll introduce you to the CSS properties that let you control the margin, padding, and border and control the appearance of the content overall.

An element can contain other elements. In this case, the parent element's context box is known as the child element's *container block* (or sometimes just *container*). This relationship is shown in Figure 16-2.

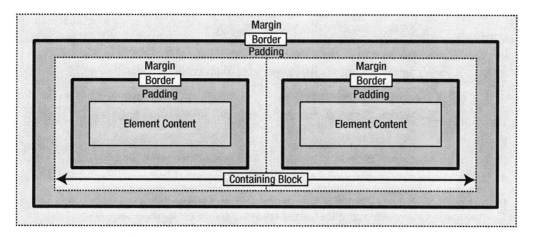

Figure 16-2. The box model relationship between parent and child elements

You can use the characteristics of the containing block to determine the appearance of an element. This is true not only for cascading and inherited properties, but also for explicitly defined properties, as you'll see in Chapter 21 when you look at layouts for elements.

Selectors Quick Reference

I describe the CSS selectors in depth in Chapters 17 and 18. For quick reference, Table 16-2 summarizes the selectors and shows in which version of CSS they were added.

Table 16-2. The CSS Selectors

Selector	Description	CSS Level
*	Selects all elements.	2
<type>	Selects elements of the specified type.	1
.<class>	Selects elements of the specified class.	1
#<id>	Selects elements with the specified value for the id attribute.	1
[attr]	Selects elements that define the attribute attr, regardless of the value assigned to the attribute.	2
[attr="val"]	Selects elements that define attr and whose value for this attribute is val.	2

`[attr^="val"]`	Selects elements that define `attr` and whose value for this attribute starts with the string `val`.	3
`[attr$="val"]`	Selects elements that define `attr` and whose value for this attribute ends with the string `val`.	3
`[attr*="val"]`	Selects elements that define `attr` and whose value for this attribute contains the string `val`.	3
`[attr~="val"]`	Selects elements that define `attr` and whose value for this attribute contains multiple values, once of which is `val`.	2
`[attr|="val"]`	Selects elements that define `attr` and whose value is a hyphen-separated list of values, the first of which is `val`.	2
`<selector>, <selector>`	Selects the union of the elements matched by each individual selector.	1
`<selector> <selector>`	Selects elements that match the second selector and that are arbitrary descendants of the elements matched by the first selector.	1
`<selector> > <selector>`	Selects elements that match the second selector and that are immediate descendants of the elements matched by the first selector.	2
`<selector> + <selector>`	Selects elements that match the second selector and that immediately follow an element that matches the first selector.	2
`<selector> ~ <selector>`	Selects elements that match the second selector and that follow an element that matches the first selector.	3
`::first-line`	Selects the first line of a block of text.	1
`::first-letter`	Selects the first letter of a block of text.	1
`:before` `:after`	Inserts content before or after the selected element.	2
`:root`	Selects the root element in the document.	3
`:first-child`	Selects elements that are the first children of their containing elements.	2
`:last-child`	Selects elements that are the last children of their containing elements.	3

`:only-child`	Selects elements that are the sole element defined by their containing element.	3
`:only-of-type`	Selects elements that are the sole element of their type defined by their containing element.	3
`:nth-child(n)`	Selects elements that are the nth child of their parent.	3
`:nth-last-child(n)`	Selects elements that are the nth from last child of their parent.	3
`:nth-of-type(n)`	Selects elements that are the nth child of their type defined by their parent.	3
`:nth-last-of-type(n)`	Selects elements that are the nth from last child of their type defined by their parent.	3
`:enabled`	Selects elements that are in their enabled state.	3
`:disabled`	Selects elements that are in their disabled state.	3
`:checked`	Selects elements that are in a checked state.	3
`:default`	Selects default elements.	3
`:valid` `:invalid`	Selects input elements that are valid or invalid based on input validation.	3
`:in-range` `:out-of-range`	Selects constrained input elements that are within or outside the specified range.	3
`:required` `:optional`	Selects input elements based on the presence of the required attribute.	3
`:link`	Selects link elements.	1
`:visited`	Selects link elements the user has visited.	1
`:hover`	Selects elements that occupy the position on screen under the mouse pointer.	2
`:active`	Selects elements that are presently activated by the user. This usually means elements that are under the pointer when the mouse button is pressed.	2
`:focus`	Selects the element that has the focus	2

`:not(<selector>)`	Negates a selection (for example, selects all elements that are not matches by `<selector>`).	3
`:empty`	Selects elements that contain no child elements.	3
`:lang(<language>)`	Selects elements based on the value of the `lang` attribute.	2
`:target`	Selects the element referred to by the URL fragment identifier.	3

Properties Quick Reference

In Chapters 19–24, I describe the CSS properties. For quick reference, the following sections summarize those properties and the version of CSS to which they were added.

Border and Background Properties

Table 16-3 summarizes the properties that can be used to apply borders and backgrounds to an element. These properties are described in full in Chapter 19.

Table 16-3. *The Border and Background Properties*

Property	Description	CSS Level
`background`	Shorthand property to set all background values.	1
`background-attachment`	Sets the attachment of the background to the element. This is useful when dealing with elements that have scrolling regions.	1
`background-clip`	Sets the area in which the background color and image are visible.	3
`background-color`	Sets the background color.	1
`background-image`	Sets the image for the background.	1
`background-origin`	Sets the point at which the background image will be drawn.	3
`background-position`	Positions the image in the element's box.	1
`background-repeat`	Specifies the repeat style for the background image.	1
`background-size`	Specifies the size at which the background image will be drawn.	3

border	Shorthand property to set all border values for all edges.	1
border-bottom	Shorthand property to set all border values for the bottom edge.	1
border-bottom-color	Sets the color for the bottom edge border.	1
border-bottom-left-radius	Sets the radius for a corner. It's used for curved borders.	3
border-bottom-right-radius	Sets the radius for a corner. It's used for curved borders.	3
border-bottom-style	Sets the style for the bottom edge border.	1
border-bottom-width	Sets the width for the bottom-edge border.	1
border-color	Sets the color of the border for all edges.	1
border-image	Shorthand for image-based borders.	3
border-image-outset	Specifies the area outside the border box that will be used to display the image.	3
border-image-repeat	Specifies the repeat style for the border image.	3
border-image-slice	Specifies the offsets for the image slices.	3
border-image-source	Specifies the source for the border image.	3
border-image-width	Sets the width of the image border.	3
border-left	Shorthand to set the border for the left edge.	1
border-left-color	Sets the color for the left-edge border.	1
border-left-style	Sets the style for the left-edge border.	1
border-left-width	Sets the width for the left-edge border.	1
border-radius	Shorthand for specifying curved edges for a border.	3
border-right	Shorthand to set the border for the right edge.	1
border-right-color	Sets the color for the right-edge border.	1

`border-right-style`	Sets the style for the right-edge border.	1
`border-right-width`	Sets the width of the right-edge border.	1
`border-style`	Shorthand to set the style for all border edges.	1
`border-top`	Shorthand to set the border for the top edge.	1
`border-top-color`	Sets the color of the top-edge border.	1
`border-top-left-radius`	Sets the radius for a corner. It's used for curved borders.	3
`border-top-right-radius`	Sets the radius for a corner. It's used for curved borders.	3
`border-top-style`	Sets the style for the top-edge border.	1
`border-top-width`	Sets the width for the top-edge border.	1
`border-width`	Sets the width for all borders.	1
`box-shadow`	Applies one or more drop shadows.	3
`outline-color`	Sets the color of the outline.	2
`outline-offset`	Sets the offset of the outline.	2
`outline-style`	Sets the style of the outline.	2
`outline-width`	Sets the width of the outline.	2
`outline`	Shorthand property to set the outline in a single declaration.	2

Box Model Properties

Table 16-4 summarizes the properties that can be used to configure an element's box. These properties are described in full in Chapter 20.

Table 16-4. *The Basic Box Properties*

Property	Description	CSS Level
`box-sizing`	Sets the box to which the size-related properties apply to	3
`clear`	Clears one or both edges of a floating element	1

display	Sets the type of an element's box	1
float	Shifts an element to the left or right edge of its containing block, or to the edge of another floating element	1
height	Sets the height of an element's box	1
margin	Shorthand property to set the margin for all four edges	1
margin-bottom	Sets the margin for the bottom edge of the margin box	1
margin-left	Sets the margin for the left edge of the margin box	1
margin-right	Sets the margin for the right edge of the margin box	1
margin-top	Sets the margin for the top edge of the margin box	1
max-height	Sets the maximum height for the element	2
max-width	Sets the maximum width for the element	2
min-height	Sets the minimum height for the element	2
min-width	Sets the minimum width for the element	2
overflow	Shorthand property to set the overflow style for both axes	2
overflow-x	Sets the style for handling overflowing content on the x-axis	3
overflow-y	Sets the style for handling overflowing content on the y-axis	3
padding	Shorthand property to set the padding for all four edges	1
padding-bottom	Sets the padding for the bottom edge	1
padding-left	Sets the padding for the left edge	1
padding-right	Sets the padding for the right edge	1
padding-top	Sets the padding for the top edge	1
visibility	Sets the visibility for an element	2
width	Sets the width of an element	1

Layout Properties

Table 16-5 summarizes the properties that can be used to create layouts for elements. These properties are described in full in Chapter 21.

Table 16-5. The Layout Properties

Property	Description	CSS Level
bottom	Sets the bottom-edge offset for a positioned element.	2
column-count	Specifies the number of columns in a multicolumn layout.	3
column-fill	Specifies how content should be distributed between columns in a multicolumn layout.	3
column-gap	Specifies the distance between columns in a multicolumn layout.	3
column-rule	Shorthand to define the rule between columns in a multicolumn layout.	3
column-rule-color	Specifies the color of the rule in a multicolumn layout.	3
column-rule-style	Specifies the style of the rule in a multicolumn layout.	3
column-rule-width	Specifies the width of the rule in a multicolumn layout.	3
columns	Shorthand for setting the column-span and column-width properties in a multicolumn layout.	3
column-span	Specifies how many columns an element should span in a multicolumn layout.	3
column-width	Specifies the width of columns in a multicolumn layout.	3
display	Specifies the way in which the element is displayed on the page.	1
flex-align flex-direction flex-order flex-pack	These properties are defined by the flexible box layout, but they are not yet implemented.	3
left	Sets the left-edge offset for a positioned element.	2

position	Sets the positioning method for an element.	2
right	Sets the right-edge offset for a positioned element.	2
top	Sets the top-edge offset for a positioned element.	2
z-index	Sets the front-to-back order for positioned elements.	2

Text Properties

Table 16-6 summarizes the properties that can be used to style text. These properties are described in full in Chapter 22.

Table 16-6. *The Text Properties*

Property	Description	CSS Level
@font-face	Specifies a web font for use	3
direction	Specifies the directionality of text	2
font	Shorthand property to set details of the font in a single declaration	1
font-family	Specifies the list of font families to be used, in order of preference	1
font-size	Specifies the size of the font	1
font-style	Specifies whether a font will be normal, italic, or oblique	1
font-variant	Specifies if the font should be displayed in small caps form	1
font-weight	Specifies the weight (boldness) of the text	1
letter-spacing	Specifies the space between letters	1
line-height	Specifies the height of a line of text	1
text-align	Specifies the alignment of text	1
text-decoration	Specifies the decoration of text	1
text-indent	Specifies the indentation of text	1

`text-justify`	Specifies the justification of text	3
`text-shadow`	Specifies a drop shadow for a block of text	3
`text-transform`	Applies a transformation to a block of text	1
`word-spacing`	Specifies the spacing between words	1

Transition, Animation, and Transform Properties

Table 16-7 summarizes the properties that can be used to change the appearance of elements, often over a period of time. These properties are described in full in Chapter 23.

Table 16-7. *The Transition, Animation, and Transform Properties*

Property	Description	CSS Level
`@keyframes`	Specifies one or more key frames for an animation	3
`animation`	Shorthand property for animations	3
`animation-delay`	Specifies a delay before an animation starts	3
`animation-direction`	Specifies how alternate repeats of an animation are performed	3
`animation-duration`	Specifies the duration of an animation	3
`animation-iteration-count`	Specifies the number of times an animation will be repeated	3
`animation-name`	Specifies the name of the set of key frames that will be used for an animation	3
`animation-play-state`	Specifies whether the animation is playing or is paused	3
`animation-timing-function`	Specifies the function used to calculate property values between key frames in an animation	3
`transform`	Specifies a transform to apply to an element	3
`transform-origin`	Specifies an origin for which a transform will be applied	3
`transition`	Shorthand property for transitions	3
`transition-delay`	Specifies a delay before the transition starts	3

`transition-duration`	Specifies the duration of a transition	3
`transition-property`	Specifies one or more properties that will be transitioned	3
`transition-timing-` `function`	Specifies the function used to calculate intermediate property values during the transition	3

Other Properties

Table 16-8 summarizes the properties that don't fit neatly into the other chapters. These properties are described in full in Chapter 24.

Table 16-8. Other Properties

Property	Description	CSS Level
`border-collapse`	Specifies the display style for borders on adjacent table cells	2
`border-spacing`	Specifies the spacing between table cell borders	2
`caption-side`	Specifies the position of a table caption	2
`color`	Sets the foreground color for an element	1
`cursor`	Sets the style of the cursor	2
`empty-cells`	Specifies how borders are drawn on empty table cells	2
`list-style`	Shorthand property to specify a list style	1
`list-style-image`	Specifies an image to be used as a list marker	1
`list-style-position`	Specifies the position of a list marker relative to a list item	1
`list-style-type`	Specifies the type of marker used in a list	1
`opacity`	Sets the transparency for an element	3
`table-layout`	Specifies how the size of a table is determined	2

Summary

In this chapter, I provided some context for the chapters that follow, in which I describe the CSS properties. I also provided quick reference tables that will let you find the property you seek when you use CSS in a real project. It is important that you take into account the CSS version in which a property was defined when considering CSS features for use in your projects. As I explained at the start of the chapter, some CSS3 modules are still unstable and others are not as widely implemented as we might like.

CHAPTER 17

Using the CSS Selectors—Part I

In Chapter 4, I explained that you use CSS selectors to identify which elements you want to apply a style to when using the style element or an external stylesheet. In this chapter and the next, I describe and demonstrate the core CSS3 selectors. You will see how easy it is to make selections and how you can tailor those selections to meet broad or very specific conditions.

These selectors were introduced over time and in different versions of CSS. The mainstream browsers have fairly good support for all of the selectors, but you might find that coverage in less popular browsers is a little patchy. To help you work out what you can rely on, I have indicated in which version of CSS each selector was introduced. Table 17-1 provides the summary for this chapter.

Table 17-1. Chapter Summary

Problem	Solution	Listing
Select all of the elements.	Use the universal selector.	17-1
Select elements by type.	Use the type selector.	17-2
Select elements by the value of the class global attribute.	Use the class selector.	17-3, 17-4
Select elements by the value of the id global attribute.	Use the id selector.	17-5
Select elements based on attributes.	Use the attributes selectors.	17-6 through 17-8
Create a union of selectors.	Separate the selectors with a comma.	17-9
Select descendants of an element.	Separate the selectors with a space.	17-10, 17-11
Select children of an element.	Use the > selector.	17-12

Select sibling elements.	Use the + or ~ selectors.	17-13, 17-14
Select the first line of a block of text.	Use the ::first-line selector.	17-15
Select the first letter of a block of text.	Use the ::first-letter selector.	17-16
Insert content into an element.	Use the :before and :after selectors.	17-17
Insert numeric content into an element.	Use the counter function.	17-18

Using the Basic CSS Selectors

There are a set of selectors that are very straightforward to use. Think of them as the *basic selectors*. You can use these selectors for making wide selections in a document, or as the foundation for more narrow matches when combined together (a technique I describe later in this chapter). In each of the following sections, I show you how to use one of the basic selectors.

Selecting All Elements

The *universal selector* matches every element in the document. This is the most fundamental of the CSS selectors, but is rarely used because it matches so widely. Table 17-2 summarizes the selector.

Table 17-2. The Universal Selector

Selector:	*
Matches:	All elements
Since CSS Version:	2

Listing 17-1 shows an example of a style that uses the universal selector.

Listing 17-1. Using the Universal Selector

```
<!DOCTYPE HTML>
<html>
    <head>
        <title>Example</title>
        <style type="text/css">
            * {
                border: thin black solid;
                padding: 4px;
            }
        </style>
```

```
    </head>
    <body>
        <a href="http://apress.com">Visit the Apress website</a>
        <p>I like <span>apples</span> and oranges.</p>
        <a href="http://w3c.org">Visit the W3C website</a>
    </body>
</html>
```

The style that I have defined in Listing 17-1 puts a thin black box around the selected elements. This is one of the styles I'll use to demonstrate the way that selectors match in this chapter. You can see the effect of this selector in Figure 17-1.

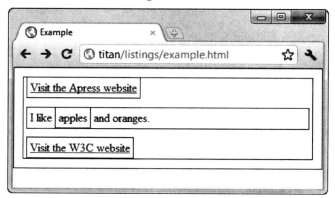

Figure 17-1. Using the universal CSS selector

If the figure looks a little odd it is because the universal selector really does match *every* element in the document, including the html and body elements. This selector is an effective, but somewhat brutal, tool and you should use it with caution.

Selecting Elements by Type

You can select all of the instances of an element in a document by specifying the element type as the selector (e.g., if you want to select all of the a elements then you use a as the selector). Table 17-3 provides a summary of the element type selector.

Table 17-3. The Element Type Selector

Selector:	`<element type>`
Matches:	All elements of the specified type
Since CSS Version:	1

Listing 17-2 provides an example.

413

Listing 17-2. Using the Element Type Selector

```
<!DOCTYPE HTML>
<html>
    <head>
        <title>Example</title>
        <style type="text/css">
            a {
                border: thin black solid;
                padding: 4px;
            }
        </style>
    </head>
    <body>
        <a href="http://apress.com">Visit the Apress website</a>
        <p>I like <span>apples</span> and oranges.</p>
        <a href="http://w3c.org">Visit the W3C website</a>
    </body>
</html>
```

You can see the effect of this selector in Figure 17-2.

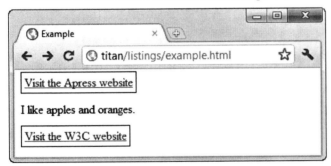

Figure 17-2. Selecting elements by type

■ **Tip** You can apply a style to multiple element types by separating the types with a comma. See the section "Combining Selectors," later in this chapter, for an example.

Selecting Elements by Class

The class selector allows us to select elements that have been assigned to a particular class using the class global attribute. Table 17-4 describes this selector. I describe the class attribute in Chapter 3.

Table 17-4. *The Element Class Selector*

Selector:	.*<classname>* (or *.*<classname>*) *<element type>*.*<classname>*
Matches:	Elements that belong to the specified class. When used with an element type, all elements of the specified type that belong to the specified class are selected.
Since CSS Version:	1

Listing 17-3 provides a demonstration of this selector.

Listing 17-3. Selecting Elements by Class

```
<!DOCTYPE HTML>
<html>
    <head>
        <title>Example</title>
        <style type="text/css">
            .class2 {
                border: thin black solid;
                padding: 4px;
            }
        </style>
    </head>
    <body>
        <a class="class1 class2" href="http://apress.com">Visit the Apress website</a>
        <p>I like <span class="class2">apples</span> and oranges.</p>
        <a href="http://w3c.org">Visit the W3C website</a>
    </body>
</html>
```

In Listing 17-3, I have used the selector .class2. This has the effect of selecting all elements of any type that have been assigned to the class class2.

There are two ways of expressing this selector: with and without the universal selector. The selectors *.class2 and .class are equivalent. The first form is more descriptive, but the second form is the one that is most commonly used. This is a recurring pattern in CSS selectors. As you proceed through the available selectors, you will see that each of them is effectively a filter that narrows the scope of the selector so that it matches fewer elements. You can combine these selectors to create focused matches. I'll show you different techniques for combining selectors in the section "Combining Selectors," later in this chapter.

In Listing 17-3, there are two elements assigned to the target class: an a element and a span element. You can see the effect of the style in Figure 17-3.

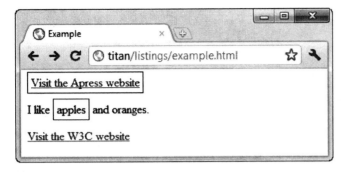

Figure 17-3. Using the class selector

You can be more specific and limit the selection to a single type of element that has been assigned to a class. You do this by replacing the universal selector with the element type, as shown in Listing 17-4.

Listing 17-4. Using the Class Selector for a Single Element Type

```
<!DOCTYPE HTML>
<html>
    <head>
        <title>Example</title>
        <style type="text/css">
            span.class2 {
                border: thin black solid;
                padding: 4px;
            }
        </style>
    </head>
    <body>
        <a class="class1 class2" href="http://apress.com">Visit the Apress website</a>
        <p>I like <span class="class2">apples</span> and oranges.</p>
        <a href="http://w3c.org">Visit the W3C website</a>
    </body>
</html>
```

In this case, I have narrowed the scope of the selector so that it will match only span elements that have been assigned to class2. You can see the effect of this narrowed scope in Figure 17-4.

Figure 17-4. Narrowing the scope of the class selector

■ **Tip** If you want to select elements that have membership in multiple classes, you can specify the class names separated with a period (e.g., `span.class1.class2`). This will select only elements that are assigned to both `class1` and `class2`.

Selecting Elements by ID

The ID selector lets you select elements by the value of the global `id` attribute, which I described in Chapter 3. Table 17-5 summarizes this selector.

Table 17-5. The Element id Selector

Selector:	`#<idvalue>` `<element type>.#<idvalue>`
Matches:	The element that has the specified value for the `id` global attribute
Since CSS Version:	1

As I explained in Chapter 3, the value of an element's `id` attribute must be unique within the HTML document. This means that when you use the ID selector, you are looking for a single element. Listing 17-5 demonstrates the use of the `id` selector.

Listing17- 5. Using the id Selector

```
<!DOCTYPE HTML>
<html>
    <head>
        <title>Example</title>
```

```
        <style type="text/css">
            #w3canchor {
                border: thin black solid;
                padding: 4px;
            }
        </style>
    </head>
    <body>
        <a id="apressanchor" class="class1 class2" href="http://apress.com">
            Visit the Apress website
        </a>
        <p>I like <span class="class2">apples</span> and oranges.</p>
        <a id="w3canchor" href="http://w3c.org">Visit the W3C website</a>
    </body>
</html>
```

In this example, I have selected the element with the id of w3canchor. You can see the effect of this in Figure 17-5.

Figure 17-5. Selecting an element by ID

It might seem that if you are targeting an individual element for a style, you could achieve the same effect by using the element's style attribute. This is true, but the real value of this selector comes when you combine it with other selectors, a technique I demonstrate later in this chapter.

Selecting Elements by Attribute

The attribute selector allows you to match attributes based on different aspects of attributes, as described in Table 17-6.

Table 17-6. The Element Attribute Selector

Selector:	`[<condition>]` `<element type>[<condition>]`
Matches:	Elements that have attributes that match the specified condition (see Table 17-7 for the supported condition

types)

Since CSS Version:	Various (see Table 17-7)

You can choose to match all of the elements (or all elements of a given type) whose attributes meet the condition by using the universal selector (*) or, in the more common form, by omitting the universal selector and putting the condition inside of the square braces (the [and] characters). Listing 17-6 demonstrates the attribute selector in use.

Listing 17-6. Using the Element Attribute Selector

```
<!DOCTYPE HTML>
<html>
    <head>
        <title>Example</title>
        <style type="text/css">
            [href] {
                border: thin black solid;
                padding: 4px;
            }
        </style>
    </head>
    <body>
        <a id="apressanchor" class="class1 class2" href="http://apress.com">
            Visit the Apress website
        </a>
        <p>I like <span class="class2">apples</span> and oranges.</p>
        <a id="w3canchor" href="http://w3c.org">Visit the W3C website</a>
    </body>
</html>
```

In Listing 17-6, I have used the simplest form of the attribute selector, which matches any element that has an href attribute, irrespective of the value assigned to the attribute. In the example HTML document, this means that both the a elements will be selected, as shown in Figure 17-6.

Figure 17-6. Selecting elements based on the presence of an attribute

You can create more sophisticated conditions to match attributes, as shown in Table 17-7. These conditions have been added to CSS in two waves, so I have indicated in which version of CSS each is supported.

Table 17-7. Conditions for the Element Attribute Selector

Condition	Description	CSS Version
[attr]	Selects elements that define the attribute attr, irrespective of the value assigned to the attribute (this is the condition shown in Listing 17-6).	2
[attr="val"]	Selects elements that define attr and whose value for this attribute is val.	2
[attr^="val"]	Selects elements that define attr and whose value for this attribute starts with the string val.	3
[attr$="val"]	Selects elements that define attr and whose value for this attribute ends with the string val.	3
[attr*="val"]	Selects elements that define attr and whose value for this attribute contains the string val.	3
[attr~="val"]	Selects elements that define attr and whose value for this attribute contains multiple values, one of which is val. See Listing 17-7 for an example of using this selector.	2
[attr|="val"]	Selects elements that define attr and whose value is a hyphen-separated list of values, the first of which is val. See Listing 17-8 for an example of using this selector.	2

The last two conditions bear additional explanation. The ~= condition is useful for dealing with attributes that support multiple values that are separated by a space character, such as the class global attribute. Listing 17-7 gives a demonstration.

Listing 17-7. Selecting Based on One of Multiple Values

```
<!DOCTYPE HTML>
<html>
    <head>
        <title>Example</title>
        <style type="text/css">
            [class~="class2"] {
                border: thin black solid;
                padding: 4px;
            }
        </style>
```

```
        </head>
        <body>
            <a id="apressanchor" class="class1 class2" href="http://apress.com">
                Visit the Apress website
            </a>
            <p>I like <span class="class2">apples</span> and oranges.</p>
            <a id="w3canchor" href="http://w3c.org">Visit the W3C website</a>
        </body>
</html>
```

In Listing 17-7, I've used the class global attribute because it is the only attribute I have introduced so far that accepts multiple values. You don't need to use the attribute selector to match class values; the class selector handles multiple class memberships automatically.

The condition that I have used in the selector is to match elements who define the class attribute and whose value for this attribute includes class2. I have highlighted the class attributes of the content elements and you can see the effect of the selector in Figure 17-7.

Figure 17-7. Selecting based on a multivalue attribute

The |= condition is useful when several pieces of information are expressed in an attribute value and separated by hyphens. A good example of this is the lang global attribute, which can be used with language specifiers that contain regional subtags (for example, en-us is English as spoken in the United States, and en-gb is English as spoken in the United Kingdom). Listing 17-8 shows how you can select all of the English tags, without having to enumerate all of the regional variations (of which there are many).

Listing 17-8. Using the |= Attribute Condition

```
<!DOCTYPE HTML>
<html>
    <head>
        <title>Example</title>
        <style type="text/css">
            [lang|="en"] {
                border: thin black solid;
                padding: 4px;
            }
        </style>
    </head>
    <body>
```

```
        <a lang="en-us" id="apressanchor" class="class1 class2" href="http://apress.com">
            Visit the Apress website
        </a>
        <p>I like <span lang="en-gb" class="class2">apples</span> and oranges.</p>
        <a lang="en" id="w3canchor" href="http://w3c.org">Visit the W3C website</a>
    </body>
</html>
```

You can see the effect of this selector in Figure 17-8. Notice that the selector matches the second a element, which has no regional subtag (i.e., the value of the lang element is en and not en-us or en-gb), as well those that do have subtags.

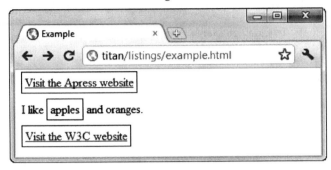

Figure 17-8. Selecting elements based on lang attributes

Combining Selectors

You can be much more specific in the elements that you select by creating combinations of selectors. These either broaden the range of elements that a style will be applied to or do the opposite: allow you to be incredibly specific in what you select. In the following sections, I'll show you the different ways you can combine selectors.

Creating Selector Unions

Creating a list of comma-separated selectors means that the style is applied to the union of all of the elements that each of the individual selectors matches. Table 17-8 summarizes unions of selectors.

Table 17-8. The Selector Union

Selector:	`<selector>, <selector>, <selector>`
Matches:	Selects the union of the elements matched by each individual selector
Since CSS Version:	1

Listing 17-9 provides an example of creating a union of selectors.

Listing 17-9. Creating Selector Unions

```
<!DOCTYPE HTML>
<html>
    <head>
        <title>Example</title>
        <style type="text/css">
            a, [lang|="en"] {
                border: thin black solid;
                padding: 4px;
            }
        </style>
    </head>
    <body>
        <a id="apressanchor" class="class1 class2" href="http://apress.com">
            Visit the Apress website
        </a>
        <p>I like <span lang="en-uk" class="class2">apples</span> and oranges.</p>
        <a id="w3canchor" href="http://w3c.org">Visit the W3C website</a>
    </body>
</html>
```

In Listing 17-9, I have specified a type selector (a) and an attribute selector ([lang|="en"]) separated by a comma (a, [lang|="en"]). The browser will evaluate each selector in turn and apply the style to the selected elements. You can mix and match different types of selectors freely and there doesn't need to be any commonality between the elements that are matched. You can see the effect of the selector from Listing 17-9 in Figure 17-9.

Figure 17-9. Creating selector unions

You can combine as many selectors as you require, each separated from the last by a comma.

Selecting Descendant Elements

You can use the *descendant selector* to select elements that are contained within another element. Table 17-9 provides a summary.

Table 17-9. The Descendant Selector

Selector:	⟨*first selector*⟩ ⟨*second selector*⟩
Matches:	Selects elements that match the second selector and are descendants of the elements matched by the first selector
Since CSS Version:	1

The first selector is applied and then the *descendants* of the matched elements are evaluated against the second selector. The descendant selector will match *any* element contained within the elements matched by the first selector, not just the immediate children. Listing 17-10 provides a demonstration.

Listing 17-10. Selecting Descendants

```
<!DOCTYPE HTML>
<html>
    <head>
        <title>Example</title>
        <style type="text/css">
            p span {
                border: thin black solid;
                padding: 4px;
            }
        </style>
    </head>
    <body>
        <a id="apressanchor" class="class1 class2" href="http://apress.com">
            Visit the Apress website
        </a>
        <p>I like <span lang="en-uk" class="class2">apples</span> and oranges.</p>
        <a id="w3canchor" href="http://w3c.org">Visit the W3C website</a>
    </body>
</html>
```

The selector in Listing 17-10 selects span elements that are descendants of p elements. Given the HTML in the example, I could just have selected the span element directly to get the same result, but this approach is more flexible, as the following example demonstrates.

Listing 17-11. A More Complex Descendant Selector Example

```
<!DOCTYPE HTML>
<html>
    <head>
        <title>Example</title>
        <style type="text/css">
            #mytable td {
                border: thin black solid;
                padding: 4px;
            }
```

```
        </style>
    </head>
    <body>
        <table id="mytable">
            <tr><th>Name</th><th>City</th></tr>
            <tr><td>Adam Freeman</td><td>London</td></tr>
            <tr><td>Joe Smith</td><td>New York</td></tr>
            <tr><td>Anne Jones</td><td>Paris</td></tr>
        </table>

        <p>I like <span lang="en-uk" class="class2">apples</span> and oranges.</p>

        <table id="othertable">
            <tr><th>Name</th><th>City</th></tr>
            <tr><td>Peter Pererson</td><td>Boston</td></tr>
            <tr><td>Chuck Fellows</td><td>Paris</td></tr>
            <tr><td>Jane Firth</td><td>Paris</td></tr>
        </table>
    </body>
</html>
```

In Listing 17-11, I have defined two simple tables, each of which defines the id attribute. Using the ID selector, I select the table with the id value of mytable and then select the td elements that it contains. You can see the effect in Figure 17-10.

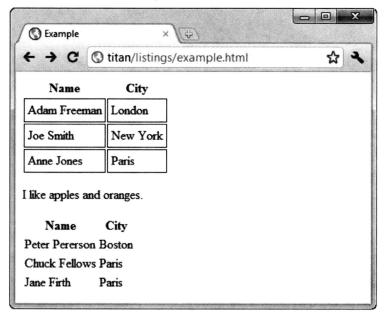

Figure 17-10. Selecting descendant elements

Notice that I am not selecting direct descendants in this example. I am skipping over the tr elements to select the td elements.

Selecting Child Elements

The counterpart to the descendant selector is the *child selector,* which will only match elements that are directly contained in matched elements. Table 17-10 summarizes the child selector.

Table 17-10. The Child Selector

Selector:	*<first selector> > <second selector>*
Matches:	Selects elements that match the second selector and are immediate descendants of the elements matched by the first selector
Since CSS Version:	2

Listing 17-12 provides a demonstration of how you can select child elements.

Listing 17-12. Selecting Child Elements

```
<!DOCTYPE HTML>
<html>
    <head>
        <title>Example</title>
        <style type="text/css">
            body > * > span, tr > th {
                border: thin black solid;
                padding: 4px;
            }
        </style>
    </head>
    <body>
        <table id="mytable">
            <tr><th>Name</th><th>City</th></tr>
            <tr><td>Adam Freeman</td><td>London</td></tr>
            <tr><td>Joe Smith</td><td>New York</td></tr>
            <tr><td>Anne Jones</td><td>Paris</td></tr>
        </table>

        <p>I like <span lang="en-uk" class="class2">apples</span> and oranges.</p>

        <table id="othertable">
            <tr><th>Name</th><th>City</th></tr>
            <tr><td>Peter Pererson</td><td>Boston</td></tr>
            <tr><td>Chuck Fellows</td><td>Paris</td></tr>
            <tr><td>Jane Firth</td><td>Paris</td></tr>
        </table>
```

```
    </body>
</html>
```

In this selector, I have created a union of child selectors. In the first, I am looking for span elements that are children of *any* element that is a child of the body element. In the second, I am looking for th elements that are children of tr elements. You can see which elements are matched in Figure 17-11.

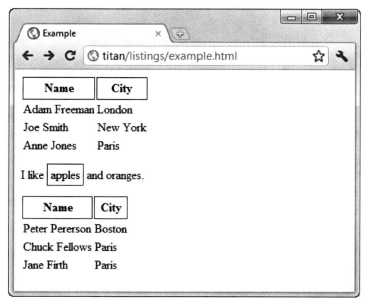

Figure 17-11. Selecting child elements

Selecting Sibling Elements

You can select elements that immediately follow other elements using the *immediate sibling selector*. Table 17-11 summarizes this selector.

Table 17-11. *The Immediate Sibling Selector*

Selector:	*<first selector> + <second selector>*
Matches:	Selects elements that match the second selector and immediately follow an element that matches the first selector
Since CSS Version:	2

Listing 17-13 shows how you can select immediate sibling elements.

Listing 17-13. Using the Immediate Sibling Selector

```
<!DOCTYPE HTML>
<html>
    <head>
        <title>Example</title>
        <style type="text/css">
            p + a {
                border: thin black solid;
                padding: 4px;
            }
        </style>
    </head>
    <body>
        <a href="http://apress.com">Visit the Apress website</a>
        <p>I like <span lang="en-uk" class="class2">apples</span> and oranges.</p>
        <a href="http://w3c.org">Visit the W3C website</a>
        <a href="http://google.com">Visit Google</a>
    </body>
</html>
```

In Listing 17-13, the selector will match a elements that immediately follow a p element. As you can see in Figure 17-12, there is only one such element in the listing and it is the a element, which creates a hyperlink to the W3C website.

Figure 17-12. Selecting an immediate sibling

You can make the selection a little looser by using the *general sibling selector,* which selects elements that follow another specified element, but not necessarily immediately. Table 17-12 describes this element.

Table 17-12. The General Sibling Selector

Selector:	*<first selector> ~ <second selector>*
Matches:	Selects elements that match the second selector and

follow an element that matches the first selector

Since CSS Version:	3

Listing 17-14 shows how you can use the general sibling selector.

Listing 17-14. Using the General Sibling Selector

```
<!DOCTYPE HTML>
<html>
    <head>
        <title>Example</title>
        <style type="text/css">
            p ~ a {
                border: thin black solid;
                padding: 4px;
            }
        </style>
    </head>
    <body>
        <a href="http://apress.com">Visit the Apress website</a>
        <p>I like <span lang="en-uk" class="class2">apples</span> and oranges.</p>
        <a href="http://w3c.org">Visit the W3C website</a>
        <a href="http://google.com">Visit Google</a>
    </body>
</html>
```

We are not limited to elements that immediately follow an element matched by the first selector, which means that the second selector will match against two a elements in this example. The excluded a element (the one that links to http://apress.com) is not selected because it precedes the p element; we can only select siblings that follow on). You can see the effect of this selector in Figure 17-13.

Figure 17-13. Using the general sibling selector

Using Pseudo-Element Selectors

So far, you have seen selections using the elements defined in the HTML document. CSS also includes *pseudo-selectors*, which provide more complex functionality but don't directly correspond to the elements defined in the document. There are two kinds of pseudo-selectors: *pseudo-elements* and *pseudo-classes*. In this section, I describe and demonstrate the pseudo-element selectors. As their name suggests, pseudo-elements don't really exist; they are a convenience provided by CSS to let you make helpful selections.

Using the ::first-line Selector

The `::first-line` selector matches the first line of a block of text. Table 17-13 summarizes the `::first-line` selector.

Table 17-13. The ::first-line Pseudo-Element Selector

Selector:	*::first-line*
Matches:	The first line of text content
Since CSS Version:	1

Listing 17-15 shows an example of using the `::first-line` selector.

Listing 17-15. Using the ::first-line Pseudo-Element Selector

```
<!DOCTYPE HTML>
<html>
    <head>
        <title>Example</title>
        <style type="text/css">
            ::first-line {
                background-color:grey;
                color:white;
            }
        </style>
    </head>
    <body>
        <p>Fourscore and seven years ago our fathers brought forth
            on this continent a new nation, conceived in liberty, and
            dedicated to the proposition that all men are created equal.</p>

        <p>I like <span lang="en-uk" class="class2">apples</span> and oranges.</p>

        <a href="http://w3c.org">Visit the W3C website</a>
    </body>
</html>
```

I have used the selector on its own in this example, but it can also be applied as a modifier to other selectors. For example, if I wanted to select the first line of only p elements, I could specify p::first-line as the selector.

■ **Tip** The pseudo-element selector is prefixed with two colon characters (::), but browsers will recognize the selector with just one colon (i.e., :first-line instead of ::first-line). This makes the format consistent with the pseudo-class selectors I described earlier in this chapter for purposes of backward compatibility.

The browser will reassess what the first line is as the browser window is resized. This means that the style is always correctly applied to the first line of the text, as shown in Figure 17-14.

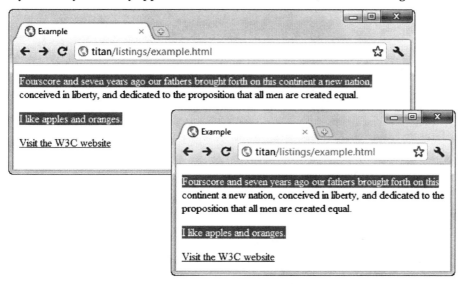

Figure 17-14. The browser ensures that the style is applied to the first line, even when the window is resized

Using the ::first-letter Selector

The ::first-letter selector does just what its name suggests: it selects the first letter in a block of text. Table 17-14 summarizes this pseudo-element selector.

Table 17-14. The ::first-letter Pseudo-Element Selector

Selector:	::first-letter
Matches:	The first letter of text content

Since CSS Version:	1

Listing 17-16 shows the selector in use.

Listing 17-16. Using the ::first-letter Pseudo-Element Selector

```
<!DOCTYPE HTML>
<html>
    <head>
        <title>Example</title>
        <style type="text/css">
            ::first-letter {
                background-color:grey;
                color:white;
                border: thin black solid;
                padding: 4px;

            }
        </style>
    </head>
    <body>
        <p>Fourscore and seven years ago our fathers brought forth
            on this continent a new nation, conceived in liberty, and
                dedicated to the proposition that all men are created equal.</p>

        <p>I like <span lang="en-uk" class="class2">apples</span> and oranges.</p>
        <a href="http://w3c.org">Visit the W3C website</a>
    </body>
</html>
```

You can see the effect of this selector in Figure 17-15.

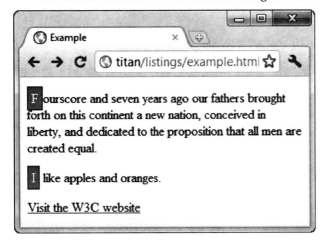

Figure 17-15. Using the ::first-letter selector

Using the :before and :after Selectors

The :before and :after selectors are unusual in that they generate content and add it to the document. I introduced the :before selector in Chapter 9, and showed you how to use it to create custom lists. The :after selector is the counterpart to :before and adds content following an element, as opposed to before an element. Table 17-15 describes these selectors.

Table 17-15. The :before and :after Selectors

Selector	Description	CSS Version
:before	Inserts content before the content of the selected elements.	2
:after	Inserts content after the content of the selected elements.	2

Listing 17-17 demonstrates these attributes in use.

Listing 17-17. Using the :before and :after Selectors

```
<!DOCTYPE HTML>
<html>
    <head>
        <title>Example</title>
        <style type="text/css">
            a:before {
                content: "Click here to "
            }
            a:after {
                content: "!"
            }
        </style>
    </head>
    <body>
        <a href="http://apress.com">Visit the Apress website</a>
        <p>I like <span>apples</span> and oranges.</p>
        <a href="http://w3c.org">Visit the W3C website</a>
    </body>
</html>
```

In Listing 17-17, I have selected the a elements and applied the :before and :after pseudo-selectors. When using these selectors, you specify the content you want to insert by setting a value for the content property. This is a special property that you may use only with these selectors. In this example, the content Click here to will be inserted before the content of the a elements, and an exclamation mark (!) will be inserted after the content. You can see the effect of these additions in Figure 17-16.

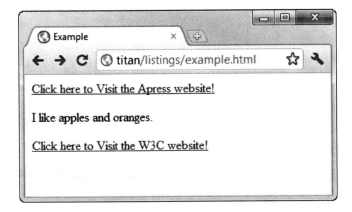

Figure 17-16. Using the :before and :after selectors

Using the CSS Counter Feature

The `:before` and `:after` selectors are often used with the CSS *counter* feature, which lets you generate numeric content. I gave an example of using these counters to create custom lists in Chapter 9. Listing 17-18 gives a demonstration.

Listing 17-18. Using the CSS Counter Feature

```
<!DOCTYPE HTML>
<html>
    <head>
        <title>Example</title>
        <style type="text/css">
            body {
                counter-reset: paracount;
            }
            p:before {
                content: counter(paracount) ". ";
                counter-increment: paracount;
            }
        </style>
    </head>
    <body>
        <a href="http://apress.com">Visit the Apress website</a>
        <p>I like <span>apples</span> and oranges.</p>
        <p>I also like <span>mangos</span> and cherries.</p>
        <a class="myclass1 myclass2" href="http://w3c.org">Visit the W3C website</a>
    </body>
</html>
```

To create a counter, you use the special counter-reset property and set the value to be the name you want to use for the counter, like this:

```
counter-reset: paracount;
```

This has the effect of initializing a counter called paracount counter and setting the value to 1. You can specify a different initial value by adding a number after the counter name, like this:

```
counter-reset: paracount 10;
```

If you want to define multiple counters, you simply add the names (and optional initial values) to the same counter-reset declaration, like this:

```
counter-reset: paracount 10 othercounter;
```

This declaration creates a counter called paracount (with an initial value of 10) and a counter called othercounter (with an initial value of 1). After you have initialized a counter, you can use it in the content property of styles that use the :before and :after selectors, like this:

```
content: counter(paracount) ". ";
```

Because this declaration has been used in a selector that includes :after, this has the effect of including the current value of the counter in the HTML before every element that the selector matches and, in this case, appending a period and a space after each value. The value is expressed as a decimal integer by default (1, 2, 3, etc.), but you can specify other numeric formats as well, like this:

```
content: counter(paracount, lower-alpha) ". ";
```

The additional argument to the counter function is the style of number you want. You may use any of the supported values for the list-style-type property, which I describe in Chapter 24.

You increment the counter using the special counter-increment property. The value for this property is the name of the counter you want to increment, like this:

```
counter-increment: paracount;
```

Counters are incremented by one by default, but you can specify a different increment by adding the step size you want to the declaration, like this:

```
counter-increment: paracount 2;
```

You can see the effect of the counter from Listing 17-18 in Figure 17-17.

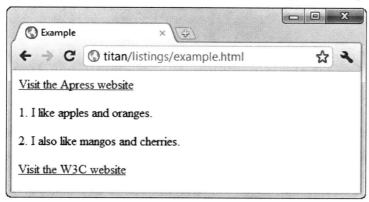

Figure 17-17. Using counters with generated content

Summary

In this chapter I have described the CSS selectors and pseudo-elements, which are the means by which you identify the elements that you want to apply a style to. The selectors allow you to match elements in broad sweeps or, by combining selectors, narrow your focus to elements in particular parts of your HTML documents. The pseudo-elements are a convenience that let you select content that doesn't really exist in the document. You'll see a similar principle in the next chapter when you examine pseudo-classes.

Learning the selectors is the key to getting the most out of CSS. In the chapters that follow, you will see lots of examples of selectors at work and I recommend that you take the time to experiment and become familiar with them yourself.

CHAPTER 18

Using the CSS Selectors—Part II

In this chapter, I continue your tour of the CSS selectors and show you the *pseudo-classes*. As with the pseudo-elements, these are not classes that have been applied to your elements, but a convenience that allows you to select elements based on some common characteristics. Table 18-1 provides the summary for this chapter.

Table 18-1. Chapter Summary

Problem	Solution	Listing
Select the root element in the document.	Use the :root selector.	18-1
Select a child element.	Use the :first-child, :last:child, :only-child, or :only-of-type selectors.	18-2 through 18-6
Select a child at a specific index.	Use the :nth-child, :nth-last-child, :nth-of-type, or :nth-last-of-type selectors.	18-7
Select elements that are enabled or disabled.	Use the :enabled or :disabled selectors.	18-8
Select radio button or check box elements that are checked.	Use the :checked selector.	18-9
Select the default element.	Use the :default selector.	18-10
Select elements based on input validation.	Use the :valid or :invalid selectors.	18-11
Select range-constrained input elements.	Use the :in-range and :out-of-range selectors.	18-12
Select input elements based on the presence of the required attribute.	Use the :required or :optional selectors.	18-13

Select a hyperlink.	Use the :link and :visited selectors.	18-14
Select the element that the mouse is currently over.	Use the :hover selector.	18-15
Select the active element.	Use the :active selector.	18-16
Select the focused element.	Use the :focus selector.	18-17
Negate another selector.	Use the negation selector.	18-18
Select elements that have no content.	Use the :empty selector.	—
Select elements based on language.	Use the :lang selector.	18-19
Selects the element referred to in a URL fragment.	Use the :target selector.	18-20

Using the Structural Pseudo-Class Selectors

The *structural pseudo-class* selectors allow you to select elements based on where they are in the document. These selectors are prefixed with a colon character (:); for example, :empty. You may use these selectors on their own or combined with another selector; for example, p:empty.

Using the :root Selector

The :root selector selects the root element in the document. This is perhaps the least useful of the pseudo-class selectors, because it will always return the html element. Table 18-2 summarizes the :root selector.

Table 18-2. The :root Selector

Selector:	:root
Matches:	Selects the root element in the document; this is the html element
Since CSS Version:	3

Listing 18-1 shows the :root selector in use.

Listing 18-1. Using the :root Selector

```
<!DOCTYPE HTML>
<html>
    <head>
        <title>Example</title>
        <style type="text/css">
            :root {
                border: thin black solid;
                padding: 4px;
            }
        </style>
    </head>
    <body>
        <a href="http://apress.com">Visit the Apress website</a>
        <p>I like <span lang="en-uk" class="class2">apples</span> and oranges.</p>
        <a href="http://w3c.org">Visit the W3C website</a>
    </body>
</html>
```

You can see the effect of this selector in Figure 18-1. It can be a little hard to make out, but there is a border around the entire document.

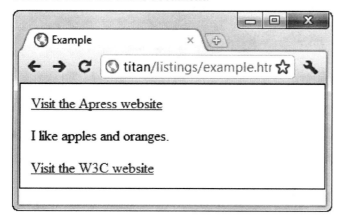

Figure 18-1. Using the :root selector

Using the Child Selectors

The *child selectors* allow you to select single elements that are directly contained inside other elements. Table 18-3 summarizes these selectors.

Table 18-3. The Child Selectors

Selector	Description	CSS Version
:first-child	Selects elements that are the first children of their containing elements.	2
:last-child	Selects elements that are the last children of their containing elements.	3
:only-child	Selects elements that are the sole element defined by their containing element.	3
:only-of-type	Selects elements that are the sole element of their type defined by their containing element.	3

Using the :first-child Selector

The :first-child selector will match elements that are the first element defined by the element that contains them (the *parent* element, as it is known). Listing 18-2 shows the :first-child selector in use.

Listing 18-2. Using the :first-child Selector

```
<!DOCTYPE HTML>
<html>
    <head>
        <title>Example</title>
        <style type="text/css">
            :first-child {
                border: thin black solid;
                padding: 4px;
            }
        </style>
    </head>
    <body>
        <a href="http://apress.com">Visit the Apress website</a>
        <p>I like <span>apples</span> and <span>oranges</span>.</p>
        <a href="http://w3c.org">Visit the W3C website</a>
    </body>
</html>
```

In Listing 18-2, I have used the :first-child selector on its own, meaning that it will match any element that is the first child of its containing element. You can see which elements are selected in Figure 18-2.

Figure 18-2. Using the :first-child selector

You can be more specific by using the :first-child selector as a modifier and, optionally, combining it with other selectors. Listing 18-3 shows how.

Listing 18-3. Combining the :first-child Selector with Other Selectors

```
<!DOCTYPE HTML>
<html>
    <head>
        <title>Example</title>
        <style type="text/css">
            p > span:first-child {
                border: thin black solid;
                padding: 4px;
            }
        </style>
    </head>
    <body>
        <a href="http://apress.com">Visit the Apress website</a>
        <p>I like <span>apples</span> and <span>oranges</span>.</p>
        <a href="http://w3c.org">Visit the W3C website</a>
    </body>
</html>
```

This selector will match any span element that is the first child of a p element. There is only one such element in the HTML in this example, and you can see the match in Figure 18-3.

Figure 18-3. Combining the :first-child selector with another selector

Using the :last-child Selector

The :last-child selector selects elements that are the last elements defined by their containing element. Listing 18-4 shows the :last-child selector in use.

Listing 18-4. Using the :last-child Selector

```
<!DOCTYPE HTML>
<html>
    <head>
        <title>Example</title>
        <style type="text/css">
            :last-child {
                border: thin black solid;
                padding: 4px;
            }
        </style>
    </head>
    <body>
        <a href="http://apress.com">Visit the Apress website</a>
        <p>I like <span>apples</span> and <span>oranges</span>.</p>
        <a href="http://w3c.org">Visit the W3C website</a>
    </body>
</html>
```

You can see which elements this selector matches in Figure 18-4. Notice that there is a border around the content area. This happens because the body element is the last child of the html element and is, therefore, matched by the selector.

Figure 18-4. Using the :last-child selector

Using the :only-child Selector

The :only-child selector matches elements that are the only elements contained by their parent. Listing 18-5 shows this selector in use.

Listing 18-5. Using the :only-child Selector

```
<!DOCTYPE HTML>
<html>
    <head>
        <title>Example</title>
        <style type="text/css">
            :only-child {
                border: thin black solid;
                padding: 4px;
            }
        </style>
    </head>
    <body>
        <a href="http://apress.com">Visit the Apress website</a>
        <p>I like <span>apples</span> and oranges.</p>
        <a href="http://w3c.org">Visit the W3C website</a>
    </body>
</html>
```

The only element that has a single child is the p element, which contains one span element. You can see that this is only element the selector matches in Figure 18-5.

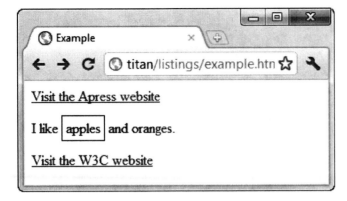

Figure 18-5. Using the :only-child selector

Using the :only-of-type selector

The :only-of-type selector matches elements that are the only child of their type defined by their parent. Listing 18-6 provides a demonstration.

Listing 18-6. Using the :only-of-type Selector

```
<!DOCTYPE HTML>
<html>
    <head>
        <title>Example</title>
        <style type="text/css">
            :only-of-type {
                border: thin black solid;
                padding: 4px;
            }
        </style>
    </head>
    <body>
        <a href="http://apress.com">Visit the Apress website</a>
        <p>I like <span>apples</span> and oranges.</p>
        <a href="http://w3c.org">Visit the W3C website</a>
    </body>
</html>
```

You can see the elements that this selector matches in Figure 18-6. You can see that this selector matches quite widely when used on its own. In any document, there are usually a number of elements that are the only ones of their type defined by their parent. Of course, you can narrow the match by combining this selector with others.

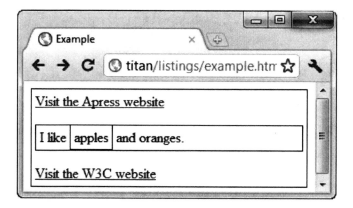

Figure 18-6. Using the :only-of-type selector

Using the nth-Child Selectors

The *nth-child selectors* are similar to the child selectors I described in the previous section, but they allow you to specify an index to match elements in a particular position. Table 18-4 summarizes the nth-child selectors.

Table 18-4. The nth-Child Selectors

Selector	Description	CSS Version
:nth-child(n)	Selects elements that are the nth child of their parent.	3
:nth-last-child(n)	Selects elements that are the nth from last child of their parent.	3
:nth-of-type(n)	Selects elements that are the nth child of their type defined by their parent.	3
:nth-last-of-type(n)	Selects elements that are the nth from last child of their type defined by their parent.	3

Each of these selectors takes an argument, which is the index of the element you are interested in; the indexes start at 1. Listing 18-7 shows the :nth-child selector in use.

Listing 18-7. Using the :nth-child Selector

```
<!DOCTYPE HTML>
<html>
    <head>
        <title>Example</title>
        <style type="text/css">
```

445

```
                    body > :nth-child(2) {
                        border: thin black solid;
                        padding: 4px;
                    }
                </style>
        </head>
        <body>
            <a href="http://apress.com">Visit the Apress website</a>
            <p>I like <span>apples</span> and oranges.</p>
            <a href="http://w3c.org">Visit the W3C website</a>
        </body>
    </html>
```

In Listing 18-7, I have selected all elements that are the second child of a body element. There is only one such element, as shown in Figure 18-7.

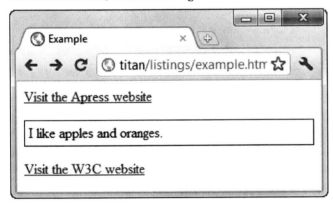

Figure 18-7. Using the :nth-child element

I am not going to demonstrate the other nth-child selectors because they function in the same way as the corresponding regular child selector, with the addition of an index value.

Using the UI Pseudo-Class Selectors

The UI pseudo-class selectors allow you to select elements based on their state. Table 18-5 describes the UI selectors.

Table 18-5. The UI Selectors

Selector	Description	CSS Version
:enabled	Selects elements that are in their enabled state.	3
:disabled	Selects elements that are in their disabled state.	3

:checked	Selects elements that are in a checked state.	3
:default	Selects default elements.	3
:valid :invalid	Selects input elements that are valid or invalid, based on input validation.	3
:in-range :out-of-range	Selects constrained input elements that are within or outside the specified range.	3
:required :optional	Selects input elements based on the presence of the required attribute.	3

Selecting Enabled/Disabled Elements

Some elements have enabled and disabled states. Those that do are the ones that can be used to collect input from the user. The :enabled and :disabled selectors will not match any element that cannot be disabled. Listing 18-8 gives an example of using the :enabled selector.

Listing 18-8. Using the :enabled Selector

```
<!DOCTYPE HTML>
<html>
    <head>
        <title>Example</title>
        <style type="text/css">
            :enabled {
               border: thin black solid;
               padding: 4px;
            }
        </style>
    </head>
    <body>
        <textarea> This is an enabled textarea</textarea>
        <textarea disabled> This is a disabled textarea</textarea>
    </body>
</html>
```

The HTML in Listing 18-8 contains two textarea elements, one of which defines the disabled attribute. The :enabled selector will select the first textarea but not the second, as you can see in Figure 18-8.

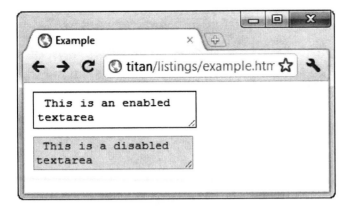

Figure 18-8. Using the :enabled selector

Selecting Checked Elements

Radio buttons and check boxes that are checked (either through the checked attribute or by the user) can be selected through the :checked selector. The problem in demonstrating this selector is that there isn't much styling that you can apply to check boxes and radio buttons. Listing 18-9 shows the application of the :checked selector.

Listing 18-9. Using the :checked Selector

```
<!DOCTYPE HTML>
<html>
    <head>
        <title>Example</title>
        <meta name="author" content="Adam Freeman"/>
        <meta name="description" content="A simple example"/>
        <link rel="shortcut icon" href="favicon.ico" type="image/x-icon" />
        <style>
            :checked + span {
                background-color: red;
                color: white;
                padding: 5px;
                border: medium solid black;
            }
        </style>
    </head>
    <body>
        <form method="post" action="http://titan:8080/form">
            <p>
                <label for="apples">Do you like apples:</label>
                <input type="checkbox" id="apples" name="apples"/>
                <span>This will go red when checked</span>
            </p>
            <input type="submit" value="Submit"/>
```

```
        </form>
    </body>
</html>
```

To get around the styling limitations, I have used the sibling selector (described in Chapter 17) to change the appearance of the span element, which adjacent to the check box. You can see the transition from unchecked to checked in Figure 18-9.

Figure 18-9. Selecting checked elements

There is no specific selector for unchecked elements, but you can combine :checked with the negation selector, which is described in the section "Using the Negation Selector," later in this chapter.

Selecting Default Elements

The :default element selects the default element from among a group of similar elements. For example, the submit button is always the default button in a form. You can see the :default selector used in Listing 18-10.

Listing 18-10. Using the :default Element

```
<!DOCTYPE HTML>
<html>
    <head>
        <title>Example</title>
        <meta name="author" content="Adam Freeman"/>
        <meta name="description" content="A simple example"/>
        <link rel="shortcut icon" href="favicon.ico" type="image/x-icon" />
        <style>
            :default {
                outline: medium solid red;
            }
```

```
            </style>
        </head>
        <body>
            <form method="post" action="http://titan:8080/form">
                <p>
                    <label for="name">Name: <input id="name" name="name"/></label>
                </p>
                <button type="submit">Submit Vote</button>
                <button type="reset">Reset</button>
            </form>
        </body>
</html>
```

This selector is most often used with the outline property, which I describe in Chapter 19. You can see the effect of this selector in Figure 18-10.

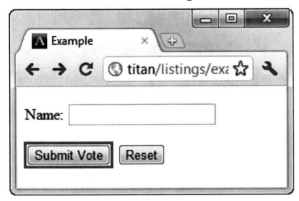

Figure 18-10. Using the :default selector

Selecting Valid and Invalid input Elements

The :valid and :invalid selectors match input elements that have met or failed their input validation requirements, respectively. You can learn more about input validation in Chapter 14. Listing 18-11 shows these selectors in use.

Listing 18-11. Using the :valid and :invalid Selectors

```
<!DOCTYPE HTML>
<html>
    <head>
        <title>Example</title>
        <meta name="author" content="Adam Freeman"/>
        <meta name="description" content="A simple example"/>
        <link rel="shortcut icon" href="favicon.ico" type="image/x-icon" />
        <style>
            :invalid {
                outline: medium solid red;
```

```
            }
            :valid {
                outline: medium solid green;
            }
        </style>
    </head>
    <body>
        <form method="post" action="http://titan:8080/form">
            <p>
                <label for="name">Name: <input required id="name" name="name"/></label>
            </p>
            <p>
                <label for="name">City: <input required id="city" name="city"/></label>
            </p>
            <button type="submit">Submit</button>
        </form>
    </body>
</html>
```

In Listing 18-11, I have applied a red outline for invalid elements and a green outline for valid elements. There are two input elements in the document, and both have the required attribute. This means that they will be valid only if a value has been entered. You can see the effect of these selectors in Figure 18-11.

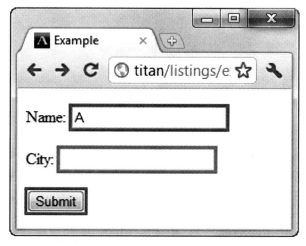

Figure 18-11. Selecting valid and invalid input elements

■ **Tip** Notice that the submit button has been affected as well, at least in Chrome. This occurs because the logic behind the :valid selector is fairly simplistic and selects any input element that is not invalid. To filter out certain input elements, you can use the attribute selectors described in Chapter 17, or a more specific selector, such as those described next.

451

Selecting input Elements with Range Limitations

A more specific variation on input validation is to select input elements that have a constraint on the range of values that they can contain. The :in-range selector matches input elements that are in range and the :out-of-range selector selects those that are not. Listing 18-12 shows these attributes in use.

Listing 18-12. Using the :in-range and :out-of-range Selectors

```
<!DOCTYPE HTML>
<html>
    <head>
        <title>Example</title>
        <meta name="author" content="Adam Freeman"/>
        <meta name="description" content="A simple example"/>
        <link rel="shortcut icon" href="favicon.ico" type="image/x-icon" />
        <style>
            :in-range {
                outline: medium solid green;
            }
            :out-of-range: {
                outline: medium solid red;
            }
        </style>
    </head>
    <body>
        <form method="post" action="http://titan:8080/form">
            <p>
                <label for="price">
                    $ per unit in your area:
                    <input type="number" min="0" max="100"
                            value="1" id="price" name="price"/>
                </label>
            </p>
            <input type="submit" value="Submit"/>
        </form>
    </body>
</html>
```

As I write this, none of the mainstream browsers implement the :out-of-range selector, and only Chrome and Opera support the :in-range selector. I expect this to change quickly because this functionality is tied to the new HTML5 support, which is likely to have very widespread adoption. You can see the effect of the :in-range selector in Figure 18-12.

Figure 18-12. The effect of the :in-range selector

Selecting Required and Optional input Elements

The :required selector matches input elements that have the required attribute. This ensures that the user must enter a value before submitting the HTML form with which the input element is associated (you can get more details about the required attribute in Chapter 14). The :optional selector selects input elements that do not have the required attribute. Both attributes are shown in Listing 18-13.

Listing 18-13. Selecting Required and Optional input Elements

```
<!DOCTYPE HTML>
<html>
    <head>
        <title>Example</title>
        <meta name="author" content="Adam Freeman"/>
        <meta name="description" content="A simple example"/>
        <link rel="shortcut icon" href="favicon.ico" type="image/x-icon" />
        <style>
            :required {
                outline: medium solid green;
            }
            :optional {
                outline: medium solid red;
            }
        </style>
    </head>
    <body>
        <form method="post" action="http://titan:8080/form">
            <p>
                <label for="price1">
                    $ per unit in your area:
                    <input type="number" min="0" max="100" required
                        value="1" id="price1" name="price1"/>
                </label>
                <label for="price2">
                    $ per unit in your area:
```

```
                    <input type="number" min="0" max="100"
                            value="1" id="price2" name="price2"/>
                </label>
            </p>
            <input type="submit" value="Submit"/>
        </form>
    </body>
</html>
```

In Listing 18-13, I have defined two number type input elements. One has the required attribute, but otherwise the two are identical. You can see the effect of the selectors and the associated styles in Figure 18-13. Note that the submit type input has also been selected. The :optional selector doesn't distinguish between types of input elements.

Figure 18-13. Selecting required and optional input elements

Using the Dynamic Pseudo-Class Selectors

The *dynamic pseudo-class* selectors are so-called because they match elements based on conditions that change, as opposed to the fixed state of the document. The division between static and dynamic selectors has blurred with the wider use of JavaScript to modify the documents contents and the state of elements, but these are still considered to be a separate category of selectors.

Using the :link and :visited Selectors

The :link selector matches hyperlinks and the :visited selector matches those hyperlinks that the user has previously visited. Table 18-6 summarizes these selectors.

Table 18-6. The :link and :visited Selectors

Selector	Description	CSS Version
:link	Selects link elements.	1
:visited	Selects link elements that the user has visited.	1

Browsers are free to decide how long a link remains visited after a user has clicked on it. When the user clears the browser history, or when the history naturally times out, links will return to the unvisited state. Listing 18-14 shows these selectors in use.

Listing 18-14. Using the :link and :visited Selectors

```
<!DOCTYPE HTML>
<html>
    <head>
        <title>Example</title>
        <style type="text/css">
            :link {
                border: thin black solid;
                background-color: lightgrey;
                padding: 4px;
                color:red;
            }
            :visited {
                background-color: grey;
                color:white;
            }
        </style>
    </head>
    <body>
        <a href="http://apress.com">Visit the Apress website</a>
        <p>I like <span>apples</span> and oranges.</p>
        <a href="http://w3c.org">Visit the W3C website</a>
    </body>
</html>
```

The only point to note in this example is that only some properties can be applied to links using the :visited selector. You can change the colors and the font, but that's about it. You can see the change when a link is visited in Figure 18-14. I start with a pair of links that have not been visited and click one of them to go to the http://apress.com web site. When I return to the example HTML, the visited link is styled differently.

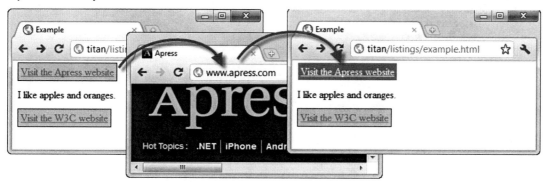

Figure 18-14. Using the :link and :visited selectors

■ **Tip** The :visited selector will match any link for which the href property is a URL that the user has visited from any page, not just your page. The most common use for the :visited selector is to apply a style so that visited links are not differentiated from unvisited ones.

Using the :hover Selector

The :hover selector will match any element that the user's mouse hovers over. The selected elements change as the user moves their mouse around the document. Table 18-7 describes this selector.

Table 18-7. The :hover Selector

Selector:	:hover
Matches:	The elements that occupy the position onscreen under the mouse pointer
Since CSS Version:	2

The browser is free to interpret the :hover selector in a way that makes sense for the display that is being used, but most browsers associate the selector with the movement of the mouse over the window. Listing 18-15 shows the selector being used.

Listing 18-15. Using the :hover Selector

```
<!DOCTYPE HTML>
<html>
    <head>
        <title>Example</title>
        <style type="text/css">
            :hover {
                border: thin black solid;
                padding: 4px;
            }
        </style>
    </head>
    <body>
        <a href="http://apress.com">Visit the Apress website</a>
        <p>I like <span>apples</span> and oranges.</p>
        <a href="http://w3c.org">Visit the W3C website</a>
    </body>
</html>
```

This selector will match multiple nested elements, as you can see in Figure 18-15.

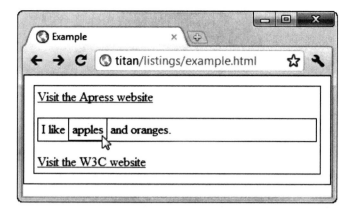

Figure 18-15. Using the :hover selector

Using the :active Selector

The :active selector matches elements during the period when the user is activating them. Once again, browsers have latitude about how they interpret this activation, but for most browsers it occurs when the mouse is pressed (or in result to a finger press on a touch screen). Table 18-8 summarizes the :active selector.

Table 18-8. *The :active Selector*

Selector:	:active
Matches:	The elements that are presently activated by the user; this usually means those elements that are under the pointer when the mouse button is pressed
Since CSS Version:	2

Listing 18-16 gives an example of using this selector.

Listing 18-16. Using the :active Selector

```
<!DOCTYPE HTML>
<html>
    <head>
        <title>Example</title>
        <style type="text/css">
            :active {
                border: thin black solid;
                padding: 4px;
            }
        </style>
```

```
    </head>
    <body>
        <a href="http://apress.com">Visit the Apress website</a>
        <p>I like <span>apples</span> and oranges.</p>
        <button>Hello</button>
    </body>
</html>
```

I have added a button to the markup in the listing, but the :active selector isn't limited to elements with which the user can interact. Any element in which the mouse has been pressed will be selected, as you can see in Figure 18-16.

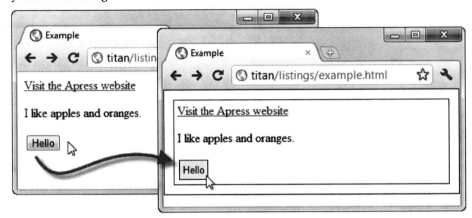

Figure 18-16. Using the :active selector

Using the :focus Selector

The last of the dynamic pseudo-class selectors is :focus, which selects elements while they have the focus. Table 18-9 summarizes this selector.

Table 18-9. The :focus Selector

Selector:	:focus
Matches:	Selects the element that has the focus
Since CSS Version:	2

Listing 18-17 demonstrates the use of this selector.

Listing 18-17. Using the :focus Selector

```
<!DOCTYPE HTML>
<html>
```

```
<head>
    <title>Example</title>
    <style type="text/css">
        :focus{
            border: thin black solid;
            padding: 4px;
        }
    </style>
</head>
<body>
    <form>
        Name: <input type="text" name="name"/>
        <p/>
        City: <input type="text" name="city"/>
        <p/>
        <input type="submit"/>
    </form>
</body>
</html>
```

The style is applied to each element, in turn, as I tab through the input elements in the markup. You can see the effect shown in Figure 18-17.

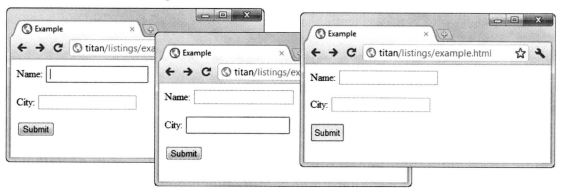

Figure 18-17. The effect of the :focus selector

Other Pseudo-Selectors

There are a few selectors that don't fit neatly into the categories I have used to group selectors in this chapter. In the following sections, I'll explain each of them in turn.

Using the Negation Selector

The negation selector lets you invert any selection. It is a surprisingly useful selector, and it is often overlooked. Table 18-10 summarizes the negation selector.

Table 18-10. The Negation Selector

Selector:	:not(<selector>)
Matches:	Inverts the selection selector
Since CSS Version:	3

Listing 18-18 shows the negation selector in use.

Listing 18-18. Using the Negation Selector

```
<!DOCTYPE HTML>
<html>
    <head>
        <title>Example</title>
        <style type="text/css">
            a:not([href*="apress"]) {
                border: thin black solid;
                padding: 4px;
            }
        </style>
    </head>
    <body>
        <a href="http://apress.com">Visit the Apress website</a>
        <p>I like <span>apples</span> and oranges.</p>
        <a href="http://w3c.org">Visit the W3C website</a>
    </body>
</html>
```

This selector matches all a elements that don't have an href element that contains the string apress. You can see the effect of this selector in Figure 18-18.

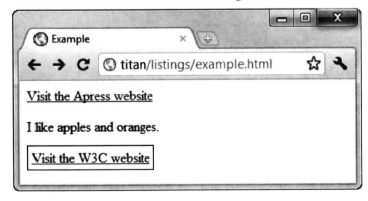

Figure 18-18. Using the negation selector

Using the :empty Selector

The :empty selector matches elements that define no children. This selector is summarized in Table 18-11. It is hard to illustrate this selector because its matches contain no content.

Table 18-11. The :empty Selector

Selector:	:empty
Matches:	Selects elements that contain no child elements
Since CSS Version:	3

Using the :lang Selector

The :lang selector matches elements based on the lang global attribute (described in Chapter 3). Table 18-12 summarizes this selector.

Table 18-12. The :lang Selector

Selector:	:lang(*<target language>*)
Matches:	Selects elements based on the value of the lang global attribute
Since CSS Version:	2

Listing 18-19 shows the lang selector in use.

Listing 18-19. Using the lang Selector

```
<!DOCTYPE HTML>
<html>
    <head>
        <title>Example</title>
        <style type="text/css">
            :lang(en) {
                border: thin black solid;
                padding: 4px;
            }
        </style>
    </head>
    <body>
        <a lang="en-us" id="apressanchor" class="class1 class2" href="http://apress.com">
            Visit the Apress website
        </a>
        <p>I like <span lang="en-uk" class="class2">apples</span> and oranges.</p>
```

```
        <a lang="en" id="w3canchor" href="http://w3c.org">Visit the W3C website</a>
    </body>
</html>
```

This selector matches elements that have a lang attribute that denotes they are written in English. The effect of the :lang selector is the same as the |= attribute selector example in Listing 17-8 in Chapter 17.

Using the :target Selector

In Chapter 3, I mention that you could append a fragment identifier to a URL to navigate directly to an element based on the value of the id global attribute. For example, if the HTML document example.html has an element with an id value of myelement, then you can navigate directly to that element by requesting example.html#myelement. The :target selector matches the element that the URL fragment identifier refers to. Table 18-13 summarizes this selector.

Table 18-13. The :target Selector

Selector:	:target
Matches:	Selects the element referred to by the URL fragment identifier
Since CSS Version:	3

Listing 18-20 shows the :target selector in action.

Listing 18-20. Using the :target Selector

```
<!DOCTYPE HTML>
<html>
    <head>
        <title>Example</title>
        <style type="text/css">
            :target {
                border: thin black solid;
                padding: 4px;
                color:red;
            }
        </style>
    </head>
    <body>
        <a href="http://apress.com">Visit the Apress website</a>
        <p id="mytarget">I like <span>apples</span> and oranges.</p>
        <a id="w3clink" href="http://w3c.org">Visit the W3C website</a>
    </body>
</html>
```

You can see how the requested URL changes the element matched by the :target selector in Figure 18-19.

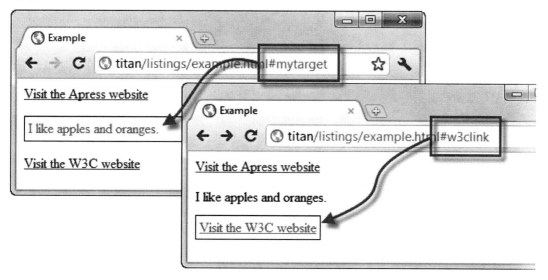

Figure 18-19. Using the :target selector

Summary

In this chapter I have described the CSS selectors, which are the means by which you identify the elements that you want to apply a style to. The selectors allow you to match elements in broad sweeps or, by combining selectors, narrow your focus to elements in particular parts of your HTML documents. Learning the selectors is the key to getting the most out of CSS.

CHAPTER 19

Using Borders and Backgrounds

In this chapter, I introduce the properties that you can use to apply background and borders to an element. These are very commonly used features that have been enhanced in CSS3. For example, you can now create borders with curved edges, use images for borders, and create drop shadows for elements. These might seem like simple things, but their omission from CSS has led to endless efforts to provide these features in other ways, with mixed success. Table 19-1 provides the summary for this chapter.

Table 19-1. Chapter Summary

Problem	Solution	Listing
Apply a border to an element.	Use the `border-width`, `border-style`, and `border-color` properties.	19-1
Apply a border to a single edge of the element box.	Use the side-specific properties, such as `border-top-width`, `border-top-style`, and `border-top-color`.	19-2
Specify the style, color, and width of a border in a single declaration.	Use the `border` property to set the border for all edges, or the `border-top`, `border-bottom`, `border-left`, and `border-right` properties to set the border for a single edge.	19-3
Create a border with rounded corners.	Use the `border-radius` shorthand property or one of the related edge-specific properties.	19-4, 19-5
Use an image to create a border.	Use the `border-image` shorthand property or one of the more specific related properties to set individual characteristics.	19-6, 19-7
Define a background color or image.	Use the `background-color` or `background-image` properties.	19-8
Specify the position of a background image.	Use the `background-position` property.	19-9

Specify the relationship between the background and the scrolling region of an element.	Use the background-attachment property.	19-10
Specify the region in which the background is drawn and the region in which it is visible.	Use the background-origin and background-clip properties.	19-11, 19-12
Set all of the background-related properties in a single declaration.	Use the background shorthand property.	19-13
Add box shadows to an element.	Use box-shadow property.	19-14, 19-15

Applying a Border

Let's start with the properties that control borders. These are very commonly applied and they will give you something visible to work with when you consider the margin and padding properties in Chapter 20. The three key properties for basic borders are border-width, border-style, and border-color. Table 19-2 describes all three properties.

Table 19-2. The Basic Border Properties

Property	Description	Values
border-width	Sets the width of the border.	See Table 19-3.
border-style	Sets the style used to draw the border.	See Table 19-4.
border-color	Sets the color of the border.	<color>

You can see these properties in use in Listing 19-1.

Listing 19-1. Defining a Basic Border

```
<!DOCTYPE HTML>
<html>
    <head>
        <title>Example</title>
        <meta name="author" content="Adam Freeman"/>
        <meta name="description" content="A simple example"/>
```

```
    <link rel="shortcut icon" href="favicon.ico" type="image/x-icon" />
    <style type="text/css">
        p {
            border-width: 5px;
            border-style: solid;
            border-color: black;
        }
    </style>
</head>
<body>
<p>
    There are lots of different kinds of fruit - there are over 500 varieties
    of banana alone. By the time we add the countless types of apples, oranges,
    and other well-known fruit, we are faced with thousands of choices.
</p>
</body>
</html>
```

In Listing 19-1, I have used a p element to denote a paragraph, and the style element to apply a border using the border-width, border-style, and border-color properties.

Defining the Border Width

You may express the border-width property as a regular CSS length, as a percentage of the width of the area that the border will be drawn around, or as one of three shortcut values. Table 19-3 describes these options. The default border-width value is medium.

Table 19-3. *Values for the border-width Property*

Value	Description
<length>	Sets the border width to a length expressed in CSS measurement units such as em, px, or cm.
<perc>%	Sets the border width to a *<perc>* percent of the *width* of the area around which the border will be drawn.
thin medium thick	Sets the border width to preset widths, the meanings of which are defined by each browser, but each of which are progressively thicker.

Defining the Border Style

The border-style property can be one of the values shown in Table 19-4. The default value is none, meaning that no border is drawn.

Table 19-4. Values for the border-style Property

Value	Description
none	No border will be drawn.
dashed	The border will be a series of rectangular dashes.
dotted	The border will be a series of circular dots.
double	The border will be two parallel lines with a gap between them.
groove	The border will appear to have be sunken into the page.
inset	The border will be such that the content looks sunken into the page.
outset	The border will be such that the content looks raised from the page.
ridge	The border will appear raised from the page.
solid	The border will be a single, unbroken line.

You can see how each of these border types appear in Figure 19-1.

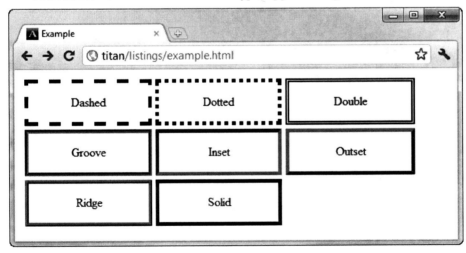

Figure 19-1. The different values for the border-style property

Some browsers have problems applying two-color border styles, such as inset and outset, when the border-color property is black. These browsers, including Google Chrome, use black for both tones, which creates an effect identical to the solid style. Smarter browsers know to use a shade of gray, including Firefox. To create the figure (which shows Chrome), I set the border-color property to gray for the groove, inset, outset, and ridge styles.

Applying a Border to a Single Side

You can apply different borders to each side of an element using properties that are more specific, as described in Table 19-5.

***Table 19-5.** The Side-Specific Border Properties*

Property	Description	Values
border-top-width border-top-style border-top-color	Defines the top border.	Values are the same as for the generic properties.
border-bottom-width border-bottom-style border-bottom-color	Defines the bottom border.	Values are the same as for the generic properties.
border-left-width border-left-style border-left-color	Defines the left border.	Values are the same as for the generic properties.
border-right-width border-right-style border-right-color	Defines the right border.	Values are the same as for the generic properties.

You can either build up the border using these properties, or use them in conjunction with their more generic counterparts to override specific edges of a border. Listing 19-2 shows the latter approach.

Listing 19-2. Using the Side-Specific Border Properties

```
<!DOCTYPE HTML>
<html>
    <head>
        <title>Example</title>
        <meta name="author" content="Adam Freeman"/>
        <meta name="description" content="A simple example"/>
        <link rel="shortcut icon" href="favicon.ico" type="image/x-icon" />
        <style type="text/css">
            p {
                border-width: 5px;
                border-style: solid;
                border-color: black;
                border-left-width: 10px;
                border-left-style: dotted;
                border-top-width: 10px;
                border-top-style: dotted;
```

```
        }
      </style>
   </head>
   <body>
   <p>
        There are lots of different kinds of fruit - there are over 500 varieties
        of banana alone. By the time we add the countless types of apples, oranges,
        and other well-known fruit, we are faced with thousands of choices.
   </p>
   </body>
</html>
```

You can see the effect of these properties in Figure 19-2.

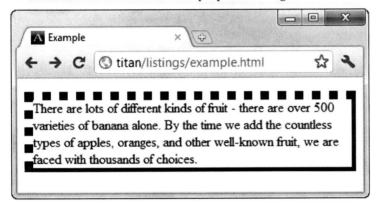

Figure 19-2. Applying borders to individual edges

Using the border Shorthand Properties

Rather than use individual properties for the style, width, and color, you can use shorthand properties that set all three values in one step. Table 19-6 describes these properties.

Table 19-6. The Shorthand border Properties

Property	Description	Values
border	Sets the border for all edges.	*<width> <style> <color>*
border-top border-bottom border-left border-right	Sets the border for a single edge.	*<width> <style> <color>*

You set the values for these properties by specifying the width, style, and color values in a single line, separated by spaces, as shown in Listing 19-3.

Listing 19-3. Using the border Shorthand Properties

```
<!DOCTYPE HTML>
<html>
    <head>
        <title>Example</title>
        <meta name="author" content="Adam Freeman"/>
        <meta name="description" content="A simple example"/>
        <link rel="shortcut icon" href="favicon.ico" type="image/x-icon" />
        <style type="text/css">
            p {
                border: medium solid black;
                border-top: solid 10px;
            }
        </style>
    </head>
    <body>
    <p>
        There are lots of different kinds of fruit - there are over 500 varieties
        of banana alone. By the time we add the countless types of apples, oranges,
        and other well-known fruit, we are faced with thousands of choices.
    </p>
    </body>
</html>
```

Notice that I have not specified a color for the border-top property. If you omit one or more of the values, the browser will use whatever value has been previously defined; in this case, the color specified by the border shorthand property. You can see the effect of these properties in Figure 19-3.

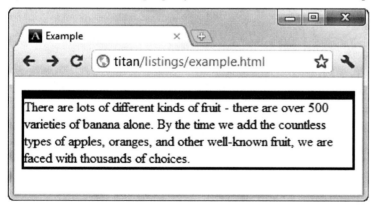

Figure 19-3. Using the border shorthand properties

Creating a Border with Rounded Corners

You can create a border with rounded corners using the border radius feature. There are five properties associated with this capability. Table 19-7 summarizes each of these.

Table 19-7. The Border radius Properties

Property	Description	Values

`border-top-left-radius`
`border-top-right-radius`
`border-bottom-left-radius`
`border-bottom-right-`
`radius`
	Sets the radius for a single corner.	A pair of length or percentage values. The percentages relate to the width and height of the border box.

`border-radius`	This shorthand property sets all corners at once.	One or four pairs of length or percentage values, separated by a / character.

You define a curved corner by specifying two radii values, either as a length or as a percentage. The first value specifies the horizontal radius, and the second specifies the vertical radius. Percentage values are of the horizontal and vertical size of the element's box. You can see how the radii values are used to determine the curve of a border in Figure 19-4.

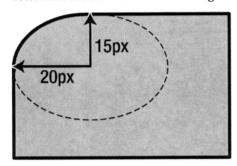

Figure 19-4. Using radii to specify the curve of a border

As you can see in the figure, the radii values are used to project an oval that intersects with the element's box, and shapes the corner of the border. Listing 19-4 shows these values expressed as part of a style declaration.

Listing 19-4. Creating a Curved Border

```
<!DOCTYPE HTML>
<html>
    <head>
        <title>Example</title>
        <meta name="author" content="Adam Freeman"/>
        <meta name="description" content="A simple example"/>
        <link rel="shortcut icon" href="favicon.ico" type="image/x-icon" />
        <style type="text/css">
            p {
                border: medium solid black;
                border-top-left-radius: 20px 15px;
            }
```

```
        </style>
    </head>
    <body>
    <p>
        There are lots of different kinds of fruit - there are over 500 varieties
        of banana alone. By the time we add the countless types of apples, oranges,
        and other well-known fruit, we are faced with thousands of choices.
    </p>
    </body>
</html>
```

If you supply only one value, then both the horizontal and vertical radii will use this value. You can see the effect, as shown by the browser, in Figure 19-5. I have magnified the curved border area to make it clearer to see.

Figure 19-5. Creating a curved border

▪ **Tip** Notice that the border touches the text in the figure. To create space between an element's content and its border, you add *padding*, which is covered in Chapter 20.

The border-radius shorthand property lets you specify one value for all four corners, or four individual values in a single value, as shown in Listing 19-5.

Listing 19-5. Using the border-radius Shorthand Property

```
<!DOCTYPE HTML>
<html>
    <head>
        <title>Example</title>
        <meta name="author" content="Adam Freeman"/>
        <meta name="description" content="A simple example"/>
        <link rel="shortcut icon" href="favicon.ico" type="image/x-icon" />
```

```
<style type="text/css">
    p {
        border: medium solid black;
    }
    #first {
        border-radius: 20px / 15px;
    }
    #second {
        border-radius: 50% 20px 25% 5em / 25% 15px 40px 55%
    }

</style>
</head>
<body>
<p id="first">
    There are lots of different kinds of fruit - there are over 500 varieties
    of banana alone. By the time we add the countless types of apples, oranges,
    and other well-known fruit, we are faced with thousands of choices.
</p>

<p id="second">
    There are lots of different kinds of fruit - there are over 500 varieties
    of banana alone. By the time we add the countless types of apples, oranges,
    and other well-known fruit, we are faced with thousands of choices.
</p>
</body>
</html>
```

In Listing 19-5, there are two paragraphs, each of which has its own border-radius declaration. The first declaration specifies just two values, which are applied to all four corners of the border. Notice that the horizontal values are separated from the vertical values by a / character. The second declaration specifies eight values. The first four values are the horizontal radius values for each corner and the last four are the horizontal counterparts. These sets of values are also separated by a / character.

You can see the effect of these declarations in Figure 19-6. The result is a little odd, but it demonstrates how you can use a single declaration to define a different curve for each corner, and how you can freely mix percentage and length values.

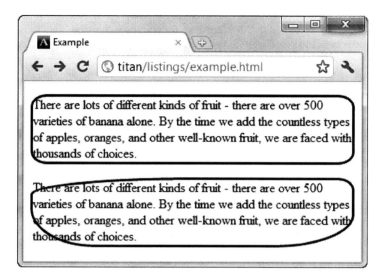

Figure 19-6. Using the border-radius shorthand property

Using Images As Borders

You are not limited to borders defined by the border-style property. You may also use images to create truly custom borders for your elements. There are five properties that configure individual aspects of an image border, plus a shorthand property that you may use to configure everything in a single declaration. Table 19-8 shows all six properties.

Table 19-8. *The border-image Properties*

Property	Description	Values
border-image-source	Sets the source of the image.	none or url(<*image*>)
border-image-slice	Sets the offsets for slicing the image.	1–4 <*length*> or <%> values, where the values relate to the width and height of the image
border-image-width	Sets the width of the border.	auto 1–4 <*length*> or <%> values
border-image-outset	Sets the area outside of the standard border that will be used to display the image border.	1–4 <*length*> or <%> values
border-image-repeat	The model by which the image is used to fill the border areas.	1 or 2 values from stretch, repeat, or round

| border-image | This shorthand property sets all values in one declaration. | Same as for individual properties; see the following |

The problem is that, as I write this, the mainstream browsers do not support these properties. You *can* use images as borders, but only through the shorthand property and only with the browser-specific prefixes that I described in Chapter 16 (and IE doesn't support this feature at all). This allows me to demonstrate the basic feature, but not to show you the individual properties. The browser-specific shorthand properties work in the same way as the border-image property, so you should have no problems transferring the examples in this section to the standard properties when the browsers support them.

Slicing an Image

The key to using an image as a border is *slicing*. You specify values that are offsets into the image, which the browser uses to slice the image into nine parts. To demonstrate the effect of the slices, I have created an image that will make it easy to see how the browser performs the slices, and uses each slice. You can see this image in Figure 19-7.

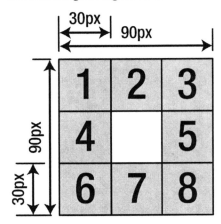

Figure 19-7. An image designed to demonstrate the border feature

This image is 90 pixels by 90 pixels, and each of the individual tiles are 30 pixels by 30 pixels. The middle tile is transparent. To slice the image, you provide insets from the top, right, bottom, and left edges of the image, expressed as lengths or percentages of the image size. You can provide different values for all four insets, or two values (which are used for the horizontal and vertical insets), or just a single value, which is then used for all four insets. For this image, I used a single value of 30px, which created the required slices, as shown in Figure 19-8.

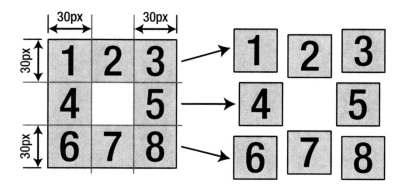

Figure19- 8. Slicing a border image

Slicing the image generates eight tiles. The tiles marked 1, 3, 6, and 8 are used to draw the corners of the border, and the tiles marked 2, 4, 5, and 7 are used to draw the border edges. Listing 19-6 shows the browser-specific properties used to slice an image and apply it as a border.

Listing 19-6. Slicing an Image and Using It As a Border

```
<!DOCTYPE HTML>
<html>
    <head>
        <title>Example</title>
        <meta name="author" content="Adam Freeman"/>
        <meta name="description" content="A simple example"/>
        <link rel="shortcut icon" href="favicon.ico" type="image/x-icon" />
        <style type="text/css">
            p {
                -webkit-border-image: url(bordergrid.png) 30 / 50px;
                -moz-border-image: url(bordergrid.png) 30 / 50px;
                -o-border-image: url(bordergrid.png) 30 / 50px;
            }
        </style>
    </head>
    <body>
    <p>
        There are lots of different kinds of fruit - there are over 500 varieties
        of banana alone. By the time we add the countless types of apples, oranges,
        and other well-known fruit, we are faced with thousands of choices.
    </p>
    </body>
</html>
```

Each property declaration has the same arguments. You have to use the url function to specify the image (this is required because the CSS specification reserves the right to implement other means of obtaining images). In each case, I have provided a single slice value of 30, matching the tile size of the example image. Note than when specifying the slice, you don't provide the units, as they are assumed to be pixels.

The / character is used to separate the slice values from the border width values. We can specify different widths for each side of the element, but I have provided a single value that will be used for all four; in this case, I have chosen a border width of 50px. Figure 19-9 shows how Chrome displays the image. Firefox and Opera look exactly the same.

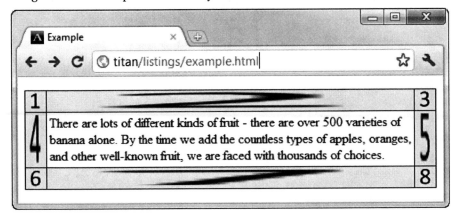

Figure 19-9. Using an image for a border

You can see how the browser has used each slice of the image. The slices marked 2 and 7 can be a little hard to make out, but they have been used for the top and bottom edges, respectively.

Controlling the Slice Repeat Style

You can see in Figure 19-10 that the slices have been stretched to fill the space available in the border. You can change the repeat style to get a different effect. This is the responsibility of the border-image-repeat property, but you can also specify the repeat style using the shorthand properties. Table 19-9 describes the values that you can use to define the repeat style.

Table 19-9. The border-image-repeat Style Values

Value	Description
stretch	The slice is stretched to fill the space (this is the default).
repeat	The slice is repeated to fill the space (this can lead to fragments of repeating).
round	The slice is stretched and repeated to fill the space without creating fragments.
space	The slice is repeated without creating fragments. Any remaining space is distributed around the slice.

As I write this, support for the repeat style values is patchy. None of the browsers support the space value, and Chrome doesn't support the round value. Listing 19-7 shows how you can use the repeat and round values with Firefox to change the border repeat style.

Listing 19-7. Controlling the Slice repeat Style

```
<!DOCTYPE HTML>
<html>
    <head>
        <title>Example</title>
        <meta name="author" content="Adam Freeman"/>
        <meta name="description" content="A simple example"/>
        <link rel="shortcut icon" href="favicon.ico" type="image/x-icon" />
        <style type="text/css">
            p {
                -moz-border-image: url(bordergrid.png) 30 / 50px round repeat;
            }
        </style>
    </head>
    <body>
    <p>
        There are lots of different kinds of fruit - there are over 500 varieties
        of banana alone. By the time we add the countless types of apples, oranges,
        and other well-known fruit, we are faced with thousands of choices.
    </p>
    </body>
</html>
```

In Listing 19-7, the first value specifies the horizontal repeat style, and the second specifies the vertical. If you provide just one value, it will be used for both the horizontal and vertical repeats. You can see the difference between these values in Figure 19-10.

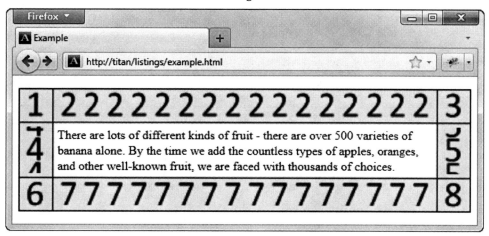

Figure 19-10. The round and repeat values for border slice repetition

Notice that the top and bottom edges don't contain any partial slices. The 2 and 7 numerals have been stretched slightly and then repeated, so that there are no broken bits. By contrast, the left and right edges, which are set to use the repeat style, are fragmented to fill the space.

Setting Element Backgrounds

The second visible area of the box model is the element's contents. In this section, I'll introduce the properties that you can use to style the background of this area. (For details of how to style the content itself, see Chapter 22.) The properties are described in Table 19-10.

Table 19-10. The background Properties

Property	Description	Values
background-color	Sets the background color for an element. The color is drawn behind any images.	`<color>`
background-image	Sets the background images for an element. If more than one image is specified, each subsequent image is drawn behind those that precede it.	none or url(image)
background-repeat	Sets the repeat style for images.	See Table 19-11.
background-size	Sets the size of a background image.	See Table 19-12.
background-position	Positions the background image.	See Table 19-13.
background-attachment	Sets the attachment style for images that are in an element that has a viewport.	See Table 19-14.
background-clip	Specifies the clipping style for images.	See Table 19-15.
background-origin	Positions the background image.	See Table 19-15.
background	Shorthand element.	See the following.

Setting the Background Color and Image

The starting point for element backgrounds is to set a background color or an image—or both—using background properties, as demonstrated in Listing 19-8.

Listing 19-8. Setting the Background Color and Image

```
<!DOCTYPE HTML>
<html>
    <head>
        <title>Example</title>
        <meta name="author" content="Adam Freeman"/>
        <meta name="description" content="A simple example"/>
        <link rel="shortcut icon" href="favicon.ico" type="image/x-icon" />
        <style type="text/css">
```

```
        p {
                border: medium solid black;
                background-color: lightgray;
                background-image: url(banana.png);
                background-size: 40px 40px;
                background-repeat: repeat-x;
        }
    </style>
</head>
<body>
<p>
    There are lots of different kinds of fruit - there are over 500 varieties
    of banana alone. By the time we add the countless types of apples, oranges,
    and other well-known fruit, we are faced with thousands of choices.
</p>
</body>
</html>
```

In this example, I have set the background-color to lightgray, and used the url function to load an image called banana.png for the background-image property. You can see the effect of this image in Figure 19-11. The background image is always drawn over the background color.

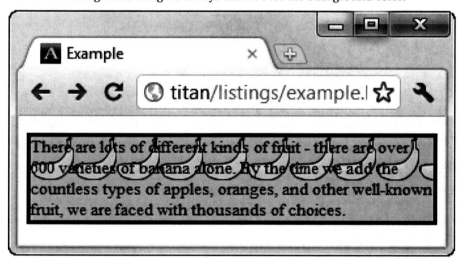

Figure 19-11. Using a background color and image

This image overwhelms the element's text somewhat, but then background images tend to do that unless chosen very carefully. Notice that the image is repeated horizontally across the element in the figure. This is achieved through the background-repeat property, the allowed values for which are described in Table 19-11.

481

Table 19-11. The background-repeat Values

Value	Description
repeat-x	Repeats the image horizontally; the image may be fragmented.
repeat-y	Repeats the image vertically; the image may be fragmented.
repeat	Repeats the image in both directions; the image may be fragmented.
space	The image is repeated to fill the space without creating fragments, and the remaining area is allocated evenly around the images.
round	The image is scaled so that it can be repeated without creating fragments.
no-repeat	The image is not repeated.

You can specify a value for both the horizontal and vertical repeats, but if you provide only one value, the browser will use that style of repeat in both directions. The exceptions are repeat-x and repeat-y, where the browser will use the no-repeat style for the second value.

Setting the Background Image Size

The image I have specified is too large for the element, so I have used the background-size property to specify that the image should be resized to 40 pixels by 40 pixels. In addition to lengths, you can specify percentages (which are derived from the width and height of the image), and some predefined values, described in Table 19-12.

Table 19-12. The background-size Values

Value	Description
contain	Scales the image, preserving the aspect ratio, to the largest size that can fit inside the display area.
cover	Scales the image, preserving the aspect ratio, to the smallest size that can fit inside the display area.
auto	This is the default value. The image will be displayed at full size.

The contain value ensures that the image is scaled so that all of it can be seen inside of the element. The browser determines if the image length or height is larger, and uses this as the axis for scaling. By contract, for the cover value, the browser selects the smallest value, and scales the image along this axis. This means that not all of the image will be displayed. You can see the two different size styles in Figure 19-12.

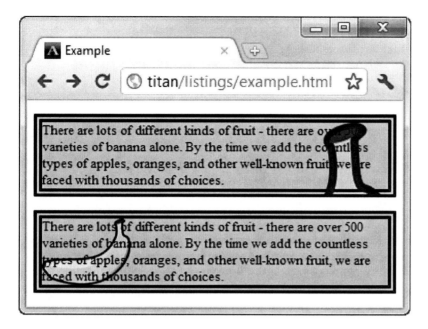

Figure 19-12. The contain and cover size styles

The banana image is taller than it is wide. This means that when you use the cover value, the image will be scaled so that the width is displayed fully, even if not all of the image height can be displayed. You can see this effect in the uppermost element Figure 19-12. When using the contain value, the image is scaled so that the largest axis is visible in its entirety, meaning that the entire image will be displayed, even if it doesn't cover the entire background area. You can see this effect in the lower element in Figure 19-12.

Setting the Background Image Position

The background-position property lets you instruct the browser as to where the background image should be located. This is most useful when you are not repeating the image. You can see this property in use in Listing 19-9.

Listing 19-9. Positioning the Background Image

```
<!DOCTYPE HTML>
<html>
    <head>
        <title>Example</title>
        <meta name="author" content="Adam Freeman"/>
        <meta name="description" content="A simple example"/>
        <link rel="shortcut icon" href="favicon.ico" type="image/x-icon" />
        <style type="text/css">
            p {
```

```
                border: 10px double black;
                background-color: lightgray;
                background-image: url(banana.png);
                background-size: 40px 40px;
                background-repeat: no-repeat;
                background-position: 30px 10px;
            }
        </style>
    </head>
    <body>
        <p>
            There are lots of different kinds of fruit - there are over 500 varieties
            of banana alone. By the time we add the countless types of apples, oranges,
            and other well-known fruit, we are faced with thousands of choices.
        </p>
    </body>
</html>
```

This declaration tells the browser to draw the background image 30 pixels from the left edge and 10 pixels from the top edge. I specified the position using lengths, but you can also use the predefined values shown in Table 19-13.

Table 19-13. The background-position Values

Value	Description
top	Positions the image at the top edge.
left	Positions the image at the left edge.
right	Positions the image at the right edge.
bottom	Positions the image at the bottom edge.
center	Positions the image at the mid-point.

The first value controls the vertical position and can be top, bottom, or center. The second value controls the horizontal position and can be left, right, or center. You can see the effect of positioning the image in Figure 19-13.

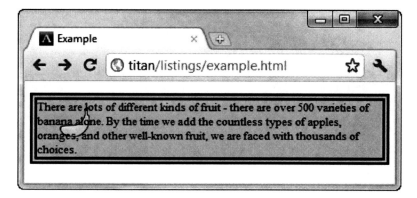

Figure 19-13. Positioning the background image

Setting the Attachment for the Background

When you apply a background to an element that has a viewport, you can specify how the background is attached to the content. A good example of an element with a viewport is textarea (described in Chapter 14), which will automatically add scrollbars to display content. Another common example is the body element, which can have scrollbars when the content is longer than the browser window (you can find details of the body element in Chapter 7). You control the background attachment using the background-attachment property. Table 19-14 describes the allowed values.

Table 19-14. The background-attachment Values

Value	Description
fixed	The background is fixed to the viewport, meaning that the background doesn't move when the content is scrolled.
local	The background is attached to the content, meaning that the background moves with the content when scrolled.
scroll	The background is fixed to the element, and does not scroll with the content.

Listing 19-10 shows the textarea element used with the border-attachment property.

Listing 19-10. Using the border-attachment Property

```
<!DOCTYPE HTML>
<html>
    <head>
        <title>Example</title>
        <meta name="author" content="Adam Freeman"/>
        <meta name="description" content="A simple example"/>
        <link rel="shortcut icon" href="favicon.ico" type="image/x-icon" />
```

```
<style type="text/css">
    textarea {
        border: medium solid black;
        background-color: lightgray;
        background-image: url(banana.png);
        background-size: 60px 60px;
        background-repeat: repeat;
        background-attachment: scroll;
    }
</style>
</head>
<body>
<p>
    <textarea rows="8" cols="30">
    There are lots of different kinds of fruit - there are over 500 varieties
    of banana alone. By the time we add the countless types of apples, oranges,
    and other well-known fruit, we are faced with thousands of choices.
    </textarea>
</p>
</body>
</html>
```

I can't demonstrate the different attachment modes in figures. This is something that you have to see in the browser yourself. To see the difference between the fixed and scroll modes, use the example HTML document, resize the browser window so that the textarea isn't fully shown, and then scroll using the browser scrollbar (not the textarea one).

Setting the Background Image Origin and Clipping Style

The origin of the background specifies where the background color and image are applied. The clipping style determines the region where the background color and image are drawn in the element's box. The background-origin and background-clip properties control these features, and each has the same three allowed values, which are described in Table 19-15.

Table 19-15. The background-origin and background-clip Values

Value	Description
border-box	The background color and image are drawn within the border box.
padding-box	The background color and image are drawn within the padding box.
content-box	The background color and image are drawn within the content box.

Listing 19-11 shows the use of the background-origin property.

Listing 19-11. Using the background-origin Property

```
<!DOCTYPE HTML>
<html>
    <head>
        <title>Example</title>
        <meta name="author" content="Adam Freeman"/>
        <meta name="description" content="A simple example"/>
        <link rel="shortcut icon" href="favicon.ico" type="image/x-icon" />
        <style type="text/css">
            p {
                border: 10px double black;
                background-color: lightgray;
                background-image: url(banana.png);
                background-size: 40px 40px;
                background-repeat: repeat;
                background-origin: border-box;
            }
        </style>
    </head>
    <body>
    <p>
        There are lots of different kinds of fruit - there are over 500 varieties
        of banana alone. By the time we add the countless types of apples, oranges,
        and other well-known fruit, we are faced with thousands of choices.
    </p>
    </body>
</html>
```

In Listing 19-11, I have selected the border-box value, which means that the browser will draw the background color and image under the border. I say under, because the border is always drawn over the background. You can see the effect in Figure 19-14.

Figure 19-14. Using the background-origin property

The background-clip property determines which portion of the background is visible by applying a *clipping box*. Anything outside the box is discarded and not shown. You have the same three values available as for the background-origin property, and you can see the effect of combining these properties in Listing 19-12.

Listing 19-12. Using the background-clip Property

```
<!DOCTYPE HTML>
<html>
    <head>
        <title>Example</title>
        <meta name="author" content="Adam Freeman"/>
        <meta name="description" content="A simple example"/>
        <link rel="shortcut icon" href="favicon.ico" type="image/x-icon" />
        <style type="text/css">
            p {
                border: 10px double black;
                background-color: lightgray;
                background-image: url(banana.png);
                background-size: 40px 40px;
                background-repeat: repeat;
                background-origin: border-box;
                background-clip: content-box;
            }
        </style>
    </head>
    <body>
    <p>
        There are lots of different kinds of fruit - there are over 500 varieties
        of banana alone. By the time we add the countless types of apples, oranges,
        and other well-known fruit, we are faced with thousands of choices.
    </p>
    </body>
</html>
```

This combination tells the browser to draw the background within the border box, but discard anything outside of the content box. You can see the effect, which is quite subtle, in Figure 19-15.

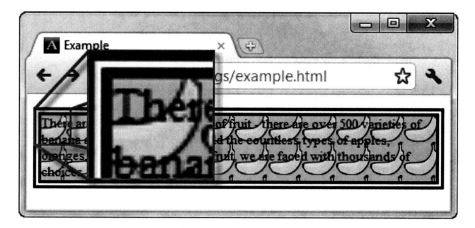

Figure 19-15. Using the border-origin and border-clip properties together

Using the background Shorthand Property

The background property allows you to set all of the different background values in a single declaration. Here is the format for the value of this property, referencing the individual properties:

background: <background-color> <background-position> <background-size>
    <background-repeat> <background-origin> <background-clip> <background-attachment>
    <background-image>

This is quite a lengthy value declaration, but you may omit values. If you do, then the browser will use the defaults. Listing 19-13 shows the border shorthand property in use.

Listing 19-13. Using the border Shorthand Property

```
<!DOCTYPE HTML>
<html>
    <head>
        <title>Example</title>
        <meta name="author" content="Adam Freeman"/>
        <meta name="description" content="A simple example"/>
        <link rel="shortcut icon" href="favicon.ico" type="image/x-icon" />
        <style type="text/css">
            p {
                border: 10px double black;
                background: lightgray top right no-repeat border-box content-box
                    local url(banana.png);
            }
        </style>
    </head>
    <body>
        <p>
        There are lots of different kinds of fruit - there are over 500 varieties
```

```
        of banana alone. By the time we add the countless types of apples, oranges,
        and other well-known fruit, we are faced with thousands of choices.
      </p>
    </body>
</html>
```

This single property is equivalent to the following set of individual properties:

```
background-color: lightgray;
background-position: top right;
background-repeat: no-repeat;
background-origin: border-box;
background-position: content-box;
background-attachment: local;
background-image: url(banana.png);
```

■ **Tip** Not all browsers support this property, at present.

Creating a Box Shadow

One of the most keenly awaited CSS3 features is the ability to add drop shadows to an element's box. You do this using the drop-shadow property, which is described in Table 19-16.

Table 19-16. The drop-shadow Property

Property	Description	Values
drop-shadow	Specifies a shadow for an element.	See Table 19-17.

The value for the box-shadow element is made up as follows:

box-shadow: hoffset voffset blur spread color inset

These individual value elements are described in Table 19-17.

Table 19-17. The Values of the box-shadow Property

Value	Description
hoffset	The horizontal offset, which is a length value. A positive value offsets the shadow to the right, and a negative value offsets the shadow to the left.
voffset	The vertical offset, which is a length value. A positive value offsets the shadow below the element's box, and a negative value offsets the shadow above the element's box.

blur   (Optional) Specifies the blur radius, which is a length value. The larger the value, the
                     more blurred the edge of the box. For the default value, 0, the edge of the box is sharp.

spread   (Optional) Specifies the spread radius, which is a length value. Positive values make the
                     shadow expand in all directions, and negative values cause the shadow to contract
                     toward the box.

color   (Optional) The color of the shadow. If omitted, the browser will select a color.

inset   (Optional) Causes the shadow to be inset inside the box. See Listing 19-15 for an
                     example.

▩ **Caution** Take care when omitting the `color` value. This should be an optional value, allowing the browser to apply a standard color, perhaps one that is appropriate for the user's operating system or browser choice. But at the time of writing, Webkit-based browsers won't draw a border in a color is not specified. For this reason, it is worth explicitly specifying a color in the `box-shadow` value.

You can see this property used in Listing 19-14.

Listing 19-14. Creating a Drop Shadow

```
<!DOCTYPE HTML>
<html>
    <head>
        <title>Example</title>
        <meta name="author" content="Adam Freeman"/>
        <meta name="description" content="A simple example"/>
        <link rel="shortcut icon" href="favicon.ico" type="image/x-icon" />
        <style type="text/css">
            p {
                border: 10px double black;

                box-shadow: 5px 4px 10px 2px gray;
            }
        </style>
    </head>
    <body>
    <p>
        There are lots of different kinds of fruit - there are over 500 varieties
        of banana alone. By the time we add the countless types of apples, oranges,
        and other well-known fruit, we are faced with thousands of choices.
    </p>
    </body>
</html>
```

You can see the effect of this property in Figure 19-16.

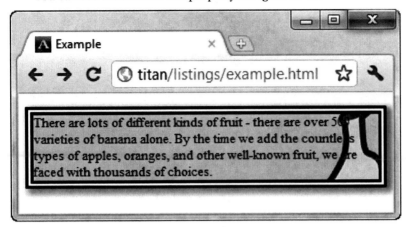

Figure 19-16. A box shadow applied to an element

You may define multiple shadows in a single box-shadow declaration. To do this, separate each declaration with a comma, as shown in Listing 19-15.

Listing 19-15. Applying Multiple Shadows to an Element

```
<!DOCTYPE HTML>
<html>
    <head>
        <title>Example</title>
        <meta name="author" content="Adam Freeman"/>
        <meta name="description" content="A simple example"/>
        <link rel="shortcut icon" href="favicon.ico" type="image/x-icon" />
        <style type="text/css">
            p {
                border: 10px double black;

                box-shadow: 5px 4px 10px 2px gray, 4px 4px 6px gray inset;
            }
        </style>
    </head>
    <body>
    <p>
        There are lots of different kinds of fruit - there are over 500 varieties
        of banana alone. By the time we add the countless types of apples, oranges,
        and other well-known fruit, we are faced with thousands of choices.
    </p>
    </body>
</html>
```

In Listing 19-15, I have defined two shadows, one of which is inset. You can see the effect in Figure 19-17.

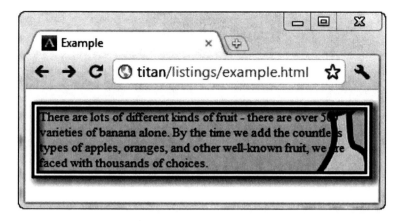

Figure 19-17. Defining multiple shadows for an element

Using Outlines

Outlines are an alternative to borders. They are most useful for temporarily drawing the attention of a user to an element, such as a button that must be pressed or an error in data entry. You draw outlines outside of the border box. The key difference between a border and an outline is that outlines are not considered to be part of the page, and so do not cause the page layout to be adjusted when you apply them. Table 19-18 describes the elements that relate to outlines.

Table 19-18. The outline Properties

Property	Description	Values
outline-color	Sets the color out the outline.	`<color>`
outline-offset	Sets the offset of the outline.	`<length>`
outline-style	Sets the style of the outline.	**This value is the same as for the `border-style` property. See Table 19-4.**
outline-width	Sets the width of the outline.	thin medium thick `<length>`
outline	This shorthand property sets the outline in a single declaration.	`<color>` `<style>` `<width>`

Listing 19-16 shows the application of an outline. I have included a simple script in this example so that I can demonstrate the way in which outlines are drawn without causing the page to be laid out again.

Listing 19-16. Using an Outline

```
<!DOCTYPE HTML>
<html>
    <head>
        <title>Example</title>
        <meta name="author" content="Adam Freeman"/>
        <meta name="description" content="A simple example"/>
        <link rel="shortcut icon" href="favicon.ico" type="image/x-icon" />
        <style>
            p {
                width: 30%;
                padding: 5px;
                border: medium double black;
                background-color: lightgray;
                margin: 2px;
                float: left;
            }
            #fruittext {
                outline: thick solid red;
            }
        </style>
    </head>
    <body>
        <p>
            There are lots of different kinds of fruit - there are over 500
            varieties of banana alone. By the time we add the countless types of
            apples, oranges, and other well-known fruit, we are faced with
            thousands of choices.
        </p>
        <p id="fruittext">
            There are lots of different kinds of fruit - there are over 500
            varieties of banana alone. By the time we add the countless types of
            apples, oranges, and other well-known fruit, we are faced with
            thousands of choices.
        </p>
        <p>
            There are lots of different kinds of fruit - there are over 500
            varieties of banana alone. By the time we add the countless types of
            apples, oranges, and other well-known fruit, we are faced with
            thousands of choices.
        </p>
        <button>Outline Off</button>
        <button>Outline On</button>
        <script>
            var buttons = document.getElementsByTagName("BUTTON");
            for (var i = 0; i < buttons.length; i++) {
```

```
            buttons[i].onclick = function(e) {
                var elem = document.getElementById("fruittext");
                if (e.target.innerHTML == "Outline Off") {
                    elem.style.outline = "none";
                } else {
                    elem.style.outlineColor = "red";
                    elem.style.outlineStyle = "solid";
                    elem.style.outlineWidth = "thick";
                }
            };
        }
    </script>
</body>
</html>
```

You can see the effect of applying an outline in Figure 19-18. Notice how the elements do not change position. This is because outlines are not assigned their own space in the page layout.

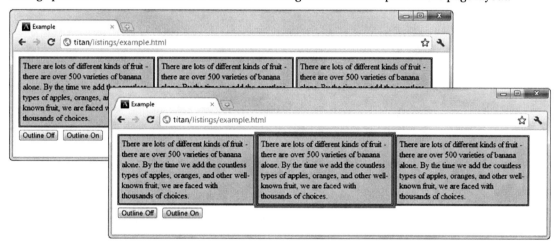

Figure 19-18. Applying an outline to an element

Summary

In this chapter, I have shown you the properties that you can use to add borders, backgrounds, and outlines to an element's box.

You can select borders from a set of simple styles, or completely customize them using images. The key technique for image borders is slicing, in which an image is divided up into sections, each of which is then used to draw part of the border.

You can use backgrounds to complement borders. I showed you how to create color or image backgrounds, and how you can configure them to relate to the rest of the element's box.

I finished this chapter by demonstrating drop shadows, which, along with curved borders, are the main new features that CSS3 adds to the area of borders and backgrounds.

CHAPTER 20

Working with the Box Model

In this chapter, I cover the CSS properties you can use to configure an element's box model. As I explained in Chapter 16, the box model is one of the fundamental concepts in CSS, and you use it to configure the appearance of elements and the overall layout of your documents. Table 20-1 provides the summary for this chapter.

Table 20-1. Chapter Summary

Problem	Solution	Listing
Set the size of the box padding area.	Use the padding shorthand element or the padding-top, padding-bottom, padding-left, or padding-right properties.	20-1, 20-2
Set the size of the box margin area.	Use the margin shorthand element or the margin-top, margin-bottom, margin-left, or margin-right properties.	20-3
Set the size of an element.	Use the width and height properties.	20-4
Set which part of the box sizes apply to.	Use the box-sizing property.	20-4
Setting bounds for an element's size.	Use the max-width, min-width, max-height, and min-height properties.	20-5
Set the manner in which overflowing content is handled.	Use the overflow, overflow-x, or overflow-y properties.	20-6, 20-7
Set the visibility of an element.	Use the visibility property (also see the none value for the display property).	20-8
Set the type of box for an element.	Use the display property.	—
Set the box type so an element is displayed with vertical distinctiveness.	Use the block value of the display property.	20-9

Set the box type so an element is displayed as a word in a paragraph.	Use the `inline` value of the `display` property.	20-10
Set the box type so that an element is treated like an inline element on the outside, but a block element on the inside.	Use the `inline-block` value of the `display` property.	20-11
Set the box type so that the way in which an element is displayed depends on the elements around it.	Use the `run-in` value of the `display` property.	20-12, 20-13
Hide an element and its contents.	Use the `none` value of the `display` property.	20-14
Shift an element to the left or right so that it is positioned against the edge of the containing box or another floating element.	Use the `float` property.	20-15
Prevent a floating element from being placed against another floating element.	Use the `clear` property.	20-16

Applying Padding to an Element

Padding adds space between an element's contents and its border. You can set padding for individual edges of the content box, or use a shorthand `padding` property to apply values in a single declaration. The padding properties are listed in Table 20-2.

Table 20-2. The padding Properties

Property	Description	Values
`padding-top`	Sets the padding for the top edge.	`<length>` or `<%>`
`padding-right`	Sets the padding for the right edge.	`<length>` or `<%>`
`padding-bottom`	Sets the padding for the bottom edge.	`<length>` or `<%>`
`padding-left`	Sets the padding for the left edge.	`<length>` or `<%>`
`padding`	This shorthand property sets the padding for all edges in a single declaration.	1–4 `<length>` or `<%>` values

When specifying padding using percentage values, the percentage is always derived from the *width* of the containing block; the height isn't taken into account. Listing 20-1 shows how you can apply padding to an element.

Listing 20-1. Applying Padding to an Element

```
<!DOCTYPE HTML>
<html>
    <head>
        <title>Example</title>
        <meta name="author" content="Adam Freeman"/>
        <meta name="description" content="A simple example"/>
        <link rel="shortcut icon" href="favicon.ico" type="image/x-icon" />
        <style type="text/css">
            p {
                border: 10px double black;
                background-color: lightgray;
                background-clip: content-box;
                padding-top: 0.5em;
                padding-bottom: 0.3em;
                padding-right: 0.8em;
                padding-left: 0.6em;
            }
        </style>
    </head>
    <body>
    <p>
        There are lots of different kinds of fruit - there are over 500 varieties
        of banana alone. By the time we add the countless types of apples, oranges,
        and other well-known fruit, we are faced with thousands of choices.
    </p>
    </body>
</html>
```

In Listing 20-1, I have applied a different amount of padding to each side of the box. You can see the effect this has in Figure 20-1. I have set the background-clip property (described in Chapter 19) so that the background color doesn't cover the padding area, which will emphasize the effect of the padding.

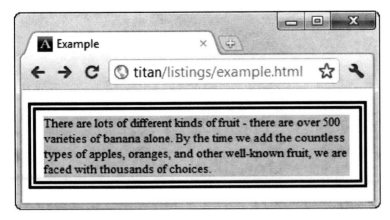

Figure 20-1. Applying padding to an element

You can use the padding shorthand property to set the padding for all four edges in a single declaration. You can specify one to four values for this property. When you supply four values, they are used to set the padding for the top, right, bottom, and left edges, respectively. As you omit values, the best-matching specified value is used: if you omit the left value, it is the same as the right; if you omit the bottom value, it is the same as the top. If you omit all but one value, then all four edges take on that same padding value.

Listing 20-2 shows how you use the padding shorthand property. I have added a curved border to this example to show how you can use padding to ensure that the border doesn't get drawn over the element content.

Listing 20-2. Using the padding Shorthand Property

```
<!DOCTYPE HTML>
<html>
    <head>
        <title>Example</title>
        <meta name="author" content="Adam Freeman"/>
        <meta name="description" content="A simple example"/>
        <link rel="shortcut icon" href="favicon.ico" type="image/x-icon" />
        <style type="text/css">
            p {
                border: 10px solid black;
                background: lightgray;
                border-radius: 1em 4em 1em 4em;
                padding: 5px 25px 5px 40px;
            }
        </style>
    </head>
    <body>
<p>
        There are lots of different kinds of fruit - there are over 500 varieties
        of banana alone. By the time we add the countless types of apples, oranges,
        and other well-known fruit, we are faced with thousands of choices.
```

```
    </p>
    </body>
</html>
```

You can see how the browser displays the border and padding in Figure 20-2.

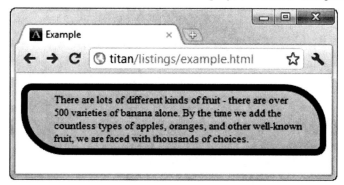

Figure 20-2. Using the shorthand padding property

Without the padding, the border would have been drawn over the text, as it was in Chapter 19. With the padding, you can ensure that there is sufficient space between the content and the border to prevent this from happening.

Appling Margin to an Element

Margin is space between the element border and whatever surrounds it on the page. This includes other elements and the parent element. Table 20-3 summarizes the properties that control margin.

Table 20-3. The margin Properties

Property	Description	Values
margin-top	Sets the margin for the top edge.	auto <length> <%>
margin-right	Sets the margin for the right edge.	auto <length> <%>
margin-bottom	Sets the margin for the bottom edge.	auto <length> <%>
margin-left	Sets the margin for the left edge.	auto <length> <%>

margin	This shorthand property sets the margin for all edges in a single declaration.	1–4 auto, *‹length›*, or *‹%›*

As with the padding properties, the percentage values are always derived from the width of the containing block, even when used for padding the top and bottom edge. Listing 20-3 shows the effect of adding margin.

Listing 20-3. Adding Margin to Elements

```
<!DOCTYPE HTML>
<html>
    <head>
        <title>Example</title>
        <meta name="author" content="Adam Freeman"/>
        <meta name="description" content="A simple example"/>
        <link rel="shortcut icon" href="favicon.ico" type="image/x-icon" />
        <style type="text/css">
            img {
                border: 4px solid black;
                background: lightgray;
                padding: 4px;
                margin:4px 20px;
            }
        </style>
    </head>
    <body>
        <img src="banana-small.png" alt="small banana">
        <img src="banana-small.png" alt="small banana">
    </body>
</html>
```

In Listing 20-3, there are two img elements. I have specified 4 pixels of margin for the top and bottom edges, and 20 pixels of margin for the left and right edges. You can see how the margin creates space around the element in Figure 20-3, which shows the img elements with and without margin.

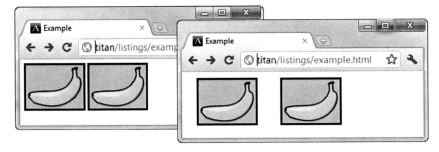

Figure 20-3. The effect of applying margin to elements

Margin isn't always drawn, even when you apply it with one of the margin properties. For example, if you apply margin to an element that has the display value inline, margin isn't displayed at the top and bottom edges. I explain the display property in the section "Setting an Element Box Type," later in this chapter.

Controlling the Size of an Element

Browsers will set the sizes of elements based on the flow of content on the page. There are some horrifically detailed rules that browsers must follow about how to allocate size. You can override this behavior by using the size-related properties, which are described in Table 20-4.

Table 20-4. The size Properties

Property	Description	Values
width height	Set the width and height for the element.	auto *<length>* *<%>*
min-width min-height	Set the minimum acceptable width or height for the element.	auto *<length>* *<%>*
max-width max-height	Set the maximum acceptable width or height for the element.	auto *<length>* *<%>*
box-sizing	Sets which part of an element's box is used for sizing.	content-box padding-box border-box margin-box

The default value for all these properties is auto, meaning that the browser will figure out the width and height of the element. You can specify sizes explicitly using lengths or percentages. The percentage values are calculated from the width of the containing block (even when dealing with height). Listing 20-4 shows how you can set the size of an element.

Listing 20-4. Setting the Size of an Element

```
<!DOCTYPE HTML>
<html>
    <head>
        <title>Example</title>
        <meta name="author" content="Adam Freeman"/>
        <meta name="description" content="A simple example"/>
        <link rel="shortcut icon" href="favicon.ico" type="image/x-icon" />
        <style type="text/css">
            div {
                width: 75%;
                height: 100px;
                border: thin solid black;
```

```
            }
            img {
                background: lightgray;
                border: 4px solid black;
                margin: 2px;
                height: 50%;
            }
            #first {
                box-sizing: border-box;
                width: 50%;
            }
            #second {
                box-sizing: content-box;
            }
        </style>
    </head>
    <body>
        <div>
            <img id="first" src="banana-small.png" alt="small banana">
            <img id="second" src="banana-small.png" alt="small banana">
        </div>
    </body>
</html>
```

There are three key elements in this example. A div element contains two img elements. You can see how the browser displays these elements in Figure 20-4.

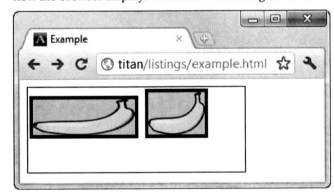

Figure 20-4. Setting the size of element

The div element is a child of the body element. When I express the width of the div element as 75%, I am telling the browser that I want the div element to be 75 percent of the width of the containing block (the body content box in this case), whatever that might be. If the user resizes the browser window, the body element will be resized and this will lead to my div element being resized to preserve the 75% relationship. You can see the effect that resizing the browser window has in Figure 20-5. I added a border to the div element to make it easy to see its size.

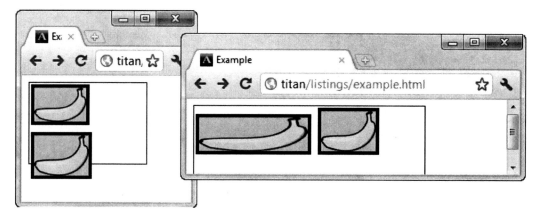

Figure 20-5. Resizing the browser window to demonstrate a relative size relationship

You can see that the div is always 75 percent of the width of the body element, which fills the browser window. I specified the height of the div element to be 100px, which is an absolute value and which won't change as the containing block is resized. You can see how part of the div element is hidden when I resized the browser window to be long and short.

I have done much the same thing with the img elements. One has a width value that is expressed as 50% of the containing block, meaning that the image is resized to maintain that relationship, even though this means that the aspect ratio of the image is not preserved. I have not set a width value for the second img element, which leaves the browser to figure it out. By default, the width will be derived from the height, set so that the aspect ratio is maintained.

■ **Tip** Notice how the images spill over the edge of the div elements Figure 20-5. This is known as *overflow*. I'll show you how to control overflow later in this chapter.

Setting the Sized Box

The two img elements in my example have the same height value (50%), but they look different on the screen. This is because I have used the box-sizing property to change the part of the element's box that the size properties apply to for one of the elements.

By default, the height and width are calculated and applied for the element's content box. This means that if you set an element's height property to 100px, for example, then the real height onscreen will be 100 pixels, plus the top and bottom padding, border, and margin values. The box-sizing property lets you specify which of the element's box areas will be sized to apply styling, meaning that you don't have to account for the variation yourself. Table 20-4 shows the allowed values.

■ **Tip** A common use for the size properties is to try and create a grid layout. It works, but a much better way is to use the table layout feature instead. You can get details of how this works in Chapter 21.

Setting Minimum and Maximum Sizes

You can use the min- and max- properties to set limits in which the browser is free to size the element. This allows the browser some latitude in how sizing is applied. Listing 20-5 gives a demonstration.

Listing 20-5. Setting min and max Ranges for Size

```
<!DOCTYPE HTML>
<html>
    <head>
        <title>Example</title>
        <meta name="author" content="Adam Freeman"/>
        <meta name="description" content="A simple example"/>
        <link rel="shortcut icon" href="favicon.ico" type="image/x-icon" />
        <style type="text/css">
            img {
                background: lightgray;
                border: 4px solid black;
                margin: 2px;
                box-sizing: border-box;
                min-width: 100px;
                width:50%;
                max-width: 200px;
            }
        </style>
    </head>
    <body>
            <img src="banana-small.png" alt="small banana">
    </body>
</html>
```

In Listing 20-5, I have applied the min-width and max-width properties to a single img element, and set the initial width to be 50 percent of the containing block. This gives the browser some leeway to resize the image to maintain the 50 percent relationship within the upper and lower bounds I have defined. The browser will use this leeway to preserve the aspect ratio of the image, as shown in Figure 20-6.

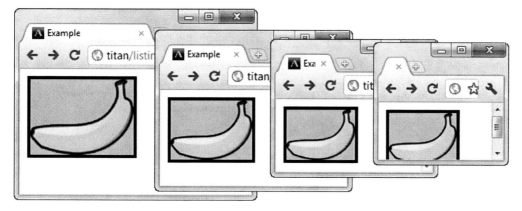

Figure 20-6. Setting bounds for element size using the min-width property

Figure 20-6 shows what happens when I resize the browser window to make it smaller. As the window gets smaller, the browser resizes the image to preserve the percentage relationship between the img element and the body element. When the minimum width is reached, the browser can no longer resize the image. You can see this in the last frame of the figure, where the image is clipped by the bottom of the browser window.

■ **Note** The browser support for the box-sizing property is variable.

Dealing with Overflowing Content

When you start to change the size of elements, you quickly arrive at a point where the content is too large to be displayed within an element's content box. The default behavior is for the content to spill out and be drawn anyway. Listing 20-6 creates an element that has a fixed size that is too small to display its content.

Listing 20-6. Creating an Element That Is Too Small to Fully Display Its Content

```
<!DOCTYPE HTML>
<html>
    <head>
        <title>Example</title>
        <meta name="author" content="Adam Freeman"/>
        <meta name="description" content="A simple example"/>
        <link rel="shortcut icon" href="favicon.ico" type="image/x-icon" />
        <style type="text/css">
            p {
                width: 200px;
                height: 100px;
                border: medium double black;
```

```
            }
        </style>
    </head>
    <body>
        <p>
            There are lots of different kinds of fruit - there are over 500 varieties
            of banana alone. By the time we add the countless types of apples, oranges,
            and other well-known fruit, we are faced with thousands of choices.
        </p>
    </body>
</html>
```

I have specified absolute values for the width and height properties, which creates the effect you can see in Figure 20-7.

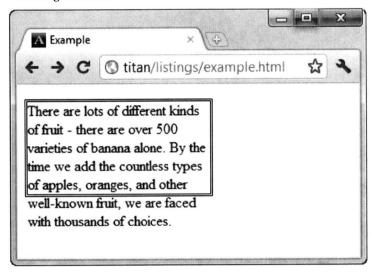

Figure 20-7. The default appearance of an element whose content is too large to display

We can change this behavior by using the overflow properties, which are described in Table 20-5.

Table 20-5. The overflow Properties

Property	Description	Values
overflow-x overflow-y	Set the horizontal or vertical overflow style.	See Table 20-6.
overflow	Shorthand property.	overflow overflow-x overflow-y

The overflow-x and overflow-y properties set the style for horizontal and vertical overflows, and the overflow shorthand property lets you define the style for both directions in a single declaration. Table 20-6 shows the allowed values for these properties.

Table 20-6. The overflow Property Values

Value	Description
auto	This value leaves the browser to work out what to do. Typically, this means that a scrollbar is displayed when the content is clipped, but not otherwise (this is in contrast to the scroll value, which displays a scrollbar whether or not it is required).
hidden	The content is clipped so that only the portion inside the content box is displayed. No mechanism is provided for the user to see the clipped part of the content.
no-content	The content is removed if it cannot be displayed completely. This value is not supported by any of the mainstream browsers.
no-display	The content is hidden if it cannot be displayed completely. This value is not supported by any of the mainstream browsers.
scroll	The browser will add a scrolling mechanism so that the user can see the content. This is typically a scrollbar, but this is dependent on the platform and browser. The scrollbar will be visible even if the content doesn't overflow.
visible	This is the default value. The element's content is displayed, even though it overflows the content box.

Listing 20-7 shows the overflow properties in use.

Listing 20-7. Controlling Content Overflow

```
<!DOCTYPE HTML>
<html>
    <head>
        <title>Example</title>
        <meta name="author" content="Adam Freeman"/>
        <meta name="description" content="A simple example"/>
        <link rel="shortcut icon" href="favicon.ico" type="image/x-icon" />
        <style type="text/css">
            p {
                width: 200px;
                height: 100px;
                border: medium double black;
            }

            #first {overflow: hidden;}
            #second { overflow: scroll;}
```

```
            </style>
        </head>
        <body>
            <p id="first">
                There are lots of different kinds of fruit - there are over 500 varieties
                of banana alone. By the time we add the countless types of apples, oranges,
                and other well-known fruit, we are faced with thousands of choices.
            </p>

            <p id="second">
                There are lots of different kinds of fruit - there are over 500 varieties
                of banana alone. By the time we add the countless types of apples, oranges,
                and other well-known fruit, we are faced with thousands of choices.
            </p>
        </body>
</html>
```

In Listing 20-7, the first paragraph has the hidden value for the overflow property, and the second paragraph has the scroll value. You can see the effect of these values in Figure 20-8.

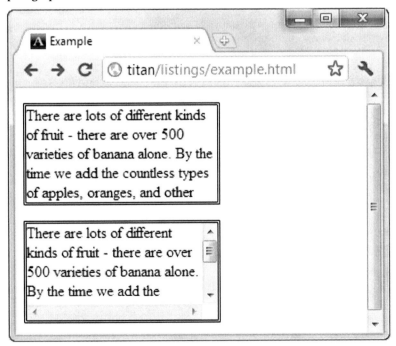

Figure 20-8. Using the hidden and scroll values for the overflow property

■ **Tip** This is an area for which the CSS module has yet to settle down. There are proposals to extend the set of overflow-related properties so that marquee behavior is supported (this is where the contents of the element span across the display so that all of the content is visible over time). The following properties are defined by CSS3, but have yet to be implemented by any of the mainstream browsers: `overflow-style`, `marquee-direction`, `marquee-loop`, `marquee-play-count`, `marquee-speed`, and `marquee-style`.

Controlling Element Visibility

You can control the visibility of your elements using the `visibility` property, which is described in Table 20-7. This might seem like an odd thing to do, but you can create some sophisticated effects by using this property with JavaScript.

Table 20-7. The visibility Property

Property	Description	Values
visibility	Sets the visibility of an element.	collapse hidden visible

Table 20-8 describes the allowed values for the `visibility` property.

Table 20-8. The visibility Property Values

Value	Description
collapse	The element isn't visible and doesn't occupy space in the page layout.
hidden	The element isn't visible, but it still occupies space in the page layout.
visible	This is the default value. The element is visible on the page.

Listing 20-8 demonstrates changing the visibility of an element using JavaScript and some `button` elements (which are described in Chapter 12).

Listing 20-8. Using the visibility Property

```
<!DOCTYPE HTML>
<html>
    <head>
        <title>Example</title>
        <meta name="author" content="Adam Freeman"/>
        <meta name="description" content="A simple example"/>
        <link rel="shortcut icon" href="favicon.ico" type="image/x-icon" />
```

```
    <style type="text/css">
        tr > th { text-align:left; background:gray; color:white}
        tr > th:only-of-type {text-align:right; background: lightgray; color:gray}
    </style>
</head>
<body>
    <table>
        <tr>
            <th>Rank</th><th>Name</th><th>Color</th><th>Size</th>
        </tr>
        <tr id="firstchoice">
            <th>Favorite:</th><td>Apples</td><td>Green</td><td>Medium</td>
        </tr>
        <tr>
            <th>2nd Favorite:</th><td>Oranges</td><td>Orange</td><td>Large</td>
        </tr>
    </table>
    <p>
        <button>Visible</button>
        <button>Collapse</button>
        <button>Hidden</button>
    </p>
    <script>
        var buttons = document.getElementsByTagName("BUTTON");
        for (var i = 0; i < buttons.length; i++) {
            buttons[i].onclick = function(e) {
                document.getElementById("firstchoice").style.visibility =
                    e.target.innerHTML;
            };
        }
    </script>
</body>
</html>
```

The script in this example locates the element with the id value of firstchoice and sets the value of the visibility property based on which of the button elements has been pressed. In this way, you can toggle between the visible, hidden, and collapse values. You can see the effect of each value in Figure 20-9.

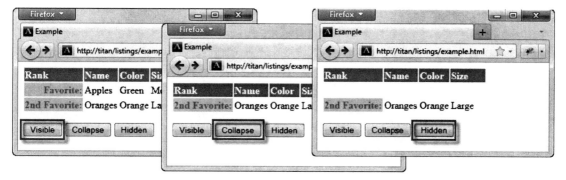

Figure 20-9. The effect of the values for the visibility property

The collapse value is only applicable to table-related elements, such as tr and td. You can learn more about these elements in Chapter 11. Some browsers, such as Chrome, don't implement the collapse value at all (which is why I have used Firefox for Figure 20-9).

■ **Tip** You can use the none value for the display property to get the same effect as the collapse value on nontable elements or in browsers that don't implement this feature. I cover the display property next.

Setting an Element Box Type

The display property provides a way for you to change the type of box for an element, which changes the way that an element is laid out on the page. In Part II of this book, you will have noticed that some of the elements have a style convention that includes a value for the display property. Many elements use the default value, inline, but some specify other values. The set of allowed values for the display property are described in Table 20-9.

Table 20-9. The display Property Values

Value	Description
inline	The box is displayed like a word in a line of text.
block	The box is displayed like a paragraph.
inline-block	The box is displayed like a line of text.
list-item	The box is displayed as a list item, typically with a bullet or some other kind of marker (such as an index number).
run-in	The type of box is dependent on the surrounding elements. See Listings

20-12 and 20-13 for an example.

compact	The type of box is either a block or a marker box (similar to that produced by the `list-item` type). At the time of this writing, mainstream browsers do not support this value.
flexbox	This value relates to the flexible box layout, described in Chapter 21.
table inline-table table-row-group table-header-group table-footer-group table-row table-column-group table-column table-cell table-caption	These values relate to laying out elements in a table. See Chapter 21 for details.
ruby ruby-base ruby-text ruby-base-group ruby-text-group	These values relate to laying out text with ruby annotations.
none	The element isn't visible and takes no space in the layout.

These values cause a lot of confusion, and they have a profound effect on the layout of your documents. I explain each kind of box type in the sections that follow.

Understanding Block-Level Elements

When you use the block value, you create a *block-level element*. This is an element that is vertically distinct from those that surround it. You would usually achieve this effect by placing a line break before and after the element, creating a sense of separation between the element and its surroundings, much like a paragraph appears in a book. The p element, which denotes a paragraph, includes the block value for the display property in its default style convention, but you may apply this value to any element, as shown in Listing 20-9.

Listing 20-9. Using the block Value of the display Property

```
<!DOCTYPE HTML>
<html>
    <head>
        <title>Example</title>
        <meta name="author" content="Adam Freeman"/>
        <meta name="description" content="A simple example"/>
        <link rel="shortcut icon" href="favicon.ico" type="image/x-icon" />
        <style type="text/css">
```

```
        p {border: medium solid black}
        span {
            display: block;
            border: medium double black;
            margin: 2px;
        }
    </style>
</head>
<body>
    <p>
        There are lots of different kinds of fruit - there are over 500 varieties
        of banana alone. By the time we add the countless types of apples, oranges,
        and other well-known fruit, we are faced with thousands of choices.
    </p>
    <p>
        One of the most interesting aspects of fruit is the variety available in
        each country. <span>I live near London</span>, in an area which is known for
        its apples. When travelling in Asia, I was struck by how many different
        kinds of banana were available - many of which had unique flavours and
        which were only avaiable within a small region.
    </p>
</body>
</html>
```

You can see the effect that block-level elements have on the layout through two different element types. The first is the p element, which, as I mentioned, uses the block value for the display property in its default style convention (you can learn more about the p element in Chapter 9). I also wanted to demonstrate that you can apply this property value to any element, so I have included a span element and explicitly set the display property for this element type in the style element. You can see the visual effect of this box type in Figure 20-10.

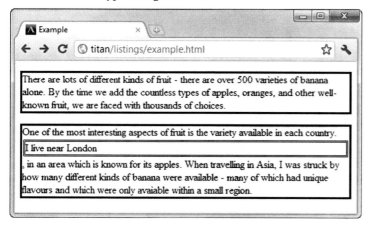

Figure 20-10. Using the block value of the display property

515

You have seen how the p element is displayed before. I have added a border to the elements in this example to make the vertical spacing more evident. Notice that the span element, to which I applied the block value, is also visually distinct within the box of the containing p element.

Understanding Inline-Level Elements

When you use the inline value, you create *inline-level elements*, which are displayed without being visually distinct from the surrounding content, such as a word in a line of text. Listing 20-10 shows how you can apply this value, even to elements such as p, which are block-level elements by default.

Listing 20-10. Using the inline Value for the display Property

```
<!DOCTYPE HTML>
<html>
    <head>
        <title>Example</title>
        <meta name="author" content="Adam Freeman"/>
        <meta name="description" content="A simple example"/>
        <link rel="shortcut icon" href="favicon.ico" type="image/x-icon" />
        <style type="text/css">
            p {
                display: inline;
            }
            span {
                display: inline;
                border: medium double black;
                margin: 2em;
                width: 10em;
                height: 2em;
            }
        </style>
    </head>
    <body>
        <p>
            There are lots of different kinds of fruit - there are over 500 varieties
            of banana alone. By the time we add the countless types of apples, oranges,
            and other well-known fruit, we are faced with thousands of choices.
        </p>
        <p>
            One of the most interesting aspects of fruit is the variety available in
            each country. <span>I live near London</span>, in an area which is known for
            its apples. When travelling in Asia, I was struck by how many different
            kinds of banana were available - many of which had unique flavours and
            which were only avaiable within a small region.
        </p>
    </body>
</html>
```

I have applied the inline property to both the p and span elements, and you can see the effect in Figure 20-11. You can see that there is no separation between the p elements and that the span element is shown inline with the rest of the text.

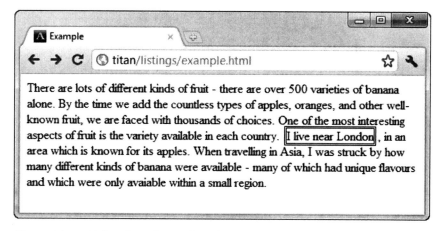

Figure 20-11. Using the inline value of the display property

When using the `inline` value, the browser will ignore certain properties, such as `width`, `height`, and `margin`. I have defined values for all three properties to the `span` element in the listing, but you can see that they have not been applied in the layout.

Understanding Inline-Block Elements

The `inline-block` value creates an element whose box is a mix of `block` and `inline` characteristics. The outside of the box is treated like an `inline` element. This means that there is no vertical distinctiveness and the content appears alongside the surrounding content. However, the inside of the box is treated like a `block` element, and properties such as `width`, `height`, and `margin` are applied. You can see the effect of this in Listing 20-11.

Listing 20-11. Using the inline-block Value

```
<!DOCTYPE HTML>
<html>
    <head>
        <title>Example</title>
        <meta name="author" content="Adam Freeman"/>
        <meta name="description" content="A simple example"/>
        <link rel="shortcut icon" href="favicon.ico" type="image/x-icon" />
        <style type="text/css">
            p {
                display: inline;
            }
            span {
                display: inline-block;
                border: medium double black;
                margin: 2em;
                width: 10em;
                height: 2em;
            }
```

```
        </style>
    </head>
    <body>
        <p>
            There are lots of different kinds of fruit - there are over 500 varieties
            of banana alone. By the time we add the countless types of apples, oranges,
            and other well-known fruit, we are faced with thousands of choices.
        </p>
        <p>
            One of the most interesting aspects of fruit is the variety available in
            each country. <span>I live near London</span>, in an area which is known for
            its apples. When travelling in Asia, I was struck by how many different
            kinds of banana were available - many of which had unique flavours and
            which were only avaiable within a small region.
        </p>
    </body>
</html>
```

The only change in this listing is the new display property value for the span element, but the visual effect is significant because the properties that were ignored previously (when the display value was inline) are now applied. You can see the effect in Figure 20-12.

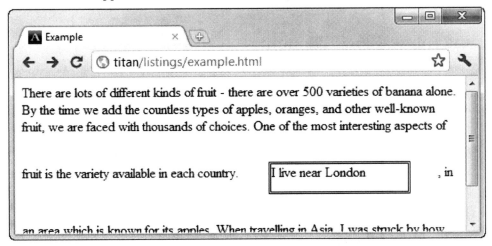

Figure 20-12. Using the inline-block value for the display property

Understanding Run-In Elements

The run-in value creates a box whose type depends on the surrounding elements. There are three situations that the browser must evaluate to determine the nature of a run-in box.

1. If a run-in element contains an element whose display value is block, then the run-in element becomes a block-level element.

2. Otherwise, if the next sibling element to a run-in element is a block element, then the run-in element becomes the first inline-level element in the sibling. I demonstrate this condition in Listing 20-12.

3. Otherwise, the run-in element is treated as a block-level element.

Of these three conditions, the second one bears demonstration. Listing 20-12 shows a run-in element whose sibling is a block-level element.

Listing 20-12. A run-in Element with a Block-Level Sibling

```
<!DOCTYPE HTML>
<html>
    <head>
        <title>Example</title>
        <meta name="author" content="Adam Freeman"/>
        <meta name="description" content="A simple example"/>
        <link rel="shortcut icon" href="favicon.ico" type="image/x-icon" />
        <style type="text/css">
            p {
                display: block;
            }
            span {
                display: run-in;
                border: medium double black;
            }
        </style>
    </head>
    <body>
        <span>
            There are lots of different kinds of fruit - there are over 500 varieties
            of banana alone.
        </span>
        <p>
            By the time we add the countless types of apples, oranges,
            and other well-known fruit, we are faced with thousands of choices.
        </p>
    </body>
</html>
```

You can see how the run-in element is treated as part of the block that follows in Figure 20-13 (although I should note that not all of the browsers correctly support this property).

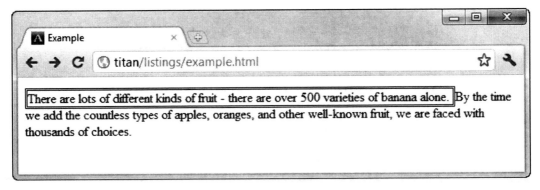

Figure 20-13. A run-in element with a block-level sibling

If the sibling element isn't a block-level element, then the run-in is treated as a block. An example of this relationship is shown in Listing 20-13.

Listing 20-13. A run-in Element with an Inline Sibling

```
<!DOCTYPE HTML>
<html>
    <head>
        <title>Example</title>
        <meta name="author" content="Adam Freeman"/>
        <meta name="description" content="A simple example"/>
        <link rel="shortcut icon" href="favicon.ico" type="image/x-icon" />
        <style type="text/css">
            p {
                display: inline;
            }
            span {
                display: run-in;
                border: medium double black;
            }
        </style>
    </head>
    <body>
        <span>
            There are lots of different kinds of fruit - there are over 500 varieties
            of banana alone.
        </span>
        <p>
            By the time we add the countless types of apples, oranges,
            and other well-known fruit, we are faced with thousands of choices.
        </p>
    </body>
</html>
```

In this example, the run-in element is displayed as a block, as shown in Figure 20-14.

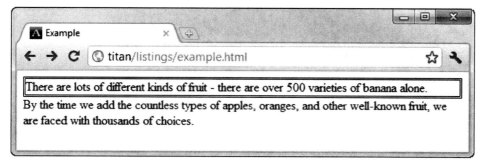

Figure 20-14. A run-in element displayed as a block-level element

Hiding Elements

The none value tells the browser not to create any kind of box for an element, or for any descendent
elements. When the display property is set to none, the element doesn't occupy any space in the page
layout. Listing 20-14 shows an HTML document that has a simple script that toggles the display
property of a p element between block and none.

Listing 20-14. Using the none Value of the display Property

```
<!DOCTYPE HTML>
<html>
    <head>
        <title>Example</title>
        <meta name="author" content="Adam Freeman"/>
        <meta name="description" content="A simple example"/>
        <link rel="shortcut icon" href="favicon.ico" type="image/x-icon" />
    </head>
    <body>
        <p id="toggle">
            There are lots of different kinds of fruit - there are over 500 varieties
            of banana alone. By the time we add the countless types of apples, oranges,
            and other well-known fruit, we are faced with thousands of choices.
        </p>
        <p>
            One of the most interesting aspects of fruit is the variety available in
            each country. <span>I live near London</span>, in an area which is known for
            its apples. When travelling in Asia, I was struck by how many different
            kinds of banana were available - many of which had unique flavours and
            which were only avaiable within a small region.
        </p>
        <p>
            <button>Block</button>
            <button>None</button>
        </p>

        <script>
            var buttons = document.getElementsByTagName("BUTTON");
```

```
        for (var i = 0; i < buttons.length; i++) {
            buttons[i].onclick = function(e) {
                document.getElementById("toggle").style.display=
                    e.target.innerHTML;
            };
        }
    </script>
</body>
</html>
```

You can see how the none value causes the element to be removed from the layout in Figure 20-15.

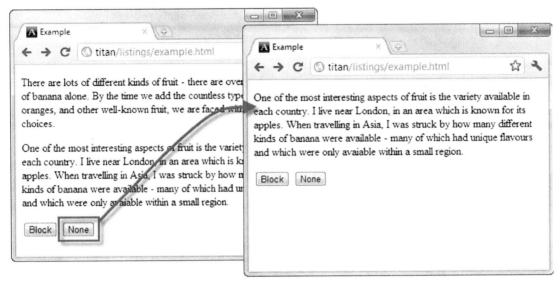

Figure 20-15. The effect of the none value for the display property

Creating Floating Boxes

You can use the float property to create *floating boxes*, which are shifted to one side until the left or right edge touches the edge of the containing block or another floating box. Table 20-10 summarizes the property.

Table 20-10. The float Property

Property	Description	Values
float	Sets the floating style for an element.	left right none

Table 20-11 describes the allowed values for the float property.

Table 20-11. The display Property Values

Value	Description
left	The element is shifted so that the left edge touches the left edge of the containing block or the right edge of another floating block.
right	The element is shifted so that the right edge touches the right edge of the containing block or the left edge of another floating block.
none	The element is not floated.

Listing 20-15 shows the float property in use.

Listing 20-15. Using the float Property

```
<!DOCTYPE HTML>
<html>
    <head>
        <title>Example</title>
        <meta name="author" content="Adam Freeman"/>
        <meta name="description" content="A simple example"/>
        <link rel="shortcut icon" href="favicon.ico" type="image/x-icon" />
        <style>
            p.toggle {
                float:left;
                border: medium double black;
                width: 40%;
                margin: 2px;
                padding: 2px;
            }
        </style>
    </head>
    <body>
        <p class="toggle">
            There are lots of different kinds of fruit - there are over 500 varieties
            of banana alone. By the time we add the countless types of apples, oranges,
            and other well-known fruit, we are faced with thousands of choices.
        </p>
        <p class="toggle">
            One of the most interesting aspects of fruit is the variety available in
            each country. I live near London, in an area which is known for
            its apples.
        </p>
        <p>
            When travelling in Asia, I was struck by how many different
            kinds of banana were available - many of which had unique flavours and
            which were only avaiable within a small region.
        </p>
        <p>
```

```
            <button>Left</button>
            <button>Right</button>
            <button>None</button>
        </p>
        <script>
            var buttons = document.getElementsByTagName("BUTTON");
            for (var i = 0; i < buttons.length; i++) {
                buttons[i].onclick = function(e) {
                    var elements = document.getElementsByClassName("toggle");
                    for (var j = 0; j < elements.length; j++) {
                        elements[j].style.cssFloat = e.target.innerHTML;
                    }
                };
            }
        </script>
    </body>
</html>
```

In this example, there are a number of p elements, two of which have a float value of left. This means that they will be shifted to the left until they hit the edge of the containing box or another floating element. Because there are two elements that are shifted, the first will be moved to the containing block edge and the second will abut the first. You can see this effect in Figure 20-16.

▓ **Tip** Notice that when I refer to the float property in JavaScript, I have to use cssFloat. You'll get into styling elements with JavaScript in Chapter 29

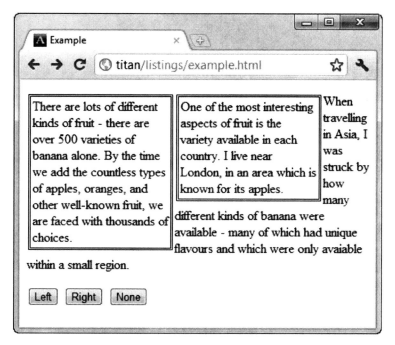

Figure 20-16. Using the left value of the float property

Notice how the rest of the content flows around the floating elements. In this example, I also added some button elements and a simple script that changes the float value for the two p elements based on which button is pressed. If you press the Right button, you can see how the elements are shifted to the right, as shown in Figure 20-17. Notice the order in which the elements appear: the first element defined in the document is furthest to the right.

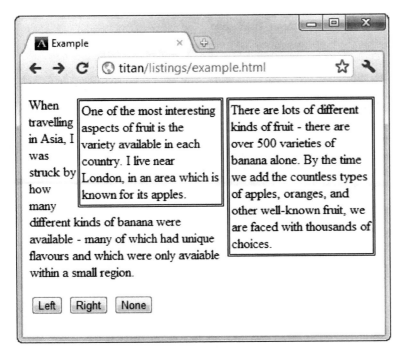

Figure 20-17. Using the right value of the float property

The final button, None, disables the float effect by setting the float value to none. This restores the default box behavior of the element. The p element is a block-level element by default, and you can see the effect in Figure 20-18.

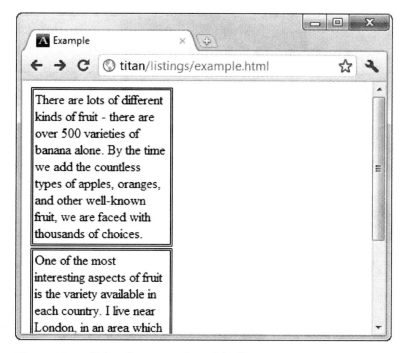

Figure 20-18. Using the none value of the float property

Preventing Floating Elements from Stacking Up

By default, floating elements will stack up next to one another. You can prevent this from happening by using the clear property, which specifies that one or both edges of a floating element must not adjoin the edge of another floating element. Table 20-12 summarizes the clear property.

Table 20-12. The clear Property

Property	Description	Values
clear	Specifies whether the element can be floated next to another floating element.	left right both none

Table 20-13 describes the allowed values of the clear element.

Table 20-13. The clear Property Values

Value	Description
left	The left edge of the element may not adjoin another floating element.
right	The right edge of the element may not adjoin another floating element.
both	Neither edge may adjoin another floating element.
none	The element is not cleared and either edge may adjoin another floating element.

Listing 20-16 shows the clear property in use.

Listing 20-16. Using the clear Property

```
<!DOCTYPE HTML>
<html>
    <head>
        <title>Example</title>
        <meta name="author" content="Adam Freeman"/>
        <meta name="description" content="A simple example"/>
        <link rel="shortcut icon" href="favicon.ico" type="image/x-icon" />
        <style>
            p.toggle {
                float:left;
                border: medium double black;
                width: 40%;
                margin: 2px;
                padding: 2px;
            }

            p.cleared {
                clear:left;
            }

        </style>
    </head>
    <body>
        <p class="toggle">
            There are lots of different kinds of fruit - there are over 500 varieties
            of banana alone. By the time we add the countless types of apples, oranges,
            and other well-known fruit, we are faced with thousands of choices.
        </p>
        <p class="toggle cleared">
            One of the most interesting aspects of fruit is the variety available in
            each country. I live near London, in an area which is known for
            its apples.
        </p>
```

```
<p>
    When travelling in Asia, I was struck by how many different
    kinds of banana were available - many of which had unique flavours and
    which were only avaiable within a small region.
</p>

<p>
    <button>Left</button>
    <button>Right</button>
    <button>None</button>
</p>

<script>
    var buttons = document.getElementsByTagName("BUTTON");
    for (var i = 0; i < buttons.length; i++) {
        buttons[i].onclick = function(e) {
            var elements = document.getElementsByClassName("toggle");
            for (var j = 0; j < elements.length; j++) {
                elements[j].style.cssFloat = e.target.innerHTML;
            }
        };
    }
</script>
    </body>
</html>
```

This is a simple extension of the previous example, with the addition of a new style that clears the left edge of the second p element. You can see how this changes the page layout in Figure 20-19 (the elements are floating left in this figure).

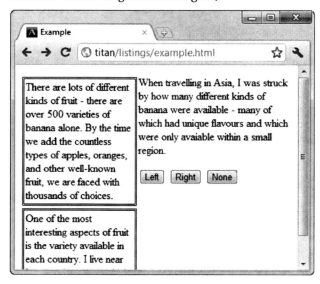

Figure 20-19. Clearing the left edge of a floating element

The left edge of the p element isn't allowed to be next to another floating element, and so the browser moves the element down the page. The right edge remains uncleared, which means that when you float the elements to the right, they can touch one another, as shown in Figure 20-20.

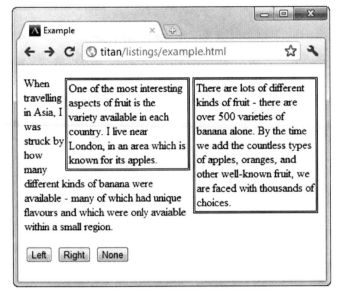

Figure 20-20. The uncleared right edge of a right-floating element

Summary

In this chapter, I have shown how you can perform the basic configuration of an element's box model, changing the way that it appears in the page layout. You started with the basic properties, such as padding and margin, and continued through into more complex concepts, such as ranges for widths and heights and overflowing content.

The most important concept in this chapter is the effect of the different kinds of box that you can create for an element. Understanding the relationship between block- and inline-level elements is essential to mastering HTML5 layouts, and floating elements and clearing edges are very widely used techniques to create flexibility in pages.

In the next chapter, I'll show you some more complex models that CSS supports for creating element layouts.

CHAPTER 21

Creating Layouts

In this chapter, I will show you the different options available for controlling the layout of elements on the page. With the increased emphasis separating the semantic significance of HTML elements from their presentational impact, the role of CSS in laying out elements has become more important in HTML5. There are some very useful layout features in CSS3 and, of course, you can use the existing facility from earlier versions of CSS.

There are two proposed layout models for CSS3 that have yet to mature enough for me to cover in this chapter. The first, template layouts, allows you to create flexible to contain elements. None of the browsers implement this module, but you can experiment with the functionality through a jQuery plugin available at http://a.deveria.com/?p=236. The other new module creates flexible grids for layouts. Unfortunately, as I write this, the specification is not yet complete and there is no implementation available.

The entire area of layouts in CSS3 remains volatile. One of the layout styles that I *do* cover in this chapter—the flexible box model—offers excellent features, but the standard keeps changing and I have had to demonstrate the approach to layouts using browser-specific properties that were implemented against an early draft of the standard.

Given the early nature of these new features, I suggest considering using a CSS framework for creating sophisticated page layouts. I recommend Blueprint, which you can download from www.blueprintcss.org. A CSS framework may give you the functionality you require until the CSS3 layout features mature. Table 21-1 provides the summary for this chapter.

Table 21-1. Chapter Summary

Problem	Solution	Listing
Change the way that an element is positioned inside its container block.	Use the position property.	21-1
Offset a positioned element from the edges of its container block.	Use the top, bottom, left, or right properties.	21-1
Set the front-to-back order for a positioned element.	Use the z-index property.	21-2
Create a layout similar to a newspaper page.	Use a multicolumn layout.	21-3, 21-4
Fluidly allocate space to elements within a	Use the flexbox layout.	21-5 through

Positioning Content

The simplest way of directing content is through *positioning*, which allows you to change the way that an element is laid out by the browser. Table 21-2 describes the positioning properties.

Table 21-2. The Positioning Properties

Property	Description	Values
position	Sets the positioning method.	See Table 21-3.
left right top bottom	Sets offset values for positioned elements.	*<length>* <%> auto
z-index	Sets the front-to-back ordering of elements.	number

Setting the Position Type

The position property sets the method by which an element is positioned. The allowed values are described in Table 21-3.

Table 21-3. The position Property Values

Value	Description
static	The element is laid out as normal (this is the default value).
relative	The element is positioned relative to its normal position.
absolute	The element is positioned relative to its first ancestor that has a position value other than static.
fixed	The element is positioned relative to the browser window.

The different values for the position property specify different elements against which the element is positioned. You use the top, bottom, left, and right properties to offset the element from the element specified by the position property. Listing 21-1 demonstrates the effect of the different values.

Listing 21-1. Using the position Property

```
<!DOCTYPE HTML>
<html>
    <head>
        <title>Example</title>
        <meta name="author" content="Adam Freeman"/>
        <meta name="description" content="A simple example"/>
        <link rel="shortcut icon" href="favicon.ico" type="image/x-icon" />
        <style>
            img {
                top: 5px;
                left:150px;
                border: medium double black;
            }
        </style>
    </head>
    <body>
        <p>
            There are lots of different kinds of fruit - there are over 500 varieties
            of banana alone. By the time we add the countless types of apples, oranges,
            and other well-known fruit, we are faced with thousands of choices.
        </p>
        <p>
            One of the most interesting aspects of fruit is the variety available in
            each country. I live near London, in an area which is known for
            its apples.

        </p>
        <img id="banana" src="banana-small.png" alt="small banana"/>
        <p>
            When travelling in Asia, I was struck by how many different
            kinds of banana were available - many of which had unique flavours and
            which were only avaiable within a small region.
        </p>
        <p>
            <button>Static</button>
            <button>Relative</button>
            <button>Absolute</button>
            <button>Fixed</button>
        </p>
        <script>
            var buttons = document.getElementsByTagName("BUTTON");
            for (var i = 0; i < buttons.length; i++) {
                buttons[i].onclick = function(e) {
                    document.getElementById("banana").style.position =
                        e.target.innerHTML;
                };
            }
        </script>
    </body>
```

```
</html>
```

In this example, I have added a small script to the page that changes the value of the position property on an img element based on button presses. Notice that I have set the left property to 150px and the top property to 5px. This means that the img element will be offset by 150 pixels along the horizontal axis, and 5 pixels along the vertical axis when any position value other than static is applied. Figure 21-1 shows the transition from static (the default value) to relative.

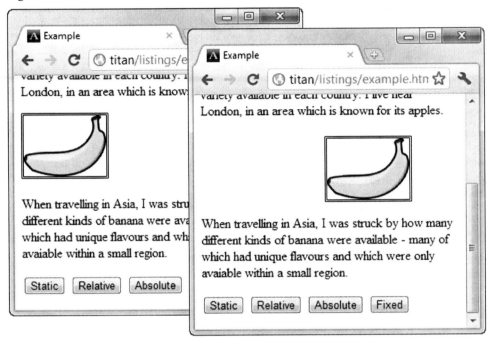

Figure 21-1. The static and relative values for the position property

The relative value applies the top, bottom, left, and right properties to position the element relative to where it would be under the static value. As you can see in the figure, the left and top values of 150px cause the img element to be moved down and to the right.

The absolute value causes the element to be positioned relative to the nearest ancestor that has a position value other than static. There is no such element in this example, which means that the element is positioned relative to the body element, as shown in Figure 21-2.

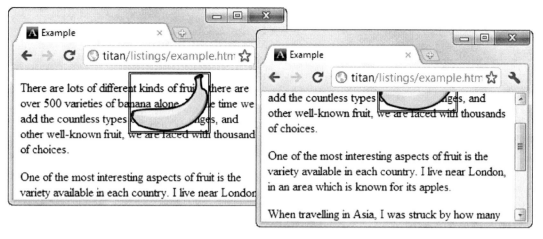

Figure 21-2. The absolute value of the position property

Notice that when I scroll the browser page, the img element moves with the rest of the content. This is in contrast to how the fixed value works, as shown in Figure 21-3.

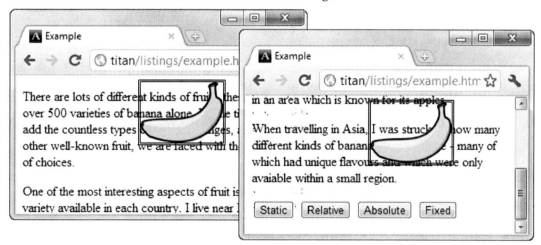

Figure 21-3. The fixed value of the position property

When you use the fixed value, the element is placed relative to the browser window. This means that the element occupies the same location, even when the rest of the content is scrolled up or down.

Setting the Z-Order

The z-index property lets you specify the front-to-back order in which elements are drawn. This property is summarized in Table 21-4.

Table 21-4. The float Property

Property	Description	Values
z-index	Sets the relative front-to-back order of an element.	*<number>*

The value for the z-index value is a number, and negative values are allowed. The smaller the value, the further to the back the element will be drawn. This property has utility only when elements overlap, as is the case in Listing 21-2.

Listing 21-2. Using the z-index Property

```
<!DOCTYPE HTML>
<html>
    <head>
        <title>Example</title>
        <meta name="author" content="Adam Freeman"/>
        <meta name="description" content="A simple example"/>
        <link rel="shortcut icon" href="favicon.ico" type="image/x-icon" />
        <style>
            img {
                border: medium double black;;
                background-color: lightgreay;
                position: fixed;
            }

            #banana {
                z-index: 1;
                top: 15px;
                left:150px;
            }

            #apple {
                z-index: 2;
                top: 25px;
                left:120px;
            }
        </style>
    </head>
    <body>
        <p>
            There are lots of different kinds of fruit - there are over 500 varieties
            of banana alone. By the time we add the countless types of apples, oranges,
            and other well-known fruit, we are faced with thousands of choices.
        </p>
        <p>
            One of the most interesting aspects of fruit is the variety available in
            each country. I live near London, in an area which is known for
            its apples.
```

```
            </p>
            <img id="banana" src="banana-small.png" alt="small banana"/>
            <img id="apple" src="apple.png" alt="small banana"/>
            <p>
                When travelling in Asia, I was struck by how many different
                kinds of banana were available - many of which had unique flavours and
                which were only avaiable within a small region.
            </p>
        </body>
</html>
```

In this example, I have created two fixed position img elements and set the top and left values so that the elements overlap. The z-index value of the img element with the id value of apple is the larger of the two values and, therefore, will be drawn over the banana image, as shown in Figure 21-4.

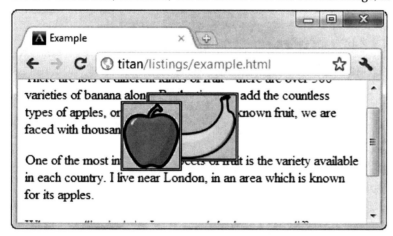

Figure 21-4. Using the z-index property

The default value for the z-index property is zero, which is why the browser has drawn the images over the p elements.

Creating Multicolumn Layouts

The multicolumn feature allows you to lay out content in multiple vertical columns, much like you would see in a newspaper. Table 21-5 describes the multicolumn properties.

Table 21-5. The Multicolumn Properties

Property	Description	Values
column-count	Specifies the ideal number of columns.	*<number>*
column-fill	Specifies how the content should be distributed between columns. The balance value means that the browser	balance auto

	should minimize variations in column lengths, and the auto value means that columns should be filled sequentially.	
column-gap	Specifies the distance between columns.	*<length>*
column-rule	Shorthand property for setting the column-rule-* properties in a single declaration.	*<width> <style> <color>*
column-rule-color	Specifies the color of the rule between columns.	*<color>*
column-rule-style	Specifies the style of the rule between columns.	**Same as for the** border-style **property**
column-rule-width	Specifies the width of the rule between columns.	*<length>*
columns	Shorthand property for setting the column-span and column-width properties.	*<length> <number>*
column-span	Specifies how many columns an element should span.	none all
column-width	Specifies the width of the columns.	*<length>*

Listing 21-3 shows the multicolumn layout applied to an HTML document.

Listing 21-3. Using the Multicolumn Layout

```
<!DOCTYPE HTML>
<html>
    <head>
        <title>Example</title>
        <meta name="author" content="Adam Freeman"/>
        <meta name="description" content="A simple example"/>
        <link rel="shortcut icon" href="favicon.ico" type="image/x-icon" />
        <style>
            p {
                column-count: 3;
                column-fill: balance;
                column-rule: medium solid black;
                column-gap: 1.5em;
            }

            img {
```

```
                float: left;
                border: medium double black;
                background-color: lightgray;
                padding: 2px;
                margin: 2px;
            }
        </style>
    </head>
    <body>
        <p>
            There are lots of different kinds of fruit - there are over 500 varieties
            of banana alone. By the time we add the countless types of apples, oranges,
            and other well-known fruit, we are faced with thousands of choices.
            <img src="apple.png" alt="apple"/>
            One of the most interesting aspects of fruit is the variety available in
            each country. I live near London, in an area which is known for
            its apples.
            <img src="banana-small.png" alt="banana"/>
            When travelling in Asia, I was struck by how many different
            kinds of banana were available - many of which had unique flavours and
            which were only avaiable within a small region.

            And, of course, there are fruits which are truely unique - I am put in mind
            of the durian, which is widely consumed in SE Asia and is known as the
            "king of fruits". The durian is largely unknown in Europe and the USA - if
            it is known at all, it is for the overwhelming smell, which is compared
            to a combination of almonds, rotten onions and gym socks.
        </p>
    </body>
</html>
```

In this example, I have applied some of the multicolumn properties to a p element. This element contains a mix of text and img elements, and you can see the column effect in Figure 21-5.

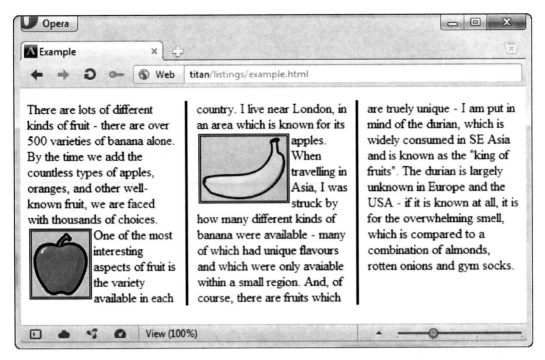

Figure 21-5. A multicolumn layout

■ **Note** The figure shows Opera, which is the only browser that supports the multicolumn layout at the time of writing. Not all of the properties are implemented, but the basic functionality is present.

As Figure 21-5 shows, the content of the p element flows from one column to the next, much as in the style of a newspaper page. I applied the float property to the img elements in this example so that the text content of the p element will flow nicely around the images. Details of the float property can be found in Chapter 20.

I used the column-count property to specify three columns in this layout. The browser will adjust the width of the columns as the window is resized to preserve the number of columns. An alternative is to specify the desired width of the columns instead, as shown in Listing 21-4.

Listing 21-4. Setting the Width of the Columns

```
...
<style>
    p {
        column-width: 10em;
        column-fill: balance;
        column-rule: medium solid black;
```

```
        column-gap: 1.5em;
    }

    img {
        float:left;
        border: medium double black;
        background-color: lightgray;
        padding: 2px;
        margin: 2px;
    }
</style>
...
```

When you apply this property, the browser preserves the specified column width by adding and removing columns to the element, as shown in Figure 21-6.

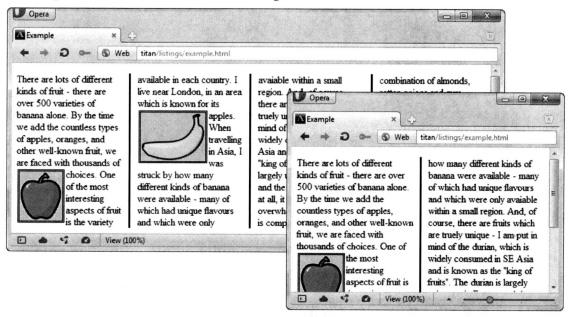

Figure 21-6. Defining columns by width, rather than count

Creating Flexible Box Layouts

The *flexible box layout* (also known as *flexbox*) is a CSS3 enhancement that adds a new value for the display property (flexbox), and defines some additional properties. The flexible layout lets you create fluid interfaces that respond well when the browser window is resized. This is done by distributing unused space in a container block among the contained elements. The specification for flexbox defines the following new properties:

- flex-align
- flex-direction

- flex-order

- flex-pack

As I write this, the standard for the flexible box layout remains volatile. The names of the properties and their values have recently changed. The mainstream browsers have implemented the core functionality of this feature using browser-specific properties and values, based on the previous property names.

The flexbox is a useful and important addition to CSS, and so I am going to show you the functionality based on the earlier draft of the standard and using the –webkit prefixed properties. This is not ideal, but it will give you a sense of what the flexbox does and, hopefully, leave you in a position to easily transition to the finished standard when it becomes available and widely implemented. Given the difference between the specification and the implementation, let's start with a definition of the problem that the flexbox sets out to solve. Listing 21-5 shows a simple layout with a problem.

Listing 21-5. An HTML Document with a Layout Problem

```
<!DOCTYPE HTML>
<html>
    <head>
        <title>Example</title>
        <meta name="author" content="Adam Freeman"/>
        <meta name="description" content="A simple example"/>
        <link rel="shortcut icon" href="favicon.ico" type="image/x-icon" />
        <style>
            p {
                float:left;
                width: 150px;
                border: medium double black;
                background-color: lightgray;
            }
    </style>
    </head>
    <body>
        <div id="container">
            <p id="first">
                There are lots of different kinds of fruit - there are over 500 varieties
                of banana alone. By the time we add the countless types of apples,
                oranges, and other well-known fruit, we are faced with thousands
                of choices.
            </p>
            <p id="second">
                One of the most interesting aspects of fruit is the variety available in
                each country. I live near London, in an area which is known for
                its apples.
            </p>
            <p id="third">
                When travelling in Asia, I was struck by how many different kinds of
                banana were available - many of which had unique flavours and which
                were only avaiable within a small region.
            </p>
        </div>
```

```
    </body>
</html>
```

There are three p elements contained within a div. I want to display the p elements in a horizontal row, which is easily done using the float property (described in Chapter 20). You can see how the browser displays this HTML in Figure 21-7.

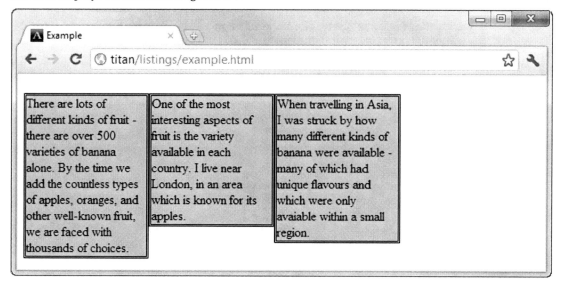

Figure 21-7. An element with undistributed empty space

The problem you can use the flexbox to solve is how you deal with the block of empty space that appears to the right of the p elements. There are several ways that you can solve this problem. For example, you could use percentage widths, but the flexbox gives you a much more fluid and elegant alternative. Table 21-6 shows the three -webkit properties that implement the core of flexbox functionality (I have omitted the -webkit prefix for brevity).

Table 21-6. The –webkit Flexbox Properties

Property	Description	Values
box-align	Tells the browser how to deal with additional space when the height of the content elements is less than the height of the container.	start end center baseline stretch
box-flex	Specifies the flexibility of an element; applied to individual elements within the flexbox container.	*<number>*
box-pack	Tells the browser how to allocate space when	start

543

the flexible elements have reached their maximum size.	end center justify

Creating a Simple Flexbox

You create a flexbox using the display property. The standard value will be flexbox, but you must use -webkit-box until the standard is completed and implemented. You tell the browser how to allocate the unused space between elements using the box-flex property. You can see the new display values and the box-flex property in Listing 21-6.

Listing 21-6. Creating a Simple Flexbox

```
<!DOCTYPE HTML>
<html>
    <head>
        <title>Example</title>
        <meta name="author" content="Adam Freeman"/>
        <meta name="description" content="A simple example"/>
        <link rel="shortcut icon" href="favicon.ico" type="image/x-icon" />
        <style>
            p {
                width: 150px;
                border: medium double black;
                background-color: lightgray;
                margin: 2px;
            }
            #container {
                display: -webkit-box;
            }
            #second {
                -webkit-box-flex: 1;
            }
        </style>
    </head>
    <body>
        <div id="container">
            <p id="first">
                There are lots of different kinds of fruit - there are over 500 varieties
                of banana alone. By the time we add the countless types of apples,
                oranges, and other well-known fruit, we are faced with thousands
                of choices.
            </p>
            <p id="second">
                One of the most interesting aspects of fruit is the variety available in
                each country. I live near London, in an area which is known for
                its apples.
            </p>
            <p id="third">
                When travelling in Asia, I was struck by how many different kinds of
```

```
            banana were available - many of which had unique flavours and which
            were only avaiable within a small region.
        </p>
    </div>
  </body>
</html>
```

The display property is applied to the flexbox container. This is the element that will have the additional space and whose contents you want to lay out flexibly. The box-flex property is applied to elements inside the flexbox container and tells the browser which elements should be flexed in size as the size of the container changes. In this case, I have selected the p element, which has an id value of second.

⬛ **Tip** Notice that I have removed the float property from the style declaration for the p elements. Flexbox elements cannot contain floating elements.

You can see how the browser flexes the size of the selected element in Figure 21-8.

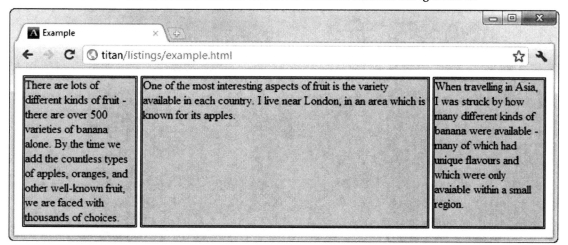

Figure 21-8. A flexing element

I have expanded the browser window in Figure 21-8, which has caused the div container to expand and the second paragraph to flex to take up the additional space. Flexing isn't just about additional space; when I shrink the browser window, the flexing element is the one that is resized to accommodate the space loss, as shown in Figure 21-9. Notice that the elements to which the box-flex property is applied do not change in size.

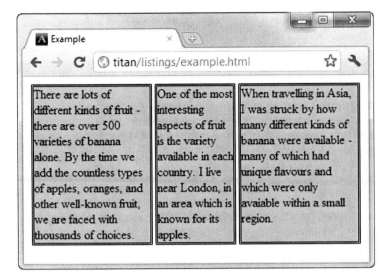

Figure 21-9. A flexing element resized to accommodate less space

Flexing Multiple Elements

You can tell the browser to flex the sizes of more than one element by applying the box-flex property. The values that you set determine the ratio that the browser will use to allocate space. Listing 21-7 shows changes to the style element of the previous example.

Listing 21-7. Creating Multiple Flex Elements

```
...
<style>
    p {
        width: 150px;
        border: medium double black;
        background-color: lightgray;
        margin: 2px;
    }
    #container {
        display: -webkit-box;
    }

    #first {
        -webkit-box-flex: 3;
    }

    #second {
        -webkit-box-flex: 1;
    }
</style>
...
```

I have applied the box-flex property to the p element with the id of first. The value of this property is 3, meaning that the browser will allocate three times of the additional space to the first element as it will to the second element. When you create ratios like this, you are referring to only the flexibility of the element. You use the ratio to allocate additional space or to reduce the size of the element, not to change its preferred size. You can see how the ratio is applied in Figure 21-10.

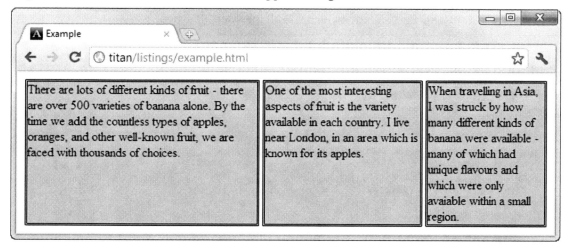

Figure 21-10. Creating a flexibility ratio

Dealing with Vertical Space

The box-align property lets you tell the browser what to do with any additional vertical space. This element is summarized in Table 21-7.

Table 21-7. The box-align Property

Property	Description	Values
box-align	Specifies how the browser should handle excess vertical space.	start end stretch center

The default is to stretch the elements vertically so that they fill the space. You can see this in Figure 21-10, where the first two p elements have been sized so that there is empty space under their contents. Table 21-8 shows the allowed values for the box-align property.

Table 21-8. The box-align Property Values

Value	Description
start	The elements are placed along the top edge of the container, and any empty space will be shown beneath them.

end	The elements are placed along the bottom edge of the container, and any empty space will be shown above them.
center	Any additional space is divided equally and shown above and below the elements.
stretch	Adjust the height of the elements to fill the available space.

Listing 21-8 shows the style element changes to apply the box-align property. Note that this property is applied to the flex container and not the content elements.

Listing 21-8. Applying the box-align Property

```
...
<style>
    p {
        width: 150px;
        border: medium double black;
        background-color: lightgray;
        margin: 2px;
    }
    #container {
        display: -webkit-box;
        -webkit-box-direction: reverse;
        -webkit-box-align: end;
    }
    #first {
        -webkit-box-flex: 3;
    }
    #second {
        -webkit-box-flex: 1;
    }
</style>
...
```

In this example, I have selected the end value, which will mean that the content elements are placed on the bottom edge of the container element, and any vertical space will be displayed above them. You can see the effect of this value in Figure 21-11.

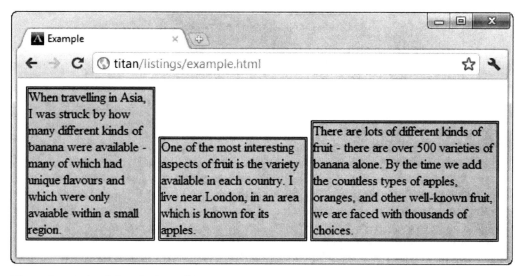

Figure 21-11. Applying the box-align property

Dealing with Maximum Sizes

The flexbox model will respect maximum size values for content elements. The browser will flex the size of elements to fill additional space until the maximum sizes are reached. The box-pack property tells the browser what to do if all of the flexible elements have reached their maximum sizes before all of the additional space has been allocated. This property is summarized in Table 21-9.

Table 21-9. The box-pack Property

Property	Description	Values
box-pack	Specifies how to deal with additional space if it cannot be allocated to flexible elements.	start end justify center

Table 21-10 describes the allowed values for this property.

Table 21-10. The box-pack Property Values

Value	Description
start	The elements are laid out from the left edge and any unallocated space is displayed to the right of the final element.
end	The elements are laid out from the right edge and any unallocated space is displayed to the left of the first element.

center	Any unallocated additional space is allocated evenly on the left side of the first element and the right side of the final element.
justify	Any unallocated space is spread evenly between the elements.

Listing 21-9 shows the box-pack property in use. Notice that I have defined max-width values for the p elements (you can learn more about the max-width in Chapter 20).

Listing 21-9. Using the box-pack Property

```
<!DOCTYPE HTML>
<html>
    <head>
        <title>Example</title>
        <meta name="author" content="Adam Freeman"/>
        <meta name="description" content="A simple example"/>
        <link rel="shortcut icon" href="favicon.ico" type="image/x-icon" />
<style>
    p {
        width: 150px;
        max-width: 250px;
        border: medium double black;
        background-color: lightgray;
        margin: 2px;
    }
    #container {
        display: -webkit-box;
        -webkit-box-direction: reverse;
        -webkit-box-align: end;
        -webkit-box-pack: justify;
    }
    #first {
        -webkit-box-flex: 3;
    }
    #second {
        -webkit-box-flex: 1;
    }
</style>
    </head>
    <body>
        <div id="container">
            <p id="first">
                There are lots of different kinds of fruit - there are over 500 varieties
                of banana alone. By the time we add the countless types of apples,
                oranges, and other well-known fruit, we are faced with thousands
                of choices.
            </p>
            <p id="second">
                One of the most interesting aspects of fruit is the variety available in
                each country. I live near London, in an area which is known for
```

```
            its apples.
        </p>
        <p id="third">
            When travelling in Asia, I was struck by how many different kinds of
            banana were available - many of which had unique flavours and which
            were only avaiable within a small region.
        </p>
    </div>
</body>
</html>
```

You can see the effect of this property in Figure 21-12. After the flexible p elements have reached their maximum widths, the browser starts allocating the additional space between the elements. Notice that the space is only *between* the content elements; no space is placed before the first element or after the last.

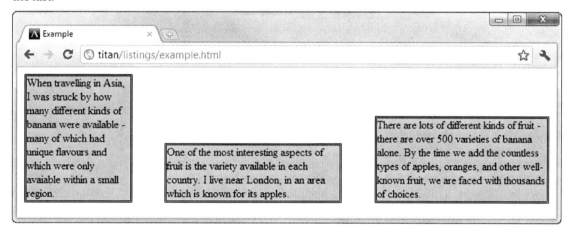

Figure 21-12. Using the box-pack property

Creating Table Layouts

For many years, the HTML table element has been widely used for laying out web pages, but the increased emphasis on the semantic significance of HTML elements makes this undesirable, and in HTML5 you must be careful only to use the table element to present tabular data (see Chapter 11 for details).

Of course, the reason that using the table element has been so popular is because it solves a very common layout problem: creating simple grids to hold content. Fortunately, you can use the CSS table layout feature to lay out your pages much as you would using the table element, but without abusing its semantic significance. You create CSS table layouts by using the display property. The values that relate to this feature are described in Table 21-11. Each of the values shown in the table corresponds to an HTML element.

Table 21-11. The display Property Values That Relate to Table Layouts

Value	Description
table	Behaves like the table element.
inline-table	Behaves like the table element, but creates an inline-level element (see Chapter 20 for details of block- and inline-level elements).
table-caption	Behaves like the caption element.
table-column	Behaves like the col element.
table-column-group	Behaves like the colgroup element.
table-header-group	Behaves like the thead element.
table-row-group	Behaves like the tbody element.
table-footer-group	Behaves like the tfoot element.
table-row	Behaves like the tr element.
table-cell	Behaves like the td element.

The process of applying these values is demonstrated in Listing 21-10.

Listing 21-10. Creating a CSS Table Layout

```
<!DOCTYPE HTML>
<html>
    <head>
        <title>Example</title>
        <meta name="author" content="Adam Freeman"/>
        <meta name="description" content="A simple example"/>
        <link rel="shortcut icon" href="favicon.ico" type="image/x-icon" />
        <style>

            #table {
                display: table;
            }
            div.row {
                display: table-row;
                background-color: lightgray;
            }

            p {
                display: table-cell;
```

```
                    border: thin solid black;
                    padding: 15px;
                    margin: 15px;
                }

                img {
                    float:left;
                }

        </style>
    </head>
    <body>
        <div id="table">
            <div class="row">
                <p>
                    There are lots of different kinds of fruit - there are over 500
                    varieties of banana alone. By the time we add the countless types of
                    apples, oranges, and other well-known fruit, we are faced with
                    thousands of choices.
                </p>
                <p>
                    One of the most interesting aspects of fruit is the variety available
                    in each country. I live near London, in an area which is known for
                    its apples.
                </p>
                <p>
                    When travelling in Asia, I was struck by how many different kinds of
                    banana were available - many of which had unique flavours and which
                    were only avaiable within a small region.
                </p>
            </div>
            <div class="row">
                <p>
                    This is an apple. <img src="apple.png" alt="apple"/>
                </p>
                <p>
                    This is a banana. <img src="banana-small.png" alt="banana"/>
                </p>
                <p>
                    No picture here
                </p>
            </div>
        </div>
    </body>
</html>
```

You can see the effect of these values in Figure 21-13.

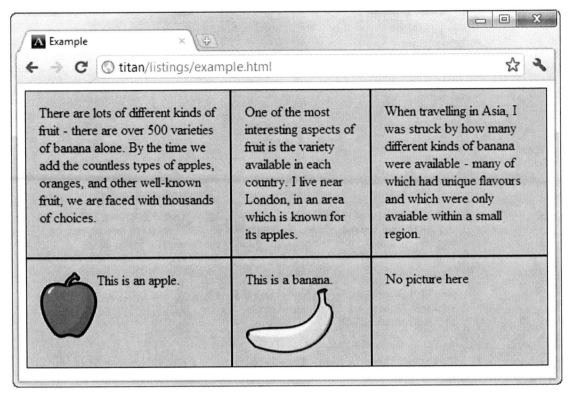

Figure 21-13. A simple CSS table layout

The behavior that table layouts are prized for is the automatic sizing of cells so that the widest or tallest content sets the size for the entire column or row. You can see this effect in Figure 21-13.

Summary

In this chapter, I have shown you the CSS features for creating layouts, ranging from the simple positioning of elements to the fluidity of the flexible box layout. I also showed you how to create table layouts without needing to abuse the `table` HTML element.

Layouts are an area that is receiving much attention in various CSS3 modules, but it is still early days and not all the feature sets are properly defined or implemented by the browsers. There is plenty to work within the interim (especially if you adopt a CSS layout framework), and I recommend you keep a close eye as CSS new layout modules gain acceptance.

CHAPTER 22

Styling Text

In this chapter, I show you the CSS properties you can use to style text. This is a volatile area for CSS3. There are some very useful new features that have been widely adopted (and which I explain in the sections that follow). There are also some very speculative proposals whose future is uncertain. These tend to deal with very technical typographic details, and it is not certain that there is sufficient demand to drive these proposals into standards. That said, the features that have been embraced by the mainstream browsers make working with text a lot more flexible and pleasant. Table 22-1 provides the summary for this chapter.

Table 22-1. *Chapter Summary*

Problem	Solution	Listing
Align a block of text.	Use the `text-align` and `text-justify` properties.	1
Define how white space is processed.	Use the `whitespace` property.	2, 3
Specify the direction that text should be drawn in.	Use the `direction` property.	4
Specify the spacing between words, letters, and lines of text.	Use the `letter-spacing`, `word-spacing`, and `line-height` properties.	5
Specify how overflowing text should be broken.	Use the `word-wrap` property.	6
Specify the indentation of text.	Use the `text-indent` property.	7
Decorate or transform text.	Use the `text-decoration` or `text-transform` property.	8
Apply a drop shadow to a block of text.	Use the `text-shadow` property.	9

| Specify and configure a font. | Use the font, font-family, font-size, font-style, font-variant, and font-weight properties. | 10-12 |
| Use a custom font. | Use @font-face. | 13 |

■ **Tip** The `color` property can be used to set the color of text. This property is described in Chapter 24.

Applying Basic Text Styles

In the following sections, I'll show you how to use the properties that apply basic text styling.

Aligning and Justifying Text

There are properties available for managing the alignment and justification of textual content, as described in Table 22-2.

Table 22-2. The Alignment and Justification Properties

Property	Description	Values
text-align	Specifies the alignment for a block of text	start end left right center justify
text-justify	Specifies the technique that will be used to justify the text when the justify value for the text-align property is used	See Table 22-3.

The `text-align` property is simple enough, although it is important to note that you can align text to an explicitly named edge (using the `left` and `right` values) or to the edges that are innate to the language being used (with the `start` and `end` values). This is an important distinction when dealing with right-to-left languages. Listing 22-1 shows the `text-align` property applied to blocks of text.

Listing 22-1. Aligning Text

```
<!DOCTYPE HTML>
<html>
    <head>
        <title>Example</title>
        <meta name="author" content="Adam Freeman"/>
        <meta name="description" content="A simple example"/>
        <link rel="shortcut icon" href="favicon.ico" type="image/x-icon" />
```

```
        <style>
            #fruittext {
                width: 400px;
                margin: 5px;
                padding: 5px;
                border: medium double black;
                background-color: lightgrey;
            }
        </style>
    </head>
    <body>
        <p id="fruittext">
            There are lots of different kinds of fruit - there are over 500
            varieties of banana alone. By the time we add the countless types of
            apples, oranges, and other well-known fruit, we are faced with
            thousands of choices.
            One of the most interesting aspects of fruit is the
            variety available in each country. I live near London, in an area which is
            known for its apples.
        </p>
        <p>
            <button>Start</button>
            <button>End</button>
            <button>Left</button>
            <button>Right</button>
            <button>Justify</button>
            <button>Center</button>
        </p>
        <script>
            var buttons = document.getElementsByTagName("BUTTON");
            for (var i = 0; i < buttons.length; i++) {
                buttons[i].onclick = function(e) {
                    document.getElementById("fruittext").style.textAlign =
                        e.target.innerHTML;
                };
            }
        </script>
    </body>
</html>
```

In this example, I added a simple script that changes the value of the text-align property for a p element based on button presses. Figure 22-1 shows the effect of some of the property values on the alignment of the text.

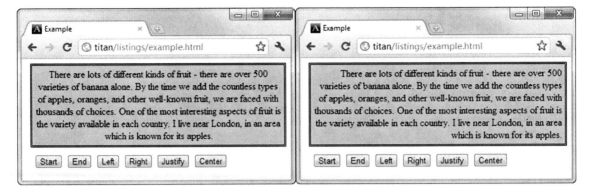

Figure 22-1. The effect of the center and right values for the text-align property

When using the justify value, you can use the text-justify property to specify how spacing is added to the text. The allowed values for this property are described in Table 22-3.

Table 22-3. The text-justify Property Values

Value	Description
auto	The browser will select the justification technique. This is the simplest approach, but it can lead to slight presentation differences between browsers.
none	Justification of the text is disabled.
inter-word	Spacing is distributed between words. This is suited to languages that use word separators, such as English.
inter-ideograph	Spacing is distributed between words and at inter-graphemic boundaries. This is suited to languages such as Japanese and Korean.
inter-cluster	Spacing is distributed between words and at grapheme cluster boundaries. This is suited to languages such as Thai.
distribute	Spacing is distributed between words and at grapheme cluster boundaries in all scripts except those that use connected or cursive styles.
kashida	Justification is applied by elongating characters (applies only to cursive scripts).

Dealing with Whitespace

Whitespace is usually collapsed or ignored in HTML. This allows you to separate the layout of your HTML documents from the appearance on the page. Listing 22-2 shows an HTML document with a text block that contains white space.

Listing 22-2. An HTML Document with White Space

```
<!DOCTYPE HTML>
<html>
    <head>
        <title>Example</title>
        <meta name="author" content="Adam Freeman"/>
        <meta name="description" content="A simple example"/>
        <link rel="shortcut icon" href="favicon.ico" type="image/x-icon" />
        <style>
            #fruittext {
                width: 400px;
                margin: 5px;
                padding: 5px;
                border: medium double black;
                background-color: lightgrey;
            }
        </style>
    </head>
    <body>
        <p id="fruittext">
            There are lots of different kinds of fruit - there are over 500
            varieties

            of banana alone. By the time we add the countless types of
            apples, oranges, and other well-known fruit, we are faced with
            thousands of choices.

            One     of the      most interesting aspects of fruit is the
            variety available    in each country. I live near London,

            in an area which is
            known for its apples.

        </p>
    </body>
</html>
```

I introduced some spaces, tabs, and line breaks into the text. When the browser encounters multiple white-space characters (such as multiple spaces), they are *collapsed*, meaning that they are replaced with a single space character. Other types of white space, such as line breaks, are simply ignored and the browser *wraps* the text so that individual lines fit within the boundaries of the element. You can see the way that the browser displays the text in the example in Figure 22-2.

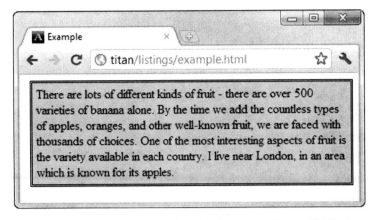

Figure 22-2. The default handling of white space in an HTML document

This isn't always convenient—sometimes you want to preserve the formatting of the text as it is in the source HTML document. You can control the handling of white space characters with the whitespace property, which is summarized in Table 22-4.

Table 22-4. The whitespace Property

Property	Description	Values
whitespace	Specifies how white-space characters will be processed	**See Table 22-5**

The allowed values for the whitespace property are described in Table 22-5.

Table 22-5. The whitespace Property Values

Value	Description
normal	This is the default value. Whitespace is collapsed, and lines are wrapped.
nowrap	Whitespace is collapsed, but lines are not wrapped.
pre	Whitespace is preserved, and text will wrap only on line breaks. This is the same effect that the pre element has (described in Chapter 8).
pre-line	Whitespace is collapsed, and text will wrap to make lines fit or when a line break is encountered.
pre-wrap	Whitespace is preserved, and text will wrap to make lines fit or when a line break is encountered.

Listing 22-3 demonstrates the application of the whitespace property.

Listing 22-3. Using the whitespace Property

```
<!DOCTYPE HTML>
<html>
    <head>
        <title>Example</title>
        <meta name="author" content="Adam Freeman"/>
        <meta name="description" content="A simple example"/>
        <link rel="shortcut icon" href="favicon.ico" type="image/x-icon" />
        <style>
            #fruittext {
                width: 400px;
                margin: 5px;
                padding: 5px;
                border: medium double black;
                background-color: lightgrey;
                white-space: pre-line;
            }
        </style>
    </head>
    <body>
        <p id="fruittext">
            There are lots of different kinds of fruit - there are over 500
            varieties

            of banana alone. By the time we add the countless types of
            apples, oranges, and other well-known fruit, we are faced with
            thousands of choices.

            One      of the      most interesting aspects of fruit is the
            variety available  in each country. I live near London,

            in an area which is
            known for its apples.

        </p>
    </body>
</html>
```

You can see the effect of the pre-line value in Figure 22-3. The text is wrapped so that the contents fit into the element, but the line breaks are preserved.

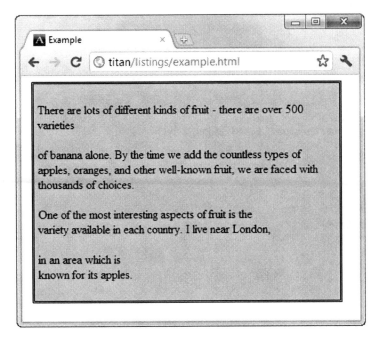

Figure 22-3. Using the pre-line value for the whitespace property

▪ **Tip** The CSS3 module for text defines the whitespace property as shorthand for two other properties: bikeshedding and text-wrap. Neither of these properties has been implemented yet, and the definition of the bikeshedding property is incomplete. (One of the outstanding issues is to pick a more meaningful name.)

Specifying Text Direction

The direction property lets you tell the browser about the directionality of a block of text, as described in Table 22-6.

Table 22-6. The direction Property

Property	Description	Values
direction	Sets the direction for the text	ltr rtl

You can see a simple application of the direction property in Listing 22-4.

Listing 22-4. Using the direction Property

```
<!DOCTYPE HTML>
<html>
    <head>
        <title>Example</title>
        <meta name="author" content="Adam Freeman"/>
        <meta name="description" content="A simple example"/>
        <link rel="shortcut icon" href="favicon.ico" type="image/x-icon" />
        <style>
            #first {
                direction: ltr;
            }

            #second {
                direction: rtl;
            }
        </style>
    </head>
    <body>
        <p id="first">
            This is left-to-right text
        </p>
        <p id="second">
            This is right-to-lefttext
        </p>
    </body>
</html>
```

You can see the effect of this property in Figure 22-4.

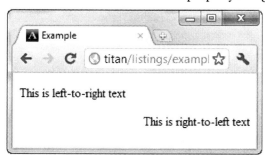

Figure 22-4. Using the direction property

■ **Caution** The direction property has been removed from the latest draft of the relevant CSS module, although no reason has been given and it may be restored before the module is finalized.

Specifying the Space Between Words, Letters, and Lines

You can tell the browser how much space to place between words, letters, and lines. The relevant properties are described in Table 22-7.

Table 22-7. The spacing Properties

Property	Description	Values
letter-spacing	Sets the space between letters	normal <length>
word-spacing	Sets the space between words	normal <length>
line-height	Sets the height of each line	normal <number> <length> <%>

Listing 22-5 shows all three properties applied to a block of text.

Listing 22-5. Using the letter-spacing and word-spacing Properties

```
<!DOCTYPE HTML>
<html>
    <head>
        <title>Example</title>
        <meta name="author" content="Adam Freeman"/>
        <meta name="description" content="A simple example"/>
        <link rel="shortcut icon" href="favicon.ico" type="image/x-icon" />
        <style>
            #fruittext {
                margin: 5px;
                padding: 5px;
                border: medium double black;
                background-color: lightgrey;
                word-spacing: 10px;
                letter-spacing: 2px;
                line-height: 3em;
            }
        </style>
    </head>
    <body>
        <p id="fruittext">
            There are lots of different kinds of fruit - there are over 500
            varieties of banana alone. By the time we add the countless types of
            apples, oranges, and other well-known fruit, we are faced with
            thousands of choices.
        </p>
```

```
        </body>
</html>
```

You can see the effect of these properties in Figure 22-5.

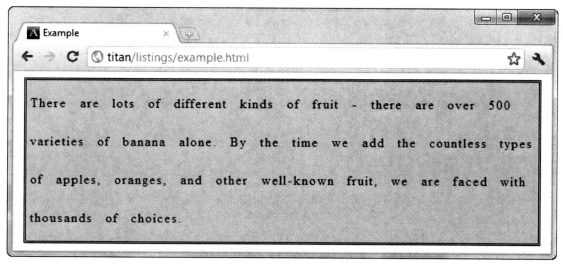

Figure 22-5. Applying the word-spacing and letter-spacing properties

Controlling Word Breaks

The word-wrap property tells the browser what to do when a word is longer than its containing block is wide. The allowed values for this property are described in Table 22-8.

Table 22-8. The word-wrap Property Values

Value	Description
normal	Words are not broken, even when they cannot be fitted into the containing element.
break-word	Words are broken to make them fit.

Listing 22-6 shows the application of the word-wrap property.

Listing 22-6. Using the word-wrap Property

```
<!DOCTYPE HTML>
<html>
    <head>
        <title>Example</title>
        <meta name="author" content="Adam Freeman"/>
        <meta name="description" content="A simple example"/>
        <link rel="shortcut icon" href="favicon.ico" type="image/x-icon" />
```

```
        <style>
            p {
                width:150px;
                margin: 15px;
                padding: 5px;
                border: medium double black;
                background-color: lightgrey;
                float:left;
            }

            #first {
                word-wrap: break-word;
            }

            #second {
                word-wrap: normal;
            }
        </style>
    </head>
    <body>
        <p id="first">
            There are lots of different kinds of fruit - there are over 500
            varieties of madeupfruitwithaverylongname alone.
        </p>
        <p id="second">
            There are lots of different kinds of fruit - there are over 500
            varieties of madeupfruitwithaverylongname alone.
        </p>
    </body>
</html>
```

There are two p elements in this example, to which I have applied the values of the word-wrap property. You can see the effect of the property in Figure 22-6.

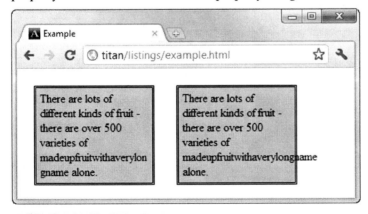

Figure 22-6. Using the word-wrap property

The left-most p element in the figure uses the break-word value, so the very long word in the text is broken and wrapped across two lines to make it fit. The other p element uses the default value, normal, which means the browser won't break the word, even though it flows over the edge of the p element.

⬛ **Tip** You can use the overflow property (described in Chapter 20) to stop the browser from displaying the overflowing text, although this will have the effect of simply not displaying the part of the word that doesn't fit.

Indenting the First Line

The text-indent property allows you to specify an indentation for the first line of a block of text, expressed either as a length or as a percentage of the width of the containing element. Table 22-9 summarizes this property.

Table 22-9. The text-indent Property

Property	Description	Values
text-indent	Sets the indentation of the first line of text	<length> <%>

Listing 22-7 shows the use of this property.

Listing 22-7. Using the text-indent Property

```
<!DOCTYPE HTML>
<html>
    <head>
        <title>Example</title>
        <meta name="author" content="Adam Freeman"/>
        <meta name="description" content="A simple example"/>
        <link rel="shortcut icon" href="favicon.ico" type="image/x-icon" />
        <style>
            p {
                margin: 15px;
                padding: 5px;
                border: medium double black;
                background-color: lightgrey;
                float:left;
                text-indent: 15%;
            }
        </style>
    </head>
    <body>
        <p>
            There are lots of different kinds of fruit - there are over 500
            varieties of banana alone. By the time we add the countless types of
```

```
        apples, oranges, and other well-known fruit, we are faced with
        thousands of choices.
        One of the most interesting aspects of fruit is the
        variety available in each country. I live near London, in an area which is
        known for its apples.
      </p>
    </body>
</html>
```

You can see the effect that this property has in Figure 22-7.

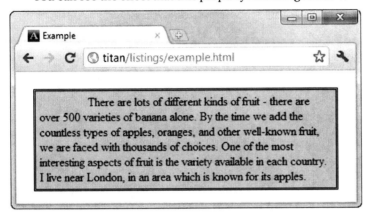

Figure 22-7. Indenting the first line in a block of text

Decorating and Transforming Text

There are two properties, text-decoration and text-transform, that allow you to decorate and transform text. These are described in Table 22-10.

Table 22-10. The Decoration and Tranformation Properties

Property	Description	Values
text-decoration	Applies a décor to a block of text	none underline overline line-through blink
text-transform	Applies a transformation to a block of text	none capitalize uppercase lowercase

The text-decoration property applies an effect to a block of text, such as underlining it. The default value is none (meaning no decoration is applied). The text-transform property changes the case of a block of text and, once again, the default value is none. You can see both properties applied, along with a script to switch between them, in Listing 22-8.

Listing 22-8. Using the text-decoration and text-transform Properties

```
<!DOCTYPE HTML>
<html>
    <head>
        <title>Example</title>
        <meta name="author" content="Adam Freeman"/>
        <meta name="description" content="A simple example"/>
        <link rel="shortcut icon" href="favicon.ico" type="image/x-icon" />
        <style>
            p {
                border: medium double black;
                background-color: lightgrey;
                text-decoration: line-through;
                text-transform: uppercase;
            }
        </style>
    </head>
    <body>
        <p>
            There are lots of different kinds of fruit - there are over 500
            varieties of banana alone. By the time we add the countless types of
            apples, oranges, and other well-known fruit, we are faced with
            thousands of choices.
            One of the most interesting aspects of fruit is the
            variety available in each country. I live near London, in an area which is
            known for its apples.
        </p>
    </body>
</html>
```

Figure 22-8 shows the effect of the uppercase value of the text-transform property and the line-through value of the text-decoration property applied together.

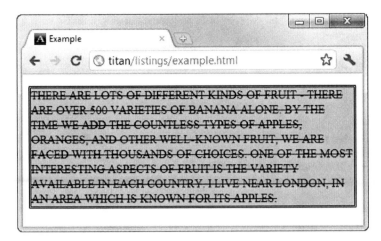

Figure 22-8. Decorating and transforming text

■ **Tip** The `blick` value for the `text-decoration` property should be used sparingly. It creates an effect that is very annoying, especially if the user will be working with the page for a protracted period. I recommend finding a less irritating way to draw a user's attention.

Creating Text Shadows

In Chapter 19, I showed you how to create shadows for elements. You can do much the same thing for text using the `text-shadow` property, which is summarized in Table 22-11.

Table 22-11. The text-shadow Property

Property	Description	Values
text-shadow	Applies a shadow to a block of text	<h-shadow> <v-shadow> <blur> <color>

The h-shadow and v-shadow values specify the offset for the shadow. Values are expressed as lengths and negative values are allowed. The blur value is another length value and specifies the degree of blur that will be applied to the shadow. This value is optional. The color value specifies the color of the shadow. Listing 22-9 shows the text-shadow property in use.

Listing 22-9. Using the text-shadow Property

```
<!DOCTYPE HTML>
<html>
    <head>
```

```
    <title>Example</title>
    <meta name="author" content="Adam Freeman"/>
    <meta name="description" content="A simple example"/>
    <link rel="shortcut icon" href="favicon.ico" type="image/x-icon" />
    <style>
        h1 {
            text-shadow: 0.1em .1em 1px lightgrey;
        }
        p {
            text-shadow: 5px 5px 20px black;
        }
    </style>
</head>
<body>
    <h1>Thoughts about Fruit</h1>
    <p>
        There are lots of different kinds of fruit - there are over 500
        varieties of banana alone. By the time we add the countless types of
        apples, oranges, and other well-known fruit, we are faced with
        thousands of choices.
    </p>
</body>
</html>
```

I applied two different shadows to the text in this example. You can see the effect in Figure 22-9. Notice that the shadow follows the shape of the text characters, rather than the containing element.

Figure 22-9. Applying shadows to text

Working with Fonts

One of the most fundamental changes you can make to text is to the font that is used to display the characters. Table 22-12 describes the font-related properties. Balance in typography is very difficult to achieve—on one hand, there are advanced users who want to control every aspect of their typography (of which there are many). On the other hand, there are regular designers and programmers who want ready access to key typographic features, but don't want to get bogged down in the detail. Sadly, CSS font support satisfies neither party. Very few of the deep technical aspects of typefaces are exposed, but those that are exposed present little use to the mainstream designer or programmer. There some proposed CSS3 modules that would enhance typeface support, but they are at an early stage and have yet to attract any mainstream implementations.

Table 22-12. *The Font Properties*

Property	Description	Values
font-family	Specifies the font family for a block of text	**See Table 22-13.**
font-size	Specifies the size of the font for a block of text	**See Table 22-14.**
font-style	Specifies the style for a font	normal italic oblique
font-variant	Specifies whether or not the text should be displayed in a small-caps font	normal smallcaps
font-weight	Specifies the weight for a font (the thickness of the characters)	normal bold bolder lighter <number 100-900>
font	Shorthand property to set fonts in a single declaration	**See sections that follow.**

The format for the font property value is as follows:

```
font: <font-style> <font-variant> <font-weight> <font-size> <font-family>
```

Selecting a Font

The font-family property specifies the fonts that will be used, in order of preference. The browser begins with the first font in the list and works its way down until it finds a font that can be used. This approach is required because you can use the fonts installed on a user's computer and, of course, different users will have different fonts installed based on operating system and preference.

As a final backstop, CSS defines some generic fonts that are available everywhere. These are broad categories of fonts, known as the *generic font families*, and there can be variations in the exact font that is used by a browser to render them. A summary of the generic font families can be found in Table 22-13.

Table 22-13. *The Generic Font Families*

Generic Font Family	Example Implementation Font
serif	Times
sans-serif	Helvetica
cursive	Zapf-Chancery
fantasy	Western
monospace	Courier

Listing 22-10 shows the font-family property applied to a block of text.

Listing 22-10. *Using the font-family Property*

```
<!DOCTYPE HTML>
<html>
    <head>
        <title>Example</title>
        <meta name="author" content="Adam Freeman"/>
        <meta name="description" content="A simple example"/>
        <link rel="shortcut icon" href="favicon.ico" type="image/x-icon" />
        <style>
            p {
                padding: 5px;
                border: medium double black;
                background-color: lightgrey;
                margin: 2px;
                float: left;
                font-family: "HelveticaNeue Condensed", monospace;
            }
        </style>
    </head>
    <body>
        <p>
            There are lots of different kinds of fruit - there are over 500
            varieties of banana alone. By the time we add the countless types of
            apples, oranges, and other well-known fruit, we are faced with
            thousands of choices.
        </p>
    </body>
</html>
```

In this example, I specified HelveticaNeue Condensed for the font-family property. This is a font that is used by Apress and isn't available on every system. I specified the generic monospace as the fallback to be used if HelveticaNeue Condensed isn't available. You can see the effect this has in Figure 22-10.

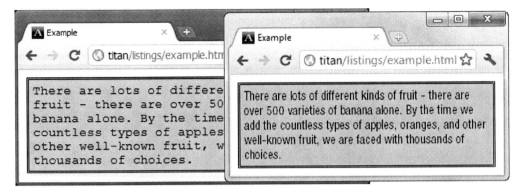

Figure 22-10. Using the font-family property

The browser on the right of the figure is running on the machine I use to write this book. It has the Apress fonts installed, so the browser is able to find and use HelveticaNeue Condensed. The browser on the left is from one of my test machines, which doesn't have HelveticaNeue Condensed installed. You can see that it has fallen back to using the generic monospace.

■ **Tip** One problem that can occur when using a fallback font is that the fonts have different sizes on screen. You can see this in the figure, where the fallback font is larger than the first-choice font. The font-size-adjust property can be used to express a scaling ratio, but this is supported only by Firefox at present.

Setting the Font Size

The font-size property lets you specify the size of the font. The allowed values for this property are described in Table 22-14.

Table 22-14. The font-size Property Values

Value	Description
xx-small x-small small medium large x-large xx-large	Sets the font size. The browser is responsible for deciding the exact size that each value represents, but the sizes are guaranteed to increase as you move down the list of values.
smaller larger	Sets the font size relative to the font size of the parent element.

\<length\>	Sets the font size precisely using a CSS length value.
\<%\>	Sets the font size as a percentage of the parent element's font size.

Listing 22-11 shows the font-size property in use.

Listing 22-11. Using the font-size Property

```
<!DOCTYPE HTML>
<html>
    <head>
        <title>Example</title>
        <meta name="author" content="Adam Freeman"/>
        <meta name="description" content="A simple example"/>
        <link rel="shortcut icon" href="favicon.ico" type="image/x-icon" />
        <style>
            p {
                padding: 5px;
                border: medium double black;
                background-color: lightgrey;
                margin: 2px;
                float: left;
                font-family: sans-serif;
                font-size: medium;
            }
            #first {
                font-size: xx-large;
            }
            #second {
                font-size: larger;
            }
        </style>
    </head>
    <body>
        <p>
            There are lots of different kinds of fruit - there are over 500
            varieties of <span id="first">banana</span> alone. By the time we add the
            countless types of <span id="second">apples, oranges, and other
            well-known fruit, we are faced with thousands of choices</span>.
        </p>
    </body>
</html>
```

In this example, I applied three font-size declarations. You can see the effect they have in Figure 22-11.

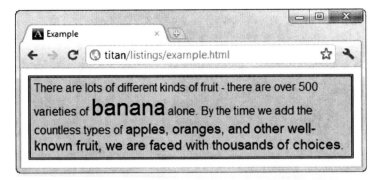

Figure 22-11. Using the font-size property

Setting the Font Style and Weight

You can set the weight of the font using the font-weight property—increasing the weight makes the text bolder. The font-style property allows you to select between normal, italic, and oblique fonts. There is a distinction between italic and oblique fonts, but it is tediously technical and for the most part makes little or no difference to the appearance of text. Listing 22-12 demonstrates these properties.

Listing 22-12. Using the font-weight and font-style Properties

```
<!DOCTYPE HTML>
<html>
    <head>
        <title>Example</title>
        <meta name="author" content="Adam Freeman"/>
        <meta name="description" content="A simple example"/>
        <link rel="shortcut icon" href="favicon.ico" type="image/x-icon" />
        <style>
            p {
                padding: 5px;
                border: medium double black;
                background-color: lightgrey;
                margin: 2px;
                float: left;
                font-family: sans-serif;
                font-size: medium;
            }
            #first {
                font-weight: bold;
            }
            #second {
                font-style: italic;
            }
        </style>
    </head>
    <body>
        <p>
```

```
        There are lots of different kinds of fruit - there are over 500
        varieties of <span id="first">banana</span> alone. By the time we add the
        countless types of <span id="second">apples, oranges, and other
        well-known fruit, we are faced with thousands of choices</span>.
      </p>
  </body>
</html>
```

You can see the effect of these properties in Figure 22-12.

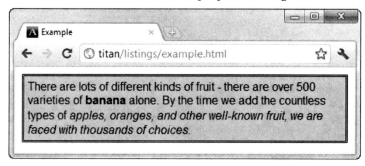

Figure 22-12. Using the font-weight and font-style properties

Using Web Fonts

I already alluded to one of the biggest problems with CSS fonts. The fact that you can't rely on the font you want to be installed on the user's machine. A solution to this problem is to use *web fonts*, where you can download a font and use it on your page without requiring any action on the part of the user. You specify web fonts using @font-face, as shown in Listing 22-13.

Listing 22-13. Using a Web Font

```
<!DOCTYPE HTML>
<html>
    <head>
        <title>Example</title>
        <meta name="author" content="Adam Freeman"/>
        <meta name="description" content="A simple example"/>
        <link rel="shortcut icon" href="favicon.ico" type="image/x-icon" />
        <style>
            @font-face {
                font-family: 'MyFont';
                font-style: normal;
                font-weight: normal;
                src: url('http://titan/listings/MyFont.woff');
            }
            p {
                padding: 5px;
                border: medium double black;
                background-color: lightgrey;
```

```
                margin: 2px;
                float: left;
                font-size: medium;
                font-family: MyFont, cursive;
            }
            #first {
                font-weight: bold;
            }
            #second {
                font-style: italic;
            }
        </style>
    </head>
    <body>
        <p>
            There are lots of different kinds of fruit - there are over 500
            varieties of <span id="first">banana</span> alone. By the time we add the
            countless types of <span id="second">apples, oranges, and other
            well-known fruit, we are faced with thousands of choices</span>.
        </p>
    </body>
</html>
```

When you use @font-face, you use the standard font properties to describe the font you are using. The font-family property defines the name by which you can refer to the downloaded font, and the font-style and font-weight properties tell the browser what the style and weight settings are for the font, which means that you can create italic and bold characters. The src property is used to specify the location of the font file. Web fonts come in many different formats, but the WOFF format seems to be the most widely supported and available.

▨ **Tip** Some web servers won't send font files to the browser by default. You may have to add the file type or MIME type to your server's configuration.

You can see the effect of the web font in Figure 22-13.

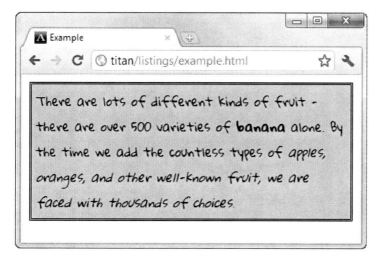

Figure 22-13. Using a web font

There are a lot of web font resources available. My favorite is provided by Google. You can see the fonts they have on offer and get instructions for how to include them in your HTML at `www.google.com/webfonts`. (this was the source for the font I used in the example.)

Summary

In this chapter, you saw the CSS properties that allow you to style text. The effects you can apply range from the simple (such as basic alignment) to the sophisticated (using custom fonts and creating text shadows). This is another volatile area for CSS. There are some interesting proposals for properties that would allow greater control over the appearance of text, but it is not yet clear if there is sufficient interest to drive adoption and it is entirely possible that these proposals will not become standards.

CHAPTER 23

Transitions, Animations, and Transforms

In this chapter, I introduce three different ways that you can apply simple special effects to HTML elements: *transitions*, *animations*, and *transforms*. I'll explain and demonstrate each of these terms later in the chapter. All three features are new in CSS3 and, as I write this, are supported only through browser-specific prefixes. This is something I expect to change reasonably quickly, because these features are going to be extremely popular with web designers and developers.

Applying effects to HTML elements isn't a new idea, and most of the good JavaScript libraries available contain at least a few of the effects that are now rolled into CSS3. The advantage of using CSS3 over JavaScript is performance. Much of the new functionality is about changing the value of CSS properties over time, and this is something that can be handled with less overhead directly in the browser engine. Despite this, these effects (even the basic ones) can take a lot of processing power, especially on complex web pages. For this reason, you should use the effects I describe in this chapter sparingly. Causing the user's computer to grind to a halt is always unwelcome, especially if you are just showing off your animation skills.

Another reason to use these effects infrequently is that they can be hugely distracting and annoying. Use these effects to enhance the task that the user is performing with your page—whatever that might be—and don't apply effects to elements that are not core to that task. Table 23-1 provides the summary for this chapter.

Table 23-1. Chapter Summary

Problem	Solution	Listing
Create a basic transition.	Use the transition-delay, transition-property, or transition-duration properties, or the transition shorthand property.	23-1, 23-2
Create an inverse transition.	Define a counter-transition in the base style for an element.	23-3
Specify how intermediate property values are calculated during a transition.	Use the transition-timing-function property.	23-4
Create a basic animation.	Use the animation-delay, animation-duration,	23-5

	animation-iteration-count, and animation-name properties. The animation-name value must correspond to a set of key frames defined using @keyframes.	
Set an initial state for an animation.	Add a from clause to the @keyframes declaration.	23-6
Specify intermediate key frames for an animation.	Add clauses to the @keyframes declaration, using the name of the clause to specify the percentage point of the animation to which the key frame pertains.	23-7
Specify the direction of alternate repeats of the animation.	Use the animation-direction property.	23-8
Preserve the final state of an animation.	Animations revert to the initial state at completion; consider using a transform instead.	23-9
Apply animations in the initial page layout.	Include the animation properties in styles that apply to elements in their base state.	23-10
Reuse key frames.	Create multiple styles that contain the animation-name property and whose values refer to the same @keyframes declaration.	23-11
Apply multiple animations to an element.	Specify multiple @keyframes declarations as the value of the animation-name property.	23-12, 23-13
Pause and resume an animation.	Use the animation-play-state property.	23-14
Apply a transform to an element.	Use the transform property.	23-15
Specify an origin for a transform.	Use the transform-origin property.	23-16
Animate or transition a transform.	Include the transform property in the transitioned style or in a @keyframes declaration.	23-17

Using Transitions

The browser normally applies changes in CSS properties to an element immediately. If you use the :hover selector, for example, the browser applies the properties you associate with the selector as soon as the user moves the mouse over the element. Listing 23-1 gives an example.

Listing 23-1. Immediately Applying a New Property Value

```
<!DOCTYPE HTML>
<html>
    <head>
        <title>Example</title>
        <meta name="author" content="Adam Freeman"/>
        <meta name="description" content="A simple example"/>
        <link rel="shortcut icon" href="favicon.ico" type="image/x-icon" />
        <style>
            p {
                padding: 5px;
                border: medium double black;
                background-color: lightgray;
                font-family: sans-serif;
            }
            #banana {
                font-size: large;
                border: medium solid black;
            }
            #banana:hover {
                font-size: x-large;
                border: medium solid white;
                background-color: green;
                color: white;
                padding: 4px;
            }
        </style>
    </head>
    <body>
        <p>
            There are lots of different kinds of fruit - there are over 500
            varieties of <span id="banana">banana</span> alone. By the time we add the
            countless types of apples, oranges, and other
            well-known fruit, we are faced with thousands of choices.
        </p>
    </body>
</html>
```

In this example, there is a span element for which there are two specific styles. One style is applied universally (with the selector #banana), and one is applied only when the user moves the mouse over the element (with the selector #banana:hover).

▓ **Tip** I have used the color property in this example. You can learn more about this property in Chapter 24.

The browser responds when the user moves the mouse over the span element, and applies the new property values immediately. You can see the change in Figure 23-1.

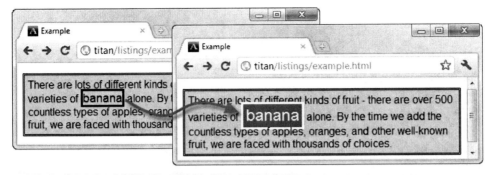

Figure 23-1. The immediate application of change CSS property values

The CSS transition feature allows you to control the rate at which new property values are applied. So, for example, you can choose to change the appearance of the span element in the example gradually, to make the effect of moving the mouse over the word banana less jarring. Table 23-2 describes the properties that let you do this.

Table 23-2. The Transition Properties

Property	Description	Values
transition-delay	Specifies a delay after which the transition will start.	*<time>*
transition-duration	Specifies the time span over which the transition will be performed.	*<time>*
transition-property	Specifies the property that the transition applies to.	*<string>*
transition-timing-function	Specifies the way that intermediate values are calculated during the transition.	See Listing 23-4.
transition	Shorthand to specify all of the details of a transition in one declaration.	See Listing 23-2.

The transition-delay and transition-duration properties are specified as CSS times, which are a number followed by either ms (to denote milliseconds) or s (to denote seconds).

The format for the transition shorthand property is as follows:

```
transition: <transition-property> <transition-duration> <transition-timing-function>
    <transition-delay>
```

Listing 23-2 shows how you can apply a transition to the example HTML document. As I write this, none of the mainstream browsers support the transition properties directly However, all but Internet Explorer implement the properties with the browser-specific prefix. I have used the –webkit prefix in the listing.

■ **Note** The animations feature is not yet implemented by any of the mainstream browsers using the standard properties. Much like transitions, all of the browsers except Internet Explorer implement the functionality using the browser-specific prefixes. In Listing 23-2, I used the -webkit prefix, meaning that this example will work with Safari and Chrome. If you want to work with Firefox or Opera, simply substitute -webkit for -moz or -o. This is another important area of enhancement in CCS3, and I expect that it will soon be implemented properly.

Listing 23-2. Using a Transition

```
<!DOCTYPE HTML>
<html>
    <head>
        <title>Example</title>
        <meta name="author" content="Adam Freeman"/>
        <meta name="description" content="A simple example"/>
        <link rel="shortcut icon" href="favicon.ico" type="image/x-icon" />
        <style>
            p {
                padding: 5px;
                border: medium double black;
                background-color: lightgray;
                font-family: sans-serif;
            }
            #banana {
                font-size: large;
                border: medium solid black;
            }
            #banana:hover {
                font-size: x-large;
                border: medium solid white;
                background-color: green;
                color: white;
                padding: 4px;
                -webkit-transition-delay: 100ms;
                -webkit-transition-property: background-color, color, padding,
                    font-size, border;
                -webkit-transition-duration: 500ms;
            }
        </style>
    </head>
    <body>
        <p>
            There are lots of different kinds of fruit - there are over 500
            varieties of <span id="banana">banana</span> alone. By the time we add the
            countless types of apples, oranges, and other
            well-known fruit, we are faced with thousands of choices.
        </p>
```

```
        </body>
    </html>
```

In this example, I have added a transition to the style that is applied through the #banana:hover selector. This transition will be started 100 milliseconds after the user moves the mouse over the span element, have a duration of 500 milliseconds, and apply to the background-color, color, padding, font-size, and border properties. Figure 23-2 shows the gradual progression of the transition.

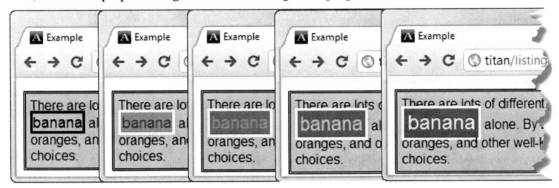

Figure 23-2. The gradual application of a transition

Notice how I specified multiple properties in the example. Each of the transition properties will take comma-separated values so that you can have concurrent transitions effects. You can specify multiple values for the delay and duration as well, which means that different property transitions start at different times and run for different durations.

Creating Inverse Transitions

Transitions take effect only when the style they are associated with is applied. My example style uses the :hover selector, which means that the style is only applied when the user's mouse is over the span element. As soon as the user moves the mouse away from the span element, only the #banana style applies and, by default, the appearance of the element instantly snaps back to its original state.

It is for this reason that most transitions come in pairs: the transition to the temporary state and the inverse transition back in the other direction. Listing 23-3 shows how you can smooth the return to the original style through the application of a second transition.

Listing 23-3. Creating a Second Transition

```
<!DOCTYPE HTML>
<html>
    <head>
        <title>Example</title>
        <meta name="author" content="Adam Freeman"/>
        <meta name="description" content="A simple example"/>
        <link rel="shortcut icon" href="favicon.ico" type="image/x-icon" />
        <style>
            p {
                padding: 5px;
                border: medium double black;
```

```
                background-color: lightgray;
                font-family: sans-serif;
            }
            #banana {
                font-size: large;
                border: medium solid black;
                -webkit-transition-delay: 10ms;
                -webkit-transition-duration: 250ms;
            }
            #banana:hover {
                font-size: x-large;
                border: medium solid white;
                background-color: green;
                color: white;
                padding: 4px;
                -webkit-transition-delay: 100ms;
                -webkit-transition-property: background-color, color, padding,
                    font-size, border;
                -webkit-transition-duration: 500ms;
            }
        </style>
    </head>
    <body>
        <p>
            There are lots of different kinds of fruit - there are over 500
            varieties of <span id="banana">banana</span> alone. By the time we add the
            countless types of apples, oranges, and other
            well-known fruit, we are faced with thousands of choices.
        </p>
    </body>
</html>
```

I have omitted the transition-property property in this example. This causes all of the property changes to be applied gradually throughout the duration of the transition. I have also specified an initial delay of 10 milliseconds and duration of 250 milliseconds. Adding a brief inverse transition makes the return to the original state less jarring.

░ **Tip** The browser doesn't apply transitions when first laying out the page. This means that the properties in the #banana style are applied immediately when the HTML document is first displayed, and then applied gradually through a transition thereafter.

Selecting How Intermediate Values Are Calculated

When you use a transition, the browser has to work out intermediate values between the initial and final values for each property. You use the transition-timing-function property to specify the way that intermediate values are determined, expressed as a set of four points representing a cubic Bezier curve. There are five preset curves to choose from, represented by the following values:

- ease (the default value)

- linear

- ease-in

- ease-out

- ease-in-out

You can see each curve in Figure 23-3. The line shows the rate at which the intermediate values progress toward the final value over time.

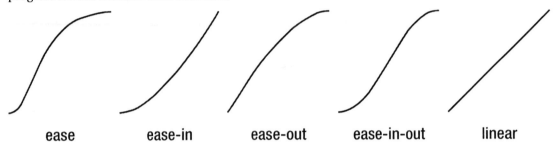

Figure 23-3. The timing function curves

The easiest way to make sense of these values is to experiment in your own HTML document. There is one additional value, cubic-bezier, that allows you to specify a custom curve. However, my experience is that the transitions are not as smooth as they could be and that a lack of granularity undermines most of these values and makes specifying a custom curve largely pointless. Hopefully the implementations will improve as they converge on the final standard. Listing 23-4 shows the application of the transition-timing-function property.

Listing 23-4. Using the transition-timing-function Property

```
<!DOCTYPE HTML>
<html>
    <head>
        <title>Example</title>
        <meta name="author" content="Adam Freeman"/>
        <meta name="description" content="A simple example"/>
        <link rel="shortcut icon" href="favicon.ico" type="image/x-icon" />
        <style>
            p {
                padding: 5px;
                border: medium double black;
                background-color: lightgray;
                font-family: sans-serif;
            }
            #banana {
                font-size: large;
                border: medium solid black;
                -webkit-transition-delay: 10ms;
```

```
                -webkit-transition-duration: 250ms;
        }
        #banana:hover {
            font-size: x-large;
            border: medium solid white;
            background-color: green;
            color: white;
            padding: 4px;
            -webkit-transition-delay: 100ms;
            -webkit-transition-property: background-color, color, padding,
                font-size, border;
            -webkit-transition-duration: 500ms;
            -webkit-transition-timing-function: linear;
        }
    </style>
</head>
<body>
    <p>
        There are lots of different kinds of fruit - there are over 500
        varieties of <span id="banana">banana</span> alone. By the time we add the
        countless types of apples, oranges, and other
        well-known fruit, we are faced with thousands of choices.
    </p>
</body>
</html>
```

I have selected the linear value, which is the one that I find gives me the least stuttering transition.

Using Animations

CSS animations are essentially enhanced transitions. You have more options, more control, and more flexibility in how you move from one CSS style to another. Table 23-3 describes the animation properties.

Table 23-3. The Animation Properties

Property	Description	Values
animation-delay	Sets a delay before the animation commences.	*<time>*
animation-direction	Specifies whether the animation should be played backward on alternate cycles.	normal alternate
animation-duration	Specifies the span of time over which the animation will be performed.	*<time>*
animation-iteration-count	Specifies the number of times that the animation will be performed.	infinite *<number>*
animation-name	Specifies the name of the animation.	none

589

		`<string>`
`animation-play-state`	Allows the animation to be paused and resumed.	`running` `paused`

`animation-timing-function`	Specifies how intermediate animation values are calculated. See the section "Using Transitions," earlier in this chapter, for details of these values.	`ease`
		`linear`
		`ease-in`
		`ease-out`
		`ease-in-out`
		`cubic-bezier`

`animation`	Shorthand property.	See the following explanation.

The format for the animation shorthand property is as follows:

```
animation: <animation-name> <animation-duration> <animation-timing-function>
    <animation-delay> <animation-iteration-count>
```

Notice that none of these properties allow you to specify the CSS properties that will be animated. This is because animations are defined in two parts. The first part is contained within the style declaration and uses the properties shown in Table 23-3. This defines the style of the animation, but not what is to be animated. The second part is created with the @key-frames rule, and is used to define the set of properties that the animation will apply to. You can see both parts of the animation in Listing 23-5.

Listing 23-5. Creating an Animation

```
<!DOCTYPE HTML>
<html>
    <head>
        <title>Example</title>
        <meta name="author" content="Adam Freeman"/>
        <meta name="description" content="A simple example"/>
        <link rel="shortcut icon" href="favicon.ico" type="image/x-icon" />
        <style>
            p {
                padding: 5px;
                border: medium double black;
                background-color: lightgray;
                font-family: sans-serif;
            }
            #banana {
                font-size: large;
                border: medium solid black;
            }

            #banana:hover {
                -webkit-animation-delay: 100ms;
                -webkit-animation-duration: 500ms;
```

```
                        -webkit-animation-iteration-count: infinite;
                        -webkit-animation-timing-function: linear;
                        -webkit-animation-name: 'GrowShrink';
                    }

                    @-webkit-keyframes GrowShrink {
                        to {
                            font-size: x-large;
                            border: medium solid white;
                            background-color: green;
                            color: white;
                            padding: 4px;
                        }
                    }
            </style>
        </head>
        <body>
            <p>
                There are lots of different kinds of fruit - there are over 500
                varieties of <span id="banana">banana</span> alone. By the time we add the
                countless types of apples, oranges, and other
                well-known fruit, we are faced with thousands of choices.
            </p>
        </body>
</html>
```

To understand what is happening in this example, you have to look at both parts of the animation. The first part is the use of the animation properties in the style with the #banana:hover selector. Let's start with the basic properties: the animation will start 100 milliseconds after the style has been applied, will have a duration of 500 milliseconds, will repeat indefinitely, and intermediate values will be calculated using the linear function. With the exception of repeating the animation, these properties have direct counterparts in transitions.

These basic properties don't describe the set of properties that will be animated. To do this, I need to use the animation-name property. By setting the value of this property to GrowShrink, I have instructed the browser to find a set of *key frames* called GrowShrink and use the values of the basic properties to animate the properties specified by the key frames. Here is the key frame declaration from the listing (I have removed the –webkit prefix):

```
@keyframes GrowShrink {
    to {
        font-size: x-large;
        border: medium solid white;
        background-color: green;
        color: white;
        padding: 4px;
    }
}
```

I start the declaration with @keyframes and then specify the name by which this set will be known. In this case, the name is GrowShrink. Inside the declaration, I specify the set of properties that will be animated. In this case, I have specified five properties and their values inside of a to declaration. This is the simplest kind of key frame set. The to declaration defines both the set of properties to animate and the final values for those properties at the end of the animation. (I'll show you more complex key frames shortly.) The initial values for the animation are taken from the property values of the animated element prior to the style being applied.

The animation in the listing is similar to the example I used for transitions earlier in the chapter, and the effect even looks the same when you view the HTML document in a browser and move the mouse over the span element. At least it looks the same initially, and then the animation repeats itself, which is the first of the differences. The span element grows in size, reaches its maximum, and then returns to its original state, at which point the animation starts over. You can see the effect in Figure 23-4.

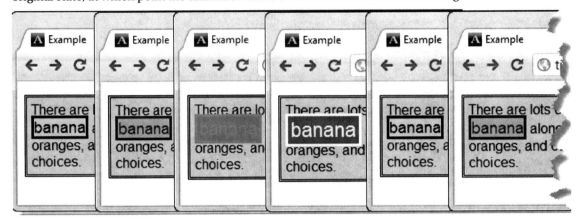

Figure 23-4. Repeating states in an animation

Working with Key Frames

The key frames aspect of CSS animations is extremely flexible and well worth exploring. In the sections that follow, I'll show some different ways to express key frames in order to create more complex effects.

Setting an Initial State

In the previous example, the initial values for the animated properties were taken from the element itself. You can specify an alternate set of initial values using the from clause, as shown in Listing 23-6.

Listing 23-6. Specifying an Alternate Initial State

```
...
<style>
    p {
        padding: 5px;
        border: medium double black;
        background-color: lightgray;
        font-family: sans-serif;
    }
    #banana {
        font-size: large;
        border: medium solid black;
```

```
}

#banana:hover {
    -webkit-animation-delay: 100ms;
    -webkit-animation-duration: 250ms;
    -webkit-animation-iteration-count: infinite;
    -webkit-animation-timing-function: linear;
    -webkit-animation-name: 'GrowShrink';
}

@-webkit-keyframes GrowShrink {
    from {
        font-size: xx-small;
        background-color: red;
    }
    to {
        font-size: x-large;
        border: medium solid white;
        background-color: green;
        color: white;
        padding: 4px;
    }
}
</style>
...
```

In this example, I have provided initial values for the font-size and background-color properties. The initial values for the other properties specified in the to clause will be taken from the element when the animation commences. You can see the effect of the new clause in Figure 23-5. The text size and background color of the span element switch to the initial values specified in the from clause at the start of the animation.

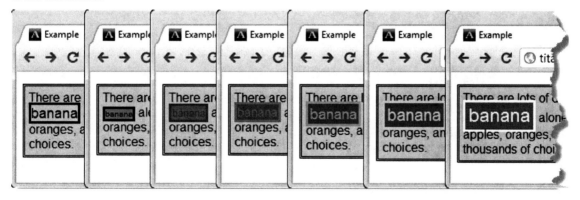

Figure 23-5. Setting an initial state with a from clause

Specifying Intermediate Key Frames

You can add additional key frames to define intermediate stages in the animation. You do this by adding *percentage clauses,* as demonstrated in Listing 23-7.

Listing 23-7. Adding Intermediate Key Frames

```
...
<style>
    p {
        padding: 5px;
        border: medium double black;
        background-color: lightgray;
        font-family: sans-serif;
    }
    #banana {
        font-size: large;
        border: medium solid black;
    }

    #banana:hover {
        -webkit-animation-delay: 100ms;
        -webkit-animation-duration: 2500ms;
        -webkit-animation-iteration-count: infinite;
        -webkit-animation-timing-function: linear;
        -webkit-animation-name: 'GrowShrink';
    }

    @-webkit-keyframes GrowShrink {
        from {
            font-size: xx-small;
            background-color: red;
        }

        50% {
            background-color: yellow;
            padding: 1px;
        }

        75% {
            color: white;
            padding: 2px;
        }

        to {
            font-size: x-large;
            border: medium solid white;
            background-color: green;
            padding: 4px;
        }
    }
```

```
</style>
...
```

For each percentage clause, you define the point in the animation where the properties and values specified in the clause should be fully applied. In this example, I have defined a 50% and a 75% clause.

There are two uses for intermediate key frames. The first is to define a new rate of change for a property. I have done this for the padding property. At the midway point (defined by the 50% clause), the padding for the animated element will be 1px. At 75%, it will be 2px, and by the end of the animation it will be set to 4px. The browser will calculate the progression of values required to move from one key frame to another using the timing function specified by the animation-timing-function property, giving a smooth progression from one key frame to the next.

■ **Tip** If you prefer, you may use 0% and 100% instead of from and to when defining the first and last key frames.

The other use for intermediate key frames is to define values to create more complex animations. I have done this with the background-color property. The initial value (red) is defined in the from clause. At the 50 percent point, the value will be yellow, and at the end of the animation, it will be green. By adding a nonsequential intermediate value, I have created two color transitions in a single animation: red to yellow, and yellow to green Notice that I have not provided an intermediate value in the 75% clause. This is because you don't have to provide values for every key frame. You can see the effect of the new key frames in Figure 23-6.

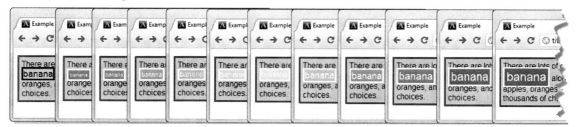

Figure 23-6. Adding intermediate key frames

Setting the Repeat Direction

When you set an animation to repeat, you have a choice about what happens when the browser reaches the end of the animation. You specify your preference using the animation-direction property, using the values that are described in Table 23-4.

Table 23-4. The animation-direction Property Values

Value	Description
normal	Every iteration of the animation is played forward. If there are multiple iterations, the element snaps back to its initial state and the animation is repeated.

alternate	The animation is played forward and then in reverse. This is two iterations of the animation for the purposes of the animation-iteration-count property..

You can see the animation-direction property in Listing 23-8.

Listing 23-8. Using the animation-direction Property

```
<style>
    p {
        padding: 5px;
        border: medium double black;
        background-color: lightgray;
        font-family: sans-serif;
    }
    #banana {
        font-size: large;
        border: medium solid black;
    }

    #banana:hover {
        -webkit-animation-delay: 100ms;
        -webkit-animation-duration: 250ms;
        -webkit-animation-iteration-count: 2;
        -webkit-animation-timing-function: linear;
        -webkit-animation-name: 'GrowShrink';
        -webkit-animation-direction: alternate;
    }

    @-webkit-keyframes GrowShrink {
        to {
            font-size: x-large;
            border: medium solid white;
            background-color: green;
            padding: 4px;
        }
    }
}
</style>
```

In this example, I have used the animation-iteration-count property to specify that the animation should be performed only twice. At the end of the second iteration, the animated element will return to its original state. I have used the alternate value for the animation-direction property so that the animation is played forward and then backward. You can see the effect in Figure 23-7.

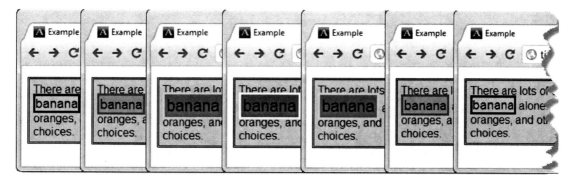

Figure 23-7. Setting the direction of the animation to alternate

If I had used the `infinite` value for the `animation-iteration-count` property, the animation would have been played forward and backward for as long as the mouse was hovering over the `span` element, creating a simple pulsing effect.

The `normal` value causes the animation to jump back to the start and each iteration is played forward. You can see the effect of this in Figure 23-8.

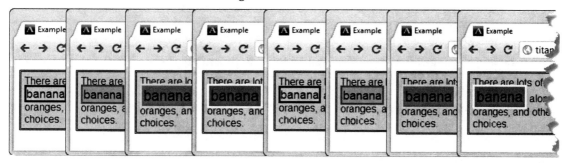

Figure 23-8. Setting the direction of the animation to normal

Understanding the End State

One of the limitations of CSS animations is that the values for the properties defined by the key frames in an animation are only applied during the animation itself. At the end of the animation, the appearance of the animated element will revert to its original state. Listing 23-9 gives an example.

Listing 23-9. Loss of Animation State at the End of the Animation

```
...
<style>
    p {
        padding: 5px;
        border: medium double black;
        background-color: lightgray;
        font-family: sans-serif;
    }
```

```
#banana {
    font-size: large;
    border: medium solid black;
}

#banana:hover {
    -webkit-animation-delay: 100ms;
    -webkit-animation-duration: 250ms;
    -webkit-animation-iteration-count: 1;
    -webkit-animation-timing-function: linear;
    -webkit-animation-name: 'GrowShrink';
}

@-webkit-keyframes GrowShrink {
    to {
        font-size: x-large;
        border: medium solid white;
        background-color: green;
        padding: 4px;
    }
}
</style>
...
```

You can see the effect this creates in Figure 23-8. Even though the mouse is still hovering over the span element, the appearance of the element is reset once the animation is complete.

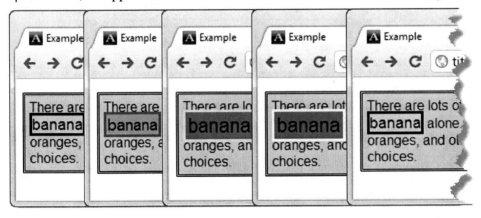

Figure 23-9. The reverted appearance of an element, after the animation is complete

The reason that this happens is because CSS animations animate the application of a new style, but don't make any persistent changes themselves. If you want to preserve the appearance of the element at the end of the animation, you must use a transition as described earlier in this chapter.

Applying Animations to the Initial Layout

One advantage that animations have over transitions is that you can apply them to the initial layout of the page. Listing 23-10 gives an example.

Listing 23-10. Animating an Element at Initial Layout

```
...
<style>
    p {
        padding: 5px;
        border: medium double black;
        background-color: lightgray;
        font-family: sans-serif;
    }
    #banana {
        font-size: large;
        border: medium solid black;
        -webkit-animation-duration: 2500ms;
        -webkit-animation-iteration-count: infinite;
        -webkit-animation-direction: alternate;
        -webkit-animation-timing-function: linear;
        -webkit-animation-name: 'ColorSwap';
    }

    @-webkit-keyframes ColorSwap {
        to {
            border: medium solid white;
            background-color: green;
        }
    }
</style>
...
```

In this example, I have defined the animation in the style with the #banana selector. This style is applied automatically when the page is loaded, which means that the animation is applied as soon as the browser displays the HTML.

▪ **Tip** You should use this approach with particular caution. Animating the page when you are not responding to a user action should be used sparingly, and the animation effects should be subtle and not prevent the user from reading or interacting with the wider page.

Reusing Key Frames

You can use the same set of key frames for multiple animations, each of which can be configured with different values for the animation properties. Listing 23-11 gives a demonstration.

Listing 23-11. Reusing Key Frames Across Multiple Animations

```
<!DOCTYPE HTML>
<html>
    <head>
        <title>Example</title>
        <meta name="author" content="Adam Freeman"/>
        <meta name="description" content="A simple example"/>
        <link rel="shortcut icon" href="favicon.ico" type="image/x-icon" />
<style>
    p {
        padding: 5px;
        border: medium double black;
        background-color: lightgray;
        font-family: sans-serif;
    }

    span {
        font-size: large;
        border: medium solid black;
    }

    #banana {
        -webkit-animation-duration: 2500ms;
        -webkit-animation-iteration-count: infinite;
        -webkit-animation-direction: alternate;
        -webkit-animation-timing-function: linear;
        -webkit-animation-name: 'ColorSwap';
    }

    #apple {
        -webkit-animation-duration: 500ms;
        -webkit-animation-iteration-count: infinite;
        -webkit-animation-direction: normal;
        -webkit-animation-timing-function: ease-in-out;
        -webkit-animation-name: 'ColorSwap';
    }

    @-webkit-keyframes ColorSwap {
        to {
            border: medium solid white;
            background-color: green;
        }
    }

</style>
    </head>
    <body>
        <p>
            There are lots of different kinds of fruit - there are over 500
            varieties of <span id="banana">banana</span> alone. By the time we add the
```

```
                countless types of <span id="apple">apples</span>, oranges, and other
                well-known fruit, we are faced with thousands of choices.
        </p>
    </body>
</html>
```

Listing 23-11 shows two styles, each of which uses the ColorSwap key frames. The animation associated with the #apple selector will be performed over a short direction, using a different timing function, and will also be played forward.

Applying Multiple Animations to Multiple Elements

A variation on the previous example is to target multiple elements with the same animation. You do this by expanding the scope of the selector for the style that contains the animation details, as shown in Listing 23-12.

Listing 23-12. Targeting Multiple Elements

```
...
<style>
    p {
        padding: 5px;
        border: medium double black;
        background-color: lightgray;
        font-family: sans-serif;
    }

    span {
        font-size: large;
        border: medium solid black;
    }

    #banana, #apple {
        -webkit-animation-duration: 2500ms;
        -webkit-animation-iteration-count: infinite;
        -webkit-animation-direction: alternate;
        -webkit-animation-timing-function: linear;
        -webkit-animation-name: 'ColorSwap';
    }

    @-webkit-keyframes ColorSwap {
        to {
            border: medium solid white;
            background-color: green;
        }
    }
</style>
...
```

In this example, both span elements in the document are matched by the selector, so both will be animated using the same key frames and the same configuration. You can see the effect in Figure 23-10.

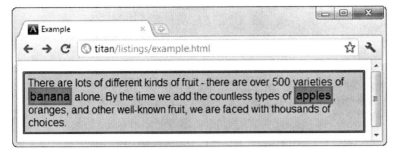

Figure 23-10. Animating multiple elements with the same animation

You can also apply multiple animations to an element by simply adding comma-separated values to the animation properties. Listing 23-13 shows how you can apply multiple key frames to a single element.

Listing 23-13. Applying Multiple Key Frames to a Single Element

```
...
<style>
    p {
        padding: 5px;
        border: medium double black;
        background-color: lightgray;
        font-family: sans-serif;
    }

    span {
        font-size: large;
        border: medium solid black;
    }

    #banana, #apple {
        -webkit-animation-duration: 1500ms;
        -webkit-animation-iteration-count: infinite;
        -webkit-animation-direction: alternate;
        -webkit-animation-timing-function: linear;
        -webkit-animation-name: 'ColorSwap', 'GrowShrink';
    }

    @-webkit-keyframes ColorSwap {
        to {
            border: medium solid white;
            background-color: green;
        }
    }

    @-webkit-keyframes GrowShrink {
        to {
            font-size: x-large;
```

```
            padding: 4px;
        }
    }
</style>
...
```

In this example, I have applied the ColorSwap and GrowShrink key frames to the #banana and #apple elements. The browser will apply both key frames simultaneously.

Stopping and Starting Animations

You can stop and resume an animation through the animation-play-state property. When this property has a value of paused, the animation will be halted. The value playing will resume the animation. Listing 23-14 shows how you can use JavaScript to change the value of this property. I'll explain more about how you can use JavaScript in similar situations in Part IV of this book.

Listing 23-14. Stopping and Starting an Animation

```
<!DOCTYPE HTML>
<html>
    <head>
        <title>Example</title>
        <meta name="author" content="Adam Freeman"/>
        <meta name="description" content="A simple example"/>
        <link rel="shortcut icon" href="favicon.ico" type="image/x-icon" />
        <style>
            #fruittext {
                padding: 5px;
                border: medium double black;
                background-color: lightgray;
                font-family: sans-serif;
            }

            #banana {
                -webkit-animation-duration: 2500ms;
                -webkit-animation-iteration-count: infinite;
                -webkit-animation-direction: alternate;
                -webkit-animation-timing-function: linear;
                -webkit-animation-name: 'GrowShrink';
            }

            @-webkit-keyframes GrowShrink {
                from {
                    font-size: large;
                    border: medium solid black;
                }
                to {
                    font-size: x-large;
                    border: medium solid white;
                    background-color: green;
                    color: white;
                    padding: 4px;
```

```
                }
            }
        </style>
    </head>
    <body>
        <p id="fruittext">
            There are lots of different kinds of fruit - there are over 500
            varieties of <span id="banana">banana</span> alone. By the time we add the
            countless types of apples, oranges, and other
            well-known fruit, we are faced with thousands of choices.
        </p>
        <p>
            <button>Running</button>
            <button>Paused</button>
        </p>
        <script>
            var buttons = document.getElementsByTagName("BUTTON");
            for (var i = 0; i < buttons.length; i++) {
                buttons[i].onclick = function(e) {
                    document.getElementById("banana").style.webkitAnimationPlayState =
                        e.target.innerHTML;
                };
            }
        </script>
    </body>
</html>
```

Using Transforms

CSS *transforms* allow you to apply linear transformations to elements, meaning that you can rotate, scale, skew, and translate elements. Table 23-5 shows the properties that you use to apply transforms.

Table 23-5. The Transforms Properties

Property	Description	Values
transform	Specifies the transform function to apply.	See Table 23-6.
transform-origin	Specifies the origin of the transform.	See Table 23-7.

Applying a Transform

You apply a transform to an element through the transform property. The allowed values for this property are a set of predefined functions, as described in Table 23-6.

Table 23-6. *The transform Property Values*

Value	Description
translate(*<length or %>*) translateX(*<length or %>*) translateY(*<length or %>*)	Translate an element in the X, Y, or both directions.
scale(*<number>*) scaleX(*<number>*) scaleY(*<number>*)	Scale an element along one or both axes.
rotate(*<angle>*)	Rotate an element.
skew(*<angle>*) skewX(*<angle>*) skewY(*<angle>*)	Skew an element along one or both axes.
matrix(*4-6 x <number>*)	Specify a custom transform. Most browsers don't yet implement z-axis scaling, so the last two numbers are ignored (and in some cases must be omitted).

You can see an example of a transform in Listing 23-15. As with the other CSS features in this chapter, the mainstream browsers don't yet implement transforms directly. I have used the –moz prefix in the listing because Firefox has the most complete implementation.

Listing 23-15. Applying a Transform to an Element

```
<!DOCTYPE HTML>
<html>
    <head>
        <title>Example</title>
        <meta name="author" content="Adam Freeman"/>
        <meta name="description" content="A simple example"/>
        <link rel="shortcut icon" href="favicon.ico" type="image/x-icon" />
        <style>
            p {
                padding: 5px;
                border: medium double black;
                background-color: lightgray;
                font-family: sans-serif;
            }
            #banana {
                font-size: x-large;
                border: medium solid white;
                background-color: green;
                color: white;
                padding: 4px;
                -moz-transform: rotate(-45deg) scaleX(1.2);
```

```
            }
        </style>
    </head>
    <body>
        <p id="fruittext">
            There are lots of different kinds of fruit - there are over 500
            varieties of <span id="banana">banana</span> alone. By the time we add the
            countless types of apples, oranges, and other
            well-known fruit, we are faced with thousands of choices.
        </p>
    </body>
</html>
```

In this example, I have added a transform property declaration to the #banana style, specifying two transforms. The first is a rotation of -45deg (i.e., a counterclockwise 45-degree rotation), and the second is a scaling with a factor of 1.2 along the x axis. You can see the effect of these transformations in Figure 23-11.

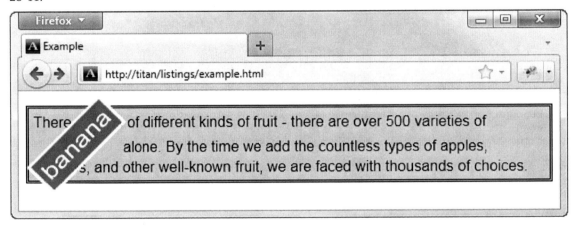

Figure 23-11. Rotating and scaling an element

As you can see, the element has been rotated and scaled as specified. Notice that the layout of the page hasn't changed to accommodate the transforms. The element overwrites some of the surrounding content.

Specifying an Origin

The transform-origin property allows you to specify the origin around which the transform will be applied. By default, the center of the element is used, but you can select a different origin using the values described in Table 23-7.

Table 23-7. The transform-origin Property Values

Value	Description
<%>	Specifies the origin of the elements x or y axis.
<length>	Specifies a distance.
left center right	Specifies a position on the x axis.
top center bottom	Specifies a position on the y axis.

To define a value, you provide a value for each of the x and y axes. If you supply only one value, the second value is assumed to be center. Listing 23-16 shows the use of the transform-origin property.

Listing 23-16. Using the transform-origin Property

```
<!DOCTYPE HTML>
<html>
    <head>
        <title>Example</title>
        <meta name="author" content="Adam Freeman"/>
        <meta name="description" content="A simple example"/>
        <link rel="shortcut icon" href="favicon.ico" type="image/x-icon" />
        <style>
            p {
                padding: 5px;
                border: medium double black;
                background-color: lightgray;
                font-family: sans-serif;
            }
            #banana {

                font-size: x-large;
                border: medium solid white;
                background-color: green;
                color: white;
                padding: 4px;
                -moz-transform: rotate(-45deg) scaleX(1.2);
                -moz-transform-origin: right top;
            }
        </style>
    </head>
    <body>
        <p id="fruittext">
```

```
            There are lots of different kinds of fruit - there are over 500
            varieties of <span id="banana">banana</span> alone. By the time we add the
            countless types of apples, oranges, and other
            well-known fruit, we are faced with thousands of choices.
        </p>
    </body>
</html>
```

In this example, I have moved the origin to the top-right corner of the element. You can see the effect this has in Figure 23-12.

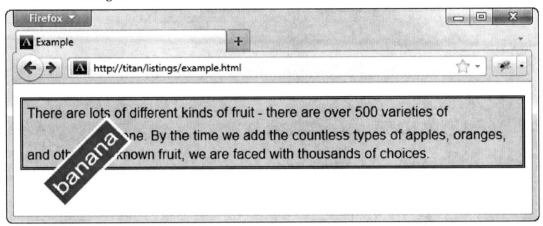

Figure 23-12. Specifying an origin for a transform

Animating and Transitioning a Transform

You can apply animations and transitions to a transform, just as you would any other CSS property. Listing 23-17 contains a demonstration.

Listing 23-17. Applying a Transition to a Transform

```
<!DOCTYPE HTML>
<html>
    <head>
        <title>Example</title>
        <meta name="author" content="Adam Freeman"/>
        <meta name="description" content="A simple example"/>
        <link rel="shortcut icon" href="favicon.ico" type="image/x-icon" />
        <style>
            p {
                padding: 5px;
                border: medium double black;
                background-color: lightgray;
                font-family: sans-serif;
            }
            #banana {
```

```
            font-size: x-large;
            border: medium solid white;
            background-color: green;
            color: white;
            padding: 4px;
        }

        #banana:hover {
            -moz-transition-duration: 1.5s;
            -moz-transform: rotate(360deg);
        }

    </style>
</head>
<body>
    <p id="fruittext">
        There are lots of different kinds of fruit - there are over 500
        varieties of <span id="banana">banana</span> alone. By the time we add the
        countless types of apples, oranges, and other
        well-known fruit, we are faced with thousands of choices.
    </p>
</body>
</html>
```

In this example, I have defined a transition that will apply a 360-degree rotation transform over a period of 1.5 seconds. This transition will be applied when the user hovers over the span element. You can see the effect in Figure 23-13.

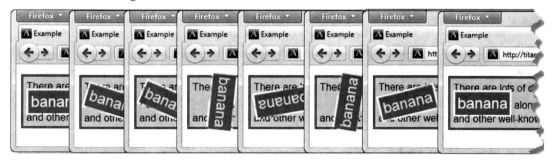

Figure 23-13. Combining transitions with transforms

Summary

In this chapter, I have shown you three new features in CSS3 that give you enormous control over the appearance of your elements. Transitions, transforms, and animation are simple to use, and deliver reasonable performance and great flexibility. I recommend using these features sparingly, but careful application can enhance the appearance and overall user experience of web pages and applications. I have used the browser-specific prefixes throughout this chapter, but the implementations are very close to the standard and I would expect the browsers to offer support for the real property names soon.

CHAPTER 24

Other CSS Properties and Features

In this chapter, I finish up my coverage of CSS with the properties that didn't fit into the other chapters. These are important and useful properties, but I couldn't find a way of incorporating them into the themes that the other chapters followed. In this chapter, you'll see how to set the foreground color and opacity of elements, and how to apply special styles to HTML table and list elements. Table 24-1 provides the summary for this chapter.

Table 24-1. Chapter Summary

Problem	Solution	Listing
Set the foreground color of an element.	Use the color property.	24-1
Set the transparency for an element.	Use the opacity property.	24-2
Specify how borders of adjacent table cells are drawn.	Use the border-collapse and border-spacing properties.	24-3 through 24-5
Specify the position of a table caption.	Use the caption-side property.	24-6
Specify how the size of a table is determined.	Use the table-layout property.	24-7
Specify the type of marker used in a list.	Use the list-style-type property.	24-8
Use an image as a list marker.	Use the list-style-image property.	24-9
Specify the position of a list marker.	Use the list-style-position property.	24-10
Specify the cursor.	Use the cursor property.	24-11

Setting Element Color and Transparency

You have seen different uses for CSS colors throughout this part of the book, with the background-color property, the border-color property, and so on. There are two additional properties that relate to colors. Table 24-2 describes these properties.

Table 24-2. The Color-Related Properties

Property	Description	Values
color	Sets the foreground color of an element.	*<color>*
opacity	Sets the transparency of an element.	*<number>*

Setting the Foreground Color

The color property sets the foreground color for the element. In principle, elements can have a different interpretation of what the color property means to them, but in practice, the color property sets the color of text. Listing 24-1 shows the color property in use.

Listing 24-1. Using the color Property

```
<!DOCTYPE HTML>
<html>
    <head>
        <title>Example</title>
        <meta name="author" content="Adam Freeman"/>
        <meta name="description" content="A simple example"/>
        <link rel="shortcut icon" href="favicon.ico" type="image/x-icon" />
        <style>
            p {
                padding: 5px;
                border: medium double black;
                background-color: lightgray;
                font-family: sans-serif;
            }
            #banana {
                font-size: x-large;
                border: medium solid white;
                background-color: green;
                color: rgba(255, 255, 255, 0.7);
            }
            a:hover {
                color: red;
            }

        </style>
    </head>
```

```
<body>
    <p id="fruittext">
        There are lots of different kinds of fruit - there are over 500
        varieties of <span id="banana">banana</span> alone. By the time we add the
        countless types of apples, oranges, and other well-known fruit, we are faced
        with thousands of choices.
        <a href="http://en.wikipedia.org/wiki/Banana">Learn more about Bananas</a>
    </p>
</body>
</html>
```

In this example, I have used the color property twice: once to set the foreground color and transparency for the span element, and once to set the foreground color of a elements when the mouse hovers over them. You can see the effect in Figure 24-1. The effect might be hard to make out on the printed page. To understand the effect, you should display the example HTML document in a browser.

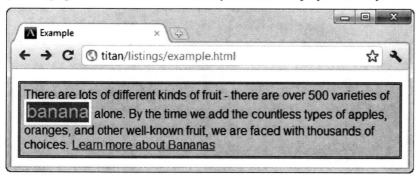

Figure 24-1. Using the color property to set the foreground

Setting Element Opacity

Notice that I used the rgba function to set the color of the span element in the previous example. I made the text slightly transparent by providing an alpha value that is less than 1. It might be difficult to see from the figure, but the effect is that the text is allowing some of the background color to show through.

You can use the opacity property to make entire elements and their text content transparent. The allowed range for this property is from zero (meaning completely transparent) to 1 (meaning completely opaque). Listing 24-2 shows the opacity property in use.

Listing 24-2. Using the opacity Property

```
<!DOCTYPE HTML>
<html>
    <head>
        <title>Example</title>
        <meta name="author" content="Adam Freeman"/>
        <meta name="description" content="A simple example"/>
        <link rel="shortcut icon" href="favicon.ico" type="image/x-icon" />
        <style>
```

```
    p {
        padding: 5px;
        border: medium double black;
        background-color: lightgray;
        font-family: sans-serif;
    }
    #banana {
        font-size: x-large;
        border: medium solid white;
        background-color: green;
        color: white;
        opacity: 0.4;
    }
    a:hover {
        color: red;
    }
  </style>
 </head>
 <body>
   <p id="fruittext">
       There are lots of different kinds of fruit - there are over 500
       varieties of <span id="banana">banana</span> alone. By the time we add the
       countless types of apples, oranges, and other well-known fruit, we are faced
       with thousands of choices.
       <a href="http://en.wikipedia.org/wiki/Banana">Learn more about Bananas</a>
   </p>
 </body>
</html>
```

In this example, I set the opacity of the span element to 0.4. The effect is shown in Figure 24-2, but might be hard to make out on the printed page.

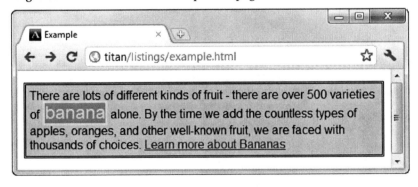

Figure 24-2. Setting the opacity of an element

Styling Tables

There are a number of properties that let you style the unique characteristics of the table element, which I introduced in Chapter 11. Table 24-3 summarizes these properties.

Table 24-3. The Table-Related Properties

Property	Description	Values
border-collapse	Specifies how borders on adjacent cells are handled.	collapse separate
border-spacing	Specifies the spacing between adjacent cell borders.	1 or 2 *<length>*
caption-side	Specifies the location of the caption element.	top bottom
empty-cells	Specifies how borders are drawn on empty cells.	hide show
table-layout	Specifies the layout style for the table.	auto fixed

Collapsing Table Borders

The border-collapse property lets you control the way that the browser draws borders for the table element. You can see the default approach in Figure 24-3.

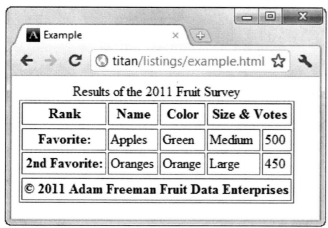

Figure 24-3. The default appearance of a table with borders

615

The browser draws a border around the table plus a border around each cell, creating a double border effect. You can address this by applying the border-collapse property, as shown in Listing 24-3.

Listing 24-3. Using the border-collapse Property

```
<!DOCTYPE HTML>
<html>
    <head>
        <title>Example</title>
        <meta name="author" content="Adam Freeman"/>
        <meta name="description" content="A simple example"/>
        <link rel="shortcut icon" href="favicon.ico" type="image/x-icon" />
        <style>
            table {
                border-collapse: collapse;
            }
            th, td {
                padding: 2px;
            }
        </style>
    </head>
    <body>
        <table border="1">
            <caption>Results of the 2011 Fruit Survey</caption>
            <colgroup id="colgroup1">
                <col id="col1And2" span="2"/>
                <col id="col3"/>
            </colgroup>
            <colgroup id="colgroup2" span="2"/>
            <thead>
                <tr>
                    <th>Rank</th><th>Name</th><th>Color</th>
                    <th colspan="2">Size & Votes</th>
                </tr>
            </thead>
            <tbody>
                <tr>
                    <th>Favorite:</th><td>Apples</td><td>Green</td>
                    <td>Medium</td><td>500</td>
                </tr>
                <tr>
                    <th>2nd Favorite:</th><td>Oranges</td><td>Orange</td>
                    <td>Large</td><td>450</td>
                </tr>
            </tbody>
            <tfoot>
                <tr>
                    <th colspan="5">&copy; 2011 Adam Freeman Fruit Data Enterprises</th>
                </tr>
            </tfoot>
        </table>
```

```
    </body>
</html>
```

The collapse value tells the browser that you don't want borders drawn on every edge of adjacent elements. You can see the effect this has in Figure 24-4.

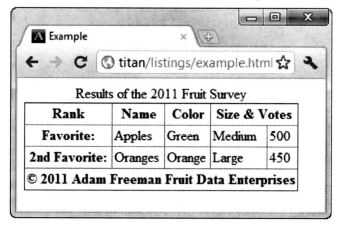

Figure 24-4. Collapsing the border for a table

Configuring Separated Borders

If you do use the default separate value for the border-collapse property, you can use some additional properties to refine the appearance. The border-spacing property defines the amount of space that will be drawn between the borders of adjacent elements, as shown in Listing 24-4.

Listing 24-4. Using the border-spacing Property

```
<!DOCTYPE HTML>
<html>
    <head>
        <title>Example</title>
        <meta name="author" content="Adam Freeman"/>
        <meta name="description" content="A simple example"/>
        <link rel="shortcut icon" href="favicon.ico" type="image/x-icon" />
        <style>
            table {
                border-collapse: separate;
                border-spacing: 10px;
            }
            th, td {
                padding: 2px;
            }
        </style>
    </head>
    <body>
```

```
<table border="1">
    <caption>Results of the 2011 Fruit Survey</caption>
    <colgroup id="colgroup1">
        <col id="col1And2" span="2"/>
        <col id="col3"/>
    </colgroup>
    <colgroup id="colgroup2" span="2"/>
    <thead>
        <tr>
            <th>Rank</th><th>Name</th><th>Color</th>
            <th colspan="2">Size & Votes</th>
        </tr>
    </thead>
    <tbody>
        <tr>
            <th>Favorite:</th><td>Apples</td><td>Green</td>
            <td>Medium</td><td>500</td>
        </tr>
        <tr>
            <th>2nd Favorite:</th><td>Oranges</td><td>Orange</td>
            <td></td><td></td>
        </tr>
    </tbody>
    <tfoot>
        <tr>
            <th colspan="5">&copy; 2011 Adam Freeman Fruit Data Enterprises</th>
        </tr>
    </tfoot>
</table>
</body>
</html>
```

In this example, I have specified a 10-pixel gap between borders. You can see the effect in Figure 24-5.

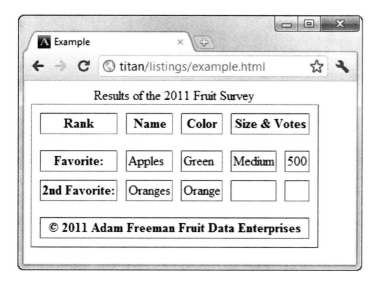

Figure 24-5. Using the border-spacing property

Dealing with Empty Cells

You can also tell the browser how to handle empty cells. By default, the browser draws a separate border when a cell is empty, as you can see in Figure 24-5. You can control this behavior using the empty-cells property. The show value, which is the default, creates the effect in Figure 24-3, while the hide value tells the browser not to draw the border. Listing 24-5 shows the addition of the empty-cells property to the style element of the previous example.

Listing 24-5. Using the empty-cells Property

```
<style>
    table {
        border-collapse: separate;
        border-spacing: 10px;
        empty-cells: hide;
    }
    th, td {
        padding: 2px;
    }
</style>
```

You can see the effect of this change in Figure 24-6.

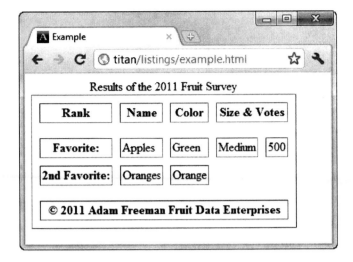

Figure 24-6. Using the empty-cells property

Positioning the Caption

As I explained in Chapter 11, when you add a caption element to a table, it is displayed at the top of the table, even when it is not the first child element. You can change this behavior using the caption-side property. This property has two values: top (the default) and bottom. Listing 24-6 shows the application of this property.

Listing 24-6. Using the caption-side Property

```
<!DOCTYPE HTML>
<html>
    <head>
        <title>Example</title>
        <meta name="author" content="Adam Freeman"/>
        <meta name="description" content="A simple example"/>
        <link rel="shortcut icon" href="favicon.ico" type="image/x-icon" />
        <style>
            table {
                border-collapse: collapse;
                caption-side: bottom;
            }
            th, td {
                padding: 5px;
            }
        </style>
    </head>
    <body>
        <table border="1">
            <caption>Results of the 2011 Fruit Survey</caption>
```

```
            <colgroup id="colgroup1">
                <col id="col1And2" span="2"/>
                <col id="col3"/>
            </colgroup>
            <colgroup id="colgroup2" span="2"/>
            <thead>
                <tr>
                    <th>Rank</th><th>Name</th><th>Color</th>
                    <th colspan="2">Size & Votes</th>
                </tr>
            </thead>
            <tbody>
                <tr>
                    <th>Favorite:</th><td>Apples</td><td>Green</td>
                    <td>Medium</td><td>500</td>
                </tr>
                <tr>
                    <th>2nd Favorite:</th><td>Oranges</td><td>Orange</td>
                    <td></td><td></td>
                </tr>
            </tbody>
            <tfoot>
                <tr>
                    <th colspan="5">&copy; 2011 Adam Freeman Fruit Data Enterprises</th>
                </tr>
            </tfoot>
        </table>
    </body>
</html>
```

You can see the effect of this property in Figure 24-7.

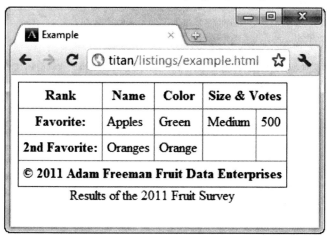

Figure 24-7. Using the caption-side property to move the caption

Specifying the Table Layout

By default, the browser sets the width of the table based on the widest cell in each column. This means that you don't have to worry about figuring out the sizes yourself, but it also means that the browser has to receive all of the table content before it can determine the layout for the page.

The approach that the browser takes to displaying tables is controlled by the table-layout property, and the default value, described above, is set by the value auto. You can disable the automatic layout by using the other allowed value fixed. In fixed mode, the size of the table is set by the width values for the table and for individual columns. If there is no column width information available, the browser will allocate the space evenly across the columns.

As a consequence, the browser is able to determine the width of each column after receiving just one row of the table data. The data for subsequent rows is wrapped to make it fit (which can cause rows to be higher than they would be in the auto mode).

Listing 24-7 shows the table-layout property in use.

Listing 24-7. Using the table-layout Property

```
<!DOCTYPE HTML>
<html>
    <head>
        <title>Example</title>
        <meta name="author" content="Adam Freeman"/>
        <meta name="description" content="A simple example"/>
        <link rel="shortcut icon" href="favicon.ico" type="image/x-icon" />
        <style>
            table {
                border-collapse: collapse;
                caption-side: bottom;
                table-layout: fixed;
                width: 100%;
            }
            th, td {
                padding: 5px;
            }
        </style>
    </head>
    <body>
        <table border="1">
            <caption>Results of the 2011 Fruit Survey</caption>
            <colgroup id="colgroup1">
                <col id="col1And2" span="2"/>
                <col id="col3"/>
            </colgroup>
            <colgroup id="colgroup2" span="2"/>
            <thead>
                <tr>
                    <th>Rank</th><th>Name</th><th>Color</th>
                    <th colspan="2">Size & Votes</th>
                </tr>
            </thead>
            <tbody>
```

```
        <tr>
            <th>Really Really Really Long Title:</th>
            <td>Apples</td><td>Green</td>
            <td>Medium</td><td>500</td>
        </tr>
        <tr>
            <th>2nd Favorite:</th><td>Oranges</td><td>Orange</td>
            <td></td><td></td>
        </tr>
    </tbody>
    <tfoot>
        <tr>
            <th colspan="5">&copy; 2011 Adam Freeman Fruit Data Enterprises</th>
        </tr>
    </tfoot>
</table>
</body>
</html>
```

In this example, I have set the width of the table element to occupy 100 percent of the available space, and set the layout style to fixed. I have also changed the contents of one of the cells in the second row to demonstrate the effect on the layout, which is shown in Figure 24-8.

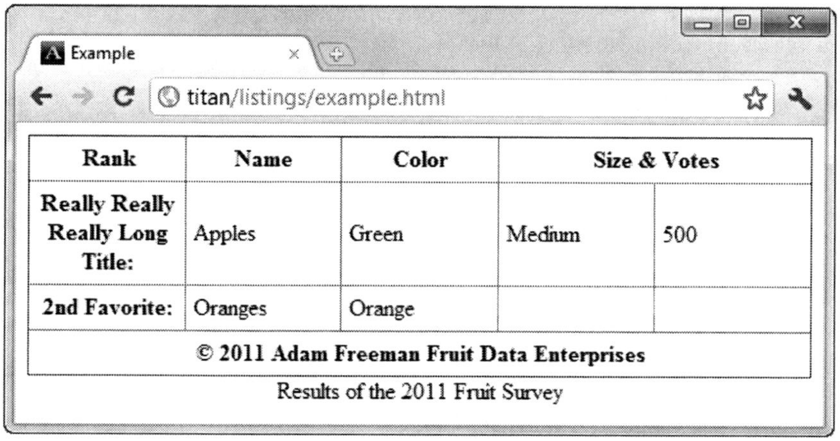

Figure 24-8. Using the table-layout property

Notice how the available space is allocated evenly across the five columns and how the long title in the second row is wrapped to make it fit, causing that row to be much higher than the others.

Styling Lists

There are a number of properties that are specific to styling lists. Table 24-4 summarizes these properties.

Table 24-4. *The List-Related Properties*

Property	Description	Values
list-style-type	Specifies the type of marker used in the list.	See Table 24-5.
list-style-image	Specifies an image for use as a marker.	*<image>*
list-style-position	Specifies the position of the marker in relation to the list item box.	inside outside
list-style	Shorthand property to set all list characteristics.	See the following explanation.

The format for the list-style shorthand property is as follows:

list-style: <list-style-type> <list-style-position> <list-style-image>

Setting the List Marker Type

You use the list-style-type property to set the style of marker (also sometimes known as the bullet) for a list. You can see the allowed values for this property in Table 24-5.

Table 24-5. *The list-style-type Property Values*

Value	Description
none	No marker will be shown.
box check circle diamond disc dash square	Use the specified shape as the marker. Note that not all browsers support all shapes.
decimal	Use decimal numbers for the markers.
binary	Use binary numbers for the markers.
lower-alpha	Use lowercase alpha characters for the markers.
upper-alpha	Use uppercase alpha characters for the markers.

Table 24-5 shows only some of the available styles. There are a great many more, representing different alphabets, symbol styles, and numeric conventions. You can find a full list at www.w3.org/TR/css3-lists. Listing 24-8 shows the list-style-type property in use.

Listing 24-8. Using the list-style-type Property

```
<!DOCTYPE HTML>
<html>
    <head>
        <title>Example</title>
        <meta name="author" content="Adam Freeman"/>
        <meta name="description" content="A simple example"/>
        <link rel="shortcut icon" href="favicon.ico" type="image/x-icon" />
        <style>
            ol {
                list-style-type: lower-alpha;
            }
        </style>
    </head>
    <body>
        I like apples and oranges.

        I also like:
        <ol>
            <li>bananas</li>
            <li>mangoes</li>
            <li style="list-style-type: decimal">cherries</li>
            <li>plums</li>
            <li>peaches</li>
            <li>grapes</li>
        </ol>
    </body>
</html>
```

You can apply this property to entire lists or individual list items. I have done both in this example (although the result isn't something that would make sense to a reader). You can see the effect in Figure 24-9.

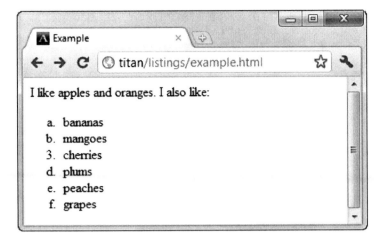

Figure 24-9. Setting the list marker type

Using an Image As a List Marker

You can use an image as the marker through the list-style-image property. Listing 24-9 shows this property in action.

Listing 24-9. Using an Image As a List Marker

```
<!DOCTYPE HTML>
<html>
    <head>
        <title>Example</title>
        <meta name="author" content="Adam Freeman"/>
        <meta name="description" content="A simple example"/>
        <link rel="shortcut icon" href="favicon.ico" type="image/x-icon" />
        <style>
            ul {
                list-style-image: url('banana-vsmall.png');
            }
        </style>
    </head>
    <body>
        I like apples and oranges.

        I also like:
        <ul>
            <li>bananas</li>
            <li>mangoes</li>
            <li>cherries</li>
            <li>plums</li>
            <li>peaches</li>
            <li>grapes</li>
```

```
        </ul>
    </body>
</html>
```

You can see the effect of applying this property in Figure 24-10.

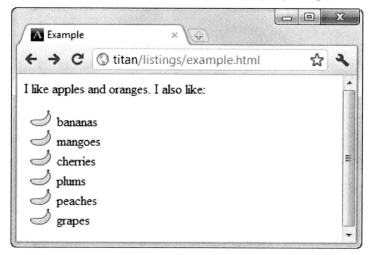

Figure 24-10. Using an image as a list marker

Positioning the Marker

You can specify the position of the marker in relation to the li element's content box using the list-style-position property. The allowed values are inside (meaning that the marker is inside the content box) and outside (meaning that the marker is outside the content box). Listing 24-10 shows the list-style-position property and its values in use.

Listing 24-10. Specifying the Position of the Marker

```
<!DOCTYPE HTML>
<html>
    <head>
        <title>Example</title>
        <meta name="author" content="Adam Freeman"/>
        <meta name="description" content="A simple example"/>
        <link rel="shortcut icon" href="favicon.ico" type="image/x-icon" />
        <style>
            li.inside {
                list-style-position: inside;
            }
            li.outside {
                list-style-position: outside;
            }
            li {
```

```
                    background-color: lightgray;
              }
        </style>
   </head>
   <body>
        I like apples and oranges.

        I also like:
        <ul>
            These are the inside items:
            <li class="inside">bananas</li>
            <li class="inside">mangoes</li>
            <li class="inside">cherries</li>
            These are the outside items:
            <li class="outside">plums</li>
            <li class="outside">peaches</li>
            <li class="outside">grapes</li>
        </ul>
   </body>
</html>
```

I have broken the li items into two classes and applied different values of the list-style-position property. You can see the effect in Figure 24-11.

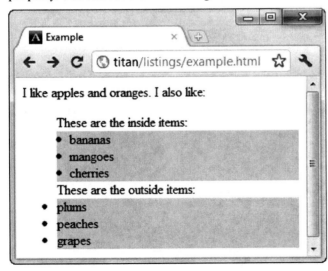

Figure 24-11. Positioning the marker

In this figure, I have set the background-color property for all of the li elements so that you can see the effect of each position value.

Styling the Cursor

The cursor property lets you change the appearance of the cursor. Table 24-6 summarizes this element.

Table 24-6. The cursor Property

Property	Description	Values
cursor	Sets the style for the cursor.	auto, crosshair, default, help, move, pointer, progress, text, wait, n-resize, s-resize, e-resize, w-resize, ne-resize, nw-resize, se-resize, and sw-resize

The different values for the cursor property cause the browser to display different styles of cursor when the mouse passes over the styled element. You can see the property in use in Listing 24-11.

Listing 24-11. Using the cursor Property

```
<!DOCTYPE HTML>
<html>
    <head>
        <title>Example</title>
        <meta name="author" content="Adam Freeman"/>
        <meta name="description" content="A simple example"/>
        <link rel="shortcut icon" href="favicon.ico" type="image/x-icon" />
        <style>
            p {
                padding: 5px;
                border: medium double black;
                background-color: lightgray;
                font-family: sans-serif;
            }
            #banana {
                font-size: x-large;
                border: medium solid white;
                background-color: green;
                color: rgba(255, 255, 255, 0.7);
                cursor: progress;
            }

        </style>
    </head>
    <body>
        <p id="fruittext">
            There are lots of different kinds of fruit - there are over 500
            varieties of <span id="banana">banana</span> alone. By the time we add the
            countless types of apples, oranges, and other well-known fruit, we are faced
            with thousands of choices.
        </p>
    </body>
```

629

```
</html>
```

You can see the effect in Figure 24-12. I have magnified the cursor to show that it switches to the Windows 7 wait cursor when I pass the mouse over the span element.

Figure 24-12. Setting the cursor style

Summary

In this chapter, I have described the CSS properties that don't really fit anywhere else. That's not to say that these properties are not important, just that they didn't fit into the theme of the earlier chapters. The properties in this chapter allow you to set the color and opacity of all elements, and apply specific styles to lists and tables, which are essential HTML features in their own right.

PART IV

Working with the DOM

The *Domain Object Model* (DOM) allows you to use JavaScript to explore and manipulate the contents of an HTML document. It is an essential set of features for creating rich content. In the chapters that follow, I'll show you how to gain access to the DOM, how to find and change JavaScript objects that represent elements in the document, and how to respond to user interactions using events.

C H A P T E R   25

The DOM in Context

In this part of the book, you will explore the *Document Object Model* (the *DOM*). You can achieve some complex effects using the elements and CSS properties I have shown you so far, but if you want to get total control of your HTML, you need to use JavaScript. The DOM is the connection between JavaScript and the contents of your HTML document. Using the DOM, you can add, remove, and manipulate elements. You can respond to user interaction using *events* and you can take complete control of CSS.

From this point on, you are at the programming end of HTML5. Until now, you've created content using element and CSS declarations, but it is time to put on your programmer hat and start using JavaScript. Chapter 5 gives a tour of the JavaScript basics, if you need a refresher.

Understanding the Document Object Model

The DOM is a collection of objects representing the elements in your HTML document. The name says it all: the DOM is quite literally a *model*, which is comprised of *objects* that represent your *document*. The DOM is a key tool in web development and provides the bridge between the structure and content of your HTML documents and JavaScript. To give an example, Listing 25-1 shows a simple HTML document.

Listing 25-1. A Simple HTML Document

```
<!DOCTYPE HTML>
<html>
    <head>
        <title>Example</title>
        <meta name="author" content="Adam Freeman"/>
        <meta name="description" content="A simple example"/>
    </head>
    <body>
        <p id="fruittext">
            There are lots of different kinds of fruit - there are over 500
            varieties of <span id="banana">banana</span> alone. By the time we add the
            countless types of apples, oranges, and other well-known fruit, we are faced
            with thousands of choices.
        </p>
        <p id="apples">
            One of the most interesting aspects of fruit is the
```

```
            variety available in each country. I live near London, in an area which is
            known for its apples.
        </p>
    </body>
</html>
```

You can see how the browser displays the sample HTML document in Figure 25-1.

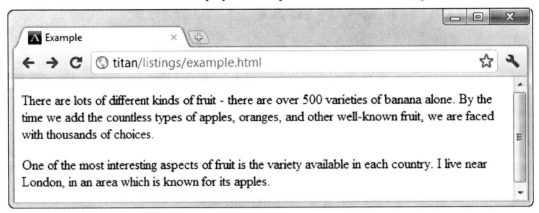

Figure 25-1. Displaying the basic HTML document

As part of the process of displaying your HTML document, the browser parses the HTML and creates a model. The model preserves the hierarchy of the HTML elements, as shown in Figure 25-2, and each element is represented by a JavaScript object.

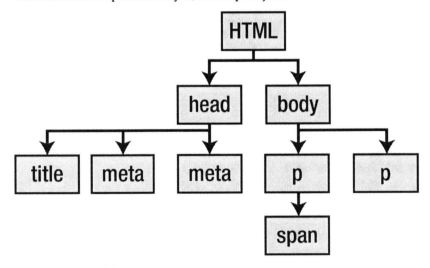

Figure 25-2. The hierarchy of elements in an HTML document

As you'll see in the chapters that follow, you can use the DOM to get information about the document or to make changes to it. This is the foundation of modern web applications.

Each model object in the model has properties and methods. When you use these to change the state of the object, the browser reflects the changes in the corresponding HTML element and updates your document.

All of the DOM objects that represent elements support the same set of basic features. These are HTMLElement objects and the core functionality defined by HTMLElement is always available to use, irrespective of the kind of element that an object represents. In addition, some objects define extra functionality that let you perform operations that reflect the unique characteristics of specific HTML elements. I describe these extra features in Chapter 31. This is an important point to note: every object in the document model that represents an element supports *at least* the HTMLElement features and, in some cases, extra features.

Not all of the objects available to you represent HTML elements. As you'll soon see, there are objects that represent collections of elements, objects that represent information about the DOM itself and, of course, the Document object, which is our gateway into the DOM and the subject of Chapter 26.

▨ **Note** I am skipping over some detail here. If you are familiar with the concepts of object-oriented programming, then it may help you to know that HTMLElement is an interface that is implemented by the objects contained in the DOM. The objects used to represent more specific elements are interfaces that are derived from HTMLElement, meaning that you can treat an object either as an implementation or HTMLElement, or its more specific subtype. Don't worry if you are *not* familiar with object-oriented concepts. It isn't important to understand them for mainstream web programming. I won't be referring to them again and I will be referring to everything as an *object* for simplicity.

Understanding DOM Levels and Compliance

As you start to work with the DOM, you will encounter web articles and tutorials that mention DOM levels (that a certain feature is defined by DOM Level 3, for example). The DOM levels are the version numbers for the standardization process and, for the most part, you should ignore them.

The standardization process for the DOM has been a mixed success. There *are* standards and documents that describe each DOM level, but they are not fully implemented and the browsers have simply cherry-picked useful features and ignored others. Worse, there is a degree of inconsistency between the features that are implemented.

Part of the problem has been that the DOM specification has been developed separately from the HTML standard. HTML5 attempts to address this problem by including a core set of DOM features that should be implemented. However, this has yet to take effect and fragmentation remains.

There are a number of ways that you can deal with variability in DOM features. The first is to use a JavaScript library, such as jQuery, which irons out the differences between browser implementation. The advantage of using a library is consistency, but the disadvantage is that you are limited to the features that the library supports. If you want to go outside of the library features, you are back to using the DOM directly and face the same issue anyway. (That's not to say that jQuery and its alternatives don't have value; they can be very useful and are well worth a look.)

The second approach is conservatism: use only the features that you know are widely supported. This is the most sensible approach for the most part, although it does require careful and thorough testing. Furthermore, you have to be careful about testing new releases of browsers to make sure that support for features hasn't changed or been removed.

Testing for DOM Features

A third approach is to test for the presence of the property or method on the DOM object that is associated with a feature. Listing 25-2 contains a simple example.

■ **Tip** Don't worry about the detail in the script in Listing 25-2. I'll explain all of the objects and features that it uses in the chapters that follow.

Listing 25-2. Testing for a Feature

```
<!DOCTYPE HTML>
<html>
    <head>
        <title>Example</title>
    </head>
    <body>
        <p id="paratext">
            There are lots of different kinds of fruit - there are over 500 varieties
            of banana alone. By the time we add the countless types of apples, oranges,
            and other well-known fruit, we are faced with thousands of choices.
            <img src="apple.png" alt="apple"/>
        </p>
        <script>
            var images;
            if (document.querySelectorAll) {
                images = document.querySelectorAll("#paratext > img");
            } else {
                images = document.getElementById("paratext").getElementsByTagName("img");
            }

            for (var i = 0; i < images.length; i++) {
                images[i].style.border = "thick solid black";
                images[i].style.padding = "4px";
            }
        </script>
    </body>
</html>
```

In this example, the script uses an if clause to determine whether the document object defines a method called querySelectorAll. If the clause evaluates to true, then the browser supports the feature, and I can go on and use it. If the clause evaluates to false, then I can take an alternative approach to achieve the same goal.

This is advice that you will often see when it comes to the DOM, but it is usually given glibly and without pointing out the drawbacks, which can be serious.

The first drawback is that there isn't always an alternative approach to achieve the effect of a given feature. My neat example in Listing 25-2 works because the feature I am testing for is a convenience enhancement built on top of other functions, but this isn't always the case.

The second drawback is that I am only testing for the *presence* of the feature, and not the quality and consistency of its implementation. Many features, especially when they are new, take several browser releases to stabilize and achieve consistency. This is less of a problem than it used to be, but you can easily end up with unexpected results because of variations in the way that browsers implement a feature you rely on.

The third drawback is that you have to test every feature that you rely on. This requires extreme diligence and produces code that is littered with endless tests. That's not to say that this can't be a useful technique, but it has flaws and should not be taken as a substitute for proper testing.

The DOM Quick Reference

The following sections provide a quick reference for the objects, methods, properties, and events that I describe in the chapters that follow.

The Document Members

Chapter 26 describes the Document object, which represents the current document and is your gateway into the DOM. Table 25-1 summarizes the members that this object defines.

Table 25-1. The Document Object

Name	Description	Returns
activeElement	Returns an object representing the currently focused element in the document.	HTMLElement
body	Returns an object representing the body element in the document.	HTMLElement
characterSet	Returns the document character set encoding. This is a read-only property.	string
charset	Gets or sets the document character set encoding.	string
childNodes	Returns the set of child elements.	HTMLElement[]
compatMode	Gets compatibility mode for the document.	string
cookie	Gets or sets the cookies for the current document.	string

defaultCharset	Gets the default character encoding used by the browser.	string
defaultView	Returns the Window object for the current document. See Chapter 26 for details of this object.	Window
dir	Gets or sets the text direction for the document.	string
domain	Gets or sets the domain for the current document.	string
embeds plugins	Returns objects representing all the embed elements in the document.	HTMLCollection
firstChild	Returns the first child element of an element.	HTMLElement
forms	Returns objects representing all the form elements in the document.	HTMLCollection
getElementById(<id>)	Returns the element with the specified id value.	HTMLElement
getElementsByClassName(<class s>)	Returns the elements with the specified class value.	HTMLElement[]
getElementsByName(<name>)	Returns the elements with the specified name value.	HTMLElement[]
getElementsByTagName(<tag>)	Returns the elements of the specified type.	HTMLElement[]
hasChildNodes()	Returns true if the current element has child elements.	boolean
head	Returns an object representing the head element.	HTMLHeadElement
images	Returns objects representing all the img elements.	HTMLCollection
implementation	Provides information about the DOM features that are available.	DOMImplementation
lastChild	Returns the last child element.	HTMLElement
lastModified	Returns the last modified time of the	string

	document.	
links	Returns objects representing all the a and area elements in the document that have href attributes.	HTMLCollection
location	Provides information about the URL of the current document.	Location
nextSibling	Returns the sibling element defined after the current element.	HTMLElement
parentNode	Returns the parent element.	HTMLElement
previousSibling	Returns the sibling element defined before the current element.	HTMLElement
querySelector(<selector>)	Returns the first element that matches the specified CSS selector.	HTMLElement
querySelectorAll(<selector>)	Returns all of the elements that match the specified CSS selector.	HTMLElement[]
readyState	Returns the state of the current document.	string
referrer	Returns the URL of the document that linked to the current document (this is the value of the corresponding HTTP header).	string
scripts	Returns objects representing all the script elements.	HTMLCollection
title	Gets or sets the title of the current document.	string

Chapter 26 also describes the Location object, which is summarized in Table 25-2.

Table 25-2. The Location Object

Name	Description	Returns
assign(<URL>)	Navigates to the specified URL.	void
hash	Gets or sets the hash component of the document URL.	string
host	Gets or sets the host component of the document URL.	string

hostname	Gets or sets the host name component of the document URL.	string
href	Gets or sets the current document's location.	string
pathname	Gets or sets the path component of the document URL.	string
port	Gets or sets the port component of the document URL.	string
protocol	Gets or sets the protocol component of the document URL.	string
reload()	Reloads the current document.	void
replace(<URL>)	Removes the current document and navigates to the one specified by the URL.	void
resolveURL(<URL>)	Resolves the specified relative URL to an absolute one.	string
search	Gets or sets the query component of the document URL.	string

The Window Members

Chapter 27 describes the Window object, which defines a wide range of features. Table 25-3 summarizes the members that this object defines.

Table 25-3. The Window Object

Name	Description	Returns
alert(<msg>)	Displays a dialog window to the user and waits for it to be dismissed.	void
blur()	Unfocuses the window.	void
clearInterval(<id>)	Cancels an interval timer.	void
clearTimeout(<id>)	Cancels a timeout timer.	void
close()	Closes the window.	void

`confirm(<msg>)`	Displays a dialog window with an OK/Cancel prompt.	`boolean`
`defaultView`	Returns the `Window` for the active document.	`Window`
`document`	Returns the `Document` object associated with this window.	`Document`
`focus()`	Focuses the window.	`void`
`frames`	Returns an array of the `Window` objects for the nested `iframe` elements in the document.	`Window[]`
`history`	Provides access to the browser history.	`History`
`innerHeight`	Gets the height of the window content area.	`number`
`innerWidth`	Gets the width of the window content area.	`number`
`length`	Returns the number of nested `iframe` elements in the document.	`number`
`location`	Provides details of the current document's location.	`Location`
`opener`	Returns the `Window` that opened the current browsing context.	`Window`
`outerHeight`	Gets the height of the window, including borders, menu bars, etc.	`number`
`outerWidth`	Gets the width of the window, including borders, menu bars, etc.	`number`
`pageXOffet`	Gets the number of pixels that the window has been scrolled horizontally from the top-left corner.	`number`
`pageYOffset`	Gets the number of pixels that the window has been scrolled vertically from the top-left corner.	`number`
`parent`	Returns the parent of the current `Window`.	`Window`
`postMessage(<msg>, <origin>)`	Sends the message to another document.	`void`

print()	Prompts the user to print the page.	void
prompt(<msg>, <val>)	Displays a dialog prompting the user to enter a value.	string
screen	Returns a Screen object describing the screen.	Screen
screenLeft screenX	Gets the number of pixels from the left edge of the window to the left edge of the screen.	number
screenTop screenY	Gets the number of pixels from the top edge of the window to the top edge of the screen.	number
scrollBy(<x>, <y>)	Scrolls the document relative to its current position.	void
scrollTo(<x>, <y>)	Scrolls to the specified position.	void
self	Returns the Window for the current document.	
setInterval(<function>, <time>)	Creates a timer that will call the specified function every time milliseconds.	int
setTimeout(<function>, <time>)	Creates a timer that will call the specified function once after time milliseconds.	int
showModalDialog(<url>)	Displays a pop-up window showing the specified URL.	void
stop()	Stops the document loading.	void
top	Returns the top-most Window.	Window

Chapter 27 also describes the History object, whose members are summarized in Table 25-4.

Table 25-4. The History Object

Name	Description	Returns
back()	Goes one step back in the history.	void
forward()	Goes one step forward in the history.	void
go(<index>)	Goes to a position in the history relative to the current document. Positive values are forward, negative are backward.	void

length	Returns the number of items in the history.	number
pushState(<state>, <title>, <url>)	Adds an entry to the browser history.	void
replaceState(<state>, <title>, <url>)	Replaces the current entry in the browser history.	void
state	Returns the state data associated with the current document in the browser history.	object

Chapter 27 also describes the Screen object, whose members are summarized in Table 25-5.

Table 25-5. The Screen Object

Name	Description	Returns
availHeight	Returns the height of the portion of the screen available for displaying windows (excludes toolbars, etc.).	number
availWidth	Returns the width of the portion of the screen available for displaying windows (excludes toolbars, etc.)	number
colorDepth	Returns the color depth of the screen.	number
height	Returns the height of the screen.	number
width	Returns the width of the screen.	number

The HTMLElement Members

Chapter 28 describes the HTMLElement object, which represents the HTML elements in the document. Table 25-6 summarizes the members that this object defines.

Table 25-6. The HTMLElement Object

Name	Description	Returns
checked	Gets or sets the presence of the checked attribute.	boolean

classList	Gets or sets the list of classes that the element belongs to.	DOMTokenList
className	Gets or sets the list of classes that the element belongs to.	string
dir	Gets or sets the value of the dir attribute.	string
disabled	Gets or sets the presence of the disabled attribute.	boolean
hidden	Gets or sets the presence of the hidden attribute.	boolean
id	Gets or sets the value of the id attribute.	string
lang	Gets or sets the value of the lang attribute.	string
spellcheck	Gets or sets the presence of the spellcheck attribute.	boolean
tabIndex	Gets or sets the value of the tabindex attribute.	number
tagName	Returns the tag name (indicating the element type).	string
title	Gets or sets the value of the title attribute.	string
add(<class>)	Adds the specified class to the element.	void
contains(<class>)	Returns true if the element belongs to the specified class.	boolean
length	Returns the number of classes to which the element belongs.	number
remove(<class>)	Removes the specified class from the element.	boid
toggle(<class>)	Adds the class if it is not present, and removes it if it is present.	boolean
attributes	Returns the attributes applied to the element.	Attr[]
dataset	Returns the data-* attributes.	string[<name>]

`getAttribute(<name>)`	Returns the value of the specified attribute.	`string`
`hasAttribute(<name>)`	Returns true if the element has the specified attribute.	`boolean`
`removeAttribute(<name>)`	Removes the specified attribute from the element.	`void`
`setAttribute(<name>, <value>)`	Applies an attribute with the specified name and value.	`void`
`appendChild(HTMLElement)`	Appends the specified element as a child of the current element.	`HTMLElement`
`cloneNode(boolean)`	Copies an element.	`HTMLElement`
`compareDocumentPosition(HTML Element)`	Determines the relative position of an element.	`number`
`innerHTML`	Gets or sets the element's content.	`string`
`insertAdjacentHTML(<pos>, <text>)`	Inserts HTML relative to the element.	`void`
`insertBefore(<newelem>, <childElem>)`	Inserts the first element before the second (child) element.	`HTMLElement`
`isEqualNode(<HTMLElement>)`	Determines whether the specified element is equal to the current element.	`boolean`
`isSameNode(HTMLElement)`	Determines whether the specified element is the same as the current element.	`boolean`
`outerHTML`	Gets or sets an element's HTML and contents.	`string`
`removeChild(HTMLElement)`	Removes the specified child of the current element.	`HTMLElement`
`replaceChild(HTMLElement, HTMLElement)`	Replaces a child of the current element.	`HTMLElement`
`createElement(<tag>)`	Creates a new `HTMLElement` object with the specified tag type.	`HTMLElement`
`createTextNode(<text>)`	Creates a new Text object with the specified content.	`Text`

Chapter 28 also describes the Text object, which is used to represent text content in a document. Table 25-7 describes the members of the Text object.

Table 25-7. The Text Object

Name	Description	Returns
appendData(<string>)	Appends the specified string to the end of the block of text.	void
data	Gets or sets the text.	string
deleteData(<offset>, <count>)	Removes the text from the string. The first number is the offset, and the second is the number of characters to remove.	void
insertData(<offset>, <string>)	Inserts the specified string at the specified offset.	void
length	Returns the number of characters.	number
replaceData(<offset>, <count>, <string>)	Replaces a region of text with the specified string.	void
replaceWholeText(<string>)	Replaces all of the text.	Text
splitText(<number>)	Splits the existing Text element into two at the specified offset. See the section "Inserting an Element into a Text Block," later in this chapter, for a demonstration of this method.	Text
substringData(<offset>, <count>)	Returns a substring from the text.	string
wholeText	Gets the text.	string

DOM CSS Properties

Chapter 29 describes how you can use the DOM to work with CSS styles in a document. The properties of the CSSStyleDeclaration object and the styles they correspond to (and the chapters in which they are described) are listed in Table 25-8.

Table 25-8. *The Members of the CSSStyleDeclaration Object*

Member	Corresponds To	See Chapter
background	background	19
backgroundAttachment	background-attachment	19
backgroundColor	background-color	19
backgroundImage	background-image	19
backgroundPosition	background-position	19
backgroundRepeat	background-repeat	19
border	border	19
borderBottom	border-bottom	19
borderBottomColor	border-bottom-color	19
borderBottomStyle	border-bottom-style	19
borderBottomWidth	border-bottom-width	19
borderCollapse	border-collapse	24
borderColor	border-color	19
borderLeft	border-left	19
borderLeftColor	border-left-color	19
borderLeftStyle	border-left-style	19
borderLeftWidth	border-left-width	19
borderRight	border-right	19
borderRightColor	border-right-color	19
borderRightStyle	border-right-style	19
borderRightWidth	border-right-width	19

borderSpacing	border-spacing	24
borderStyle	border-style	19
borderTop	border-top	19
borderTopColor	border-top-color	19
borderTopStyle	border-top-style	19
borderTopWidth	border-top-width	19
borderWidth	border-width	19
captionSide	caption-side	24
clear	clear	20
color	color	24
cssFloat	float	20
cursor	cursor	24
direction	direction	22
display	display	20
emptyCells	empty-cells	24
font	font	22
fontFamily	font-family	22
fontSize	font-size	22
fontStyle	font-style	22
fontVariant	font-variant	22
fontWeight	font-weight	22
height	height	20
letterSpacing	letter-spacing	22

lineHeight	line-height	22
listStyle	list-style	24
listStyleImage	list-style-image	24
listStylePosition	list-style-position	24
listStyleType	list-style-type	24
margin	margin	20
marginBottom	margin-bottom	20
marginLeft	margin-left	20
marginRight	margin-right	20
marginTop	margin-top	20
maxHeight	max-height	20
maxWIdth	max-width	20
minHeight	min-height	20
minWidth	min-width	20
outline	outline	19
outlineColor	outline-color	19
outlineStyle	outline-style	19
outlineWidth	outline-width	19
overflow	overflow	20
padding	padding	20
paddingBottom	padding-bottom	20
paddingLeft	padding-left	20
paddingRight	padding-right	20

paddingTop	padding-top	20
tableLayout	table-layout	24
textAlign	text-align	22
textDecoration	text-decoration	22
textIndent	text-indent	22
textShadow	text-shadow	22
textTransform	text-transform	22
visibility	visibility	20
whiteSpace	whitespace	22
width	width	20
wordSpacing	word-spacing	22
zIndex	z-index	21

The DOM Events

Chapter 30 explains the DOM event system. There are a number of different events available, as described in Table 25-9.

Table 25-9. The DOM Events

Name	Description
blur	Triggered when the element loses the focus.
click	Triggered when the mouse button is pressed and released.
dblclick	Triggered when the mouse button is pressed and released twice.
focus	Triggered when the element gains the focus.
focusin	Triggered when the element is just about to gain the focus.
focusout	Triggered when the element is just about to lose the focus.

keydown	Triggered when the user presses a key.
keypress	Triggered when a user presses and releases a key.
keyup	Triggered when the use releases a key.
mousedown	Triggered when the mouse button is pressed.
mouseenter	Triggered when the pointer is moved to be within the screen region occupied by the element or one of its descendants.
mouseleave	Triggered when the pointer is moved to be outside the screen region occupied by the element and all its descendants.
mousemove	Triggered when the pointer is moved while over the element.
mouseout	The same as for mouseleave, except that this event will trigger while the pointer is still over a descendant element.
mouseover	The same as for mouseenter, except that this event will trigger while the pointer is still over a descendant element.
mouseup	Triggered when the mouse button is released.
onabort	Triggered when the loading of a document or resource is aborted.
onafterprint	Triggered when the Window.print() method is called, before the user is presented with the print options.
onbeforeprint	Triggered after the user has printed the document.
onerror	Triggered when there is an error loading a document or resource.
onhashchange	Triggered when the has fragment changes.
onload	Triggered when the loading of a document or resource is complete.
onpopstate	Triggered to provide a state object associated with the browser history. See Chapter 26 for a demonstration of this event.
onresize	Triggered when the window is resized.
onunload	Triggered when the document is unloaded from the window/browser.
readystatechange	Triggered when the value of the readyState property changes.

| reset | Triggered when a form is reset. |
| submit | Triggered when a form is submitted. |

Summary

In this chapter, I have provided some context for the DOM and the role it plays in HTML documents. I have also explained how DOM specification levels bear little relationship to the features implemented by the mainstream browsers, and the different approaches you can take to ensure that the DOM features you rely on are available in the browsers you target. Although, it must be said, none of these approaches replace diligent and thorough testing.

This chapter also included some quick reference tables for the objects, members, and events that I describe in the chapters that follow.

Working with the Document Object

In this chapter, I introduce you to one of its key components of the DOM: the Document object. The Document object is the gateway to the functionality of the DOM and provides you with information about the current document and a set of features to explore, navigate, search, and otherwise manipulate the structure and content. Table 26-1 provides the summary for this chapter.

Table 26-1. *Chapter Summary*

Problem	Solution	Listing
Perform basic DOM tasks.	Use the basic DOM API features.	1
Getting information about the document.	Use the document metadata properties.	2
Get information about the document location.	Use the document.location property.	3
Navigate to a new document.	Change a property value of the Location object.	4, 5
Read and write cookies.	Use the document.cookie property.	6
Determine how the browser is progressing in processing the document.	Use the document.readystate property.	7
Get details of the DOM features implemented by the browser.	Use the document.implementation property.	8
Obtain objects representing specific element types.	Use the document properties, such as images, links, and scripts.	9, 10
Search for elements in the document.	Use the document.getElement* methods.	11

Search for elements in the document using a CSS selector.	Use the document.querySelector or document.querySelectorAll methods.	12
Chain searches for elements together.	Call the search methods on the result of an earlier search.	13
Navigate the DOM tree.	Use the document/element methods and properties such as hasChildNodes(), firstChild, and lastChild.	14

You access the Document object through the global document variable; this is one of the key objects that the browser creates for us. The Document object provides you with information about the document as a whole and gives you access to the individual objects in the model. The best way to get started with the DOM is with an example. Listing 26-1 shows the example document from the previous chapter, with the addition of a script that demonstrates some basic DOM features.

Listing 26-1. Using the Document Object

```
<!DOCTYPE HTML>
<html>
    <head>
        <title>Example</title>
        <meta name="author" content="Adam Freeman"/>
        <meta name="description" content="A simple example"/>
    </head>
    <body>
        <p id="fruittext">
            There are lots of different kinds of fruit - there are over 500
            varieties of <span id="banana">banana</span> alone. By the time we add the
            countless types of apples, oranges, and other well-known fruit, we are faced
            with thousands of choices.
        </p>
        <p id="apples">
            One of the most interesting aspects of fruit is the
            variety available in each country. I live near London, in an area which is
            known for its apples.
        </p>
        <script>
            document.writeln("<pre>URL: " + document.URL);
            var elems = document.getElementsByTagName("p");
            for (var i = 0; i < elems.length; i++) {
                document.writeln("Element ID: " + elems[i].id);
                elems[i].style.border = "medium double black";
                elems[i].style.padding = "4px";
            }
            document.write("</pre>");
        </script>
    </body>
</html>
```

The script is short and simple, but it neatly captures many of the different uses of the DOM. I'll break down the script into pieces and explain what is going on. One of the most basic things we can do with the Document object is get information about the HTML document that we are working with. The first line in the script does just that:

```
document.writeln("<pre>URL: " + document.URL);
```

In this case, I have read the value of the document.URL property, which returns the URL of the current document. This is the URL that the browser used to load the document in which the script is running. I'll show you the different pieces of information you can get from the Document object in the "Getting Information from the Document" section, later in this chapter.

The statement also calls the writeln method:

```
document.writeln("<pre>URL: " + document.URL);
```

This method appends content to the end of the HTML document. In this case, I have written the opening tag of a pre element and the value of the URL property. This is a very simple example of *modifying the DOM*, meaning that I have changed the structure of the document. I describe manipulating the DOM in more detail in Chapter 28.

Next, I select some elements from the document:

```
var elems = document.getElementsByTagName("p");
```

There is a range of methods for selecting elements, which I'll explain in the "Obtaining HTML Element Objects" section, later in this chapter. The getElementsByTagName selects all of the elements of a given type, in this case, p elements. Any p elements that are contained in the document are returned from the method and placed in the variable called elems. As I explained, all elements are represented by the HTMLElement object, which provides the basic functionality to represent HTML elements. The result from the getElementsByTagName method is a collection of HTMLElement objects.

Now that I have a collection of HTMLElement objects to work with, I use a for loop to enumerate the contents of the collection and process each p element that the browser has found in the HTML document:

```
for (var i = 0; i < elems.length; i++) {
    document.writeln("Element ID: " + elems[i].id);
    elems[i].style.border = "medium double black";
    elems[i].style.padding = "4px";
}
```

For each HTMLElement in the collection, I read the id property to get the value of the id attribute and use the document.writeln method to append the result to the contents of the pre element that I started earlier:

```
for (var i = 0; i < elems.length; i++) {
    document.writeln("Element ID: " + elems[i].id);
    elems[i].style.border = "medium double black";
    elems[i].style.padding = "4px";
}
```

The id property is one of a number of properties defined by HTMLElement. I'll show you the other properties in Chapter 28. You can use these properties to obtain information about an element or to modify it (and, by doing so, the HTML element that it represents). In this case, I have used the style property to change the value of the CSS border and padding properties:

```
for (var i = 0; i < elems.length; i++) {
```

655

```
        document.writeln("Element ID: " + elems[i].id);
        elems[i].style.border = "medium double black";
        elems[i].style.padding = "4px";
}
```

These changes create an inline style for each of the elements that you found using the getElementsByTagName earlier (I described inline styles in Chapter 4). When you change an object, the browser applies the change to the corresponding element immediately, in this case, by adding padding and a border to the p elements.

The last line of the script writes the end tag for the pre element that I opened back at the start of the script. I use the write method to do this, which is just like writeln but doesn't append end-of-line characters to the string that is added to the document. This doesn't make much of difference unless you are writing preformatted content or content for which you have specified nonstandard whitespace handling (see Chapter 22 for details).

The use of the pre element means that the end-of-line characters added by the writeln method will be used to structure the content. You can see the effect on the display of the document in Figure 26-1.

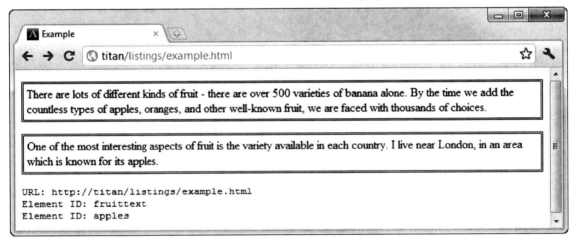

Figure 26-1. The effect of the script on the basic HTML document

Working with Document Metadata

As I explained in the previous section, one use for the Document object is to provide you with information about the document. Table 26-2 describes the properties you can use to get document metadata.

Table 26-2. Document Metadata Properties

Property	Description	Returns
characterSet	Returns the document character set encoding. This is a read-only property.	string

charset	Gets or sets the document character set encoding.	string
compatMode	Gets the compatibility mode for the document.	string
cookie	Gets or sets the cookies for the current document.	string
defaultCharset	Gets the default character encoding used by the browser.	string
defaultView	Returns the Window object for the current document; see Chapter 27 for details of this object.	Window
dir	Gets or sets the text direction for the document.	string
domain	Gets or sets the domain for the current document.	string
implementation	Provides information about the DOM features that are available.	DOMImplementation
lastModified	Returns the last modified time of the document (or the current time if no modification time is available).	string
location	Provides information about the URL of the current document.	Location
readyState	Returns the state of the current document. This is a read-only property.	string
referrer	Returns the URL of the document that linked to the current document (this is the value of the corresponding HTTP header).	string
title	Gets or sets the title of the current document (the contents of the title element, described in Chapter 7).	string

Getting Information from the Document

You can get some useful information about the document using the metadata properties, as demonstrated by Listing 26-2.

Listing 26-2. Using the Document Object to Obtain Metadata

```
<!DOCTYPE HTML>
<html>
    <head>
        <title>Example</title>
        <meta name="author" content="Adam Freeman"/>
```

```
            <meta name="description" content="A simple example"/>
        </head>
        <body>
            <script>
                document.writeln("<pre>");

                document.writeln("characterSet: " + document.characterSet);
                document.writeln("charset: " + document.charset);
                document.writeln("compatMode: " + document.compatMode);
                document.writeln("defaultCharset: " + document.defaultCharset);
                document.writeln("dir: " + document.dir);
                document.writeln("domain: " + document.domain);
                document.writeln("lastModified: " + document.lastModified);
                document.writeln("referrer: " + document.referrer);
                document.writeln("title: " + document.title);

                document.write("</pre>");
            </script>
        </body>
    </html>
```

These properties provide you with some useful insights into the document that you are working with. You can see the values for these properties as displayed by the browser in Figure 26-2.

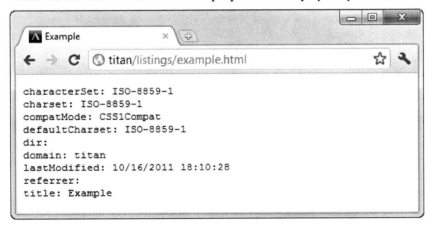

Figure 26-2. Basic information about the document

Understanding Quirks Mode

The compatMode property tells you how the browser has handled the content in the document. There is a lot of nonstandard HTML in the world, and browsers try to display such pages even when they don't conform to the HTML specification. Some of this content relies on features that date back to the days when browsers competed on their unique differences, rather than standards compliance. The compatMode property will return one of two values, as described in Table 26-3.

Table 26-3. The compatMode Property Values

Value	Description
CSS1Compat	The document conforms to a valid HTML specification (although this need not be HTML5; valid HTML4 documents will return this value, too).
BackCompat	The document contains nonstandard features and has triggered the quirks mode.

Using the Location Object

The document.location property returns a Location object that gives you fine-grained information about the document's address and allows you to navigate to other documents. Table 26-4 describes the functions and properties of the Location object.

Table 26-4. Location Methods and Properties

Property	Description	Returns
protocol	Gets or sets the protocol component of the document URL	string
host	Gets or sets the host component of the document URL	string
href	Gets or sets the current document's location	string
hostname	Gets or sets the host name component of the document URL	string
port	Gets or sets the port component of the document URL	string
pathname	Gets or sets the path component of the document URL	string
search	Gets or sets the query component of the document URL	string
hash	Gets or sets the hash component of the document URL	string
assign(<URL>)	Navigates to the specified URL	void
replace(<URL>)	Removes the current document and navigates to the one specified by the URL.	void
reload()	Reloads the current document	void
resolveURL(<URL>)	Resolves the specified relative URL to an absolute one	string

The simplest use for the document.location property is to get information about the location of the current object, as shown in Listing 26-3.

Listing 26-3. Using the Location Object to Get Information About the Document

```
<!DOCTYPE HTML>
<html>
    <head>
        <title>Example</title>
        <meta name="author" content="Adam Freeman"/>
        <meta name="description" content="A simple example"/>
    </head>
    <body>
        <script>
            document.writeln("<pre>");

            document.writeln("protocol: " + document.location.protocol);
            document.writeln("host: " + document.location.host);
            document.writeln("hostname: " + document.location.hostname);
            document.writeln("port: " + document.location.port);
            document.writeln("pathname: " + document.location.pathname);
            document.writeln("search: " + document.location.search);
            document.writeln("hash: " + document.location.hash);

            document.write("</pre>");
        </script>
    </body>
</html>
```

The search property returns the query string portion of the URL, and the hash property returns the URL fragment. Figure 26-3 shows the values returned by the Location properties for the URL http://titan/listings/example.html?query=apples#apples.

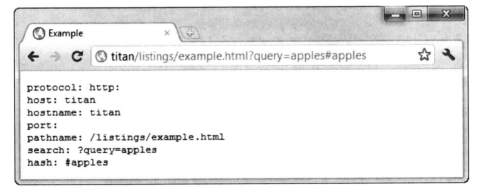

Figure 26-3. Using the Location object to get information

■ **Tip** Notice that the property doesn't return a value when the port is 80, the default for HTTP.

Using the Location Object to Navigate Elsewhere

You can also use the Location object available through the document.location property to navigate elsewhere. There are a couple of different ways of doing this. First, you can assign a new value to one of the properties that I used in the previous example, as shown in Listing 26-4.

Listing 26-4. Navigating to a Document by Assigning a New Value to a Location Property

```
<!DOCTYPE HTML>
<html>
    <head>
        <title>Example</title>
        <meta name="author" content="Adam Freeman"/>
        <meta name="description" content="A simple example"/>
    </head>
    <body>
        <p>
            There are lots of different kinds of fruit - there are over 500 varieties
            of banana alone. By the time we add the countless types of apples, oranges,
            and other well-known fruit, we are faced with thousands of choices.
        </p>
        <button id="pressme">Press Me</button>
        <p>
            One of the most interesting aspects of fruit is the variety available in
            each country. I live near London, in an area which is known for
            its apples.

        </p>
        <img id="banana" src="banana-small.png" alt="small banana"/>
        <script>
            document.getElementById("pressme").onclick = function() {
                document.location.hash = "banana";
            }
        </script>
    </body>
</html>
```

This example contains a button element that, when clicked, causes a new value to be assigned to the document.location.hash property. The association between the button and the JavaScript function that will be executed when it is clicked is made using an *event*. This is the purpose of the onclick property, and you can learn more about events in Chapter 30.

This change causes the browser to navigate to the element whose id attribute value matches the hash value, the img element in this case. You can see the effect of this navigation in Figure 26-4.

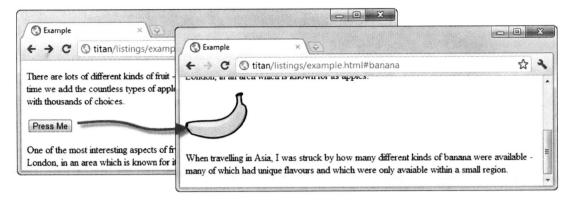

Figure 26-4. Using the Location object to navigate

Although I navigated to a different location within the same document, you can use the properties of the Location object to navigate to other documents as well. However, this is usually done through the href property, since you can set the complete URL. You can also use the *methods* that the Location object defines.

The difference between the assign and replace methods is that replace removes the current document from the browser's history, meaning that when the user clicks the back button, for example, the browser will skip over the current document, as though it had never been visited. Listing 26-5 shows the use of the assign method.

Listing 26-5. Navigating Using the assign Method of the Location Object

```
<!DOCTYPE HTML>
<html>
    <head>
        <title>Example</title>
        <meta name="author" content="Adam Freeman"/>
        <meta name="description" content="A simple example"/>
    </head>
    <body>
        <button id="pressme">Press Me</button>
        <script>
            document.getElementById("pressme").onclick = function() {
                document.location.assign("http://apress.com");
            }
        </script>
    </body>
</html>
```

When the user clicks the button element, the browser will navigate to the specified URL, which in this case is http://apress.com.

Reading and Writing Cookies

The cookie property allows you to read, add to, and update the cookies associated with the document. Listing 26-6 gives a demonstration.

Listing 26-6. Reading and Creating Cookies

```
<!DOCTYPE HTML>
<html>
    <head>
        <title>Example</title>
        <meta name="author" content="Adam Freeman"/>
        <meta name="description" content="A simple example"/>
    </head>
    <body>
        <p id="cookiedata">

        </p>
        <button id="write">Add Cookie</button>
        <button id="update">Update Cookie</button>
        <script>

            var cookieCount = 0;
            document.getElementById("update").onclick = updateCookie;
            document.getElementById("write").onclick = createCookie;
            readCookies();

            function readCookies() {
                document.getElementById("cookiedata").innerHTML = document.cookie;
            }

            function createCookie() {
                cookieCount++;
                document.cookie = "Cookie_" + cookieCount + "=Value_" + cookieCount;
                readCookies();
            }

            function updateCookie() {
                document.cookie = "Cookie_" + cookieCount + "=Updated_" + cookieCount;
                readCookies();
            }
        </script>
    </body>
</html>
```

The cookie property works in a slightly odd way. When you read the value of the property, you get back all of the cookies that are associated with the document. Cookies are name/value pairs in the form name=value. If multiple cookies are available, all are returned as the result of the cookie property, separated by a semicolon, for example: name1=value1;name2=value2.

By contrast, when you want to create a new cookie, you assign a new name/value pair as the value of the cookie property, and it is added to the set of cookies for the document. You can set only one cookie

663

at a time. If you set a value whose name portion corresponds to an existing cookie, then the value portion is used to update the cookie.

To demonstrate this, the listing contains a script that reads, creates, and updates cookies. The readCookies function reads the value of the document.cookie property and sets the result as the content of a paragraph (p) element.

There are two button elements in the document. When the Add Cookie button is clicked, the createCookie function assigns a new value to the cookie property, which will be added to the cookie collection. The Update Cookie button causes the updateCookie function to be invoked. This function provides a new value for an existing cookie. You can see the effect of this script in Figure 26-5, but to truly get a feel for what's happening, I recommend you load this document and play around.

Figure 26-5. Adding and updating cookies

In this case, I have added three cookies, one of which has been updated to have a new value. Although the name=value form is the default for adding cookies, you can apply some additional data that changes the way the cookie is handled. These additions are described in Table 26-5.

***Table 26-5.** The Additional Fields That Can Be Added to a Cookie*

Addition	Description
path=<path>	Sets the path associated with the cookie; this default to the path of the current document if not specified.
domain=<domain>	Sets the domain associated with the cookie; this defaults to the domain of the current document if not specified.
max-age=<seconds>	Sets the life of the cookie in terms of the number of seconds from the moment it was created.
expires=<date>	Sets the life of the cookie using a GMT-format date.
secure	The cookie will be sent only over a secure (HTTPS) connection.

Each of these additional items is prepended to the name/value pair and separated with a semicolon, like this:

```
document.cookie = "MyCookie=MyValue;max-age=10";
```

Understanding the Ready State

The document.readyState property gives you information about the current stage in the process of loading and parsing the HTML document. Remember that, by default, the browser executes your scripts as soon as it encounters the script element in the document, but that script execution can be deferred using the defer attribute (as described in Chapter 7). As you have already seen in some of the examples and as I'll explain in detail in Chapter 30, you can use the JavaScript event system to execute individual functions in response to changes in the document or user actions.

In all of these situations, it can be useful to know what stage the browser has got to in loading and processing the HTML. The readyState property returns three different values, which are described in Table 26-6.

Table 26-6. *The Values Returned by the readyState Property*

Value	Description
loading	The browser is loading and processing the document.
interactive	The document has been parsed, but the browser is still loading linked resources (images, media files, and so on).
complete	The document has been parsed and all of the resources have been loaded.

The value of the readyState property moves from loading to interactive to complete as the browser loads and processes the document. This property is most useful in conjunction with the readystatechange event, which is triggered each time the value of the readyState property changes. I'll explain events in Chapter 30, but Listing 26-7 shows how you can use the event and the property together to achieve a common task.

Listing 26-7. *Using the Document Ready State to Defer Script Execution*

```
<!DOCTYPE HTML>
<html>
    <head>
        <title>Example</title>
        <meta name="author" content="Adam Freeman"/>
        <meta name="description" content="A simple example"/>
        <script>
            document.onreadystatechange = function() {
                if (document.readyState == "interactive") {
                    document.getElementById("pressme").onclick = function() {
                        document.getElementById("results").innerHTML = "Button Pressed";
                    }
                }
            }
        </script>
    </head>
    <body>
        <button id="pressme">Press Me</button>
```

```
        <pre id="results"></pre>
    </body>
</html>
```

This script uses the document ready state to defer execution of a function until the document reaches the `interactive` stage. This script relies on being able to find elements in the document that have not been loaded by the browser at the point where the script is being executed. By deferring execution until the document has been completely loaded, I can be sure that the elements will be found. This is an alternative to putting the `script` element at the end of the document. I explain how to find elements in the "Obtaining HTML Element Objects" section, later in this chapter. I explain how to use events in Chapter 30.

Getting DOM Implementation Details

The `document.implementation` property provides you with information about the browser implementation of the DOM features. This property returns a `DOMImplementation` object, which has one method that you are interested in: the `hasFeature` method. You can use this method to determine which DOM features are implemented, as demonstrated in Listing 26-8.

Listing 26-8. Using the document.implementation.hasFeature Method

```
<!DOCTYPE HTML>
<html>
    <head>
        <title>Example</title>
        <meta name="author" content="Adam Freeman"/>
        <meta name="description" content="A simple example"/>
    </head>
    <body>
        <script>

            var features = ["Core", "HTML", "CSS", "Selectors-API"];
            var levels = ["1.0", "2.0", "3.0"];

            document.writeln("<pre>");
            for (var i = 0; i < features.length; i++) {
                document.writeln("Checking for feature: " + features[i]);
                for (var j = 0; j < levels.length; j++) {
                    document.write(features[i] + " Level " + levels[j] + ": ");
                    document.writeln(document.implementation.hasFeature(features[i],
                        levels[j]));
                }
            }
            document.write("</pre>")
        </script>
    </body>
</html>
```

This script checks some of the different DOM features and the defined feature levels. This isn't as useful as it might appear. First, browsers don't always report the features they implement correctly. Some implement features but don't report them through the `hasFeature` method, and others claim to implement features but don't. Second, a browser reporting that a feature doesn't mean that it is implemented in a useful way. This is less of a problem than it has been, but there are some differences between DOM implementations.

If you are intending to write code that works on all mainstream browsers (and you should be), then the hasFeature method is not much use. Instead, check your code thoroughly during the testing phase, test for the support and fallback when you need to, and, optionally, consider using a JavaScript library (such as jQuery), which can help smooth out differences in the DOM implementations.

Obtaining HTML Element Objects

One of the key functions of the Document object is to act as a gateway to the objects that represent the elements in your document. You can perform this task in a few different ways. There are properties that return objects that represent specific types of element in the document, there are some handy methods that let you match for elements using search criteria, and you can treat the DOM as a tree and navigate through its structure. In the sections that follow, I introduce these techniques.

■ **Tip** Obviously, you want to obtain these objects in order to do interesting things with them. I'll describe how to use these objects in Chapter 38, in which I describe the features of the HTMLElement object.

Using Properties to Obtain Element Objects

The Document object provides you with a set of properties that return objects that represent specific elements or types of elements in the document. These properties are summarized in Table 26-7.

Table 26-7. Element Properties of the Document Object

Property	Description	Returns
activeElement	Returns an object representing the currently focused element	HTMLElement
body	Returns an object representing the body element	HTMLElement
embeds plugins	Returns objects representing all the embed elements	HTMLCollection
forms	Returns objects representing all the form elements	HTMLCollection
head	Returns an object representing the head element	HTMLHeadElement
images	Returns objects representing all the img elements	HTMLCollection
links	Returns objects representing all the a and area elements in	HTMLCollection

<table>
<tr><td></td><td>the document that have href attributes</td><td></td></tr>
<tr><td>scripts</td><td>Returns objects representing all the script elements</td><td>HTMLCollection</td></tr>
</table>

Most of the properties described in Table 26-7 return an HTMLCollection object. This is the way that the DOM represents a collection of objects that represent elements. Listing 26-9 demonstrates the two ways in which you can access the objects contained in the collection.

Listing 26-9. Working with the HTMLCollection Object

```html
<!DOCTYPE HTML>
<html>
    <head>
        <title>Example</title>
        <meta name="author" content="Adam Freeman"/>
        <meta name="description" content="A simple example"/>
        <link rel="shortcut icon" href="favicon.ico" type="image/x-icon" />
        <style>
            pre {border: medium double black;}
        </style>
    </head>
    <body>
        <pre id="results"></pre>
        <img id="lemon" src="lemon.png" alt="lemon"/>
        <p>
            There are lots of different kinds of fruit - there are over 500 varieties
            of banana alone. By the time we add the countless types of apples, oranges,
            and other well-known fruit, we are faced with thousands of choices.
        </p>
        <img id="apple" src="apple.png" alt="apple"/>
        <p>
            One of the most interesting aspects of fruit is the variety available in
            each country. I live near London, in an area which is known for
            its apples.
        </p>
        <img id="banana" src="banana-small.png" alt="small banana"/>
        <script>
            var resultsElement = document.getElementById("results");

            var elems = document.images;

            for (var i = 0; i < elems.length; i++) {
                resultsElement.innerHTML += "Image Element: " + elems[i].id + "\n";
            }

            var srcValue = elems.namedItem("apple").src;
            resultsElement.innerHTML += "Src for apple element is: " + srcValue + "\n";
        </script>
    </body>
```

```
</html>
```

The first way of working with an HTMLCollection is to treat it like an array. The length property returns the number of items in the collection, and the standard JavaScript array indexer is supported (the element[i] notation) to provide direct access to individual objects in the collection. This is the first approach I use in the example, having used the document.images property to get an HTMLCollection containing object representing all of the img elements in the document.

▪ **Tip** Notice that I used the innerHTML property to set the contents of the pre element. I'll explain this property in more detail in Chapter 38.

The second approach is to use the namedItem method, which returns the item in the collection that has the specified id or name attribute value (if there is one). This is the second approach I use in the example, where I use the namedItem method to retrieve the object representing the img element with the id attribute value of apple.

▪ **Tip** Notice that I read the value of the src property on one of the objects. This is a property that is implemented by HTMLImageElement objects, which are used to represent img elements. I explain more about this kind of object in Chapter 31. The other property I use, id, is part of HTMLElement and so is available for all types of element.

Using Array Notation to Obtain a Named Element

You can also use array-style notation to obtain an object representing a *named element*. This is an element that has an id or name attribute value. Listing 26-10 provides an example.

Listing 26-10. Obtaining Named Element Objects

```HTML
<!DOCTYPE HTML>
<html>
    <head>
        <title>Example</title>
        <meta name="author" content="Adam Freeman"/>
        <meta name="description" content="A simple example"/>
        <link rel="shortcut icon" href="favicon.ico" type="image/x-icon" />
        <style>
            pre {border: medium double black;}
        </style>
    </head>
    <body>
        <pre id="results"></pre>
        <img id="lemon" name="image" src="lemon.png" alt="lemon"/>
        <p>
```

```
        There are lots of different kinds of fruit - there are over 500 varieties
        of banana alone. By the time we add the countless types of apples, oranges,
        and other well-known fruit, we are faced with thousands of choices.
    </p>
    <img id="apple" name="image" src="apple.png" alt="apple"/>
    <p>
        One of the most interesting aspects of fruit is the variety available in
        each country. I live near London, in an area which is known for
        its apples.

    </p>
    <img id="banana" src="banana-small.png" alt="small banana"/>
    <script>
        var resultsElement = document.getElementById("results");
        var elems = document["apple"];

        if (elems.namedItem) {
            for (var i = 0; i < elems.length; i++) {
                resultsElement.innerHTML += "Image Element: " + elems[i].id + "\n";
            }
        } else {
            resultsElement.innerHTML += "Src for element is: " + elems.src + "\n";
        }
    </script>
</body>
</html>
```

You can see how I have used the array-style indexer to obtain an object representing the element with an id value of apple. An oddity of obtaining elements this way is that you can get different kinds of results, depending on the contents of the document and the order of the elements.

The browser looks at all of the elements in the document in a depth-first order, trying to match either the id or name attribute to the specified value. If the first match is an id attribute, then the browser stops searching (because id values must be unique in documents) and returns an HTMLElement representing the matched element.

If the first match is against a name attribute value, then you will receive either an HTMLElement (if there is only one matching element) or an HTMLCollection (if there is more than one). The browser won't match id values once it has started to match name values.

You can see how I use the namedItem property as a test to see which kind of result I have received. In the example I receive an HTMLElement because the value I specified matches an id value.

■ **Tip** You can also refer to named elements as properties. So, for example, document[apple] and document.apple have the same meaning. I tend to prefer the dot-notation format because it makes it clearer that I am trying to obtain element objects, but it is a matter of personal preference.

Searching for Elements

The Document object defines a number of methods that you can use to search for elements in the document. These methods are described in Table 26-8.

Table 26-8. Document Methods to Find Elements

Property	Description	Returns
getElementById(<id>)	Returns the element with the specified id value	HTMLElement
getElementsByClassName(<class>)	Returns the elements with the specified class value	HTMLElement[]
getElementsByName(<name>)	Returns the elements with the specified name value	HTMLElement[]
getElementsByTagName(<tag>)	Returns the elements of the specified type	HTMLElement[]
querySelector(<selector>)	Returns the first element that matches the specified CSS selector	HTMLElement
querySelectorAll(<selector>)	Returns all of the elements that match the specified CSS selector	HTMLElement[]

As you might expect, some of these methods return multiple elements. I have shown these as returning an array of HTMLElement objects in the table, but this isn't strictly true. In fact, these methods return a NodeList, which is part of the underlying DOM specification that deals with generic structured document formats and not just HTML. However, for these purposes, you can treat them like arrays and keep the focus on HTML5.

The search methods can be broken into two categories. Listing 26-11 shows demonstrates the first of these categories—those methods whose name begins with getElement.

Listing 26-11. Using the document.getElement* Methods

```
<!DOCTYPE HTML>
<html>
    <head>
        <title>Example</title>
        <meta name="author" content="Adam Freeman"/>
        <meta name="description" content="A simple example"/>
        <link rel="shortcut icon" href="favicon.ico" type="image/x-icon" />
        <style>
            pre {border: medium double black;}
        </style>
    </head>
    <body>
        <pre id="results"></pre>
```

```
<img id="lemon" class="fruits" name="apple" src="lemon.png" alt="lemon"/>
<p>
    There are lots of different kinds of fruit - there are over 500 varieties
    of banana alone. By the time we add the countless types of apples, oranges,
    and other well-known fruit, we are faced with thousands of choices.
</p>
<img id="apple" class="fruits images" name="apple"  src="apple.png" alt="apple"/>
<p>
    One of the most interesting aspects of fruit is the variety available in
    each country. I live near London, in an area which is known for
    its apples.

</p>
<img id="banana" src="banana-small.png" alt="small banana"/>
<script>
    var resultsElement = document.getElementById("results");

    var pElems = document.getElementsByTagName("p");
    resultsElement.innerHTML += "There are " + pElems.length + " p elements\n";

    var fruitsElems = document.getElementsByClassName("fruits");
    resultsElement.innerHTML += "There are " + fruitsElems.length
        + " elements in the fruits class\n";

    var nameElems = document.getElementsByName("apple");
    resultsElement.innerHTML += "There are " + nameElems.length
        + " elements with the name 'apple'";
</script>
    </body>
</html>
```

These methods work just as you might expect, and there is only one behavior to note. When using the getElementById method, the browser will return null if no element can be found with the specified id value. By contrast, the other methods will always return an array of HTMLElement objects, but the length property will return 0 to indicate no matches.

Searching with CSS Selectors

A useful alternative is to search using CSS selectors. Selectors allow you to find a broader range of elements in the document. I describe CSS selectors in Chapters 17 and 18. Listing 26-12 demonstrates obtaining element objects in this way.

Listing 26-12. Obtaining Element Objects Using CSS Selectors

```
<!DOCTYPE HTML>
<html>
    <head>
        <title>Example</title>
        <meta name="author" content="Adam Freeman"/>
        <meta name="description" content="A simple example"/>
        <link rel="shortcut icon" href="favicon.ico" type="image/x-icon" />
```

```
        <style>
            pre {border: medium double black;}
        </style>
    </head>
    <body>
        <pre id="results"></pre>
        <img id="lemon" class="fruits" name="apple" src="lemon.png" alt="lemon"/>
        <p>
            There are lots of different kinds of fruit - there are over 500 varieties
            of banana alone. By the time we add the countless types of apples, oranges,
            and other well-known fruit, we are faced with thousands of choices.
        </p>
        <img id="apple" class="fruits images" name="apple"  src="apple.png" alt="apple"/>
        <p>
            One of the most interesting aspects of fruit is the variety available in
            each country. I live near London, in an area which is known for
            its apples.

        </p>
        <img id="banana" src="banana-small.png" alt="small banana"/>
        <script>
            var resultsElement = document.getElementById("results");

            var elems = document.querySelectorAll("p, img#apple")
            resultsElement.innerHTML += "The selector matched " + elems.length
                + " elements\n";
        </script>
    </body>
</html>
```

In this example, I have used a selector that will match all p elements and the img element that has an id value of apple. It is hard to achieve the same effect using the other document methods, and I find that I use the selectors more frequently than the getElement methods.

Chaining Searches Together

A nice DOM feature is that all but one of the search methods the Document object implements are also implemented by HTMLElement objects, allowing you to chain searches together. The exception is the getElementById method, which is available only through the Document object. Listing 26-13 provides a demonstration of chaining searches.

Listing 26-13. Chaining Searches Together

```
<!DOCTYPE HTML>
<html>
    <head>
        <title>Example</title>
        <meta name="author" content="Adam Freeman"/>
        <meta name="description" content="A simple example"/>
        <link rel="shortcut icon" href="favicon.ico" type="image/x-icon" />
        <style>
```

```
            pre {border: medium double black;}
        </style>
    </head>
    <body>
        <pre id="results"></pre>
        <p id="tblock">
            There are lots of different kinds of fruit - there are over 500 varieties
            of <span id="banana">banana</span> alone. By the time we add the countless
            types of <span id="apple">apples</span>,
            <span="orange">oranges</span="orange">, and other well-known fruit, we are
            faced with thousands of choices.
        </p>
        <script>
            var resultsElement = document.getElementById("results");

            var elems = document.getElementById("tblock").getElementsByTagName("span");
            resultsElement.innerHTML += "There are " + elems.length + " span elements\n";

            var elems2 = document.getElementById("tblock").querySelectorAll("span");
            resultsElement.innerHTML += "There are " + elems2.length
                + " span elements (Mix)\n";

            var selElems = document.querySelectorAll("#tblock > span");
            resultsElement.innerHTML += "There are " + selElems.length
                + " span elements (CSS)\n";

        </script>
    </body>
</html>
```

There are two chained searches in this example, both of which I have started with the getElementById method (which gives me a single object to work with). In the first example, I chain a search using the getElementsByTagName method, and in the second I use a very simple CSS selector through the querySelectorAll method. Each of these examples returns the collection of span elements contained in the p element whose id is tblock.

Of course, you can achieve the same effect using the CSS selector methods applied solely to the Document object (which I have shown as the third part of the example), but this feature can be convenient when you are dealing with HTMLElement objects that have been produced by another function in your script (or by a third-party script). You can see the results of the searches in Figure 26-6.

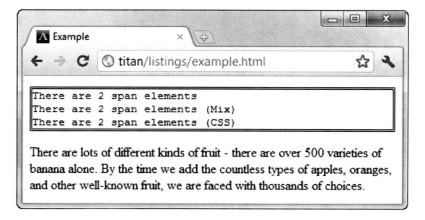

Figure 26-6. Chaining searches together

Navigating the DOM Tree

An alternative approach to searching for elements is to treat the DOM like a tree and navigate its hierarchical structure. There are a set of properties and methods that are supported by all DOM objects that let us do just that; they are described in Table 26-9.

Table 26-9. Tree navigation Properties and Methods

Property	Description	Returns
childNodes	Returns the set of child elements	HTMLElement[]
firstChild	Returns the first child element	HTMLElement
hasChildNodes()	Returns true if the current element has child elements	boolean
lastChild	Returns the last child element	HTMLElement
nextSibling	Returns the sibling element defined after the current element	HTMLElement
parentNode	Returns the parent element	HTMLElement
previousSibling	Returns the sibling element defined before the current element	HTMLElement

Listing 26-14 shows a script that lets you navigate around the document, displaying information about the currently selected element in a pre element.

Listing 26-14. Navigating the DOM Tree

```
<!DOCTYPE HTML>
<html>
    <head>
        <title>Example</title>
        <meta name="author" content="Adam Freeman"/>
        <meta name="description" content="A simple example"/>
        <link rel="shortcut icon" href="favicon.ico" type="image/x-icon" />
        <style>
            pre {border: medium double black;}
        </style>
    </head>
    <body>
        <pre id="results"></pre>
        <p id="tblock">
            There are lots of different kinds of fruit - there are over 500 varieties
            of <span id="banana">banana</span> alone. By the time we add the countless
            types of <span id="apple">apples</span>,
            <span="orange">oranges</span="orange">, and other well-known fruit, we are
            faced with thousands of choices.
        </p>
        <img id="apple" class="fruits images" name="apple"  src="apple.png" alt="apple"/>
        <img id="banana" src="banana-small.png" alt="small banana"/>
        <p>
            One of the most interesting aspects of fruit is the variety available in
            each country. I live near London, in an area which is known for
            its apples.
        </p>
        <p>
            <button id="parent">Parent</button>
            <button id="child">First Child</button>
            <button id="prev">Prev Sibling</button>
            <button id="next">Next Sibling</button>
        </p>

        <script>
            var resultsElem = document.getElementById("results");
            var element = document.body;

            var buttons = document.getElementsByTagName("button");
            for (var i = 0; i < buttons.length; i++) {
                buttons[i].onclick = handleButtonClick;
            }

            processNewElement(element);

            function handleButtonClick(e) {
                if (element.style) {
                    element.style.backgroundColor = "white";
                }
```

```
            if (e.target.id == "parent" && element != document.body) {
                element = element.parentNode;
            } else if (e.target.id == "child" && element.hasChildNodes()) {
                element = element.firstChild;
            } else if (e.target.id == "prev" && element.previousSibling) {
                element = element.previousSibling;
            } else if (e.target.id == "next" && element.nextSibling) {
                element = element.nextSibling;
            }
            processNewElement(element);
            if (element.style) {
                element.style.backgroundColor = "lightgrey";
            }
        }

        function processNewElement(elem) {
            resultsElem.innerHTML = "Element type: " + elem + "\n";
            resultsElem.innerHTML += "Element id: " + elem.id + "\n";
            resultsElem.innerHTML += "Has child nodes: "
                + elem.hasChildNodes() + "\n";
            if (elem.previousSibling) {
                resultsElem.innerHTML += ("Prev sibling is: "
                    + elem.previousSibling + "\n");
            } else {
                resultsElem.innerHTML += "No prev sibling\n";
            }
            if (elem.nextSibling) {
                resultsElem.innerHTML += "Next sibling is: "
                    + elem.nextSibling + "\n";
            } else {
                resultsElem.innerHTML += "No next sibling\n";
            }
        }
    </script>
  </body>
</html>
```

The important part of the script is shown in bold; this is the section that does the actual navigation. The rest of the script deals with the setup, processing button clicks and display information about the currently selected element. You can see the effect of the script in Figure 26-7.

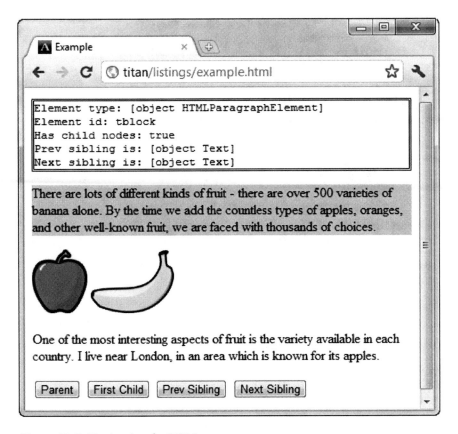

Figure 26-7. Navigating the DOM tree

Summary

In this chapter, I introduced you to the Document object, which the browser creates for you and which acts as the gateway into the Document Object Model (DOM). I explained how you get information about the document, how you find and obtain objects that represent elements in the document, and how you can navigate the DOM as a tree structure.

CHAPTER 27

Working with the Window Object

The Window object has been added to the HTML specification as part of HTML5. Prior to this, it has been an unofficial standard; browsers have implemented roughly the same set of features in a broadly consistent way. With HTML5, the Window object in the specification incorporates the de facto functionality and a few enhancements. Implementation of this object is mixed; different browsers have different levels of compliance. This chapter focuses on the features that have a reasonable level of support.

■ **Note** Some of the advanced features described in this chapter rely on DOM *events*, which are the topic of Chapter 30. If you are unfamiliar with events, you may wish to read that chapter and then return to the examples in this one.

The Window object has been a bit of a dumping ground for features that don't have a natural home elsewhere. You will see what I mean as we tour the features of this object. Table 27-1 provides the summary for this chapter.

Table 27-1. Chapter Summary

Problem	Solution	Listing
Obtain a Window object	Use document.defaultView or the window global variable	1
Get information about a window	Use the Window informational properties	2
Interact with the window	Use the methods defined by the Window object	3
Prompt the user with a modal dialog window	Use the alert, confirm, prompt, and showModalDialog methods on a Window	4

	object	
Perform simple operations on the browser history	Use the back, forward, and go methods on the History object returned by the Window.history property	5
Manipulate the browser history	Use the pushState and replaceState methods on the History object returned by the Window.history property	6–11
Send a message to a script running in a different document	Use the cross-document messaging feature	12–15
Set one-off or repeating timers	Use the setInterval, setTimeout, clearInterval, and clearTimeout methods on the Window object	16

Obtaining a Window Object

You can get a Window object in two ways. The official HTML5 way is to use the defaultView property on the Document object. Another approach is to use the window global variable, which all of the browsers support. Listing 27-1 demonstrates both techniques.

Listing 27-1. Obtaining a Window Object

```
<!DOCTYPE HTML>
<html>
    <head>
        <title>Example</title>
    </head>
    <body id="bod">
        <table>
            <tr><th>outerWidth:</th><td id="owidth"></td></tr>
            <tr><th>outerHeight:</th><td id="oheight"></td></tr>
        </table>

        <script type="text/javascript">
            document.getElementById("owidth").innerHTML = window.outerWidth;
            document.getElementById("oheight").innerHTML
                = document.defaultView.outerHeight;
        </script>
    </body>
</html>
```

In the script I use the Window object to read the value of a pair of properties, outerWidth and outerHeight, which are explained in the following section.

Getting Information about the Window

As its name suggests, the basic functionality of the Window object relates to the window in which the document is currently displayed. Table 27-2 lists the properties and methods that handle this functionality. For the purposes of HTML, tabs within a browser window are treated as windows in their own right.

Table 27-2. Window-Related Members

Name	Description	Returns
innerHeight	Gets the height of the window content area	number
innerWidth	Gets the width of the window content area	number
outerHeight	Gets the height of the window, including borders, menu bars, and so on	number
outerWidth	Gets the width of the window, including borders, menu bars, and so on	number
pageXOffset	Gets the number of pixels that the window has been scrolled horizontally from the top-left corner	number
pageYOffset	Gets the number of pixels that the window has been scrolled vertically from the top-left corner	number
screen	Returns a Screen object describing the screen	Screen
screenLeft screenX	Gets the number of pixels from the left edge of the window to the left edge of the screen (not all browsers implement both properties or calculate this value in the same way)	number
screenTop screenY	Gets the number of pixels from the top edge of the window to the top edge of the screen (not all browsers implement both properties or calculate this value in the same way)	number

Listing 27-2 shows how to use these properties to get information about the window.

Listing 27-2. Getting Information About the Window

```
<!DOCTYPE HTML>
<html>
    <head>
        <title>Example</title>
        <style>
            table { border-collapse: collapse; border: thin solid black;}
            th, td { padding: 4px; }
```

```
        </style>
    </head>
    <body>
        <table border="1">
            <tr>
                <th>outerWidth:</th><td id="ow"></td><th>outerHeight:</th><td id="oh">
            </tr>
            <tr>
                <th>innerWidth:</th><td id="iw"></td><th>innerHeight:</th><td id="ih">
            </tr>
            <tr>
                <th>screen.width:</th><td id="sw"></td>
                <th>screen.height:</th><td id="sh">
            </tr>
        </table>

        <script type="text/javascript">
            document.getElementById("ow").innerHTML = window.outerWidth;
            document.getElementById("oh").innerHTML = window.outerHeight;
            document.getElementById("iw").innerHTML = window.innerHeight;
            document.getElementById("ih").innerHTML = window.innerHeight;
            document.getElementById("sw").innerHTML = window.screen.width;
            document.getElementById("sh").innerHTML = window.screen.height;
        </script>
    </body>
</html>
```

The script in this example displays the value of various Window properties in a table. Notice that I used the screen property to obtain a Screen object. This object provides information about the screen that the window is displayed on and defines the properties shown in Table 27-3.

Table 27-3. The Screen Object Properties

Name	Description	Returns
availHeight	The height of the portion of the screen available for displaying windows (excludes toolbars, menu bars, and so on)	number
availWidth	The width of the portion of the screen available for displaying windows (excludes toolbars, menu bars, and so on)	number
colorDepth	The color depth of the screen	number
height	The height of the screen	number
width	The width of the screen	number

You can see the effect of the script in Figure 27-1.

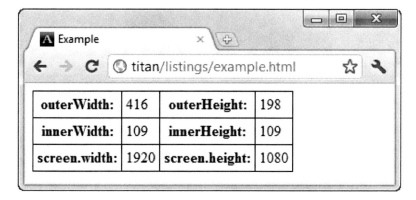

Figure 27-1. Displaying information about the window and screen

Interacting with the Window

The Window object provides a set of methods through which you can interact with the window that contains your document. These methods are described in Table 27-4.

Table 27-4. The Window Interaction Features

Name	Description	Returns
blur()	Unfocuses the window	void
close()	Closes the window (not all browsers allow a script to close the window)	void
focus()	Focuses the window	void
print()	Prompts the user to print the page	void
scrollBy(<x>, <y>)	Scrolls the document relative to its current position	void
scrollTo(<x>, <y>)	Scrolls to the specified position	void
stop()	Stops the document from loading	void

All of these methods should be used with caution because they take the control of the browser window away from the user. Users have very fixed expectations of how applications should behave, and windows that scroll, print, and close themselves are largely unwelcome. If you must use these methods, put control in the hands of the user, and provide clear visual cues about what is going to happen.

Listing 27-3 shows some of the window interaction methods in use.

Listing 27-3. Interacting with the Window

```
<!DOCTYPE HTML>
<html>
    <head>
        <title>Example</title>
    </head>
    <body>
        <p>
            <button id="scroll">Scroll</button>
            <button id="print">Print</button>
            <button id="close">Close</button>
        </p>
        <p>
            There are lots of different kinds of fruit - there are over 500 varieties
            of banana alone. By the time we add the countless types of apples, oranges,
            and other well-known fruit, we are faced with thousands of choices.
            <img src="apple.png" alt="apple"/>
            One of the most interesting aspects of fruit is the variety available in
            each country. I live near London, in an area which is known for
            its apples.
            <img src="banana-small.png" alt="banana"/>
            When traveling in Asia, I was struck by how many different
            kinds of banana were available - many of which had unique flavors and
            which were only available within a small region.

            And, of course, there are fruits which are truly unique - I am put in mind
            of the durian, which is widely consumed in SE Asia and is known as the
            "king of fruits." The durian is largely unknown in Europe and the USA - if
            it is known at all, it is for the overwhelming smell, which is compared
            to a combination of almonds, rotten onions and gym socks.
        </p>
        <script>
            var buttons = document.getElementsByTagName("button");
            for (var i = 0; i < buttons.length; i++) {
                buttons[i].onclick = handleButtonPress;
            }

            function handleButtonPress(e) {
                if (e.target.id == "print") {
                    window.print();
                } else if (e.target.id == "close") {
                    window.close();
                } else {
                    window.scrollTo(0, 400);
                }
            }
        </script>
    </body>
</html>
```

The script in this example prints, closes, and scrolls the window in response to button presses.

Prompting the User

The Window object contains a set of methods for prompting the user in different ways, as described in Table 27-5.

Table 27-5. The Prompting Features

Name	Description	Returns
alert(<msg>)	Displays a dialog window to the user and waits for it to be dismissed	void
confirm(<msg>)	Displays a dialog window with an OK/Cancel prompt	boolean
prompt(<msg>, <val>)	Displays a dialog prompting the user to enter a value	string
showModalDialog(<url>)	Displays a popup window showing the specified URL	void

Each of these methods presents a different kind of prompt. Listing 27-4 demonstrates how they can be used.

Listing 27-4. Prompting the User

```
<!DOCTYPE HTML>
<html>
    <head>
        <title>Example</title>
        <style>
            table { border-collapse: collapse; border: thin solid black;}
            th, td { padding: 4px; }
        </style>
    </head>
    <body>

        <button id="alert">Alert</button>
        <button id="confirm">Confirm</button>
        <button id="prompt">Prompt</button>
        <button id="modal">Modal Dialog</button>

        <script type="text/javascript">

            var buttons = document.getElementsByTagName("button");
            for (var i = 0 ; i < buttons.length; i++) {
                buttons[i].onclick = handleButtonPress;
            }
```

```
            function handleButtonPress(e) {
                if (e.target.id == "alert") {
                    window.alert("This is an alert");
                } else if (e.target.id == "confirm") {
                    var confirmed
                        = window.confirm("This is a confirm - do you want to proceed?");
                    alert("Confirmed? " + confirmed);
                } else if (e.target.id == "prompt") {
                    var response = window.prompt("Enter a word", "hello");
                    alert("The word was " + response);
                } else if (e.target.id == "modal") {
                    window.showModalDialog("http://apress.com");
                }
            }
        }
    </script>
  </body>
</html>
```

These features should be used with caution. Each browser handles the prompts differently and creates a different experience for the user.

As an example, consider Figure 27-2, which shows the different approaches taken by Chrome and Firefox for the alert prompt. The prompts may look similar, but the effect is quite different. Chrome takes the specification literally and creates a modal dialog. This means that the browser won't do anything else until the user has clicked the OK button and dismissed the prompt. The user can't switch tabs, close the current tab, or do anything else with the browser. Firefox takes a more liberal view and limits the effect of the prompt to the current tab. This is a more sensible approach, but it is a *different* approach, and inconsistency is something to consider carefully when selecting features to use in a web application.

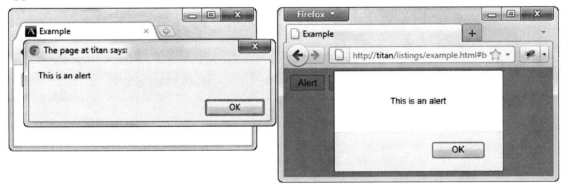

Figure 27-2. Chrome and Firefox showing an alert prompt

The showModalDialog method creates a popup window—a feature that has been much abused by advertisers. In fact, it's has been so abused that all of the browsers make efforts to limit the use of this feature to sites that the user has previously approved. If you are relying on a popup to present the user with critical information, you run the risk that the message simply won't be seen.

▨ **Tip** If you want to attract the user's attention, consider using inline dialog boxes provided by a JavaScript library such as jQuery. They are simple to use, less intrusive, and behaviorally and visually consistent across browsers. For more information about jQuery, see my book *Pro jQuery*, published by Apress.

Getting General Information

The Window object provides access to objects that return more general information, including details of the current location (the URL from which the document was loaded) and the user's browsing history. These properties are described in Table 27-6.

Table 27-6. The Informational Object Properties

Name	Description	Returns
document	Returns the Document object associated with this window	Document
history	Provides access to the browser history	History
location	Provides details of the current document's location	Location

The Document object is the subject of Chapter 26. The Location object that is returned by the Window.location property is the same as for the Document.location property, which I also described in Chapter 26. We'll look at working with the browser history next.

Working with the Browser History

The Window.history property returns a History object, which you can use to perform basic operations on the browser history. Table 27-7 describes the properties and methods that the History object defines.

Table 27-7. The History Object Properties and Methods

Name	Description	Returns
back()	Goes one step back in the history	void
forward()	Goes one step forward in the history	void
go(<index>)	Goes to a position in the history relative to the current document; positive values are forward, and negative values are backward	void
length	Returns the number of items in the history	number

pushState(\<state>, \<title>, \<url>)	Adds an entry to the browser history	void
replaceState(\<state>, \<title>, \<url>)	Replaces the current entry in the browser history	void
state	Returns the state data associated with the current document in the browser history	object

Navigating Within the Browsing History

The back, forward, and go methods tell the browser to navigate to a URL in the history. The back and forward methods have the same effect as the browser back and forward buttons. The go method navigates to a place in the history relative to the current document. A positive value specifies the browser should go forward in the history, and a negative value specifies to move backward. The magnitude of the value specifies how many steps. For example, a value of -2 tells the browser to navigate to the document before last in the history. Listing 27-5 demonstrates the use of these three methods.

Listing 27-5. Navigating Within the Browser History

```
<!DOCTYPE HTML>
<html>
    <head>
        <title>Example</title>
    </head>
    <body>
        <button id="back">Back</button>
        <button id="forward">Forward</button>
        <button id="go">Go</button>

        <script type="text/javascript">

            var buttons = document.getElementsByTagName("button");
            for (var i = 0 ; i < buttons.length; i++) {
                buttons[i].onclick = handleButtonPress;
            }

            function handleButtonPress(e) {
                if (e.target.id == "back") {
                    window.history.back();
                } else if (e.target.id == "forward") {
                    window.history.forward();
                } else if (e.target.id == "go") {
                    window.history.go("http://www.apress.com");
                }
            }
        </script>
    </body>
</html>
```

In addition to these basic functions, HTML5 provides support for changing the browser history, within certain constraints. The best place to start is with an example of the kind of problem that changing the history can help solve, as provided by Listing 27-6.

Listing 27-6. Dealing with the Browser History

```html
<!DOCTYPE HTML>
<html>
    <head>
        <title>Example</title>
    </head>
    <body>
        <p id="msg"></p>
        <button id="banana">Banana</button>
        <button id="apple">Apple</button>

        <script type="text/javascript">

            var sel = "No selection made";
            document.getElementById("msg").innerHTML = sel;

            var buttons = document.getElementsByTagName("button");
            for (var i = 0; i < buttons.length; i++) {
                buttons[i].onclick = function(e) {
                    document.getElementById("msg").innerHTML = e.target.innerHTML;
                };
            }
        </script>
    </body>
</html>
```

This example contains a script that displays a message based on which button the user clicks. It's all very simple. The problem is that when the user navigates away from the example document, the information about which button was clicked is lost. You can see this effect in Figure 27-3.

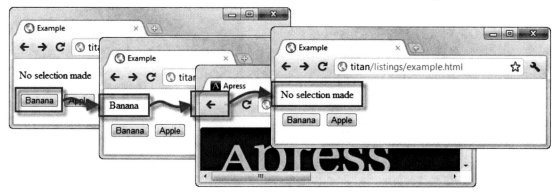

Figure 27-3. The regular history sequence

The sequence of events is as follows:

1. I navigate to the example document. The No selection made message is displayed.

2. I click the Banana button. The Banana message is displayed.

3. I navigate to http://apress.com.

4. I click the back button to return to the example document.

At the end of this sequence, I am back at the example document, and no record of my previous selection is available. This is the regular behavior of a browser—the browsing history is handled using URLs. When I click the back button, the browser returns to the URL of my example, and I start all over again. The history of my session looks like this:

- http://titan/listings/example.html

- http://apress.com

Inserting an Entry into the History

The History.pushState method lets you add a URL to the browser history, with some constraints. The URL must be from the same server name and port as the current document. One approach to adding URLs is to use just the query string or hash fragment appended to the current document, as shown in Listing 27-7.

Listing 27-7. Adding an Entry to the Browser History

```
<!DOCTYPE HTML>
<html>
    <head>
        <title>Example</title>
    </head>
    <body>
        <p id="msg"></p>
        <button id="banana">Banana</button>
        <button id="apple">Apple</button>

        <script type="text/javascript">

            var sel = "No selection made";
            if (window.location.search == "?banana") {
                sel = "Selection: Banana";
            } else if (window.location.search == "?apple") {
                sel = "Selection: Apple";
            }
            document.getElementById("msg").innerHTML = sel;

            var buttons = document.getElementsByTagName("button");
            for (var i = 0; i < buttons.length; i++) {
                buttons[i].onclick = function(e) {
```

```
                document.getElementById("msg").innerHTML = e.target.innerHTML;
                window.history.pushState("", "", "?" + e.target.id);
            };
        }
    </script>
</body>
</html>
```

The script in this example uses the pushState method to add an item to the browser history. The URL that it added is the URL of the current document plus a query string indicating which button the user clicked. I also added some code that uses the Location object (described in Chapter 26) to read the query string and the selected value. Two user-discernible changes arise from this script. The first occurs when the user clicks one of the buttons, as shown in Figure 27-4.

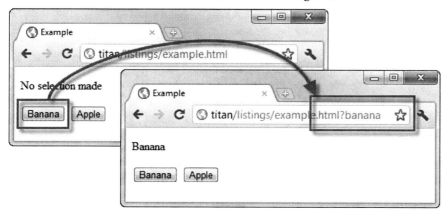

Figure 27-4. The effect of pushing an item into the browser history

When the user clicks the Banana button, the browser navigation bar shows the URL I pushed into the browsing history. The document isn't reloaded; only the history and the displayed URL change. At this point, the browser history looks like this:

- http://titan/listings/example.html

- http://titan/listings/example.html?banana

Each time a button is clicked, a new URL is added to the history, creating a record of the user's path through the navigation. The benefit of these additional entries comes when the user navigates elsewhere and then returns to the document, as shown in Figure 27-5.

Figure 27-5. Preserving application breadcrumbs through the browser history

This time, when the user clicks the back button, the URL that I inserted into the history is loaded, and the script uses the query string to preserve some simple application state. This is a simple but useful technique.

Adding an Entry for a Different Document

You don't need to use the query string or the document fragment as the URL when you add an item to the browser history. You can specify any URL that comes from the same source as the current document. However, there is an oddity to note. Listing 27-8 provides a demonstration.

Listing 27-8. Using a Different URL in a History Entry

```html
<!DOCTYPE HTML>
<html>
    <head>
        <title>Example</title>
    </head>
    <body>
        <p id="msg"></p>
        <button id="banana">Banana</button>
        <button id="apple">Apple</button>

        <script type="text/javascript">

            var sel = "No selection made";
            if (window.location.search == "?banana") {
                sel = "Selection: Banana";
            } else if (window.location.search == "?apple") {
                sel = "Selection: Apple";
            }
            document.getElementById("msg").innerHTML = sel;

            var buttons = document.getElementsByTagName("button");
```

```
            for (var i = 0; i < buttons.length; i++) {
                buttons[i].onclick = function(e) {
                    document.getElementById("msg").innerHTML = e.target.innerHTML;
                    window.history.pushState("", "", "otherpage.html?" + e.target.id);
                };
            }
        </script>
    </body>
</html>
```

This script has only one change: I set the URL argument to the pushState method to be otherpage.html. Listing 27-9 shows the contents of otherpage.html.

Listing 27-9. The Contents of otherpage.html

```
<!DOCTYPE HTML>
<html>
    <head>
        <title>Other Page</title>
    </head>
    <body>
        <h1>Other Page</h1>
        <p id="msg"></p>
        <script>
            var sel = "No selection made";
            if (window.location.search == "?banana") {
                sel = "Selection: Banana";
            } else if (window.location.search == "?apple") {
                sel = "Selection: Apple";
            }
            document.getElementById("msg").innerHTML = sel;
        </script>
    </body>
</html>
```

I still use the query string to maintain the user's selection, but the document itself has changed. And this is where the oddity comes in. Figure 27-6 shows what you can expect when you run this example.

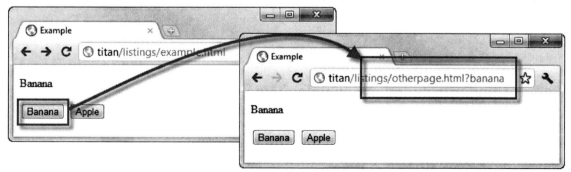

Figure 27-6. Using a different URL in a history entry

As the figure shows, the other document's URL is displayed in the navigation box, but the document itself doesn't change. And here's the catch: if the user navigates away to another document and then clicks the back button, the browser can choose either to display the original document (example.html in this case) or the document specified (otherpage.html). You have no way of controlling which one will be used. And what's worse is that different browsers operate in different ways.

Storing Complex State in the History

Notice that when I used the pushState method in the last couple of examples, I used empty strings ("") for the first two arguments. The middle argument is ignored by all of the mainstream browsers and is of no interest here. But the first argument can be very useful, because it allows you to associate a complex state object with a URL in the browser history.

In the previous examples, I used the query string to represent the user's choice, which is fine for such a simple piece of data, but not much help if you have more complex data to preserve. Listing 27-10 demonstrates how to use the first pushState argument to store something more complex.

Listing 27-10. Storing a State Object in the Browser History

```
<!DOCTYPE HTML>
<html>
    <head>
        <title>Example</title>
        <style>
            * { margin: 2px; padding: 4px; border-collapse: collapse;}
        </style>
    </head>
    <body>
        <table border="1">
            <tr><th>Name:</th><td id="name"></td></tr>
            <tr><th>Color:</th><td id="color"></td></tr>
            <tr><th>Size:</th><td id="size"></td></tr>
            <tr><th>State:</th><td id="state"></td></tr>
            <tr><th>Event:</th><td id="event"></td></tr>
        </table>
        <button id="banana">Banana</button>
        <button id="apple">Apple</button>

        <script type="text/javascript">

            if (window.history.state) {
                displayState(window.history.state);
                document.getElementById("state").innerHTML = "Yes";
            } else {
                document.getElementById("name").innerHTML = "No Selection";
            }

            window.onpopstate = function(e) {
                displayState(e.state);
                document.getElementById("event").innerHTML = "Yes";
            }
```

```
                var buttons = document.getElementsByTagName("button");
                for (var i = 0; i < buttons.length; i++) {
                    buttons[i].onclick = function(e) {
                        var stateObj;
                        if (e.target.id == "banana") {
                            stateObj = {
                                name: "banana",
                                color: "yellow",
                                size: "large"
                            }
                        } else {
                            stateObj = {
                                name: "apple",
                                color: "red",
                                size: "medium"
                            }
                        }
                        window.history.pushState(stateObj, "");
                        displayState(stateObj);
                    };
                }

            function displayState(stateObj) {
                document.getElementById("name").innerHTML = stateObj.name;
                document.getElementById("color").innerHTML = stateObj.color;
                document.getElementById("size").innerHTML = stateObj.size;
            }
        </script>
    </body>
</html>
```

In this example, I represent the user's selection using an object with three properties, containing the name, color, and size of the fruit that the user has picked, like this:

```
stateObj = { name: "apple", color: "red", size: "medium"}
```

When the user makes a selection, I use the History.pushState method to create a new history entry and associate the state object with it, like this:

```
window.history.pushState(stateObj, "");
```

I haven't specified a URL in this example, which means that the state object is associated with the current document. (I did this to demonstrate the possibility; I could have specified a URL as in the previous examples.)

You can use two ways to retrieve the state object when the user returns to your document. The first is through the history.state property, like this:

```
...
if (window.history.state) {
    displayState(window.history.state);
...
```

695

The problem you face is that not all browsers make the state object available through this property (Chrome doesn't, for example). To deal with this, you must listen for the popstate event as well. I explain events in Chapter 30, but this example is important for working with the history feature, so you may want to return to this section after you have read that chapter. Here is the code that listens and responds to the popstate event:

```
window.onpopstate = function(e) {
    displayState(e.state);
    document.getElementById("event").innerHTML = "Yes";
}
```

Notice that I display the state information in a table element, along with details of how the state object was obtained: via the property or the event. You can see how this appears in Figure 27-7, but this an example that really needs to be experimented with firsthand.

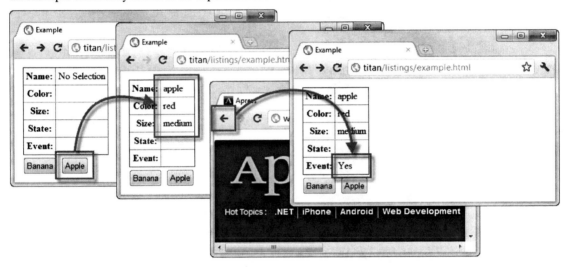

Figure 27-7. Using a state object in the browser history

■ **Caution** You must be careful not to rely on the state information being available. The browser's history can be lost in a number of different situations, including the user explicitly deleting it.

Replacing an Item in the History

The previous examples have all focused on adding items to the history in addition to the current document, but you can use the replaceState method to replace the entry for the current document. Listing 27-11 provides a demonstration.

Listing 27-11. Replacing the Current Entry in the Browser History

```
<!DOCTYPE HTML>
<html>
    <head>
        <title>Example</title>
    </head>
    <body>
        <p id="msg"></p>
        <button id="banana">Banana</button>
        <button id="apple">Apple</button>

        <script type="text/javascript">

            var sel = "No selection made";
            if (window.location.search == "?banana") {
                sel = "Selection: Banana";
            } else if (window.location.search == "?apple") {
                sel = "Selection: Apple";
            }
            document.getElementById("msg").innerHTML = sel;

            var buttons = document.getElementsByTagName("button");
            for (var i = 0; i < buttons.length; i++) {
                buttons[i].onclick = function(e) {
                    document.getElementById("msg").innerHTML = e.target.innerHTML;
                    window.history.replaceState("", "", "otherpage?" + e.target.id);
                };
            }
        </script>
    </body>
</html>
```

Using Cross-Document Messaging

The `Window` object is a gateway to another new feature in HTML5 called *cross-document messaging*. Under normal circumstances, scripts from different sources (known as *origins*) are not allowed to communicate, although communication between scripts is such a sought-after feature that there have been endless hacks and workarounds to bypass the browser security measures.

■ **Note** This is an advanced topic that uses *events*, which are described in Chapter 30. You may wish to read that chapter before reading this section.

UNDERSTANDING SCRIPT ORIGINS

Browsers use components of a URL to determine the origin of a resource such as a script. Limitations are placed on interaction and communication between scripts from different origins. If the protocol, hostname, and port are the same, then two scripts are considered to be from the same origin, even if other parts of the URL are different. The following table gives some examples, each of which is compared to the URL `http://titan.mydomain.com/example.html`.

URL	Result
`http://titan.mydomain.com/apps/other.html`	Same origin
`https``://titan.mydomain.com/apps/other.html`	Different origin; protocol differs
`http://titan:`**`81`**`.mydomain.com/apps/example.html`	Different origin; port differs
`http://`**`myserver`**`.mydomain.com/doc.html`	Different origin; host differs

Scripts can use the `document.domain` property to change their origin, although only to widen the focus of the current URL. For example, scripts that originate from `http://server1.domain.com` and `http://server2.domain.com` can both set the `domain` property to `domain.com` in order to have the same origin.

HTML5 provides a specification for this kind of communication through the `Window` method described in Table 27-8.

Table 27-8. The Cross-Document Messaging Method

Name	Description	Returns
`postMessage(<msg>, <origin>)`	Sends the specified message to another document	`void`

To set the scene for this feature, Listing 27-12 shows the problem I'm trying to solve.

Listing 27-12. The Cross-Document Problem

```
<!DOCTYPE HTML>
<html>
    <head>
        <title>Example</title>
    </head>
    <body>
        <p id="status">Ready</p>
        <button id="send">Send Message</button>
        <p>
```

```
        <iframe name="nested" src="http://titan:81/otherdomain.html" width="90%"
                height="75px"></iframe>
    </p>
    <script>
        document.getElementById("send").onclick = function() {

            document.getElementById("status").innerHTML = "Message Sent";
        }
    </script>
</body>
</html>
```

This document contains an `iframe` element that loads a document from a different source. Scripts are from the same source only if they come from the same host and port. I will be loading this document from port 80 on the server called `titan`, so a second server on port 81 is considered a different source. Listing 27-13 shows the content of the `otherdomain.html` document, which will be loaded by the `iframe`.

Listing 27-13. The otherdomain.html Document

```
<!DOCTYPE HTML>
<html>
    <head>
        <title>Other Page</title>
    </head>
    <body>
        <h1 id="banner">This is the nested document</h1>
        <script>
            function displayMessage(msg) {
                document.getElementById("banner").innerHTML = msg;
            }
        </script>
    </body>
</html>
```

The goal is for the main document, `example.html`, to be able to call the `displayMessage` function defined in the `script` element of the embedded document, `otherdomain.html`.

I use the `postMessage` method, but I need to call that method on the `Window` that contains the document I want to target. Fortunately, the `Window` object provides the support needed to find embedded documents, as described in Table 27-9.

Table 27-9. Finding Embedded Windows

Name	Description	Returns
defaultView	Returns the Window for the active document	Window
frames	Returns an array of the Window objects for the nested iframe elements in the document	Window[]
opener	Returns the Window that opened the current browsing context	Window

parent	Returns the parent of the current Window	Window
self	Returns the Window for the current document	Window
top	Returns the topmost Window	Window
length	Returns the number of nested iframe elements in the document	number
[<index>]	Returns the Window for the nested document at the specified index	Window
[<name>]	Returns the Window for the nested document with the specified name	Window

For this example, I am going to use the array-style notation to locate the Window object I want, so that I can call the postMessage method. Listing 27-14 shows the required additions to the example.html document.

Listing 27-14. Locating a Window Object and Invoking the postMessage Method

```
<!DOCTYPE HTML>
<html>
    <head>
        <title>Example</title>
    </head>
    <body>
        <p id="status">Ready</p>
        <button id="send">Send Message</button>
        <p>
            <iframe name="nested" src="http://titan:81/otherdomain.html" width="90%"
                    height="75px"></iframe>
        </p>
        <script>
            document.getElementById("send").onclick = function() {
                window["nested"].postMessage("I like apples", "http://titan:81");
                document.getElementById("status").innerHTML = "Message Sent";
            }
        </script>
    </body>
</html>
```

I find the Window object that contains the script that I want to send the message to (window["nested"]), and then call the postMessage method. The two arguments are the message that I want to send and the origin of the target script, which in this case is http://titan:81, but will differ for your environment if you are following this example.

___

■ **Caution** As a security measure, the browser will discard the message if the postMessage method is called with the wrong target origin.

___

To receive the message, I need to listen for the message event in the other script. (As noted earlier, I explain events in Chapter 30, and you may wish to read that chapter now if you are unfamiliar with events and their operation.) The browser passes a MessageEvent object, which defines the properties shown in Table 27-10.

Table 27-10. MessageEvent Properties

Name	Description	Returns
data	Returns the message sent by the other script	object
origin	Returns the origin of the sending script	string
source	Returns the window associated with the sending script	Window

Listing 27-15 shows how to use the message event to receive a cross-document message.

Listing 27-15. Listening for the Message Event

```
<!DOCTYPE HTML>
<html>
    <head>
        <title>Other Page</title>
    </head>
    <body>
        <h1 id="banner">This is the nested document</h1>
        <script>
            window.addEventListener("message", receiveMessage, false);

            function receiveMessage(e) {
                if (e.origin == "http://titan") {
                    displayMessage(e.data);
                } else {
                    displayMessage("Message Discarded");
                }
            }

            function displayMessage(msg) {
                document.getElementById("banner").innerHTML = msg;
            }
        </script>
    </body>
</html>
```

You can learn about the addEventListener method in Chapter 30. Note that when a message event is received, I check the origin property of the MessageEvent object to make sure I recognize and trust the other script. This is an important precaution that prevents messages from unknown and untrusted scripts being acted on. I now have a simple mechanism for sending a message from one script to another, even though they have different origins. You can see the effect in Figure 27-8.

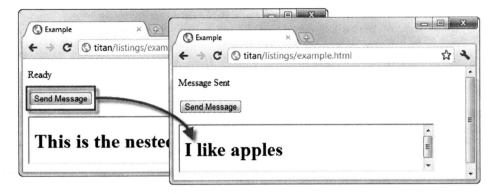

Figure 27-8. Using the cross-document messaging feature

Using Timers

A useful feature provided by the Window object is the ability to set one-off and recurring timers. These timers are used to execute a function after a preset period. Table 27-11 summarizes the methods that support this feature.

Table 27-11. Timing Methods

Name	Description	Returns
clearInterval(<id>)	Cancels an interval timer	void
clearTimeout(<id>)	Cancels a timeout timer	void
setInterval(<function>, <time>)	Creates a timer that will call the specified function every time milliseconds	int
setTimeout(<function>, <time>)	Creates a timer that will call the specified function once after time milliseconds	int

The setTimeout method creates a timer that executes the specified function just once, whereas the setInterval method creates a timer that executes a function repeatedly. These methods return a unique identifier that can later be used as an argument to the clearTimeout and clearInterval methods to cancel the timer. Listing 27-16 shows the use of the timer methods.

Listing 27-16. Using the Timing Methods

```
<!DOCTYPE HTML>
<html>
    <head>
        <title>Example</title>
    </head>
```

```
<body>
    <p id="msg"></p>
    <p>
        <button id="settime">Set Time</button>
        <button id="cleartime">Clear Time</button>
        <button id="setinterval">Set Interval</button>
        <button id="clearinterval">Clear Interval</button>
    </p>

    <script>
        var buttons = document.getElementsByTagName("button");
        for (var i = 0; i < buttons.length; i++) {
            buttons[i].onclick = handleButtonPress;
        }

        var timeID;
        var intervalID;
        var count = 0;

        function handleButtonPress(e) {
            if (e.target.id == "settime") {
                timeID = window.setTimeout(function() {
                    displayMsg("Timeout Expired");
                }, 5000);
                displayMsg("Timeout Set");
            } else if (e.target.id == "cleartime") {
                window.clearTimeout(timeID);
                displayMsg("Timeout Cleared");
            } else if (e.target.id == "setinterval") {
                intervalID = window.setInterval(function() {
                    displayMsg("Interval expired. Counter: " + count++);
                }, 2000);
                displayMsg("Interval Set");
            } else if (e.target.id == "clearinterval") {
                window.clearInterval(intervalID);
                displayMsg("Interval Cleared");
            }
        }

        function displayMsg(msg) {
            document.getElementById("msg").innerHTML = msg;
        }

    </script>
</body>
</html>
```

The script in this example sets and cancels timers and intervals that call the displayMsg function to set the content of a p element. You can see the effect in Figure 27-9.

Figure 27-9. Using timers and intervals

Timers and intervals can be useful, but you should consider their use carefully. Users expect an application's state to remain consistent except when they are directly interacting with it. If you find yourself using timers to change the application state automatically, then you may wish to consider if the result is helpful to the user or just plain annoying.

Summary

In this chapter, I have shown you the odd collection of functionality that is grouped together through the Window object. Some of the features are directly related to windows, such as the ability to get the inner and outer size of the browser window and the screen on which it is displayed. Other functions are less directly related. These include the history and cross-document messaging features, which are important HTML5 features.

CHAPTER 28

Working with DOM Elements

In the previous chapter, some of the features of the HTMLElement object leaked through into the discussion of the document-level features. We can now turn our focus toward the element object itself and give it the attention it deserves. In this chapter, I'll show you the different HTMLElement properties and methods, and demonstrate how to use them. Table 28-1 provides the summary for this chapter. Please note that not all of the examples work in all of the mainstream browsers.

Table 28-1. Chapter Summary

Problem	Solution	Listing
Get information about an element	Use the HTMLElement metadata properties	1
Get or set a single string containing all of the classes to which an element belongs	Use the className property	2
Inspect or modify individual element classes	Use the classList property	3
Get or set an element's attributes	Use the attribute, getAttribute, setAttribute, removeAttribute, and hasAttribute methods	4, 6
Get or set an element's custom attributes	Use the dataset property	5
Work with an element's text content	Use Text objects	7–9
Create or delete elements	Use the document.create* methods and the HTMLElement methods for managing child elements	10
Duplicate an element	Use the cloneNode method	11
Move an element	Use the appendChild method	12

Compare two objects for equality	Use the isSameNode method	13
Compare two elements for equality	Use the isEqualNode method	14
Work directly with HTML fragments	Use the innerHTML and outerHTML properties and the insertAdjacentHTML method	15–17
Insert an element into a text block	Use the splitText and appendChild methods	18

Working with Element Objects

HTMLElement objects provide a set of properties that you can use to read and modify data about the element that is being represented. Table 28-2 describes these properties.

Table 28-2. Element Data Properties

Property	Description	Returns
checked	Gets or sets the presence of the checked attribute	boolean
classList	Gets or sets the list of classes to which the element belongs	DOMTokenList
className	Gets or sets the list of classes to which the element belongs	string
dir	Gets or sets the value of the dir attribute	string
disabled	Gets or sets the presence of the disabled attribute	boolean
hidden	Gets or sets the presence of the hidden attribute	boolean
id	Gets or sets the value of the id attribute	string
lang	Gets or sets the value of the lang attribute	string
spellcheck	Gets or sets the presence of the spellcheck attribute	boolean
tabIndex	Gets or sets the value of the tabindex attribute	number
tagName	Returns the tag name (indicating the element type)	string
title	Gets or sets the value of the title attribute	string

Listing 28-1 shows the use of some of the basic properties listed in the table.

Listing 28-1. Using the Basic Element Data Properties

```html
<!DOCTYPE HTML>
<html>
    <head>
        <title>Example</title>
        <meta name="author" content="Adam Freeman"/>
        <meta name="description" content="A simple example"/>
        <link rel="shortcut icon" href="favicon.ico" type="image/x-icon" />
        <style>
            p {border: medium double black;}
        </style>
    </head>
    <body>

        <p id="textblock" dir="ltr" lang="en-US">
            There are lots of differentß kinds of fruit - there are over 500 varieties
            of <span id="banana">banana</span> alone. By the time we add the countless
            types of <span id="apple">apples</span>,
            <span="orange">oranges</span>, and other well-known fruit, we are
            faced with thousands of choices.
        </p>
        <pre id="results"></pre>
        <script>
            var results = document.getElementById("results");
            var elem = document.getElementById("textblock");

            results.innerHTML += "tag: " + elem.tagName + "\n";
            results.innerHTML += "id: " + elem.id + "\n";
            results.innerHTML += "dir: " + elem.dir + "\n";
            results.innerHTML += "lang: " + elem.lang + "\n";
            results.innerHTML += "hidden: " + elem.hidden + "\n";
            results.innerHTML += "disabled: " + elem.disabled + "\n";
        </script>
    </body>
</html>
```

You can see the results that the browser provides for these properties in Figure 28-1.

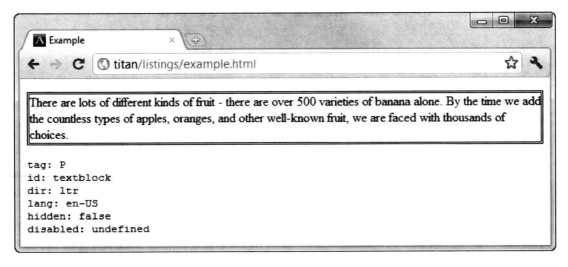

Figure 28-1. Getting information about an element

Working with Classes

You can deal with the classes that an element belongs to in two ways. The first is to use the `className` property, which returns a list of the classes. You add or remove classes by changing the value of the string. You can see both reading and modifying the classes in this way in Listing 28-2.

■ **Tip** A common use for classes is to target elements with styles. You'll learn how to work with styles in the DOM in Chapter 29.

Listing 28-2. Using the className Property

```html
<!DOCTYPE HTML>
<html>
    <head>
        <title>Example</title>
        <meta name="author" content="Adam Freeman"/>
        <meta name="description" content="A simple example"/>
        <link rel="shortcut icon" href="favicon.ico" type="image/x-icon" />
        <style>
            p {
                border: medium double black;
            }
            p.newclass {
                background-color: grey;
                color: white;
```

```
                }
            </style>
    </head>
    <body>
        <p id="textblock" class="fruit numbers">
            There are lots of different kinds of fruit - there are over 500 varieties
            of banana alone. By the time we add the countless types of apples, oranges,
            and other well-known fruit, we are faced with thousands of choices.
        </p>
        <button id="pressme">Press Me</button>
        <script>
            document.getElementById("pressme").onclick = function(e) {
                document.getElementById("textblock").className += " newclass";
            };
        </script>
    </body>
</html>
```

In this example, clicking the button triggers the script, which appends a new class to the list for the element. Notice that I need to add a leading space to the value I appended to the className property value. This is because the browser expects a list of classes, each separated by a space. The browser will apply styles whose selectors are class-based when I make a change like this, meaning that there is a clear visual change in this example, as shown in Figure 28-2.

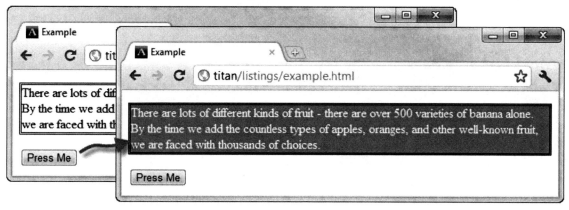

Figure 28-2. Using the className property

The className property is easy to use when you want to quickly add classes to an element, but it becomes hard work if you want to do anything else, such as removing a class. Fortunately, you can use the classList property, which returns a DOMTokenList object. This object defines some useful methods and properties that allow you to manage the class list, as described in Table 28-3.

709

Table 28-3. DOMTokenList Members

Member	Description	Returns
add(<class>)	Adds the specified class to the element	void
contains(<class>)	Returns true if the element belongs to the specified class	boolean
length	Returns the number of classes to which the element belongs	number
remove(<class>)	Removes the specified class from the element	boid
toggle(<class>)	Adds the class if it is not present and removes it if it is present	boolean

In addition to these properties and methods, you can also retrieve classes by index, using array-style notation. The use of the DOMTokenList object is shown in Listing 28-3.

Listing 28-3. Using the classList Property

```
<!DOCTYPE HTML>
<html>
    <head>
        <title>Example</title>
        <meta name="author" content="Adam Freeman"/>
        <meta name="description" content="A simple example"/>
        <link rel="shortcut icon" href="favicon.ico" type="image/x-icon" />
        <style>
            p {
                border: medium double black;
            }
            p.newclass {
                background-color: grey;
                color: white;
            }
        </style>
    </head>
    <body>
        <p id="textblock" class="fruit numbers">
            There are lots of different kinds of fruit - there are over 500 varieties
            of banana alone. By the time we add the countless types of apples, oranges,
            and other well-known fruit, we are faced with thousands of choices.
        </p>
        <pre id="results"></pre>
        <button id="toggle">Toggle Class</button>
        <script>
            var results = document.getElementById("results");
            document.getElementById("toggle").onclick = toggleClass;

            listClasses();
```

```
function listClasses() {
    var classlist = document.getElementById("textblock").classList;
    results.innerHTML = "Current classes: "
    for (var i = 0; i < classlist.length; i++) {
        results.innerHTML += classlist[i] + " ";
    }
}

function toggleClass() {
    document.getElementById("textblock").classList.toggle("newclass");
    listClasses();
}
</script>
</body>
</html>
```

In this example, the listClasses function uses the classList property to obtain and enumerate the classes that the p element belongs to, using the array-style indexer to retrieve class names.

The toggleClass function, which is invoked when the button is clicked, uses the toggle method to add and remove a class called newclass. A style is associated with this class, and you can see the visual effect of the class change in Figure 28-3.

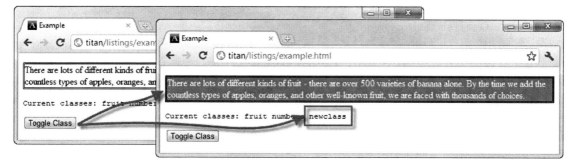

Figure 28-3. Enumerating and toggling a class

Working with Element Attributes

There are properties for some of the most important global attributes, but there is also support for reading and setting any attribute on an element. Table 28-4 describes the available methods and properties defined by the HTMLElement object for this purpose.

Table 28-4. Attribute-Related Properties and Methods

Member	Description	Returns
attributes	Returns the attributes applied to the element	Attr[]

dataset	Returns the data-* attributes	string[<name>]
getAttribute(<name>)	Returns the value of the specified attribute	string
hasAttribute(<name>)	Returns true if the element has the specified attribute	boolean
removeAttribute(<name>)	Removes the specified attribute from the element	void
setAttribute(<name>, <value>)	Applies an attribute with the specified name and value	void

The four methods for working with attributes are easy to use and behave just as you might expect. Listing 28-4 demonstrates the use of these methods.

Listing 28-4. Using the Attribute Methods

```
<!DOCTYPE HTML>
<html>
    <head>
        <title>Example</title>
        <meta name="author" content="Adam Freeman"/>
        <meta name="description" content="A simple example"/>
        <link rel="shortcut icon" href="favicon.ico" type="image/x-icon" />
        <style>
            p {border: medium double black;}
        </style>
    </head>
    <body>
        <p id="textblock" class="fruit numbers">
            There are lots of different kinds of fruit - there are over 500 varieties
            of banana alone. By the time we add the countless types of apples, oranges,
            and other well-known fruit, we are faced with thousands of choices.
        </p>
        <pre id="results"></pre>
        <script>
            var results = document.getElementById("results");
            var elem = document.getElementById("textblock");

            results.innerHTML = "Element has lang attribute: "
                + elem.hasAttribute("lang") + "\n";
            results.innerHTML += "Adding lang attribute\n";
            elem.setAttribute("lang", "en-US");
            results.innerHTML += "Attr value is : " + elem.getAttribute("lang") + "\n";
            results.innerHTML += "Set new value for lang attribute\n";
            elem.setAttribute("lang", "en-UK");
            results.innerHTML += "Value is now: " + elem.getAttribute("lang") + "\n";
        </script>
```

```
    </body>
</html>
```

In this example, I check for, add, and change the value of the lang attribute. You can see the results produced by this script in Figure 28-4.

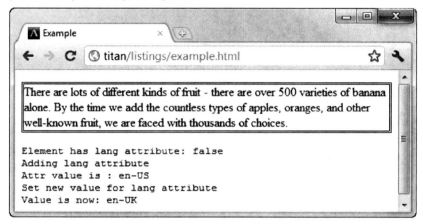

Figure 28-4. Using the attribute methods

Working with the data-* Attributes

In Chapter 3, I described how HTML5 supports custom attributes that are prefixed with data-, such as data-mycustomattribute. You can work with these custom attributes in the DOM via the dataset property, which returns an array of values, indexed by the custom part of the name. Listing 28-5 contains an example.

Listing 28-5. Using the dataset Property

```
<!DOCTYPE HTML>
<html>
    <head>
        <title>Example</title>
        <meta name="author" content="Adam Freeman"/>
        <meta name="description" content="A simple example"/>
        <link rel="shortcut icon" href="favicon.ico" type="image/x-icon" />
        <style>
            p {border: medium double black;}
        </style>
    </head>
    <body>
        <p id="textblock" class="fruit numbers" data-fruit="apple" data-sentiment="like">
            There are lots of different kinds of fruit - there are over 500 varieties
            of banana alone. By the time we add the countless types of apples, oranges,
            and other well-known fruit, we are faced with thousands of choices.
        </p>
```

```
<pre id="results"></pre>
<script>
    var results = document.getElementById("results");
    var elem = document.getElementById("textblock");

    for (var attr in elem.dataset) {
        results.innerHTML += attr + "\n";
    }

    results.innerHTML += "Value of data-fruit attr: " + elem.dataset["fruit"];
</script>
</body>
</html>
```

The array of values that the dataset property returns isn't indexed by position as in regular arrays. If you want to enumerate the data-* attributes, you can do so using a for...in statement, as shown in the listing. Alternatively, you can request a value by name. Note that you need to provide only the custom part of the attribute name. For example, if you want the value of the data-fruit attribute, you request the value dataset["fruit"]. You can see the effect of this script in Figure 28-5.

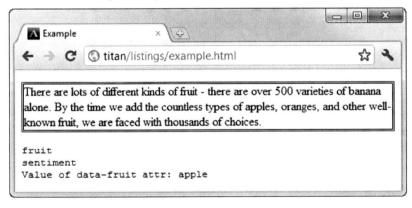

Figure 28-5. Using the dataset property

Working with All Attributes

You can obtain a collection containing all of the attributes for an element through the attributes property, which returns an array of Attr objects. The properties of the Attr object are described in Table 28-5.

Table 28-5. Properties of the Attr Object

Properties	Description	Returns
name	Returns the name of the attribute	string
value	Gets or sets the value of the attribute	string

Listing 28-6 shows how to use the attributes property and the Attr object to read and modify an element's attributes.

Listing 28-6. Working with the attributes Property

```
<!DOCTYPE HTML>
<html>
    <head>
        <title>Example</title>
        <meta name="author" content="Adam Freeman"/>
        <meta name="description" content="A simple example"/>
        <link rel="shortcut icon" href="favicon.ico" type="image/x-icon" />
        <style>
            p {border: medium double black;}
        </style>
    </head>
    <body>
        <p id="textblock" class="fruit numbers" data-fruit="apple" data-sentiment="like">
            There are lots of different kinds of fruit - there are over 500 varieties
            of banana alone. By the time we add the countless types of apples, oranges,
            and other well-known fruit, we are faced with thousands of choices.
        </p>
        <pre id="results"></pre>
        <script>
            var results = document.getElementById("results");
            var elem = document.getElementById("textblock");

            var attrs = elem.attributes;

            for (var i = 0; i < attrs.length; i++) {
                results.innerHTML += "Name: " + attrs[i].name + " Value: "
                    + attrs[i].value + "\n";
            }

            attrs["data-fruit"].value = "banana";

            results.innerHTML += "Value of data-fruit attr: "
                + attrs["data-fruit"].value;
        </script>
    </body>
</html>
```

As you can see from the listing, the attributes in the array of Attr objects are indexed by position and name. In this example, I enumerate the names and values of the attributes applied to an element, and then modify the value of one of them. You can see the effect of this script in Figure 28-6.

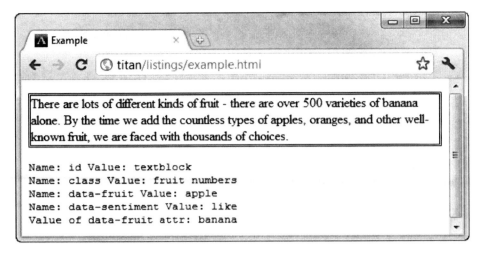

Figure 28-6. Using the attributes property

Working with Text

The text content of an element is represented by a Text object, which is presented as a child of the element in the document model. Listing 28-7 shows an element with some text content.

Listing 28-7. An Element with Text Content

```
...
<p id="textblock" class="fruit numbers" data-fruit="apple" data-sentiment="like">
    There are lots of different kinds of fruit - there are over 500 varieties
    of banana alone. By the time we add the countless types of apples, oranges,
    and other well-known fruit, we are faced with thousands of choices.
</p>
...
```

When the browser represents the p element in the document model, there will be an HTMLElement object for the element itself and a Text object for the content, as shown in Figure 28-7.

Figure 28-7. The relationship between the objects representing an element and its content

If an element has children and they contain text, each will be handled in the same way. Listing 28-8 adds an element to the paragraph.

Listing 28-8. Adding an Element to the Paragraph

```
...
<p id="textblock" class="fruit numbers" data-fruit="apple" data-sentiment="like">
    There are lots of different kinds of fruit - there are over <b>500</b> varieties
    of banana alone. By the time we add the countless types of apples, oranges,
    and other well-known fruit, we are faced with thousands of choices.
</p>
...
```

The addition of the b element changes the hierarchy of nodes used to represent the p element and its contents, as illustrated by Figure 28-8.

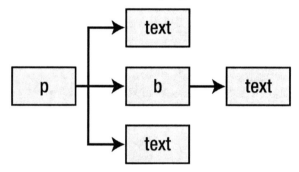

Figure 28-8. The effect of adding an element to the paragraph

The first child of the p element is a Text object that represents the text from the start of the block to the b element. Then there is the b element, which has its own child Text object representing the text contained between the start and end tags. Finally, the last child of the p element is a Text object representing the text that follows the b element through to the end of the block. Table 28-6 describes the members supported by the Text object.

Table 28-6. Members of the Text Object

Member	Description	Returns
appendData(<string>)	Appends the specified string to the end of the block of text	void
data	Gets or sets the text	string
deleteData(<offset>, <count>)	Removes the text from the string; the first number is the offset, and the second is the number of characters to remove	void
insertData(<offset>, <string>)	Inserts the specified string at the specified offset	void

length	Returns the number of characters	number
replaceData(\<offset\>, \<count\>, \<string\>)	Replaces a region of text with the specified string	void
replaceWholeText(\<string\>)	Replaces all of the text	Text
splitText(\<number\>)	Splits the existing Text element into two at the specified offset (see the "Inserting an Element into a Text Block" section later in this chapter for a demonstration of this method)	Text
substringData(\<offset\>, \<count\>)	Returns a substring from the text	string
wholeText	Gets the text	string

Unfortunately, there are no convenient ways to locate Text elements, other than by finding their parent element object and navigating through their children. This makes working with the Text elements harder than it should be. Listing 28-9 shows some of the Text element methods and properties in use.

Listing 28-9. Dealing with Text

```
<!DOCTYPE HTML>
<html>
    <head>
        <title>Example</title>
        <meta name="author" content="Adam Freeman"/>
        <meta name="description" content="A simple example"/>
        <link rel="shortcut icon" href="favicon.ico" type="image/x-icon" />
        <style>
            p {border: medium double black;}
        </style>
    </head>
    <body>
        <p id="textblock" class="fruit numbers" data-fruit="apple" data-sentiment="like">
            There are lots of different kinds of fruit - there are over <b>500</b>
            varieties of banana alone. By the time we add the countless types of apples,
            oranges, and other well-known fruit, we are faced with thousands of choices.
        </p>
        <button id="pressme">Press Me</button>
        <pre id="results"></pre>
        <script>
            var results = document.getElementById("results");
            var elem = document.getElementById("textblock");

            document.getElementById("pressme").onclick = function() {
                var textElem = elem.firstChild;
                results.innerHTML = "The element has " + textElem.length + " chars\n";
```

```
                    textElem.replaceWholeText("This is a new string ");
                };
            </script>
        </body>
    </html>
```

When the button element is pressed, I display the number of characters in the first Text child of the p element and change its content using the replaceWholeText method.

■ **Caution** An important point to note when working with text is that whitespace is not collapsed. This means that any spaces or other whitespace characters that have been used to add structure to the HTML are counted as part of the text.

Modifying the Model

In the previous sections, I have shown you how to use the DOM to modify individual elements. You can change the attributes and the text content, for example. You can do this because there is a live link between the DOM and the document itself. As soon as you make a change to the DOM, the browser makes a corresponding change in the document. You can use this link to go further and change the structure of the document itself. You can add, remove, duplicate, and copy elements in any way you please. You do this by altering the DOM hierarchy, and since the link is live, the changes you make to the hierarchy are immediately reflected in the browser. Table 28-7 describes the properties and methods that are available for altering the DOM hierarchy.

Table 28-7. DOM Manipulation Members

Member	Description	Returns
appendChild(HTMLElement)	Appends the specified element as a child of the current element	HTMLElement
cloneNode(boolean)	Copies an element	HTMLElement
compareDocumentPosition(HTMLElement)	Determines the relative position of an element	number
innerHTML	Gets or sets the element's contents	string
insertAdjacentHTML(<pos>, <text>)	Inserts HTML relative to the element	void
insertBefore(<newElem>, <childElem>)	Inserts the first element before the second (child) element	HTMLElement
isEqualNode(<HTMLElement>)	Determines if the specified element is	boolean

	equal to the current element	
isSameNode(HTMLElement)	Determines if the specified element is the same as the current element	boolean
outerHTML	Gets or sets an element's HTML and contents	string
removeChild(HTMLElement)	Removes the specified child of the current element	HTMLElement
replaceChild(HTMLElement, HTMLElement)	Replaces a child of the current element	HTMLElement

These properties and methods are available on all element objects. In addition, the document object defines two methods that allow you to create new elements. This is essential when you want to add content to your document. These creation methods are described in Table 28-8.

Table 28-8. DOM Manipulation Members

Member	Description	Returns
createElement(<tag>)	Creates a new HTMLElement object with the specific tag type	HTMLElement
createTextNode(<text>)	Creates a new Text object with the specified content	Text

Creating and Deleting Elements

You create new elements through the document object, and then insert them by finding an existing HTMLElement and using one of the methods described previously. Listing 28-10 provides a demonstration.

Listing 28-10. Creating and Deleting Elements

```
<!DOCTYPE HTML>
<html>
    <head>
        <title>Example</title>
        <meta name="author" content="Adam Freeman"/>
        <meta name="description" content="A simple example"/>
        <link rel="shortcut icon" href="favicon.ico" type="image/x-icon" />
        <style>
            table {
                border: solid thin black;
                border-collapse: collapse;
                margin: 10px;
            }
```

```
              td { padding: 4px 5px; }
          </style>
      </head>
      <body>
          <table border="1">
              <thead><th>Name</th><th>Color</th></thead>
              <tbody id="fruitsBody">
                  <tr><td>Banana</td><td>Yellow</td></tr>
                  <tr><td>Apple</td><td>Red/Green</td></tr>
              </tbody>
          </table>

          <button id="add">Add Element</button>
          <button id="remove">Remove Element</button>

          <script>
              var tableBody = document.getElementById("fruitsBody");

              document.getElementById("add").onclick = function() {
                var row = tableBody.appendChild(document.createElement("tr"));
                row.setAttribute("id", "newrow");
                row.appendChild(document.createElement("td"))
                  .appendChild(document.createTextNode("Plum"));
                row.appendChild(document.createElement("td"))
                  .appendChild(document.createTextNode("Purple"));
              };

              document.getElementById("remove").onclick = function() {
                  var row = document.getElementById("newrow");
                  row.parentNode.removeChild(row);
              }
          </script>
      </body>
</html>
```

The script in this example uses the DOM to add and remove rows from an HTML table (which is described in Chapter 11). When adding the row, I start by creating a tr element, and then use it as the parent for the td and Text objects. Notice how I use the method results to chain the calls together and (slightly) simplify the code.

As you can see, the process of creating elements is laborious. You need to create the element, associate it with its parent, and repeat the process for any child elements or text content. The process for removing elements is also awkward. You must find the element, navigate to the parent element, and then use the removeChild method. You can see the effect of this script in Figure 28-9.

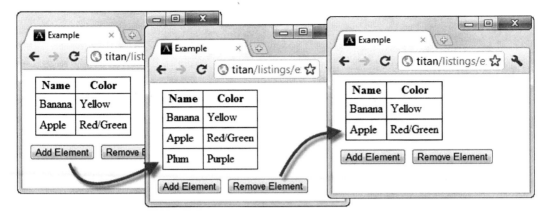

Figure 28-9. Using the DOM to create and remove elements

Duplicating Elements

You can use the cloneNode method to duplicate existing elements. This can be a convenient way to avoid the process of creating the elements you want from scratch. Listing 28-11 demonstrates this technique.

Listing 28-11. Duplicating Elements

```
<!DOCTYPE HTML>
<html>
    <head>
        <title>Example</title>
        <meta name="author" content="Adam Freeman"/>
        <meta name="description" content="A simple example"/>
        <link rel="shortcut icon" href="favicon.ico" type="image/x-icon" />
        <style>
            table {
                border: solid thin black;
                border-collapse: collapse;
                margin: 10px;
            }
            td { padding: 4px 5px; }
        </style>
    </head>
    <body>
        <table border="1">
            <thead><tr><th>Multiply</th><th>Result</th></tr></thead>
            <tbody id="fruitsBody">
                <tr><td class="sum">1 x 1</td><td class="result">1</td></tr>
            </tbody>
        </table>

        <button id="add">Add Row</button>
```

```
    <script>
        var tableBody = document.getElementById("fruitsBody");

        document.getElementById("add").onclick = function() {
            var count = tableBody.getElementsByTagName("tr").length + 1;

            var newElem = tableBody.getElementsByTagName("tr")[0].cloneNode(true);
            newElem.getElementsByClassName("sum")[0].firstChild.data = count
                + " + " + count;
            newElem.getElementsByClassName("result")[0].firstChild.data =
                count * count;

            tableBody.appendChild(newElem);
        };
    </script>
    </body>
</html>
```

In this example, I duplicate an existing row in a table to create more rows. The Boolean argument to the cloneNode method specifies whether the child elements of the element should be duplicated as well. In this case, I have specified true, because I want the td elements that are contained in the tr element to form the structure of my new row.

░ **Tip** Note the awkward way that I need to set the text for the table cells in this example. Dealing with Text objects really is a pain. For a simpler approach, see the "Working with HTML Fragments" section later in this chapter.

Moving Elements

When moving elements from one part of the document to another, you simply need to associate the element you want to move with its new parent. You don't need to dislocate the element from its starting position. Listing 28-12 provides a demonstration by moving a row from one table to another.

Listing 28-12. Moving Elements

```
<!DOCTYPE HTML>
<html>
    <head>
        <title>Example</title>
        <meta name="author" content="Adam Freeman"/>
        <meta name="description" content="A simple example"/>
        <link rel="shortcut icon" href="favicon.ico" type="image/x-icon" />
        <style>
            table {
                border: solid thin black;
                border-collapse: collapse;
                margin: 10px;
```

```
                float: left;
            }
            td { padding: 4px 5px; }
            p { clear:left; }
        </style>
    </head>
    <body>
        <table border="1">
            <thead><tr><th>Fruit</th><th>Color</th></tr></thead>
            <tbody>
                <tr><td>Banana</td><td>Yellow</td></tr>
                <tr id="apple"><td>Apple</td><td>Red/Green</td></tr>
            </tbody>
        </table>

        <table border="1">
            <thead><tr><th>Fruit</th><th>Color</th></tr></thead>
            <tbody id="fruitsBody">
                <tr><td>Plum</td><td>Purple</td></tr>
            </tbody>
        </table>

        <p>
            <button id="move">Move Row</button>
        </p>
        <script>
            document.getElementById("move").onclick = function() {
                var elem = document.getElementById("apple");
                document.getElementById("fruitsBody").appendChild(elem);
            };
        </script>
    </body>
</html>
```

When the button element is pressed, the script moves the tr element with the id of apple and calls the appendChild element on the tbody element with the id of fruitsBody. This has the effect of moving the row from one table to another, as shown in Figure 28-10.

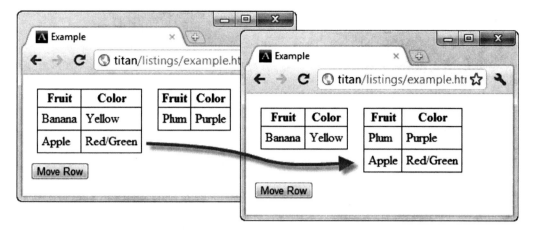

Figure 28-10. Moving an element from one part of a document to another

Comparing Element Objects

You can compare element objects in two ways. The first is simply to see if they represent the same element, which you can do using the isSameNode method. This allows you to compare objects that you have obtained from different queries, as shown in Listing 28-13.

Listing 28-13. Comparing Element Objects

```
<!DOCTYPE HTML>
<html>
    <head>
        <title>Example</title>
        <meta name="author" content="Adam Freeman"/>
        <meta name="description" content="A simple example"/>
        <link rel="shortcut icon" href="favicon.ico" type="image/x-icon" />
        <style>
            table {
                border: solid thin black;
                border-collapse: collapse;
            }
            td { padding: 4px 5px; }
        </style>
    </head>
    <body>
        <table border="1">
            <thead><tr><th>Fruit</th><th>Color</th></tr></thead>
            <tbody id="fruitsBody">
                <tr id="plumrow"><td>Plum</td><td>Purple</td></tr>
            </tbody>
        </table>
        <pre id="results"></pre>
```

```
<script>

    var elemByID = document.getElementById("plumrow");
    var elemByPos
        = document.getElementById("fruitsBody").getElementsByTagName("tr")[0];

    if (elemByID.isSameNode(elemByPos)) {
        document.getElementById("results").innerHTML = "Objects are the same";
    }

</script>
    </body>
</html>
```

The script in this example locates element objects using two different techniques: by searching for a specific id and by searching by tag type from the parent element. The isSameNode method returns true when these objects are compared because they represent the same element.

The alternative is to test to see if element objects are equal , which you can do by using the isEqualNode method. Elements are equal if they are of the same type, have the same attribute values, and each of their children is also equal and in the same order. Listing 28-14 demonstrates a pair of equal elements.

Listing 28-14. Working with Equal Elements

```
<!DOCTYPE HTML>
<html>
    <head>
        <title>Example</title>
        <meta name="author" content="Adam Freeman"/>
        <meta name="description" content="A simple example"/>
        <link rel="shortcut icon" href="favicon.ico" type="image/x-icon" />
        <style>
            table {
                border: solid thin black;
                border-collapse: collapse;
                margin: 2px 0px;
            }
            td { padding: 4px 5px; }
        </style>
    </head>
    <body>
        <table border="1">
            <thead><tr><th>Fruit</th><th>Color</th></tr></thead>
            <tbody>
                <tr class="plumrow"><td>Plum</td><td>Purple</td></tr>
            </tbody>
        </table>

        <table border="1">
            <thead><tr><th>Fruit</th><th>Color</th></tr></thead>
            <tbody>
                <tr class="plumrow"><td>Plum</td><td>Purple</td></tr>
```

```
                </tbody>
            </table>

            <pre id="results"></pre>
            <script>
                var elems = document.getElementsByClassName("plumrow");

                if (elems[0].isEqualNode(elems[1])) {
                    document.getElementById("results").innerHTML = "Elements are equal";
                } else {
                    document.getElementById("results").innerHTML = "Elements are NOT equal";
                }
            </script>
        </body>
</html>
```

In this example, the two tr elements are equal, even though they are distinct elements in different parts of the document. If I changed any of the attributes or the content of the child td element, then the elements would no longer be equal.

Working with HTML Fragments

The innerHTML and outerHTML properties and the insertAdjacentHTML method are convenient syntax shortcuts that allow you to work with fragments of HTML, thus avoiding the need to create elaborate hierarchies of element and text objects. Listing 28-15 demonstrates using the innerHTML and outerHTML properties to get the HTML from elements.

Listing 28-15. Using the innerHTML and outerHTML Properties

```
<!DOCTYPE HTML>
<html>
    <head>
        <title>Example</title>
        <meta name="author" content="Adam Freeman"/>
        <meta name="description" content="A simple example"/>
        <link rel="shortcut icon" href="favicon.ico" type="image/x-icon" />
        <style>
            table {
                border: solid thin black;
                border-collapse: collapse;
                margin: 5px 2px;
                float: left;
            }
            td { padding: 4px 5px; }
            p {clear: left};
        </style>
    </head>
    <body>
        <table border="1">
            <thead><tr><th>Fruit</th><th>Color</th></tr></thead>
            <tbody>
```

```
                    <tr id="applerow"><td>Plum</td><td>Purple</td></tr>
                </tbody>
            </table>
            <textarea  rows="3" id="results"></textarea>
            <p>
                <button id="inner">Inner HTML</button>
                <button id="outer">Outer HTML</button>
            </p>
            <script>
                var results = document.getElementById("results");
                var row = document.getElementById("applerow");

                document.getElementById("inner").onclick = function() {
                    results.innerHTML = row.innerHTML;
                };

                document.getElementById("outer").onclick = function() {
                    results.innerHTML = row.outerHTML;
                }
            </script>
        </body>
</html>
```

The outerHTML property returns a string containing the HTML defining the element and the HTML of all of its children. The innerHTML property returns just the HTML of the children. In this example, I defined a pair of buttons that display the inner and outer HTML for a table row. I displayed the content in a textarea element, so that the browser treats the strings returned by these properties as text and not HTML. You can see the effect of the script in Figure 28-11.

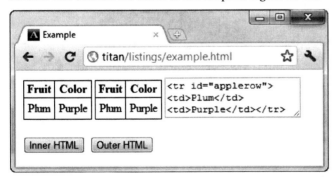

Figure 28-11. Displaying the outerHTML property for a table row

Changing the Document Structure

You can use the outerHTML and innerHTML properties to change the structure of the document as well. I have been using the innerHTML property in many of the examples in this part of the book as a convenient way of setting the content of elements, because I can use the property to set text content without needing to create Text elements. Listing 28-16 shows how to use these properties to modify the document model.

Listing 28-16. Modifying the Document Model

```
<!DOCTYPE HTML>
<html>
    <head>
        <title>Example</title>
        <meta name="author" content="Adam Freeman"/>
        <meta name="description" content="A simple example"/>
        <link rel="shortcut icon" href="favicon.ico" type="image/x-icon" />
        <style>
            table {
                border: solid thin black;
                border-collapse: collapse;
                margin: 10px;
                float: left;
            }
            td { padding: 4px 5px; }
            p { clear:left; }
        </style>
    </head>
    <body>
        <table border="1">
            <thead><tr><th>Fruit</th><th>Color</th></tr></thead>
            <tbody>
                <tr><td>Banana</td><td>Yellow</td></tr>
                <tr id="apple"><td>Apple</td><td>Red/Green</td></tr>
            </tbody>
        </table>

        <table border="1">
            <thead><tr><th>Fruit</th><th>Color</th></tr></thead>
            <tbody id="fruitsBody">
                <tr><td>Plum</td><td>Purple</td></tr>
                <tr id="targetrow"><td colspan="2">This is the placeholder</td></tr>
            </tbody>
        </table>

        <p>
            <button id="move">Move Row</button>
        </p>
        <script>
            document.getElementById("move").onclick = function() {
                var source = document.getElementById("apple");
                 var target = document.getElementById("targetrow");
                target.innerHTML = source.innerHTML;
                source.outerHTML = '<tr id="targetrow"><td colspan="2">' +
                    'This is the placeholder</td>';
            };
        </script>
    </body>
</html>
```

In this example, I used the innerHTML property to set the child elements of a table row and the outerHTML to replace an element inline. These properties work on strings, meaning that you can obtain HTML fragments by reading the property values or by creating strings from scratch, as shown in the listing. You can see the effect in Figure 28-12.

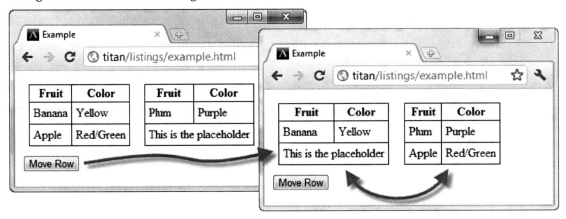

Figure 28-12. Using the innerHTML and outerHTML properties

Inserting HTML Fragments

The innerHTML and outerHTML properties are useful for replacing existing elements, but if you want to use an HTML fragment to insert new elements, you must use the insertAdjacentHTML method. This method takes two arguments. The first is a value from Table 28-9 indicating where the fragment should be inserted relative to the current element, and the second is the fragment to insert.

Table 28-9. Position Parameter Values for the insertAdjacentHTML Method

Value	Description
afterbegin	Inserts the fragment as the first child of the current element
afterend	Inserts the fragment immediately before the current element
beforebegin	Inserts the fragment immediately before the current element
beforeend	Inserts the fragment as the last child of the current element

Listing 28-17 shows the use of the insertAdjacentHTML method to insert fragments of HTML in and around a table row element.

Listing 28-17. Using the insertAdjacentHTML Method

```
<!DOCTYPE HTML>
<html>
    <head>
        <title>Example</title>
        <meta name="author" content="Adam Freeman"/>
        <meta name="description" content="A simple example"/>
        <link rel="shortcut icon" href="favicon.ico" type="image/x-icon" />
    </head>
    <body>
        <table border="1">
            <thead><tr><th>Fruit</th><th>Color</th></tr></thead>
            <tbody id="fruitsBody">
                <tr id="targetrow"><td>Placeholder</td></tr>
            </tbody>
        </table>

        <p>
            <button id="ab">After Begin</button>
            <button id="ae">After End</button>
            <button id="bb">Before Begin</button>
            <button id="be">Before End</button>
        </p>
        <script>
            var target = document.getElementById("targetrow");
            var buttons = document.getElementsByTagName("button");
            for (var i = 0; i < buttons.length; i++) {
                buttons[i].onclick = handleButtonPress;
            }

            function handleButtonPress(e) {
                if (e.target.id == "ab") {
                    target.insertAdjacentHTML("afterbegin", "<td>After Begin</td>");
                } else if (e.target.id == "be") {
                    target.insertAdjacentHTML("beforeend", "<td>Before End</td>");
                } else if (e.target.id == "bb") {
                    target.insertAdjacentHTML("beforebegin",
                        "<tr><td colspan='2'>Before Begin</td></tr>");
                } else {
                    target.insertAdjacentHTML("afterend",
                        "<tr><td colspan='2'>After End</td></tr>");
                }
            }

        </script>
    </body>
</html>
```

731

In this example, I use the different position values to demonstrate how to insert HTML fragments in different locations. This example is best to experiment with in a browser, but you can see the basic effect in Figure 28-13.

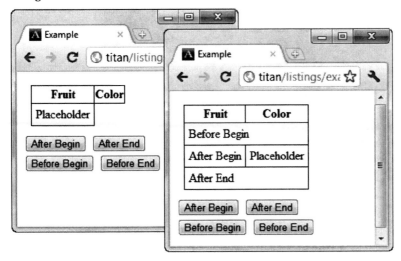

Figure 28-13. Inserting HTML fragments into a document

Inserting an Element into a Text Block

An important variation on modifying the model is to add an element to a text block, represented by a Text object. Listing 28-18 shows how this is done.

Listing 28-18. Inserting an Element into a Text Block

```
<!DOCTYPE HTML>
<html>
    <head>
        <title>Example</title>
        <meta name="author" content="Adam Freeman"/>
        <meta name="description" content="A simple example"/>
        <link rel="shortcut icon" href="favicon.ico" type="image/x-icon" />
    </head>
    <body>
        <p id="textblock">There are lots of different kinds of fruit - there are over
            500 varieties of banana alone. By the time we add the countless types of
            apples, oranges, and other well-known fruit, we are faced with thousands of
            choices.
        </p>
        <p>
            <button id="insert">Insert Element</button>
        </p>
        <script>
```

```
document.getElementById("insert").onclick = function() {
    var textBlock = document.getElementById("textblock");
    textBlock.firstChild.splitText(10);
    var newText = textBlock.childNodes[1].splitText(4).previousSibling;
    textBlock.insertBefore(document.createElement("b"),
        newText).appendChild(newText);
}
    </script>
  </body>
</html>
```

In this example, I have done the slightly difficult task of taking a word from the existing text and making it a child of a new b element. As with the previous examples, dealing with the model means some verbose code. Figure 28-14 shows the result.

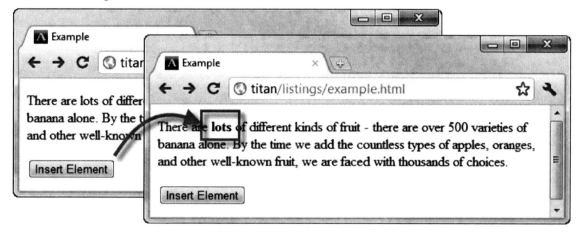

Figure 28-14. Inserting an element into a block of text

Summary

This chapter introduced the functionality of the HTMLElement and Text objects, which represent elements and content, respectively, in HTML documents. You saw how to get information about elements from objects; how to work with text content; and how to use the capabilities of the DOM to add, modify, duplicate, move, and delete elements. Working with the DOM can require verbose scripts, but the live link between the object model and the way that the document is displayed to the user makes the effort worthwhile.

CHAPTER 29

Styling DOM Elements

As you will recall from Chapter 4, you can apply styles to an element indirectly (through a stylesheet or the style element) or directly (through the style attribute). In this chapter, I show how you can use the DOM to work with the CSS styles in your document—both the ones you have explicitly defined, as well as the *computed style* that the browser uses to actually display elements. The specification for working with CSS in the DOM contains some deep hierarchies of object types, many of which are not implemented by the browsers. I have simplified the objects in this chapter to focus on those that the browsers use. Table 29-1 provides the summary for this chapter. Please note that not all of the examples work in all of the mainstream browsers.

Table 29-1. Chapter Summary

Problem	Solution	Listing
Get basic information about a stylesheet.	Use the CSSStyleSheet properties.	29-1
Get details of the media constraints applied to a stylesheet.	Use the MediaList object.	29-2
Enable or disable a stylesheet.	Use the disabled property of the CSSStyleSheet object.	29-3
Get details of individual styles defined within a stylesheet.	Use the CSSRuleList and CSSStyleRule objects.	29-4
Obtain the style from an elements style attribute.	Use the HTML.style property.	29-5
Get or set values for core CSS properties.	Use the convenience properties of the CSSStyleDeclaration object.	29-6
Get or set properties for all CSS properties.	Use the setProperty and getPropertyValue methods.	29-7

Explore the properties in a style.	Enumerate the styles using the `length` property and `getPropertyValue` method.	29-8
Get or set property priority.	Use the `getPropertyPriority` and `setProperty` methods.	29-9
Work with the fine-grained CSS DOM objects.	Use the `getPropertyCSSValue` method.	29-10
Obtain the computed style for an element.	Use the `document.defaultView.getComputedStyle` method.	29-11

Working with Stylesheets

You access the CSS stylesheets available in your document using the `document.styleSheets` property, which returns a collection of objects representing the stylesheets associated with the document. Table 29-2 summarizes the `document.styleSheets` property.

Table 29-2. Accessing Stylesheets

Property	Description	Returns
`document.stylesheets`	Returns the collection of stylesheets.	`CSSStyleSheet[]`

Each stylesheet is represented by a `CSSStyleSheet` object, which provides the set of properties and methods for manipulating the styles in the document. Table 29-3 summarizes the `CSSStyleSheet` members.

Table 29-3. The Members of the CSSStyleSheet Object

Member	Description	Returns
`cssRules`	Returns the set of rules in the stylesheet.	`CSSRuleList`
`deleteRule(<pos>)`	Removes a rule from the stylesheet.	`void`
`disabled`	Gets or sets the disabled state of the stylesheet.	`boolean`
`href`	Returns the `href` for linked stylesheets.	`string`
`insertRule(<rule>, <pos>)`	Inserts a new rule into the stylesheet.	`number`
`media`	Returns the set of media constraints applied to the stylesheet.	`MediaList`

ownerNode	Returns the element in which the style is defined.	HTMLElement
title	Returns the value of the title attribute.	string
type	Returns the value of the type attribute.	string

Getting Basic Information About Stylesheets

The place to start is to get some basic information about the stylesheets defined in the document. Listing 29-1 gives a demonstration.

Listing 29-1. Getting Basic Information About the Stylesheets in a Document

```html
<!DOCTYPE HTML>
<html>
    <head>
        <title>Example</title>
        <meta name="author" content="Adam Freeman"/>
        <meta name="description" content="A simple example"/>
        <link rel="shortcut icon" href="favicon.ico" type="image/x-icon" />
        <style title="core styles">
            p {
                border: medium double black;
                background-color: lightgray;
            }
            #block1 { color: white;}
            table {border: thin solid black; border-collapse: collapse;
                    margin: 5px; float: left;}
                    td {padding: 2px;}
        </style>
        <link rel="stylesheet" type="text/css" href="styles.css"/>
        <style media="screen AND (min-width:500px)" type="text/css">
            #block2 {color:yellow; font-style:italic}
        </style>
    </head>
    <body>
        <p id="block1">There are lots of different kinds of fruit - there are over
            500 varieties of banana alone. By the time we add the countless types of
            apples, oranges, and other well-known fruit, we are faced with thousands of
            choices.
        </p>
        <p id="block2">
            One of the most interesting aspects of fruit is the variety available in
            each country. I live near London, in an area which is known for
            its apples.
        </p>
        <div id="placeholder"/>
        <script>
```

```
        var placeholder = document.getElementById("placeholder");
        var sheets = document.styleSheets;

        for (var i = 0; i < sheets.length; i++) {
            var newElem = document.createElement("table");
            newElem.setAttribute("border", "1");
            addRow(newElem, "Index", i);
            addRow(newElem, "href", sheets[i].href);
            addRow(newElem, "title", sheets[i].title);
            addRow(newElem, "type", sheets[i].type);
            addRow(newElem, "ownerNode", sheets[i].ownerNode.tagName);
            placeholder.appendChild(newElem);
        }

        function addRow(elem, header, value) {
            elem.innerHTML += "<tr><td>" + header + ":</td><td>"
                + value + "</td></tr>";
        }
    </script>
  </body>
</html>
```

The script in this example enumerates the stylesheets defined in the document and creates a table element containing the basic information available for each. In this document, there are three stylesheets. Two are defined using script elements and the other is contained in an external file called styles.css and is imported into the document using the link element. You can see the output from the script in Figure 29-1.

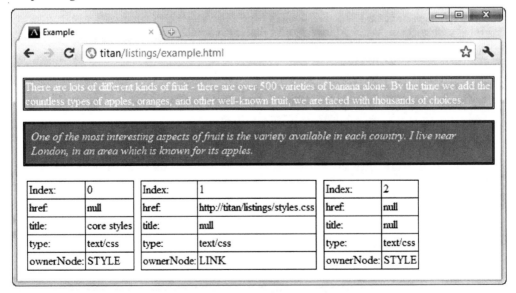

Figure 29-1. Getting information about the stylesheets in the document

Note that not all properties have values. As an example, the href property will only return a value if the stylesheet has been loaded as an external file.

Working with Media Constraints

As I demonstrated in Chapter 7, you can use the media attribute when defining stylesheets to restrict the circumstances under which the styles will be applied. You can access those constraints through the CSSStyleSheet.media property, which returns a MediaList object. The methods and properties of the MediaList object are described in Table 29-4.

Table 29-4. *The Members of the MediaList Object*

Member	Description	Returns
appendMedium(<medium>)	Adds a new medium to the list.	void
deleteMedium(<medium>)	Removes a medium from the list.	void
item(<pos>)	Returns the media at the specified index.	string
length	Returns the number of media.	number
mediaText	Returns the text value of the media attribute.	string

Listing 29-2 demonstrates the use of the MediaList object.

Listing 29-2. *Using the MediaList Object*

```
<!DOCTYPE HTML>
<html>
    <head>
        <title>Example</title>
        <meta name="author" content="Adam Freeman"/>
        <meta name="description" content="A simple example"/>
        <link rel="shortcut icon" href="favicon.ico" type="image/x-icon" />
        <style title="core styles">
            p {
                border: medium double black;
                background-color: lightgray;
            }
            #block1 { color: white;}
            table {border: thin solid black; border-collapse: collapse;
                    margin: 5px; float: left;}
                    td {padding: 2px;}
        </style>
        <link rel="stylesheet" type="text/css" href="styles.css"/>
        <style media="screen AND (min-width:500px), PRINT" type="text/css">
            #block2 {color:yellow; font-style:italic}
```

```
            </style>
        </head>
        <body>
            <p id="block1">There are lots of different kinds of fruit - there are over
                500 varieties of banana alone. By the time we add the countless types of
                apples, oranges, and other well-known fruit, we are faced with thousands of
                choices.
            </p>
            <p id="block2">
                One of the most interesting aspects of fruit is the variety available in
                each country. I live near London, in an area which is known for
                its apples.
            </p>
            <div id="placeholder"/>
            <script>
                var placeholder = document.getElementById("placeholder");
                var sheets = document.styleSheets;

                for (var i = 0; i < sheets.length; i++) {
                    if (sheets[i].media.length > 0) {
                        var newElem = document.createElement("table");
                        newElem.setAttribute("border", "1");
                        addRow(newElem, "Media Count", sheets[i].media.length);
                        addRow(newElem, "Media Text", sheets[i].media.mediaText);
                        for (var j =0; j < sheets[i].media.length; j++) {
                            addRow(newElem, "Media " + j, sheets[i].media.item(j));
                        }
                        placeholder.appendChild(newElem);
                    }
                }

                function addRow(elem, header, value) {
                    elem.innerHTML += "<tr><td>" + header + ":</td><td>"
                        + value + "</td></tr>";
                }
            </script>
        </body>
    </html>
```

In this example, I create a table for any stylesheet that has a media attribute, enumerating the individual media, the total number of media in the attribute value, and the overall media string. You can see the effect of the script in Figure 29-2.

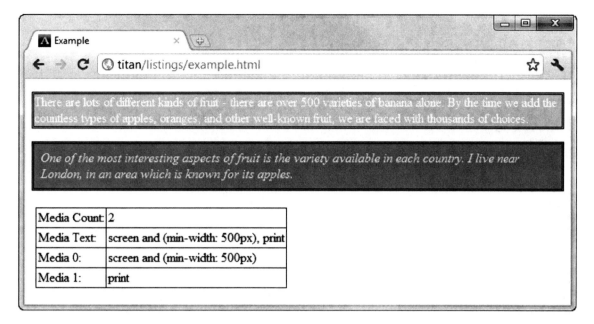

Figure 29-2. Working with the MediaList object

Disabling Stylesheets

The CSSStyleSheet.disabled property lets you enable and disable all of the styles in a stylesheet in a single step. Listing 29-3 gives a demonstration of using this property to toggle a stylesheet on and off.

Listing 29-3. Enabling and Disabling a Stylesheet

```
<!DOCTYPE HTML>
<html>
    <head>
        <title>Example</title>
        <meta name="author" content="Adam Freeman"/>
        <meta name="description" content="A simple example"/>
        <link rel="shortcut icon" href="favicon.ico" type="image/x-icon" />
        <style title="core styles">
            p {
                border: medium double black;
                background-color: lightgray;
            }
            #block1 { color: white; border: thick solid black; background-color: gray;}
        </style>
    </head>
    <body>
        <p id="block1">There are lots of different kinds of fruit - there are over
            500 varieties of banana alone. By the time we add the countless types of
```

```
        apples, oranges, and other well-known fruit, we are faced with thousands of
        choices.
    </p>
    <div><button id="pressme">Press Me </button></div>
    <script>
        document.getElementById("pressme").onclick = function() {
            document.styleSheets[0].disabled = !document.styleSheets[0].disabled;
        }
    </script>
</body>
</html>
```

In this example, clicking the button toggles the value of the disabled property on the (sole) stylesheet. When a stylesheet is disabled, none of the styles within the stylesheet are applied to elements, as you can see in Figure 29-3.

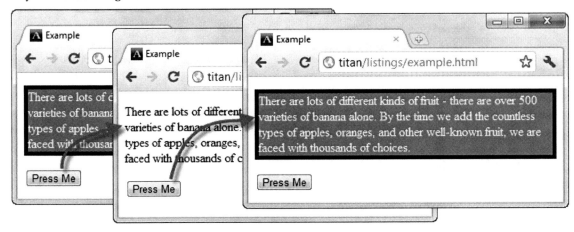

Figure 29-3. Disabling and enabling a stylesheet

Working with Individual Styles

The CSSStyleSheet.cssRules property returns a CSSRuleList object that provides access to the individual styles in the stylesheet. The members of this object are described in Table 29-5.

Table 29-5. The Members of the CSSRuleList Object

Member	Description	Returns
item(<pos>)	Returns the CSS style at the specified index.	CSSStyleRule
length	Returns the number of styles in the stylesheet.	number

Each CSS style in the stylesheet is represented by a CSSStyleRule object (ignore, if you will, the inconsistency in terminology). The members of the CSSStyleRule are shown in Table 29-6.

Table 29-6. *The Members of the CSSStyleRule Object*

Member	Description	Returns
cssText	Gets or sets the text (including the selector) for the style.	string
parentStyleSheet	Gets the stylesheet to which this style belongs.	CSSStyleSheet
selectorText	Gets or sets the selector text for the style.	string
style	Gets an object representing the styles.	CSSStyleDeclaration

Listing 29-4 shows the use of the CSSRuleList object and the basic properties of the CSSStyleRule object. I say basic, because the style property returns a CSSStyleDeclaration property, which lets you dig deeply into a style and which is the same object you use when applying styles to an individual element. You can learn more about the CSSStyleDeclaration object in the section "Working with CSSStyleDeclaration Objects," later in this chapter.

Listing 29-4. Working with the CSSRuleList and CSSStyleRule Objects

```
<!DOCTYPE HTML>
<html>
    <head>
        <title>Example</title>
        <meta name="author" content="Adam Freeman"/>
        <meta name="description" content="A simple example"/>
        <link rel="shortcut icon" href="favicon.ico" type="image/x-icon" />
        <style title="core styles">
            p {
                border: medium double black;
                background-color: lightgray;
            }
            #block1 { color: white; border: thick solid black; background-color: gray;}
            table {border: thin solid black; border-collapse: collapse;
                    margin: 5px; float: left;}
            td {padding: 2px;}
        </style>
    </head>
    <body>
        <p id="block1">There are lots of different kinds of fruit - there are over
            500 varieties of banana alone. By the time we add the countless types of
            apples, oranges, and other well-known fruit, we are faced with thousands of
            choices.
        </p>
        <p id="block2">
            One of the most interesting aspects of fruit is the variety available in
            each country. I live near London, in an area which is known for
            its apples.
        </p>
        <div><button id="pressme">Press Me </button></div>
```

```
            <div id="placeholder"></div>
            <script>
                var placeholder = document.getElementById("placeholder");
                processStyleSheet();

                document.getElementById("pressme").onclick = function() {

                    document.styleSheets[0].cssRules.item(1).selectorText = "#block2";

                    if (placeholder.hasChildNodes()) {
                        var childCount = placeholder.childNodes.length;
                        for (var i = 0; i < childCount; i++) {
                            placeholder.removeChild(placeholder.firstChild);
                        }
                    }
                    processStyleSheet();
                }

                function processStyleSheet() {
                    var rulesList = document.styleSheets[0].cssRules;

                    for (var i = 0; i < rulesList.length; i++) {
                        var rule = rulesList.item(i);

                        var newElem = document.createElement("table");
                        newElem.setAttribute("border", "1");

                        addRow(newElem, "parentStyleSheet", rule.parentStyleSheet.title);
                        addRow(newElem, "selectorText", rule.selectorText);
                        addRow(newElem, "cssText", rule.cssText);
                        placeholder.appendChild(newElem);
                    }
                }

                function addRow(elem, header, value) {
                    elem.innerHTML += "<tr><td>" + header + ":</td><td>"
                        + value + "</td></tr>";
                }
            </script>
        </body>
    </html>
```

This example does two things with these objects. The first is simply to get information about the defined styles, reporting on the parent stylesheet, the selector, and the individual declarations contained in the style. You can see this in Figure 29-4.

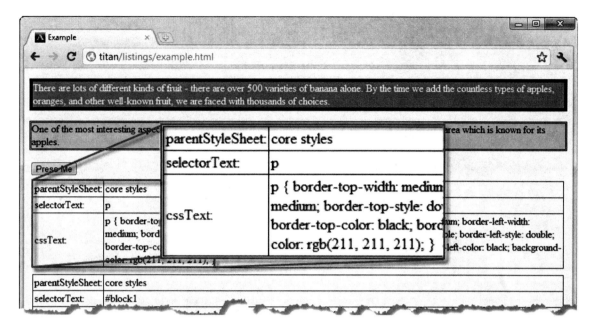

Figure 29-4. Getting information about a style

⬛ Tip Notice how the shorthand properties I used in the style declarations have been expanded by the browser to their constituent properties. Not all browsers do this. Some will display the shorthand properties if they have been used (Firefox, for example, displays the shorthand properties; Chrome, as you can see in the figure, does not). If you are trying to parse the CSS as a string, then you need to take this into account. Although, in general, working directly with CSS values like this is a bad idea. See the section on the CSSStyleDeclaration object ("Working with CSSStyleDeclaration Objects"), later in this chapter, for a better approach.

The script also demonstrates how easily you can change a style. When the button is clicked, the selector for one of the styles is changed from #block1 to #block2, which has the effect of changing which of the p elements the style applies to. As with other changes to the DOM, the browser reflects the new selector immediately and updates the way that styles are applied, as shown in Figure 29-5.

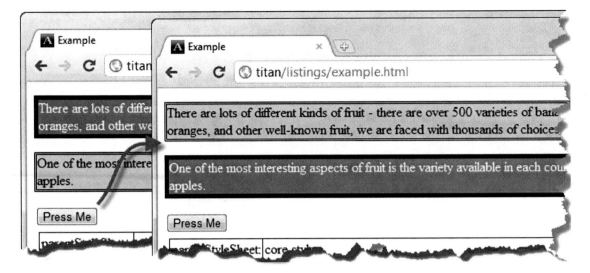

Figure 29-5. Changing the selector for a style

Working with Element Styles

To obtain the properties defined in an element's style attribute, you read the value of the style property defined by HTMLElement objects (you can learn more about the HTMLElement objects in Chapter 28). The style property returns a CSSStyleDeclaration object, which is the same kind of object that you can obtain through stylesheets. I describe this object in detail in the next section. To demonstrate the HTMLElement.style property, I have used the CSSStyleDeclaration.cssText property in Listing 29-5 to display and modify the style properties that are applied to an element.

Listing 29-5. Obtaining a CSSStyleDeclaration Object from an HTMLElement

```
<!DOCTYPE HTML>
<html>
    <head>
        <title>Example</title>
        <meta name="author" content="Adam Freeman"/>
        <meta name="description" content="A simple example"/>
        <link rel="shortcut icon" href="favicon.ico" type="image/x-icon" />
    </head>
    <body>
        <p id="block1"
            style="color:white; border: thick solid black; background-color: gray">
            There are lots of different kinds of fruit - there are over
            500 varieties of banana alone. By the time we add the countless types of
            apples, oranges, and other well-known fruit, we are faced with thousands of
            choices.
        </p>
        <div><button id="pressme">Press Me </button></div>
```

```
        <div id="placeholder"></div>
        <script>
            var placeholder = document.getElementById("placeholder");
            var targetElem = document.getElementById("block1");
            displayStyle();

            document.getElementById("pressme").onclick = function() {
                targetElem.style.cssText = "color:black";
                displayStyle();
            }

            function displayStyle() {
                if (placeholder.hasChildNodes()) {
                    placeholder.removeChild(placeholder.firstChild);
                }
                var newElem = document.createElement("table");
                addRow(newElem, "Element CSS", targetElem.style.cssText);
                placeholder.appendChild(newElem);
            }

            function addRow(elem, header, value) {
                elem.innerHTML += "<tr><td>" + header + ":</td><td>"
                    +  value + "</td></tr>";
            }
        </script>
    </body>
</html>
```

This script displays the value of the style attribute for an element and, when the button is clicked, changes that value to apply a different style. You can see the effect in Figure 29-6.

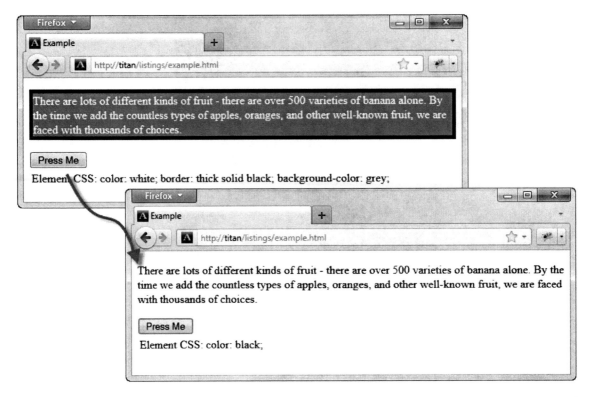

Figure 29-6. Reading and changing the style applied to an element

I have used Firefox in this figure because it displays the shorthand property names in the cssText value.

■ **Tip** In the section on stylesheets, I explained that it isn't a good idea to try and parse the value of the cssText property. The same applies when working with individual elements. See the section on the CSSStyleDeclaration object that follows for a more robust approach to digging into the detail of CSS property values.

Working with CSSStyleDeclaration Objects

It doesn't matter if you are dealing with stylesheets or an element's style attribute. To get complete control of CSS via the DOM, you have to use the CSSStyleDeclaration object. Table 29-7 describes the members of this important object.

Table 29-7. The Members of the CSSStyleDeclaration Object

Member	Description	Returns
cssText	Gets or sets the text of the style.	string
getPropertyCSSValue(<name>)	Gets the specified property.	CSSPrimitiveValue
getPropertyPriority(<name>)	Gets the priority of the specified property.	string
getPropertyValue(<name>)	Gets the specified value as a string.	string
item(<pos>)	Gets the item at the specified position.	string
length	Gets the number of items.	number
parentRule	Gets the style rule if there is one.	CSSStyleRule
removeProperty(<name>)	Removes the specified property.	string
setProperty(<name>, <value>, <priority>)	Sets the value and priority for the specified property.	void
<style>	Convenience property to get or set the specified CSS property.	string

In addition to the item method, most browsers support array-style notation, so that item(4) and item[4] are equivalent.

Working with the Convenience Properties

The easiest way to work with a CSSStyleDeclaration object is through the convenience properties, which correspond to individual CSS properties. You can determine the current value for a CSS property by reading the corresponding object property, and change the CSS value by assigning a new value to the object property.

▪ **Tip** The values that I read and modify in this section are the *configured values*. You are effectively reading and modifying the values defined in the HTML document, either in a stylesheet or applied directly to an element. When the browser comes to display an element, it will generated a set of *computed values*, where the browser styles, the stylesheets, and style attributes are allowed to cascade and inherit using the model I described in Chapter 4.

See the section "Working with Computed Styles" for details of how to obtain the computed CSS values for an element.

Listing 29-6 provides a demonstration.

Listing 29-6. Working with CSSStyleDeclaration Object Convenience Properties

```html
<!DOCTYPE HTML>
<html>
    <head>
        <title>Example</title>
        <meta name="author" content="Adam Freeman"/>
        <meta name="description" content="A simple example"/>
        <link rel="shortcut icon" href="favicon.ico" type="image/x-icon" />
        <style title="core styles">
            #block1 { color: white; border: thick solid black; background-color: gray;}
            p {
                border: medium double black;
                background-color: lightgray;
            }
            table {border: thin solid black; border-collapse: collapse;
                    margin: 5px; float: left;}
            td {padding: 2px;}
        </style>
    </head>
    <body>
        <p id="block1">There are lots of different kinds of fruit - there are over
            500 varieties of banana alone. By the time we add the countless types of
            apples, oranges, and other well-known fruit, we are faced with thousands of
            choices.
        </p>
        <p id="block2" style="border: medium dashed blue; color: red; padding: 2px">
            One of the most interesting aspects of fruit is the variety available in
            each country. I live near London, in an area which is known for
            its apples.
        </p>
        <div><button id="pressme">Press Me </button></div>
        <div id="placeholder"></div>
        <script>
            var placeholder = document.getElementById("placeholder");
            displayStyles();

            document.getElementById("pressme").onclick = function() {
                document.styleSheets[0].cssRules.item(1).style.paddingTop = "10px";
                document.styleSheets[0].cssRules.item(1).style.paddingRight = "12px";
                document.styleSheets[0].cssRules.item(1).style.paddingLeft = "5px";
                document.styleSheets[0].cssRules.item(1).style.paddingBottom = "5px";
                displayStyles();
            }
```

```
        function displayStyles() {
            if (placeholder.hasChildNodes()) {
                var childCount = placeholder.childNodes.length;
                for (var i = 0; i < childCount; i++) {
                    placeholder.removeChild(placeholder.firstChild);
                }
            }
            displayStyleProperties(document.styleSheets[0].cssRules.item(1).style);
            displayStyleProperties(document.getElementById("block2").style);
        }

        function displayStyleProperties(style) {
            var newElem = document.createElement("table");
            newElem.setAttribute("border", "1");

            addRow(newElem, "border", style.border);
            addRow(newElem, "color", style.color);
            addRow(newElem, "padding", style.padding);
            addRow(newElem, "paddingTop", style.paddingTop);

            placeholder.appendChild(newElem);
        }

        function addRow(elem, header, value) {
            elem.innerHTML += "<tr><td>" + header + ":</td><td>"
                + value + "</td></tr>";
        }
    </script>
  </body>
</html>
```

The script in Listing 29-6 displays the values of four CSSStyleDeclaration convenience properties. These are read from objects obtained from a stylesheet and from an element's style attribute to demonstrate the two different ways you can get these objects. You can see how the values are displayed in Figure 29-7.

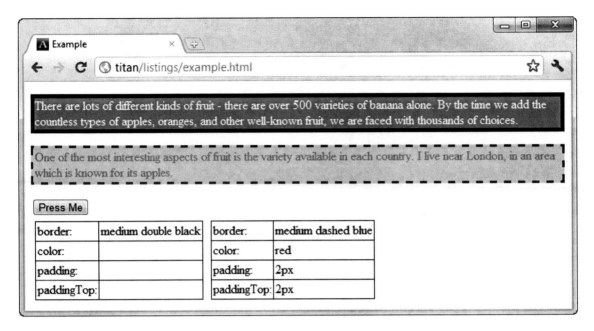

Figure 29-7. Reading values from style convenience properties

The border, color, and padding convenience properties correspond to the CSS properties with the same name. The paddingTop convenience property corresponds to the padding-top CSS property. This is the general naming pattern for multiword CSS properties: remove the hyphens and capitalize the first letter of the second and subsequent words. As you can see, there are convenience properties for both shorthand and individual CSS properties (padding and paddingTop, for example). The convenience properties return an empty string ("") when there is no value set for the corresponding CSS property.

When the button is clicked, the script modifies the value of the individual padding properties using the paddingTop, paddingBottom, paddingLeft, and paddingRight convenience properties on the CSSStyleDeclaration object obtained from the first stylesheet in the document. You can see the effect in Figure 29-8. Not only do the changed values have an immediate effect on the appearance of the document, but the shorthand and individual convenience properties are synchronized to reflect the new values.

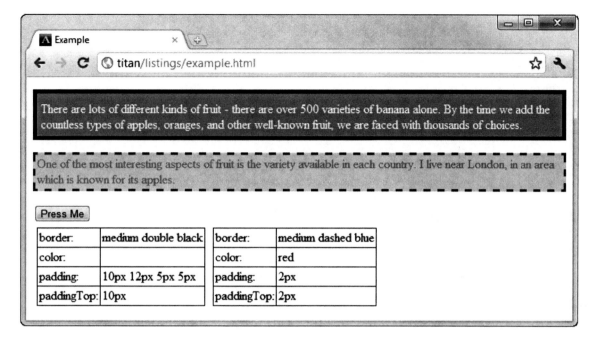

Figure 29-8. Changing CSS properties via a CSSStyleDeclaration object

Working with the Regular Properties

The convenience properties are simple to use if you already know the name of the CSS properties you need to work with, and there is a convenience property available for it. If you need to explore the CSS properties programmatically, or get/set a CSS property for which there is no corresponding convenience property, then the other members of the CSSStyleDeclaration object can be very useful. Listing 29-7 shows some of these properties in use.

Listing 29-7. Using the Regular Properties of the CSSStyleDeclaration Object

```
<!DOCTYPE HTML>
<html>
    <head>
        <title>Example</title>
        <meta name="author" content="Adam Freeman"/>
        <meta name="description" content="A simple example"/>
        <link rel="shortcut icon" href="favicon.ico" type="image/x-icon" />
        <style title="core styles">
            p {
                color: white;
                border: medium double black;
                background-color: gray;
                padding-top: 5px;
            }
```

```
            table {border: thin solid black; border-collapse: collapse;
                    margin: 5px; float: left;}
            td {padding: 2px;}
        </style>
    </head>
    <body>
        <p id="block1">There are lots of different kinds of fruit - there are over
            500 varieties of banana alone. By the time we add the countless types of
            apples, oranges, and other well-known fruit, we are faced with thousands of
            choices.
        </p>
        <div><button id="pressme">Press Me </button></div>
        <div id="placeholder"></div>
        <script>
            var placeholder = document.getElementById("placeholder");
            displayStyles();

            document.getElementById("pressme").onclick = function() {
                var styleDeclr = document.styleSheets[0].cssRules[0].style;
                styleDeclr.setProperty("background-color", "lightgray");
                styleDeclr.setProperty("padding-top", "20px");
                styleDeclr.setProperty("color", "black");
                displayStyles();
            }

            function displayStyles() {
                if (placeholder.hasChildNodes()) {
                    var childCount = placeholder.childNodes.length;
                    for (var i = 0; i < childCount; i++) {
                        placeholder.removeChild(placeholder.firstChild);
                    }
                }

                var newElem = document.createElement("table");
                newElem.setAttribute("border", "1");

                var style = document.styleSheets[0].cssRules[0].style;

                addRow(newElem, "border", style.getPropertyValue("border"));
                addRow(newElem, "color", style.getPropertyValue("color"));
                addRow(newElem, "padding-top", style.getPropertyValue("padding-top"));
                addRow(newElem, "background-color",
                        style.getPropertyValue("background-color"));

                placeholder.appendChild(newElem);
            }

            function addRow(elem, header, value) {
                elem.innerHTML += "<tr><td>" + header + ":</td><td>"
                    + value + "</td></tr>";
            }
        </script>
```

```
        </body>
</html>
```

In this example, I read the style properties from only one source: the stylesheet. I use the getPropertyValue method to retrieve a value for a CSS property, and the setProperty method to define new values. Notice that you use the real CSS property names with these methods, and not the names of the convenience properties.

Exploring Properties Programmatically

In the examples so far, I have explicitly named the CSS properties I wanted to work with. If I want to obtain information about which properties have been applied without prior knowledge, I must explore via the CSSStyleDeclaration members, as shown in Listing 29-8.

Listing 29-8. Programmatically Exploring CSS Properties

```
<!DOCTYPE HTML>
<html>
    <head>
        <title>Example</title>
        <meta name="author" content="Adam Freeman"/>
        <meta name="description" content="A simple example"/>
        <link rel="shortcut icon" href="favicon.ico" type="image/x-icon" />
        <style title="core styles">
            p {
                color: white;
                background-color: gray;
                padding: 5px;
            }
            table {border: thin solid black; border-collapse: collapse;
                    margin: 5px; float: left;}
            td {padding: 2px;}
        </style>
    </head>
    <body>
        <p id="block1">There are lots of different kinds of fruit - there are over
            500 varieties of banana alone. By the time we add the countless types of
            apples, oranges, and other well-known fruit, we are faced with thousands of
            choices.
        </p>
        <div id="placeholder"></div>
        <script>
            var placeholder = document.getElementById("placeholder");
            displayStyles();

            function displayStyles() {
                var newElem = document.createElement("table");
                newElem.setAttribute("border", "1");

                var style = document.styleSheets[0].cssRules[0].style;
                for (var i = 0; i < style.length; i++) {
```

```
                addRow(newElem, style[i], style.getPropertyValue(style[i]));
            }

            placeholder.appendChild(newElem);
        }

        function addRow(elem, header, value) {
            elem.innerHTML += "<tr><td>" + header + ":</td><td>"
                + value + "</td></tr>";
        }
    </script>
</body>
</html>
```

The script in this example enumerates the properties in the first style in the stylesheet. You can see the results in Figure 29-9.

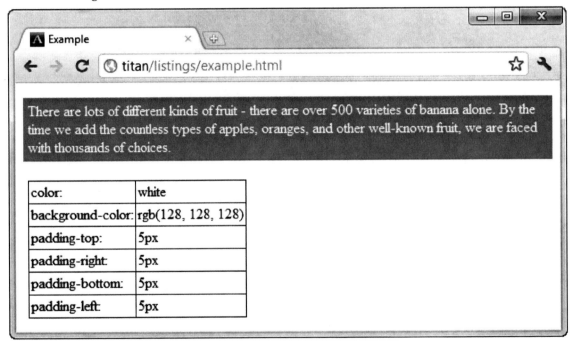

Figure 29-9. Enumerating the properties in a style

Getting Style Property Importance

As I explained in Chapter 4, you can apply !important to a property declaration to give priority to the value when the browser assesses which values are used to display an element. When working with the CSSStyleDeclaration object, you can use the getPropertyPriority method to see if !important has been applied to a property, as demonstrated in Listing 29-9.

Listing 29-9. Getting the Importance of a Property

```
<!DOCTYPE HTML>
<html>
    <head>
        <title>Example</title>
        <meta name="author" content="Adam Freeman"/>
        <meta name="description" content="A simple example"/>
        <link rel="shortcut icon" href="favicon.ico" type="image/x-icon" />
        <style title="core styles">
            p {
                color: white;
                background-color: gray !important;
                padding: 5px !important;
            }
            table {border: thin solid black; border-collapse: collapse;
                    margin: 5px; float: left;}
            td {padding: 2px;}
        </style>
    </head>
    <body>
        <p id="block1">There are lots of different kinds of fruit - there are over
            500 varieties of banana alone. By the time we add the countless types of
            apples, oranges, and other well-known fruit, we are faced with thousands of
            choices.
        </p>
        <div id="placeholder"></div>
        <script>
            var placeholder = document.getElementById("placeholder");
            displayStyles();

            function displayStyles() {
                var newElem = document.createElement("table");
                newElem.setAttribute("border", "1");

                var style = document.styleSheets[0].cssRules[0].style;

                for (var i = 0; i < style.length; i++) {
                    addRow(newElem, style[i], style.getPropertyPriority(style[i]));
                }
                placeholder.appendChild(newElem);
            }

            function addRow(elem, header, value) {
                elem.innerHTML += "<tr><td>" + header + ":</td><td>"
                    + value + "</td></tr>";
            }
        </script>
    </body>
</html>
```

The getPropertyPriority method returns important for high priority values, and the empty string ("") if no importance has been specified.

▓ **Tip** You can use the setProperty method to specify whether a value is important. I omitted the importance argument when I demonstrated the setProperty method earlier in the chapter, but if you want !important applied to a value, then specify important as the third argument to the setProperty method.

Using the Fine-Grained CSS DOM Objects

By enumerating the properties in a style and using the getPropertyValue method, you can discover which properties have been used. However, you still need to know something about each property to make use of it. For example, you have to know that values for the width property are expressed as lengths, and the values for the animation-delay property are expressed as time spans.

In some situations, you don't want to have this knowledge in advance, and so you can use the CSSStyleDeclaration.getPropertyCSSValue method to obtain CSSPrimitiveValue objects that represent the values defined for each property in the style. Table 29-8 describes the members of the CSSPrimitiveValue object.

Table 29-8. The Members of the CSSPrimitiveValue Object

Member	Description	Returns
cssText	Gets a text representation of the value.	string
getFloatValue(<type>)	Gets a number value.	number
getRGBColorValue()	Gets a color value.	RGBColor
getStringValue()	Gets a string value.	string
primitiveType	Gets the unit type for the value.	number
setFloatValue(<type>, <value>)	Sets a numeric value.	void
setStringValue(<type>, <value>)	Sets a value for a string-based value.	void

The key to the CSSPrimitiveValue object is the primitiveType property, which tells you the units that the value of the property has been expressed in. The set of defined unit types is shown in Table 29-9. These correspond to the CSS units I described in Chapter 4.

Table 29-9. *The Members of the CSSPrimitiveValue Object*

Primitive Unit Type	Description
CSS_NUMBER	The unit is expressed as a number.
CSS_PERCENTAGE	The unit is expressed as a percentage.
CSS_EMS	The unit is expressed in ems.
CSS_PX	The unit is expressed in CSS pixels.
CSS_CM	The unit is expressed in centimeters.
CSS_IN	The unit is expressed in inches.
CSS_PT	The unit is expressed points.
CSS_PC	The unit is expressed in picas.
CSS_DEG	The unit is expressed in degrees.
CSS_RAD	The unit is expressed in radians.
CSS_GRAD	The unit is expressed in gradians.
CSS_MS	The unit is expressed in milliseconds.
CSS_S	The unit is expressed in seconds.
CSS_STRING	The unit is expressed as string
CSS_RGBCOLOR	The unit is expressed as a color

Listing 29-10 shows how you can use this object to determine the number of units and the unit type of a CSS property value.

Listing 29-10. *Using the CSSPrimitiveValue Object*

```
<!DOCTYPE HTML>
<html>
    <head>
        <title>Example</title>
        <meta name="author" content="Adam Freeman"/>
        <meta name="description" content="A simple example"/>
        <link rel="shortcut icon" href="favicon.ico" type="image/x-icon" />
```

```
    <style title="core styles">
        p {
            color: white;
            background-color: gray !important;
            padding: 7px !important;
        }
        table {border: thin solid black; border-collapse: collapse;
                margin: 5px; float: left;}
        td {padding: 2px;}
    </style>
</head>
<body>
    <p id="block1">There are lots of different kinds of fruit - there are over
        500 varieties of banana alone. By the time we add the countless types of
        apples, oranges, and other well-known fruit, we are faced with thousands of
        choices.
    </p>
    <div id="placeholder"></div>
    <script>
        var placeholder = document.getElementById("placeholder");
        displayStyles();

        function displayStyles() {
            var newElem = document.createElement("table");
            newElem.setAttribute("border", "1");

            var style = document.styleSheets[0].cssRules[0].style;

            for (var i = 0; i < style.length; i++) {
                var val = style.getPropertyCSSValue(style[i]);

                if (val.primitiveType == CSSPrimitiveValue.CSS_PX) {
                    addRow(newElem, style[i],
                            val.getFloatValue(CSSPrimitiveValue.CSS_PX), "pixels");
                    addRow(newElem, style[i],
                            val.getFloatValue(CSSPrimitiveValue.CSS_PT), "points");
                    addRow(newElem, style[i],
                            val.getFloatValue(CSSPrimitiveValue.CSS_IN), "inches");
                } else if (val.primitiveType == CSSPrimitiveValue.CSS_RGBCOLOR) {
                    var color = val.getRGBColorValue();
                    addRow(newElem, style[i], color.red.cssText + " "
                            + color.green.cssText + " "
                            + color.blue.cssText, "(color)");
                } else {
                    addRow(newElem, style[i], val.cssText, "(other)");
                }
            }
            placeholder.appendChild(newElem);
        }

        function addRow(elem, header, value, units) {
```

```
        elem.innerHTML += "<tr><td>" + header + ":</td><td>"
            +  value + "</td><td>" + units + "</td></tr>";
      }
    </script>
  </body>
</html>
```

One of the most useful features of the `CSSPrimtiveValue` object is that it will convert between one unit and another. In Listing 29-10, the script identifies values that are expressed as pixels and requests the same values as points and inches. This means that you can work with values in the units that suit you, rather than the units as they were originally expressed.

Note that color values are obtained through the `GetRGBColorValue` method, which returns a `RGBColor` object. This object has three properties (red, green, and blue), each of which returns its own `CSSPrimitiveValue` object. You can see how the browser deals with the unit types in Figure 29-10.

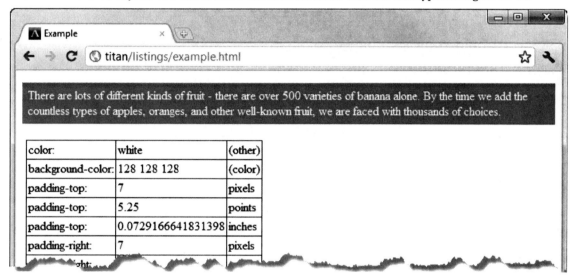

Figure 29-10. Working with the CSSPrimtiveValue object

Working with Computed Styles

All of the examples in this chapter so far have focused on the values specified for CSS properties in stylesheets or in `style` attributes. This is useful for determining what is directly contained within the document, but as I explained in Chapter 4, the browser brings together styles from a number of sources in order to work out which values it should use to display an element. These include properties for which you have not explicitly specified values, either because the values are inherited or because of a browser style convention.

The set of CSS property values that the browser uses to display an element is called the *computed style*. You can obtain a `CSSStyleDeclaration` object containing the computed style for an element using the `document.defaultView.getComputedStyle` method. The object that you get back from this method contains details of all of the properties that the browser uses to display the element, and the value for each of them.

▪ **Tip** You cannot modify the computed style through the CSSStyleDeclaration object that you get from the getComputedStyle method. Instead, you must modify a stylesheet or apply a property directly through the style attribute of an element, as shown earlier in this chapter.

Listing 29-11 demonstrates working with some computed style values.

Listing 29-11. Working with the Computed Style for an Element

```
<!DOCTYPE HTML>
<html>
    <head>
        <title>Example</title>
        <meta name="author" content="Adam Freeman"/>
        <meta name="description" content="A simple example"/>
        <link rel="shortcut icon" href="favicon.ico" type="image/x-icon" />
        <style title="core styles">
            p {
                padding: 7px !important;
            }
            table {border: thin solid black; border-collapse: collapse;
                    margin: 5px; float: left;}
            td {padding: 2px;}
        </style>
    </head>
    <body>
        <p id="block1">There are lots of different kinds of fruit - there are over
            500 varieties of banana alone. By the time we add the countless types of
            apples, oranges, and other well-known fruit, we are faced with thousands of
            choices.
        </p>
        <div id="placeholder"></div>
        <script>
            var placeholder = document.getElementById("placeholder");
            displayStyles();

            function displayStyles() {
                var newElem = document.createElement("table");
                newElem.setAttribute("border", "1");

                var targetElem = document.getElementById("block1");
                var style = document.defaultView.getComputedStyle(targetElem);
                addRow(newElem, "Property Count", style.length);
                addRow(newElem, "margin-top", style.getPropertyValue("margin-top"));
                addRow(newElem, "font-size", style.getPropertyValue("font-size"));
                addRow(newElem, "font-family", style.getPropertyValue("font-family"));

                placeholder.appendChild(newElem);
```

```
                }

        function addRow(elem, header, value) {
            elem.innerHTML += "<tr><td>" + header + ":</td><td>"
                + value + "</td></tr>";
        }
    </script>
  </body>
</html>
```

In this example, I have displayed the value of some properties that I have not explicitly defined values for. You can see the effect in Figure 29-11. You can also see why I have only displayed a few properties. The first row in the table reports how many properties there are in the computed style. The numbers vary between browsers, but the 223 that Chrome reports is typical.

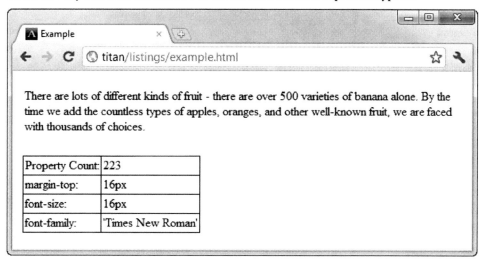

Figure 29-11. Working with the computed style

Summary

In this chapter, I have shown you the different ways that you can use the DOM to operate on the CSS properties and values in your HTML document. You can work through stylesheets or through the style attribute on individual elements, and you can use an extensive collection of objects to dig deep into the detail of styles. Not only can you work with the properties and values that you have explicitly defined, but you can also work with the computed style, which the browser uses to display elements. This allows you to compare what you defined with what is actually used.

CHAPTER 30

Working with Events

I have been using events in the examples for this part of the book to respond to button clicks. In this chapter, it is time to dig into the details, explain what events really are, show you how they work, and how they fit within the rest of the DOM. In short, events allow you to define JavaScript functions that are invoked in response to a change in the state of an element, such as when the element gains and loses the focus, or when the user clicks the mouse button over the element.

In this chapter, I focus on introducing the event mechanism and the events defined by the document and HTMLElement objects. These are the events that are used most often and apply to all documents and elements. Table 30-1 provides the summary for this chapter.

Table 30-1. Chapter Summary

Problem	Solution	Listing
Handle an event inline.	Use one of the on* attributes on an element.	30-1, 30-2
Handle an event in a function.	Define the function and use its name as the value for the on* attribute.	30-3
Use the DOM to handle events.	Use the standard DOM search techniques and assign a function using the on* properties or the addEventListener method of the HTMLElement object that represents the element.	30-4, 30-5
Distinguish between event types.	Use the Event.type property.	30-6
Process an event before it reaches a descendant element.	Use event capture.	30-7
Stop an event from being propagated.	Use the stopPropagation or stopImmediatePropagation methods on the Event object.	30-8
Process an event after it has reached a descendant element.	Use event bubbling.	30-9

Using Simple Event Handlers

There are a few different ways that you can handle events. The most direct way is to create a *simple event handler* using an *event attribute*. Elements define an event attribute for each of the event that they support. For example, the onmouseover event attribute is the event attribute for the global mouseover event, which is triggered when the user moves the pointer over the area of the browser screen that is occupied by the element. (This is a general pattern; for most events, there will be a corresponding event attribute defined as on<*eventname*>).

Implementing a Simple Inline Event Handler

The most direct way of using an event attribute is to assign the attribute a set of JavaScript statements. When the event is triggered, the browser will execute the statements you have provided. Listing 30-1 gives a simple example.

Listing 30-1. Handling an Event with Inline JavaScript

```
<!DOCTYPE HTML>
<html>
    <head>
        <title>Example</title>
        <style type="text/css">
            p {
                background: gray;
                color:white;
                padding: 10px;
                margin: 5px;
                border: thin solid black
            }
        </style>
    </head>
    <body>
        <p onmouseover="this.style.background='white'; this.style.color='black'">
            There are lots of different kinds of fruit - there are over
            500 varieties of banana alone. By the time we add the countless types of
            apples, oranges, and other well-known fruit, we are faced with thousands of
            choices.
```

```
        </p>
    </body>
</html>
```

In this example, I have specified that two JavaScript statements should be executed in response to the mouseover event by setting them at the value for the onmouseover event attribute for the p element in the document. Here are the statements:

```
this.style.background='white';
this.style.color='black'
```

These are CSS properties that are applied directly to the element's style attribute, as explained in Chapter 4. The browser sets the value of the special variable this to be the HTMLElement object representing the element that triggered the event, and the style property returns the CSSStyleDeclaration object for the element.

■ **Tip** Notice that I use double quotes to delimit the overall attribute value, and single quotes to specify the colors I want as JavaScript string literals. You can use them in the other order if you prefer, but this is the technique for embedding quoted values in an attribute.

If you load the document into a browser, the initial style defined in the style element is applied to the p element. When you move the mouse over the element, the JavaScript statements will be executed and change the values assigned to the background and color CSS properties, using the techniques I described in Chapter 4. You can see the transition in Figure 30-1.

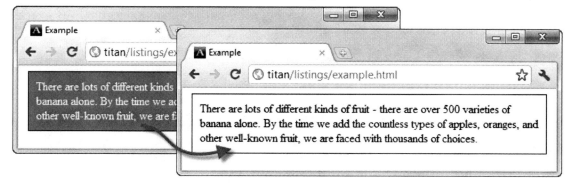

Figure 30-1. Handling the MouseOver event

This is a one-way transition; the style doesn't reset when the mouse leaves the element's screen area. Many events come in pairs. The event that is the counterpart to mouseover is called mouseout, and you handle this event through the onmouseout event attribute, as shown in Listing 30-2.

Listing 30-2. Handling the MouseOut Event

```html
<!DOCTYPE HTML>
<html>
    <head>
        <title>Example</title>
        <style type="text/css">
            p {
                background: gray;
                color:white;
                padding: 10px;
                margin: 5px;
                border: thin solid black
            }
        </style>
    </head>
    <body>
        <p onmouseover="this.style.background='white'; this.style.color='black'"
            onmouseout="this.style.removeProperty('color');
            this.style.removeProperty('background')">
            There are lots of different kinds of fruit - there are over
            500 varieties of banana alone. By the time we add the countless types of
            apples, oranges, and other well-known fruit, we are faced with thousands of
            choices.
        </p>
    </body>
</html>
```

With this addition, you have an element that responds to the mouse entering and exiting the screen space it occupies. You can see the new transition in Figure 30-2.

Figure 30-2. The transition effect of combining counterpart events

Listing 30-2 shows the first of two problems with inline event handlers: they are verbose and make the HTML very hard to read. The second problem is that the JavaScript statements apply to only one element. I have to duplicate those statements on every other p element that I want to behave in this way.

Implementing a Simple Event-Handling Function

We can address some of the verbosity and duplication by defining a function and specifying the function name as the value for the event attributes in the element. Listing 30-3 shows how you achieve this.

Listing 30-3. Using a Function to Handle an Event

```html
<!DOCTYPE HTML>
<html>
    <head>
        <title>Example</title>
        <style type="text/css">
            p {
                background: gray;
                color:white;
                padding: 10px;
                margin: 5px;
                border: thin solid black
            }
        </style>
        <script type="text/javascript">
            function handleMouseOver(elem) {
                elem.style.background='white';
                elem.style.color='black';
            }

            function handleMouseOut(elem) {
                elem.style.removeProperty('color');
                elem.style.removeProperty('background');
            }
        </script>
    </head>
    <body>
        <p onmouseover="handleMouseOver(this)" onmouseout="handleMouseOut(this)">
            There are lots of different kinds of fruit - there are over
            500 varieties of banana alone. By the time we add the countless types of
            apples, oranges, and other well-known fruit, we are faced with thousands of
            choices.
        </p>
        <p onmouseover="handleMouseOver(this)" onmouseout="handleMouseOut(this)">
            One of the most interesting aspects of fruit is the variety available in
            each country. I live near London, in an area which is known for
            its apples.
        </p>
    </body>
</html>
```

In this example, I define JavaScript functions that contain the statements I want performed in response to the mouse events and specify those functions in the onmouseover and onmouseout attributes. The special value this refers to the element that has triggered the event.

This approach is an improvement over the previous technique. There is less duplication and the code is somewhat easier to read. But I like to separate out my events from the HTML elements, and to do this I need to revisit our old friend, the DOM.

Using the DOM and the Event Object

The simple handlers I demonstrated in the earlier sections are fine for basic tasks, but if you want to perform more sophisticated handling (and more elegant definition of event handlers), switch to working with the DOM and the JavaScript Event object. Listing 30-4 shows how you can use the Event object and how you can use the DOM to associate a function with an event.

Listing 30-4. Using the DOM to Set Up Event Handling

```
<!DOCTYPE HTML>
<html>
    <head>
        <title>Example</title>
        <style type="text/css">
            p {
                background: gray;
                color:white;
                padding: 10px;
                margin: 5px;
                border: thin solid black
            }
        </style>
    </head>
    <body>
        <p>
            There are lots of different kinds of fruit - there are over
            500 varieties of banana alone. By the time we add the countless types of
            apples, oranges, and other well-known fruit, we are faced with thousands of
            choices.
        </p>
        <p>
            One of the most interesting aspects of fruit is the variety available in
            each country. I live near London, in an area which is known for
            its apples.
        </p>
        <script type="text/javascript">

            var pElems = document.getElementsByTagName("p");
            for (var i = 0; i < pElems.length; i++) {
                pElems[i].onmouseover = handleMouseOver;
                pElems[i].onmouseout = handleMouseOut;
            }

            function handleMouseOver(e) {
                e.target.style.background='white';
                e.target.style.color='black';
```

```
        }

        function handleMouseOut(e) {
            e.target.style.removeProperty('color');
            e.target.style.removeProperty('background');
        }
    </script>
</body>
</html>
```

This is the approach that you have seen in the examples in previous chapters. The script (which I have had to move to the bottom of the page, because I am working with the DOM), finds all of the elements that I want to handle events for, and sets a function name for the event handler property. There are properties like this for all the events. They are all named in the same way: on, followed by the name of the event. You can learn more about the available events in the Working with the HTML Events section later in this chapter.

■ **Tip** Notice that I use the *name* of the function to register it as an event listener. A common mistake is to put parentheses after the function name, so `handleMouseOver()` is used instead of `handleMouse`. This has the effect of calling your function when the script is executed and not when the event is triggered.

The functions that handle events in the listing define a parameter called e. This will be set to an Event object created by the browser and that represents the event when it is triggered. The Event objects provide you with information about what's happened and let you respond to user interactions with more flexibility than including code in element attributes. In this example, I have used the target property to obtain the HTMLElement that triggered the event so I can use the style property and change its appearance.

Before I show you the event object, I want to demonstrate an alternative approach to specifying which functions are used to process events. The event properties (the ones that are named on*) are generally the easiest approach, but you can also use the addEventListener method, which is implemented by the HTMLElement object. You can also use the removeEventListener method to disassociate a function and an event. Both methods let you express the event type and the functions that handle them as arguments, as shown in Listing 30-5.

Listing 30-5. Using the addEventListener and removeEventListener Methods

```
<!DOCTYPE HTML>
<html>
    <head>
        <title>Example</title>
        <style type="text/css">
            p {
                background: gray;
                color:white;
                padding: 10px;
                margin: 5px;
```

```
                    border: thin solid black
                }
        </style>
    </head>
    <body>
        <p>
            There are lots of different kinds of fruit - there are over
            500 varieties of banana alone. By the time we add the countless types of
            apples, oranges, and other well-known fruit, we are faced with thousands of
            choices.
        </p>
        <p id="block2">
            One of the most interesting aspects of fruit is the variety available in
            each country. I live near London, in an area which is known for
            its apples.
        </p>
        <button id="pressme">Press Me</button>
        <script type="text/javascript">

            var pElems = document.getElementsByTagName("p");
            for (var i = 0; i < pElems.length; i++) {
                pElems[i].addEventListener("mouseover", handleMouseOver);
                pElems[i].addEventListener("mouseout", handleMouseOut);
            }

            document.getElementById("pressme").onclick = function() {
                document.getElementById("block2").removeEventListener("mouseout",
                    handleMouseOut);
            }

            function handleMouseOver(e) {
                e.target.style.background='white';
                e.target.style.color='black';
            }

            function handleMouseOut(e) {
                e.target.style.removeProperty('color');
                e.target.style.removeProperty('background');
            }
        </script>
    </body>
</html>
```

The script in this example uses the addEventListener method to register the handleMouseOver and handleMouseOut functions as event handlers for the p elements. When the button is clicked, the removeEventListener method is used to disassociate the handleMouseOut function for the p element with the id value of block2. Notice that I have used the onclick property to set up the handler for the click event on the button element to demonstrate that you can freely mix and match techniques in the same script.

The advantage of the addEventListener method is that it allows you access to some of the advanced event features, as I describe shortly. The members of the Event object are described in Table 30-2.

Table 30-2. Functions and Properties of the Event Object

Name	Description	Returns
type	The name of the event (e.g., mouseover).	string
target	The element at which the event is targeted.	HTMLElement
currentTarget	The element whose event listeners are currently being invoked.	HTMLElement
eventPhase	The phase in the event life cycle.	number
bubbles	Returns true if the event will bubble through the document, false otherwise.	boolean
cancelable	Returns true if the event has a default action that can be cancelled, false otherwise.	boolean
timeStamp	The time at which the event was created, or 0 if the time isn't available.	string
stopPropagation()	Halts the flow of the event through the element tree after the event listeners for the current element have been triggered.	void
stopImmediatePropagation()	Immediately halts the flow of the event through the element tree; untriggered event listeners for the current element will be ignored.	void
preventDefault()	Prevents the browser from performing the default action associated with the event.	void
defaultPrevented	Returns true if preventDefault() has been called.	boolean

▓ **Tip** The Event object defines the functionality that is common to all events. However, as you'll see when I show you the basic events later in this chapter, there are other event-related objects that define extra functionality that is specified to a particular kind of event.

Distinguishing Events by Type

The type property tells you which kind of event you are dealing with. This value is provided as a string, such as mouseover. Being able to detect the type of event allows you to use one function to deal with multiple types, as shown in Listing 30-6.

Listing 30-6. Using the type Property

```
<!DOCTYPE HTML>
<html>
    <head>
        <title>Example</title>
        <style type="text/css">
            p {
                background: gray;
                color:white;
                padding: 10px;
                margin: 5px;
                border: thin solid black
            }
        </style>
    </head>
    <body>
        <p>
            There are lots of different kinds of fruit - there are over
            500 varieties of banana alone. By the time we add the countless types of
            apples, oranges, and other well-known fruit, we are faced with thousands of
            choices.
        </p>
        <p id="block2">
            One of the most interesting aspects of fruit is the variety available in
            each country. I live near London, in an area which is known for
            its apples.
        </p>
        <script type="text/javascript">

            var pElems = document.getElementsByTagName("p");
            for (var i = 0; i < pElems.length; i++) {
                pElems[i].onmouseover = handleMouseEvent;
                pElems[i].onmouseout = handleMouseEvent;
            }

            function handleMouseEvent(e) {
                if (e.type == "mouseover") {
                    e.target.style.background='white';
                    e.target.style.color='black';
                } else {
                    e.target.style.removeProperty('color');
                    e.target.style.removeProperty('background');
                }
            }
```

```
        </script>
    </body>
</html>
```

In the script for this example, I use the `type` property to work out what kind of event I am dealing with inside of a single event-handling function, `handleMouseEvent`.

Understanding Event Flow

An event has three phases to its life cycle: *capture, target,* and *bubbling.* In this section, I'll explain each of these phases and show you how they work and how you can use event listener functions to get control of them.

Understanding the Capture Phase

When an event is triggered, the browser identifies the element that the event relates to, which is referred to as the *target* for the event. The browser identifies all of the elements between the body element and the target and checks each of them to see if they have any event handlers that have asked to be notified of events of their descendants. The browser triggers any such handler before triggering the handlers on the target itself. Listing 30-7 provides a demonstration.

Listing 30-7. Capturing Events

```
<!DOCTYPE HTML>
<html>
    <head>
        <title>Example</title>
        <style type="text/css">
            p {
                background: gray;
                color:white;
                padding: 10px;
                margin: 5px;
                border: thin solid black
            }
            span {
                background: white;
                color: black;
                padding: 2px;
                cursor: default;
            }
        </style>
    </head>
    <body>
        <p id="block1">
            There are lots of different kinds of fruit - there are over
            500 varieties of <span id="banana">banana</span> alone. By the time we add
            the countless types of apples, oranges, and other well-known fruit, we are
            faced with thousands of choices.
        </p>
```

```
<script type="text/javascript">

    var banana = document.getElementById("banana");
    var textblock = document.getElementById("block1");

    banana.addEventListener("mouseover", handleMouseEvent);
    banana.addEventListener("mouseout", handleMouseEvent);
    textblock.addEventListener("mouseover", handleDescendantEvent, true);
    textblock.addEventListener("mouseout", handleDescendantEvent, true);

    function handleDescendantEvent(e) {
      if (e.type == "mouseover" && e.eventPhase == Event.CAPTURING_PHASE) {
          e.target.style.border = "thick solid red";
          e.currentTarget.style.border = "thick double black";
      } else if (e.type == "mouseout" && e.eventPhase == Event.CAPTURING_PHASE) {
          e.target.style.removeProperty("border");
          e.currentTarget.style.removeProperty("border");
      }
    }

    function handleMouseEvent(e) {
        if (e.type == "mouseover") {
            e.target.style.background='white';
            e.target.style.color='black';
        } else {
            e.target.style.removeProperty('color');
            e.target.style.removeProperty('background');
        }
    }
</script>
</body>
</html>
```

In this example, I have defined a span element as a child of the p element and registered handlers for the mouseover and mouseout events. Notice that when I registered with the parent (the p element), I added a third argument to the addEventListener method, like this:

```
textblock.addEventListener("mouseover", handleDescendantEvent, true);
```

This additional argument tells the browser that I want the p element to receive events for its descendant elements during the capture phase. When the mouseover event is triggered, the browser starts at the root of the HTML document and starts working its way down the DOM toward the target (the element that triggered the event). For each element in the hierarchy, the browser checks to see if it has registered an interest in captured events. You can see the sequence for the example document in Figure 30-3.

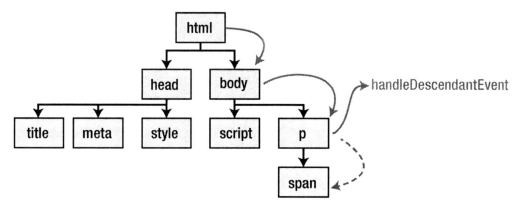

Figure 30-3. The capture event flow

At each element, the browser invokes any capture-enabled listeners. In this case, the browser will find and invoke the handleDescendantEvent function that I registered with the p element. When the handleDescendantEvent function is called, the Event object contains information about the target element (via the target property), and the element that has led the function to be invoked, via the currentTarget property. I use both of these properties so that I can change the style of the p element and the span child. You can see the effect in Figure 30-4.

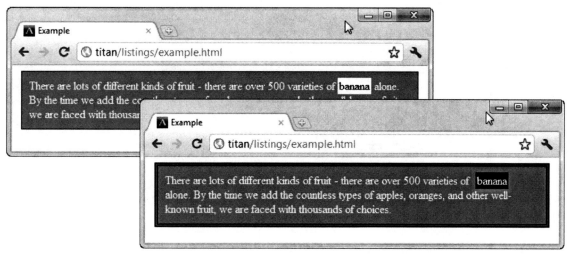

Figure 30-4. Dealing with event capture

Event capture gives each of an element's ancestors a chance to react to an event before it is passed to the element itself. A parent element event handler can stop flow of the event down toward the target by calling the stopPropagation or stopImmediatePropagation functions on the Event object. The difference between these functions is that stopPropagation will ensure that all of the event listeners registered for the current element will be invoked, whereas stopImmediatePropagation ignores any untriggered listeners. Listing 30-8 shows the addition of the stopPropagation function to the handleDescendantEvent event handler.

Listing 30-8. Preventing Further Event Flow

```
...
function handleDescendantEvent(e) {
    if (e.type == "mouseover" && e.eventPhase == Event.CAPTURING_PHASE) {
        e.target.style.border = "thick solid red";
        e.currentTarget.style.border = "thick double black";
    } else if (e.type == "mouseout" && e.eventPhase == Event.CAPTURING_PHASE) {
        e.target.style.removeProperty("border");
        e.currentTarget.style.removeProperty("border");
    }
    e.stopPropagation();
}
...
```

With this change, the browser capture phase ends when the handler on the p element is invoked. No other elements will be inspected, and the target and bubble phases (described shortly) will be skipped. In terms of the example, this means that the style changes in the handleMouseEvent function will not be applied in response to the mouseover event, as you can see in Figure 30-5.

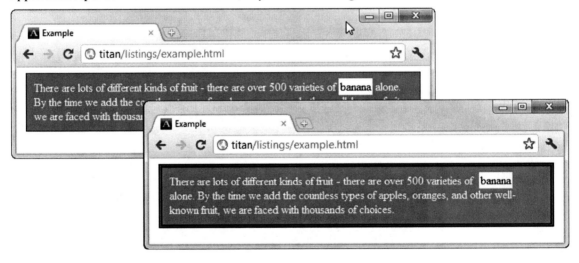

Figure 30-5. Stopping event propagation

Notice that in the handler, I check the event type and establish which phase the event is in by using the eventPhase property, like this:

```
...
if (e.type == "mouseover" && e.eventPhase == Event.CAPTURING_PHASE) {
...
```

Enabling capture events when registering an event listener doesn't stop events that are targeted at the element itself. In this case, the p element occupies space on the browser screen and will respond to mouseover events as well. To avoid this, I check to make sure that I only apply style changes when dealing with events that are in the capture phase (i.e., events that are targeted at a descendant element and that I am only processing because I have registered a capture-enabled listener). The eventPhase property will return one of the three values shown in Table 30-3, representing the three phases in the event life cycle. I explain the other two phases in the following sections.

Table 30-3. Values for the Event.eventPhase Property

Name	Description
CAPTURING_PHASE	The event is in the capture phase.
AT_TARGET	The event is in the target phase.
BUBBLING_PHASE	The event is in the bubble phase.

Understanding the Target Phase

The target phase is the simplest of the three. When the capture phase has finished, the browser triggers any listeners for the event type that have been added to the target element, as shown in Figure 30-6.

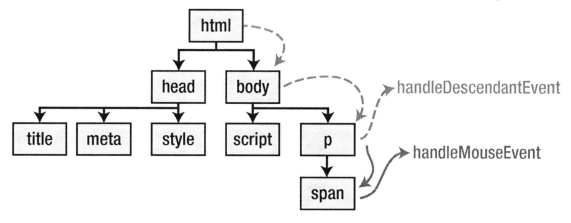

Figure 30-6. The target phase

You've already seen this phase in previous examples. The only point to note here is that you can make multiple calls to the addEventListener function, and so there can be more than one listener for a given event type.

■ **Tip** If you call the `stopPropagation` or `stopImmediatePropagation` functions during the target phase, you stop the flow of the event, and the bubble phase won't be performed.

Understanding the Bubble Phase

After the target phase has been completed, the browser starts working its way up the chain of ancestor elements back toward the body element. At each element, the browser checks to see if there are listeners for the event type that are not capture-enabled (i.e., the third argument to the addEventListener function is false). This is known as *event bubbling*. Listing 30-9 gives an example.

Listing 30-9. Event Bubbling

```
<!DOCTYPE HTML>
<html>
    <head>
        <title>Example</title>
        <style type="text/css">
            p {
                background: gray;
                color:white;
                padding: 10px;
                margin: 5px;
                border: thin solid black
            }
            span {
                background: white;
                color: black;
                padding: 2px;
                cursor: default;
            }
        </style>
    </head>
    <body>
        <p id="block1">
            There are lots of different kinds of fruit - there are over
            500 varieties of <span id="banana">banana</span> alone. By the time we add
            the countless types of apples, oranges, and other well-known fruit, we are
            faced with thousands of choices.
        </p>
        <script type="text/javascript">

            var banana = document.getElementById("banana");
            var textblock = document.getElementById("block1");

            banana.addEventListener("mouseover", handleMouseEvent);
            banana.addEventListener("mouseout", handleMouseEvent);
            textblock.addEventListener("mouseover", handleDescendantEvent, true);
```

```
            textblock.addEventListener("mouseout", handleDescendantEvent, true);
            textblock.addEventListener("mouseover", handleBubbleMouseEvent, false);
            textblock.addEventListener("mouseout", handleBubbleMouseEvent, false);

            function handleBubbleMouseEvent(e) {
                if (e.type == "mouseover" && e.eventPhase == Event.BUBBLING_PHASE) {
                    e.target.style.textTransform = "uppercase";
                } else if (e.type == "mouseout" && e.eventPhase == Event.BUBBLING_PHASE) {
                    e.target.style.textTransform = "none";
                }
            }

            function handleDescendantEvent(e) {
              if (e.type == "mouseover" && e.eventPhase == Event.CAPTURING_PHASE) {
                    e.target.style.border = "thick solid red";
                    e.currentTarget.style.border = "thick double black";
                } else if (e.type == "mouseout" && e.eventPhase == Event.CAPTURING_PHASE) {
                    e.target.style.removeProperty("border");
                    e.currentTarget.style.removeProperty("border");
                }
            }

            function handleMouseEvent(e) {
                if (e.type == "mouseover") {
                    e.target.style.background='black';
                    e.target.style.color='white';
                } else {
                    e.target.style.removeProperty('color');
                    e.target.style.removeProperty('background');
                }
            }
        </script>
    </body>
</html>
```

I have added a new function called handleBubbleMouseEvent and added it to the p element in the document. The p element has two event listeners now, one that is capture-enabled and one that is bubble-enabled. When you use the addEventListener method, you are always in one of these states, meaning that an element's listeners will always be notified about decedent element events *in addition to its own events*. The choice is whether the listener is invoked before or after the target phase for events from descendants.

The result of this new addition is that you have three listener functions that will be triggered for the mouseover event on the span element in the document. The handleDescendantEvent function will be triggered during the capture phase, the handleMouseEvent function will be invoked during the target phase, and handleBubbleMouseEvent during the bubble phase. You can see the effect of this in Figure 30-7.

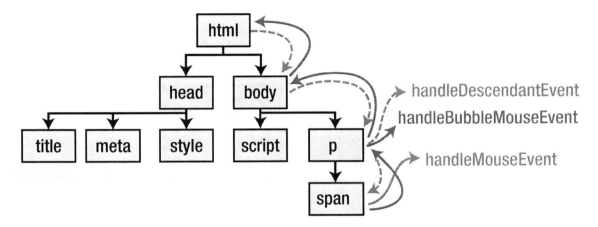

Figure 30-7. The bubble phase

The appearance of the element is now affected by the style changes in all of the listener functions, as shown in Figure 30-8.

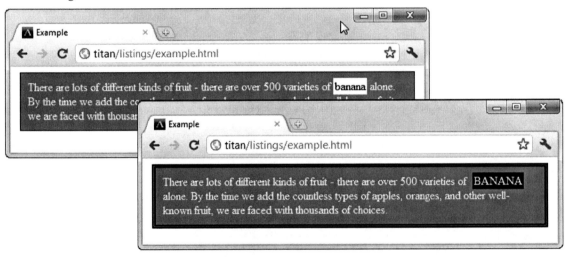

Figure 30-8. The effect of adding a handler for the bubble phase

---

■ **Tip** Not all events support bubbling. You can check to see whether an event will bubble using the `bubbles` property. A value of `true` indicates that the event will bubble, and `false` means that it won't.

Working with Cancellable Events

Some events define a default action that will be performed when an event is triggered. As an example, the default action for the click event on the a element is that the browser will load the content at the URL specified in the href attribute. When an event has a default action, the value of its cancelable property will be true. You can stop the default action from being performed by calling the preventDefault function. Listing 30-10 gives an example of working with a cancellable event in an event-handler function.

Listing 30-10. Cancelling a Default Action

```
<!DOCTYPE HTML>
<html>
    <head>
        <title>Example</title>
        <style type="text/css">
            a {
                background: gray;
                color:white;
                padding: 10px;
                border: thin solid black
            }
        </style>
    </head>
    <body>
        <p>
            <a href="http://apress.com">Visit Apress</a>
            <a href="http://w3c.org">Visit W3C</a>
        </p>

        <script type="text/javascript">

            function handleClick(e) {
                if (!confirm("Do you want to navigate to " + e.target.href + " ?")) {
                    e.preventDefault();
                }
            }

            var elems = document.querySelectorAll("a");
            for (var i = 0; i < elems.length; i++) {
                elems[i].addEventListener("click", handleClick, false);
            }

        </script>
    </body>
</html>
```

In this example, I use the confirm function to prompt the user to see whether they really want to navigate to the URL that the a element leads to. If the user clicks the Cancel button, then I call the preventDefault function. This means that the browser will no longer navigate to the URL.

Note that calling the preventDefault function doesn't stop the event from flowing through the capture, target, and bubble phases. These phases will still be performed, but the browser won't perform the default action at the end of the bubble phase. You can test to see whether the preventDefault function has been called on an event by an earlier event handler by reading the defaultPrevented property; if it returns true, then the preventDefault function has been called.

Working with the HTML Events

HTML defines a set of events, which I describe in the section that follow, grouped by type. The first section, the document and window events, are applied to the Document and Window objects, which I discussed in Chapters 25 and 26.

The other events are defined by all HTMLElement objects and are effectively generic. To support the unique characteristic of each type of event, the browser dispatches objects that have additional properties beyond those of the core Event object. This will make sense as you go through the examples.

The Document and Window Events

In addition to the features that you have seen in earlier chapters, the Document object defines the event described in Table 30-4. You can see an example of this event being used in Chapter 25.

Table 30-4. The Document Object Events

Name	Description
readystatechange	Triggered when the value of the readyState property changes.

The window object defines a wide range of events, which are described in Table 30-5. You can handle some of these events through the body element, but support for this approach is a little patchy, and using window tends to be more reliable.

Table 30-5. The Window Object Events

Name	Description
onabort	Triggered when the loading of a document or resource is aborted.
onafterprint	Triggered when the Window.print() method is called, before the user is presented with the print options.
onbeforeprint	Triggered after the user has printed the document.
onerror	Triggered when there is an error loading a document or resource.
onhashchange	Triggered when the hash fragment changes.
onload	Triggered when the loading of a document or resource is complete.

onpopstate	Triggered to provide a state object associated with the browser history. See Chapter 27 for a demonstration.
onresize	Triggered when the window is resized.
onunload	Triggered when the document is unloaded from the window/browser.

Working with Mouse Events

You already saw the mouseover and mouseout events earlier in this chapter, but the complete set of mouse-related events is shown in Table 30-6.

Table 30-6. *The Mouse-Related Events*

Name	Description
click	Triggered when the mouse button is clicked and released.
dblclick	Triggered when the mouse button is clicked and released twice.
mousedown	Triggered when the mouse button is clicked.
mouseenter	Triggered when the pointer is moved to be within the screen region occupied by the element or one of its descendants.
mouseleave	Triggered when the pointer is moved to be outside the screen region occupied by the element and all its descendants.
mousemove	Triggered when the pointer is moved while over the element.
mouseout	This is the same as for mouseleave, except that this event will trigger while the pointer is still over a descendant element.
mouseover	This is the same as for mouseenter, except that this event will trigger while the pointer is still over a descendant element.
mouseup	Triggered when the mouse button is released.

When a mouse event is triggered, the browser dispatches a MouseEvent object. This is an Event object with the additional properties and methods shown in Table 30-7.

Table 30-7. The MouseEvent Object

Name	Description	Returns
button	Indicates which button has been clicked; **0** is the main mouse button, **1** is the middle button, and **2** is the secondary/right button.	number
altKey	Returns **true** if the **alt**/**option** key was clicked when the event was triggered.	boolean
clientX	Returns the X position of the mouse when the event was triggered, relative to the element's viewport.	number
clientY	Returns the Y position of the mouse when the event was triggered, relative to the element's viewport.	number
screenX	Returns the X position of the mouse when the event was triggered, relative to the screen coordinate system.	number
screenY	Returns the Y position of the mouse when the event was triggered, relative to the screen coordinate system.	number
shiftKey	Returns **true** if the Shift key was pressed when the event was triggered.	boolean
ctrlKey	Returns **true** if the Ctrl key was pressed when the event was triggered.	boolean

Listing 30-11 shows how you can use the additional functionality provided by the MouseEvent object.

Listing 30-11. Using the MouseEvent Object to Respond to Mouse Events

```
<!DOCTYPE HTML>
<html>
    <head>
        <title>Example</title>
        <style type="text/css">
            p {
                background: gray;
                color:white;
                padding: 10px;
                margin: 5px;
                border: thin solid black
            }
            table { margin: 5px; border-collapse: collapse; }
            th, td {padding: 4px;}
        </style>
    </head>
    <body>
        <p id="block1">
            There are lots of different kinds of fruit - there are over
```

```
            500 varieties of banana alone. By the time we add the countless types of
            apples, oranges, and other well-known fruit, we are faced with thousands
            of choices.
        </p>
        <table border="1">
            <tr><th>Type:</th><td id="eType"></td></tr>
            <tr><th>X:</th><td id="eX"></td></tr>
            <tr><th>Y:</th><td id="eY"></td></tr>
        </table>

        <script type="text/javascript">
            var textblock = document.getElementById("block1");
            var typeCell = document.getElementById("eType");
            var xCell = document.getElementById("eX");
            var yCell = document.getElementById("eY");

            textblock.addEventListener("mouseover", handleMouseEvent, false);
            textblock.addEventListener("mouseout", handleMouseEvent, false);
            textblock.addEventListener("mousemove", handleMouseEvent, false);

            function handleMouseEvent(e) {
                if (e.eventPhase == Event.AT_TARGET) {
                    typeCell.innerHTML = e.type;
                    xCell.innerHTML = e.clientX;
                    yCell.innerHTML = e.clientY;

                    if (e.type == "mouseover") {
                        e.target.style.background='black';
                        e.target.style.color='white';
                    } else {
                        e.target.style.removeProperty('color');
                        e.target.style.removeProperty('background');
                    }
                }
            }
        </script>
    </body>
</html>
```

The script in this example updates cells in a table in response to two kinds of mouse events. You can see the effect in Figure 30-9.

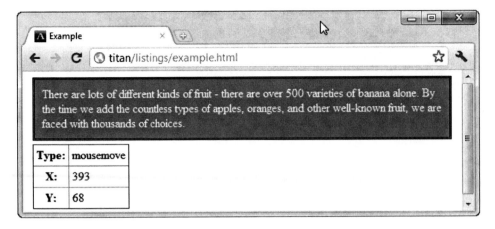

Figure 30-9. Dealing with mouse events

Working with Focus Events

The focus-related events are triggered into response to elements gaining and losing the focus. Table 30-8 summarizes these events.

Table 30-8. The Focus-Related Events

Name	Description
blur	Triggered when the element loses the focus.
focus	Triggered when the element gains the focus.
focusin	Triggered when the element is just about to gain the focus.
focusout	Triggered when the element is just about to lose the focus.

These events are represented by a FocusEvent object, which adds the property shown in Table 30-9 to the core Event object functionality.

Table 30-9. The FocusEvent Object

Name	Description	Returns
relatedTarget	The element that is about to gain or lose the focus; this property is used only by the focusin and focusout events.	HTMLElement

Listing 30-12 demonstrates the use of the focus events.

Listing 30-12. Using the Focus Events

```html
<!DOCTYPE HTML>
<html>
    <head>
        <title>Example</title>
        <style type="text/css">
            p {
                background: gray;
                color:white;
                padding: 10px;
                margin: 5px;
                border: thin solid black
            }
        </style>
    </head>
    <body>
        <form>
            <p>
                <label for="fave">Fruit: <input autofocus id="fave" name="fave"/></label>
            </p>
            <p>
                <label for="name">Name: <input id="name" name="name"/></label>
            </p>
            <button type="submit">Submit Vote</button>
            <button type="reset">Reset</button>
        </form>

        <script type="text/javascript">

            var inputElems = document.getElementsByTagName("input");
            for (var i = 0; i < inputElems.length; i++) {
                inputElems[i].onfocus = handleFocusEvent;
                inputElems[i].onblur = handleFocusEvent;
            }

            function handleFocusEvent(e) {
                if (e.type == "focus") {
                    e.target.style.backgroundColor = "lightgray";
                    e.target.style.border = "thick double red";
                } else {
                    e.target.style.removeProperty("background-color");
                    e.target.style.removeProperty("border");
                }
            }
        </script>
    </body>
</html>
```

The script in this example uses the focus and blur events to change the style of a pair of input elements. You can see the effect in Figure 30-10.

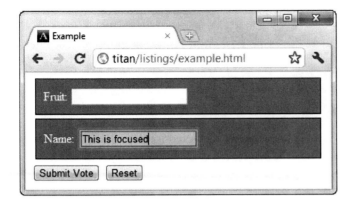

Figure 30-10. Using the focus and blur events

Working with Keyboard Events

The keyboard events are triggered in response to key presses. The set of events in this category is shown in Table 30-10.

Table 30-10. The Keyboard-Related Events

Name	Description
keydown	Triggered when the user presses a key.
keypress	Triggered when a user presses and releases a key.
keyup	Triggered when the user releases a key.

These events are represented by a FocusEvent object, which adds the property shown in Table 30-11 to the core Event object functionality.

Table 30-11. The KeyboardEvent Object

Name	Description	Returns
char	Returns the character represented by the key press.	string
key	Returns the key that was pressed.	string
ctrlKey	Returns true if the Ctrl key was down when the key was pressed.	boolean
shiftKey	Returns true if the Shift key was down when the key was	boolean

	pressed.	
altKey	Returns true if the Alt key was down when the key was pressed.	boolean
repeat	Returns true if the key is being held down.	boolean

Listing 30-13 shows some of the keyboard events in use.

Listing 30-13. Using the Keyboard Events

```
<!DOCTYPE HTML>
<html>
    <head>
        <title>Example</title>
        <style type="text/css">
            p {
                background: gray;
                color:white;
                padding: 10px;
                margin: 5px;
                border: thin solid black
            }
        </style>
    </head>
    <body>
        <form>
            <p>
                <label for="fave">Fruit: <input autofocus id="fave" name="fave"/></label>
            </p>
            <p>
                <label for="name">Name: <input id="name" name="name"/></label>
            </p>
            <button type="submit">Submit Vote</button>
            <button type="reset">Reset</button>
        </form>
        <span id="message"></span>

        <script type="text/javascript">

            var inputElems = document.getElementsByTagName("input");
            for (var i = 0; i < inputElems.length; i++) {
                inputElems[i].onkeyup = handleKeyboardEvent;
            }

            function handleKeyboardEvent(e) {
                document.getElementById("message").innerHTML = "Key pressed: " +
                    e.keyCode + " Char: " + String.fromCharCode(e.keyCode);
            }
        </script>
```

```
    </body>
</html>
```

The script in this example changes the content of a span element to display key strokes sent to a pair of input elements. Notice how I use the String.fromCharCode function to convert the value of the keyCode property into a more useful value. You can see the effect of this script in Figure 30-11.

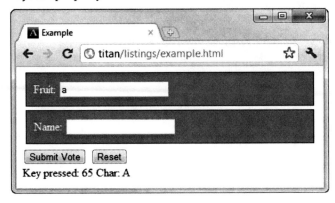

Figure 30-11. Using the key events

Working with Form Events

The form element defines two special events that are particular to that element. These are described in Table 30-12.

Table 30-12. The form Events

Name	Description
submit	Triggered when the form is submitted.
reset	Triggered when the form is reset.

You can see how the form events are used in Chapters 33 and 34, when I show you Ajax.

Summary

In this chapter, I have explained how the event system allows you to react to changes in the state of your document elements. I showed you the different ways of handling events, from the simple on* properties, using handler functions, and the addEventListener method, each of which has its own merits. I also explained the three phases of an event's life cycle—capture, at target, and bubbling—and how you can use these phases to intercept events as they are propagated. I finished this chapter with a description of the events that are available for most HTML elements.

CHAPTER 31

Using the Element-Specific Objects

The Document Object Model (DOM) defines a set of objects that represent the different types of HTML elements in a document. These objects can be treated as HTMLElement objects and, for the most part, that's what you typically do in your scripts. But if you want to access some attribute or feature that is unique to an element, you can usually do so using one of these objects.

These objects are not much use. They generally define properties that correspond to attributes supported by an element, the value of which you can access through the features of the HTMLElement. There are a couple of exceptions—the form elements have some helpful methods for use with input validation, and the table elements have some methods that can be used to build up the content of tables.

The Document and Metadata Objects

This section describes the objects that represent the data and metadata elements. You can learn more about these elements in Chapter 7.

The base Element

The base element is represented by the HTMLBaseElement object. This object doesn't define any additional events, but there are two properties, which are shown in Table 31-1.

Table 31-1. The HTMLBaseElement Object

Name	Description	Returns
href	Corresponds to the href attribute	string
target	Corresponds to the target attribute	string

The body Element

The body element is represented by the HTMLBodyElement object. This object doesn't define any additional properties, but the set of events is shown in Table 31-2.

Table 31-2. The HTMLBodyElement Events

Event	Description
error	Triggered when there is an error loading a resource, such as a script or image
load	Triggered when the document and its resources have been loaded
unload	Triggered when the browser unloads the document (typically, because the user has navigated elsewhere)

░ **Tip** Some browsers support these events through the `window` object, which I describe in Chapter 27.

The link Element

The `link` element is represented by the `HTMLLinkElement` object, which defines the properties shown in Table 31-3.

Table 31-3. The HTMLLinkElement Object

Name	Description	Returns
disabled	Corresponds to the disabled attribute	boolean
href	Corresponds to the href attribute	string
rel	Corresponds to the rel attribute	string
media	Corresponds to the media attribute	string
hreflang	Corresponds to the hreflang attribute	string
type	Corresponds to the type attribute	string

The meta Element

The `meta` element is represented by the `HTMLMetaElement` object, which defines the properties shown in Table 31-4.

Table 31-4. The HTMLMetaElement Object

Name	Description	Returns
name	Corresponds to the name attribute	string
httpEquiv	Corresponds to the http-equiv attribute	string
content	Corresponds to the content attribute	string

The script Element

The script element is represented in the DOM by the HTMLScriptElement object, which defines the additional properties described in Table 31-5.

Table 31-5. The HTMLScriptElement Object

Name	Description	Returns
src	Corresponds to the src attribute	string
async	Corresponds to the async attribute	boolean
defer	Corresponds to the defer attribute	boolean
type	Corresponds to the type attribute	string
charset	Corresponds to the charset attribute	string
text	Corresponds to the text attribute	string

The style Element

The style element is represented in the DOM by the HTMLStyleElement object, which defines the additional properties shown in Table 31-6.

Table 31-6. The HTMLStyleElement Object

Name	Description	Returns
disabled	Corresponds to the disabled attribute	boolean
media	Corresponds to the media attribute	string

| typed | Corresponds to the typed attribute | string |
| scoped | Corresponds to the scoped attribute | boolean |

The title Element

The title element is represented by the HTMLTitleElement object in the DOM. This object defines the property shown in Table 31-7.

Table 31-7. The HTMLTitleElement Object

Name	Description	Returns
text	Gets or sets the content of the title element	string

Other Document and Metadata Elements

The head and html elements are represented by the HTMLHeadElement and HTMLHtmlElement objects, respectively. These objects do not define any additional methods, properties, or events beyond those of HTMLElement. The noscript element doesn't have a special DOM object and is represented solely by HTMLElement.

The Text Elements

This section describes the objects that represent the text elements. You can learn more about these elements in Chapter 8.

The a Element

The a element is represented by the HTMLAnchorElement object, which defines the properties shown in Table 31-8. In addition to defining properties that correspond to the element attributes, this object defines a set of convenience properties that allows you to easily get or set components of the URL specified by the href attribute.

Table 31-8. The HTMLAnchorElement Object

Name	Description	Returns
href	Corresponds to the href attribute	string
target	Corresponds to the target attribute	string
rel	Corresponds to the rel attribute	string

media	Corresponds to the media attribute	string
hreflang	Corresponds to the hreflang attribute	string
type	Corresponds to the type attribute	string
text	Gets or sets the text contained by the element	string
protocol	Convenience property to get or set the protocol component of the href attribute value	string
host	Convenience property to get or set the host component of the href attribute value	string
hostname	Convenience property to get or set the host name from the href attribute value	string
port	Convenience property to get or set the port component of the href attribute value	string
pathname	Convenience property to get or set the path of the href attribute value	string
search	Convenience property to get or set the query string of the href attribute value	string
hash	Convenience property to get or set the document fragment component of the href attribute value	string

The del and ins Elements

The del and ins elements are both represented by the HTMLModElement. You can tell them apart using the tagName property defined by HTMLElement. See Chapter 26 for details. The additional properties defined by HTMLModElement are described in Table 31-9.

Table 31-9. The HTMLModElement Object

Name	Description	Returns
cite	Corresponds to the cite attribute	string
dateTime	Corresponds to the datetime attribute	string

The q Element

The q element is represented by the HTMLQuoteElement object. The property that this object defines is described in Table 31-10.

Table 31-10. The HTMLQuoteElement Object

Name	Description	Returns
cite	Corresponds to the cite attribute	string

The time Element

The time element is represented by the HTMLTimeElement object. The additional properties defined by this object are shown in Table 31-11.

Table 31-11. The HTMLTimeElement Object

Name	Description	Returns
dateTime	Corresponds to the datetime attribute	string
pubDate	Corresponds to the pubdate attribute	string
valueAsDate	Parses the time and date, and returns a Date object	Date

Other Text Elements

The br and span elements are represented by the HTMLBRElement and HTMLSpanElementobjects, respectively. These objects do not define any additional methods, properties, or events beyond those of HTMLElement. The following elements are represented solely by HTMLElement: abbr, b, cite, code, dfn, em, i, u, kbd, mark, rt, rp, ruby, s, samp, small, strong, sub, sup, var, and wbr.

The Grouping Elements

This section describes the objects that represent the grouping elements. You can learn more about these elements in Chapter 9.

The blockquote Element

The blockquote element is represented by the HTMLQuoteElement object. This is the same object that the q element uses, which I described in Table 31-10.

The li Element

The `li` element is represented by the `HTMLLIElement` object, which defines the property shown in Table 31-12.

***Table 31-12.** The HTMLLIElement Object*

Name	Description	Returns
value	Corresponds to the value attribute	number

The ol Element

The `ol` element is represented by the `HTMLOListElement` object, which defines the properties shown in Table 31-13.

***Table 31-13.** The HTMLOListElement Object*

Name	Description	Returns
reversed	Corresponds to the reversed attribute	boolean
start	Corresponds to the start attribute	number
type	Corresponds to the type attribute	string

Other Grouping Elements

Table 31-14 shows the set of grouping elements that are represented by element-specific objects that do not define any additional functionality beyond that of `HTMLElement`.

***Table 31-14.** Grouping element objects with no additional properties*

Name	DOM Object
div	HTMLDivElement
dl	HTMLDListElement
hr	HTMLHRElement
p	HTMLParagraphElement
pre	HTMLPreElement

ul	HTMLUListElement

The following elements do not have corresponding elements in the DOM and are represented by HTMLElement: dd, dt, figcaption, and figure.

The Section Elements

This section describes the objects that represent the section elements. You can learn more about these elements in Chapter 10.

The details Element

The details element is represented by the HTMLDetailsElement object. The property that this object defines is described in Table 31-15.

Table 31-15. The HTMLDetailsElement Object

Name	Description	Returns
open	Corresponds to the open attribute	boolean

Other Section Elements

The h1-h6 elements are represented by the HTMLHeadingElement object, but this object doesn't define any additional properties. The following section elements are not represented by specific objects: address, article, aside, footer, header, hgroup, nav, section, and summary.

The Table Elements

This section describes the objects that represent the table elements. You can learn more about these elements in Chapter 11.

The col and colgroup Elements

The col and colgroup elements are both represented by the HTMLTableColElement object, which defines the property shown in Table 31-16.

Table 31-16. The HTMLTableColElement Object

Name	Description	Returns
span	Corresponds to the span attribute	number

The table Element

The table element is represented by the HTMLTableElement object. This is one of the most useful of the element-specific objects. The properties and methods defined by this object are described in Table 31-17.

Table 31-17. The HTMLTableElement Object

Name	Description	Returns
border	Corresponds to the border attribute	string
caption	Returns the table's caption element	HTMLElement
createCaption()	Returns the table's caption element, creating it if required	HTMLElement
deleteCaption()	Removes the table's caption element	void
tHead	Returns the table's thead element	HTMLTableSectionElement
createTHead()	Returns the thead element, creating one if required	HTMLTableSectionElement
deleteTHead()	Removes the table's thead element	void
tFoot	Returns the table's tfoot element	HTMLTableSectionElement
createTFoot()	Returns the tfoot element, creating one if required	HTMLTableSectionElement
deleteTFoot()	Removes the table's tfoot element	void
tBodies	Returns the tbody elements	HTMLTableSectionElement[]
createTBody()	Returns the tbody element, creating one if required	HTMLTableSectionElement
rows	Returns the rows in the table	HTMLTableRowElement[]
insertRow(<index>)	Creates a new row in the table at the specified position	HTMLTableRowElement
deleteRow(<index>)	Deletes the table row at the specified index	void

The thead, tbody, and tfoot Elements

The thead, tbody, and tfoot elements are all represented by the HTMLTableSectionElement object. The property and methods defined by this object are shown in Table 31-18.

Table 31-18. The HTMLTableSectionElement Object

Name	Description	Returns
rows	Returns the set of rows for this section of the table	HTMLTableRowElement[]
insertRow(<index>)	Inserts a new row at the specified index	HTMLTableRowElement
deleteRow(<index>)	Removes the row at the specified index	void

The th Element

The th element is represented by the HTMLTableHeaderCellElement object. The property defined by this object is described in Table 31-19.

Table 31-19. The HTMLTableHeaderCellElement Object

Name	Description	Returns
rows	Returns the set of rows for this section of the table	HTMLTableRowElement[]
insertRow(<index>)	Inserts a new row at the specified index	HTMLTableRowElement
deleteRow(<index>)	Removes the row at the specified index	void

The tr Element

The tr element is represented by the HTMLTableRowElement object, which defines the properties and methods shown in Table 31-20.

Table 31-20. The HTMLTableRowElement Object

Name	Description	Returns
rowIndex	Returns the position of the row in the table	number
sectionRowIndex	Returns the position of the row in the table section	number

cells	Returns the collection of cell elements	HTMLElement[]
insertCell(<index>)	Inserts a new cell at the specified index	HTMLElement
deleteCell(<index>)	Deletes the cell at the specified index	void

Other Table Elements

Table 31-21 shows the set of table elements that are represented by element-specific objects that do not define any additional functionality beyond that of HTMLElement.

Table 31-21. Table Element Objects with No Additional Properties

Name	DOM Object
caption	HTMLTableCaptionElement
td	HTMLTableDataCellElement

The Form Elements

This section describes the objects that represent the form elements. You can learn more about these elements in Chapters 12–14.

The button Element

The button element is represented by the HTMLButtonElement object, which defines the properties and methods shown in Table 31-22.

Table 31-22. The HTMLButtonElement Object

Name	Description	Returns
autofocus	Corresponds to the autofocus attribute	boolean
disabled	Corresponds to the disabled attribute	disabled
form	Returns the form element with which the element is associated; corresponds to the form attribute	HTMLFormElement
formAction	Corresponds to the formaction attribute	string
formEncType	Corresponds to the formenctype attribute	string

formMethod	Corresponds to the formmethod attribute	string
formNoValidate	Corresponds to the formnovalidate attribute	string
formTarget	Corresponds to the formtarget attribute	string
name	Corresponds to the name attribute	string
type	Corresponds to the type attribute	string
value	Corresponds to the value attribute	string
labels	Returns the label elements whose attribute refers to this button element	HTMLLabelElement[]

The datalist Element

The datalist element is represented by the HTMLDataListElement object, which defines the property shown in Table 31-23.

Table 31-23. The HTMLDataListElement Object

Name	Description	Returns
options	Returns the collection of option elements contained within the datalist element	HTMLOptionElement[]

The fieldset Element

The fieldset element is represented by the HTMLFieldSetElement object, which defines the properties shown in Table 31-24.

Table 31-24. The HTMLFieldSetElement Object

Name	Description	Returns
disabled	Corresponds to the disabled attribute	boolean
form	Corresponds to the form attribute	HTMLFormElement
name	Corresponds to the name attribute	string
elements	Returns a collection containing the form controls within the fieldset	HTMLElement[]

The form Element

The form element is represented by the HTMLFormElement object, which defines the properties and methods shown in Table 31-25.

Table 31-25. The HTMLFormElement Object

Name	Description	Returns
acceptCharset	Corresponds to the accept-charset attribute	string
action	Corresponds to the action attribute	string
autocomplete	Corresponds to the autocomplete attribute	string
enctype	Corresponds to the enctype attribute	string
encoding	Corresponds to the enctype attribute	string
method	Corresponds to the method attribute	string
name	Corresponds to the name attribute	string
noValidate	Corresponds to the novalidate attribute	boolean
target	Corresponds to the target attribute	string
elements	Returns the elements in the form	HTMLElement[]
length	Returns the number of elements in the form	number
[<name>]	Returns the form element with the specified name	HTMLElement
[<index>]	Returns the form element at the specified index	HTMLElement
submit()	Submits the form	void
reset()	Resets the form	void
checkValidity()	Returns true if all of the form elements pass input validation; returns false otherwise	boolean

The input Element

The input element is represented by the HTMLInputElement object, which supports the properties and methods shown in Table 31-26.

Table 31-26. The HTMLInputElement Object

Name	Description	Returns
accept	Corresponds to the accept attribute	string
alt	Corresponds to the alt attribute	string
autocomplete	Corresponds to the autocomplete attribute	string
autofocus	Corresponds to the autofocus attribute	boolean
checked	Returns true if the element is checked	boolean
dirName	Corresponds to the dirname attribute	string
disabled	Corresponds to the disabled attribute	boolean
form	Corresponds to the form attribute	string
formAction	Corresponds to the formaction attribute	string
formEnctype	Corresponds to the formenctype attribute	string
formMethod	Corresponds to the formmethod attribute	string
formNoValidate	Corresponds to the formnovalidate attribute	string
formTarget	Corresponds to the formtarget attribute	string
list	Corresponds to the list attribute	HTMLElement
max	Corresponds to the max attribute	string
maxLength	Corresponds to the maxlength attribute	number
min	Corresponds to the min attribute	string
multiple	Corresponds to the multiple attribute	boolean
name	Corresponds to the name attribute	string
pattern	Corresponds to the pattern attribute	string
placeholder	Corresponds to the placeholder attribute	string

`readOnly`	Corresponds to the readonly attribute	boolean
`required`	Corresponds to the required attribute	boolean
`size`	Corresponds to the size attribute	number
`src`	Corresponds to the src attribute	string
`step`	Corresponds to the step attribute	string
`type`	Corresponds to the type attribute	string
`value`	Corresponds to the value attribute	string
`valueAsDate`	Gets or sets the value attribute as a date object	Date
`valueAsNumber`	Gets or sets the value attribute as a number	number
`selectedOption`	Gets the option element from the datalist specified by the list attribute that matches the input element's value	HTMLOptionElement
`stepUp(<step>)`	Increases the value by the specified amount	void
`stepDown(<step>)`	Decreases the value by the specified amount	void
`willValidate`	Returns true if the element will be subject to input validation when the form is submitted; returns false otherwise	boolean
`validity`	Returns an assessment of the validity of the input	ValidityState
`validationMessage`	Returns the error message that would be shown to the user if input validation was applied	string
`checkValidity()`	Performs input validation on the element	boolean
`setCustomValidity(<msg>)`	Sets a custom validation message	void
`labels`	Returns the label elements associated with this element	HTMLLabelElement[]

The label Element

The label element is represented by the HTMLLabelElement object, which defines the properties shown in Table 31-27.

Table 31-27. The HTMLLabelElement Object

Name	Description	Returns
form	Returns the form associated with this element	HTMLFormElement
htmlFor	Corresponds to the for attribute	string
control	Returns the element specified by the for attribute	HTMLElement

The legend Element

The legend element is represented by the HTMLLegendElement object, which defines the property shown in Table 31-28.

Table 31-28. The HTMLLegendElement Object

Name	Description	Returns
form	Returns the form associated with this element	HTMLFormElement

The optgroup Element

The optgroup element is represented by the HTMLOptGroupElement object, which defines the properties shown in Table 31-29.

Table 31-29. The HTMLOptGroupElement Object

Name	Description	Returns
disabled	Corresponds to the disabled attribute	boolean
label	Corresponds to the label attribute	string

The option Element

The option element is represented by the HTMLOptionElement object, which defines the properties shown in Table 31-30.

Table 31-30. The HTMLOptionElement Object

Name	Description	Returns
disabled	Corresponds to the disabled attribute	boolean
form	Returns the form this element is associated with	HTMLFormElement
label	Corresponds to the label attribute	string
selected	Corresponds to the selected attribute	boolean
value	Corresponds to the value attribute	string
text	Corresponds to the text attribute	string
index	Returns the index of this element in the parent select element	number

The output Element

The output element is represented by the HTMLOutputElement object, which defines the properties shown in Table 31-31.

Table 31-31. The HTMLOutputElement Object

Name	Description	Returns
htmlFor	Corresponds to the for attribute	string
form	Returns the form this element is associated with	HTMLFormElement
name	Corresponds to the name attribute	string
type	Corresponds to the type attribute	string
value	Corresponds to the value attribute	string
willValidate	Returns true if the element will be subject to input validation when the form is submitted; returns false otherwise	boolean
validationMessage	Returns the error message that would be shown to the user if input validation was applied	string
checkValidity()	Performs input validation on the element	boolean

| setCustomValidity(<msg>) | Sets a custom validation message | void |
| labels | Returns the label elements associated with this element | HTMLLabelElement[] |

The select Element

The select element is represented by the HTMLSelectElement object, which implements the properties and methods shown in Table 31-32.

Table 31-32. The HTMLSelectElement Object

Name	Description	Returns
autofocus	Corresponds to the autofocus attribute	boolean
disabled	Corresponds to the disabled attribute	boolean
form	Returns the form that this element is associated with	HTMLFormElement
multiple	Corresponds to the multiple attribute	boolean
name	Corresponds to the name attribute	string
required	Corresponds to the required attribute	boolean
size	Corresponds to the size attribute	number
type	Returns select-multiple if the element has the multiple attribute, and select-one otherwise	string
options	Returns the collection of option elements	HTMLOptionElement[]
length	Gets or sets the number of option elements	number
[<index>]	Gets the element at the specified index	HTMLElement
selectedOptions	Returns the selected option elements	HTMLOptionElement[]
selectedIndex	Returns the index of the first selected option element	number
value	Gets or sets the selected value	string

willValidate	Returns true if the element will be subject to input validation when the form is submitted; returns false otherwise	boolean
validationMessage	Returns the error message that would be shown to the user if input validation was applied	string
checkValidity()	Performs input validation on the element	boolean
setCustomValidity(<msg>)	Sets a custom validation message	void
labels	Returns the label elements associated with this element	HTMLLabelElement[]

The textarea Element

The textarea element is represented by the HTMLTextAreaElement object, which defines the methods and properties described in Table 31-33.

Table 31-33. The HTMLTextAreaElement Object

Name	Description	Returns
autofocus	Corresponds to the autofocus attribute	boolean
cols	Corresponds to the cols attribute	number
dirName	Corresponds to the dirName attribute	string
disabled	Corresponds to the disabled attribute	boolean
form	Returns the form that this element is associated with	HTMLFormElement
maxLength	Corresponds to the maxlength attribute	number
name	Corresponds to the name attribute	string
placeholder	Corresponds to the placeholder attribute	string
readOnly	Corresponds to the readonly attribute	boolean
required	Corresponds to the required attribute	boolean
rows	Corresponds to the rows attribute	number

wrap	Corresponds to the wrap attribute	string
type	Returns textarea	string
value	Returns the content of the element	string
textLength	Returns the length of the value attribute	number
willValidate	Returns true if the element will be subject to input validation when the form is submitted; returns false otherwise	boolean
validationMessage	Returns the error message that would be shown to the user if input validation was applied	string
checkValidity()	Performs input validation on the element	boolean
setCustomValidity(<msg>)	Sets a custom validation message	void
labels	Returns the label elements associated with this element	HTMLLabelElement[]

The Content Elements

This section describes the objects that represent the elements used to embed content in a document. You can learn more about these elements in Chapter 15.

▪ **Note** The other content elements, such as canvas and video, are described later in Chapter 34.

The area Element

The area element is represented by the HTMLAreaElement, which implements the properties shown in Table 31-34.

Table 31-34. The HTMLAreaElement Object

Name	Description	Returns
alt	Corresponds to the alt attribute	string
coords	Corresponds to the coords attribute	string

shape	Corresponds to the shape attribute	string
href	Corresponds to the href attribute	string
target	Corresponds to the target attribute	string
rel	Corresponds to the rel attribute	string
media	Corresponds to the media attribute	string
hrefLang	Corresponds to the hreflang attribute	string
type	Corresponds to the type attribute	string
protocol	Convenience property to get or set the protocol component of the href attribute value	string
host	Convenience property to get or set the host component of the href attribute value	string
hostname	Convenience property to get or set the host name from the href attribute value	string
port	Convenience property to get or set the port component of the href attribute value	string
pathname	Convenience property to get or set the path of the href attribute value	string
search	Convenience property to get or set the query string of the href attribute value	string
hash	Convenience property to get or set the document fragment component of the href attribute value	string

The embed Element

The embed element is represented by the HTMLEmbedElement object, which implements the properties shown in Table 31-35.

Table 31-35. The HTMLEmbedElement Object

Name	Description	Returns
src	Corresponds to the src attribute	string

813

type	Corresponds to the type attribute	string
width	Corresponds to the width attribute	string
height	Corresponds to the height attribute	string

The iframe Element

The iframe element is represented by the HTMLIFrameElement object, which implements the properties described in Table 31-36.

Table 31-36. The HTMLIFrameElement Object

Name	Description	Returns
src	Corresponds to the src attribute	string
srcdoc	Corresponds to the srcdoc attribute	string
name	Corresponds to the name attribute	string
sandbox	Corresponds to the sandox attribute	string
seamless	Corresponds to the seamless attribute	string
width	Corresponds to the width attribute	string
height	Corresponds to the height attribute	string
contentDocument	Returns the document object	Document
contentWindow	Returns the window object	Window

The img Elements

The img element is represented by the HTMLImageElement object, which implements the properties described in Table 31-37.

Table 31-37. The HTMLImageElement Object

Name	Description	Returns
alt	Corresponds to the alt attribute	string

src	Corresponds to the src attribute	string
useMap	Corresponds to the usemap attribute	string
isMap	Corresponds to the ismap attribute	boolean
width	Corresponds to the width attribute	number
height	Corresponds to the height attribute	number
complete	Returns true if the image has been downloaded	boolean

The map Element

The map element is represented by the HTMLMapElement object, which implements the properties shown in Table 31-38.

Table 31-38. The HTMLMapElement Object

Name	Description	Returns
name	Corresponds to the name attribute	string
areas	Returns the area elements in the map	HTMLAreaElement[]
images	Returns the img and object elements in the map	HTMLElement[]

The meter Element

The meter element is represented by the HTMLMeterElement object, which implements the properties shown in Table 31-39.

Table 31-39. The HTMLMeterElement Object

Name	Description	Returns
value	Corresponds to the value attribute	number
max	Corresponds to the max attribute	number
form	Returns the form that this element is associated with	HTMLFormElement
labels	Returns the label elements associated with this element	HTMLLabelElement[]

The object Element

The object element is represented by the HTMLObjectElement object, which implements the properties shown in Table 31-40.

Table 31-40. *The HTMLObjectElement Object*

Name	Description	Returns
data	Corresponds to the data attribute	string
type	Corresponds to the type attribute	string
form	Returns the form that this element is associated with	HTMLFormElement
name	Corresponds to the name attribute	string
useMap	Corresponds to the usemap attribute	string
width	Corresponds to the width attribute	string
height	Corresponds to the height attribute	string
contentDocument	Returns the document object	Document
contentWindow	Returns the window object	Window
willValidate	Returns true if the element will be subject to input validation when the form is submitted; returns false otherwise	boolean
validationMessage	Returns the error message that would be shown to the user if input validation was applied	string
checkValidity()	Performs input validation on the element	boolean
setCustomValidity(<msg>)	Sets a custom validation message	void
labels	Returns the label elements associated with this element	HTMLLabelElement[]

The param Element

The param element is represented by the HTMLParamElement object, which implements the properties shown in Table 31-41.

Table 31-41. *The HTMLParamElement Object*

Name	Description	Returns
name	Corresponds to the name attribute	string
value	Corresponds to the value attribute	string

The progress Element

The progress element is represented by the HTMLProgressElement object, which implements the properties shown in Table 31-42.

Table 31-42. *The HTMLProgressElement Object*

Name	Description	Returns
value	Corresponds to the value attribute	number
max	Corresponds to the max attribute	number
position	Corresponds to the position attribute	number
form	Returns the form that this element is associated with	HTMLFormElement
labels	Returns the label elements associated with this element	HTMLLabelElement[]

Summary

In this chapter, I listed the set of objects that are used to represent different types of elements in the DOM. For the most part, these are not especially useful—with two exceptions. The first exception is the form elements, which provide some useful control over validation and form submission. The second exception is the table elements, which provide methods for managing the content of tables. These exceptions aside, the objects described in this chapter are largely a collection of properties that represent specific attributes—the values of which can be accessed through the ubiquitous HTMLElement object.

PART V

Advanced Features

In this final part of the book, I'll show you some of the advanced features available in HTML5. These include Ajax (for making requests to the web server in the background) and the canvas element (which allows us to use JavaScript to perform drawing operations).

CHAPTER 32

Using Ajax – Part I

Ajax is a key tool in modern web application development. It allows you to send and retrieve data from a server asynchronously and process the data using JavaScript. Ajax is an acronym for *Asynchronous JavaScript and XML.* The name arose when XML was the data transfer format of choice although, as I'll explain later, this is no longer the case.

Ajax is another one of those contentious technologies. It is so useful in creating rich web applications that designers and developers have created a lore around its use and regularly engage in vicious sniping contests about the *right* way to do Ajax. This is largely rubbish and not needed. Ajax is surprisingly simple when you get down to the details, and you'll be making requests like a master in no time at all. My standard advice for dealing with zealots applies when dealing with Ajax zealots: nod politely, back away, and do the right thing for your project.

Tip You will see Ajax capitalized in a number of different ways. "Ajax" seems to be the most widely used at the moment, but AJAX is pretty common, and some people even use AJaX (picky people who believe that you never capitalize "and"). They all refer to the same technologies and techniques. I have tried to consistently use Ajax in this book.

The key specification for Ajax is named after the JavaScript object you use to set up and make requests: XMLHttpRequest. There are two levels of this specification. All of the mainstream browsers implement Level 1, which is the base level of functionality. Level 2 extends the original specification to include additional events, some features that make it easier to work with form elements, and support for some related specifications, such as CORS (which I'll explain later in this chapter).

In this chapter, I explain the Ajax basics, showing you how to create, configure, and execute simple requests. I'll show you how the progress of a request is signaled through events, how to deal with request and application errors, and how to make requests across origins.

All of the examples in this chapter are about getting data from the server. The next chapter is all about sending data—particularly, form data, which is one of the most common uses for Ajax. Table 32-1 provides the summary for this chapter.

Table 32-1. Chapter Summary

Problem	Solution	Listing
Make an Ajax request.	Create an XMLHttpRequest object, and call the open and send methods.	1-3
Use the one-off events to track request progress.	Use the Level 2 events, such as onload, onloadstart, and onloadend.	4
Detect and deal with errors.	Respond to error events, or use try...catch statements.	5
Set headers for an Ajax request.	Use the setRequestHeader method.	6-7
Read the headers from the server response.	Use the getResponseHeader and getAllResponseHeaders methods.	8
Make a cross-origin Ajax request.	Set the Access-Control-Allow-Origin header in the server response.	9-12
Abort a request.	Use the abort method.	13, 14

Getting Started with Ajax

The key to Ajax is the XMLHttpRequest object, and the best way to understand this object is through an example. Listing 32-1 shows the basic use of the XMLHttpRequest object.

Listing 32-1. Using the XMLHttpRequest Object

```
<!DOCTYPE HTML>
<html>
    <head>
        <title>Example</title>
    </head>
    <body>
        <div>
            <button>Apples</button>
            <button>Cherries</button>
            <button>Bananas</button>
        </div>
        <div id="target">
            Press a button
        </div>
        <script>
            var buttons = document.getElementsByTagName("button");
            for (var i = 0; i < buttons.length; i++) {
                buttons[i].onclick = handleButtonPress;
```

```
        }

        function handleButtonPress(e) {
            var httpRequest = new XMLHttpRequest();
            httpRequest.onreadystatechange = handleResponse;
            httpRequest.open("GET", e.target.innerHTML +  ".html");
            httpRequest.send();
        }

        function handleResponse(e) {
            if (e.target.readyState == XMLHttpRequest.DONE &&
                e.target.status == 200) {
                    document.getElementById("target").innerHTML
                        = e.target.responseText;
            }
        }
    </script>
    </body>
</html>
```

In this example, there are three button elements, each of which is labeled for a different fruit: Apples, Cherries, and Bananas. There is also a div element which, as you begin, displays a simple message telling the user to press one of the buttons. You can see the appearance of this document in Figure 32-1.

Figure 32-1. The starting state of a simple Ajax example

When one of the buttons is pressed, the script in the example loads another HTML document and sets it as the content inside of the div element. There are three other documents, and they correspond to the labels on the button elements: apples.html, cherries.html, and bananas.html. Figure 32-2 shows one of these documents being displayed in response to a button press.

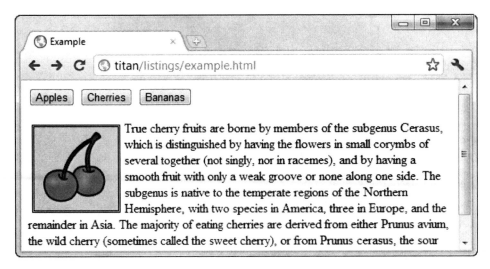

Figure 32-2. Displaying an asynchronously loaded document

The three additional documents are pretty simple—there is an image and a paragraph of text taken from the Wikipedia page for the relevant fruit. For reference, Listing 32-2 shows the contents of cherries.html, but all three documents follow the same structure (and are included in the source code download for this book, freely available at apress.com).

Listing 32-2. The Contents of cherries.html

```
<!DOCTYPE HTML>
<html>
    <head>
        <title>Cherries</title>
        <style>
            img {
                float: left; padding: 2px; margin: 5px;
                border: medium double black; background-color: lightgrey;
            }
        </style>
    </head>
    <body>
        <p>
            <img src="cherries.png" alt="cherry"/>
            True cherry fruits are borne by members of the subgenus Cerasus, which is
            distinguished by having the flowers in small corymbs of several together
            (not singly, nor in racemes), and by having a smooth fruit with only a weak
            groove or none along one side. The subgenus is native to the temperate
            regions of the Northern Hemisphere, with two species in America,
            three in Europe, and the remainder in Asia. The majority of eating cherries
            are derived from either Prunus avium, the wild cherry (sometimes called the
            sweet cherry), or from Prunus cerasus, the sour cherry.
        </p>
```

```
    </body>
</html>
```

As the user presses each fruit button, the browser goes off and retrieves the requested documents asynchronously, without reloading the main document. This is archetypal Ajax behavior.

If you turn your attention to the script, you can see how this is achieved. You start with the handleButtonPress function, which is called in response to the click event from the button controls:

```
function handleButtonPress(e) {
    var httpRequest = new XMLHttpRequest();
    httpRequest.onreadystatechange = handleResponse;
    httpRequest.open("GET", e.target.innerHTML + ".html");
    httpRequest.send();
}
```

The first step is to create a new XMLHttpRequest object. Unlike most of the objects you saw in the DOM, you don't access this kind of object through a global variable defined by the browser. Instead, you use the new keyword, like this:

```
var httpRequest = new XMLHttpRequest();
```

The next step is to set an event handler for the readystatechange event. This event is triggered several times through the request process, giving you updates about how things are going. I'll come back to this event (and the others that are defined by the XMLHttpRequest object) later in this chapter. I set the value of the onreadystatechange property to handleResponse, a function that we'll come to shortly:

```
httpRequest.onreadystatechange = handleResponse;
```

Now you can tell the XMLHttpRequest object what you want it to do. You use the open method, specifying the HTTP method (GET in this case) and the URL that should be requested:

```
httpRequest.open("GET", e.target.innerHTML + ".html");
```

■ **Tip** I showed the simplest form of the open method here. You can also provide the browser with credentials to use when making the request to the server, like this: httpRequest.open("GET", e.target.innerHTML + ".html", true, "adam", "secret"). The last two arguments are the username and password that should be sent to the server. The other argument specifies whether the request should be performed asynchronously. This should always be set to true.

I am composing the request URL based on which button the user pressed. If the Apples button is pressed, I request the URL Apples.html. The browser is smart enough to deal with relative URLs, and it uses the location of the current document as needed. In this case, my main document is loaded from the URL http://titan/listings/example.html, so Apples.html is assumed to refer to http://titan/listings/Apples.html. The URLs for your environment will be different, but the effect is the same.

■ **Tip** It is important to select the right HTTP method for your request. As I explained in Chapter 12, GET requests are for safe interactions, such that you can make the same request over and over without causing any side effects. POST requests are for *unsafe interactions*, where each request leads to some kind of change at the server and repeated requests are likely to be problematic. There are other HTTP methods, but GET and POST are the most widely used—so much so that if you want to use a different method, you must use the convention described in the "Overriding the Request HTTP Method" section of this chapter to ensure that your request passes through firewalls.

The final step in this function is to call the send method, like this:

```
httpRequest.send();
```

I am not sending any data to the server in this example, so there is no argument for the send method. I'll show you how to send data later in this chapter, but in this simple example, you are only requesting HTML documents from the server.

Dealing with the Response

As soon as the script calls the send method, the browser makes the background request to the server. Because the request is handled in the background, Ajax relies on events to notify you about how the request progresses. In this example, I handle these events with the handleResponse function:

```
function handleResponse(e) {
    if (e.target.readyState == XMLHttpRequest.DONE && e.target.status == 200) {
        document.getElementById("target").innerHTML = e.target.responseText;
    }
}
```

When the readystatechange event is triggered, the browser passes an Event object to the specified handler function. This is the same Event object that I described in Chapter 30, and the target property is set to the XMLHttpRequest that the event relates to.

A number of different stages are signaled through the readystatechange event, and you can determine which one you are dealing with by reading the value of the XMLHttpRequest.readyState property. The set of values for this property are shown in Table 32-2.

Table 32-2. Values for the XMLHttpRequest readyState Property

Value	Numeric Value	Description
UNSENT	0	The XMLHttpRequest object has been created.
OPENED	1	The open method has been called.
HEADERS_RECEIVED	2	The headers of the server response have been received.

LOADING	3	The response from the server is being received.
DONE	4	The response is complete or has failed.

The DONE status doesn't indicate that the request was successful—only that it has been completed. You get the HTTP status code through the status property, which returns a numerical value—for example, a value of 200 indicates success. Only by combining the readyState and status property values can you determine the outcome of a request.

You can see how I check for both properties in the handleResponse function. I set the content of the div element only if the readyState value is DONE and the status value is 200. I get the data that the server sent using the XMLHttpRequest.responseText property, like this:

```
document.getElementById("target").innerHTML = e.target.responseText;
```

The responseText property returns a string representing the data retrieved from the server. I use this property to set the value of the innerHTML property of the div element, so as to display the requested document's content. And with that, you have a simple Ajax example—the user clicks on a button, the browser requests a document from the server in the background and, when it arrives, you handle an event and display the requested document's content. Figure 32-3 shows the effect of this script and the different documents it displays.

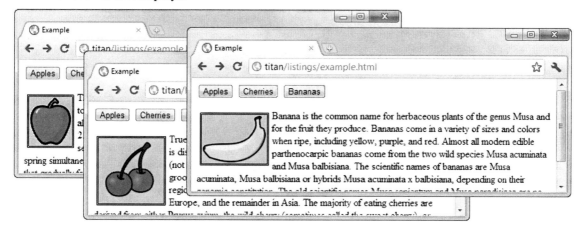

Figure 32-3. The effect of the script in the basic Ajax example

The Lowest Common Dominator: Dealing with Opera

Before we move on, we must spend a moment dealing with Opera's implementation of the XMLHttpRequest standard, which is...well, not as good or complete as the other browsers. The example shown at the start of this chapter will work perfectly well for the other mainstream browsers, but you need to make some changes to deal with a couple of problems in Opera. Listing 32-3 shows the example, which has the required changes.

Listing 32-3. Modifying the Example to Support Opera

```
<!DOCTYPE HTML>
<html>
    <head>
        <title>Example</title>
    </head>
    <body>
        <div>
            <button>Apples</button>
            <button>Cherries</button>
            <button>Bananas</button>
        </div>
        <div id="target">
            Press a button
        </div>
        <script>
            var buttons = document.getElementsByTagName("button");
            for (var i = 0; i < buttons.length; i++) {
                buttons[i].onclick = handleButtonPress;
            }

            var httpRequest;

            function handleButtonPress(e) {
                httpRequest = new XMLHttpRequest();
                httpRequest.onreadystatechange = handleResponse;
                httpRequest.open("GET", e.target.innerHTML +  ".html");
                httpRequest.send();
            }

            function handleResponse() {
                if (httpRequest.readyState == 4 && httpRequest.status == 200) {
                    document.getElementById("target").innerHTML
                        = httpRequest.responseText;
                }
            }
        </script>
    </body>
</html>
```

The first problem is that Opera doesn't dispatch an Event object when it triggers the readystatechange event. This means that you must assign the XMLHttpRequest object to a global variable in order to refer to it later. I defined a var called httpRequest, which I refer to when I create the object in the handleButtonPress function and again when I process the finished request in the handleResponse function.

This may not seem like a big deal, but if the user presses a button when a request is being processed, a new XMLHttpRequest object will be assigned to the global variable and you will lose the ability to interact with the original request.

The second problem is that Opera doesn't define the ready state constants on the XMLHttpRequest object. This means that you have to check the value of the readyState property using the numeric values I showed in Table 32-2. Instead of XMLHttpRequest.DONE, you have to check for the value 4.

I hope Opera will have upgraded and improved its XMLHttpRequest implementation by the time you read this book, but if not, you need to write your scripts to accommodate this bad behavior.

Using the Ajax Events

Now that you have built and explored a simple example, you can start to dig into the features that the XMLHttpRequest object supports and how you can use them in your requests. The place to start is with the additional events that are defined in the Level 2 specification. You saw one of these already—readystatechange, which was carried over from Level 1—but there are others as well, as described in Table 32-3.

Table 32-3. *Events Defined by the XMLHttpRequest Object*

Name	Description	Event Type
abort	Triggered when the requested is aborted	ProgressEvent
error	Triggered when the request fails	ProgressEvent
load	Triggered when the request completes successfully	ProgressEvent
loadend	Triggered when the request completes, either successfully or with an error	ProgressEvent
loadstart	Triggered when the request starts	ProgressEvent
progress	Triggered to indicate progress during the request	ProgressEvent
readystatechange	Triggered at different stages in the request life cycle	Event
timeout	Triggered if the request times out	ProgressEvent

Most of these events are triggered at a particular point in the request. The exceptions are readystatechange (which I described previously) and progress, which can be triggered several times to give progress updates.

Aside from readystatechange, the events shown in the table are defined in Level 2 of the XMLHttpRequest specification. As I write this, support for these events varies. Firefox has the most complete support, for example. Opera doesn't support them at all, and Chrome supports some of them, but not in a way that matches the specification.

▨ **Caution** The readystatechange event is the only reliable way to track request progress at this time, given the patchy implementation of the Level 2 events

---

When dispatching the events, the browser uses the regular Event object (described in Chapter 30) for the readystatechange event and the ProgressEvent object for the others. The ProgressEvent object defines all of the members of the Event object, plus the additions described in Table 32-4.

Table 32-4. Additional Properties Defined by ProgressEvent

Name	Description	Event Type
lengthComputable	Returns true if the total length of the data stream can be calculated	boolean
loaded	Returns the amount of data that has been loaded so far	number
total	Returns the total amount of data available	number

Listing 32-4 shows how these events can be used. I have shown Firefox here, which has the most complete and correct implementation.

Listing 32-4. Using the One-Off Events Defined by XMLHttpRequest

```
<!DOCTYPE HTML>
<html>
    <head>
        <title>Example</title>
        <style>
            table { margin: 10px; border-collapse: collapse; float: left}
            div {margin: 10px;}
            td, th { padding: 4px; }
        </style>
    </head>
    <body>
        <div>
            <button>Apples</button>
            <button>Cherries</button>
            <button>Bananas</button>
        </div>
        <table id="events" border="1">

        </table>
        <div id="target">
            Press a button
        </div>
        <script>
            var buttons = document.getElementsByTagName("button");
```

```
    for (var i = 0; i < buttons.length; i++) {
        buttons[i].onclick = handleButtonPress;
    }

    var httpRequest;

    function handleButtonPress(e) {
        clearEventDetails();
        httpRequest = new XMLHttpRequest();
        httpRequest.onreadystatechange = handleResponse;
        httpRequest.onerror = handleError;
        httpRequest.onload = handleLoad;
        httpRequest.onloadend = handleLoadEnd;
        httpRequest.onloadstart = handleLoadStart;
        httpRequest.onprogress = handleProgress;
        httpRequest.open("GET", e.target.innerHTML +  ".html");
        httpRequest.send();
    }

    function handleResponse(e) {
        displayEventDetails("readystate(" + httpRequest.readyState + ")");
        if (httpRequest.readyState == 4 && httpRequest.status == 200) {
                document.getElementById("target").innerHTML
                    = httpRequest.responseText;
        }
    }

    function handleError(e) { displayEventDetails("error", e);}
    function handleLoad(e) { displayEventDetails("load", e);}
    function handleLoadEnd(e) { displayEventDetails("loadend", e);}
    function handleLoadStart(e) { displayEventDetails("loadstart", e);}
    function handleProgress(e) { displayEventDetails("progress", e);}

    function clearEventDetails() {
        document.getElementById("events").innerHTML
            = "<tr><th>Event</th><th>lengthComputable</th>"
            + "<th>loaded</th><th>total</th></tr>"
    }

    function displayEventDetails(eventName, e) {
        if (e) {
            document.getElementById("events").innerHTML +=
            "<tr><td>" + eventName + "</td><td>" + e.lengthComputable
            + "</td><td>" + e.loaded + "</td><td>" + e.total
            + "</td></tr>";
        } else {
            document.getElementById("events").innerHTML +=
            "<tr><td>" + eventName
                + "</td><td>NA</td><td>NA</td><td>NA</td></tr>";
        }
    }
}
</script>
```

```
    </body>
</html>
```

This is a variation of the previous example. I registered handler functions for some of events, and I created a record of each event that I process in a `table` element. You can see how Firefox triggers the events in Figure 32-4.

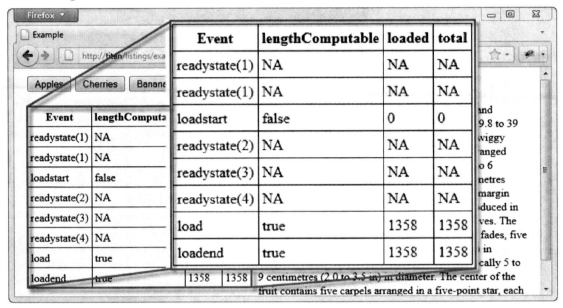

Event	lengthComputable	loaded	total
readystate(1)	NA	NA	NA
readystate(1)	NA	NA	NA
loadstart	false	0	0
readystate(2)	NA	NA	NA
readystate(3)	NA	NA	NA
readystate(4)	NA	NA	NA
load	true	1358	1358
loadend	true	1358	1358

Figure 32-4. Level 2 events as triggered by Firefox

Dealing with Errors

When working with Ajax, you have to be aware of two kinds of errors. The difference between them is driven by different perspectives.

The first kind of error is a problem from the point of view of the XMLHttpRequest object—some issue that prevents a request being made to a server, such as the hostname not resolving in the DNS, the connection request being refused, or a URL being invalid.

The second kind of error is a problem from the point of view of our application, but *not* the XMLHttpRequest object. This occurs when a request was successfully made to the server and the server accepted the request, processed it, and generated a response, but that response didn't lead to the content you were hoping for. This can arise if the URL you requested doesn't exist, for example.

There are three ways you can deal with these errors, as demonstrated by Listing 32-5.

Listing 32-5. Dealing with Ajax Errors

```
<!DOCTYPE HTML>
<html>
    <head>
        <title>Example</title>
```

```
</head>
<body>
    <div>
        <button>Apples</button>
        <button>Cherries</button>
        <button>Bananas</button>
        <button>Cucumber</button>
        <button id="badhost">Bad Host</button>
        <button id="badurl">Bad URL</button>
    </div>
    <div id="target">Press a button</div>
    <div id="errormsg"></div>
    <div id="statusmsg"></div>
    <script>
        var buttons = document.getElementsByTagName("button");
        for (var i = 0; i < buttons.length; i++) {
            buttons[i].onclick = handleButtonPress;
        }

        var httpRequest;

        function handleButtonPress(e) {
            clearMessages();
            httpRequest = new XMLHttpRequest();
            httpRequest.onreadystatechange = handleResponse;
            httpRequest.onerror = handleError;
            try {
                switch (e.target.id) {
                    case "badhost":
                        httpRequest.open("GET", "http://a.nodomain/doc.html");
                        break;
                    case "badurl":
                        httpRequest.open("GET", "http://");
                        break;
                    default:
                        httpRequest.open("GET", e.target.innerHTML + ".html");
                        break;
                }
                httpRequest.send();
            } catch (error) {
                displayErrorMsg("try/catch", error.message);
            }
        }

        function handleError(e) {
            displayErrorMsg("Error event", httpRequest.status
                            + httpRequest.statusText);
        }

        function handleResponse() {
            if (httpRequest.readyState == 4) {
                var target = document.getElementById("target");
```

```
                            if (httpRequest.status == 200) {
                                    target.innerHTML = httpRequest.responseText;
                            } else {
                                document.getElementById("statusmsg").innerHTML =
                                    "Status: " + httpRequest.status + " "
                                        + httpRequest.statusText;
                            }
                        }
                    }

                    function displayErrorMsg(src, msg) {
                        document.getElementById("errormsg").innerHTML = src + ": " + msg;
                    }

                    function clearMessages() {
                        document.getElementById("errormsg").innerHTML = "";
                        document.getElementById("statusmsg").innerHTML = "";
                    }

                </script>
            </body>
        </html>
```

Dealing with Setup Errors

The first kind of error you need to deal with occurs when you pass bad data to the XMLHttpRequest object, such as a malformed URL. This is surprisingly easy to do when generating the URL based on user input. To simulate this kind of problem, I added a button labeled Bad URL to the example document. Pressing this button leads to the following call to the open method:

```
httpRequest.open("GET", "http://");
```

I have lost count of the number of times that I have seen this problem (and, sadly, the number of times I have caused it). Typically, the user is prompted to enter a value into an input element, the contents of which are used to generate a URL for an Ajax request. When the user triggers the request without entering a value, the open method is passed a partial URL or, as in this case, just the protocol part.

This is an error that prevents the request from being performed, and the XMLHttpRequest object will throw an error when this sort of thing happens. This means you need to use a try...catch statement around the code that sets up the request, like this:

```
try {
    ...
    httpRequest.open("GET", "http://");
    ...
    httpRequest.send();
} catch (error) {
    displayErrorMsg("try/catch", error.message);
}
```

The catch clause is your opportunity to recover from the error. You might choose to prompt the user to enter a value, fall back to a default URL, or simply abandon the request. For this example, I simply display the error message by calling the `displayErrorMsg` function. This function is defined in the example script and displays the `Error.message` property in the `div` element with the ID of `errormsg`.

Dealing with Request Errors

The second kind of error arises when the request is made but something goes wrong with it. To simulate this kind of problem, I added a button labeled `Bad Host` to the example. When this button is pressed, the open method is called with a URL that cannot be used:

```
httpRequest.open("GET", "http://a.nodomain/doc.html");
```

There are two problems with this URL. The first is that the hostname won't resolve in the DNS, so the browser won't be able to make the connection to a server. This problem won't be apparent to the `XMLHttpRequest` object until after it starts to make the request, so it signals the problem in two ways. If you have registered a listener for the `error` event, the browser will dispatch an `Event` object to your listener function. Here is my function from the example:

```
function handleError(e) {
    displayErrorMsg("Error event", httpRequest.status + httpRequest.statusText);
}
```

The degree of information you get from the `XMLHttpRequest` object when this kind of error occurs can vary between browsers and, sadly, you most often get a `status` of 0 and an empty `statusText` value.

The second problem is that the URL has a different origin from the script that is making the request—and this isn't allowed by default. Usually, you are allowed to make Ajax requests only to the URLs with the same origin that the script was loaded from. The browser can report this problem by throwing an `Error` or by triggering an `error` event—it differs between browsers. Different browsers check the origin at different times, which means that you don't always see the same problem highlighted by the browser. (You can use the Cross Site Resource Specification, or CORS, to overcome the same-origin limitation. See the "Making Cross-Origin Ajax Requests" section later in this chapter).

Dealing with Application Errors

The final kind of error arises when the request succeeds from the point of view of the `XMLHttpRequest` object, but it doesn't give you the data you were hoping for. To create this kind of problem, I added a button labeled `Cucumber` to the example document. Pressing this button causes the requested URL to be generated as for the `Apples`, `Cherries`, and `Bananas` buttons, except that there is no `cucumber.html` document on the server.

When this happens there is no error as such (because the request itself succeeds), and you determine what happened from the `status` property. When you request a document that doesn't exist, you get a status code of 404, meaning that the server cannot find the requested document. You can see how I handle any code that is not 200 (meaning `OK`):

```
if (httpRequest.status == 200) {
    target.innerHTML = httpRequest.responseText;
} else {
    document.getElementById("statusmsg").innerHTML =
        "Status: " + httpRequest.status + " " + httpRequest.statusText;
}
```

For this example, I simply display the status and statusText values. In a real application, you would need to recover in a useful and meaningful way—perhaps by displaying some fallback content or alerting the user to the problem, depending on what makes sense for the application.

Getting and Setting Headers

The XMLHttpRequest object lets you set headers for the request to the server and read the headers from the server's response. Table 32-5 describes the header-related methods.

Table 32-5. Header-Related Methods of the XMLHttpRequest Object

Method	Description	Returns
setRequestHeader(<header>, <value>)	Sets the header to the specified value	void
getResponseHeader(<header>)	Gets the value of the specified header	string
getAllResponseHeaders()	Gets all of the headers in a single string	string

Overriding the Request HTTP Method

You don't often need to add to or change the headers in Ajax requests. The browser knows what it needs to send, and the server knows how to respond. But there are a couple of exceptions. The first is the X-HTTP-Method-Override header.

The HTTP standard, which is typically used to request and transport HTML documents over the Internet, defines a number of *methods*. Most people know about GET and POST because they are by far the most widely used. But there are others, including PUT and DELETE, and there is a growing trend to use these HTTP methods to give meaning to the URLs that are requested from a server. So, as a simple example, if you wanted to view, say, a user record, you would make a request like this:

```
httpRequest.open("GET", "http://myserver/records/freeman/adam");
```

I am just showing the HTTP method and the request URL here. For this request to work, there would have to be a server-side application that knows how to understand this request and turn it into a suitable piece of data to send back to the server. If you wanted to delete the data, you might do the following:

```
httpRequest.open("DELETE", "http://myserver/records/freeman/adam");
```

The key here is to express what you want the server to do through the HTTP method, rather than by encoding it in the URL in some way. This is part of a trend called *RESTful APIs*. The rest of what makes up a RESTful API is a topic of frequent and vociferous debate, which I am not going to get into here.

The *problem* with using the HTTP method in this way is that a lot of mainstream web technologies support only GET and POST and many firewalls allow only GET and POST requests to pass through. There is a convention to avoid this restriction, which is to use the X-HTTP-Method-Override header to specify the HTTP method you want to use, while actually sending a POST request. Listing 32-6 gives a demonstration.

Listing 32-6. Setting a Request Header

```
<!DOCTYPE HTML>
<html>
    <head>
        <title>Example</title>
    </head>
    <body>
        <div>
            <button>Apples</button>
            <button>Cherries</button>
            <button>Bananas</button>
        </div>
        <div id="target">Press a button</div>
        <script>
            var buttons = document.getElementsByTagName("button");
            for (var i = 0; i < buttons.length; i++) {
                buttons[i].onclick = handleButtonPress;
            }

            var httpRequest;

            function handleButtonPress(e) {
                httpRequest = new XMLHttpRequest();
                httpRequest.onreadystatechange = handleResponse;
                httpRequest.open("GET", e.target.innerHTML + ".html");
                httpRequest.setRequestHeader("X-HTTP-Method-Override", "DELETE");
                httpRequest.send();
            }

            function handleError(e) {
                displayErrorMsg("Error event", httpRequest.status
                                + httpRequest.statusText);
            }

            function handleResponse() {
                if (httpRequest.readyState == 4 && httpRequest.status == 200) {
                    document.getElementById("target").innerHTML
                        = httpRequest.responseText;
                }
            }

        </script>
    </body>
</html>
```

In this example, I used the setRequestHeader method on the XMLHttpRequest object to indicate that I want this request to be processed as though I had used the HTTP DELETE method. Notice that I set the header *after* calling the open method. The XMLHttpRequest object will throw an error if you try to use the setRequestHeader method before the open method.

▓ **Tip** Overriding the HTTP method works only if the server-side web application framework understands the X-HTTP-Method-Override convention and your server-side application is set up to look for and understand the less-used HTTP methods.

Disabling Content Caching

The second header that can be useful to add to an Ajax request is Cache-Control, especially when writing and debugging scripts. Some browsers will cache the content that is obtained via an Ajax request and not request it again during the browsing session. In the context of the example I have been using in this chapter, this means that any changes to apples.html, cherries.html, and bananas.html would not immediately be reflected in the browser. Listing 32-7 shows how you can set the header to avoid this.

Listing 32-7. Disabling Content Caching

```
...
function handleButtonPress(e) {
    httpRequest = new XMLHttpRequest();
    httpRequest.onreadystatechange = handleResponse;
    httpRequest.open("GET", e.target.innerHTML + ".html");
    httpRequest.setRequestHeader("Cache-Control", "no-cache");
    httpRequest.send();
}
...
```

You set the header value in the same way as for the previous example, but the header you are interested in is Cache-Control and the value you want is no-cache. With this statement in place, changes to the content you request through Ajax are shown when the documents are next requested.

Reading Response Headers

You can read the HTTP headers that the server sends in the response to an Ajax request through the getResponseHeader and getAllResponseHeaders methods. For the most part, you don't care what the headers say because they are part of the transaction between the browser and server. Listing 32-8 shows how you can use these properties.

Listing 32-8. Reading Response Headers

```
<!DOCTYPE HTML>
<html>
    <head>
        <title>Example</title>
        <style>
            #allheaders, #ctheader {
                border: medium solid black;
                padding: 2px; margin: 2px;

            }
```

```
            </style>
        </head>
        <body>
            <div>
                <button>Apples</button>
                <button>Cherries</button>
                <button>Bananas</button>
            </div>
            <div id="ctheader"></div>
            <div id="allheaders"></div>
            <div id="target">Press a button</div>
            <script>
                var buttons = document.getElementsByTagName("button");
                for (var i = 0; i < buttons.length; i++) {
                    buttons[i].onclick = handleButtonPress;
                }

                var httpRequest;

                function handleButtonPress(e) {
                    httpRequest = new XMLHttpRequest();
                    httpRequest.onreadystatechange = handleResponse;
                    httpRequest.open("GET", e.target.innerHTML + ".html");
                    httpRequest.send();
                }

                function handleResponse() {
                    if (httpRequest.readyState == 2) {
                        document.getElementById("allheaders").innerHTML =
                            httpRequest.getAllResponseHeaders();
                        document.getElementById("ctheader").innerHTML =
                            httpRequest.getResponseHeader("Content-Type");

                    } else if (httpRequest.readyState == 4 && httpRequest.status == 200) {
                        document.getElementById("target").innerHTML
                            = httpRequest.responseText;
                    }
                }

            </script>
        </body>
    </html>
```

The response headers are available when the readyState changes to HEADERS_RECEIVED (which has the numerical value of 2). The headers are the first thing that the server sends back in a response, which is why you can read them before the content itself is available. In this example, I set the contents of two div elements to the value of one header (Content-Type) and all of the headers, obtained with the getResponseHeader and getAllResponseHeader methods. You can see the result in Figure 32-5.

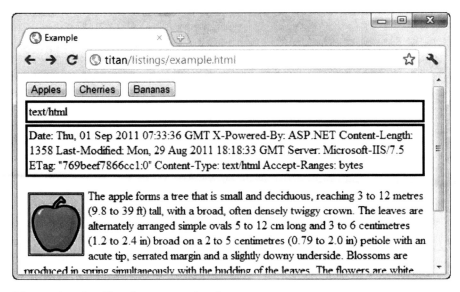

Figure 32-5. Reading the response headers

From this, you can tell that titan, my development server, is running version 7.5 of the IIS web server (which is what you would expect from a Windows Server 2008 R2 server owned by someone who does a lot of .NET development) and that I last modified the apples.html document on August 29 (but took the screenshot on September 1).

Making Cross-Origin Ajax Requests

By default, browsers limit scripts to making Ajax requests within the origin of the document that contains them. As you will recall, an origin is the combination of the protocol, hostname, and port of a URL. This means that when I load a document from http://titan, a script contained within the document cannot usually make a request to http://titan:8080 because the port in the second URL is different and, therefore, outside of the document origin. An Ajax request from one origin to another is called a *cross-origin request.*

■ **Tip** This policy is intended to reduce the risks of a *cross-site scripting* (CSS) attack, where the browser (or user) is tricked into executing a malicious script. CSS attacks are outside the scope of this book, but there is a nice Wikipedia article at http://en.wikipedia.org/wiki/Cross-site_scripting that provides a good introduction to the topic.

The problem with this policy is that it is a blanket ban—no cross-origin requests. This has led to the use of some very ugly tricks to trick the browser into making requests that contravene the policy.

Fortunately, there is now a legitimate means of making cross-origin requests, defined in the *Cross-Origin Resource Sharing* (CORS) specification.

■ **Note** This is an advanced topic that requires some basic knowledge about HTTP headers. Since this is a book about HTML5, I am not going to go into any real detail about HTTP. My suggestion is that if you are unfamiliar with HTTP, you should skip over this section.

To set the scene, let us look at the problem we are trying to fix. Listing 32-9 shows an HTML document that contains a script that wants to make a cross-origin request.

Listing 32-9. A Script That Wants to Make a Cross-Origin Request

```
<!DOCTYPE HTML>
<html>
    <head>
        <title>Example</title>
    </head>
    <body>
        <div>
            <button>Apples</button>
            <button>Cherries</button>
            <button>Bananas</button>
        </div>
        <div id="target">Press a button</div>
        <script>
            var buttons = document.getElementsByTagName("button");
            for (var i = 0; i < buttons.length; i++) {
                buttons[i].onclick = handleButtonPress;
            }

            var httpRequest;

            function handleButtonPress(e) {
                httpRequest = new XMLHttpRequest();
                httpRequest.onreadystatechange = handleResponse;
                httpRequest.open("GET", "http://titan:8080/" + e.target.innerHTML);
                httpRequest.send();
            }

            function handleResponse() {
                if (httpRequest.readyState == 4 && httpRequest.status == 200) {
                    document.getElementById("target").innerHTML
                        = httpRequest.responseText;
                }
            }
        </script>
    </body>
```

```
</html>
```

The script in this example appends the contents of the button that the user has pressed, appends it to http://titan:8080, and tries to make an Ajax request (for example, http://titan:8080/Apples). I will be loading this document from http://titan/listings/example.html, which means that the script is trying to make a cross-origin request.

The server that the script is trying to reach is running under Node.js. Listing 32-10 shows the code, which I saved in a file called fruitselector.js. (See Chapter 2 for details of obtaining Node.js.)

Listing 32-10. The fruitselector.js Node.js Script

```
var http = require('http');

http.createServer(function (req, res) {
    console.log("[200] " + req.method + " to " + req.url);

    res.writeHead(200, "OK", {"Content-Type": "text/html"});
    res.write('<html><head><title>Fruit Total</title></head><body>');
    res.write('<p>');
    res.write('You selected ' + req.url.substring(1));
    res.write('</p></body></html>');
    res.end();

}).listen(8080);
```

This is a very simple server—it generates a short HTML document based on the URL that the client has requested. If the client requests http://titan:8080/Apples, for example, the following HTML document will be generated and returned by the server:

```
<html>
    <head>
        <title>Fruit Total</title>
    </head>
    <body>
        <p>You selected Apples</p>
    </body>
</html>
```

As it stands, the script in example.html won't be able to get the data it wants from the server. The way you fix this is to add a header to the response that the server sends back to the browser, as shown in Listing 32-11.

Listing 32-11. Adding the Cross-Origin Header

```
var http = require('http');

http.createServer(function (req, res) {
    console.log("[200] " + req.method + " to " + req.url);

    res.writeHead(200, "OK", {
                    "Content-Type": "text/html",
                    "Access-Control-Allow-Origin": "http://titan"
                    });
```

```
    res.write('<html><head><title>Fruit Total</title></head><body>');
    res.write('<p>');

    res.write('You selected ' + req.url.substring(1));
    res.write('</p></body></html>');
    res.end();

}).listen(8080);
```

The `Access-Control-Allow-Origin` header specifies an origin that should be allowed to make cross-origin requests to this document. If the origin specified by the header matches the origin of the current document, the browser will load and process the data contained in the response.

■ **Tip** Supporting CORS means that the browser has to apply the cross-origin security policy after it has contacted the server and has obtained the response header, meaning that the request is made even if the response is discarded because the required header is missing or specified a different domain. This is a very different approach from browsers that don't implement CORS and that simply block the request, never contacting the server.

With the addition of this header to the response from the server, the script in the `example.html` document is able to request and receive the data from the server, as demonstrated by Figure 32-6.

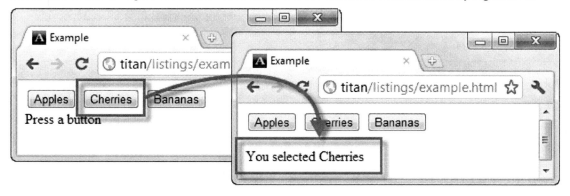

Figure 32-6. Enabling cross-origin Ajax requests

Using the Origin Request Header

As part of CORS, the browser will add an `Origin` header to the request that specifies the origin of the current document. You can use this to be more flexible about how you set the value of the `Access-Control-Allow-Origin` header, as shown in Listing 32-12.

Listing 32-12. Using the Origin Request Header

```
var http = require('http');

http.createServer(function (req, res) {
    console.log("[200] " + req.method + " to " + req.url);

    res.statusCode = 200;
    res.setHeader("Content-Type", "text/html");

    var origin = req.headers["origin"];
    if (origin.indexOf("titan") > -1) {
        res.setHeader("Access-Control-Allow-Origin", origin);
    }

    res.write('<html><head><title>Fruit Total</title></head><body>');
    res.write('<p>');

    res.write('You selected ' + req.url.substring(1));
    res.write('</p></body></html>');
    res.end();

}).listen(8080);
```

I modified the server script to set the Access-Control-Allow-Origin response header only when the request includes an Origin header whose value contains titan. This is a very slack way of checking the source of the request, but you can tailor this approach to be more rigorous within the context of your own projects.

■ **Tip** You can also set the Access-Control-Allow-Origin header to an asterisk (*), which means that cross-origin requests from *any* origin will be permitted. You should think carefully about the security implications before using this setting.

Advanced CORS Features

The CORS specification defines a number of additional headers that can be used to enforce fine-grained control over cross-origin requests, including limiting requests to specific HTTP methods. These advanced features require a *preflight request*, where the browser makes a request to the server to determine what the constraints are and then a second request to obtain the data itself. As I write this, these advanced features are not reliably implemented.

Aborting Requests

The XMLHttpRequest object defines a method that allows you to abort a request, as described in Table 32-6.

Table 32-6. XMLHttpRequest abort Method

Member	Description	Returns
abort()	Terminates the current request	void

To demonstrate this feature, I modified the `fruitselector.js` Node.js script to introduce a 10-second delay, as shown in Listing 32-13.

Listing 32-13. Introducing a Delay at the Server

```
var http = require('http');

http.createServer(function (req, res) {
    console.log("[200] " + req.method + " to " + req.url);

    res.statusCode = 200;
    res.setHeader("Content-Type", "text/html");

    setTimeout(function() {
        var origin = req.headers["origin"];
        if (origin.indexOf("titan") > -1) {
            res.setHeader("Access-Control-Allow-Origin", origin);
        }

        res.write('<html><head><title>Fruit Total</title></head><body>');
        res.write('<p>');
        res.write('You selected ' + req.url.substring(1));
        res.write('</p></body></html>');
        res.end();
    }, 10000);

}).listen(8080);
```

When the server receives a request, it writes the initial response headers, pauses for 10 seconds, and then completes the response. Listing 32-14 shows how you can use the aborting features of the XMLHttpRequest at the browser.

Listing 32-14. Aborting Requests

```
<!DOCTYPE HTML>
<html>
    <head>
        <title>Example</title>
    </head>
    <body>
        <div>
            <button>Apples</button>
            <button>Cherries</button>
            <button>Bananas</button>
        </div>
```

```
    <div>
        <button id="abortbutton">Abort</button>
    </div>
    <div id="target">Press a button</div>
    <script>
        var buttons = document.getElementsByTagName("button");
        for (var i = 0; i < buttons.length; i++) {
            buttons[i].onclick = handleButtonPress;
        }
        var httpRequest;

        function handleButtonPress(e) {
            if (e.target.id == "abortbutton") {
                httpRequest.abort();
            } else {
                httpRequest = new XMLHttpRequest();
                httpRequest.onreadystatechange = handleResponse;
                httpRequest.onabort = handleAbort;
                httpRequest.open("GET", "http://titan:8080/" + e.target.innerHTML);
                httpRequest.send();
                document.getElementById("target").innerHTML = "Request Started";
            }
        }

        function handleResponse() {
            if (httpRequest.readyState == 4 && httpRequest.status == 200) {
                document.getElementById("target").innerHTML
                    = httpRequest.responseText;
            }
        }

        function handleAbort() {
            document.getElementById("target").innerHTML = "Request Aborted";
        }
    </script>
</body>
</html>
```

I added an Abort button to the document, which calls the abort method on the XMLHttpRequest object to abort an inflight request. We have plenty of time to do this now that I have introduced a delay at the server.

The XMLHttpRequest signals an abort through the abort event and the readystatechange event. In this example, I respond to the abort event and update the contents of the div element with an id of target to indicate that the request has been aborted. You can see the effect in Figure 32-7.

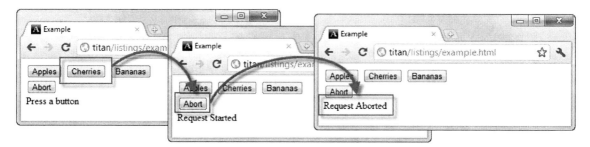

Figure 32-7. Aborting a request

Summary

In this chapter, I introduced you to Ajax through the XMLHttpRequest object. Ajax allows you to make background requests and create a smoother experience for users. I explained how the XMLHttpRequest object signals progress of a request through a series of events, how you can detect and deal with different kinds of errors, and how you can set request headers to give direction to either the browser or the server as to the kind of operation you require. As a more advanced topic, I introduced the Cross Origin Request Specification (CORS) – a set of response headers which allows a script to make an Ajax request to another origin. This is a useful technique – as long as you have the ability to add headers to the response from the server.

All of the examples in this chapter have been about retrieving data from the server. In the next chapter, I'll show you how to send data as well.

CHAPTER 33

Using Ajax—Part II

In this chapter, I will continue describing how Ajax works, showing you how to send data to the client. Sending forms and files are two common uses for Ajax, which allow web applications to create a richer experience for the user. I'll also show you how to monitor progress as you send data to the server and how to deal with different response formats sent back by the server in response to an Ajax request. Table 33-1 provides the summary for this chapter. The first three listings set up the server and HTML document used in the other examples.

Table 33-1. Chapter Summary

Problem	Solution	Listing
Send form data to the server	Use the DOM to get individual values and concatenate them in the URL-encoded format	4
Encode and send form data without using the DOM	Use a FormData object	5
Send additional form values or send form data selectively	Use the append method on the FormData object	6
Send JSON data	Use the JSON.stringify method and set the content type for the request to application/json	7
Send a file to the server	Add an input element to a form whose type is file and use a FormData object	8
Track progress as data is uploaded to the server	Use the XMLHttpRequestUpload object	9
Receive HTML fragments from the server	Read the responseText property	10, 11
Override the MIME type sent by the server	Use the overrideMimeType method	12

Receive XML from the server	Use the responseXML property	13, 14
Receive JSON data from the server	Use the JSON.parse method	15, 16

Getting Ready to Send Data to the Server

One of the most common uses of Ajax is to send data to the server. Most typically, clients send form data—the values entered into input elements contained by a form element. Listing 33-1 shows a simple form, which will be the basis for this part of the chapter. I saved this HTML into a file named example.html.

Listing 33-1. A Basic Form

```
<!DOCTYPE HTML>
<html>
    <head>
        <title>Example</title>
        <style>
            .table {display:table;}
            .row {display:table-row;}
            .cell {display: table-cell; padding: 5px;}
            .label {text-align: right;}
        </style>
    </head>
    <body>
        <form id="fruitform" method="post" action="http://titan:8080/form">
            <div class="table">
                <div class="row">
                    <div class="cell label">Bananas:</div>
                    <div class="cell"><input name="bananas" value="2"/></div>
                </div>
                <div class="row">
                    <div class="cell label">Apples:</div>
                    <div class="cell"><input name="apples" value="5"/></div>
                </div>
                <div class="row">
                    <div class="cell label">Cherries:</div>
                    <div class="cell"><input name="cherries" value="20"/></div>
                </div>
                <div class="row">
                    <div class="cell label">Total:</div>
                    <div id="results" class="cell">0 items</div>
                </div>
            </div>
            <button id="submit" type="submit">Submit Form</button>
        </form>
    </body>
</html>
```

The form in this example contains three input elements and a submit button. The input elements allow the user to specify how many of three different kinds of fruit to order, and the button submits the form to the server. For more information about these elements, see Chapters 12, 13, and 14.

Defining the Server

For the examples, you need to create the server that will process requests. Once again, I used Node.js, largely because it is simple and it uses JavaScript. See Chapter 2 for details on obtaining Node.js. I won't go into how this script works, but since it is written in JavaScript, you should be able to get a fair idea of what's going on. That said, understanding the server script isn't essential to understanding Ajax, and you can readily treat the server as a black box if you like. Listing 33-2 shows the fruitcalc.js script.

Listing 33-2. The fruitcalc.js Script for Node.js

```
var http = require('http');
var querystring = require('querystring');
var multipart = require('multipart');

function writeResponse(res, data) {
    var total = 0;
    for (fruit in data) {
        total += Number(data[fruit]);
    }
    res.writeHead(200, "OK", {
        "Content-Type": "text/html",
        "Access-Control-Allow-Origin": "http://titan"});
    res.write('<html><head><title>Fruit Total</title></head><body>');
    res.write('<p>' + total + ' items ordered</p></body></html>');
    res.end();
}

http.createServer(function (req, res) {
    console.log("[200] " + req.method + " to " + req.url);
    if (req.method == 'OPTIONS') {
        res.writeHead(200, "OK", {
            "Access-Control-Allow-Headers": "Content-Type",
            "Access-Control-Allow-Methods": "*",
            "Access-Control-Allow-Origin": "*"
            });
        res.end();
    } else if (req.url == '/form' && req.method == 'POST') {
        var dataObj = new Object();
        var contentType = req.headers["content-type"];
        var fullBody = '';

        if (contentType) {
            if (contentType.indexOf("application/x-www-form-urlencoded") > -1) {

                req.on('data', function(chunk) { fullBody += chunk.toString();});
                req.on('end', function() {
```

```
                        var dBody = querystring.parse(fullBody);
                        dataObj.bananas = dBody["bananas"];
                        dataObj.apples = dBody["apples"];
                        dataObj.cherries= dBody["cherries"];
                        writeResponse(res, dataObj);
                    });

            } else if (contentType.indexOf("application/json") > -1) {
                    req.on('data', function(chunk) { fullBody += chunk.toString();});
                    req.on('end', function() {
                        dataObj = JSON.parse(fullBody);
                        writeResponse(res, dataObj);
                    });

            } else if (contentType.indexOf("multipart/form-data") > -1) {
                    var partName;
                    var partType;
                    var parser = new multipart.parser();
                    parser.boundary = "--" + req.headers["content-type"].substring(30);

                    parser.onpartbegin = function(part) {
                        partName = part.name; partType = part.contentType};
                    parser.ondata = function(data) {
                        if (partName != "file") {
                            dataObj[partName] = data;
                        }
                    };
                    req.on('data', function(chunk) { parser.write(chunk);});
                    req.on('end', function() { writeResponse(res, dataObj);});
            }
        }
    }
}).listen(8080);
```

I have highlighted the section of the script that requires attention: the writeResponse function. This function is called after the form values have been extracted from the request, and it is responsible for generating the response to the browser. At the moment, this function produces a simple HTML document such as the one shown in Listing 33-3, but we will change and enhance this function as we deal with different formats later in the chapter.

Listing 33-3. The Simple HTML Document Generated by the writeResponse Function

```
<html>
    <head>
        <title>Fruit Total</title>
    </head>
    <body>
        <p>27 items ordered</p>
    </body>
</html>
```

This is a simple response, but it's a good place to start. The effect is that the server totals the number of fruit that the user has ordered through the input elements in the form. The rest of the server-side script is responsible for decoding the various data formats that the client may be sending using Ajax. You can start the server like this:

```
bin\node.exe fruitcalc.js
```

This script is intended for use only in this chapter. It isn't a general-purpose server, and I don't recommend you use any part of it for a production service. Many assumptions and shortcuts are tied to the examples that follow in this chapter, and the script is not suitable for any kind of serious use.

Understanding the Problem

The problem I want to use Ajax to solve is illustrated neatly in Figure 33-1.

Figure 33-1. Submitting a simple form

When you submit a form, the browser displays the result as a new page. This has two implications:

- The user must wait for the server to process the data and generate the response.
- Any document context is lost, as the results are displayed as a new document.

This is an ideal situation in which to apply Ajax. You can make the request asynchronously, so the user can continue to interact with the document while the form is processed.

Sending Form Data

The most basic way to send data to a server is to collect and format it yourself. Listing 33-4 shows the addition of a script to the example.html document that uses this approach.

Listing 33-4. Manually Collecting and Sending Data

```
<!DOCTYPE HTML>
<html>
    <head>
        <title>Example</title>
        <style>
            .table {display:table;}
            .row {display:table-row;}
            .cell {display: table-cell; padding: 5px;}
            .label {text-align: right;}
        </style>
    </head>
    <body>
        <form id="fruitform" method="post" action="http://titan:8080/form">
            <div class="table">
                <div class="row">
                    <div class="cell label">Bananas:</div>
                    <div class="cell"><input name="bananas" value="2"/></div>
                </div>
                <div class="row">
                    <div class="cell label">Apples:</div>
                    <div class="cell"><input name="apples" value="5"/></div>
                </div>
                <div class="row">
                    <div class="cell label">Cherries:</div>
                    <div class="cell"><input name="cherries" value="20"/></div>
                </div>
                <div class="row">
                    <div class="cell label">Total:</div>
                    <div id="results" class="cell">0 items</div>
                </div>
            </div>
            <button id="submit" type="submit">Submit Form</button>
        </form>
        <script>
            document.getElementById("submit").onclick = handleButtonPress;

            var httpRequest;

            function handleButtonPress(e) {
                e.preventDefault();

                var form = document.getElementById("fruitform");

                var formData = "";
                var inputElements = document.getElementsByTagName("input");
                for (var i = 0; i < inputElements.length; i++) {
                    formData += inputElements[i].name + "="
                        + inputElements[i].value + "&";
```

```
                }

                httpRequest = new XMLHttpRequest();
                httpRequest.onreadystatechange = handleResponse;
                httpRequest.open("POST", form.action);
                httpRequest.setRequestHeader('Content-Type',
                                        'application/x-www-form-urlencoded');
                httpRequest.send(formData);
            }

            function handleResponse() {
                if (httpRequest.readyState == 4 && httpRequest.status == 200) {
                    document.getElementById("results").innerHTML
                        = httpRequest.responseText;
                }
            }
        </script>
    </body>
</html>
```

This script looks more complicated than it is. To explain, I'll break down the individual steps. All of the action happens in the handleButtonPress function, which is called in response to the click event of the button element.

The first thing I do is call the preventDefault method on the Event object that the browser has dispatched to the function. I described this method in Chapter 30, when I explained that some events have default actions associated with them. For a button element in a form, the default action is to post the form using the regular, non-Ajax approach. I don't want this to happen—hence the call to the preventDefault method.

▓ **Tip** I like to place the call to the preventDefault method at the start of my event handler function because it makes debugging easier. If I called this method at the end of the function, any uncaught error in the script would cause execution to terminate and the default action to be performed. This happens so quickly that it can be impossible to read the details of the error from the browser script console.

The next step is to gather and format the values of the input elements, like this:

```
var formData = "";
var inputElements = document.getElementsByTagName("input");
for (var i = 0; i < inputElements.length; i++) {
    formData += inputElements[i].name + "=" + inputElements[i].value + "&";
}
```

I use the DOM to obtain the set of input elements and create a string that contains the name and value attributes of each. The name and value are separated by an equal sign (=), and information about each input element is separated by an ampersand (&). The result looks like this:

```
bananas=2&apples=5&cherries=20&
```

If you look back to Chapter 12, you will see that this is the default way of encoding form data—the application/x-www-form-urlencoded encoding. Even though this is default encoding used by the form element, it isn't the default encoding used by Ajax, so I need to add a header to tell the server which data format to expect, like this:

```
httpRequest.setRequestHeader('Content-Type','application/x-www-form-urlencoded');
```

The rest of the script is a regular Ajax request, just like the ones in the previous chapter, with a couple of exceptions.

First, I use the HTTP POST method when I call the open method on the XMLHttpRequest object. As a rule, data is always sent to the server using the POST method rather than the GET method. For the URL to make the request to, I read the action property of the HTMLFormElement:

```
httpRequest.open("POST", form.action);
```

The form action will cause a cross-origin request, which I deal with at the server using the CORS technique described in the previous chapter.

The second point of note is that I pass the string I want to send to the server as an argument to the send method, like this:

```
httpRequest.send(formData);
```

When I get the response back from the server, I use the DOM to set the contents of the div element with the id of results. You can see the effect in Figure 33-2.

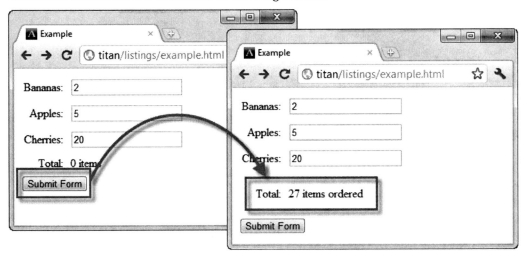

Figure 33-2. Using Ajax to post a form

The HTML document that the server returns in response to the form post is displayed on the same page, and the request is performed asynchronously. This is a much nicer effect than we started with.

Sending Form Data Using a FormData Object

A neater way of gathering form data is to use a FormData object, which is defined as part of the XMLHttpRequest Level 2 specification.

■ **Note** As I write this, Chrome, Safari, and Firefox support the FormData object, but Opera and Internet Explorer do not.

Creating a FormData Object

When you create a FormData object, you can pass an HTMLFormElement object (described in Chapter 31), and the value of all of the elements in the form will be gathered up automatically. Listing 33-5 gives an example. The listing shows only the script because the HTML remains the same.

Listing 33-5. Using a FormData Object

```
...
<script>
    document.getElementById("submit").onclick = handleButtonPress;

    var httpRequest;

    function handleButtonPress(e) {
        e.preventDefault();

        var form = document.getElementById("fruitform");

        var formData = new FormData(form);

        httpRequest = new XMLHttpRequest();
        httpRequest.onreadystatechange = handleResponse;
        httpRequest.open("POST", form.action);
        httpRequest.send(formData);
    }

    function handleResponse() {
        if (httpRequest.readyState == 4 && httpRequest.status == 200) {
            document.getElementById("results").innerHTML
                = httpRequest.responseText;
        }
    }
}
</script>
...
```

Of course, the key change is the use of the FormData object:

```
var formData = new FormData(form);
```

The other change to be aware of is that I no longer set the value of the Content-Type header. When using the FormData object, the data is always encoded as multipart/form-data (as described in Chapter 12).

Modifying a FormData Object

The FormData object defines a method that lets you add name/value pairs to the data that will be sent to the server. The method is described in Table 33-2.

Table 33-2. Header-Related Method of the XMLHttpRequest Object

Method	Description	Returns
append(<name>, <value>)	Appends a name and value to the data set	void

You can use the append method to supplement the data that is gathered from the form, but you can also create FormData objects without using an HTMLFormElement. This means that you can use the append method to be selective about which data values are sent to the client. Listing 33-6 provides a demonstration. Once again, I show only the script element, since the other HTML elements are unchanged.

Listing 33-6. Selectively Sending Data to the Server Using the FormData Object

```
...
<script>
    document.getElementById("submit").onclick = handleButtonPress;

    var httpRequest;

    function handleButtonPress(e) {
        e.preventDefault();

        var form = document.getElementById("fruitform");

        var formData = new FormData();
        var inputElements = document.getElementsByTagName("input");
        for (var i = 0; i < inputElements.length; i++) {
            if (inputElements[i].name != "cherries") {
                formData.append(inputElements[i].name, inputElements[i].value);
            }
        }

        httpRequest = new XMLHttpRequest();
        httpRequest.onreadystatechange = handleResponse;
        httpRequest.open("POST", form.action);
        httpRequest.send(formData);
    }

    function handleResponse() {
```

```
        if (httpRequest.readyState == 4 && httpRequest.status == 200) {
            document.getElementById("results").innerHTML
                = httpRequest.responseText;
        }
    }
</script>
...
```

In this script, I create a `FormData` object without providing an `HTMLFormElement` object. I then use the DOM to find all of the `input` elements in the document and add name/value pairs for all of those whose name attribute doesn't have a value of `cherries`. You can see the effect in Figure 33-3, where the total value returned by the server excludes the value supplied by the user for cherries.

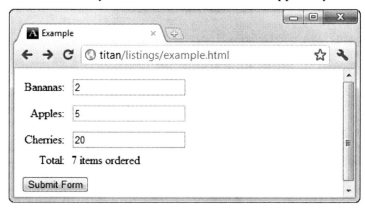

Figure 33-3. Selectively sending data using a FormData object

Sending JSON Data

You are not limited to sending just form data with Ajax. You can send pretty much anything, including JavaScript Object Notation (JSON) data, which has emerged as a popular data format. The roots of Ajax are in XML, but that is a verbose format. When you are running a web application that must transmit a high number of XML documents, verbosity translates into real costs in terms of bandwidth and system capacity.

JSON is often referred to as the fat-free alternative to XML. JSON is easy to read and write, is more compact than XML, and has gained incredibly wide support. JSON has grown beyond its roots in JavaScript, and a huge number of packages and systems understand and use the format.

Here is how a simple JavaScript object looks when represented using JSON:

```
{"bananas":"2","apples":"5","cherries":"20"}
```

This object has three properties: `bananas`, `apples`, and `cherries`. The values for these properties are 2, 5, and 20, respectively.

JSON doesn't have all of the functional richness of XML, but for many applications, those features aren't used. JSON is simple, lightweight, and expressive. Listing 33-7 demonstrates how easily you can send JSON data to the server.

Listing 33-7. Sending JSON Data to the Server

```
...
<script>
    document.getElementById("submit").onclick = handleButtonPress;

    var httpRequest;

    function handleButtonPress(e) {
        e.preventDefault();

        var form = document.getElementById("fruitform");

        var formData = new Object();
        var inputElements = document.getElementsByTagName("input");
        for (var i = 0; i < inputElements.length; i++) {
            formData[inputElements[i].name] =  inputElements[i].value;
        }

        httpRequest = new XMLHttpRequest();
        httpRequest.onreadystatechange = handleResponse;
        httpRequest.open("POST", form.action);
        httpRequest.setRequestHeader("Content-Type", "application/json");
        httpRequest.send(JSON.stringify(formData));
    }

    function handleResponse() {
        if (httpRequest.readyState == 4 && httpRequest.status == 200) {
            document.getElementById("results").innerHTML
                = httpRequest.responseText;
        }
    }
}
</script>
...
```

In this script, I create a new Object and define properties that correspond to the name attribute values of the input elements in the form. I could use any data, but the input elements are convenient and consistent with the earlier examples.

In order to tell the server that I am sending JSON data, I set the Content-Type header on the request to application/json, like this:

```
httpRequest.setRequestHeader("Content-Type", "application/json");
```

I use the JSON object to convert to and from the JSON format. (Most browsers support this object directly, but you can add the same functionality to older browsers with the script available at https://github.com/douglascrockford/JSON-js/blob/master/json2.js.) The JSON object provides two methods, as described in Table 33-3.

Table 33-3. Methods Defined by the JSON Object

Method	Description	Returns
parse(<json>)	Parses a JSON-encoded string and creates an object	object
stringify(<object>)	Creates a JSON-encoded representation of the specified object	string

In Listing 33-7, I use the `stringify` method and pass the result to the `send` method of the `XMLHttpRequest` object. Only the data encoding in this example has changed. The effect of submitting the form in the document remains the same.

Sending Files

You can send a file to the server by using a `FormData` object and an `input` element whose type attribute is `file`. When the form is submitted, the `FormData` object will automatically ensure that the contents of the file that the user has selected are uploaded along with the rest of the form values. Listing 33-8 shows how to use the `FormData` object in this way.

■ **Note** Using Ajax to upload files is tricky for browsers that don't yet support the `FormData` object. There are a lot of hacks and workarounds—some using Flash and others involving complicated sequences of posting forms to hidden `iframe` elements. They all have serious drawbacks and should be used with caution.

Listing 33-8. Sending a File to the Server Using the FormData Object

```
<!DOCTYPE HTML>
<html>
    <head>
        <title>Example</title>
        <style>
            .table {display:table;}
            .row {display:table-row;}
            .cell {display: table-cell; padding: 5px;}
            .label {text-align: right;}
        </style>
    </head>
    <body>
        <form id="fruitform" method="post" action="http://titan:8080/form">
            <div class="table">
                <div class="row">
                    <div class="cell label">Bananas:</div>
                    <div class="cell"><input name="bananas" value="2"/></div>
```

```
                    </div>
                    <div class="row">
                        <div class="cell label">Apples:</div>
                        <div class="cell"><input name="apples" value="5"/></div>
                    </div>
                    <div class="row">
                        <div class="cell label">Cherries:</div>
                        <div class="cell"><input name="cherries" value="20"/></div>
                    </div>
                    <div class="row">
                        <div class="cell label">File:</div>
                        <div class="cell"><input type="file" name="file"/></div>
                    </div>
                    <div class="row">
                        <div class="cell label">Total:</div>
                        <div id="results" class="cell">0 items</div>
                    </div>

                </div>
                <button id="submit" type="submit">Submit Form</button>
            </form>
            <script>
                document.getElementById("submit").onclick = handleButtonPress;

                var httpRequest;

                function handleButtonPress(e) {
                    e.preventDefault();

                    var form = document.getElementById("fruitform");

                    var formData = new FormData(form);
                    httpRequest = new XMLHttpRequest();
                    httpRequest.onreadystatechange = handleResponse;
                    httpRequest.open("POST", form.action);
                    httpRequest.send(formData);
                }

                function handleResponse() {
                    if (httpRequest.readyState == 4 && httpRequest.status == 200) {
                        document.getElementById("results").innerHTML
                            = httpRequest.responseText;
                    }
                }
            </script>
        </body>
</html>
```

In this example, the significant change occurs in the form element. The addition of the input element leads to the FormData object uploading whatever file the user selects. You can see the effect of the addition in Figure 33-4.

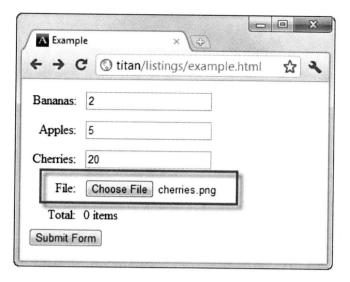

Figure 33-4. Adding an input element to upload files through the FormData object

___

■ **Tip** In Chapter 37, I show you how to use the drag-and-drop API to allow users to drag files to be uploaded from the operating system, rather than using a file chooser.

___

Tracking Upload Progress

You can track the progress of your data upload as it is sent to the server. You do this through the upload property of the XMLHttpRequest object, which is described in Table 33-4.

Table 33-4. The upload Property

Name	Description	Returns
upload	Returns an object that can be used to monitor progress	XMLHttpRequestUpload

The XMLHttpRequestUpload object that the upload property returns defines only the attributes required to register handlers for the events described in the previous chapter: onprogress, onload, and so on. Listing 33-9 shows how to use these events to display upload progress to the user.

Listing 33-9. Monitoring and Displaying Upload Progress

```
<!DOCTYPE HTML>
<html>
    <head>
```

```
        <title>Example</title>
        <style>
            .table {display:table;}
            .row {display:table-row;}
            .cell {display: table-cell; padding: 5px;}
            .label {text-align: right;}
        </style>
    </head>
    <body>
        <form id="fruitform" method="post" action="http://titan:8080/form">
            <div class="table">
                <div class="row">
                    <div class="cell label">Bananas:</div>
                    <div class="cell"><input name="bananas" value="2"/></div>
                </div>
                <div class="row">
                    <div class="cell label">Apples:</div>
                    <div class="cell"><input name="apples" value="5"/></div>
                </div>
                <div class="row">
                    <div class="cell label">Cherries:</div>
                    <div class="cell"><input name="cherries" value="20"/></div>
                </div>
                <div class="row">
                    <div class="cell label">File:</div>
                    <div class="cell"><input type="file" name="file"/></div>
                </div>
                <div class="row">
                    <div class="cell label">Progress:</div>
                    <div class="cell"><progress id="prog" value="0"/></div>
                </div>
                <div class="row">
                    <div class="cell label">Total:</div>
                    <div id="results" class="cell">0 items</div>
                </div>

            </div>

            <button id="submit" type="submit">Submit Form</button>
        </form>
        <script>
            document.getElementById("submit").onclick = handleButtonPress;

            var httpRequest;

            function handleButtonPress(e) {
                e.preventDefault();

                var form = document.getElementById("fruitform");
                var progress = document.getElementById("prog");

                var formData = new FormData(form);
```

```
        httpRequest = new XMLHttpRequest();

        var upload = httpRequest.upload;
        upload.onprogress = function(e) {
            progress.max = e.total;
            progress.value = e.loaded;

        }
        upload.onload = function(e) {
            progress.value = 1;
            progress.max = 1;
        }

        httpRequest.onreadystatechange = handleResponse;
        httpRequest.open("POST", form.action);
        httpRequest.send(formData);
    }

    function handleResponse() {
        if (httpRequest.readyState == 4 && httpRequest.status == 200) {
            document.getElementById("results").innerHTML
                = httpRequest.responseText;
        }
    }
    </script>
    </body>
</html>
```

In this example, I added a progress element (described in Chapter 15) and used it to provide data upload progress information to the user. I obtain an XMLHttpRequestUpload object by reading the XMLHttpRequest.upload property, and register functions to respond to the progress and load events.

The browser won't give progress information for small data transfers, so the best way to test this example is to select a large file. Figure 33-5 shows the progress of a movie file being sent to the server.

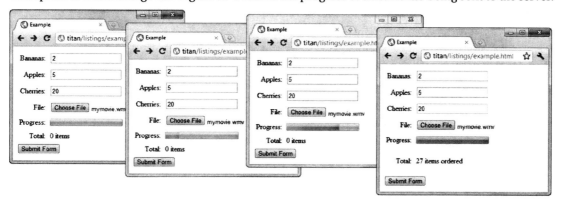

Figure 33-5. Displaying progress as data is uploaded to the server

865

Requesting and Processing Different Content Types

So far, all of the Ajax examples return a complete HTML document, including the head, title, and body elements. These elements are overhead and, given how little data is actually being transmitted from the server, the ratio of useful to useless information isn't ideal.

Fortunately, you don't need to return complete HTML documents. In fact, you don't need to return HTML at all. In the following sections, I'll show you how to deal with different kinds of data and, in doing so, reduce the amount of overhead that Ajax requests incur.

Receiving HTML Fragments

The simplest change to make is to have the server return an HTML fragment instead of the entire document. To do this, I first need to make a change to the writeResponse of the Node.js server script, as shown in Listing 33-10.

Listing 33-10. Modifying the Server to Send Back an HTML Fragment

```
...
function writeResponse(res, data) {
    var total = 0;
    for (fruit in data) {
        total += Number(data[fruit]);
    }
    res.writeHead(200, "OK", {
        "Content-Type": "text/html",
        "Access-Control-Allow-Origin": "http://titan"});
    res.write('You ordered <b>' + total + '</b> items');
    res.end();
}
...
```

Instead of a fully formed document, the server now sends just a fragment of HTML. Listing 33-11 shows the client HTML document.

Listing 33-11. Working with HTML Fragments

```
<!DOCTYPE HTML>
<html>
    <head>
        <title>Example</title>
        <style>
            .table {display:table;}
            .row {display:table-row;}
            .cell {display: table-cell; padding: 5px;}
            .label {text-align: right;}
        </style>
    </head>
    <body>
        <form id="fruitform" method="post" action="http://titan:8080/form">
            <div class="table">
```

```
            <div class="row">
                <div class="cell label">Bananas:</div>
                <div class="cell"><input name="bananas" value="2"/></div>
            </div>
            <div class="row">
                <div class="cell label">Apples:</div>
                <div class="cell"><input name="apples" value="5"/></div>
            </div>
            <div class="row">
                <div class="cell label">Cherries:</div>
                <div class="cell"><input name="cherries" value="20"/></div>
            </div>
            <div class="row">
                <div class="cell label">Total:</div>
                <div id="results" class="cell">0 items</div>
            </div>
        </div>
        <button id="submit" type="submit">Submit Form</button>
    </form>
    <script>
        document.getElementById("submit").onclick = handleButtonPress;

        var httpRequest;

        function handleButtonPress(e) {
            e.preventDefault();

            var form = document.getElementById("fruitform");

            var formData = new Object();
            var inputElements = document.getElementsByTagName("input");
            for (var i = 0; i < inputElements.length; i++) {
                formData[inputElements[i].name] =  inputElements[i].value;
            }

            httpRequest = new XMLHttpRequest();
            httpRequest.onreadystatechange = handleResponse;
            httpRequest.open("POST", form.action);
            httpRequest.setRequestHeader("Content-Type", "application/json");
            httpRequest.send(JSON.stringify(formData));
        }

        function handleResponse() {
            if (httpRequest.readyState == 4 && httpRequest.status == 200) {
                document.getElementById("results").innerHTML
                    = httpRequest.responseText;
            }
        }
    </script>
  </body>
</html>
```

I have removed some of the recent additions for uploading files and monitoring progress. I send the data to the server as JSON and receive an HTML fragment in return (although there is no relationship between the data format that I used to send data to the server and the data format that I get back from the server).

Since I have control of the server, I made sure that the Content-Type header is set to text/html, which tells the browser that it is dealing with HTML, even though the data it gets doesn't start with a DOCTYPE or an html element. You can use the overrideMimeType method if you want to override the Content-Type header and specify the data type yourself, as shown in Listing 33-12.

Listing 33-12. Overriding the Data Type

```
<script>
    document.getElementById("submit").onclick = handleButtonPress;

    var httpRequest;

    function handleButtonPress(e) {
        e.preventDefault();

        var form = document.getElementById("fruitform");

        var formData = new Object();
        var inputElements = document.getElementsByTagName("input");
        for (var i = 0; i < inputElements.length; i++) {
            formData[inputElements[i].name] =  inputElements[i].value;
        }

        httpRequest = new XMLHttpRequest();
        httpRequest.onreadystatechange = handleResponse;
        httpRequest.open("POST", form.action);
        httpRequest.setRequestHeader("Content-Type", "application/json");
        httpRequest.send(JSON.stringify(formData));
    }

    function handleResponse() {
        if (httpRequest.readyState == 4 && httpRequest.status == 200) {
            httpRequest.overrideMimeType("text/html");
            document.getElementById("results").innerHTML
                = httpRequest.responseText;
        }
    }
</script>
```

Specifying the data type can be useful if the server doesn't classify the data the way you want it. This most often happens when you are delivering fragments of content from files and the server has preconfigured notions of how the Content-Type header should be set.

Receiving XML Data

XML is less popular in web applications than it used to be, having largely been replaced by JSON. That said, it can still be useful to deal with XML data, especially when working with legacy data sources. Listing 33-13 shows the changes to the server script required to send XML to the browser.

Listing 33-13. Sending XML Data from the Server

```
function writeResponse(res, data) {
    var total = 0;
    for (fruit in data) {
        total += Number(data[fruit]);
    }
    res.writeHead(200, "OK", {
        "Content-Type": "application/xml",
        "Access-Control-Allow-Origin": "http://titan"});

    res.write("<?xml version='1.0'?>");
    res.write("<fruitorder total='" + total + "'>");
    for (fruit in data) {
        res.write("<item name='" + fruit + "' quantity='" + data[fruit] + "'/>")
        total += Number(data[fruit]);
    }
    res.write("</fruitorder>");
    res.end();
}
```

This revised function generates a short XML document, like this one:

```
<?xml version='1.0'?>
<fruitorder total='27'>
    <item name='bananas' quantity='2'/>
    <item name='apples' quantity='5'/>
    <item name='cherries' quantity='20'/>
</fruitorder>
```

This is a superset of the information that I need to display in the client, but it is no longer in a format that I can just display using the DOM innerHTML property. Fortunately, the XMLHttpRequest object makes it easy to work with XML, which is not surprising since XML is the *x* in *Ajax*. Listing 33-14 shows how to work with XML in the browser.

Listing 33-14. Working with an XML Ajax Response

```
<script>
    document.getElementById("submit").onclick = handleButtonPress;

    var httpRequest;

    function handleButtonPress(e) {
        e.preventDefault();

        var form = document.getElementById("fruitform");
```

```
        var formData = new Object();
        var inputElements = document.getElementsByTagName("input");
        for (var i = 0; i < inputElements.length; i++) {
            formData[inputElements[i].name] =  inputElements[i].value;
        }

        httpRequest = new XMLHttpRequest();
        httpRequest.onreadystatechange = handleResponse;
        httpRequest.open("POST", form.action);
        httpRequest.setRequestHeader("Content-Type", "application/json");
        httpRequest.send(JSON.stringify(formData));
    }

    function handleResponse() {
        if (httpRequest.readyState == 4 && httpRequest.status == 200) {
            httpRequest.overrideMimeType("application/xml");
            var xmlDoc = httpRequest.responseXML;
            var val = xmlDoc.getElementsByTagName("fruitorder")[0].getAttribute("total");
            document.getElementById("results").innerHTML = "You ordered "
                + val + " items";
        }
    }
}
</script>
```

All of the changes to the script to work with the XML data occur in the handleResponse function. The first thing that I do when the request has completed successfully is override the MIME type of the response:

```
httpRequest.overrideMimeType("application/xml");
```

This isn't really needed in this example, because the server is sending a complete XML document. But when dealing with XML fragments, it is important to explicitly tell the browser that you are working with XML; otherwise, the XMLHttpRequest object won't properly support the responseXML property, which I use in the following statement:

```
var xmlDoc = httpRequest.responseXML;
```

The responseXML property is an alternative to responseText. It parses the XML that has been received and returns it as a Document object. You can then employ this technique to navigate through the XML using the DOM features for HTML (described in Chapter 26), like this:

```
var val = xmlDoc.getElementsByTagName("fruitorder")[0].getAttribute("total");
```

This statement obtains the value of the total attribute in the first fruitorder element, which I then use with the innerHTML property to display a result to the user:

```
document.getElementById("results").innerHTML = "You ordered "+ val + " items";
```

HTML VS. XML IN THE DOM

It is time for an admission. In Part IV of this book, I deliberately smoothed over the relationship between HTML, XML. and the DOM. All of the features that I described for navigating and dealing with elements in an HTML document are equally available for dealing with XML.

In fact, the objects that represent HTML elements are derived from some core objects that arise from XML support. For the most part, and for most readers of the book, the HTML support is what matters. If you are working with XML, you may wish to spend some time reading up on the core XML support, which you can find defined at www.w3.org/standards/techs/dom.

Having said that, if you are doing a lot of work with XML, you might want to consider an alternative encoding strategy. XML is verbose and performing complex processing at the browser isn't always ideal. A more tailored and terse format, such as JSON, may serve you better.

Receiving JSON Data

JSON data is generally easier to work with than XML because you end up with a JavaScript object that you can interrogate and manipulate using the core language features. Listing 33-15 shows the changes required to the server script to generate a JSON response.

Listing 33-15. Generating a JSON Response at the Server

```
function writeResponse(res, data) {
    var total = 0;
    for (fruit in data) {
        total += Number(data[fruit]);
    }
    data.total = total;
    var jsonData = JSON.stringify(data);

    res.writeHead(200, "OK", {
        "Content-Type": "application/json",
        "Access-Control-Allow-Origin": "http://titan"});
    res.write(jsonData);
    res.end();
}
```

All I need to do to generate a JSON response is define the total property on the object that is passed as the data parameter to the function and use JSON.stringify to represent the object as a string. The server sends a response to the browser, like this:

```
{"bananas":"2","apples":"5","cherries":"20","total":27}
```

Listing 33-16 shows the script changes required at the browser to deal with this response.

Listing 33-16. Receiving a JSON Response from the Server

```
<script>
    document.getElementById("submit").onclick = handleButtonPress;

    var httpRequest;

    function handleButtonPress(e) {
        e.preventDefault();

        var form = document.getElementById("fruitform");

        var formData = new Object();
        var inputElements = document.getElementsByTagName("input");
        for (var i = 0; i < inputElements.length; i++) {
            formData[inputElements[i].name] =  inputElements[i].value;
        }

        httpRequest = new XMLHttpRequest();
        httpRequest.onreadystatechange = handleResponse;
        httpRequest.open("POST", form.action);
        httpRequest.setRequestHeader("Content-Type", "application/json");
        httpRequest.send(JSON.stringify(formData));
    }

    function handleResponse() {
        if (httpRequest.readyState == 4 && httpRequest.status == 200) {
            var data = JSON.parse(httpRequest.responseText);
            document.getElementById("results").innerHTML = "You ordered "
                + data.total + " items";
        }
    }
</script>
```

JSON is exceptionally easy to work with, as these two listings demonstrate. This ease of use, plus the compactness of the representation, is why JSON has become so popular.

Summary

In this chapter, I finished explaining the intricacies of Ajax. I showed you how to send data to the server, both manually and using the FormData object. You learned how to send a file and how to monitor progress as the data is uploaded to the server. I also covered how to deal with different data formats sent by the server: HTML, fragments of HTML, XML, and JSON.

Working with Multimedia

HTML5 includes support for playing back audio and video files in the browser without the use of plugins such as Adobe Flash. Browser plugins are a major cause of browser crashes and Flash, in particular, is a notorious cause of problems.

As a related aside, I have come to loathe Flash for media playback. I like to listen to podcasts when I am writing, and Chrome uses Flash to play these by default. I like the ease of integration, but every now and again something goes wrong and I have a locked-up machine. It drives me crazy and makes me curse Adobe every time. The ubiquity of Flash is useful; the quality of the software leaves a lot to be desired.

As you'll see in this chapter, the HTML support for native audio and video has a lot of potential, but there are still some wrinkles to be ironed out. These are largely related to the formats each browser supports and the different interpretations browsers have about their ability to play file formats. Table 34-1 provides the summary for this chapter.

■ **Tip** If you want to re-create the examples in this chapter, you may need to add some MIME types to your web server. You can see which ones are required in Listing 34-7.

Table 34-1. Chapter Summary

Problem	Solution	Listing
Include a video in an HTML document.	Use the video element.	1
Specify if a video file should be loaded before the user starts playback.	Use the preload attribute.	2
Specify an image that will be shown until video playback starts.	Use the poster attribute.	3
Set the size of the video on screen.	Use the width and height attributes.	4
Specify the video source.	Use the src attribute.	5

Specify multiple formats of the same video source.	Use the source element.	6, 7
Include audio in an HTML document.	Use the audio element.	8, 9
Manipulate media elements through the DOM.	Use the `HTMLMediaElement`, `HTMLVideoElement`, or `HTMLAudioElement` object.	10
Obtain an indication of whether a media format is supported by the browser.	Use the `canPlayType` method.	11
Control media playback.	Use the play and pause methods of the `HTMLMediaElement`, and the properties that provide playback details.	12, 13

Using the video Element

You use the video element to embed video content into a web page. Table 34-2 describes the video element.

Table 34-2. The video Element

Element:	video
Element Type:	Flow/Phrasing
Permitted Parents:	Any element that can contain flow or phrasing elements
Local Attributes:	autoplay, preload, controls, loop, poster, height, width, muted, src
Contents:	source and track elements, plus phrasing and flow content
Tag Style:	Start and end tags
New in HTML5?	**Yes**
Changes in HTML5	N/A
Style Convention	None

Listing 34-1 shows the basic use of this element.

Listing 34-1. Using the video Element

```
<!DOCTYPE HTML>
<html>
    <head>
        <title>Example</title>
    </head>
    <body>
        <video width="360" height="240" src="timessquare.webm"
                autoplay controls preload="none" muted>
            Video cannot be displayed
        </video>
    </body>
</html>
```

If you have ever seen video in a web page before, the result of using the video element will be familiar, as shown in Figure 34-1.

Figure 34-1. Using the video element

If the browser doesn't support the video element or cannot play the video, the fallback content (the content between the start and end tags) will be displayed instead. In this example, I provided a simple text message, but a common technique is to offer video playback using a non-HTML5 technique (such as Flash) to support older browsers.

There are a number of attributes for the video element, which I describe in Table 34-3.

Table 34-3. Attributes for the video Element

Attribute	Description
autoplay	If present, this attribute causes the browser to start playing the video as soon as it is able to do so.
preload	Tells the browser whether or not to load the video in advance. See the next section for details.
controls	The browser will not display controls unless this attribute is present.
loop	If present, this attribute tells the browser to repeat the video.
poster	Specifies an image to display when the video data is being loaded. See the "Displaying a Placeholder Image" section for details.
height	Specifies the height of the video. See the "Setting the Video Size" section for details.
width	Specifies the width of the video. See the "Setting the Video Size" section for details.
muted	If this attribute is present, the video will be muted initially.
src	Specifies the video to display. See the "Setting the Video Source (and Format)" section for details.

Preloading the Video

The preload attribute tells the browser whether it should optimistically download the video when the page that contains the video element is first loaded. Preloading the video reduces the initial delay when the user starts playback, but can be a waste of network bandwidth if the user doesn't view the video. The allowed values for this attribute are described in Table 34-4.

Table 34-4. The Allowed Values for the preload Attribute

Value	Description
none	The video will not be loaded until the user starts playback.
metadata	Only the metadata for the video (width, height, first frame, duration, and other such information) should be loaded before the user starts playback.
auto	Requests that the browser download the video in its entirety as soon as possible. The browser is free to ignore this request. This is the default behavior.

The decision about preemptively loading video should be driven by the likelihood that the user will want to watch the video, balanced against the bandwidth required to automatically load the video content. Automatically loading the video results in a smoother user experience, but it can drive up capacity costs significantly, which are wasted when the user navigates away from the page without viewing the video.

The metadata value for this attribute can be used to strike a modest balance between the none and auto values. The problem with the none value is that the video content is shown as a blank region of the screen. The metadata value causes the browser to get enough information to show the user the first frame of the video, without having to download all of the content. Listing 34-2 shows the none and metadata values in use in the same document.

Listing 34-2. Using the none and metadata Values for the preload Attribute

```
<!DOCTYPE HTML>
<html>
    <head>
        <title>Example</title>
    </head>
    <body>
        <video width="360" height="240" src="timessquare.webm"
                controls preload="none" muted>
            Video cannot be displayed
        </video>
        <video width="360" height="240" src="timessquare.webm"
                controls preload="metadata" muted>
            Video cannot be displayed
        </video>
    </body>
</html>
```

You can see how these values affect the display shown to the user in Figure 34-2.

Figure 34-2. Using the none and metadata values for the preload attribute

---

▨ **Caution** The metadata value gives a nice preview to the user, but some caution is required. In playing around with this property and using a network analyzer, I found that browsers tended to preemptively download the entire video, even though only the metadata was requested. In all fairness, the preload attribute expresses a preference that the browser is free to ignore. However, if you need to constrain bandwidth consumption, the poster attribute may provide a better alternative. See the next section for details.

Displaying a Placeholder Image

You can present the user with a placeholder image by using the poster attribute. This image will be shown in place of the video until the user starts playback. Listing 34-3 shows the poster attribute in use.

Listing 34-3. Using the poster Attribute to Specify a Placeholder Image

```
<!DOCTYPE HTML>
<html>
    <head>
        <title>Example</title>
    </head>
    <body>
        <video width="360" height="240" src="timessquare.webm"
                controls preload="none" poster="poster.png">
            Video cannot be displayed
        </video>
        <img src="poster.png"/>
    </body>
</html>
```

I took a screenshot of the first frame of the video file and superimposed the word Poster on top of it. This picture includes the video controls to indicate to the user that the poster represents a video clip. I also included an img element in this example to demonstrate that the poster image is shown by the video element without modification. Figure 34-3 shows the poster in both forms.

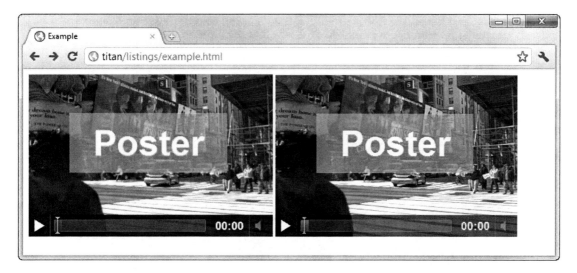

Figure 34-3. Using a poster for a video clip

Setting the Video Size

If the width and height attributes are omitted, the browser displays a small placeholder element that is resized to the intrinsic dimensions of the video when the metadata becomes available (that is, when the user starts playback or if the preload attribute is set to metadata). This can create a jarring effect as the page layout is adjusted to accommodate the video.

   If you do specify the width and height attributes, the browser preserves the video's aspect ratio—you don't have to worry about the video being stretched in either direction. Listing 34-4 shows the application of the width and height attributes.

Listing 34-4. Applying the width and height Attributes

```
<!DOCTYPE HTML>
<html>
    <head>
        <title>Example</title>
        <style>
            video {
                background-color: lightgrey;
                border: medium double black;
            }
        </style>
    </head>
    <body>
        <video src="timessquare.webm" controls preload="auto" width="600" height="240">
            Video cannot be displayed
        </video>
    </body>
</html>
```

In this example, I set the width attribute so that it is out of ratio with the height attribute. I also applied a style to the video element to emphasize the way that the browser uses only some of the space allocated to the element to preserve the aspect ratio of the video. Figure 34-4 shows the result.

Figure 34-4. The browser preserving the aspect ratio of a video

Specifying the Video Source (and Format)

The simplest way of specifying the video is to use the src attribute, giving the URL of the video file that is required. This is the approach I took in the previous examples and which is shown again in Listing 34-5.

Listing 34-5. Specifying a Video Source Using the src Attribute

```
<!DOCTYPE HTML>
<html>
    <head>
        <title>Example</title>
    </head>
    <body>
        <video src="timessquare.webm" controls width="360" height="240">
            Video cannot be displayed
        </video>
    </body>
</html>
```

In this listing, I used the source element to specify the file timessquare.webm. This is a file encoded in the WebM format. And with this, you enter the difficult world of video formats. Earlier in the book, I mentioned the browser wars—an attempt by several companies to assert control over the browser market through nonstandard additions to HTML and related technologies. Happily, those days have passed and compliance with standards is seen as a selling point for browsers, along with speed, ease of use, and a catchy logo.

Sadly, the same point has not been reached when it comes to video formats. There is the potential for some parties to make a lot of money if they can establish their own formats as the dominant ones for HTML5. License fees can be charged, royalties can be levied, and patent portfolios can grow in value. As such, there is no universally supported video format, and if you want to use video to target a wide range of HTML5 users, you can expect to encode your video in a number of formats. Table 34-5 shows the formats that have strong support at the moment (although this will almost certainly change over time).

Table 34-5. *Video Formats with Significant Browser Support*

Format	Description	Support
WebM	This is a format backed by Google with a goal of creating a patent-free, royalty-free format. The people behind the MP4/H.264 format have been openly seeking a patent pool to use to begin litigation against WebM (or at least to worry people enough to prevent them from using it).	Opera Chrome Firefox
Ogg/Theora	Ogg Theora is an open, royalty-free, and patent-free format.	Opera Chrome Firefox
MP4/H.264	This is a format that is presently free to use until 2015 because the licensor has publically waived its usual distribution fee schedule.	Internet Explorer Chrome Safari

The sad fact is that there isn't a single format that can be used to target all of the mainstream browsers—until there is, encoding the same video in multiple formats is required.

▪ **Note** There is a whole level of detail in video encoding I am going to skip right over. It involves containers, codecs, and other exciting concepts. The upshot is that there are options and choices within each format that trade off quality or compactness for compatibility—given the shifting landscape of browser support for video, the combinations change frequently. I recommend that you consult the release notes for the mainstream browsers to determine support levels or, as I do, just encode in every possible permutation and see what gives the broadest support.

You use the source element to specify multiple formats. This element is described in Table 34-6.

Table 34-6. The source Element

Element:	source
Element Type:	N/A
Permitted Parents:	video, audio
Local Attributes:	src, type, media
Contents:	None
Tag Style:	Void element
New in HTML5?	**Yes**
Changes in HTML5	N/A
Style Convention	None

Listing 34-6 shows how you can use the source element to provide the browser with a choice of video formats.

Listing 34-6. Using the source Element

```
<!DOCTYPE HTML>
<html>
    <head>
        <title>Example</title>
    </head>
    <body>
        <video controls width="360" height="240">
            <source src="timessquare.webm"/>
            <source src="timessquare.ogv"/>
            <source src="timessquare.mp4"/>
            Video cannot be displayed
        </video>
    </body>
</html>
```

The browser works its way down the list in sequence looking for a video file it can play. This may mean multiple requests for the server to get additional information about each file. One of the ways the browser works out whether it can play a video is through the MIME type returned by the server. You can provide a hint to the user by applying the type attribute to the source element, specifying the MIME type of the file, as shown in Listing 34-7.

Listing 34-7. Applying the type Attribute on the source Element

```
<!DOCTYPE HTML>
<html>
    <head>
        <title>Example</title>
    </head>
    <body>
        <video controls width="360" height="240">
            <source src="timessquare.webm" type="video/webm" />
            <source src="timessquare.ogv" type="video/ogg" />
            <source src="timessquare.mp4" type="video/mp4" />
            Video cannot be displayed
        </video>
    </body>
</html>
```

▓ **Tip** The media attribute provides the browser with guidance about the kind of device that the video is best suited for. See Chapter 7 for details of how to define values for this attribute.

The track Element

The HTML5 specification includes the track element, which provides a mechanism for additional content related to the video. This includes subtitles, captions, and the chapter title. Table 34-7 describes this element, but none of the mainstream browsers currently implement this element.

Table 34-7. *The track Element*

Element:	source
Element Type:	N/A
Permitted Parents:	video, audio
Local Attributes:	kind, src, srclang, label, default
Contents:	None
Tag Style:	Void element
New in HTML5?	**Yes**
Changes in HTML5	N/A
Style Convention	None

Using the audio Element

The audio element allows you to embed audio content into an HTML document. This element is described in Table 34-8.

Table 34-8. The audio Element

Element:	audio
Element Type:	Flow/Phrasing
Permitted Parents:	Any element that can contain flow or phrasing elements
Local Attributes:	autoplay, preload, controls, loop, muted, src
Contents:	source and track elements, plus phrasing and flow content
Tag Style:	Start and end tags
New in HTML5?	**Yes**
Changes in HTML5	N/A
Style Convention	None

You can see that the audio element has a lot in common with the video element. Listing 34-8 shows the audio element in use.

Listing 34-8. Using the audio Element

```
<!DOCTYPE HTML>
<html>
    <head>
        <title>Example</title>
    </head>
    <body>
        <audio controls src="mytrack.mp3" autoplay>
            Audio content cannot be played
        </audio>
    </body>
</html>
```

You specify the audio source using the src attribute. Even though the world of audio formats is less contentious than video, there *still* isn't a format that all of the browsers can play natively, although I am more hopeful this will change for audio than video.

■ **Tip** By applying the `autoplay` attribute and omitting the `controls` attributes, you can create a situation where audio is played automatically and the user has no way to stop it. On behalf of all of your users, I beg you not to do this—especially if you intend to play dreary, synthetic, anonymous, and essentially unidentifiable music. Inflicting music like this on your users makes every transaction reminiscent of an interminable elevator ride, and this is especially true if your audio tracks have no discernible instruments involved. Please don't inflict bland, soulless, and pointless music on your users, and certainly don't make it start automatically and leave the user without the means to disable it.

Listing 34-9 shows how you can use the source element to provide multiple formats.

Listing 34-9. Using the source Element to Provide Multiple Audio Formats

```
<!DOCTYPE HTML>
<html>
    <head>
        <title>Example</title>
    </head>
    <body>
        <audio controls autoplay>
            <source src="mytrack.ogg" />
            <source src="mytrack.mp3" />
            <source src="mytrack.wav" />
            Audio content cannot be played
        </audio>
    </body>
</html>
```

In both of these examples, I used the `controls` attribute so that the browser will display the default controls to the user. There are some variations between browsers, but Figure 34-5 gives you an idea of what to expect.

Figure 34-5. The default controls for an audio element in Google Chrome

Working with Embedded Media via the DOM

The audio and video elements have enough in common that the HTMLMediaElement object defines the core functionality for both of them in the DOM. The audio element is represented in the DOM by the HTMLAudioElement object, but this defines no additional functionality beyond HTMLMediaElement. The video element is represented by the HTMLVideoElement object. This does define some additional properties, which I describe later in this chapter.

■ **Tip** The audio and video elements have so much in common that the only difference is the amount of screen space they occupy. The audio element isn't laid out with a chunk of screen to display video images. You can actually use the audio element to play video files (although you get only the soundtrack, obviously), and you can use the video element to play audio files (although the video display remains blank). Strange but true.

Getting Information About the Media

The HTMLMediaElement object defines a number of members you can use to get and modify information about the element and the media associated with it. These are described in Table 34-9.

Table 34-9. Basic Members of the HTMLMediaElement Object

Member	Description	Returns
autoplay	Gets or sets the presence of the autoplay attribute	boolean
canPlayType(<type>)	Gets an indication of whether the browser can play a particular MIME type	string
currentSrc	Gets the current source	string
controls	Gets or sets the presence of the controls attribute	boolean
defaultMuted	Gets or sets the initial presence of the muted attribute	boolean
loop	Gets or sets the presence of the loop attribute	boolean
muted	Gets or sets the presence of the muted attribute	boolean
preload	Gets or sets the value of the preload attribute	string
src	Gets or sets the value of the src attribute	string
volume	Gets or sets the volume on a scale from 0.0 to 1.0	number

The HTMLVideoElement object defines the additional properties shown in Table 34-10.

Table 34-10. Properties Defined by the HTMLVideoElement Object

Member	Description	Returns
height	Gets or sets the value of the height attribute	number
poster	Gets or sets the value of the poster attribute	string
videoHeight	Gets the intrinsic height of the video	number
videoWidth	Gets the intrinsic width of the video	number
width	Gets or sets the value of the width attribute	number

Listing 34-10 shows some of the HTMLMediaElement properties being used to get basic information about a media element.

Listing 34-10. Getting Basic Information About a Media Element

```
<!DOCTYPE HTML>
<html>
    <head>
        <title>Example</title>
        <style>
            table {border: thin solid black; border-collapse: collapse;}
            th, td {padding: 3px 4px;}
            body > * {float: left; margin: 2px;}
        </style>
    </head>
    <body>
        <video id="media" controls width="360" height="240" preload="metadata">
            <source src="timessquare.webm"/>
            <source src="timessquare.ogv"/>
            <source src="timessquare.mp4"/>
            Video cannot be displayed
        </video>
        <table id="info" border="1">
            <tr><th>Property</th><th>Value</th></tr>
        </table>
        <script>
            var mediaElem = document.getElementById("media");
            var tableElem = document.getElementById("info");

            var propertyNames = ["autoplay", "currentSrc", "controls", "loop", "muted",
                                 "preload", "src", "volume"];
```

```
            for (var i = 0; i < propertyNames.length; i++) {
                tableElem.innerHTML +=
                    "<tr><td>" + propertyNames[i] + "</td><td>" +
                    mediaElem[propertyNames[i]] + "</td></tr>";
            }
        </script>
    </body>
</html>
```

The script in this example displays the value of a number of the properties in a table, alongside the video element. You can see the results in Figure 34-6.

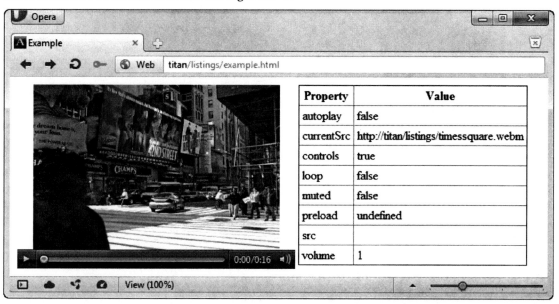

Figure 34-6. Displaying basic information about a video element

I showed Opera in the figure because it is the only browser that properly implements the currentSrc property. This property displays the value of the src attribute, either from the media element itself or from the source element in use when there is a choice of formats available.

Assessing Playback Capabilities

The canPlayType method can be used to get an idea of whether the browser can play a particular media format. This method returns one of the values shown in Table 34-11.

Table 34-11. *The Allowed Values for the canPlayType Attribute*

Value	Description
"" (empty string)	The browser cannot play the media type.
maybe	The browser might be able to play the media type.
probably	The browser is reasonably confident that it can play the media type.

These values are obviously vague—and this goes back to the complexity around some media formats and the encoding options that can be used when creating them. Listing 34-11 shows the canPlayType method in use.

Listing 34-11. *Using the canPlayType Method*

```
<!DOCTYPE HTML>
<html>
    <head>
        <title>Example</title>
        <style>
            table {border: thin solid black; border-collapse: collapse;}
            th, td {padding: 3px 4px;}
            body > * {float: left; margin: 2px;}
        </style>
    </head>
    <body>
        <video id="media" controls width="360" height="240" preload="metadata">
            Video cannot be displayed
        </video>
        <table id="info" border="1">
            <tr><th>Property</th><th>Value</th></tr>
        </table>
        <script>
            var mediaElem = document.getElementById("media");
            var tableElem = document.getElementById("info");

            var mediaFiles = ["timessquare.webm", "timessquare.ogv", "timessquare.mp4"];
            var mediaTypes = ["video/webm", "video/ogv", "video/mp4"];

            for (var i = 0; i < mediaTypes.length; i++) {
                var playable = mediaElem.canPlayType(mediaTypes[i]);
                if (!playable) {
                    playable = "no";
                }

                tableElem.innerHTML +=
                    "<tr><td>" + mediaTypes[i] + "</td><td>" + playable + "</td></tr>";
```

```
            if (playable == "probably") {
                mediaElem.src = mediaFiles[i];
            }
        }
    }
    </script>
    </body>
</html>
```

In the script in this example, I use the canPlayType method to assess a set of media types. If I receive a probably response, I set the src attribute value for the video element. Along the way, I record the response for each media type in a table.

Some caution is required when trying to select media in this way, because the way that browsers assess their ability to play a format differs. For example, Figure 34-7 shows the response from Firefox.

Figure 34-7. Assessing media format support in Firefox

Firefox is very bullish about WebM and certain that the Ogg and MP4 files can't be played—yet, Firefox seems to handle Ogg video files very well. Figure 34-8 shows the response from Chrome.

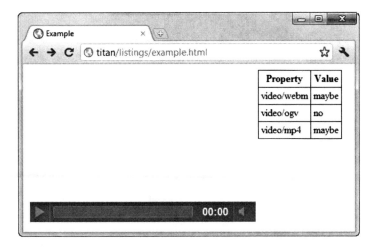

Figure 34-8. Assessing media format support in Chrome

Chrome takes a much more conservative view, yet it will happily play all three of my media files. In fact, Chrome is so conservative that I don't get a probably response from the canPlayType method and so don't make a media selection.

It is hard to criticize the browsers for the inconsistency of their responses. There are too many variables to be able to give definitive answers, but the different ways in which support is assessed means that the canPlayType method should be used very carefully.

Controlling Media Playback

The HTMLMediaElement object defines a number of members that allow you to control playback and get information about playback. These properties and methods are described in Table 34-12.

Table 34-12. Playback Members of the HTMLMediaElement Object

Member	Description	Returns
currentTime	Returns the current playback point in the media file	number
duration	Returns the total length of the media file	number
ended	Returns true if the media file has finished playing	boolean
pause()	Pauses playback of the media	void
paused	Returns true if playback is paused; returns false otherwise	boolean
play()	Starts playback of the media	void

Listing 34-12 shows how you can use the properties in the table to get information about playback.

Listing 34-12. Using HTMLMediaElement Properties to Get Details of Media Playback

```
<!DOCTYPE HTML>
<html>
    <head>
        <title>Example</title>
        <style>
            table {border: thin solid black; border-collapse: collapse;}
            th, td {padding: 3px 4px;}
            body > * {float: left; margin: 2px;}
            div {clear: both;}
        </style>
    </head>
    <body>
        <video id="media" controls width="360" height="240" preload="metadata">
            <source src="timessquare.webm"/>
            <source src="timessquare.ogv"/>
            <source src="timessquare.mp4"/>
            Video cannot be displayed
        </video>
        <table id="info" border="1">
            <tr><th>Property</th><th>Value</th></tr>
        </table>
        <div>
            <button id="pressme">Press Me</button>
        </div>
        <script>
            var mediaElem = document.getElementById("media");
            var tableElem = document.getElementById("info");

            document.getElementById("pressme").onclick = displayValues;

            displayValues();

            function displayValues() {
                var propertyNames = ["currentTime", "duration", "paused", "ended"];
                tableElem.innerHTML = "";
                for (var i = 0; i < propertyNames.length; i++) {
                    tableElem.innerHTML +=
                        "<tr><td>" + propertyNames[i] + "</td><td>" +
                        mediaElem[propertyNames[i]] + "</td></tr>";
                }
            }
        </script>
    </body>
</html>
```

This example includes a button element which, when pressed, causes the current values of the currentTime, duration, paused, and ended properties to be displayed in a table. You can see the effect in Figure 34-9.

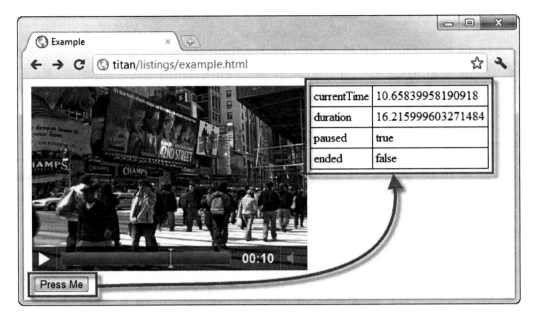

Figure 34-9. Taking a snapshot of playback property values in response to a button press

You can use the playback methods to replace the default media controls. Listing 34-13 provides a demonstration.

Listing 34-13. Replacing the Default Media Controls

```
<!DOCTYPE HTML>
<html>
    <head>
        <title>Example</title>
    </head>
    <body>
        <video id="media" width="360" height="240" preload="auto">
            <source src="timessquare.webm"/>
            <source src="timessquare.ogv"/>
            <source src="timessquare.mp4"/>
            Video cannot be displayed
        </video>
        <div>
            <button>Play</button>
            <button>Pause</button>
        </div>
        <script>
            var mediaElem = document.getElementById("media");

            var buttons = document.getElementsByTagName("button");
            for (var i = 0; i < buttons.length; i++) {
```

```
                buttons[i].onclick = handleButtonPress;
            }

            function handleButtonPress(e) {
                switch (e.target.innerHTML) {
                    case 'Play':
                        mediaElem.play();
                        break;
                    case 'Pause':
                        mediaElem.pause();
                        break;
                }
            }
        }
    </script>
  </body>
</html>
```

In this example, I omitted the controls attribute from the video element and use the play and pause methods, triggered by button presses, to start and stop the media playback. You can see the effect in Figure 34-10.

Figure 34-10. Replacing the default media controls

■ **Tip** The HTML specification defines a series of events related to loading and playing media, exposed through the `controller` property of the `HTMLMediaElement` object. As I write this, none of the mainstream browsers support this property or the `MediaController` object that it should return.

Summary

In this chapter, I showed you how HTML5 supports native media playback through the `video` and `audio` elements and how you can control those elements using the DOM. Native media support has a lot of potential, given the difficulties with plugins like Flash, but it is an approach that is still at an early stage of adoption. You will be stuck with a mix-and-match approach until the format support issues are resolved and there is a critical mass of browser support for this approach.

CHAPTER 35

Using the Canvas Element – Part I

In the previous chapter I alluded to (and briefly ranted about) the love/hate relationship that most web application developers and designers have with Adobe Flash. The hate comes from the lack of stability and security because Adobe recently has been accused of poor software quality. The love for Flash comes from its ubiquity of installation and the way that it can be used to produce rich content.

As a native alternative to Flash, HTML5 defines the canvas element. If you have read any description of the new capabilities in HTML5, the canvas was likely to have been one of the first features mentioned and it was probably described as a Flash-killer.

As is often the case, the hype and the reality don't match up. The canvas element is a drawing surface that we configure and drive using JavaScript. It is flexible, relatively easy to use and it provides enough features that it can replace Flash for some kinds of rich content. But calling the canvas element a Flash-killer (or even a Flash-replacement) is premature, as it will be a while before the canvas takes over.

This is the first of two chapters on the canvas element. In this chapter, I show you how to get set up with the canvas element and introduce the objects that we use in JavaScript to interact with the canvas. I also show you the support for basic shapes, how to use solid colors and gradients and how to draw images on the canvas. The next chapter shows you how to draw more complex shapes and how to apply effects and transformations. Table 35-1 provides the summary for this chapter.

Table 35-1. Chapter Summary

Problem	Solution	Listing
Prepare a canvas for drawing	Find the canvas element in the DOM and call the getContext method on the HTMLCanvasObject	1,2
Draw a rectangle	Use the fillRect or strokeRect methods	3
Clear a rectangle	Use the clearRect method	4
Set the style for a drawing operation	Set the values for the drawing state properties (such as lineWidth and lineJoin) prior to performing the operation	5, 6
Use solid colors in drawing operations	Set the fillStyle or strokeStyle properties to a color value or name	7

Create a linear gradient	Call the `createLinearGradient` method and add colors to the gradient by calling the `addColorStop` method	8-11
Create a radial gradient	Call the `createRadialGradient` method and add colors to the gradient by calling the `addColorStop` method	12, 13
Create a pattern	Call the `createPattern` method, specifying the source of the pattern image and the repeat style	14, 15
Save and restore the drawing state	Use the `save` and `restore` methods	16
Draw an image on the canvas	Use the `drawImage` method, specifying an `img`, `canvas` or `video` element as the source	17-20

Getting Started with the Canvas Element

The `canvas` element is pretty simple in that all of its functionality is exposed through a JavaScript object, so the element itself only has two attributes, as shown in Table 35-2.

Table 35-2. The canvas element

Element:	`canvas`
Element Type:	Phrasing/Flow
Permitted Parents:	Any element that can contain phrasing or flow elements
Local Attributes:	`height`, `width`
Contents:	Phrasing or flow content
Tag Style:	Start and end tag.
New in HTML5?	**Yes**
Changes in HTML5	N/A
Style Convention	None

The content of a canvas element is used as a fallback if the browser doesn't support the element itself. Listing 35-1 shows the canvas element and some simple fallback content.

Listing 35-1. Using the canvas element with basic fallback content

```
<!DOCTYPE HTML>
<html>
    <head>
        <title>Example</title>
        <style>
            canvas {border: medium double black; margin: 4px}
        </style>
    </head>
    <body>
        <canvas width="500" height="200">
            Your browser doesn't support the <code>canvas</code> element
        </canvas>
    </body>
</html>
```

As you might imagine, the width and height attributes specify the size of the element on screen. You can see how the browser displays this example in Figure 35-1 (although, of course, there isn't much to see at this point).

■ **Tip** I applied a style to the canvas element in this example to set a border. Otherwise there would be no way to see the canvas in the browser window. I'll show a border in all of the examples in this chapter, so it is always clear how the operations I describe relate to the canvas coordinates.

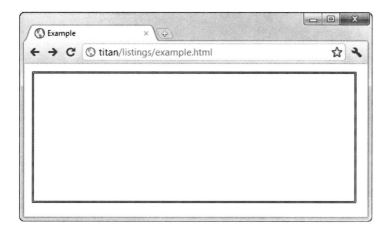

Figure 35-1. Adding the canvas element to an HTML document

Getting a Canvas Context

In order to draw on a canvas element, we need to get a context object, which is an object that exposes drawing functions for a particular style of graphics. In our case, we will be working with the 2d context, which is used to perform two-dimensional operations. Some browsers provide support for an experimental 3D context, but this is still at an early stage.

We get a context through the object that represents the canvas element in the DOM. This object, HTMLCanvasElement, is described in Table 35-3.

Table 35-3. *The HTMLCanvasElement object*

Member	Description	Returns
height	Corresponds to the height attribute	number
width	Corresponds to the width attribute	number
getContext(<context>)	Returns a drawing context for the canvas	object

The key method is getContext – to get the two-dimensional context object, we request pass the 2d argument to the method. Once we have the context, we can begin drawing. Listing 35-2 provides a demonstration.

Listing 35-2. Obtaining a two-dimensional context object for a canvas

```
<!DOCTYPE HTML>
<html>
    <head>
        <title>Example</title>
        <style>
            canvas {border: medium double black; margin: 4px}
        </style>
    </head>
    <body>
        <canvas id="canvas" width="500" height="100">
            Your browser doesn't support the <code>canvas</code> element
        </canvas>
        <script>
            var ctx = document.getElementById("canvas").getContext("2d");
            ctx.fillRect(10, 10, 50, 50);
        </script>
    </body>
</html>
```

I have emphasized the key statement in this listing. I use the document object to find the object representing the canvas element in the DOM and call the getContext method, using the argument 2d. You will see this statement, or a close variation, in all of the examples in this chapter.

Once I have the context object, I can begin to draw. In this example, I have called the fillRect method, which draws a filled rectangle on the canvas. You can see the (simple) effect in Figure 35-2.

Figure 35-2. Obtaining a context object and performing a simple drawing operations

Drawing Rectangles

Let us begin with the `canvas` support for rectangles. Table 35-4 describes the relevant methods, all of which we apply to the context object (and not the canvas itself).

▪ **Tip** We can draw more complex shapes, but I don't show you how to do that until Chapter 36. We can use rectangles to explore some of the canvas features without getting bogged down in how the other shapes work.

Table 35-4. The simple shapes methods

Name	Description	Returns
clearRect(x, y, w, h)	Clears the specified rectangle	void
fillRect(x, y, w, h)	Draws a filled rectangle	void
strokeRect(x, y, w, h)	Draws an unfilled rectangle	void

All three of these methods take four arguments. The first two (x and y as shown in the table) are the offset from the top-left corner of the canvas element. The w and h arguments specify the width and height of the rectangle to draw. Listing 35-3 shows the use of the `fillRect` and `strokeRect` methods.

Listing 35-3. Using the fillRect and strokeRect methods

```
<!DOCTYPE HTML>
<html>
    <head>
        <title>Example</title>
        <style>
```

```
                canvas {border: thin solid black; margin: 4px}
            </style>
        </head>
        <body>
            <canvas id="canvas" width="500" height="140">
                Your browser doesn't support the <code>canvas</code> element
            </canvas>
            <script>
                var ctx = document.getElementById("canvas").getContext("2d");

                var offset = 10;
                var size = 50;
                var count = 5;

                for (var i = 0; i < count; i++) {
                    ctx.fillRect(i * (offset + size) + offset, offset, size, size);
                    ctx.strokeRect(i * (offset + size) + offset, (2 * offset) + size,
                        size, size);
                }
            </script>
        </body>
    </html>
```

The script in this example uses the `fillRect` and `strokeRect` methods to create a series of filled and unfilled rectangles. You can see the result in Figure 35-3.

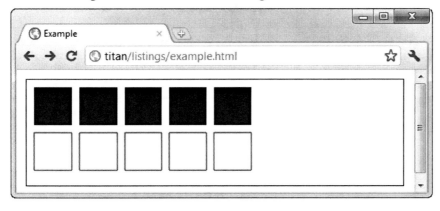

Figure 35-3. Drawing filled and unfilled rectangles

I wrote the script this way to emphasize the programmatic nature of the **canvas** element. I used a JavaScript **for** loop to draw these rectangles. I could have used ten individual statements, all with specific coordinate parameters, but one of the joys of the **canvas** is that we don't need to do this. It can be hard to get your head around this aspect of the canvas if you are not from a programming background.

The **clearRect** method removes whatever has been drawn in the specified rectangle. Listing 35-4 provides a demonstration.

Listing 35-4. Using the clearRect method

```
<!DOCTYPE HTML>
<html>
    <head>
        <title>Example</title>
        <style>
            canvas {border: thin solid black; margin: 4px}
        </style>
    </head>
    <body>
        <canvas id="canvas" width="500" height="140">
            Your browser doesn't support the <code>canvas</code> element
        </canvas>
        <script>
            var ctx = document.getElementById("canvas").getContext("2d");

            var offset = 10;
            var size = 50;
            var count = 5;

            for (var i = 0; i < count; i++) {
                ctx.fillRect(i * (offset + size) + offset, offset, size, size);
                ctx.strokeRect(i * (offset + size) + offset, (2 * offset) + size,
                            size, size);
                ctx.clearRect(i * (offset + size) + offset, offset + 5, size, size -10);
            }
        </script>
    </body>
</html>
```

In this example, I use the `clearRect` method to clear an area of the canvas that has previously been drawn on by the `fillRect` method. You can see the effect in Figure 35-4.

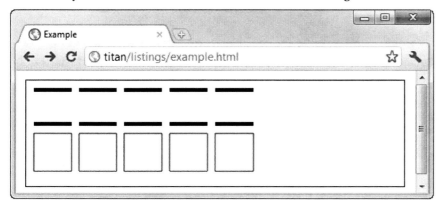

Figure 35-4. Using the clearRect method

Setting the Canvas Drawing State

Drawing operations are configured by the *drawing state*. This is a set of properties that specify everything from line width to fill color. When we draw a shape, the current settings in the drawing state are used. Listing 35-5 provides a demonstration, using the lineWIdth property, which is part of the drawing state and sets the width of lines used for shapes such as those produced by the strokeRect method.

Listing 35-5. Setting the drawing state before performing an operation

```
<!DOCTYPE HTML>
<html>
    <head>
        <title>Example</title>
        <style>
            canvas {border: thin solid black; margin: 4px}
        </style>
    </head>
    <body>
        <canvas id="canvas" width="500" height="70">
            Your browser doesn't support the <code>canvas</code> element
        </canvas>
        <script>
            var ctx = document.getElementById("canvas").getContext("2d");

            ctx.lineWidth = 2;
            ctx.strokeRect(10, 10, 50, 50);
            ctx.lineWidth = 4;
            ctx.strokeRect(70, 10, 50, 50);
            ctx.lineWidth = 6;
            ctx.strokeRect(130, 10, 50, 50);
            ctx.strokeRect(190, 10, 50, 50);
        </script>
    </body>
</html>
```

When I use the strokeRect method, the current value of the lineWidth property is used to draw the rectangle. In the example, I set the property value to 2, 4, and finally 6 pixels, which has the effect of making the lines of the rectangles thicker. Note that I have not changed the value between the last two calls to strokeRect. I have done this to demonstrate that the value of the drawing state properties do not change between drawing operations, as shown in Figure 35-5.

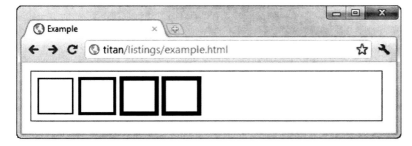

Figure 35-5. Changing a drawing state value between drawing operations

Table 35-5 shows the basic drawing state properties. There are other properties, which we will encounter as we look at more advanced features.

Table 35-5. The basic drawing state properties

Name	Description	Default
fillStyle	Gets or sets the style used for filled shapes	black
lineJoin	Gets or sets the style used when lines meet in a shape	miter
lineWidth	Gets or sets the width of lines	1.0
strokeStyle	Gets or sets the style used for lines	black

Setting the Line Join Style

The lineJoin property determines how lines that join one another are drawn. There are three values: round, bevel, and miter. The default value is miter. Listing 35-6 shows the three styles in use.

Listing 35-6. Setting the lineJoin property

```
<!DOCTYPE HTML>
<html>
    <head>
        <title>Example</title>
        <style>
            canvas {border: thin solid black; margin: 4px}
        </style>
    </head>
    <body>
        <canvas id="canvas" width="500" height="140">
            Your browser doesn't support the <code>canvas</code> element
        </canvas>
        <script>
```

```
                var ctx = document.getElementById("canvas").getContext("2d");
                ctx.lineWidth = 20;

                ctx.lineJoin = "round";
                ctx.strokeRect(20, 20, 100, 100);

                ctx.lineJoin = "bevel";
                ctx.strokeRect(160, 20, 100, 100);

                ctx.lineJoin = "miter";
                ctx.strokeRect(300, 20, 100, 100);
            </script>
        </body>
    </html>
```

In this example, I have used the lineWidth property so that the strokeRect method will draw rectangles with very thick lines and then used each of the lineJoin style values in turn. You can see the result in Figure 35-6.

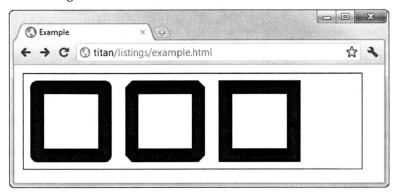

Figure 35-6. The lineJoin property

Setting the Fill & Stroke Styles

When we set a style using the fillStyle or strokeStyle properties, we can specify a color using the CSS color values that I described in Chapter 35-4, using either a name or a color model. Listing 35-7 provides an example.

Listing 35-7. Setting colors using the fillStyle and strokeStyle properties

```
<!DOCTYPE HTML>
<html>
    <head>
        <title>Example</title>
        <style>
            canvas {border: thin solid black; margin: 4px}
        </style>
```

```
    </head>
    <body>
        <canvas id="canvas" width="500" height="140">
            Your browser doesn't support the <code>canvas</code> element
        </canvas>
        <script>
            var ctx = document.getElementById("canvas").getContext("2d");

            var offset = 10;
            var size = 50;
            var count = 5;
            ctx.lineWidth = 3;
            var fillColors = ["black", "grey", "lightgrey", "red", "blue"];
            var strokeColors = ["rgb(0,0,0)", "rgb(100, 100, 100)",
                                "rgb(200, 200, 200)", "rgb(255, 0, 0)",
                                "rgb(0, 0, 255)"];

            for (var i = 0; i < count; i++) {
                ctx.fillStyle = fillColors[i];
                ctx.strokeStyle = strokeColors[i];

                ctx.fillRect(i * (offset + size) + offset, offset, size, size);
                ctx.strokeRect(i * (offset + size) + offset, (2 * offset) + size,
                               size, size);
            }
        </script>
    </body>
</html>
```

In this example, I define two arrays of colors using the CSS color names and the rgb model. I then assign these colors to the fillStyle and strokeStyle properties in the for loop which calls the fillRect and strokeRect methods. You can see the effect in Figure 35-7.

Figure 35-7. Setting the fill and stroke style using CSS colors

---

■ **Note** Of course, anything that involves colors loses something when reproduced in shades of grey on the printed page, so you may wish to load the example in a browser to see the effect. If so, you can get all of the code samples for this book free-of-charge from `apress.com`.

Using Gradients

We can also set the fill and stroke styles using gradients, rather than solid colors. A gradient is a gradual progression between two or more colors. The `canvas` element supports two kinds of gradients: linear and radial, using the methods described in Table 35-6.

Table 35-6. The gradient methods

Name	Description	Returns
`createLinearGradient(x0, y0, x1, y1)`	Creates a linear gradient	`CanvasGradient`
`createRadialGradient(x0, y0, r0, x1, y1, r1)`	Creates a radial gradient	`CanvasGradient`

Both of these methods return a `CanvasGradient` object, which defines the method shown in Table 35-7. The arguments describe the line or circle used by the gradient, which is explained in the following examples.

Table 35-7. The CanvasGradient method

Name	Description	Returns
`addColorStop(<position>, <color>)`	Adds a solid color to the gradient line	`void`

Using a Linear Gradient

A *linear gradient* is one in which we specify the colors we want along a line. Listing 35-8 shows how we can create a simple linear gradient.

Listing 35-8. Creating a linear gradient

```
<!DOCTYPE HTML>
<html>
    <head>
        <title>Example</title>
        <style>
            canvas {border: thin solid black; margin: 4px}
        </style>
    </head>
    <body>
```

```
<canvas id="canvas" width="500" height="140">
    Your browser doesn't support the <code>canvas</code> element
</canvas>
<script>
    var ctx = document.getElementById("canvas").getContext("2d");

    var grad = ctx.createLinearGradient(0, 0, 500, 140);
    grad.addColorStop(0, "red");
    grad.addColorStop(0.5, "white");
    grad.addColorStop(1, "black");

    ctx.fillStyle = grad;
    ctx.fillRect(0, 0, 500, 140);
</script>
</body>
</html>
```

When we use the createLinearGradient method, we supply four values that are used as the start and end coordinates of a line on the canvas. In this example, I have used coordinates to describe a line that starts at the point 0, 0 and ends at 500, 140. These points correspond to the top-left and bottom-right corners of the canvas, as shown in Figure 35-8.

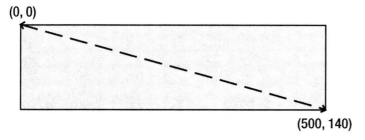

Figure 35-8. The line in a linear gradient

The line represents the gradient. We can now use the addColorStop method on the CanvasGradient returned by the createLinearGradient method to add colors along the gradient line, like this:

```
grad.addColorStop(0, "red");
grad.addColorStop(0.5, "white");
grad.addColorStop(1, "black");
```

The first argument to the addColorStop method is the position on the line that we want to apply the color, which we specify using the second argument. The start of the line (the coordinate 0, 0 in this example) is represented by the value 0 and the end of the line by the value 1. In the example, I have told the canvas that I want the color red at the start of the line, the color white half way along the line, and the color black at the end of the line. The canvas will then work out how to gradually transition between those colors at those points. We can specify as many color stops as we like (but if we get carried away, we end up with something that looks like a rainbow).

Once we have defined the gradient and added the color stops, we can assign the CanvasGradient object to set the fillStyle or strokeStyle properties, like this:

```
ctx.fillStyle = grad;
```

Finally, we can draw a shape. In this example, I drew a filled rectangle, like this:

```
ctx.fillRect(0, 0, 500, 140);
```

This rectangle fills the canvas, showing the entire gradient, as you can see in Figure 35-9.

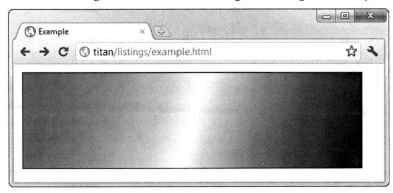

Figure 35-9. Using a linear gradient in a filled rectangle

You can see that the colors change along the line of the gradient. There is solid red in the top-left corner, solid white in the middle of the line, and solid black in the bottom-right corner, and the color gradually shifts between these points.

Using a Linear Gradient with a Smaller Shape

When we define the gradient line, we do so relative to the canvas – not the shapes that we draw. This tends to cause some confusion at first. Listing 35-9 contains a demonstration of what I mean.

Listing 35-9. Using a gradient with a shape that doesn't fill the canvas

```
<!DOCTYPE HTML>
<html>
    <head>
        <title>Example</title>
        <style>
            canvas {border: thin solid black; margin: 4px}
        </style>
    </head>
    <body>
        <canvas id="canvas" width="500" height="140">
            Your browser doesn't support the <code>canvas</code> element
        </canvas>
        <script>
            var ctx = document.getElementById("canvas").getContext("2d");

            var grad = ctx.createLinearGradient(0, 0, 500, 140);
            grad.addColorStop(0, "red");
            grad.addColorStop(0.5, "white");
```

```
            grad.addColorStop(1, "black");

            ctx.fillStyle = grad;
            ctx.fillRect(10, 10, 50, 50);
        </script>
    </body>
</html>
```

The change in this example is simply to make the rectangle smaller. You can see the result in Figure 35-10.

Figure 35-10. Missing the gradations in a gradient

This is what I mean about the gradient line relating to the canvas. I have drawn my rectangle in a region that is solid red. (In fact, if we were able to zoom in close enough, we might be able to detect tiny gradations toward white, but the general appearance is of a solid color.) The best way to think about this is that when we draw a shape, we are allowing part of the underlying gradient show through, which means we have to think about how the gradient line relates to the area we are going to expose. Listing 35-10 shows how we can target the gradient line for a shape.

Listing 35-10. Making the gradient line match a desired shape

```
<!DOCTYPE HTML>
<html>
    <head>
        <title>Example</title>
        <style>
            canvas {border: thin solid black; margin: 4px}
        </style>
    </head>
    <body>
        <canvas id="canvas" width="500" height="140">
            Your browser doesn't support the <code>canvas</code> element
        </canvas>
        <script>
            var ctx = document.getElementById("canvas").getContext("2d");
```

```
            var grad = ctx.createLinearGradient(10, 10, 60, 60);
            grad.addColorStop(0, "red");
            grad.addColorStop(0.5, "white");
            grad.addColorStop(1, "black");

            ctx.fillStyle = grad;
            ctx.fillRect(0, 0, 500, 140);
        </script>
    </body>
</html>
```

In this example, I have set the gradient line so that it starts and stops within the area that I want to reveal with my smaller rectangle. However, I have drawn the rectangle to reveal *all* of the gradient so you can see the effect of the change, as shown in Figure 11.

Figure 35-11. The effect of moving and shortening the gradient line

You can see how the gradations have been shifted to the area I am going to expose with the smaller rectangle. The last step is to match the rectangle to the gradient, as shown in Listing 35-11.

Listing 35-11. Matching the shape to the gradient

```
<!DOCTYPE HTML>
<html>
    <head>
        <title>Example</title>
        <style>
            canvas {border: thin solid black; margin: 4px}
        </style>
    </head>
    <body>
        <canvas id="canvas" width="500" height="140">
            Your browser doesn't support the <code>canvas</code> element
        </canvas>
        <script>
            var ctx = document.getElementById("canvas").getContext("2d");
```

```
            var grad = ctx.createLinearGradient(10, 10, 60, 60);
            grad.addColorStop(0, "red");
            grad.addColorStop(0.5, "white");
            grad.addColorStop(1, "black");

            ctx.fillStyle = grad;
            ctx.fillRect(10, 10, 50, 50);
        </script>
    </body>
</html>
```

■ **Tip** Notice that the numeric values I used as arguments in the `createLinearGradient` method are different from the parameters I used in the `fillRect` method. The `createLinearGradient` values represent a pair of coordinates in the canvas, whereas the `fillRect` values represent the width and height of a rectangle relative to a single coordinate. If you find that the gradient and shape don't line up, this is likely to be the cause of the problem.

Now the shape and the gradient are perfectly aligned, as shown in Figure 35-12. Of course, we don't always want them perfectly aligned. We might want to expose a specific region of a larger gradient in order to get a different effect. Whatever the goal, it is important to understand the relationship between the gradient and the shapes that we use it with.

Figure 35-12. Aligning shape and gradient

Using a Radial Gradient

We define radial gradients using two circles. The start of the gradient is defined by the first circle, the end of the gradient by the second circle and we add color stops between them. Listing 35-12 provides an example.

Listing 35-12. Using a radial gradient

```html
<!DOCTYPE HTML>
<html>
    <head>
        <title>Example</title>
        <style>
            canvas {border: thin solid black; margin: 4px}
        </style>
    </head>
    <body>
        <canvas id="canvas" width="500" height="140">
            Your browser doesn't support the <code>canvas</code> element
        </canvas>
        <script>
            var ctx = document.getElementById("canvas").getContext("2d");

            var grad = ctx.createRadialGradient(250, 70, 20, 200, 60, 100);
            grad.addColorStop(0, "red");
            grad.addColorStop(0.5, "white");
            grad.addColorStop(1, "black");

            ctx.fillStyle = grad;
            ctx.fillRect(0, 0, 500, 140);
        </script>
    </body>
</html>
```

The six arguments to the `createRadialGradient` method represent:

- The coordinate for the center of the start circle (the first and second arguments)

- The radius of the start circle (the third argument)

- The coordinate for the center of the finish circle (the fourth and fifth arguments)

- The radius of the finish circle (the sixth argument)

The values in the example give the start and end circles as shown in Figure 35-13. Notice that we can specify gradients that are outside of the canvas (this is true for linear gradients as well).

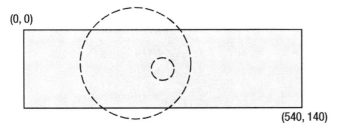

Figure 35-13. The start and end circles in a radial gradient

In this example, the start circle is the smaller one and is encompassed by the finish circle. When we add color stops on this gradient, they are placed on a line between the edge of the start circle (a stop value of 0.0) and the edge of the finish circle (a stop value of 1.0).

■ **Tip** Be careful when specifying circles such that one does not contain the other. There are some inconsistencies between browsers in how to derive the gradations and the results are messy.

Since we are able to specify the position of both circles, the distance between the circle edges can vary and the rate of gradation between colors will also vary. You can see the effect in Figure 35-14.

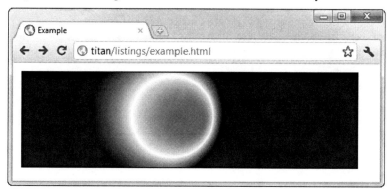

Figure 35-14. Using a radial gradiation

The figure shows the whole gradient, but the same rules apply for how the gradient relates to drawing shapes. Listing 35-13 creates a pair of smaller shapes that reveal subsections of the gradient.

Listing 35-13. Using smaller shapes with a radial gradient

```
<!DOCTYPE HTML>
<html>
    <head>
        <title>Example</title>
        <style>
            canvas {border: thin solid black; margin: 4px}
        </style>
    </head>
    <body>
        <canvas id="canvas" width="500" height="140">
            Your browser doesn't support the <code>canvas</code> element
        </canvas>
        <script>
            var ctx = document.getElementById("canvas").getContext("2d");
```

```
            var grad = ctx.createRadialGradient(250, 70, 20, 200, 60, 100);
            grad.addColorStop(0, "red");
            grad.addColorStop(0.5, "white");
            grad.addColorStop(1, "black");

            ctx.fillStyle = grad;
            ctx.fillRect(150, 20, 75, 50);

            ctx.lineWidth = 8;
            ctx.strokeStyle = grad;
            ctx.strokeRect(250, 20, 75, 50);
        </script>
    </body>
</html>
```

Notice that I am able to use the gradient for both the `fillStyle` and `strokeStyle` properties, enabling us to use gradients for lines as well as solid shapes, as shown by Figure 35-15.

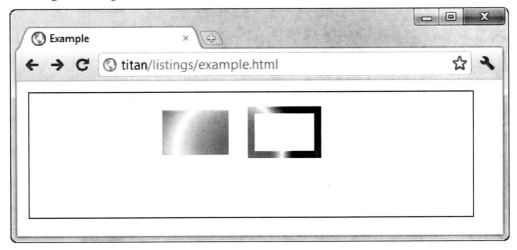

Figure 35-15. Using a radial gradient for both fills and strokes

Using Patterns

In addition to solid colors and gradients, we can create *patterns*. We do this using the `createPattern` method, which is defined by the canvas context object. The 2D drawing context defines support for three types of pattern – image, video, and canvas – but only the image pattern is implemented (and only by Firefox and Opera. As I write this, the other browsers ignore this pattern type.).

To use an image pattern, we pass an `HTMLImageElement` object as the first argument to the `createPattern` method. The second argument is the repeat style, which must be one of the values shown in Table 35-8.

Table 35-8. The pattern repeat values

Value	Description
repeat	The image should be repeated vertically and horizontally
repeat-x	The image should be repeated horizontally
repeat-y	The image should be repeated vertically
no-repeat	The image should not be repeated in the pattern

Listing 35-14 shows how we can create and use an image pattern.

Listing 35-14. Using an image pattern

```
<!DOCTYPE HTML>
<html>
    <head>
        <title>Example</title>
        <style>
            canvas {border: thin solid black; margin: 4px}
        </style>
    </head>
    <body>
        <canvas id="canvas" width="500" height="140">
            Your browser doesn't support the <code>canvas</code> element
        </canvas>
        <img id="banana" hidden src="banana-small.png"/>
        <script>
            var ctx = document.getElementById("canvas").getContext("2d");
            var imageElem = document.getElementById("banana");

            var pattern = ctx.createPattern(imageElem, "repeat");

            ctx.fillStyle = pattern;
            ctx.fillRect(0, 0, 500, 140);
        </script>
    </body>
</html>
```

The document in this example contains an `img` element, which isn't visible to the user because I have applied the `hidden` attribute (described in Chapter 4). In the script, I use the DOM to locate the `HTMLImageElement` object that represents the `img` element as the first argument to the `createPattern` method. For the second argument, I use the `repeat` value, which causes the image to be repeated in both directions. Finally, I set the pattern as the value for the `fillStyle` property and use the `fillRect` method to draw a filled rectangle which is the same size as the canvas. You can see the result in Figure 35-16.

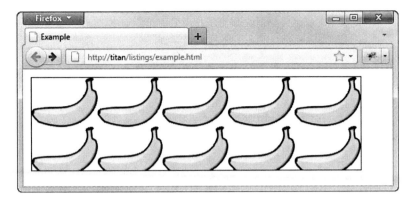

Figure 35-16. Creating an image pattern

The pattern is copied from the current state of the img element, meaning the pattern won't change if we use JavaScript and the DOM to change the value of the src attribute value of the img element.

As with gradients, the pattern applies to the entire canvas and we decide which portions of the pattern are shown by the shapes we draw. Listing 35-15 shows using the pattern for smaller fill and stroke shapes.

Listing 35-15. Using smaller shapes with an image pattern

```
<!DOCTYPE HTML>
<html>
    <head>
        <title>Example</title>
        <style>
            canvas {border: thin solid black; margin: 4px}
        </style>
    </head>
    <body>
        <canvas id="canvas" width="500" height="140">
            Your browser doesn't support the <code>canvas</code> element
        </canvas>
        <img id="banana" hidden src="banana-small.png"/>
        <script>
            var ctx = document.getElementById("canvas").getContext("2d");
            var imageElem = document.getElementById("banana");

            var pattern = ctx.createPattern(imageElem, "repeat");

            ctx.fillStyle = pattern;
            ctx.fillRect(150, 20, 75, 50);

            ctx.lineWidth = 8;
            ctx.strokeStyle = pattern;
            ctx.strokeRect(250, 20, 75, 50);
        </script>
```

```
        </body>
</html>
```

You can see the result in Figure 35-17.

Figure 35-17. Using smaller shapes with an image pattern

Saving and Restoring Drawing State

We can save the drawing state and return to it later using the methods described in Table 35-9.

Table 35-9. Saving and restoring state

Value	Description
save()	Saves the values for the drawing state properties and pushes them on the state stack
restore()	Pops the first set of values from the state stack and uses them to set the drawing state

The saved drawing states are stored in a last-in, first-out (LIFO) stack, such that the last state we saved using the **save** method is the first one restored by the **restore** method. Listing 35-16 shows these methods in use.

Listing 35-16. Saving and restoring state

```
<!DOCTYPE HTML>
<html>
    <head>
        <title>Example</title>
        <style>
            canvas {border: thin solid black; margin: 4px}
        </style>
    </head>
    <body>
```

```
<canvas id="canvas" width="500" height="140" preload="auto">
    Your browser doesn't support the <code>canvas</code> element
</canvas>
<div>
    <button>Save</button>
    <button>Restore</button>
</div>
<script>
    var ctx = document.getElementById("canvas").getContext("2d");

    var grad = ctx.createLinearGradient(500, 0, 500, 140);
    grad.addColorStop(0, "red");
    grad.addColorStop(0.5, "white");
    grad.addColorStop(1, "black");

    var colors = ["black", grad, "red", "green", "yellow", "black", "grey"];

    var cIndex = 0;

    ctx.fillStyle = colors[cIndex];
    draw();

    var buttons = document.getElementsByTagName("button");
    for (var i = 0; i < buttons.length; i++) {
        buttons[i].onclick = handleButtonPress;
    }

    function handleButtonPress(e) {
        switch (e.target.innerHTML) {
            case 'Save':
                ctx.save();
                cIndex = (cIndex + 1) % colors.length;
                ctx.fillStyle = colors[cIndex];
                draw();
                break;
            case 'Restore':
                cIndex = Math.max(0, cIndex -1);
                ctx.restore();
                draw();
                break;
        }
    }
    function draw() {
        ctx.fillRect(0, 0, 500, 140);
    }
</script>
</body>
</html>
```

In this example, I have defined an array that contains CSS color names and a linear gradient. The current drawing state is saved using the save method when the Save button is pressed. When the Restore button is pressed, the previous drawing state is restored. After either button press, the draw function is called, which uses the `fillRect` method to draw a filled rectangle. The `fillStyle` property is advanced and retarded in the array and saved and restored when the buttons are pressed because this property is part of the drawing state. You can see the effect in Figure 35-18.

Figure 35-18. Saving and restoring the drawing state

The contents of the canvas are not saved or restored; only the property values for the drawing state are saved or restored. This includes properties we have seen in this chapter, such as `lineWidth`, `fillStyle`, and `strokeStyle`, and some additional properties that I describe in Chapter 36.

Drawing Images

We can draw images on the canvas by using the `drawImage` method. This method takes three, five, or nine arguments. The first argument is always the source of the image, which can be the DOM object that represents an `img`, `video,` or another `canvas` element. Listing 35-17 gives an example, using an `img` element as the source.

Listing 35-17. Using the drawImage method

```
<!DOCTYPE HTML>
<html>
    <head>
        <title>Example</title>
        <style>
            canvas {border: thin solid black; margin: 4px}
        </style>
    </head>
    <body>
        <canvas id="canvas" width="500" height="140" preload="auto">
            Your browser doesn't support the <code>canvas</code> element
        </canvas>
        <img id="banana" hidden src="banana-small.png"/>
        <script>
```

921

```
        var ctx = document.getElementById("canvas").getContext("2d");
        var imageElement = document.getElementById("banana");

        ctx.drawImage(imageElement, 10, 10);
        ctx.drawImage(imageElement, 120, 10, 100, 120);
        ctx.drawImage(imageElement, 20, 20, 100, 50, 250, 10, 100, 120);
    </script>
</body>
</html>
```

When using three arguments, the second and third arguments give the coordinate on the canvas at which the image should be drawn. The image is drawn at its intrinsic width and height. When using five arguments, the additional arguments specify the width and height at which the image should be drawn, overriding the intrinsic size.

When using nine arguments:

- The second and third arguments are the offset into the source image.

- The fourth and fifth arguments are the width and height of the region of the source image that will be used.

- The sixth and seventh arguments specify the canvas coordinate at which the top-left corner of the selected region will be drawn.

- The eighth and ninth arguments specify the width and height to which the selected region will be draw.

You can see the effect of these arguments in Figure 35-19.

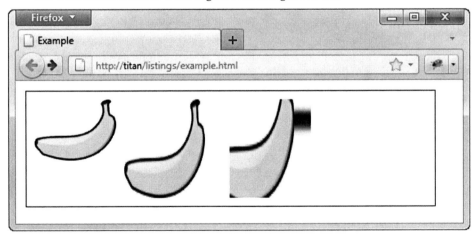

Figure 35-19. Drawing an image

Using Video Images

We can use a **video** element as the source of the image for the **drawImage** method. When we do this, we take a snapshot of the video. Listing 35-18 provides a demonstration.

Listing 35-18. Using video as the source for the drawImage element

```
<!DOCTYPE HTML>
<html>
    <head>
        <title>Example</title>
        <style>
            canvas {border: thin solid black}
            body > * {float:left;}
        </style>
    </head>
    <body>
        <video id="vid" src="timessquare.webm" controls preload="auto"
            width="360" height="240">
            Video cannot be displayed
        </video>
        <div>
            <button id="pressme">Snapshot</button>
        </div>
        <canvas id="canvas" width="360" height="240">
            Your browser doesn't support the <code>canvas</code> element
        </canvas>
        <script>
            var ctx = document.getElementById("canvas").getContext("2d");
            var imageElement = document.getElementById("vid");

            document.getElementById("pressme").onclick = function(e) {
                ctx.drawImage(imageElement, 0, 0, 360, 240);
            }
        </script>
    </body>
</html>
```

In this example, I have a video element, a button, and a canvas element. When the button is pressed, the current video frame is used to paint the canvas using the drawImage method. You can see the result in Figure 35-20.

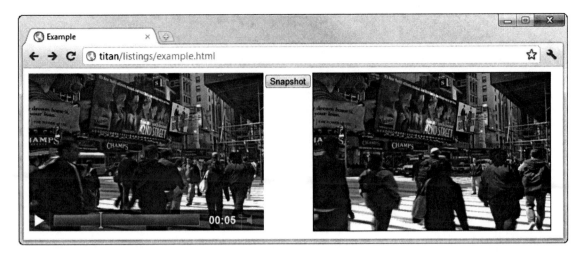

Figure 35-20. Using a video as the source for the canvas drawImage method

If you find yourself looking at HTML5 demos, you will often see the canvas used to draw over a video. This is done using the technique I just showed you, combined with a timer (such as that described in Chapter 27). Listing 35-19 shows how to put this together. This is not a technique I am particularly fond of. If you want to know why, just watch the CPU load on the machine displaying a document of this type.

Listing 35-19. Using the canvas to display and draw on video

```
<!DOCTYPE HTML>
<html>
    <head>
        <title>Example</title>
        <style>
            canvas {border: thin solid black}
            body > * {float:left;}
        </style>
    </head>
    <body>
        <video id="vid" hidden src="timessquare.webm" preload="auto"
            width="360" height="240" autoplay></video>
        <canvas id="canvas" width="360" height="240">
            Your browser doesn't support the <code>canvas</code> element
        </canvas>
        <script>
            var ctx = document.getElementById("canvas").getContext("2d");
            var imageElement = document.getElementById("vid");

            var width = 100;
            var height = 10;
            ctx.lineWidth = 5;
            ctx.strokeStyle = "red";
```

```
        setInterval(function() {
            ctx.drawImage(imageElement, 0, 0, 360, 240);
            ctx.strokeRect(180 - (width/2),120 - (height/2), width, height);
        }, 25);

        setInterval(function() {
            width = (width + 1) % 200;
            height = (height + 3) % 200;
        }, 100);

    </script>
    </body>
</html>
```

In this example, there is a `video` element to which I have applied the `hidden` attribute, so that it is not visible to the user. I have used two timers – the first fires every 25 milliseconds and draws the current video frame and then a stroked rectangle. The second timer fires every 100 milliseconds and changes the values used for the rectangle. The effect is that the rectangle changes size and is superimposed over the video image. You can get a sense of the effect in Figure 35-21, although to fully appreciate what is happening, you should load the example document into a browser.

Figure 35-21. Using timers to recreate overlaid video on a canvas

We can't use the built-in controls when using a video element like this. I have used the `autoplay` attribute to keep the example simple, but a more useful solution is to implement custom controls as shown in Chapter 34.

Using Canvas Images

We can use the contents of one canvas as the source for the `drawImage` method on another, as shown in Listing 35-20.

Listing 35-20. Using a canvas as the source for the drawImage method

```
<!DOCTYPE HTML>
<html>
    <head>
        <title>Example</title>
        <style>
            canvas {border: thin solid black}
            body > * {float:left;}
        </style>
    </head>
    <body>
        <video id="vid" hidden src="timessquare.webm" preload="auto"
            width="360" height="240" autoplay></video>
        <canvas id="canvas" width="360" height="240">
            Your browser doesn't support the <code>canvas</code> element
        </canvas>
        <div>
            <button id="pressme">Press Me</button>
        </div>
        <canvas id="canvas2" width="360" height="240">
            Your browser doesn't support the <code>canvas</code> element
        </canvas>
        <script>
            var srcCanvasElement = document.getElementById("canvas");
            var ctx = srcCanvasElement.getContext("2d");
            var ctx2= document.getElementById("canvas2").getContext("2d");
            var imageElement = document.getElementById("vid");

            document.getElementById("pressme").onclick = takeSnapshot;

            var width = 100;
            var height = 10;
            ctx.lineWidth = 5;
            ctx.strokeStyle = "red";
            ctx2.lineWidth = 30;
            ctx2.strokeStyle = "black;"

            setInterval(function() {
                ctx.drawImage(imageElement, 0, 0, 360, 240);
                ctx.strokeRect(180 - (width/2),120 - (height/2), width, height);
            }, 25);

            setInterval(function() {
                width = (width + 1) % 200;
                height = (height + 3) % 200;
            }, 100);

            function takeSnapshot() {
                ctx2.drawImage(srcCanvasElement, 0, 0, 360, 240);
```

```
            ctx2.strokeRect(0, 0, 360, 240);
        }
    </script>
    </body>
</html>
```

In this example, I have added a second `canvas` element and a `button`. When the button is pressed, I use the `HTMLCanvasElement` object that represents the original `canvas` as the first argument in a call to the `drawImage` method on the context object of the second `canvas`. In essence, pressing the button takes a snapshot of the left-hand canvas and displays it on the right-hand canvas. We copy everything on the canvas, including the red overlaid rectangle. We can perform further drawing operations, which is why I have drawn a thick black border on the second canvas as part of the snapshot. You can see the effect in Figure 22.

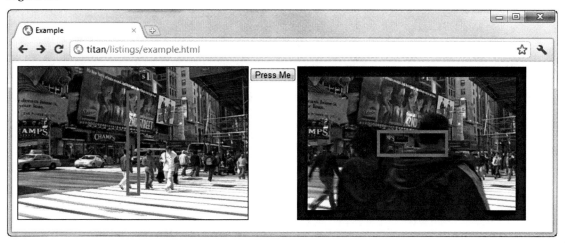

Figure 35-22. Using one canvas as the source for the drawImage method on another canvas

Summary

In this chapter, I have introduced the `canvas` element, showing how to draw basic shapes, how to configure, save, and restore the drawing state, and how to use solid colors and gradients in drawing operations. I also showed how we can draw images using the contents of `img`, `video`, or other `canvas` elements as the image source. In Chapter 36, I'll show how to draw more complex shapes and how to apply effects and transformations.

CHAPTER 36

Using the Canvas
Element – Part II

In this chapter, I continue describing the features of the canvas element, showing how we can draw more complex shapes (including arcs and curves), how we can limit operations using a clipping region and how we can draw text. I also describe the effects and transformations that we can apply to the canvas, including shadows, transparency, rotations, and translations. Table 36-1 provides the summary for this chapter.

Table 36-1. Chapter Summary

Problem	Solution	Listing
Draw a shape using lines	Use the beginPath, moveTo, lineTo and, optionally, the closePath methods	1
Set the style used to draw the end of lines	Set the lineCap property	2
Draw rectangles as part of a path	Use the rect method	3, 4
Draw an arc	Use the arc or arcTo methods	5-7
Draw a cubic or quadratic Bezier curve	Use the bezierCurveTo or quadraticCurveTo methods	8-9
Limit the effect of drawing operations to a particular region of the canvas	Use the clip method	10
Draw text on the canvas	Use the fillText or strokeText methods	11
Add shadows to text or shapes	Use the shadow properties	12
Set a general transparency value	Use the globalAlpha property	13

| Set the composition style | Use the globalCompositeOperation property | 14 |
| Transform the canvas | Use one of the transformation methods, such as rotate or scale. | 15 |

Drawing Using Paths

The examples in the Chapter 35 all relied on our ability to draw rectangles. Rectangles are a useful shape, but they are not always what's required. Fortunately, the canvas element and its context provide a set of methods that allow us to draw shapes using *paths*. Paths are essentially a set of individual lines (known as sub-paths) which cumulatively form a shape. We draw sub-paths much as we would use a pen to draw on a piece of paper without lifting the nib from the page - each sub-path starts from the point on the canvas where the last sub-path ended. Table 2 shows the methods that are available for drawing basic paths.

Table 2. The basic path methods

Name	Description	Returns
beginPath()	Begins a new path	void
closePath()	Attempts to close the existing path by drawing a line from the end of the last line to the initial coordinates	void
fill()	Fills the shape described by the sub-paths	void
isPointInPath(x, y)	Returns true if the specified point is contained by the shape described by the current path	boolean
lineTo(x, y)	Draws a sub-path to the specified coordinates	void
moveTo(x, y)	Moves to the specified coordinates without drawing a sub-path	void
rect(x, y, w, h)	Draws a rectangle whose top-left corners is at (x, y) with width w and height h.	void
stroke()	Draws the outline of the shape as described by the sub-paths	void

The basic sequence for drawing a path is as follows:

- Call the beginPath method
- Move to the start position using the moveTo method
- Draw sub-paths with methods such as arc, lineTo, etc.

- Optionally call the closePath method

- Call the fill or stoke methods

In the sections that follow, I'll show you how to use this sequence with the different sub-path methods.

Drawing Paths with Lines

The simplest paths are those made up of straight lines. Listing 36-1 provides a demonstration.

Listing 36-1. Creating a path from straight-lines

```
<!DOCTYPE HTML>
<html>
    <head>
        <title>Example</title>
        <style>
            canvas {border: thin solid black}
            body > * {float:left;}
        </style>
    </head>
    <body>
        <canvas id="canvas" width="500" height="140">
            Your browser doesn't support the <code>canvas</code> element
        </canvas>
        <script>
            var ctx = document.getElementById("canvas").getContext("2d");

            ctx.fillStyle = "yellow";
            ctx.strokeStyle = "black";
            ctx.lineWidth = 4;

            ctx.beginPath();
            ctx.moveTo(10, 10);
            ctx.lineTo(110, 10);
            ctx.lineTo(110, 120);
            ctx.closePath();
            ctx.fill();

            ctx.beginPath();
            ctx.moveTo(150, 10);
            ctx.lineTo(200, 10);
            ctx.lineTo(200, 120);
            ctx.lineTo(190, 120);

            ctx.fill();
            ctx.stroke();

            ctx.beginPath();
            ctx.moveTo(250, 10);
```

931

```
                ctx.lineTo(250, 120);
                ctx.stroke();
            </script>
        </body>
    </html>
```

In this example, I have created three paths. You can see how they appear on the canvas in Figure 36-1.

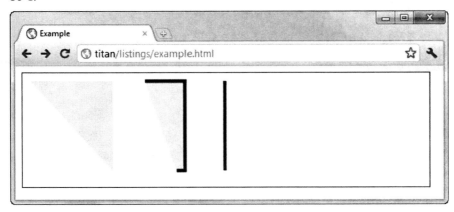

Figure 36-1. Creating simple paths with the lineTo method

For the first path, I explicitly drew two lines and then used the closePath method. The canvas will close the path. I then call the fill method to fill the shape with the style specified by the fillStyle property (I have used a solid color in this example, but we can use any of the gradients and patterns described in Chapter 35).

For the second shape, I specified three sub-paths, but didn't close the shape. You can see that I called both the fill and stroke methods to fill the shape with color and draw a line along the path. Notice that the fill color is drawn as though the shape were closed. The canvas element assumes a sub-path from the last point to the first and uses this to fill the shape. By contrast, the stroke method only follows sub-paths that have been defined.

▪ **Tip** For the second shape, I called the fill method before the stroke method, which causes the canvas to fill the shape with solid color and then draw a line that follows the path. We get a different visual effect if the lineWidth property is greater than 1 and we call the stroke method first. Wider lines are drawn on both sides of the path, so part of the line is covered by the fill method when it is called, effectively narrowing the line width.

For the third shape, I have simply drawn a line between two points because paths don't have to have multiple sub-paths. When we draw lines or leave shapes open, we can use the lineCap property to set the style for how the line is terminated. The three allowed values for this property are: butt, round, and square (butt is the default). Listing 36-2 shows this property and each of its values in use.

Listing 36-2. Setting the lineCap property

```
<!DOCTYPE HTML>
<html>
    <head>
        <title>Example</title>
        <style>
            canvas {border: thin solid black}
            body > * {float:left;}
        </style>
    </head>
    <body>
        <canvas id="canvas" width="200" height="140">
            Your browser doesn't support the <code>canvas</code> element
        </canvas>
        <script>
            var ctx = document.getElementById("canvas").getContext("2d");

            ctx.strokeStyle = "red";
            ctx.lineWidth = "2";
            ctx.beginPath();
            ctx.moveTo(0, 50);
            ctx.lineTo(200, 50);
            ctx.stroke();

            ctx.strokeStyle = "black";
            ctx.lineWidth = 40;

            var xpos = 50;
            var styles = ["butt", "round", "square"];
            for (var i = 0; i < styles.length; i++) {
                ctx.beginPath();
                ctx.lineCap = styles[i];
                ctx.moveTo(xpos, 50);
                ctx.lineTo(xpos, 150);
                ctx.stroke();
                xpos += 50;
            }
        </script>
    </body>
</html>
```

The script in this example draws a very thick line for each of the styles. I have also added a guide line to demonstrate that the round and square styles are drawn beyond the end of the line, as shown in Figure 36-2.

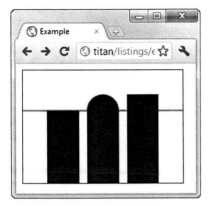

Figure 36-2. The three lineCap styles

Drawing Rectangles

The rect method adds a rectangular sub-path to the current path. If you need a stand-alone rectangle, then the fillRect and strokeRect methods described in Chapter 35 are more suitable. The rect method is useful when you need to add a rectangle to a more complex shape, as demonstrated by Listing 36-3.

Listing 36-3. Drawing a rectangle with the rect method

```
<!DOCTYPE HTML>
<html>
    <head>
        <title>Example</title>
        <style>
            canvas {border: thin solid black}
            body > * {float:left;}
        </style>
    </head>
    <body>
        <canvas id="canvas" width="500" height="140">
            Your browser doesn't support the <code>canvas</code> element
        </canvas>
        <script>
            var ctx = document.getElementById("canvas").getContext("2d");

            ctx.fillStyle = "yellow";
            ctx.strokeStyle = "black";
            ctx.lineWidth = 4;

            ctx.beginPath();
            ctx.moveTo(110, 10);

            ctx.lineTo(110, 100);
            ctx.lineTo(10, 10);
```

```
        ctx.closePath();

        ctx.rect(110, 10, 100, 90);
        ctx.rect(110, 100, 130, 30);

        ctx.fill();
        ctx.stroke();
    </script>
  </body>
</html>
```

We don't have to use the moveTo method when using the rect method because we specify the coordinates of the rectangle as the first two method arguments. In the listing, I have drawn a pair of lines, called closePath to create a triangle and then drawn two adjoining rectangles. You can see the result in Figure 36-3.

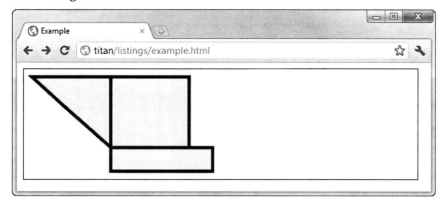

Figure 36-3. Using the rect method to draw rectangles

Sub-paths don't have to touch to form part of a path. We can have several disconnected sub-paths and they are still treated as being part of the same shape. Listing 36-4 gives a demonstration.

Listing 36-4. Working with disconnected sub-paths

```
...
<script>
    var ctx = document.getElementById("canvas").getContext("2d");

    ctx.fillStyle = "yellow";
    ctx.strokeStyle = "black";
    ctx.lineWidth = 4;

    ctx.beginPath();
    ctx.moveTo(110, 10);

    ctx.lineTo(110, 100);
    ctx.lineTo(10, 10);
    ctx.closePath();
```

```
    ctx.rect(120, 10, 100, 90);
    ctx.rect(150, 110, 130, 20);

    ctx.fill();
    ctx.stroke();
</script>
...
```

In this example, the sub-paths are not connected, but the overall result is still a single path. When I call the stroke or fill methods, the effects are applied to all of the sub-paths I created, as you can see in Figure 36-4.

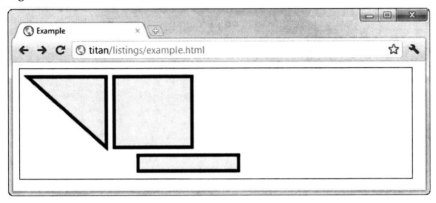

Figure 36-4. Using disconnected sub-paths

Drawing Arcs

We use the arc and arcTo methods to draw arcs on the canvas, although each method draws the arc in a different way. Table 36-3 describes the arc-related methods in the canvas.

Table 36-3. The arc methods

Name	Description	Returns
arc(x, y, rad, startAngle, endAngle,direction)	Draws an arc to (x, y) with radius rad, start angle startAngle, and finish angle endAngle. The optional direction parameter specifies the direction of the arc	void
arcTo(x1, y1, x2, y2,rad)	Draw an arc to (x2, y2) that passes (x1, y1) and has radius rad	void

Using the arcTo Method

Listing 36-5 demonstrates using the arcTo method.

Listing 36-5. Using the arcTo method

```
<!DOCTYPE HTML>
<html>
    <head>
        <title>Example</title>
        <style>
            canvas {border: thin solid black}
            body > * {float:left;}
        </style>
    </head>
    <body>
        <canvas id="canvas" width="500" height="140">
            Your browser doesn't support the <code>canvas</code> element
        </canvas>
        <script>
            var ctx = document.getElementById("canvas").getContext("2d");

            var point1 = [100, 10];
            var point2 = [200, 10];
            var point3 = [200, 110];

            ctx.fillStyle = "yellow";
            ctx.strokeStyle = "black";
            ctx.lineWidth = 4;

            ctx.beginPath();
            ctx.moveTo(point1[0], point1[1]);
            ctx.arcTo(point2[0], point2[1], point3[0], point3[1], 100);
            ctx.stroke();

            drawPoint(point1[0], point1[1]);
            drawPoint(point2[0], point2[1]);
            drawPoint(point3[0], point3[1]);

            ctx.beginPath();
            ctx.moveTo(point1[0], point1[1]);
            ctx.lineTo(point2[0], point2[1]);
            ctx.lineTo(point3[0], point3[1]);
            ctx.stroke();

            function drawPoint(x, y) {
                ctx.lineWidth = 1;
                ctx.strokeStyle = "red";
                ctx.strokeRect(x -2, y-2, 4, 4);
            }
        </script>
```

```
        </body>
</html>
```

The arc drawn by the arcTo method depends on two lines. The first line is drawn from the end of the last sub-path to the point described by the first two method arguments. The second line is drawn from the point described by the first two arguments to the point described by the third and fourth arguments. The arc is then drawn as the shortest line between the end of the last sub-path and the second point that describes an arc of a circle with the radius specified by the last argument. To make this easier to understand, I have added some additional paths to the canvas to provide some context, as shown in Figure 36-5.

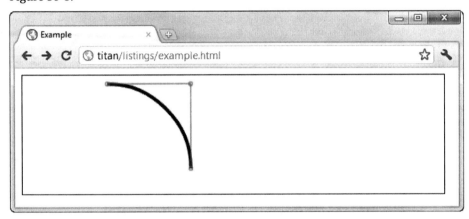

Figure 36-5. Using the arcTo method

You can see the two lines drawn in red. I have specified a radius and the length of both lines are all the same, which means that we end up with a neat curve that just touches the last point of the previous sub-path and the point described by the third and fourth method arguments. The radius and the line lengths are not always so conveniently sized, so the canvas will adjust the arc it draws as required. As a demonstration, Listing 36-6 uses the events described in Chapter 30 to monitor mouse movements and draw arc lines for different points as the mouse is moved across the screen.

Listing 36-6. Drawing arcs in response to mouse movements

```
<!DOCTYPE HTML>
<html>
    <head>
        <title>Example</title>
        <style>
            canvas {border: thin solid black}
            body > * {float:left;}
        </style>
    </head>
    <body>
        <canvas id="canvas" width="500" height="140">
            Your browser doesn't support the <code>canvas</code> element
        </canvas>
```

```
<script>
    var canvasElem = document.getElementById("canvas");
    var ctx = canvasElem.getContext("2d");

    var point1 = [100, 10];
    var point2 = [200, 10];
    var point3 = [200, 110];

    draw();

    canvasElem.onmousemove = function (e) {
        if (e.ctrlKey) {
            point1 = [e.clientX, e.clientY];
        } else if(e.shiftKey) {
            point2 = [e.clientX, e.clientY];
        } else {
            point3 = [e.clientX, e.clientY];
        }
        ctx.clearRect(0, 0, 540, 140);
        draw();
    }

    function draw() {

        ctx.fillStyle = "yellow";
        ctx.strokeStyle = "black";
        ctx.lineWidth = 4;

        ctx.beginPath();
        ctx.moveTo(point1[0], point1[1]);
        ctx.arcTo(point2[0], point2[1], point3[0], point3[1], 50);
        ctx.stroke();

        drawPoint(point1[0], point1[1]);
        drawPoint(point2[0], point2[1]);
        drawPoint(point3[0], point3[1]);

        ctx.beginPath();
        ctx.moveTo(point1[0], point1[1]);
        ctx.lineTo(point2[0], point2[1]);
        ctx.lineTo(point3[0], point3[1]);
        ctx.stroke();
    }

    function drawPoint(x, y) {
        ctx.lineWidth = 1;
        ctx.strokeStyle = "red";
        ctx.strokeRect(x -2, y-2, 4, 4);
    }
</script>
</body>
</html>
```

The script in this example moves different points based on which key is pressed as the mouse is moved. If the control key is pressed, the first point is moved (the one that represents the end of the previous sub-path). If the shift key is pressed, the second point is moved (the point represented by the first two arguments to the arcTo method). If neither key is pressed, the third point is moved (the one represented by the third and fourth method arguments). It is worth spending a moment playing with this example to get a sense for how the arc relates to the position of the two lines. You can see a snapshot of this in Figure 36-6.

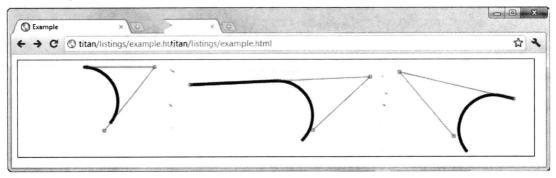

Figure 36-6. The relationship between the lines and the arc

Using the arc Method

The arc method is a little simpler to work with. We specify a point on the canvas using the first two method arguments. We specify the radius of the arc with the third argument and then we specify the start and end angle for the arc. The final argument specifies whether the arc is drawn in the clockwise or anticlockwise direction. Listing 36-7 gives some examples.

Listing 36-7. Using the arc method

```
<!DOCTYPE HTML>
<html>
    <head>
        <title>Example</title>
        <style>
            canvas {border: thin solid black}
            body > * {float:left;}
        </style>
    </head>
    <body>
        <canvas id="canvas" width="500" height="140">
            Your browser doesn't support the <code>canvas</code> element
        </canvas>
        <script>
            var ctx = document.getElementById("canvas").getContext("2d");
            ctx.fillStyle = "yellow";
            ctx.lineWidth = "3";
```

```
        ctx.beginPath();
        ctx.arc(70, 70, 60, 0, Math.PI * 2, true);
        ctx.stroke();

        ctx.beginPath();
        ctx.arc(200, 70, 60, Math.PI/2, Math.PI, true);
        ctx.fill();
        ctx.stroke();

        ctx.beginPath();
        var val = 0;
        for (var i = 0; i < 4; i++) {
            ctx.arc(350, 70, 60, val, val + Math.PI/4, false);
            val+= Math.PI/2;
        }
        ctx.closePath();
        ctx.fill();
        ctx.stroke();
    </script>
  </body>
</html>
```

You can see the shapes that are described by these arcs in Figure 36-7.

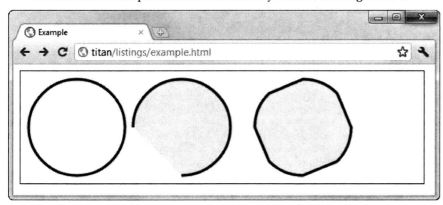

Figure 36-7. Using the arc method

As the first and second arcs show, we can use the arc method to draw complete circles or regular arcs, just as you would expect. However, as the third shape shows, we can use the arc method to create more complex paths. If we use the arc method and we have already drawn a sub-path, then a line is drawn directly from the end of the previous sub-path to the coordinates described by the first two arguments to the arc method. This line is drawn in addition to the arc we described. I use this quirk in conjunction with a for loop to connect together four small arcs drawn around the same point, leading to the shape shown in the Figure 36-7.

Drawing Bezier Curves

The canvas supports drawing two kinds of Bezier curves: cubic and quadratic. You have probably used Bezier curves in a drawing package. We pick a start and end point and then add one or more control points that shape the curve. The problem with Bezier curves on the canvas is that we don't have any visual feedback, which makes it harder to get the curves we want. In the examples that follow, I'll add some code to the script to provide some context, but in a real project you'll have to experiment to get the curves you require. Table 36-4 shows the methods we can use to draw curves.

Table 36-4. The curve methods

Name	Description	Returns
bezierCurveTo(cx1, cy1, cx2, cy2, x, y)	Draws a Bezier curve to the point (x, y) with the control points (cx1, cy1) and (cx2, cy2).	void
quadraticCurveTo(cx, xy, x, y)	Draws a quadratic Bezier curve to (x, y) with the control point (cx, cy).	void

Drawing Cubic Bezier Curves

The bezierCurveTo method draws a curve from the end of the previous sub-path to the point specified by the 5th and 6th method arguments. There are two controls points – these are specified by the first four arguments. Listing 36-8 shows the use of this method (and with some additional paths to make it easier to understand the relationship between the argument values and the curve that is produced).

Listing 36-8. Drawing cubic Bezier curves

```
<!DOCTYPE HTML>
<html>
    <head>
        <title>Example</title>
        <style>
            canvas {border: thin solid black}
            body > * {float:left;}
        </style>
    </head>
    <body>
        <canvas id="canvas" width="500" height="140">
            Your browser doesn't support the <code>canvas</code> element
        </canvas>
        <script>
            var canvasElem = document.getElementById("canvas");
            var ctx = canvasElem.getContext("2d");

            var startPoint = [50, 100];
            var endPoint = [400, 100];
            var cp1 = [250, 50];
```

```
        var cp2 = [350, 50];

        canvasElem.onmousemove = function(e) {
            if (e.shiftKey) {
                cp1 = [e.clientX, e.clientY];
            } else if (e.ctrlKey) {
                cp2 = [e.clientX, e.clientY];
            }
            ctx.clearRect(0, 0, 500, 140);
            draw();
        }

        draw();

        function draw() {
            ctx.lineWidth = 3;
            ctx.strokeStyle = "black";
            ctx.beginPath();
            ctx.moveTo(startPoint[0], startPoint[1]);
            ctx.bezierCurveTo(cp1[0], cp1[1], cp2[0], cp2[1],
                endPoint[0], endPoint[1]);
            ctx.stroke();

            ctx.lineWidth = 1;
            ctx.strokeStyle = "red";
            var points = [startPoint, endPoint, cp1, cp2];
            for (var i = 0; i < points.length; i++) {
                drawPoint(points[i]);
            }
            drawLine(startPoint, cp1);
            drawLine(endPoint, cp2);
        }

        function drawPoint(point) {
            ctx.beginPath();

            ctx.strokeRect(point[0] -2, point[1] -2, 4, 4);
        }

        function drawLine(from, to) {
            ctx.beginPath();
            ctx.moveTo(from[0], from[1]);
            ctx.lineTo(to[0], to[1]);
            ctx.stroke();
        }
    </script>
  </body>
</html>
```

To give you a sense of how the curves are drawn, the script in this example moves the control points on a Bezier curve in response to mouse movement. If the shift key is pressed then the first control point is moved. The second control point is moved if the control key is pressed. You can see the effect in Figure 36-8.

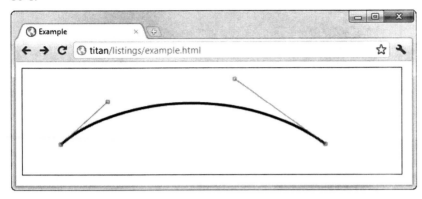

Figure 36-8. Drawing a cubic Bezier curve

Drawing Quadratic Bezier Curves

A quadratic Bezier curve has only one control point and so the quadraticCurveTo method has two fewer arguments than the bezierCurveTo method. Listing 36-9 shows the previous example reworked to display a quadratic curve, drawn with the quadraticCurveTo method.

Listing 36-9. Drawing a quadratic Bezier curve

```
<!DOCTYPE HTML>
<html>
    <head>
        <title>Example</title>
        <style>
            canvas {border: thin solid black}
            body > * {float:left;}
        </style>
    </head>
    <body>
        <canvas id="canvas" width="500" height="140">
            Your browser doesn't support the <code>canvas</code> element
        </canvas>
        <script>
            var canvasElem = document.getElementById("canvas");
            var ctx = canvasElem.getContext("2d");

            var startPoint = [50, 100];
            var endPoint = [400, 100];
            var cp1 = [250, 50];

            canvasElem.onmousemove = function(e) {
                if (e.shiftKey) {
```

```
                cp1 = [e.clientX, e.clientY];
            }
            ctx.clearRect(0, 0, 500, 140);
            draw();
        }

        draw();

        function draw() {
            ctx.lineWidth = 3;
            ctx.strokeStyle = "black";
            ctx.beginPath();
            ctx.moveTo(startPoint[0], startPoint[1]);
            ctx.quadraticCurveTo(cp1[0], cp1[1], endPoint[0], endPoint[1]);
            ctx.stroke();

            ctx.lineWidth = 1;
            ctx.strokeStyle = "red";
            var points = [startPoint, endPoint, cp1];
            for (var i = 0; i < points.length; i++) {
                drawPoint(points[i]);
            }
            drawLine(startPoint, cp1);
            drawLine(endPoint, cp1);
        }

        function drawPoint(point) {
            ctx.beginPath();

            ctx.strokeRect(point[0] -2, point[1] -2, 4, 4);
        }

        function drawLine(from, to) {
            ctx.beginPath();
            ctx.moveTo(from[0], from[1]);
            ctx.lineTo(to[0], to[1]);
            ctx.stroke();
        }
    </script>
  </body>
</html>
```

You can see an example curve in Figure 36-9.

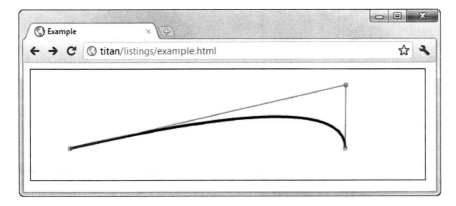

Figure 36-9. A quadratic Bezier curve

Creating a Clipping Region

As demonstrated earlier in this chapter, we can use the stroke and fill methods to draw or fill a path. There is an alternative, which is to use the method described in Table 36-5.

Table 36-5. The clip method

Name	Description	Returns
clip()	Creates a new clipping region	void

Once we define a clipping region, only paths that occur inside of the region are shown on the screen. Listing 36-10 gives a demonstration.

Listing 36-10. Using a clipping region

```
<!DOCTYPE HTML>
<html>
    <head>
        <title>Example</title>
        <style>
            canvas {border: thin solid black}
            body > * {float:left;}
        </style>
    </head>
    <body>
        <canvas id="canvas" width="500" height="140">
            Your browser doesn't support the <code>canvas</code> element
        </canvas>
        <script>
            var ctx = document.getElementById("canvas").getContext("2d");
```

```
        ctx.fillStyle = "yellow";
        ctx.beginPath();
        ctx.rect(0, 0, 500, 140);
        ctx.fill();

        ctx.beginPath();
        ctx.rect(100, 20, 300, 100);
        ctx.clip();

        ctx.fillStyle = "red";
        ctx.beginPath();
        ctx.rect(0, 0, 500, 140);
        ctx.fill();

    </script>
  </body>
</html>
```

The script in this example draws a rectangle that fills the canvas, creates a smaller clipping region and then draws another canvas-filling rectangle. As you can see in Figure 36-10, only the part of the second rectangle which fits within the clipping region is drawn.

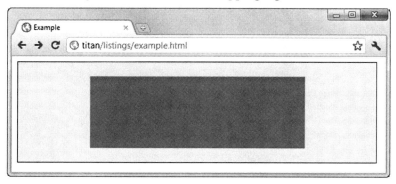

Figure 36-10. The effect of a clipping region

Drawing Text

We can draw text on the canvas, although the support for doing so is pretty basic. Table 36-6 shows the methods available.

Table 36-6. The text methods

Name	Description	Returns
fillText(<text>, x, y, width)	Draws and fills the specified text at the position (x, y). The optional width argument sets an upper limit on the width of the text	void

strokeText(<text>, x, y, width)	Draws and strokes the specified text at the position (x, y). The optional width argument sets an upper limit on the width of the text	void

There are three drawing state properties that we can use to control the way that text is drawn, as shown in Table 36-7.

Table 36-7. The text drawing state properties

Name	Description	Returns
font	Sets the font used when text is drawn	string
textAlign	Sets the alignment of the text: start, end, left, right, center	string
textBaseline	Sets the text baseline: top, hanging, middle, alphabetic, ideographic, bottom	string

Listing 36-11 shows how we can fill and stroke text. We specify the value for the font property using the same format string as for the CSS font shorthand property, which I described in Chapter 22.

Listing 36-11. Drawing text on the canvas

```
<!DOCTYPE HTML>
<html>
    <head>
        <title>Example</title>
        <style>
            canvas {border: thin solid black}
            body > * {float:left;}
        </style>
    </head>
    <body>
        <canvas id="canvas" width="350" height="140">
            Your browser doesn't support the <code>canvas</code> element
        </canvas>
        <script>
            var ctx = document.getElementById("canvas").getContext("2d");

            ctx.fillStyle = "lightgrey";
            ctx.strokeStyle = "black";
            ctx.lineWidth = 3;

            ctx.font = "100px sans-serif";
            ctx.fillText("Hello", 50, 100);
            ctx.strokeText("Hello", 50, 100);
        </script>
    </body>
</html>
```

Text is drawn using the fillStyle and strokeStyle properties, meaning that we have the same set of colors, gradients and patterns as for shapes. In this example, I have filled and stroked the text in two solid colors. You can see the effect in Figure 36-11.

Figure 36-11. Filling and stroking text

Using Effects and Transformations

We can apply a number of effects and transformations to the canvas, as described in the following sections.

Using Shadows

There are four drawing state properties that we can use to add shadows to the shapes and text we draw on the canvas. These properties are described in Table 36-8.

Table 36-8. The shadow properties

Name	Description	Returns
shadowBlur	Sets the degree of blur in the shadow	number
shadowColor	Sets the color of the shadow	string
shadowOffsetX	Sets the x-offset for the shadow	number
shadowOffsetY	Sets the y-offset for the shadow	number

Listing 36-12 shows how we can apply shadows using these properties.

Listing 36-12. Applying shadows to shapes and text

```
<!DOCTYPE HTML>
<html>
    <head>
        <title>Example</title>
        <style>
            canvas {border: thin solid black}
            body > * {float:left;}
        </style>
    </head>
    <body>
        <canvas id="canvas" width="500" height="140">
            Your browser doesn't support the <code>canvas</code> element
        </canvas>
        <script>
            var ctx = document.getElementById("canvas").getContext("2d");

            ctx.fillStyle = "lightgrey";
            ctx.strokeStyle = "black";
            ctx.lineWidth = 3;

            ctx.shadowOffsetX = 5;
            ctx.shadowOffsetY = 5;
            ctx.shadowBlur = 5;
            ctx.shadowColor = "grey";

            ctx.strokeRect(250, 20, 100, 100);

            ctx.beginPath();
            ctx.arc(420, 70, 50, 0, Math.PI, true);
            ctx.stroke();

            ctx.beginPath();
            ctx.arc(420, 80, 40, 0, Math.PI, false);
            ctx.fill();

            ctx.font = "100px sans-serif";
            ctx.fillText("Hello", 10, 100);
            ctx.strokeText("Hello", 10, 100);
        </script>
    </body>
</html>
```

This example applies shadows to text, a rectangle, a complete circle. and two arcs. As shown in Figure 36-12, the shadows are applied to shapes irrespective of whether they are open, closed, filled, or stroked.

Figure 36-12. Applying shadows to text and shapes

Using Transparency

We can set the transparency of the text and shapes we draw in two ways. The first is to specify a fillStyle or strokeStyle value using the rgba function (instead of rgb), as described in Chapter 4. We can also use the globalAlpha drawing state property, which is applied universally. Listing 36-13 shows the use of the globalAlpha property.

Listing 36-13. Using the globalAlpha property

```
<!DOCTYPE HTML>
<html>
    <head>
        <title>Example</title>
        <style>
            canvas {border: thin solid black}
            body > * {float:left;}
        </style>
    </head>
    <body>
        <canvas id="canvas" width="300" height="120">
            Your browser doesn't support the <code>canvas</code> element
        </canvas>
        <script>
            var ctx = document.getElementById("canvas").getContext("2d");

            ctx.fillStyle = "lightgrey";
            ctx.strokeStyle = "black";
            ctx.lineWidth = 3;

            ctx.font = "100px sans-serif";
            ctx.fillText("Hello", 10, 100);
            ctx.strokeText("Hello", 10, 100);

            ctx.fillStyle = "red";
```

```
            ctx.globalAlpha = 0.5;
            ctx.fillRect(100, 10, 150, 100);
        </script>
    </body>
</html>
```

The value for the globalAlpha values may range from 0 (completely transparent) to 1 (completely opaque, which is the default value). In this example, I draw some text, set the globalAlpha property to 0.5 and then fill a rectangle partly over the text. You can see the result in Figure 36-13.

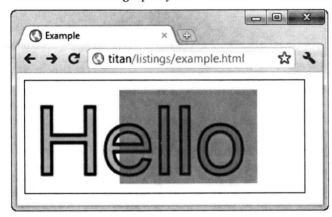

Figure 36-13. Using transparency through the globalAlpha property

Using Composition

We can use transparency in conjunction with the globalCompositeOperation property to control the way that shapes and text are drawn onto the canvas. The allowed values for this property are described in Table 36-9. For this property, the *source* consists of any operations performed once the property has been set and the destination image is the state of the canvas at the time that the property was set

Table 36-9. The allowed globalCompositeOperation values

Value	Description
copy	Draw the source over the destination, ignoring any transparency
destination-atop	Show the canvas where the
destination-in	Same as source-in but using the destination image instead of the source image and vice versa
destination-over	Same as source-over but using the destination image instead of the source image and vice versa

distination-out	Same as source-out but using the destination image instead of the source image and vice versa
lighter	Display the sum of the source image and destination image, with color values approaching 255 (100%) as a limit.
source-atop	Display the source image wherever both images are opaque. Display the destination image wherever the destination image is opaque but the source image is transparent. Display transparency elsewhere
source-in	Display the source image wherever both the source image and destination image are opaque. Display transparency elsewhere.
source-out	Display the source image wherever the source image is opaque and the destination image is transparent. Display transparency elsewhere
source-over	Display the source image wherever the source image is opaque. Display the destination image elsewhere
xor	Exclusive OR of the source image and destination image.

The values for the globalCompositeOperation property can create some striking effects. Listing 36-14 contains a select element that contains options for all of the composition values. It is worth spending a moment playing with this example to see how each composition mode works.

Listing 36-14. Using the globalCompositeOperation property

```
<!DOCTYPE HTML>
<html>
    <head>
        <title>Example</title>
        <style>
            canvas {border: thin solid black; margin: 4px;}
            body > * {float:left;}
        </style>
    </head>
    <body>
        <canvas id="canvas" width="300" height="120">
            Your browser doesn't support the <code>canvas</code> element
        </canvas>
        <label>Composition Value:</label><select id="list">
            <option>copy</option>
            <option>destination-atop</option><option>destination-in</option>
            <option>destination-over</option><option>distination-out</option>
            <option>lighter</option><option>source-atop</option>
            <option>source-in</option><option>source-out</option>
            <option>source-over</option><option>xor</option>
        </select>
        <script>
```

```
        var ctx = document.getElementById("canvas").getContext("2d");

        ctx.fillStyle = "lightgrey";
        ctx.strokeStyle = "black";
        ctx.lineWidth = 3;

        var compVal = "copy";

        document.getElementById("list").onchange = function(e) {
            compVal = e.target.value;
            draw();
        }

        draw();

        function draw() {
            ctx.clearRect(0, 0, 300, 120);
            ctx.globalAlpha = 1.0;
            ctx.font = "100px sans-serif";
            ctx.fillText("Hello", 10, 100);
            ctx.strokeText("Hello", 10, 100);

            ctx.globalCompositeOperation = compVal;

            ctx.fillStyle = "red";
            ctx.globalAlpha = 0.5;
            ctx.fillRect(100, 10, 150, 100);
        }
    </script>
  </body>
</html>
```

You can see the source-out and destination-over values in Figure 36-14. Some browsers interpret the styles in slightly different ways, so you may not see exactly what the figure shows.

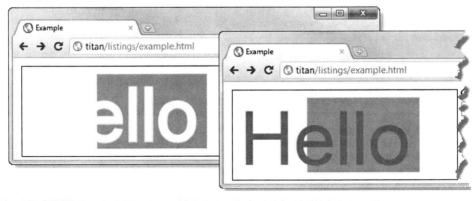

Figure 36-14. Using the globalCompositeOperation property

Using a Transformation

We can apply a transformation to the canvas, which is then applied to any subsequent drawing operations. Table 36-10 describes the transformation methods.

Table 36-10. The transformation methods

Name	Description	Returns
scale(<xScale>, <yScale>)	Scales the canvas by xScale in the x-axis and yScale in the y-axis	void
rotate(<angle>)	Rotates the canvas clockwise around the point (0, 0) by the specified number of radians.	void
translate(<x>, <y>)	Translates the canvas by x along the x-axis and y along the y-axis.	void
transform(a, b, c, d, e, f)	Combines the existing transformation with the matrix specified by the values a-f.	void
setTransform(a, b, c, d, e, f)	Replaces the existing transformation with the matrix specified by the values a-f.	void

The transformations created by these methods only apply to subsequent drawing operations – the existing contents of the canvas remain unchanged. Listing 36-15 shows how we can use the scale, rotate, and translate methods.

Listing 36-15. Using transformations

```
<!DOCTYPE HTML>
<html>
    <head>
        <title>Example</title>
        <style>
            canvas {border: thin solid black; margin: 4px;}
            body > * {float:left;}
        </style>
    </head>
    <body>
        <canvas id="canvas" width="400" height="200">
            Your browser doesn't support the <code>canvas</code> element
        </canvas>
        <script>
            var ctx = document.getElementById("canvas").getContext("2d");

            ctx.fillStyle = "lightgrey";
            ctx.strokeStyle = "black";
            ctx.lineWidth = 3;
```

```
            ctx.clearRect(0, 0, 300, 120);
            ctx.globalAlpha = 1.0;
            ctx.font = "100px sans-serif";
            ctx.fillText("Hello", 10, 100);
            ctx.strokeText("Hello", 10, 100);

            ctx.scale(1.3, 1.3);
            ctx.translate(100, -50);
            ctx.rotate(0.5);

            ctx.fillStyle = "red";
            ctx.globalAlpha = 0.5;
            ctx.fillRect(100, 10, 150, 100);

            ctx.strokeRect(0, 0, 300, 200);
        </script>
    </body>
</html>
```

In this example, I fill and stroke some text and then scale, translate, and rotate the canvas, which affects the filled rectangle and the stroked rectangle that I draw subsequently. You can see the effect in Figure 36-15.

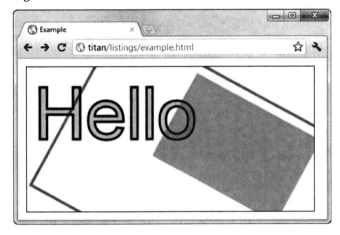

Figure 36-15. Transforming the canvas

Summary

In this chapter, I have shown how to draw on the canvas using different kinds of paths, including lines, rectangles, arc, and curves. I also demonstrated the canvas text facilities and how we can apply effects such as shadows and transparency. I finished this chapter by demonstrating the different composition modes and transformations that the canvas supports.

Using Drag & Drop

HTML5 adds support for drag and drop. This is something that we had to rely on JavaScript libraries such as jQuery to handle previously. The advantage of having drag and drop built into the browser is that it is properly integrated into the operating system and, as you will see, works between browsers.

It is still early days for this feature and there is a significant gap between the specification and the implementations offered by the mainstream browsers. Not all parts of the specification are implemented by all browsers and some features are implemented in substantially different ways. In this chapter, I have showed you what currently works. This isn't the complete set of features defined by the HTML5 standard, but it is enough to get up and running. Table 37-1 provides the summary for this chapter.

Table 37-1. Chapter Summary

Problem	Solution	Listing
Enable dragging for an HTML element	Set the draggable attribute to true	1
Manage the dragging lifecycle	Handle the dragstart, drag and dragend events	2
Create a drop zone	Handle the dragenter and dragover events	3
Receive a dropped element in the drop zone	Handle the drop event	4
Transfer data from the dropped element to the drop zone	Use the DataTransfer object	5
Filter items based on the content they carry	Use the getData method of the DataTransfer object	6
Process files dragged from the operating system and dropped in the drop zone	Use the files property of the DataTransfer object	7
Upload files dragged from the operating system and dropped in the drop zone as	Use the append method of the FormData object, passing the File	8

part of an Ajax form submission   object as the second argument

Creating the Source Items

We tell the browser which elements in the document can be dragged through the draggable attribute. There are three permitted values for this attribute, which are described in Table 37-2.

Table 37-2. *Values for the draggable attribute*

Value	Description
true	The element can be dragged
false	The element cannot be dragged
auto	The browser may decide if an element can be dragged

The default is the auto value, which leaves the decision up to the browser, which typically means that all elements can be dragged by default and that we have to explicitly disable dragging by setting the draggable attribute to false. When using the drag and drop feature, I tend to explicitly set the draggable attribute to true, even though the mainstream browsers consider all elements to be draggable by default. Listing 37-1 shows a simple HTML document that has some elements that can be dragged.

Listing 37-1. Defining the draggable items

```html
<!DOCTYPE HTML>
<html>
    <head>
        <title>Example</title>
        <style>
            #src > * {float:left;}
            #target, #src > img {border: thin solid black; padding: 2px; margin:4px;}
            #target {height: 81px; width: 81px; text-align: center; display: table;}
            #target > p {display: table-cell; vertical-align: middle;}
            #target > img {margin: 1px;}

        </style>
    </head>
    <body>
        <div id="src">
            <img draggable="true" id="banana" src="banana100.png" alt="banana"/>
            <img draggable="true" id="apple" src="apple100.png" alt="apple"/>
            <img draggable="true" id="cherries" src="cherries100.png" alt="cherry"/>
            <div id="target">
                <p>Drop Here</p>
            </div>
        </div>
```

```
    <script>
        var src = document.getElementById("src");
        var target = document.getElementById("target");
    </script>
    </body>
</html>
```

In this example, there are three img elements, each of which has the draggable attribute set to true. I have also created a div element with an id of target, which we will shortly set up to be the recipient of our dragged img elements. You can see how this document appears in the browser in Figure 37-1.

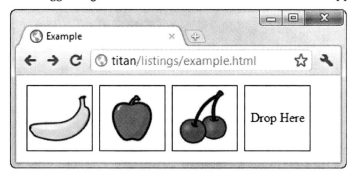

Figure 37-1. Three draggable images and a target

We can drag the fruit images without doing any further work, but the browser will indicate that we can't drop them anywhere. This is usually done by showing a no-entry sign as the cursor, as shown in Figure 37-2.

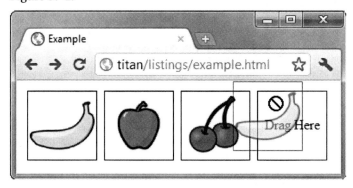

Figure 37-2. The browser showing that the dragged item cannot be dropped

Handling the Drag Events

We take advantage of the drag and drop feature through a series of events. These are events that are targeted at the dragged element and events that are targeted at potential drop zones. Table 37-3 describes those events that are for the dragged element.

Table 37-3. The dragged element events

Name	Description
dragstart	Triggered when the element is first dragged
drag	Triggered repeatedly as the element is being dragged
dragend	Triggered when the drag operation is completed

We can use these events to emphasize the drag operation visually, as demonstrated in Listing 37-2.

Listing 37-2. Using the events targeted at the dragged element

```html
<!DOCTYPE HTML>
<html>
    <head>
        <title>Example</title>
        <style>
            #src > * {float:left;}
            #target, #src > img {border: thin solid black; padding: 2px; margin:4px;}
            #target {height: 81px; width: 81px; text-align: center; display: table;}
            #target > p {display: table-cell; vertical-align: middle;}
            #target > img {margin: 1px;}
            img.dragged {background-color: lightgrey;}

        </style>
    </head>
    <body>
        <div id="src">
            <img draggable="true" id="banana" src="banana100.png" alt="banana"/>
            <img draggable="true" id="apple" src="apple100.png" alt="apple"/>
            <img draggable="true" id="cherries" src="cherries100.png" alt="cherry"/>
            <div id="target">
                <p id="msg">Drop Here</p>
            </div>
        </div>

        <script>
            var src = document.getElementById("src");
            var target = document.getElementById("target");
            var msg = document.getElementById("msg");

            src.ondragstart = function(e) {
                e.target.classList.add("dragged");
            }

            src.ondragend = function(e) {
                e.target.classList.remove("dragged");
                msg.innerHTML = "Drop Here";
```

```
        }

        src.ondrag = function(e) {
            msg.innerHTML = e.target.id;
        }
    </script>
</body>
</html>
```

I have defined a new CSS style that is applied to elements in the dragged class. I add the element that has been dragged to this class in response to the dragstart event and remove it from the class in response to the dragend event. In response to the drag event, I set the text displayed in the drop zone to be the id value of the dragged element. The drag event is called every few milliseconds during the drag operation, so this is not the most efficient technique, but it does demonstrate the event. You can see the effect in Figure 3. Note that we still don't have a working drop zone, but we are getting closer.

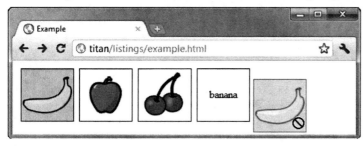

Figure 37-3. Using the dragstart, dragend, and drag events

Creating the Drop Zone

To make an element a drop zone, we need to handle the dragenter and dragover events. These are two of the events which are targeted at the drop zone. The complete set is described in Table 37-4.

Table 37-4. The dragged element events

Name	Description
dragenter	Triggered when a dragged element enters the screen space occupied by the drop zone
dragover	Triggered when a dragged element moves within the drop zone
dragleave	Triggered when a dragged element leaves the drop zone without being dropped
drop	Triggered when a dragged element is dropped in the drop zone

The default action for the dragenter and dragover events is to refuse to accept any dragged items, so the most important thing we must do is prevent the default action from being performed. Listing 37-3 contains an example.

▓ **Note** The specification for drag and drop tells us that we must also apply the dropzone attribute to the element we want to make into a drop zone, and that the value of the attribute should contain details of the operations and data types that we are willing to accept. This is not how the browsers actually implement the feature. For this chapter, I have described the way things really work, rather than how they have been specified.

Listing 37-3. Creating a drop zone by handling the dragenter and dragover events

```
<!DOCTYPE HTML>
<html>
    <head>
        <title>Example</title>
        <style>
            #src > * {float:left;}
            #target, #src > img {border: thin solid black; padding: 2px; margin:4px;}
            #target {height: 81px; width: 81px; text-align: center; display: table;}
            #target > p {display: table-cell; vertical-align: middle;}
            #target > img {margin: 1px;}
            img.dragged {background-color: lightgrey;}

        </style>
    </head>
    <body>
        <div id="src">
            <img draggable="true" id="banana" src="banana100.png" alt="banana"/>
            <img draggable="true" id="apple" src="apple100.png" alt="apple"/>
            <img draggable="true" id="cherries" src="cherries100.png" alt="cherry"/>
            <div id="target">
                <p id="msg">Drop Here</p>
            </div>
        </div>

        <script>
            var src = document.getElementById("src");
            var target = document.getElementById("target");
            var msg = document.getElementById("msg");

            target.ondragenter = handleDrag;
            target.ondragover = handleDrag;

            function handleDrag(e) {
                e.preventDefault();
            }
```

```
            src.ondragstart = function(e) {
                e.target.classList.add("dragged");
            }

            src.ondragend = function(e) {
                e.target.classList.remove("dragged");
                msg.innerHTML = "Drop Here";
            }

            src.ondrag = function(e) {
                msg.innerHTML = e.target.id;
            }
        </script>
    </body>
</html>
```

With these additions, we have an active drop zone. When we drag an item over the drop zone element, the browser will indicate that it will be accepted if we drop it, as shown in Figure 37-4.

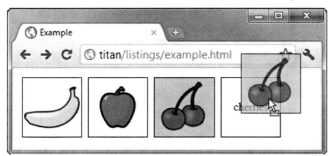

Figure 37-4. The browser indicating that an item can be dropped

Receiving the Drop

We receive the dropped element by handling the drop event, which is triggered when an item is dropped on the drop zone element. Listing 37-4 shows how we can respond to the drop event using a global variable as a conduit between the dragged element and the drop zone.

Listing 37-4. Handling the drop event

```
<!DOCTYPE HTML>
<html>
    <head>
        <title>Example</title>
        <style>
            #src > * {float:left;}
            #src > img {border: thin solid black; padding: 2px; margin:4px;}
            #target {border: thin solid black; margin:4px;}
            #target { height: 81px; width: 81px; text-align: center; display: table;}
```

```
            #target > p {display: table-cell; vertical-align: middle;}
            img.dragged {background-color: lightgrey;}
        </style>
    </head>
    <body>
        <div id="src">
            <img draggable="true" id="banana" src="banana100.png" alt="banana"/>
            <img draggable="true" id="apple" src="apple100.png" alt="apple"/>
            <img draggable="true" id="cherries" src="cherries100.png" alt="cherry"/>
            <div id="target">
                <p id="msg">Drop Here</p>
            </div>
        </div>

        <script>
            var src = document.getElementById("src");
            var target = document.getElementById("target");
            var msg = document.getElementById("msg");

            var draggedID;

            target.ondragenter = handleDrag;
            target.ondragover = handleDrag;

            function handleDrag(e) {
                e.preventDefault();
            }

            target.ondrop = function(e) {
                var newElem = document.getElementById(draggedID).cloneNode(false);
                target.innerHTML = "";
                target.appendChild(newElem);
                e.preventDefault();
            }

            src.ondragstart = function(e) {
                draggedID = e.target.id;
                e.target.classList.add("dragged");
            }

            src.ondragend = function(e) {
                var elems = document.querySelectorAll(".dragged");
                for (var i = 0; i < elems.length; i++) {
                    elems[i].classList.remove("dragged");
                }
            }
        </script>
    </body>
</html>
```

I set the value of the draggedID variable when the dragstart event is triggered. This allows me to keep a note of the id attribute value of the element that has been dragged. When the drop event is triggered, I use this value to clone the img element that was dragged and add it as a child of the drop zone element.

▨ **Tip** In the example, I prevented the default action for the drop event. Without this, the browser can do some unexpected things. For example, in this scenario, Firefox navigates away from the page and displays the image referenced by the src attribute of the dragged img element.

You can see the effect in Figure 37-5.

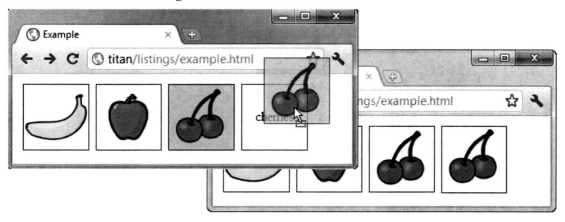

Figure 37-5. Responding to the drag event

Working with the DataTransfer Object

The object dispatched along with the events triggered for drag and drop is DragEvent, which is derived from MouseEvent. The DragEvent object defines all of the functionality of the Event and MouseEvent objects (which is described in Chapter 30), with the additional property shown in Table 37-5.

Table 37-5. The property defined by the DragEvent object

Name	Description	Returns
dataTransfer	Returns the object used to transfer data to the drop zone	DataTransfer

We use the DataTransfer object to transfer arbitrary data from the dragged element to the drop zone element. The properties and methods that the DataTransfer object defines are described in Table 37-6.

Table 37-6. *The properties defined by the DataTransfer object*

Name	Description	Returns
types	Returns the formats for the data	string[]
getData(<format>)	Returns the data for a specific format	string
setData(<format>, <data>)	Sets the data for a given format	void
clearData(<format>)	Removes the data for a given format	void
files	Returns a list of the files that have been dragged	FileList

In the previous example, I cloned the element itself; however, the DataTransfer object allows us a more sophisticated approach. The first thing we can do is to use the DataTransfer object to transfer data from the dragged element to the drop zone, as demonstrated in Listing 37-5.

Listing 37-5. Using the DataTransfer object to transfer data

```
<!DOCTYPE HTML>
<html>
    <head>
        <title>Example</title>
        <style>
            #src > * {float:left;}
            #src > img {border: thin solid black; padding: 2px; margin:4px;}
            #target {border: thin solid black; margin:4px;}
            #target { height: 81px; width: 81px; text-align: center; display: table;}
            #target > p {display: table-cell; vertical-align: middle;}
            img.dragged {background-color: lightgrey;}
        </style>
    </head>
    <body>
        <div id="src">
            <img draggable="true" id="banana" src="banana100.png" alt="banana"/>
            <img draggable="true" id="apple" src="apple100.png" alt="apple"/>
            <img draggable="true" id="cherries" src="cherries100.png" alt="cherry"/>
            <div id="target">
                <p id="msg">Drop Here</p>
            </div>
        </div>

        <script>
            var src = document.getElementById("src");
            var target = document.getElementById("target");

            target.ondragenter = handleDrag;
            target.ondragover = handleDrag;
```

```
        function handleDrag(e) {
            e.preventDefault();
        }

        target.ondrop = function(e) {
            var droppedID = e.dataTransfer.getData("Text");
            var newElem = document.getElementById(droppedID).cloneNode(false);
            target.innerHTML = "";
            target.appendChild(newElem);
            e.preventDefault();
        }

        src.ondragstart = function(e) {
            e.dataTransfer.setData("Text", e.target.id);
            e.target.classList.add("dragged");
        }

        src.ondragend = function(e) {
            var elems = document.querySelectorAll(".dragged");
            for (var i = 0; i < elems.length; i++) {
                elems[i].classList.remove("dragged");
            }
        }
    </script>
</body>
</html>
```

I use the setData method when responding to the dragstart event to set the data that I want to transfer. There are only two supported values for the first argument which specifies the type of data—Text or Url (and only Text is reliably supported by the browsers). The second argument is the data we want to transfer: in this case, the id attribute of the dragged element. To retrieve the value, I use the getData method, using the data type as the argument.

You might be wondering why this is a better approach than using a global variable. The answer is that it works across browsers, and by this, I don't mean across windows or tabs in the same browsers, but across different *types* of browser. This means that I can drag an element from a Chrome document and drop it in a Firefox document because the drag and drop support is integrated with the same feature in the operating system. If you open a text editor, type the word banana, select it and then drag it to the drop zone in the browser, you will see the banana image being displayed, just as it was when we dragged one of the img elements in the same document.

Filtering Dragged Items by Data

We can use the data stored in the DataTransfer object to be selective about the kinds of elements that we are willing to accept in the drop zone. Listing 37-6 shows how.

Listing 37-6. Using the DataTransfer object to filter dragged elements

```
...
<script>
    var src = document.getElementById("src");
```

```
        var target = document.getElementById("target");

        target.ondragenter = handleDrag;
        target.ondragover = handleDrag;

        function handleDrag(e) {
            if (e.dataTransfer.getData("Text") == "banana") {
                e.preventDefault();
            }
        }

        target.ondrop = function(e) {
            var droppedID = e.dataTransfer.getData("Text");
            var newElem = document.getElementById(droppedID).cloneNode(false);
            target.innerHTML = "";
            target.appendChild(newElem);
            e.preventDefault();
        }

        src.ondragstart = function(e) {
            e.dataTransfer.setData("Text", e.target.id);
            e.target.classList.add("dragged");
        }

        src.ondragend = function(e) {
            var elems = document.querySelectorAll(".dragged");
            for (var i = 0; i < elems.length; i++) {
                elems[i].classList.remove("dragged");
            }
        }
</script>
...
```

In this example, I get the data value from the DataTransfer object and check to see what it is. I indicate that I am willing to accept the dragged element only if the data value is banana. This has the effect of filtering out the apple and cherry images. When the user drags these over the drop-zone, the browser will indicate that they cannot be dropped.

■ **Tip** This kind of filtering doesn't work in Chrome, as the getData method doesn't work when called in handlers for the dragenter and dragover events.

Dragging and Dropping Files

Hidden deep in the browser is another new HTML5 feature, called the *File API*, which allows us to work with files on the local machine, albeit in a tightly controlled manner. Part of the control is that we don't usually interact with the File API directly. Instead, it is exposed through other features, including drag and drop. Listing 37-7 shows how we can use the File API to respond when the use drags files from the operating system and drops them in our drop zone.

Listing 37-7. Dealing with files

```
<!DOCTYPE HTML>
<html>
    <head>
        <title>Example</title>
        <style>
            body > * {float: left;}
            #target {border: medium double black; margin:4px; height: 75px;
                width: 200px; text-align: center; display: table;}
            #target > p {display: table-cell; vertical-align: middle;}
            table {margin: 4px; border-collapse: collapse;}
            th, td {padding: 4px};
        </style>
    </head>
    <body>
        <div id="target">
            <p id="msg">Drop Files Here</p>
        </div>
        <table id="data" border="1">
        </table>

        <script>
            var target = document.getElementById("target");

            target.ondragenter = handleDrag;
            target.ondragover = handleDrag;

            function handleDrag(e) {
                e.preventDefault();
            }

            target.ondrop = function(e) {
                var files = e.dataTransfer.files;
                var tableElem = document.getElementById("data");
                tableElem.innerHTML = "<tr><th>Name</th><th>Type</th><th>Size</th></tr>";
                for (var i = 0; i < files.length; i++) {
                    var row = "<tr><td>" + files[i].name + "</td><td>" +
                        files[i].type+ "</td><td>" +
                        files[i].size + "</td></tr>";
                    tableElem.innerHTML += row;
                }
                e.preventDefault();
            }
        </script>
    </body>
</html>
```

When the user drops files on our drop zone, the files property of the DataTransfer object returns a FileList object. We can treat this as an array of File objects, each of which represents a file that the user has dropped (the user can select multiple files and drop them in one go). Table 37-7 shows the properties of the File object.

Table 37-7. The properties defined by the File object

Name	Description	Returns
name	Gets the name of the file	string
type	Gets the type of file, expressed as a MIME type	string
size	Gets the size (in bytes) of the file	number

In the example, the script enumerates the files that are dropped on the drop zone and displays the values of the File properties in a table. You can see the effect in Figure 37-6, where I have dropped some of example files on the drop zone.

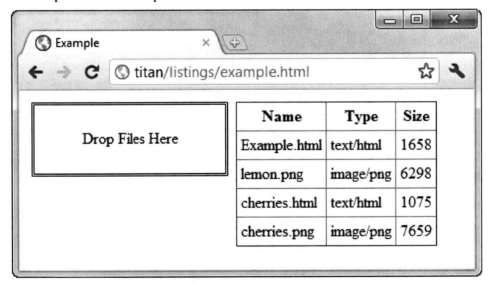

Figure 37-6. Displaying data about files

Uploading Dropped Files in a Form

We can combine the drag and drop feature, the File API and uploading data using an Ajax request to allow users to drag the files that want included in a form submission from the operating system. Listing 37-8 contains a demonstration.

970

Listing 37-8. Combining drag and drop, the File API and the FormData object

```html
<!DOCTYPE HTML>
<html>
    <head>
        <title>Example</title>
        <style>
            .table {display:table;}
            .row {display:table-row;}
            .cell {display: table-cell; padding: 5px;}
            .label {text-align: right;}
            #target {border: medium double black; margin:4px; height: 50px;
                width: 200px; text-align: center; display: table;}
            #target > p {display: table-cell; vertical-align: middle;}
        </style>
    </head>
    <body>
        <form id="fruitform" method="post" action="http://titan:8080/form">
            <div class="table">
                <div class="row">
                    <div class="cell label">Bananas:</div>
                    <div class="cell"><input name="bananas" value="2"/></div>
                </div>
                <div class="row">
                    <div class="cell label">Apples:</div>
                    <div class="cell"><input name="apples" value="5"/></div>
                </div>
                <div class="row">
                    <div class="cell label">Cherries:</div>
                    <div class="cell"><input name="cherries" value="20"/></div>
                </div>
                <div class="row">
                    <div class="cell label">File:</div>
                    <div class="cell"><input type="file" name="file"/></div>
                </div>
                <div class="row">
                    <div class="cell label">Total:</div>
                    <div id="results" class="cell">0 items</div>
                </div>
            </div>
            <div id="target">
                <p id="msg">Drop Files Here</p>
            </div>
            <button id="submit" type="submit">Submit Form</button>
        </form>
        <script>
            var target = document.getElementById("target");
            var httpRequest;
            var fileList;

            document.getElementById("submit").onclick = handleButtonPress;
```

```
                    target.ondragenter = handleDrag;
                    target.ondragover = handleDrag;

                    function handleDrag(e) {
                        e.preventDefault();
                    }

                    target.ondrop = function(e) {
                        fileList = e.dataTransfer.files;
                        e.preventDefault();
                    }

                    function handleButtonPress(e) {
                        e.preventDefault();

                        var form = document.getElementById("fruitform");
                        var formData = new FormData(form);

                        if (fileList || true) {
                            for (var i = 0; i < fileList.length; i++) {
                                formData.append("file" + i, fileList[i]);
                            }
                        }

                        httpRequest = new XMLHttpRequest();
                        httpRequest.onreadystatechange = handleResponse;
                        httpRequest.open("POST", form.action);
                        httpRequest.send(formData);
                    }

                    function handleResponse() {
                        if (httpRequest.readyState == 4 && httpRequest.status == 200) {
                            var data = JSON.parse(httpRequest.responseText);
                            document.getElementById("results").innerHTML = "You ordered "
                                + data.total + " items";
                        }
                    }
                }
            </script>
        </body>
</html>
```

In this example, I have added a drop zone to an example taken from Chapter 33, where I demonstrated how to use the FormData object to upload form data to a server. We can include files dropped in the drop zone by using the FormData.append method, passing in a File object as the second argument to the method. When the form is submitted, the contents of the files will automatically be uploaded to the server as part of the form request.

Summary

In this chapter, I showed you the support for dragging and dropping elements. The implementation of this feature leaves a lot to be desired, but it holds promise and I expect that the mainstream browsers will start to address the inconsistencies before long. If you can't wait until then (or you don't care about dragging to and from other browsers and the operating system), then you should consider using a JavaScript library such as jQuery and jQuery UI.

CHAPTER 38

Using Geolocation

The Geolocation API allows us to obtain information about the current geographic position of the user (or at least the position of the system on which the browser is running). This isn't part of the HTML5 specification, but it is usually grouped up as part of the new features associated with HTML5. Table 38-1 provides the summary for this chapter.

Table 38-1. Chapter Summary

Problem	Solution	Listing
Get the current position	Use the getCurrentPosition method, supplying a function that will be invoked when the position data is available	1
Handle geolocation errors	Pass a second argument to the getCurrentPosition method, specifying a function that will be invoked if there is an error	2
Specify options for geolocation requests	Pass a third argument to the getCurrentPosition method, specifying the options required	3
Monitor the position	Use the watchPosition and clearWatch methods	4

Using Geolocation

We access the geolocation feature through the global navigator.geolocation property, which returns a Geolocation object – the methods of this object are described in Table 38-2.

Table 38-2. The Geolocation object

Name	Description	Returns
getCurrentPosition(callback, errorCallback, options)	Get the current position	void

watchPosition(callback, error, options)	Start monitoring the current position	number
clearWatch(id)	Stop monitoring the current position	void

Getting the Current Position

As its name suggests the getCurrentPosition method obtains the current position, although the position information isn't returned as the result of the method itself. Instead, we supply a success callback function which is invoked when the position information is available – this allows for the fact that there can be a delay between requesting the position and it becoming available. Listing 38-1 shows how we can get the position information using this method.

Listing 38-1. Obtaining the current position

```
<!DOCTYPE HTML>
<html>
    <head>
        <title>Example</title>
        <style>
            table {border-collapse: collapse;}
            th, td {padding: 4px;}
            th {text-align: right;}
        </style>
    </head>
    <body>
        <table border="1">
            <tr>
                <th>Longitude:</th><td id="longitude">-</td>
                <th>Latitude:</th><td id="latitude">-</td>
            </tr>
            <tr>
                <th>Altitude:</th><td id="altitude">-</td>
                <th>Accuracy:</th><td id="accuracy">-</td>
            </tr>
            <tr>
                <th>Altitude Accuracy:</th><td id="altitudeAccuracy">-</td>
                <th>Heading:</th><td id="heading">-</td>
            </tr>
            <tr>
                <th>Speed:</th><td id="speed">-</td>
                <th>Time Stamp:</th><td id="timestamp">-</td>
            </tr>
        </table>
        <script>
            navigator.geolocation.getCurrentPosition(displayPosition);

            function displayPosition(pos) {
                var properties = ["longitude", "latitude", "altitude", "accuracy",
```

```
                        "altitudeAccuracy", "heading", "speed"];

            for (var i = 0; i < properties.length; i++) {
                var value = pos.coords[properties[i]];
                document.getElementById(properties[i]).innerHTML = value;
            }
            document.getElementById("timestamp").innerHTML = pos.timestamp;
        }
    </script>
</body>
</html>
```

The script in this example calls the getCurrentPosition, passing the displayPosition function as the method argument. When the position information is available, the nominated function is invoked and the browser passes in a Position object which gives the details of the position – the details are displayed in the cells of a table element. The Position object is pretty simple, as you can see in Table 38-3.

Table 38-3. The Position object

Name	Description	Returns
coords	Returns the coordinates for the current position	Coordinates
timestamp	Returns the time that the coordinate information was obtained	string

We are really interested in the Coordinates object, which is returned by the Position.coords property. Table 38-4 describes the properties of the Coordinates object.

Table 38-4. The Coordinates object

Name	Description	Returns
latitude	Returns the latitude in decimal degrees	number
longitude	Returns the longitude in decimal degrees	number
altitude	Returns the height in meters	number
accuracy	Returns the accuracy of the coordinates in meters	number
altitudeAccuracy	Returns the accuracy of the altitude in meters	number
heading	Returns the direction of travel in degrees	number
speed	Returns the speed of travel in meters/second	number

Not all of the data values in the Coordinates object will be available all of the time. The mechanism by which the browser obtains the location information is unspecified and there are a number of techniques that are used. Mobile devices increasingly have GPS, accelerometer, and compass facilities, which means that the most accurate and complete data will be available on those platforms.

We can still get location information for other devices – the browsers use a geolocation service that tries to determine location based on network information. If your system has a Wi-Fi adaptor, then the networks that are in range are compared with a catalogue of networks taken as part of the surveys done for street-level views, such as Google Street View. If Wi-Fi isn't available, then the IP address provided by your ISP can be used to get a general idea of location.

The accuracy of locations inferred from network information varies, but it can be startlingly accurate. When I started testing this feature, I was surprised by just how narrowly my location was reported. In fact, it was so accurate, that I have substituted the location of the Empire State Building in the screenshots – with the real location information (derived from my and nearby Wi-Fi networks) you can easily find my house and see photos of my car on the driveway. Scary stuff – so much so that the first thing that all of the browsers do when a document uses the geolocation feature is ask the user to grant permission – you can see how Chrome does this in Figure 38-1.

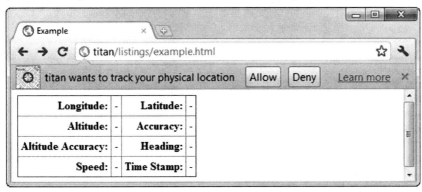

Figure 38-1. Granting permission for the geolocation feature

If the user approves the request, then the location information is obtained and, when it is available, the callback function is invoked. You can see the kind of data available from my desktop machine in Figure 38-2.

Longitude:	-73.986171	**Latitude:**	40.748716
Altitude:		**Accuracy:**	69
Altitude Accuracy:		**Heading:**	
Speed:		**Time Stamp:**	1315990791832

Figure 38-2. Displaying location information provided by the geolocation service

The computer that I use to write books doesn't have any kind of specialized location hardware installed – no GPS, compass, altimeter, or accelerometer. For that reason, the only data that is available is latitude and longitude and the accuracy of those values. For my location, Chrome estimates that I am within 69 meters (which is about 75 yards) of the position that has been reported (which is an underestimation in my case).

■ **Tip** Chrome, Firefox, and Opera all use the Google geolocation service. Internet Explorer and Safari use their own. I can only report on my location, but the Microsoft service reported accuracy to around 48,000 meters (about 30 miles). I found that the data was accurate to about 3 miles. The Apple service reported an accuracy of 500 meters, but provided the best data of all – it identified my location within a few feet. Wow!

Handling Geolocation Errors

We can provide a second argument to the getCurrentPosition method, which allows us to supply a function that will be invoked if there is an error obtaining the location. The function is passed a PositionError object, which defines the properties described in Table 38-5.

Table 38-5. The PositionError object

Name	Description	Returns
code	Returns a code indicating the type of error	number
message	Returns a string that describes the error	string

There are three possible values for the code property. These properties are described in Table 38-6.

Table 38-6. Values for the PositionError.code property

Value	Description
1	The user did not grant permission to use the geolocation feature
2	The position could not be determined
3	The attempt to request the location timed out

Listing 38-2 shows how we can receive errors using the PositionError object.

Listing 38-2. Handling errors with the PositionError object

```
<!DOCTYPE HTML>
```

```html
<html>
    <head>
        <title>Example</title>
        <style>
            table {border-collapse: collapse;}
            th, td {padding: 4px;}
            th {text-align: right;}
        </style>
    </head>
    <body>
        <table border="1">
            <tr>
                <th>Longitude:</th><td id="longitude">-</td>
                <th>Latitude:</th><td id="latitude">-</td>
            </tr>
            <tr>
                <th>Altitude:</th><td id="altitude">-</td>
                <th>Accuracy:</th><td id="accuracy">-</td>
            </tr>
            <tr>
                <th>Altitude Accuracy:</th><td id="altitudeAccuracy">-</td>
                <th>Heading:</th><td id="heading">-</td>
            </tr>
            <tr>
                <th>Speed:</th><td id="speed">-</td>
                <th>Time Stamp:</th><td id="timestamp">-</td>
            </tr>
            <tr>
                <th>Error Code:</th><td id="errcode">-</td>
                <th>Error Message:</th><td id="errmessage">-</td>
            </tr>
        </table>

        <script>
            navigator.geolocation.getCurrentPosition(displayPosition, handleError);

            function displayPosition(pos) {
                var properties = ["longitude", "latitude", "altitude", "accuracy",
                                  "altitudeAccuracy", "heading", "speed"];

                for (var i = 0; i < properties.length; i++) {
                    var value = pos.coords[properties[i]];
                    document.getElementById(properties[i]).innerHTML = value;
                }
                document.getElementById("timestamp").innerHTML = pos.timestamp;
            }

            function handleError(err) {
                document.getElementById("errcode").innerHTML = err.code;
                document.getElementById("errmessage").innerHTML = err.message;
            }
```

```
        </script>
    </body>
</html>
```

The simplest way to create an error is to refuse permission when prompted by the browser. The script in this example displays the details of the error in the `table` element and you can see the effect in Figure **38**-3.

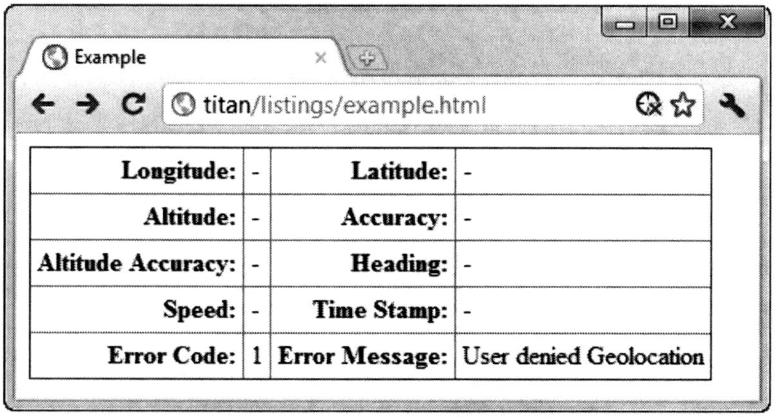

Figure 38-3. Displaying details of a geolocation error

Specifying Geolocation Options

The third argument we can provide to the `getCurrentPosition` method is a `PositionOptions` object. This feature allows us to exert some control over the way that locations are obtained. Table **38**-7 shows the properties that this object defines.

Table 38-7. The `PositionOptions` object

Name	Description	Returns
enableHighAccuracy	Tells the browser that we would like the best possible result	boolean
timeout	Sets a limit on how many milliseconds a position request can take before a timeout error is reported	number
maximumAge	Tells the browser that we are willing to accept a cached location, as long as it is no older than the specified number of milliseconds	number

Setting the `highAccuracy` property to `true` only asks the browser to give the best possible result – there are no guarantees that it will lead to a more accurate location. For mobile devices, a more accurate location may be available if a power-saving mode is disabled or, in some cases, the GPS feature is switched on (low accuracy locations may be derived from Wi-Fi or cell tower data). For other devices, there may not be higher-accuracy data available. Listing 38-3 shows how we can use the PositionOptions object when requesting a location.

Listing 38-3. Specifying options when requesting location data

```
<!DOCTYPE HTML>
<html>
    <head>
        <title>Example</title>
        <style>
            table {border-collapse: collapse;}
            th, td {padding: 4px;}
            th {text-align: right;}
        </style>
    </head>
    <body>
        <table border="1">
            <tr>
                <th>Longitude:</th><td id="longitude">-</td>
                <th>Latitude:</th><td id="latitude">-</td>
            </tr>
            <tr>
                <th>Altitude:</th><td id="altitude">-</td>
                <th>Accuracy:</th><td id="accuracy">-</td>
            </tr>
            <tr>
                <th>Altitude Accuracy:</th><td id="altitudeAccuracy">-</td>
                <th>Heading:</th><td id="heading">-</td>
            </tr>
            <tr>
                <th>Speed:</th><td id="speed">-</td>
                <th>Time Stamp:</th><td id="timestamp">-</td>
            </tr>
            <tr>
                <th>Error Code:</th><td id="errcode">-</td>
                <th>Error Message:</th><td id="errmessage">-</td>
            </tr>
        </table>
        <script>

            var options = {
                enableHighAccuracy: false,
                timeout: 2000,
                maximumAge: 30000
            };

            navigator.geolocation.getCurrentPosition(displayPosition,
                                            handleError, options);

            function displayPosition(pos) {
                var properties = ["longitude", "latitude", "altitude", "accuracy",
```

```
                                        "altitudeAccuracy", "heading", "speed"];

                    for (var i = 0; i < properties.length; i++) {
                        var value = pos.coords[properties[i]];
                        document.getElementById(properties[i]).innerHTML = value;
                    }
                    document.getElementById("timestamp").innerHTML = pos.timestamp;
                }

                function handleError(err) {
                    document.getElementById("errcode").innerHTML = err.code;
                    document.getElementById("errmessage").innerHTML = err.message;
                }

        </script>
    </body>
</html>
```

There is an oddity here in that we don't create a new PositionOptions object. Instead, we create a plain Object and define properties that match those in the table. In this example, I have indicated that I don't require the best level of resolution, that I am prepared to wait for 2 seconds before the request should timeout and I am willing to accept data that has been cached for up to 30 seconds.

Monitoring the Position

We can receive ongoing updates about the position by using the watchPosition method. This method takes the same arguments as the getCurrentPosition method and works in the same way – the difference is that the callback functions will be repeatedly called as the position changes. Listing 38-4 shows how we can use the watchPosition method.

Listing 38-4. Using the watchPosition method

```
<!DOCTYPE HTML>
<html>
    <head>
        <title>Example</title>
        <style>
            table {border-collapse: collapse;}
            th, td {padding: 4px;}
            th {text-align: right;}
        </style>
    </head>
    <body>
        <table border="1">
            <tr>
                <th>Longitude:</th><td id="longitude">-</td>
                <th>Latitude:</th><td id="latitude">-</td>
            </tr>
            <tr>
                <th>Altitude:</th><td id="altitude">-</td>
```

```
            <th>Accuracy:</th><td id="accuracy">-</td>
        </tr>
        <tr>
            <th>Altitude Accuracy:</th><td id="altitudeAccuracy">-</td>
            <th>Heading:</th><td id="heading">-</td>
        </tr>
        <tr>
            <th>Speed:</th><td id="speed">-</td>
            <th>Time Stamp:</th><td id="timestamp">-</td>
        </tr>
        <tr>
            <th>Error Code:</th><td id="errcode">-</td>
            <th>Error Message:</th><td id="errmessage">-</td>
        </tr>
    </table>
    <button id="pressme">Cancel Watch</button>
    <script>

        var options = {
            enableHighAccuracy: false,
            timeout: 2000,
            maximumAge: 30000
        };

        var watchID = navigator.geolocation.watchPosition(displayPosition,
                                                handleError,
                                                options);

        document.getElementById("pressme").onclick = function(e) {
            navigator.geolocation.clearWatch(watchID);
        };

        function displayPosition(pos) {
            var properties = ["longitude", "latitude", "altitude", "accuracy",
                            "altitudeAccuracy", "heading", "speed"];

            for (var i = 0; i < properties.length; i++) {
                var value = pos.coords[properties[i]];
                document.getElementById(properties[i]).innerHTML = value;
            }
            document.getElementById("timestamp").innerHTML = pos.timestamp;
        }

        function handleError(err) {
            document.getElementById("errcode").innerHTML = err.code;
            document.getElementById("errmessage").innerHTML = err.message;
        }

    </script>
    </body>
</html>
```

In this example, the script uses the `watchPosition` method to monitor the location. This method returns an ID value which we can pass to the `clearWatch` method when we want to stop monitoring. I do this when the `button` element is pressed.

■ **Caution** The current versions of the mainstream browsers don't implement the `watchPosition` method very well and updated locations are not always forthcoming. You may be better served using a timer (which I described in Chapter 27) and periodically calling the `getCurrentPosition` method.

Summary

In this chapter, I have described the Geolocation API, which provides information about the current location of the system that the browser is hosted by. I explained that the mechanism used by the browser to obtain location data varies and that location data isn't restricted only to those devices that have GPS support.

CHAPTER 39

Using Web Storage

Web storage allows us to store simple key/value data in the browser. Wen storage is similar to cookies, but better implemented and we can store greater amounts of data. There are two kinds of web storage – local storage and session storage. Both types share the same mechanism, but the visibility of the stored data and its longevity differ. Table 39-1 provides the summary for this chapter.

> **Tip** There is another storage specification, the Indexed Database API, which allows richer data storage and SQL-like queries. This specification is still volatile and the browser implementations are experimental and unstable as I write this.

Table 39-1. Chapter Summary

Problem	Solution	Listing
Store persistent data in the browser	Use the localStorage property to obtain a Storage object	1
Monitor changes in storage caused by other documents from the same origin	Handle the storage event	2
Store short-lived data in the browser	Use the sessionStorage property to obtain a Storage object	3
Monitor changes in storage in the top-level browsing context	Handle the storage event	4

Using Local Storage

We access the local storage feature through the localStorage global property – this property returns a Storage object, which is described in Table 39-2. The Storage object is used to store pairs of strings, organized in key/value form.

Table 39-2. The Storage object

Name	Description	Returns
clear()	Removes the stored key/value pairs	void
getItem(<key>)	Retrieves the value associated with the specified key	string
key(<index>)	Retrieves the key at the specified index	string
length	Returns the number of stored key/value pairs	number
removeItem(<key>)	Removes the key/value pair with the specified key	string
setItem(<key>, <value>)	Adds a new key/value pair or updates the value if the key has already been used	void
[<key>]	Array-style access to retrieve the value associated with the specified key	string

The Storage object allows us to store key/value pairs where both the key and the value are strings. Keys must be unique, which means the value is updated if we call the setItem method using a key that already exists in the Storage object. Listing 39-1 shows how we can add, modify, and clear the data in the local storage.

Listing 39-1. Working with local storage

```html
<!DOCTYPE HTML>
<html>
    <head>
        <title>Example</title>
        <style>
            body > * {float: left;}
            table {border-collapse: collapse; margin-left: 50px}
            th, td {padding: 4px;}
            th {text-align: right;}
            input {border: thin solid black; padding: 2px;}
            label {min-width: 50px; display: inline-block; text-align: right;}
            #countmsg, #buttons {margin-left: 50px; margin-top: 5px; margin-bottom: 5px;}
        </style>
    </head>
    <body>
```

```
<div>
    <div><label>Key:</label><input id="key" placeholder="Enter Key"/></div>
    <div><label>Value:</label><input id="value" placeholder="Enter Value"/></div>
    <div id="buttons">
        <button id="add">Add</button>
        <button id="clear">Clear</button>
    </div>
    <p id="countmsg">There are <span id="count"></span> items</p>
</div>

<table id="data" border="1">
    <tr><th>Item Count:</th><td id="count">-</td></tr>
</table>

<script>
    displayData();

    var buttons = document.getElementsByTagName("button");
    for (var i = 0; i < buttons.length; i++) {
        buttons[i].onclick = handleButtonPress;
    }

    function handleButtonPress(e) {
        switch (e.target.id) {
            case 'add':
                var key = document.getElementById("key").value;
                var value = document.getElementById("value").value;
                localStorage.setItem(key, value);
                break;
            case 'clear':
                localStorage.clear();
                break;
        }
        displayData();
    }

    function displayData() {
        var tableElem = document.getElementById("data");
        tableElem.innerHTML = "";
        var itemCount = localStorage.length;
        document.getElementById("count").innerHTML = itemCount;
        for (var i = 0; i < itemCount; i++) {
            var key = localStorage.key(i);
            var val = localStorage[key];
            tableElem.innerHTML += "<tr><th>" + key + ":</th><td>"
                + val + "</td></tr>";
        }
    }
</script>
</body>
</html>
```

989

In this example, I report on the number of items in the local storage and enumerate the set of stored name/value pairs to populate a table element. I have added two input elements, and I use their contents to store items when the Add button is pressed. In response to the Clear button, I clear the contents of the local storage. You can see the effect in Figure 39-1.

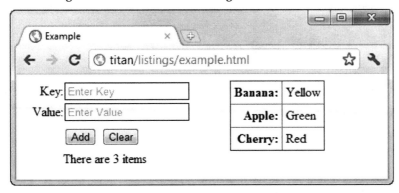

Figure 39-1. Working with local storage

The browser won't delete the data we add using the localStorage object unless the user clears the browsing data. (The specification also allows the data to be removed for security reasons, but the kind of security problems that require local data to be deleted are not articulated.)

Listening for Storage Events

The data stored via the local storage feature is available to any document that has the same origin. The storage event is triggered when one document makes a change to the local storage and we can listen to this event in other documents from the same origin to make sure that we stay abreast of changes.

The object dispatched with the storage event is a StorageEvent object, whose members are described in Table 39-3.

Table 39-3. The StorageEvent object

Name	Description	Returns
key	Returns the key that has been changed	string
oldValue	Returns the old value associated with the key	string
newValue	Returns the new value associated with the key	string
url	Returns the URL of the document that made the change	string
storageArea	Returns the Storage object which has changed	Storage

Listing 39-2 shows a document, which I have saved as storage.html, that listens and catalogues the events issued by the local storage object.

Listing 39-2. Cataloguing local storage events

```
<!DOCTYPE HTML>
<html>
    <head>
        <title>Storage</title>
        <style>
            table {border-collapse: collapse;}
            th, td {padding: 4px;}
        </style>
    </head>
    <body>
        <table id="data" border="1">
            <tr>
                <th>key</th>
                <th>oldValue</th>
                <th>newValue</th>
                <th>url</th>
                <th>storageArea</th>
            </tr>
        </table>
        <script>
            var tableElem = document.getElementById("data");

            window.onstorage = handleStorage;

            function handleStorage(e) {
                var row = "<tr>";
                row += "<td>" + e.key + "</td>";
                row += "<td>" + e.oldValue + "</td>";
                row += "<td>" + e.newValue + "</td>";
                row += "<td>" + e.url + "</td>";
                row += "<td>" + (e.storageArea == localStorage) + "</td></tr>";
                tableElem.innerHTML += row;
            };
        </script>
    </body>
</html>
```

The storage event is triggered through the Window object of any document that shares the changed storage. In this example, I add a new row to a table element each time an event is received – you can see the effect in Figure 39-2.

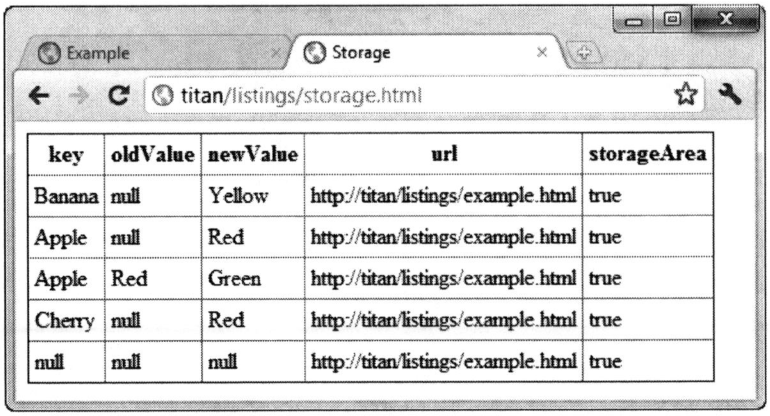

Figure 39-2. Displaying the details of storage events

The events in the figure show me adding new items to local storage. The sequence was:

- Add a new pair: Banana/Yellow
- Add a new pair: Apple/Red
- Update the value associated with Apple to Green
- Add a new pair: Cherry/Red
- Press the Clear button (which calls the clear method)

You can see that null is used when there is no value to report in the event. For example, when I add a new item to storage, the oldValue property returns null. The last event in the table has the key, oldValue, and newValue properties as null. This is the event that was triggered in response to the clear method being called, which removes all of the items from storage.

The url property helpfully tells us which document has triggered the change. The storageArea property returns the Storage object that has changed, which can be the local or session storage objects (I'll explain session storage shortly). For this example, we only receive events from the local storage object.

▓ **Note** Events are not dispatched within the document that made the change. I guess it is assumed that we already know what happened. The events are only available in *other* documents from the same origin.

Using Session Storage

Session storage works just like local storage, except that the data is private to each browsing context and is removed when the document is closed. We access session storage through the sessionStorage global variable, which returns a Storage object (previously described in Table 39-2). You can see session storage in use in Listing 39-3.

Listing 39-3. Using session storage

```
<!DOCTYPE HTML>
<html>
    <head>
        <title>Example</title>
        <style>
            body > * {float: left;}
            table {border-collapse: collapse; margin-left: 50px}
            th, td {padding: 4px;}
            th {text-align: right;}
            input {border: thin solid black; padding: 2px;}
            label {min-width: 50px; display: inline-block; text-align: right;}
            #countmsg, #buttons {margin-left: 50px; margin-top: 5px; margin-bottom: 5px;}
        </style>
    </head>
    <body>
        <div>
            <div><label>Key:</label><input id="key" placeholder="Enter Key"/></div>
            <div><label>Value:</label><input id="value" placeholder="Enter Value"/></div>
            <div id="buttons">
                <button id="add">Add</button>
                <button id="clear">Clear</button>
            </div>
            <p id="countmsg">There are <span id="count"></span> items</p>
        </div>

        <table id="data" border="1">
            <tr><th>Item Count:</th><td id="count">-</td></tr>
        </table>

        <script>
            displayData();

            var buttons = document.getElementsByTagName("button");
            for (var i = 0; i < buttons.length; i++) {
                buttons[i].onclick = handleButtonPress;
            }

            function handleButtonPress(e) {
                switch (e.target.id) {
                    case 'add':
                        var key = document.getElementById("key").value;
                        var value = document.getElementById("value").value;
                        sessionStorage.setItem(key, value);
                        break;
                    case 'clear':
                        sessionStorage.clear();
```

```
                    break;
                }
                displayData();
            }

        function displayData() {
            var tableElem = document.getElementById("data");
            tableElem.innerHTML = "";
            var itemCount = sessionStorage.length;
            document.getElementById("count").innerHTML = itemCount;
            for (var i = 0; i < itemCount; i++) {
                var key = sessionStorage.key(i);
                var val = sessionStorage[key];
                tableElem.innerHTML += "<tr><th>" + key + ":</th><td>"
                    + val + "</td></tr>";
            }
        }
        }
    </script>
    </body>
</html>
```

This example works in the same way as the one for local storage, except the visibility and life are restricted. These restrictions have a consequence on how the storage event is dealt with – remember that storage events are only triggered for documents that share storage. In the case of session storage, this means that the events will be triggered only for embedded documents, such as those in an iframe. Listing 39-4 shows an iframe added to the previous example which contains the storage.html document.

Listing 39-4. Using storage events with session storage

```
<!DOCTYPE HTML>
<html>
    <head>
        <title>Example</title>
        <style>
            body > * {float: left;}
            table {border-collapse: collapse; margin-left: 50px}
            th, td {padding: 4px;}
            th {text-align: right;}
            input {border: thin solid black; padding: 2px;}
            label {min-width: 50px; display: inline-block; text-align: right;}
            #countmsg, #buttons {margin-left: 50px; margin-top: 5px; margin-bottom: 5px;}
            iframe {clear: left;}
        </style>
    </head>
    <body>
        <div>
            <div><label>Key:</label><input id="key" placeholder="Enter Key"/></div>
            <div><label>Value:</label><input id="value" placeholder="Enter Value"/></div>
            <div id="buttons">
                <button id="add">Add</button>
                <button id="clear">Clear</button>
            </div>
```

```
            <p id="countmsg">There are <span id="count"></span> items</p>
        </div>

        <table id="data" border="1">
            <tr><th>Item Count:</th><td id="count">-</td></tr>
        </table>

        <iframe src="storage.html" width="500" height="175"></iframe>

        <script>
            displayData();

            var buttons = document.getElementsByTagName("button");
            for (var i = 0; i < buttons.length; i++) {
                buttons[i].onclick = handleButtonPress;
            }

            function handleButtonPress(e) {
                switch (e.target.id) {
                    case 'add':
                        var key = document.getElementById("key").value;
                        var value = document.getElementById("value").value;
                        sessionStorage.setItem(key, value);
                        break;
                    case 'clear':
                        sessionStorage.clear();
                        break;
                }
                displayData();
            }

            function displayData() {
                var tableElem = document.getElementById("data");
                tableElem.innerHTML = "";
                var itemCount = sessionStorage.length;
                document.getElementById("count").innerHTML = itemCount;
                for (var i = 0; i < itemCount; i++) {
                    var key = sessionStorage.key(i);
                    var val = sessionStorage[key];
                    tableElem.innerHTML += "<tr><th>" + key + ":</th><td>"
                        + val + "</td></tr>";
                }
            }
        </script>
    </body>
</html>
```

You can see how the events are reported in Figure 39-3.

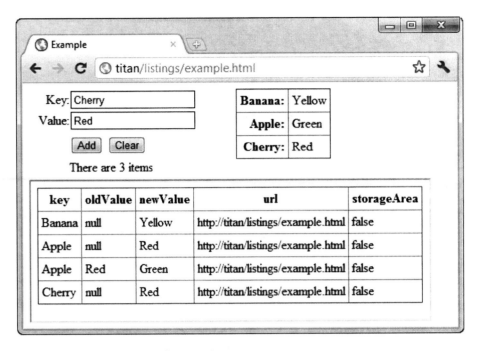

Figure 39-3. Storage events from session storage

Summary

In this chapter, I have described the web storage feature, which allows us to store key/value pairs in the browser. This is a simple feature, but the longevity of local storage can make it especially useful, particularly for storing simple user preferences.

Creating Offline Web Applications

The offline application cache feature lets us specify all of the resources that our web application requires, so that the browser can download them all when the HTML document is loaded. By doing this, we enable the user to continue to use our application even when they do not have network access.

At the time of writing, the support for the features in this chapter is exceptionally variable – I recommend you consider this chapter as a signpost for the direction that offline applications are generally following, rather than as a proscriptive reference. Table 40-1 provides the summary for this chapter.

Table 40-1. Chapter Summary

Problem	Solution	Listing
Enable offline caching	Create a manifest file and refer to it in the manifest attribute of the html element	1-3
Specify the resources to be cached in an offline application	List the resources at the top or in the CACHE section of the manifest file	4
Specify fallback content to be used when resources are not available	List the content in the FALLBACK section of the manifest file	5-8
Specify resources which are always requested from the server	List the content in the NETWORK section of the manifest file	9
Determine if the browser is offline	Read the value of the window.navigator.onLine property	10
Work with the offline cache directly	Get an ApplicationCache object by reading the window.applicationCache property	11-13

Defining the Problem

To understand the kind of problem we can solve by creating an offline web application, we need an example. Listing 40-1 shows a very simple application that relies on resources which are loaded from the server as-needed.

Listing 40-1. A simple web application

```
<!DOCTYPE HTML>
<html>
    <head>
        <title>Example</title>
        <style>
            img {border: medium double black; padding: 5px; margin: 5px;}
        </style>
    </head>
    <body>
        <img id="imgtarget" src="banana100.png"/>
        <div>
            <button id="banana">Banana</button>
            <button id="apple">Apple</button>
            <button id="cherries">Cherries</button>
        </div>
        <script>
            var buttons = document.getElementsByTagName("button");
            for (var i = 0; i < buttons.length; i++) {
                buttons[i].onclick = handleButtonPress;
            }

            function handleButtonPress(e) {
                document.getElementById("imgtarget").src = e.target.id + "100.png";
            }
        </script>
    </body>
</html>
```

There is an img element, whose src attribute is set in response to button presses. Different buttons will cause the browser to request different images from the web server. There are three images that may be required through the life of the application:

- banana100.png

- apple100.png

- cherries100.png

One of the images, banana100.png is loaded when the document loads, since it is specified as the initial value of the src attribute of the img element. You can see how the document appears in the browser in Figure 40-1.

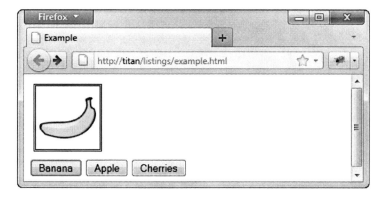

Figure 40-1. A simple web application

I have used Firefox in this chapter because it has an easily accessible offline mode (there is an option in the `File - Web Developer` menu). We can see the problem I am trying to fix when I switch the browser to offline, which simulates losing the network connection without my having to disable my wireless adapter, as shown in Figure 40-2.

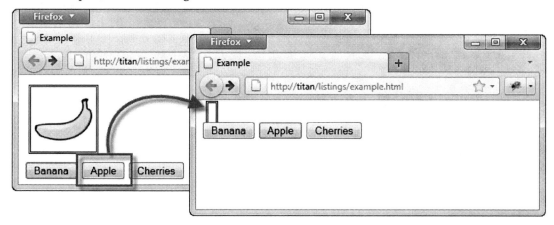

Figure 40-2. Requesting an unavailable resource when offline

When I press the `Apple` button, the browser tries to load the `apple100.png` image, but, of course, there is no network connection and the request fails. If I click on the `Banana` button, however, the correct image is displayed because `banana100.png` is in the browser cache from when the document was first loaded. Our goal in creating an offline application is to make sure that all of the resources we require are available so that the application works, even when offline.

Defining the Manifest

The manifest allows us to list all of the resources that we need to work offline. Listing 40-2 shows a manifest for the example web application.

Listing 40-2. A simple manifest

```
CACHE MANIFEST
example.html
banana100.png
apple100.png
cherries100.png
```

A manifest file is a simple text file. The first line is always CACHE MANIFEST and then we list the resources we require for the application, one per line of text.

■ **Tip** The specification for offline application recommends that we add the HTML document itself to the manifest, even though it will already be in the browser cache by the time the manifest is loaded and read.

There is no fixed naming scheme for manifest files, but the .appcache suffix is most commonly used. I saved the file in the example as fruit.appcache. Whatever naming scheme you use, you must arrange for the web server to describe the content to the browser using the text/cache-manifest MIME type.

■ **Caution** The browser will not use the cache file if the MIME type is not correctly set by the server.

We associate the manifest file with the document through the manifest attribute of the html element, as shown in Listing 40-3.

Listing 40-3. Associating a manifest file with an HTML document

```
<!DOCTYPE HTML>
<html manifest="fruit.appcache">
    <head>
        <title>Example</title>
        <style>
            img {border: medium double black; padding: 5px; margin: 5px;}
        </style>
    </head>
    <body>
        <img id="imgtarget" src="banana100.png"/>
        <div>
            <button id="banana">Banana</button>
            <button id="apple">Apple</button>
            <button id="cherries">Cherries</button>
        </div>
        <script>
            var buttons = document.getElementsByTagName("button");
            for (var i = 0; i < buttons.length; i++) {
```

```
            buttons[i].onclick = handleButtonPress;
        }

        function handleButtonPress(e) {
            document.getElementById("imgtarget").src = e.target.id + "100.png";
        }
    </script>
</body>
</html>
```

When we apply the manifest attribute to the html element, the browser may prompt the user to allow us to store the offline content locally. The way browsers handle this varies. Chrome and Opera allow us to cache offline data without the user being prompted. At the other end of the spectrum is Firefox, which requires explicit approval from the user, as shown in Figure 40-3.

Figure 40-3. Seeking user permission to store offline data

The browser will download all of the content specified in the manifest even if it hasn't yet been required. For our simple application, this means that all three of our images are downloaded. Now the application continues to work properly, even when I am offline, as shown in Figure 40-4.

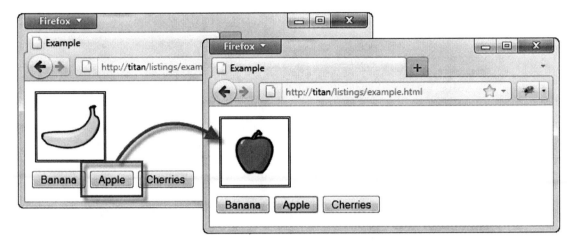

Figure 40-4. Creating an offline application

As you can see, creating an offline web application is very simple. We just create the manifest, ensure it contains the resources our application needs, and then set the value of the manifest attribute on the html element in our document.

Specifying Manifest Sections

We can add different sections to the manifest file. There are three different sections available, which I describe in the sections that follow.

Defining the Cache Section

We can list the files we need to cache at the start of the manifest, or we can create a CACHE section in the file. Listing 40-4 gives an example.

Listing 40-4. Defining a CACHE manifest file section

```
CACHE MANIFEST

example.html
banana100.png

CACHE:
apple100.png
cherries100.png
```

I have placed some of the resources in the default section at the start of the manifest file and others in the CACHE section. This is equivalent to the previous manifest, but it allows us to define the resources we want after the other sections I describe in the following section.

Defining the Fallback Section

The FALLBACK section allows us to specify how the browser should handle resources which we haven't included in the manifest. Listing 40-5 gives an example.

Listing 40-5. Defining a FALLBACK section in the manifest

```
CACHE MANIFEST

example.html
banana100.png

FALLBACK:
*.png offline.png

CACHE:
apple100.png
```

In this example, I have added a FALLBACK section. This new section contains one item, which tells the browser that it should use the offline.png file whenever it needs a png file that is not cached offline.

▪ **Tip** We don't need to add fallback resources to the CACHE section of the manifest as the browser will automatically download fallback resources.

I have removed cherries100.png from the CACHE section so that we have a resource that the application requires which is not available. You can see how the browser handles the fallback in Figure 40-5.

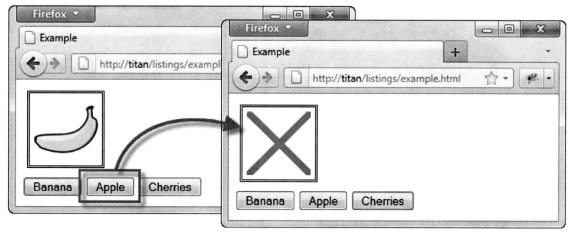

Figure 40-5. Using fallback content

The offline.png image is a simple cross. Providing fallbacks for images isn't ideal, but at least we can maintain the structure and layout of the page. Fallbacks can be much more useful for links to other documents. Listing 40-6 shows a change to our web application document that contains a link to another HTML file.

Listing 40-6. Adding a link to another file

```
<!DOCTYPE HTML>
<html manifest="fruit.appcache">
    <head>
        <title>Example</title>
        <style>
            img {border: medium double black; padding: 5px; margin: 5px;}
        </style>
    </head>
    <body>
        <img id="imgtarget" src="banana100.png"/>
        <div>
            <button id="banana">Banana</button>
            <button id="apple">Apple</button>
            <button id="cherries">Cherries</button>
        </div>
        <a href="otherpage.html">Link to another page</a>
        <script>
            var buttons = document.getElementsByTagName("button");
            for (var i = 0; i < buttons.length; i++) {
                buttons[i].onclick = handleButtonPress;
            }

            function handleButtonPress(e) {
                document.getElementById("imgtarget").src = e.target.id + "100.png";
            }
        </script>
    </body>
</html>
```

We can then create a fallback document that will be used if the HTML file that we linked to is not in the offline cache. I have called this page offline.html and its contents are shown in Listing 40-7.

Listing 40-7. The offline.html document

```
<!DOCTYPE HTML>
<html>
    <head>
        <title>Offline</title>
    </head>
    <body>
      <h1>Your browser is offline.</h1>
        Here is some placeholder content
    </body>
</html>
```

We can then add a fallback entry to the cache manifest file, as shown in Listing 40-8.

Listing 40-8. Adding a fallback entry to the manifest for HTML files

```
CACHE MANIFEST

example.html
banana100.png

FALLBACK:
*.png offline.png
* offline.html

CACHE:
apple100.png
```

The file that I have linked to (otherpage.html) is not in the manifest and so it won't be included in the offline cache. If I click on the link in the main document while offline, I am shown the fallback document instead, as illustrated by Figure 40-6. (The message that the fallback page displays isn't especially helpful, but it does demonstrate the feature. In a real application, we could display a more useful message or even define scripts that provide some kind of reduced functionality with the resources we have in the offline cache.)

Figure 40-6. Using fallback content for HTML documents

Defining the Network Section

The NETWORK section of the manifest file defines the set of resources that should not be cached, and which the browser should always request from the server, even when offline. Listing 40-9 shows the use of the NETWORK section.

Listing 40-9. Defining the NETWORK section in the manifest

```
CACHE MANIFEST

example.html
banana100.png

FALLBACK:
* offline.html

NETWORK:
cherries100.png

CACHE:
apple100.png
```

In this example, I have added the cherries100.png image to the NETWORK section. This addition means that the browser will try to request this image from the server, even when offline (although it will use a cached copy of the image if it is loaded outside of the manifest, that is, the user presses the Cherries button before the browser goes offline).

■ **Tip** Having a network section for an offline application may seem odd, but the browser will use the cached data even when it is online.

Detecting the Browser State

We can determine if the browser is online or offline through the window.navigator.onLine property, which is described in Table 40-2.

Table 40-2. The onLine property

Name	Description	Returns
window.navigator.onLine	Returns false if the browser is definitely offline and true if the browser *might* be online	boolean

This property is only definitive if the browser is sure that it is offline. A true value doesn't confirm that the browser is online but rather that it doesn't know for sure that it is offline. Listing 40-10 shows this property in use.

Listing 40-10. Detecting the state of the browser

```
<!DOCTYPE HTML>
<html>
    <head>
```

```
        <title>Example</title>
    </head>
    <body>
        The browser is: <span id="status">unknown</span>.
        <script>
            var statusValue;

            if (window.navigator.onLine) {
                statusValue = "online";
            } else {
                statusValue = "offline";
            }
            document.getElementById("status").innerHTML = statusValue;
        </script>
    </body>
</html>
```

You can see both states shown in Figure 40-7, achieved using the handy offline mode in Firefox. The state is rarely so certain in real life. The browser is free to make its own assessment of its status and most browsers don't default to offline until they have tried and failed to make a request (on the other hand, some mobile browsers will go into offline mode as soon as they lose network coverage).

Figure 40-7. Detecting the browser state

Working with the Offline Cache

We can work directly with the offline cache by calling the `window.applicationCache` property, which returns an `ApplicationCache` object. The members that this object defines are described in Table 40-3.

■ **Caution** This is an advanced topic and the caching mechanism can be incredibly frustrating to work with. Ask yourself if you really need to take control of the cache before using the objects and techniques that I describe in this section.

Table 40-3. The ApplicationCache object

Name	Description	Returns
update()	Updates the cache to ensure that the latest versions of the items in the manifest are downloaded	void
swapCache()	Swaps the current cache for a more recently updated one	void
status	Returns the status of the cache	number

The status property will return a numeric vale that corresponds to the set shown in Table 40-4.

Table 40-4. Values for the ApplicationCache status property

Value	Name	Description
0	UNCACHED	There is no caching for this document or the cached data has yet to be downloaded
1	IDLE	The cache is not performing any action
2	CHECKING	The browser is checking for updates to the manifest or the items specified in the manifest
3	DOWNLOADING	The browser is downloading manifest or content updates
4	UPDATEREADY	There updated cached data available
5	OBSOLETE	The cached data is obsolete and should not be used – this is caused by the request for the manifest file returning a 4xx HTTP code (usually indicating that the manifest file has been removed/deleted)

In addition to the methods and the status property, the ApplicationCache object defines a set of events which are triggered when the status of the cache changes. These events are described in Table 40-5.

Table 40-5. Values for the ApplicationCache status property

Name	Description
checking	The browser is obtaining the initial manifest or is checking for a manifest update
noupdate	There is no update available and the current manifest is the latest
downloading	The browser is downloading content specified in the manifest

progress	Triggered during the download phase
cached	All of the content specified in the manifest has been downloaded and cached
updateready	New resources have been downloaded and are ready for use
obsolete	The cache has become obsolete

We can combine the methods and the values of the status property to take explicit control of the offline cache, as demonstrated in Listing 40-11.

Listing 40-11. Working directly with the application cache

```
<!DOCTYPE HTML>
<html manifest="fruit.appcache">
    <head>
        <title>Example</title>
        <style>
            img {border: medium double black; padding: 5px; margin: 5px;}
            div {margin-top: 10px; margin-bottom: 10px}
            table {margin: 10px; border-collapse: collapse;}
            th, td {padding: 2px;}
            body > * {float: left;}
        </style>
    </head>
    <body>
        <div>
            <img id="imgtarget" src="banana100.png"/>
            <div>
                <button id="banana">Banana</button>
                <button id="apple">Apple</button>
                <button id="cherries">Cherries</button>
            </div>
            <div>
                <button id="update">Update</button>
                <button id="swap">Swap Cache</button>
            </div>
            The status is: <span id="status"></span>
        </div>
        <table id="eventtable" border="1">
            <tr><th>Event Type</th></tr>
        </table>
        <script>
            var buttons = document.getElementsByTagName("button");
            for (var i = 0; i < buttons.length; i++) {
                buttons[i].onclick = handleButtonPress;
            }

            window.applicationCache.onchecking =  handleEvent;
```

```
        window.applicationCache.onnoupdate = handleEvent;
        window.applicationCache.ondownloading = handleEvent;
        window.applicationCache.onupdateready = handleEvent;
        window.applicationCache.oncached = handleEvent;
        window.applicationCache.onobselete = handleEvent;

        function handleEvent(e) {
            document.getElementById("eventtable").innerHTML +=
                "<tr><td>" + e.type + "</td></td>";
            checkStatus();
        }

        function handleButtonPress(e) {
            switch (e.target.id) {
                case 'swap':
                    window.applicationCache.swapCache();
                    break;
                case 'update':
                    window.applicationCache.update();
                    checkStatus();
                    break;
                default:
                    document.getElementById("imgtarget").src = e.target.id
                        + "100.png";
            }
        }

        function checkStatus() {
            var statusNames = ["UNCACHED", "IDLE", "CHECKING", "DOWNLOADING",
                                "UPDATEREADY", "OBSOLETE"];
            var status = window.applicationCache.status;
            document.getElementById("status").innerHTML = statusNames[status];
        }

    </script>
    </body>
</html>
```

This example contains buttons that call the update and swapCache methods of the ApplicationCache object. The script also defines a listener to some of the events and displays the event type in a table element. Next, we need a manifest. Listing 40-12 shows the one used for this example.

Listing 40-12. The manifest for the cache example

```
CACHE MANIFEST

CACHE:
example.html
banana100.png
cherries100.png
apple100.png
```

```
FALLBACK:
* offline.html
```

There is nothing new in the manifest. It lists the main document, the image files it uses, and a general fallback document. You can see how the example is displayed in Figure 40-8.

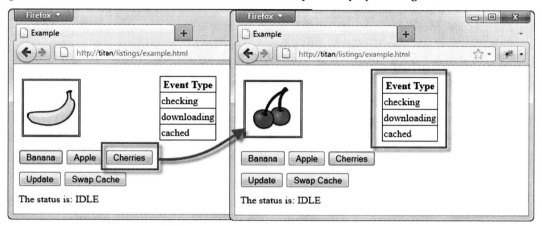

Figure 40-8. Manually controlling the cache

There are two points to note in this figure. The first is the sequence of events. When the document is loaded, the browser detects the `manifest` attribute on the `html` element and starts downloading and caching the content. You can see the effect of this in the table element—the `checking`, `downloading` and `cached` events are fired.

Making the Update

To effect a change in the cache, we have to make an update of some kind on the server. To switch the cherries for the lemon, I am simply going to overwrite the `cherries100.png` file on the server with my lemon image. To be clear: the filename is still cherries100.png but the content has been changed to a lemon.

The browser checks to see if the manifest file has changed when we call the `update` method on the `ApplicationCache` object; however, it doesn't check to see if any of the individual files specified in the manifest have been modified. So, to get the browser to load my modified image, I also need to make a change to the manifest file. For simplicity, I have changed the name of the fallback HTML file, as shown in Listing 40-13.

Listing 40-13. Making a change to the manifest file

```
CACHE MANIFEST

CACHE:
example.html
banana100.png
cherries100.png
apple100.png
```

```
FALLBACK:
* offline2.html
```

■ **Caution** A major cause of confusion when debugging the offline cache is that the browser honors the caching policy for the individual entries in the manifest file. This means that you can get into a real mess if you have set different cache expiration headers on different types of content, as the browser will check some for updates and not others. To get immediate changes in the cache (well, sort-of-immediate—see the note later in this section about that), the safest thing to do is to set your web server so that it sets the Cache-Control header to no-cache. This tells the browser not to check for updates each time a resource is required (although you won't want to do this on a production server).

Getting the Update

Now that we have made a change at the server, we can ask the browser to update the offline cache. To do this, press the Update button. The effect is shown in Figure 40-9.

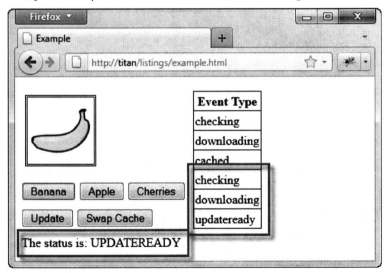

Figure 40-9. Downloading an update to the offline cache

A new sequence of events will be shown (checking, downloading, updateready) and the status of the cache will change to UPDATEREADY. At this point, the browser has downloaded the modified content, but it has not been applied to the cache we are using, which is to say that clicking on the Cherries button will still show us a picture of cherries, even though the browser has downloaded and cached the lemon substitute with the same name.

Applying the Update

When we are ready to receive the updated content, we can press the Swap Cache button, which calls the swapCache method on the ApplicationCache object. The updated content is applied to the offline cache for our application.

■ **Caution** Another cause of confusion when working with the cache is the effect that applying an update has. The changes are only used the next time that a resource is requested from the cache. This means that any stylesheets or script files that are cached will not be reloaded by the browser and you will have to explicitly reload the document that contains them to benefit from any changes.

When we press the Cherries button, we see the picture of the lemon, as shown in Figure 40-10.

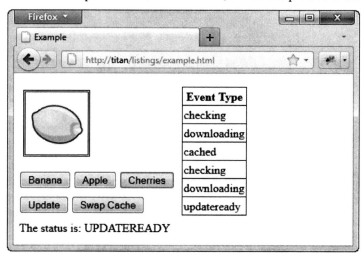

Figure 40-10. Applying an update to the offline cache

■ **Caution** The final area of frustration is that there can be a lag between applying the update and the updated content being used in a document. In writing this chapter, I encountered delays that ranged from just a few seconds to ten minutes or more.

Summary

In this chapter, I have shown you how to create offline applications that can function even when the browser cannot connect to a network. This is a really useful feature and once you get the configuration you need, the results are great; however, testing and debugging with the application cache can be a maddening process, especially if you take direct control of the cache through the `ApplicationCache` object.

Index

F

G

▓ H

■ M

■ N